BLUE GUIDE

THE MARCHE
& SAN MARINO

Ellen Grady

with photographs by Giacomo Mazza

Somerset Books • London
WW Norton • New York

Blue Guide The Marche & San Marino
First edition

Published by Blue Guides Limited, a Somerset Books Company
49–51 Causton St, London SW1P 4AT
www.blueguides.com
'Blue Guide' is a registered trademark

ISBN 1–905131–14–3

A CIP catalogue record of this book is available from the British Library

Published in the United States of America by
WW Norton and Company, Inc.
500 Fifth Avenue, New York, NY 10110
US ISBN 0–393–32888–0

The author and the publisher have made reasonable efforts to ensure the accuracy of all the information in *Blue Guide The Marche & San Marino*; however, they can accept no responsibility for any loss, injury or inconvenience sustained by any traveller as a result of information or advice contained in the guide.

Your views on this book would be much appreciated. We welcome not only specific comments, suggestions or corrections, but any more general views you may have: how this book enhanced your holiday, how it could have been more helpful. Blue Guides authors and editorial and production team work hard to bring you what we hope are the best-researched and best-presented cultural, historical and academic guide books in the English language. Please write to us by email (editorial@blueguides.com), via the comments page on our website (www.blueguides.com) or at the address given above. We will be happy to acknowledge useful contributions in the next edition, and to offer a free copy of one of our titles.

CONTENTS

INTRODUCTION

Le Marche, the region known as the Marches in English, derives its name from the German *mark*, meaning boundary or frontier. A plural name for a place with a decidedly plural personality. To look at, the area is strongly reminiscent of a patchwork quilt, casually thrown over a particularly lumpy mattress: hundreds of small farms, alternating with patches of woodland, giving different chromatic effects in the various seasons of the year. One of central Italy's more mountainous regions, it is bordered to the west by the Apennines, Umbria and Tuscany, to the east by the Adriatic, to the north by the River Marecchia and Emilia Romagna, and to the south by the River Tronto and Abruzzo: 9,693km square of hills and valleys, formed by a series of parallel rivers, all flowing west to east, from the Apennine chain to the sea. The 180 km-long coastline consists mainly of sandy beaches, interrupted only by the San Bartolo mountain north of Pesaro, and the Conero peninsula south of Ancona. About 10% of the territory is protected, under the form of nature parks and reserves. There are no big cities, and only one large industrial area, at Falconara Marittima, near the airport. Tiny townships dot the countryside, usually perched on hilltops, and often little more than a castle (which is what they originally were), with small populations, particularly jealous of their traditions and way of life, but exceedingly hospitable to visitors. San Maroto, near Camerino, has only 15 inhabitants, and Caudino, near Arcevia, has only one.

HISTORICAL SKETCH

A complicated, often extremely violent history has forged great beauty in the Marche. The first populations to leave traces of their presence were here in the Stone Age, about 100,000 years ago; tools and weapons made from pebbles have been found on Mt Conero. The Iron Age (9th century BC) saw the arrival from the west of the warlike Picenes, who were very appreciative of beautiful things, judging by the contents of their tombs. They didn't make much use of gold and silver, but they loved elegant chariots, functional, richly decorated weapons, and flamboyant jewellery of bronze and amber, which they eagerly imported from the Etruscans, from the Baltic, from Greece and from Bosnia. In the late 6th century BC the Republic of Rome began flexing its muscles; the Picenes and the Umbrians inevitably came under its sway, with the construction of the great highways, the Flaminian and the Salarian Ways. The Romans launched ambitious projects for cities, roads and bridges, many of which can still be admired; they also left the splendid Arch of Trajan in the port of Ancona; the unique 1st-century BC gilded bronze statues found at Cartoceto di Pergola (*see p. 250*); some impressive theatres and amphitheatres, city walls, water cisterns, and monumental gates. Augustus, the first emperor, divided the territory into two parts, for easier government: the north became part of Roman Umbria, while the south was known as *Picenum*. With the decline of the empire, Rome became an easy target for barbarian attacks, especially Goths and Vandals; in 476 the city was taken by the warrior Odoacer, who became the first king of Italy after the fall of the Western Empire. After him came the Ostrogoth Theodoric, who ruled for 33 years. Justinian, Emperor of the East, reconquered much, thanks to his brilliant generals Belisarius and Narses, and defeated the Gothic king Totila in 552 near the Furlo Gorge. His campaigns were militarily and financially exhausting, and his victories were short-lived. A new menace was preparing to descend into Italy: the Lombard warriors from the Danube valley. For 200 years, ruling from Lucca and Spoleto, they controlled central Italy, with the exception of Umbria and the northern Marche, which, governed from Ravenna, were still under the wing of Byzantium. Although they converted to Christianity, the Lombards made the popes uneasy, so when Pepin the Short entered Italy with his Franks in 754, he was welcomed with open arms. Pepin's son Charlemagne finally expelled the Lombards, and in 800 Pope Leo III crowned him as the first Holy Roman Emperor; in return he donated much of his territory to the papacy. His empire would survive for 1,000 years, until extinguished by Napoleon in 1806.

After Charlemagne's death in 814, poor government and rivalry between emperor and pope became more acute. The various communes, for a quiet life, paid lip service to either one or the other, while fostering loyalty among the citizens only for their own banners—a situation that would eventually lead to the Guelph-Ghibelline strife. The names of the two factions, papal and imperial, go back to the 13th century, when the pope named in the Welf (Guelph) Otto the new Holy Roman Emperor, while the supporters of his rival Frederick rallied to the Hohenstaufen battle-cry *Hie Weibling!* (Ghibelline). The pope knew he could count on the emerging middle class of merchants and artisans, while the old feudal aristocracy pinned its aspirations on the emperor's military force. The Guelphs triumphed in 1264 when Pope Urban IV invited Charles of Anjou and his French troops to enter Italy, where they became the dominant foreign power.

During the time that the popes ruled from Avignon (1305–77), local despots were quick to impose their overlordship on many small communities in central Italy. This was also the century of epidemics, like the Black Death of 1348, which claimed thousands of lives. Poignant traces of those terrible scourges can be seen in many churches: the frescoes, panel paintings, Crucifixes and statues donated by the populace as tangible prayers. In 1356 the Avignon papacy sent the determined Cardinal Albornoz to regain control over the Papal States; he built menacing fortresses which can still be seen in many towns of the Marche, but it was not until 1421, and the end of the Papal Schism, that a certain tranquillity returned to the area, thanks to the determination of Pope Martin V.

Christianity had came early to the Marche, brought by pilgrims travelling to Rome along the old roads from the coast. Monasteries following the rule of St Benedict sprang up along the routes in the 6th century. By the 10th century there was a network of flourishing religious institutions throughout the area. Romanesque architecture (11th–13th centuries), introduced by the Lombards, but often still showing traces of the old Byzantine traditions, is seen at its best in the Marche: among the many examples, the dazzling cathedral of San Ciriaco in Ancona is one of the finest of the period in Italy. And just as many tourists go to Dublin to photograph the colourful doors, a similar tour could be arranged to admire the many beautifully carved Gothic portals of the churches of Marche, built between the 12th–15th centuries. The finest is perhaps that carved by Nanni di Bartolo for the church of San Nicolò in Tolentino. The style was very popular in the Marche, and in the 14th century it was a local painter, Gentile da Fabriano, who became the foremost exponent of the International Gothic school of art.

The 15th century brought the Renaissance, a new outlook on life, and a new approach to building. Urbino, thanks to Federico da Montefeltro, became the ideal city, and his palace, venue of artists, architects, writers, poets and musicians, is the universal symbol of the Renaissance. It is the time of the really great masters, such as Piero della Francesca, Botticelli, and Raphael. The Camerino school comes into being; Giovanni Boccati paints his exquisite polyptychs, and Lorenzo d'Alessandro from San Severino Marche paints his beautiful Madonnas. The prosperity attracts artists from Venice, such as Jacobello del Fiore, Carlo Crivelli and his brother Vittore, and Lorenzo Lotto. Pottery and ceramics are inspired by the work of Raphael; Federico Brandani creates his marvellous stucco decorations in church interiors; Federico Barocci from Urbino, one of Italy's greatest artists, paints his colourful masterpieces.

In the 15th and 16th centuries wars were so frequent among the powerful aristocratic families that it became necessary to construct or rebuild the castles and fortresses, which had to be able to withstand cannon fire and attacks from other new-fangled weapons. Francesco di Giorgio Martini is a name which immediately springs to mind; he designed many of them, thought to be among the most beautiful castles anywhere: Sassocorvaro, for example, or San Leo.

The 16th century, which saw the Renaissance spreading throughout Europe, saw Italy being contested by France and Spain. The signing of a treaty between the two powers in 1559 handed most of the country over to 150 years of Spanish domination, with the exception of the Papal States. The pope was free to consolidate his control over the Marche, which he exercised through his clergy, while in Rome he concentrated his efforts on halting the spread of Protestantism by means of the Counter-Reformation movement. Churches, especially those of the Jesuits, become more and more imposing, with Mannerist-style paintings and statues, lavishly opulent, sometimes almost grotesque, but free at last from the suffocating restraint of the classical High Renaissance.

The old name of Italy was *Enotria*, from the Hebrew *Nother*, 'Trembling Land'. Frequent earthquakes mean, of necessity, frequent reconstructions; in the 17th century, that meant the Baroque style. This exuberant, decorative architecture can best be admired in some church interiors, and in some aristocratic palaces, as in Macerata; the little town of Servigliano, near Fermo, is entirely Baroque. In the 18th century, the architect Luigi Vanvitelli brought a Neoclassical influence; this was the period when every community, large or small, ardently desired an opera house, where the people could listen to concerts and operas, and plays could be performed. The dream became possible because groups of wealthy citizens paid for the construction, obtaining in exchange permanent ownership of the best boxes, and even the right to decide how the public should dress and behave when coming to the theatre (at Montefano it was forbidden to eat oranges, whistle, or enter without a jacket). The best theatre architects were probably Ireneo Aleandri (Ascoli Piceno, Macerata, Pollenza), and Vincenzo Ghinelli (Camerino, Ancona, Pesaro and Urbino), while the theatres with the best acoustics are said to be those of Recanati and Ancona.

The ideals of the French Revolution of 1789 probably sparked the Risorgimento, Italy's own republican movement, which would culminate in 1860, not with a republic, but with the Unification of Italy under Vittorio Emanuele II. The process of fragmenting the old Holy Roman Empire and conquering the city states was begun by Napoleon's invasion of Italy in 1796. He turned the Papal States into the Roman Republic, and then the Kingdom of Italy, under his brother Jerome. Pope Pius VI was forced to surrender all his possessions, cash, and most of the works of art, which were sent to the Louvre; many of them were never returned. The forging of a united nation from all these disparate states and territories was the work of the messianic reformer Giuseppe Mazzini, the guerrilla leader Giuseppe Garibaldi, and the Piedmontese statesman Camillo Cavour. Rome was the last to fall, in 1870.

THE MARCHE TODAY

The land of the Marche, well-watered and fertile, is however difficult to farm efficiently, because of the hilly terrain, so up until the Second World War, production was entrusted to the *mezzadri*, share-croppers; there was little scope for enterprise, and even less possibility of making enough money to emerge over the subsistence level. In the '50s many people emigrated to the wealthier northern regions, or overseas. But in the early '70s an interesting phenomenon developed: small industries sprang up in hundreds of tiny towns, independent among themselves, yet creating components for the town over the other side of the hill, in a kind of endless chain. The secret of their success is based on reliable quality, constant innovation and punctual deliveries. Cloth is woven in Fermignano and Osimo for the tailors of Filottrano and Recanati. In Montegiorgio they make eyelets and metal buckles for the footwear manufacturers of the Fermo area, and also electric wires for the kitchen appliances of Fabriano; the kitchens are mounted in Pesaro. Stone for the worktops of the Pesaro kitchens comes from Acqualagna and Sant'Ippolito. In Ascoli Piceno they make cardboard boxes for the shoe manufacturers of Sant'Elpidio a Mare; the soles for the shoes are made in Montegranaro. All of these enterprises are small, often not much more than a workshop, yet they can guarantee full occupation for the local people, they do not pollute the rivers or the air, they do not ruin the landscape. There are now more than 25,000 of these industries, employing about 600,000 workers, and exporting goods worth €6 billion a year, in a practically unspoilt environment. The result is a flourishing economy, with the lowest unemployment rate (less than half the national average) in Italy, and some of the wealthiest people: more luxury cars are registered in the province of Fermo than anywhere else in the country.

The farms have not been abandoned; this region has made a decided move towards low environmental impact organic farming methods, resulting in small quantities of top-quality produce. Cheese, ham, salami, olive oil and wine (13 *Denominazione d'Origine Controllata* labels) are the most important of these, together with beef, wheat for pasta, orchard fruits, spelt, lentils, jams and preserves (not to mention the exquisite truffles, which are not farmed, but found in the forests). So far no GMOs (genetically-modified organisms) are permitted. Many young people are returning to work on the farms once run by their ancestors, with enthusiasm and new ideas, and often with accommodation for tourists as well. Fishing in the Adriatic is another profitable activity; San Benedetto del Tronto is one of the busiest fishing ports in Italy, with the largest facilities for freezing and chilling in Europe; every year they sell fish worth about €200 million. Fabriano is the most important centre in Europe for the production of paper, of many different qualities: the first to manufacture tissue paper, they also make the special quality for euro notes.

Such a beautiful, interesting place could not remain a secret for ever. Now tourism is an important voice in the economy, and there is certainly much to interest visitors, apart from the splendid beaches: 250 museums and art galleries, 150 castles and fortresses; 200 Romanesque churches, 40 abbeys, and 163 sanctuaries still visited by pilgrims; 6 national and regional parks; 113 theatres, 71 of which are defined as historic (built between 1660 and 1930)—this means a theatre for every 15,000 inhabitants, the highest proportion in Italy; 170 medieval towers; 33 archaeological sites; scores of saints, dozens of ghosts, and an admirable network of efficient and friendly tourist offices, to help you make the most of your time in the area.

VER SACRUM

It was a tradition among the ancient populations of Italy to consecrate to a divinity the boy babies born during the springtime of certain years. When they grew up, these men were expected to lead groups of settlers to new lands, guided by a totem animal—the tradition was called *ver sacrum*, or 'sacred spring'. In the early Iron Age, a group of Sabines migrated east over the Apennines, and from there followed a magpie, which had perched on their banner depicting Mars, over the Tronto, where they settled. They became known as Picenes, from *picus*, magpie. Now the stylized image of the bird is the symbol of the Marche region.

ANCONA & THE CONERO PROMONTORY

Gracefully draped over the hills surrounding the harbour, Ancona—like Venice, Trieste and Dubrovnik—is one of the ancient maritime powers of the Adriatic. Capital of the province and of the region (pop. 100,100), she belies her years, and is one of Italy's most exciting cities. Ancona is also one of the few mainland sites where you can see both the sunrise and the sunset over the sea.

EXPLORING ANCONA

The port

The heart of Ancona is, of course, its port—a maze of warehouses, cranes, trucks, docks and dry-docks, railway lines, a yachting harbour, and 4km of quays; the water is up to 15m deep, allowing big ships to anchor. At the northern limit is the elegant **Arch of Trajan**, symbol of the city, and one of the finest Roman buildings of its kind in Italy. Almost 14m high, and appearing even more imposing by the 19th-century stairway in front of it, the arch was built in the year 115, by the court architect Apollodorus of Damascus, in honour of the Emperor Trajan, as a token of appreciation from the populace for the remodelling of their harbour. The plinth is of local stone, but the archway itself is built of great blocks of white Greek marble, placed in position without mortar, and then sealed with molten lead, before being completed with carvings, inscriptions (originally inlaid with gilded bronze letters), the bronze statues (now missing) of Trajan, his wife Plotina, and his sister Marciana, and the bronze rostra of captured enemy ships—you can still see where they were fixed. The concrete foundations are octagonal, and astonishingly deep—they go down several metres below the level of the sea. As a result, the arch has survived all the earthquakes and bombardments to which the city has been subjected, practically unscathed.

To the west of Trajan's Arch, at the limit of the old city walls, is the **Arco Clementino**, built in 1738 in honour of Pope Clement XII, who had just made Ancona a free port (no customs duties to pay). By doing so, the pope hoped to encourage trade, which had fallen off dramatically since the city's heyday. The architect was Luigi Vanvitelli, who worked on a number of papal projects in the Marche. His inspiration was clearly taken from the Roman arch close by.

At the bottom of the harbour is the Mole Vanvitelliana, or **Lazzaretto** (*open Tues–Fri 4.30–7.30, Sat, Sun and holidays 10–1 & 4.30–7.30; closed Mon; T: 071 2225030/1*), an enormous pentagonal construction of 1733, also built by Vanvitelli to house the quarantine for passengers and merchandise, and a hospital; it later became a barracks, a prison, a sugar factory, and a tobacco warehouse. Recently restored, it is now used for exhibitions, concerts, and as an open-air cinema. Near the Lazzaretto is **Porta Pia** (1789), built in honour of Pope Pius VI, in late Baroque style: there is a good view from here, embracing the whole city, from the Guasco Hill to the Astagno.

The 2nd-century AD Arch of Trajan, built to honour the emperor after he rebuilt and improved Ancona's harbour.

HISTORY OF ANCONA

On the spot where an elbow-shaped promontory forms a fine natural harbour (*ankon* means 'elbow' in Greek), Dionysius, tyrant of the Greek city of Syracuse, in Sicily, founded an outpost in 387 BC, a move that would give him control over the most important trade routes of the time. The position was enviable, and in fact Greeks and Sicels had maintained a tenacious foothold there since the 8th century BC, living side-by-side with the Picenes. The settlers from Syracuse built a Doric temple to Aphrodite on the acropolis, where the cathedral now stands, and for centuries Ancona was an emporium, a city of merchants dealing in amber, wool, purple dye, pottery from Greece, cosmetics and perfumes. Under the Romans the city became a *municipium* and a base for the fleet; Trajan improved the port, where he built a splendid arch of honour. The Temple of Aphrodite became the Temple of Venus, and an amphitheatre, a forum, and magnificent baths added to the town's prestige. Christianity arrived early, brought by travellers from the East. Under Byzantium Ancona became the first city of the Maritime Pentapolis (the others were Rimini, Pesaro, Fano and Senigallia), governed by Ravenna, but with considerable autonomy. By the 10th century Ancona was an independent commune and a maritime republic, rich from its commerce with Constantinople and the ports of the Adriatic. The 12th century brought three tremendous attacks: from Holy Roman Emperor Lothair II in 1137, Frederick Barbarossa in 1167, and the notorious archbishop Christian of Mainz with the Venetian fleet in 1173.

In 1348 the city was taken by the Malatesta, and forced to make act of submission to the pope's representative, Cardinal Albornoz, who built a fortress on the San Cataldo hill (destroyed by a jubilant population in 1383). In the 15th century, Ancona formed an alliance with Venice against combined Milanese and Spanish forces. After the fall of Constantinople in 1453 Ancona's commercial fortunes waned. The Medici pope Clement VII seized the city in 1532, bringing it under papal control. The maritime republic of Ancona, with its embassies in Constantinople, Alexandria and Syria; its set of maritime laws and its trading fleet, which went as far as the North Sea, was no more. In 1797 Ancona suffered the fate of her fellow republics Dubrovnik and Venice: she was occupied by the French, returning only to the Papal States in 1816, after the fall of Napoleon.

During the movement for the Unification of Italy, Ancona played an important role, and Piedmontese troops entered the city in 1860. Heavy bombing in the Second World War devastated the medieval and Renaissance quarters. An earthquake in 1972 caused serious damage to the cathedral, many ancient churches, and the Archaeological Museum.

Nowadays, Ancona is the busiest fishing and commercial port in the Adriatic. Its university is known for its faculties of Economics and Business Studies, Engineering, and Medicine.

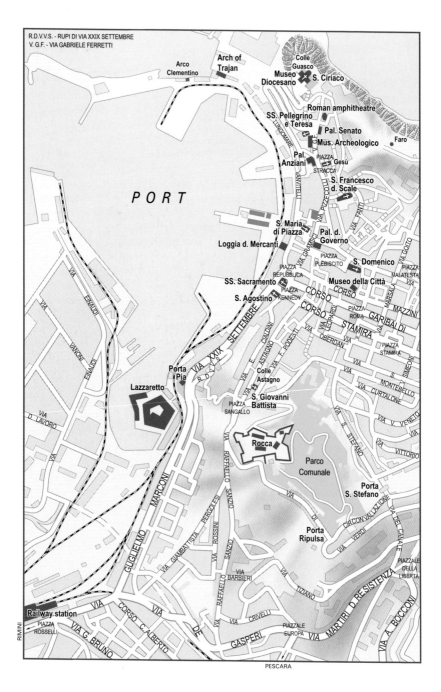

R.D.V.V.S. - RUPI DI VIA XXIX SETTEMBRE
V. G.F. - VIA GABRIELE FERRETTI

Arco
Clementino

Arch of
Trajan

Colle
Guasco

Museo
Diocesano

S. Ciriaco

Roman amphitheatre

SS. Pellegrino
e Teresa

Pal. Senato

Mus. Archeologico

Faro

Pal.
Anziani

PIAZZA
STRACCA

Gesù

S. Francesco
d. Scale

P O R T

S. Maria
di Piazza

Pal. d.
Governo

Loggia d. Mercanti

PIAZZA
PLEBISCITO

S. Domenico

PIAZZA
MALATESTA

SS. Sacramento

PIAZZA
REPUBBLICA

Museo della Città

S. Agostino

PIAZZA
KENNEDY

CORSO

CORSO

PIAZZA
ROMA

MAZZINI

GARIBALDI

STAMIRA

PIAZZA
STAMIRA

SETTEMBRE

VIA XXIX

CIALDINI

VIA E. ASTAGNO

VIA F. PODESTÀ

VIA
OBERDAN

VIA

Porta
Pia

R. D. V. V. S.

Colle
Astagno

S. Giovanni
Battista

MONTEBELLO

CURTALONE

Lazzaretto

VIA EINAUDI

VIA VANONI

VIA EINAUDI

PIAZZA
SANGALLO

Rocca

Parco
Comunale

VIA S. STEFANO

VIA V. VENETO

VITTORIO

VIA
D. LAVORO

Porta
S. Stefano

GUGLIELMO

MARCONI

RAFFAELLO SANZIO

VIA GIAMBATTISTA PERGOLESI

VIA RAFFAELLO SANZIO

ROSSINI

VIA
DI

Porta
Ripulsa

CIRCONVALLAZIONE

VIA DEL CANALE

VIA VERDI

PIAZZALE
DELLA
LIBERTÀ

Railway station

RIMINI

PIAZZA
ROSSELLI

VIA G. BRUNO

VIA

CORSO C. ALBERTO

VIA
DE

VIA
BARBIERI

CRIVELLI

TIZIANO

GASPERI

PIAZZALE
EUROPA

VIA MARTIRI D. RESISTENZA

VIA A. BOCCONI

PESCARA

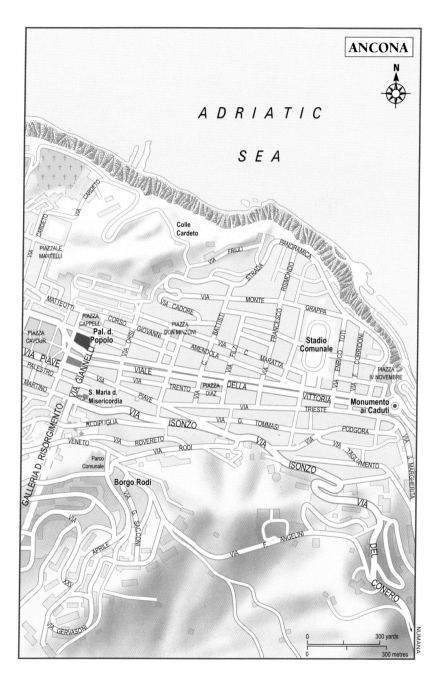

ANCONA

N

ADRIATIC

SEA

VIA CARDETO

CARDETO

Colle
Cardeto

PIAZZALE
MARTELLI

PANORAMICA

VIA FRIULI

VIA

STRADA

RISMONDO

MONTE

MATTEOTTI

VIA CADORE

VIA

GRAPPA

PIAZZA
CAPPELLI

CORSO

PIAZZA
DON MINZONI

FRANCESCO

PIAZZA
CAVOUR

**Pal. d.
Popolo**

VIA ORSI

GIOVANNI

BATTISTI

Stadio
Comunale

VIA PIAVE

VIA GIANNELLI

AMENDOLA

VIA FLZ C.

MARATTA

ENRICO TOTI

PIAZZA
IV NOVEMBRE

PALESTRO

VIALE

VIA

F. CORRIDONI

MARTINO

VIA

PIAVE

TRENTO

PIAZZA
DIAZ

DELLA

**S. Maria d.
Misericordia**

VIA

VITTORIA

**Monumento
ai Caduti**

REDIPUGLIA

ISONZO

VIA

G. TOMMASI

TRIESTE

GALLERIA D. RISORGIMENTO

VENETO

VIA

ROVERETO

VIA

RODI

VIA

PODGORA

VIA

VIA TAGLIAMENTO

Parco
Comunale

ISONZO

VIA

S. MARGHERITA

Borgo Rodi

VIA

G. SACCONI

VIA

VIA

F. ANGELINI

DEL

VIA

APRILE

VIA

CONERO

XXI

VIA GERVASONI

0   300 yards

0   300 metres

NUMANA

San Ciriaco

One of the most interesting medieval churches in Italy, the white stone Duomo di San Ciriaco (*open 8–12 & 3–6; 7 in summer*), was built between the 11th and 13th centuries, on the site of the 4th-century BC Temple of Aphrodite, protector of navigators, and a 6th-century triple-nave basilica dedicated to St Lawrence. The beautiful, harmonious structure glimmers on high, and can be seen from the whole city, with its twelve-sided copper dome (one of the oldest and best-preserved in Italy), huge Romanesque-Gothic portal (1228), in red and white stone from the Conero, with interesting carvings on the five concentric arches, and the elegant porch supported by pink granite lions (one clutching a lamb and the other a snake) and columns. The façade is perfectly balanced by a wide stairway.

The interior is a Greek cross, with the four arms forming a nave and transepts, divided by monolithic Roman columns surmounted by Byzantine capitals. The transepts are apsidal, with their altars raised over crypts. In the centre, supported by four sturdy pilasters, is the exceptional dome. Parts of the floor are of glass, in order to reveal the outlines of the pagan temple and the Palaeochristian basilica, and sections of mosaic paving. The central naves of all four arms have 15th-century painted wooden ceilings (restored), like those of the churches of San Fermo in Verona and Santo Stefano in Venice. To the left on entering, is the beautifully carved **sepulchre of Francesco Nobili**, warrior of Fermo (1530); according to legend, the knight will

The early 13th-century Romanesque-Gothic portal of San Ciriaco.

wake up in case of need. Also on the left is the chapel of the Madonna, with a rich altar designed by Vanvitelli (1738); over the altar is a small, much-venerated **canvas of the *Madonna***, by an unknown artist, donated in 1615 as an ex-voto by Bortolo, a Venetian sailor. Napoleon wanted to burn the picture, thought to be miraculous by the people, but just when he was about to throw it into the flames, he changed his mind, and told his soldiers to take it back into the cathedral.

THE STORY OF ST CYRIACUS

When St Helen, mother of Constantine, went to Jerusalem in 326 to look for the True Cross, only one man called Judas knew of its whereabouts, but he refused to divulge the secret. She had him thrown into a cistern to starve, until he was prepared to lead her to the place where the three crosses of Golgotha had been buried. When he saw the True Cross bring a dead man back to life, Judas became a Christian, changing his name to Cyriacus (Kyriakos—'dedicated to the Lord'), and went back to Italy with St Helen, where he became the first bishop of Ancona. After many years (in ?361) he returned to Palestine to carry out conversions, but was captured by the Roman governor, on behalf of the pagan emperor Julian, and gruesomely tortured: first, molten lead was poured into his mouth; then, after being liberally sprinkled with oil and salt, he was roasted on a grill, and beaten with a club at the same time. When these torments had no effect, he was placed in a cauldron of boiling oil. Still he refused to die, so a soldier cut his throat. Surprisingly, he came sailing back to Ancona again, perhaps in the 5th century. For the feast of their patron saint (4th May), the people of Ancona give one another bunches of reeds, sometimes plaited together, because they say a stone sarcophagus containing the body of Cyriacus floated into the harbour early one morning, and was drawn ashore by a reed rope. In 1979 the sarcophagus was opened, and was found to contain the 4th-century mummified body of a man aged about 60, with abundant traces of lead in the throat; a leg had been broken about 45 days before death, and the skull had received a heavy blow (probably the cause of death); the neck had also been cut.

The **crypt** under the chapel, which forms part of the old church, and is on the same level as the temple, contains the urns with the remains of the saints of Ancona—Cyriacus (centre), Liberius (left) and Marcellinus (right)—together with a vase containing the ashes of St Palatia. The right-hand arm of the cathedral, with the Chapel of the Crucifix, has been completely rebuilt, but notice the balustrade, made using 12th-century inlaid marble elements of the original one, with symbolic figures in intricate designs. The Crucifix is an 18th-century replacement of the original, destroyed in the Second World War, while the crypt underneath is the burial place of the bishops of Ancona; it gives access (*ask the priest or the sacristan*) to the

Sotterraneo, where you can see abundant traces of the preceding buildings. The **bell-tower**, to the right and a little in front of the cathedral, is completely separate from the main building, and was perhaps a medieval watch-tower. From this point there is a wonderful view over the rose-and-cream city of Ancona, surrounded by hills, with the harbour in the foreground.

From San Ciriaco to the Museo Archeologico

To the left of the cathedral, in the Episcopio, the old palace used by the bishops of the city from the 11th–18th centuries, and recently rebuilt, is situated the **Museo Diocesano** (*open May–Sept Sun and holidays 5–7; Oct–April Sun and holidays 4–6; T: 071 2074703*), illustrating in 15 rooms the vast panorama of religious art in Ancona from the 2nd century BC to the 19th century, including canvases, panel paintings and frescoes; wood, marble, terracotta and bronze statues; tapestries, silks, embroidery and religious robes; coins and medals; sarcophagi and engraved stones, and silverware. Of particular interest are the the richly carved 4th-century marble **sarcophagus of Gorgonius**, and four tapestries designed by Rubens. In front of the museum, steps lead down to a winding road (Via Giovanni XXIII) which reaches the port; immediately on the right are some Roman water-storage cisterns, one of which has a house on top of it, the *Casa del Boia*, house of the executioner, who lived here in the 19th century.

Just southeast of the cathedral is the **Roman Amphitheatre** (*T: 071 202602 to request visit, accompanied by museum staff only*), still under excavation; a Second World War bomb and the 1972 earthquake destroyed the monastery which stood over it, but it will never be possible to bring the entire structure to light, because of the 'sedimentation' of other buildings, by now also of historical importance, on top of it. Constructed in a breathtaking position overlooking the cliff, between the 1st century BC and 2nd century AD, and measuring c. 93m by 74m, it is thought there were seats for at least 8,000 people. As research continues, it is planned to create a large Archaeological Park to encompass much of the Guasco and San Cataldo (or Cappuccini) hills.

A few steps downhill from the amphitheatre is Piazza del Senato (originally the seat of the Roman Forum), with the remarkable old town hall, **Palazzo del Senato** (13th century), transformed and restored through the years, and now appearing more or less as it originally was, a lovely stone building with a double series of elegant lancet windows occupying the façade. Opposite is the church of **Santi Pellegrino e Teresa** (*open 7.30–12.30*), a round, Baroque church completed in 1738, with a large copper dome. Inside, on the main altar, is a well-preserved 12th-century wooden Crucifix.

Next to the church, at no. 6 Via Ferretti, is the **Museo Archeologico Nazionale delle Marche** (*open 8.30–7.30; closed Mon; T: 071 202602*), a particularly complete (especially the Picene exhibit) and beautifully displayed collection of objects ranging from the Palaeolithic, through the Bronze Age, to the Picene civilisation, the Celtic presence, the Roman domination and the early Middle Ages, all housed in the impressive rooms of the 16th-century Palazzo Ferretti. Built by the Mannerist architect Pellegrino Tibaldi, the palazzo is noted for the lovely ceilings, and is worth a visit in its own right. On the highest terrace of the palace is a copy of the famous group of gilded bronze statues known as the *Bronzi di Cartoceto* (1st century BC). Inside the museum you will see some more copies (not very good) of the group, but the originals are in the museum of Pergola (*see p. 250*). For a fuller understanding of the Marche, a visit to this museum is highly recommended.

The old city

Via Ferretti was the main street of old Ancona. It leads down from Colle Guasco, past a medieval tower and arch on the right, to Piazza Stracca and the dramatic ex-church of the **Gesù** (1665), with a lovely curving façade preceded by a double stairway, designed by Vanvitelli in 1743. Typical of the Counter-Reformation movement, it was the church of the Jesuits. Opposite is the 13th-century **Palazzo degli Anziani**, an impressive red-brick building, even more imposing when seen from the sea. Once the town hall, it is now used by the University as the Institute of Economics and Business Studies. Steps lead down from both sides of the palazzo to Piazza Dante Alighieri and the port.

From Piazza Stracca, the old main street continues down, as Via Pizzecolli, to Piazza San Francesco, and the 14th-century church of **San Francesco alle Scale**, sometimes called Santa Maria Maggiore; the lower part of the façade is cream plaster, surmounted by ochre-coloured brick, framing an outstanding Venetian-Gothic portal (1447) by Giorgio Orsini (*see p. 23*), white marble, with restrained, delicate carvings, and a baldachin on top. This beautiful church was humiliated when Napoleon came in 1798 and turned it into his barracks; later it was even used as a hospital. To the right of the façade are the remains of another beautiful portal, damaged in the war, which gave access to the convent (now destroyed). The interior of the church is a large single nave; in the apse is a canvas by Lorenzo Lotto of the *Assumption of the Madonna*, signed and dated 1550. It is interesting to compare this painting with that on the same subject that Lorenzo had painted two years before for the church of Santa Maria Assunta in Mogliano. Here the artist has eliminated all unnecessary detail, and uses even more subdued colours; he concentrates his attention on the Virgin, who is being carried up to Heaven; not on a fluffy cloud, but supported by cherubs, against a background of alarmingly black storm clouds. Around the tomb (now full of flower petals), disconcerted Apostles wave their arms, uselessly protesting. Over the first right-hand altar is the *Baptism of Christ* by Pellegrino Tibaldi, while over the first left-hand altar is a painting by Ancona-born artist Andrea Lilli of the *Holy House of Loreto*.

The Pinacoteca and Galleria Comunale

Continuing along Via Pizzecolli, at no. 17 is the aristocratic Palazzo Bosdari, now seat of the **Pinacoteca Francesco Podesti** (*open Tues–Sat 10–7, Sun, Mon 9–1; T: 071 2225040*), the city gallery of beautifully displayed old masters, consisting partly of the local artist Francesco Podesti's collection, bequeathed to the city on his death in 1895. Some of the outstanding works to be seen here are a *Madonna with Christ Child* (1470) by Carlo Crivelli, a tiny painting—'He used a paint brush with only one hair!' says the custodian—but full of the usual Crivelli symbolisms, the fruits and vegetables for resurrection, rebirth and the Passion, the goldfinch for the human soul, red and blue colours for the divine and the human nature of the mother and her Child. Mary is tweaking her Baby's foot—Jesus is apparently enjoying the sensation. Other works include a marvellous painting by Lorenzo Lotto called the *Pala dell'Alabarda* (1539; *pictured opposite*), where the artist, then still on the crest of the wave of his populari-ty, shows a charming Madonna accompanied by saints of Ancona, in a well-balanced composition; the lengthening shadows are those of sunset, but even the steps leading up to her throne look soft and gentle, not forbidding at all. Also represented in the collection are Guercino, Sebastiano del Piombo, Titian, Orazio Gentileschi, Giovanni Francesco Guerrieri, Carlo Maratta, and many others.

The same building also houses the modern art collection, **Galleria Comunale di Arte Moderna** (*same opening hours as above*), with about 300 works by local and Italian artists, including Adolfo de Carolis, Anselmo Bucci, Luigi Bartolini, Ivo Pannaggi, Aligi Sassu, Orfeo Tamburi, Pietro Annigoni, and Giò and Arnaldo Pomodoro.

Santa Maria di Piazza

Behind Palazzo Bosdari, Vicolo Foschi leads down to the elegant church of **Santa Maria di Piazza** (13th century), one of the most important monuments of the city. A frequently-seen feature of the buildings of Ancona, especially the churches, is the two-colour façade, ochre or brown brick for the top part, *a capanna*, literally 'like a hut', and white plaster or stone for the lower. In this case, the generously wide lower part is carved white marble, forming a triple series of little blind arches, some with figures of saints, angels, animals and birds, framing the scene-stealing portal, perhaps the loveliest in the Marche. Closer examination will reveal a wildly jungle-like Tree of Life twining around the outer arch, full of animals, birds, flowers, fruit and people, sym-bolically revealing human destiny under the benign gaze of Christ, all miraculously intact, and recently cleaned and restored. The interior, a central nave with two side aisles and a truss-beam ceiling, has a precious 16th-century wooden Crucifix over the main altar. The recent repairs have brought to light traces of two preceding churches on this spot, of the 5th and 6th centuries; parts of the mosaic floors are visible.

Outside the church, turn left along Via della Loggia, the high street of the medieval and Renaissance city, with several noteworthy 15th–16th-century palaces. At no. 5 is Palazzo Cresci-Antiqui, with a richly decorated Gothic portico; then on the right you will see the 15th-century, Venetian Gothic-style **Loggia dei Mercanti**, once the mer-chants' trading hall, with its own dock in front of it. The superb façade is by Giorgio Orsini (1451–59); in the loggia are statues representing the Cardinal Virtues (Fortitude, Temperance, Prudence and Charity); over the doorway is a knight on horseback brandishing a sword, the emblem of Ancona. Next to the loggia is the ele-gant façade of Palazzo Benincasa, built by wealthy 15th-century merchants, with two lines of Gothic double-lancet windows.

Lorenzo Lotto: *Pala dell'Alabarda* (1539).

Piazza della Repubblica and Piazza del Plebiscito

Piazza della Repubblica, in front of the main entrance to the port, is dominated by the newly-rebuilt opera house, **Teatro delle Muse** (*T: 071 207841, www.teatrodellemuse.org*), of 1827 and 2002, with 1,057 seats, excellent acoustics, and the latest theatre technology. The bas-relief in the tympanum represents *Apollo and the Nine Muses*. Opposite is the church of the **Santissimo Sacramento** (1538), with an unusual spiral cusp on top of the bell-tower, rebuilt after the 1930 earthquake, and repaired after that of 1972. The interior has a single nave surmounted by a wide dome; along the sides are statues of the Apostles by Gioacchino Varlé. This 18th-century sculptor was frequently requested by religious orders to assist in decorating their church interiors. He was prized for his skill in creating Rococo stucco details and carved wooden choirs, and for his angels and cherubs was considered unbeatable. The frescoes of the Evangelists under the dome were painted by Francesco Podesti in 1880, when he was already 80 years old. Among the other interesting works of art is a painting over the first north altar, by Filippo Bellini, of the *Sermon of the Baptist*.

By taking Via Gramsci, on the other side of the opera house, northeast out of the square, you will reach Piazza del Plebiscito, also known as *Piazza del Papa*, the favourite meeting-place of the people of Ancona, and often used for entertainment in the summer. It is a very elegant square, long and narrow, with houses finished in pink, yellow and apricot stucco, and with steps at the far end, leading up to the church of **San Domenico** (13th century and 1788), with an imposing—if unfinished—façade, the lower part in white stone, and the upper in hazelnut-coloured brick. The single-nave interior has eight side chapels, and statues and medallions of saints of the Dominican order, by Gioacchino Varlé. There are two important paintings in this church (stolen in 1972, they were fortunately recovered): in the apse, the *Crucifixion* by Titian (1558), austere and magnificent, one of his finest works; and over the first north altar, the *Annunciation* (1656) by the prolific Bolognese artist Guercino. The large convent of this church, now used as offices, was the seat of the Inquisition in the 16th century.

In front of the church is the statue of Pope Clement XII (1738), originally intended for the Arco Clementino in the port, and a semicircular fountain (19th century). The other fountain, to one side, goes back to the 15th century, and is decorated with a frieze of sculpted heads of local heroes, decapitated on this spot during the battle of 1532. To the left of the church is the **Arco di Garola** (1221), or Porta San Pietro, one of the few surviving fragments of the 13th-century fortifications, which gives access to Via Matteotti; there are still two lions' heads on it. To the right of the stairs is the ex-hospital of St Thomas à Becket (1394), incorporating the old fish market (1817), and now seat of the **Museo della Città** (*open June–Sept Sat, Sun 7–11; Oct–May Thur, Fri, Sat 10–1; Sat also 5–8, Sun 5–8; T: 071 2225037*), four really rooms illustrating the history of the city: from its earliest origins to the year 1000; from 1000–1532; from 1532–1700; and from the French occupation to the Unification of Italy.

On the south side of the square is the Prefecture, **Palazzo del Governo** (14th century, 1447, 1484 and restored after the Second World War), with a simple façade; to the left is the Arco Amoroso, giving access to the austere, beautiful courtyard, with a Gothic portico. Next to the palace is the clock tower (14th century), fitted with its clock in 1612. At no. 33 is Palazzo Mengoni-Ferretti (1592), housing the **Biblioteca Comunale Benincasa**, the city library, sadly depleted during the Second World War, but still consisting of 135,000 precious manuscripts, ancient volumes—including the famous geography book by Francesco Berlinghieri, printed in Florence in 1480—and 224 musical manuscripts of the 18th century. The library is said to be haunted by the ghost of a member of the Ferretti family with musical tastes. He can be heard playing the old piano in the director's office on certain nights of the year, but has never been seen. ·

Colle Astagno

In Piazza Kennedy, on the corner with Via Cialdini (the most important of the streets which climb up the Colle Astagno, or Capodimonte), is the church of **Sant'Agostino**, built by the Austin Fathers in 1338 as a gathering-place for travellers and pilgrims coming from Rome and from the coast, and enlarged by Vanvitelli in 1764. The splendid Venetian Gothic portal (1475; Giorgio Orsini) has some of the finest carvings of the period to be seen along the Adriatic, with baldachins and statues. Orsini, who was related to the patrician Roman family of the same name, is known on the other side of the Adriatic as George the Dalmatian (Juraj Dalmatinac). There are a number of works by his hand in Dubrovnik. His masterpiece here is the lunette, with *St Augustine Showing the Holy Scriptures to the Heretics*. The church, after being turned into a barracks in the 19th century, is now empty. Via Cialdini climbs steeply up the Astagno hill; close to the top, on the left, you will see the little Romanesque church of **San Giovanni**, severely damaged in the 1972 earthquake, as was most of this district. Inside is a beautiful canvas by Federico Zuccari of the *Ecce Homo*, a *Crucifixion* by Andrea Lilli, and a copy of the *Vision of the Blessed Gabriel Ferretti* by Carlo Crivelli, originally painted for this church, and now in the National Gallery of London.

On the top of the Astagno hill is the **Rocca**, or Citadel, built for Pope Clement VII in 1538 by Antonio da Sangallo the Younger. It will eventually house the offices of the Marche Region. At no. 12 Via Astagno, which runs parallel to Via Cialdini, in what was once the Jewish quarter, are two synagogues, one of Italian rite, the other Levantine, with beautiful old furnishings. At the height of its importance, in 1554, the community of Jewish merchants and craftsmen in Ancona numbered over 3,500.

From the port to the Passetto

From Piazza Repubblica and Piazza Kennedy depart three important parallel streets which go straight through the city, from east to west. The first is **Corso Mazzini**, where from Tuesday to Saturday the daily market for fruit, vegetables and fish is held in the morning, and where people congregate for the *passeggiata* in the evening. On the corner with Piazza Repubblica, the first building on the left on Corso Mazzini, is the huge Palazzo Jona, probably designed by Vanvitelli, now housing a particularly complete wine cellar. **Corso Garibaldi**, which becomes Viale della Vittoria (but the local people simply call the whole street *il Viale*), has expensive shops and many lovely little Art Nouveau villas. **Corso Stamira** (which becomes Via Piave and then Via

Trieste), leads to the Passetto, an airy, verdant modern district. Corso Stamira is named after a courageous widow, who during the Venetian siege of 1173 ran out from the city walls to re-ignite a primitive fire-bomb, a barrel of oil-soaked rags, which was rolled against the enemy war-machines; she is considered to be the heroine of Ancona.

These three streets pass first through the handsome Piazza Roma, with a beautiful fountain in the middle: four horses emerging from the rocks, together with playful dolphins, and a cupid on the top (18th century; Gioacchino Varlé). Close by is another lovely old fountain, Fontana del Calamo, with 13 spouts (1560; Pellegrino Tibaldi). Parallel to the fountain you can see a stretch of Roman road.

Piazza Cavour is next, a large square used as a bus station, but also for summer evening entertainment, and as a clothes market on Saturday and Tuesday mornings, with good quality merchandise. At the end of Viale della Vittoria, in Piazza IV Novembre, is the fanciful temple-like War Memorial (1933); at the foot of the cliff are beaches, which can be reached by stairs and an architecturally very interesting lift. Through the years, the local fishermen have carved a whole series of grottoes in the cliff face, to store their equipment; some of them are comfortable enough to live in.

The Homer Museum

The blind have a museum specially designed for their needs in Ancona, the **Museo Omero**, at 50 Via Tiziano, on the far side of the Citadel, no. 6 bus from Piazza Cavour (*open Tues–Sat and holidays 3.30–7.30; Sun 9.30–12.30 & 3.30–7.30; T: 071 2811935, www.museoomero.it*), where it is strictly forbidden NOT to touch the exhibits. The only one of its kind in Italy, the galleries display plaster models of all the most famous sculptures, from ancient to modern times, many of them actual size, together with models of important works of architecture. The **railway station** is also in this modern district; if you are there, don't miss the chapel, furnished entirely with objects coming from the railway: the holy water stoup is supported by a piece of track, the sacristy is an old-fashioned 2nd-class carriage, even the toilet comes from an old train.

The Cardeto Park

An interesting walk leads from Piazza Malatesta, along Via Cardeto, to a previously neglected cliff, now a park, on Colle Cardeto—literally, the Hill of the Thistles. Immersed in the maquis vegetation is a beautiful old lighthouse, the **Faro**, with an open-air theatre, the old **Jewish Cemetery** (facing Jerusalem, some tombs go back to the 15th century), the 19th-century **Polveriera**, or powder magazine, now an auditorium, the new lighthouse, and, at the foot of the cliff, an ancient mooring-place.

ANCONA'S CASTLES

On the coast west of Ancona are the sandy beaches of Torrette and Palombina, then **Falconara Marittima**, immediately recognisable by its oil refinery. This is in fact the most intensely industrialised area of the Marche, and it is also the site of the only airport in the region, and an important road and rail junction. In spite of this, the long sandy beach makes it a popular bathing resort, and it is not without charm. Two kilometres inland, on a hill, is the old city of **Falconara**, in a panoramic position dominating the Esino Valley, the coast, and Ancona. Falconara developed around the medieval castle of the Cortesi family, which certainly goes back to before the 13th century, and was later to prove an essential part of the defensive system of Ancona. Now somewhat drastically restored, it is used as the town hall and a multi-functional cultural centre, while the subterranean chambers house a museum, the Museo della Resistenza (*open Fri and Sat 5–7, or on request; T: 071 9166490*) on Piazza Carducci, exhibiting the arsenal and equipment of a band of partisans of the Apennines, together with documentation on the 1944 Liberation.

Just behind the airport, on the Chiaravalle–Jesi road, is **Castelferretti**, with the only example in the Marche of a Gonzaga-style (ie four-tower) castle, built in 1386 by Francesco Ferretti, a nobleman from Ancona. A square building, with square towers on the sides, it is similar (but on a much smaller scale) to structures in Mantua and Ferrara. Near the cemetery is the church of Santa Maria della Misericordia, with a dazzling series of 15th-century frescoes.

Offagna was one of the castles erected between the Musone and the Esino rivers to defend the city from the interior. Its aim was to frustrate the bellicose intentions of neighbouring Osimo. The windy old castle (1456), in Piazza del Maniero, is still formidable, its turrets all neatly in place; it looks wonderful at sunset. Now it houses a collection of weapons, the Museo delle Armi (*open 1–30 June Sat, Sun 10–12 & 4.30–7.30; 1 July–31 Aug 10–12 & 5–8; 1–15 Sept 10–12 & 4.30–7.30; 16–30 Sept 9–12.30 & 2.30–7.30; T: 071 710552*). Close by, in Via del Monastero, is an interesting museum dedicated to the various natural habitats of the Marche: rivers, mountains, hills, caves and coast, the Museo Luigi Paolucci (*open 1 Oct–31 May Thur–Sat 9–12, Sun and holidays 10–12 & 4–7; June and Sept 4.30–7.30, Sun and holidays 10–12 & 4.30–7.30; July and Aug 10–12 & 4.30–7.30; closed Mon; T: 071 7107611*). Offagna is an important centre for the production of DOC Rosso Conero wine; there is also an ostrich farm.

A little further west, **Polverigi**, remembered for the *Pace di Polverigi*, a peace treaty among the Guelph-Ghibelline cities of the Marche, signed here in the castle on 18th January 1202, is now well-known for hams and salami. At **Agugliano**, with sweeping views embracing much of the region, the bakers make such delicious bread that people come from Ancona to buy it. Closer to the Esino is **Camerata Picena**, a perfectly circular 14th-century castle, with a complex system of man-made caves and tunnels underneath; the inhabitants make very good cheese. The whole area is known as *Terra dei Castelli*, the Land of Castles.

THE CONERO PENINSULA

The strange, unmistakable limestone outcrop of Mount Conero (572m), just south of Ancona, and a landmark from most of the region, is protected as a nature reserve.

PARCO NATURALE DEL CONERO

Visitor centre: 30/a Via Peschiera, Sirolo; T: 071 9331879.

The park has many unique features: the lovely coastline with its typical vegetation and important wildlife; the rock formations (geologically the oldest in the region); its historical traces (people have been living on this mountain for at least 100,000 years); the traditions and occupations of the inhabitants; and the charming little towns. Eighteen nature trails of various degrees of difficulty have been laid out and signposted in the park, which covers over 600 hectares of Rosso Conero vineyards, olive groves, wheat, lavender, sunflowers, and rows of mulberry trees. The park also covers the only brackish-water coastal lakes remaining in the Marche, some breathtaking cliffs, and isolated beaches. This is just the place for birdwatchers, especially during the spring passage (Feb–April). The name derives from Greek, and means 'Mountain of Strawberry Trees'. Not many people were optimistic about this park when it was created in 1988, because of its nearness to the city, and because it is enclosed by the railway and the motorway, but the results have been excellent—the peregrine falcon flies again—and the presence of the park has made a big difference to the local economy.

Portonovo and Sirolo

When arriving from Ancona, the first place you reach is **Portonovo** (EU Blue Banner for clean sea), a beach of white stones, with a Napoleonic fort, Fortino Napoleonico (1810), built to dissuade British ships which used to stop here to stock up with spring water, now transformed into a comfortable hotel, and an 18th-century watch-tower, the Torre de Bosis, or Torre Clementina. Close by is a small, outstandingly beautiful church, **Santa Maria di Portonovo** (*should be open summer Fri, Sat, Sun 4–7*), of 1034–48, surrounded by olive trees. Unfortunately this precious gem, built by the Benedictines together with an abbey (now destroyed) in what was for centuries a totally isolated place, of the kind the monastic orders favoured, is now on private property, and it is almost impossible to visit. (*You can try asking at the Tourist Office in Ancona, or 'Italia Nostra', T: 071 56301 or 335 5316456. Good luck.*) The style is pure Romanesque, practically unique in Italy, although there are some like it in Normandy (Cérisy-la-Forêt) and in Corsica: the wonderful thing is that nobody has altered it over the centuries. The material is white stone, with red roof tiles, a Byzantine-style cupola, and a delightful series of little blind arcades going all the way around. The abbey was abandoned in the 14th century, when the monks became worried about rock falls from the cliff. For many years the church was used as a sheep-pen, but it has emerged remarkably unscathed. Close to the sea, on the other side of the fort, is the largest of the coastal lakes, Lago Grande, crowded with waterfowl during the migratory passages.

South of the mountaintop is **Sirolo**, on the cliff, with steep paths and steps going down through the maquis vegetation to the sandy beaches below; in summer there is

The beautiful sweep of sandy beach at Sirolo.

also a shuttle-bus service from the square. Sirolo has the EU Blue Banner for clean sea-water and beaches, and is often declared 'the most beautiful village of the Adriatic'. The lovely setting is unrivalled, and the little centre is traffic-free and well cared-for. Archaeologists have found traces of human habitation dating back 100,000 years, and in 1989 a Picene burial ground was discovered at I Pini (*T: 071 9331162, Numana Antiquarium, to request visit*), and is still being explored. The intact tomb has been brought to light of a Picene queen (6th century BC), who was buried together with two chariots and a rich grave treasure, including her sumptuous bed, inlaid with ivory and amber, fine vases and dishes, and a Greek *phiale*, a gold and silver dish for ritual offerings. The grave is circular, 40m in diameter, and is surrounded by a ditch, 4m wide; the queen's dress was richly decorated with glass and amber beads, and bronze threads; so far almost 2,000 of her ornaments and jewellery have been recovered (*finds on display in Numana; see overleaf*).

Sirolo was the seat of the Cortesi family, until its castle passed to Ancona in 1225. Piazza Vittorio Veneto is the tiny main square; next to it is the panoramic Piazzale Marino. On the right is the church of the Santissimo Sacramento, with the original 15th-century portal, surmounted by a carved relief of the *Madonna with Christ Child*. Corso Italia terminates in Piazza Henriquez, with the Torrione (1050), all that remains of the old castle. Next to it is the opera house, Teatro Cortesi (*T: 071 9330952*), of 1875, with 220 seats. In summer, an open-air theatre just out of town on the mountainside is used: Teatro alle Cave (*Strada del Monte, T: 071 2077190*). It was once an old quarry.

Numana

Still further south is Numana, a fishing village on the hillside, with colourful, pictur-esque little houses, and an EU Blue Banner bathing resort below, with lovely sandy beaches. Probably founded by the Sicels, Numana was an important base for the Greeks in the 8th century BC, and later became a Picene stronghold, and a Roman port. Nothing remains of the old city, which is thought to have disappeared under the sea after an earthquake in 558; although it was rebuilt, part of the town slipped into the sea again during the earthquake of 1292. In the central Piazza del Santuario is the elegant ex-Palazzo del Municipio (1773; once the summer residence of the bishops of Ancona) and the modern **Santuario del Crocifisso**; over the main altar is a mysteri-ous, very impressive life-size painted wooden Crucifix (*see box*).

CHARLEMAGNE'S CRUCIFIX

The Crucifix of Numana is thought by some scholars to be a 14th-century Byzantine carving; by others to be a Polish work, while another—probably legendary—explanation says that this is the Crucifix carved by Luke and Nicodemus as Christ was dying, using a trunk of cedar of Lebanon. On the death of St Nicodemus, the Cross was taken to Beirut; in the 8th century a man tried to chop it up for firewood, and it bled; a glass phial of the blood is still kept in St Mark's in Venice. Charlemagne was given some of the blood, and on finding that it miracu-lously healed wounded soldiers, he went to Beirut and persuaded Haroun el-Rashid to give him the Crucifix, which he probably intended to take to Rome. Returning home, however, his ship narrowly escaped disaster during a tremendous storm, so the emperor left the Crucifix at Numana, as an ex-voto, in gratitude for his life. Yet another story says that the Crucifix was fished from the sea-bed in the fishermen's nets. Often called the '*Crocifisso di Sirolo*', because in the Middle Ages Sirolo was much more important than Numana, an old proverb says: *Se vai a Loreto e non vai a Sirolo, vedi la Madre e non vedi il Figliolo* (If you go to Loreto and you don't go to Sirolo, you'll see the Mother but you won't see her Son).

On the other side of the Palazzo del Municipio is Via La Fenice, where at no. 4 the archaeological collections of Numana and the Conero area are housed at the **Antiquarium** (*open 8.30–7.30; T: 071 9330585*), one of the most complete museums of the Picene era in the region, definitely not to be missed. Numana has yielded more Picene tombs (over 2,000) than any other area in the Marche, and the well displayed finds from the burials give an excellent idea of the evolution of these people from the 9th to the 3rd centuries BC. One of the most interesting sections is that dedicated to the rich contents (including her two chariots, household goods, and some of her personal ornaments) of the 'Tomb of the Queen' at Sirolo, where excavations are still in progress (*see p. 27 above*). A rare fragment of Picene sculpture, a 7th-century BC marble head known as the *Warrior of Numana*, is displayed together with drawings which give a better understanding of the unusual decorations on his helmet. An exhibition of photographs and drawings explains how the particular position of Numana made it the ideal harbour for the Picenes, contributing to the wealth of its inhabitants.

From Numana you can take the ferry (Traghettatori Riviera del Conero, *11 Via Peschiera, T: 071 9331795*) to reach some of the otherwise inaccessible beaches, like Le Due Sorelle, renowned for its beauty, or Sirolo and Portonovo.

Camerano

On the west slope of Mt Conero is Camerano, famous for the tunnels and caves carved into the sandstone under the town. These *Grotte* (*open 14 June–18 Sept Sat, Sun 5.30 & 6.30; 19 Sept–13 June Sat, Sun 4 & 5; guided tours only; T: 071 7304018*) follow the plan of the streets above them. Their age and purpose is unknown, and many of them are decorated with carvings. According to a local saying: *ce n'è più sotto che sopra*, 'there's more of the town underneath than there is on top'. In the large, rectangular central square, Piazza Roma, is a bronze bust dedicated to the local-born painter Carlo Maratti. Maratti (better known as Carlo Maratta) became one of the most prolific Counter-Reformation artists working in Rome. From the square, Via San Francesco leads to the imposing church of San Francesco (13th century, *usually closed*), preceded by a double stairway, and said to have been founded by St Francis in person in 1215. Camerano is the most important centre for the production of the DOC Rosso Piceno wine.

PRACTICAL INFORMATION

GETTING AROUND

• **By train:** Ancona railway station (T: 071 45521) is on the main Bologna–Pescara line; the best station for Numana and Sirolo is Osimo (10km, T: 071 781195).

• **By bus:** Ancona city buses (ATMA) leave from the railway station; they also reach the Conero Peninsula.
Bus stations for the companies listed below are at Piazza Cavour, Piazza

Stamira and Piazza Ugo Bassi.
City and local buses: Services within
the city, and to Falconara, Ostra,
Chiaravalle, Senigallia, Morro d'Alba,
Osimo, Filottrano, Jesi, Recanati and
Loreto; summer services to Portonovo
(no.94) are run by Conero Bus, T: 071
2802092.
Services to Loreto, Recanati, Macerata,
Camerino, San Severino Marche,
Matelica and Fabriano are run by
Autolinee Binni, T: 0732 629592/4.
Services to Falconara, Chiaravalle, Jesi,
Ostra and Macerata are run by
Autolinee Crognaletti, T: 0731 204965,
www.autolineecrognaletti.it
Services to Senigallia, Ostra, Jesi,
Arcevia and Corinaldo are run by
Autolinee Fratelli Bucci, T: 071
7922737.
Year-round services to Camerano, Sirolo
and Porto Recanati; June–Sept also
Portonovo, Numana, Senigallia, Fano,
Pesaro, Rimini, Como and Chiasso are
run by Autolinee Reni, T: 071 8046504,
www.paginegialle.it/reni-srl
Services to Chiaravalle, Jesi and the
Esino Valley are run by SACSA, T: 0731
56536.
Services to Falconara, Chiaravalle, Jesi,
Fabriano, Arcevia, Pergola, Fano and
Pesaro are run by Autolinee Vitali, T:
0721 862515,
www.autolineevitali.191.it

INFORMATION OFFICES

There are good websites for this area:
www.conero.it; www.rivieradelconero.it;
www.coneromyst.com;
www.misaesinofrasassi.it;
www.moscioli.com (news and info on
events). There are offices at:

Ancona APTR, 4 Via Thaon de Revel,
T: 071 358991,
www.provincia.ancona.it; for informa-
tion on the museums of the province,
T: 071 64249, www.sistemamuseale.
provincia.ancona.it. **Tourist
Information Bureau**: Palazzo
Camerata, 9 Via Fanti, T: 071
2225066/67, www.comune.ancona.it
and Piazza Roma, T: 349 2149129. At
the port: IAT, Stazione Marittima,
T: 071 201183, summer only.
Camerano IAT, 22 Via Maratti, T: 071
7304018 & 071 731460; **Municipio**,
Ufficio Turismo, 24 Via San Francesco,
T: 071 7303058, www.comune.
camerano.an.it
Falconara Marittima IAT, Raffaello
Sanzio International Airport, T: 071
9156033, summer only; **IAT**, Via
Litoranea, T: 071 910458, summer
only; **Municipio**, T: 071 9166476,
www.comune.falconara-marittima.an.it
Numana IAT, Piazza del Santuario, T:
071 9330612, summer only; **Tourist
Information Bureau**, 59 Via Venezia,
T: 071 7390521.
Sirolo IAT, Via Peschiera, T: 071
9330611, summer only; **Tourist
Information Bureau**, Via Giulietti, T:
071 7390521; Parco Naturale Regionale
del Conero, 30 Via Peschiera, T: 071
9331161, www.parcoconero.it.

HOTELS

Some hotels in this area are taking a
stand to protect the environment by
reducing waste and refuse, recycling,
using organic, non-GM foods in the
restaurants, etc. They are described in
this list as eco-friendly.
Ancona

€€€€ **Grand Hotel Palace**. Situated between the port and the old centre, comfortable and elegant hotel, 16th-century building, roof garden, car park, no restaurant, shuttle-bus to private beach. 24 Lungomare Vanvitelli, T: 071 201813, www.hotelancona.it

€€€€ **Grand Hotel Passetto**. Luxurious, modern hotel in panoramic position. 1 Via Thaon de Revel, T: 071 31307, www.hotelpassetto.it

€€€ **City**. Elegant, central, car park, no restaurant. 112 Via Matteotti, T: 071 2070949.

€€€ **Fortuna**. Comfortable hotel in front of station, central, car park next door, no restaurant. 15 Piazza Rosselli, T: 071 4266, www.hotelfortuna.it

€€ **Viale**. Comfortable little hotel in villa, excellent value for money. 23 Viale della Vittoria, T: 071 201861, www.hotelviale.it

Agugliano

€€€ **Al Belvedere**. Panoramic position, restaurant, car park and garden. 3 Piazza Vittorio Emanuele, T: 071 90719, www.hotelalbelvedere.it

Camerano

€€€€ **Hotel Concorde**. Just right for the spa, with a restaurant and car park. 191 Aspio Terme, T: 071 95270, www.albergoconcorde.it

€€ **Strologo**. Central position, with a good restaurant. 89 Via Guasto, T: 071 95190.

Falconara Marittima

€€€ **Avion**. With a garden, restaurant, tennis and car park. Convenient for the airport. 6 Via delle Caserme, T: 071 9170444, hotel.avion@tin.it

€€€ **Villa Amalia**. Small quiet hotel with garden, Art Nouveau villa, with a famous restaurant. 4 Via degli Spagnoli,

T: 071 9160550, www.villa-amalia.it

Numana

€€€€ **Numana Palace**. On the lovely beach of Numana, in the Conero Park. With a very good restaurant, two pools, sauna, gym. 10 Via Litoranea, T: 071 7390155 f 071 7391160, www.hotelnumanapalace.com

€€€ **Eden Gigli**. Modern hotel on a cliff-top position, with private beach and pool, gym, restaurant and car park. Eco-friendly. 11 Via Morelli, T: 071 9330652, www.giglihotels.com

Portonovo

€€€€ **Emilia**. ■ Lovely hotel immersed in the vegetation of the Conero Park, with a private beach, garden, tennis, car park, good restaurant and internet. 149 Via Collina di Portonovo, T: 071 801145, www.hotelemilia.com

€€€ **Fortino Napoleonico**. ■ Undoubtedly one of the most unusual hotels in the region, it was once a fort (1810). Has a renowned restaurant, private beach, gym, tennis, garden, pool. Eco-friendly. 166 Via Poggio, T: 071 801450, www.hotelfortino.it;

€€€ **Internazionale**. In a peaceful hillside position, this stone building has a restaurant and car park. Eco-friendly. Collina di Portonovo, T: 071 801082, www.hotel-internazionale.com

Sirolo

€€€ **Conchiglia Verde**. Pleasant modern hotel, with a good restaurant, garage, garden and lovely pool. 12 Via Giovanni XXIII, T: 071 9330018, www.conchigliaverde.it

€€€ **Locanda Rocco**. Tiny inn on the 14th-century walls, close to the path down to beach, good restaurant. Eco-friendly. 1 Via Torrione, T: 071

9330558, www.locandarocco.it

€€€ Monteconero. Converted 11th-century Benedictine abbey of San Pietro on the top of Mt Conero, with wonderful views, pool, tennis, private beach, restaurant; perfect for trekkers. Eco-friendly. 26 Via Monteconero, T: 071 9330592, www.hotelmonteconero.it

€€€ Panoramic. Lovely little hotel, immersed in the vegetation, with restaurant, garden and pool. 8 Via San Michele, T: 071 9330659, www.mapoweb.it

€€€ Sirolo. New round hotel close to the village square, very comfortable, with a good restaurant serving organic food. Also has a garden, pool and car park. Eco-friendly. 26 Via Grilli, T: 071 9330665.

€€ Il Parco. On the hillside close to the centre, closed Nov–Feb, with a simple restaurant. 58 Via Giulietti, T: 071 9330733, winter T: 071 9331960, www.hotelilparco.it

€ Hotel Arturo. Simple accommodation right on the beach, with a restaurant; open June–Sept only. Via Spiaggia, T: 071 9330975, winter T: 071 7360641, info@conerohotels.it

BED & BREAKFAST

Massignano (Mt Conero Park)
B&B Colle Lauro. In a comfortable villa. English and French spoken. 110 Via Betelico, T: 071 731897, www.collelauro.com
La Biancarda. Nice house with garden. English, German and French spoken. Airport transfer on request. 139 Via La Biancarda, T: 071 2800503, biancarda@libero.it

FARM ACCOMMODATION

Marcelli di Numana
Le Grange del Conero. Open all year, this comfortable farm raises horses. 31/16 Via Marina II, T: 071 7391041, www.legrangedelconero.com
Massignano del Conero
Il Corbezzolo. Open summer only, farm raising horses in the heart of the park; trekking. 124 Via Piancarda, T: 071 2139039.
Offagna
L'Arcobaleno. Panoramic farm producing only organic, non-GM crops. 18th-century farmhouse, comfortable rooms, very good food, mostly home-grown (they keep their own bees too), vegetarian dishes a speciality. Closed winter. 10 Via Torre, T: 071 7107567.
Sirolo
Il Ritorno. The farm raises horses, for which it is famous. Comfortable rooms in this traditional farmhouse; meals on request. 12 Via Piani d'Aspio, Località Coppo, T: 071 9331544, www.ilritorno.com

ROOMS & APARTMENTS TO RENT

Camerano
Il Girasole. Rooms to rent over a good restaurant; home-made bread. 277/279 Via Loretana, T: 071 7304033, www.immobiliare-adriatica.it
Numana
Bar Morelli. Good value for money, rooms over a charming coffee house, open year round. 5 Via Flaminia, T: 071 9330697.
Villa Pucci. Lovely rooms; open year round.4 Via Colombo, summer T: 071 9331486, winter T: 071 9330699.

Sirolo
Residence Il Granaio di Valcastagno.
The grain stores of Villa Virginia (18th
century) have been transformed into 10
luxury apartments, just right for a quiet
holiday in a lovely setting. 12 Contrada
Valcastagno, T: 071 7391580,
www.valcastagno.it

RESTAURANTS

Ancona
€€€ **Al Rosso Agontano**. Bustling
modern restaurant with interesting
food; the menu changes regularly.
Closed Sun and Sat lunchtime. 3 Via
Marconi, T: 071 2075279.
€€€ **La Moretta**. Opened in 1897,
and always famous for fish. Lovely in
the summer when you eat out in the
square. Closed Sun. 52 Piazza
Plebiscito, T: 071 202317.
€€€ **Passetto**. Built in 1949, the
restaurant looks like a birthday cake
with the candles on the top. Renowned
for the delicious cuisine, especially fried
fish; good wine list. Closed Sun evening
and Mon. 1 Piazza IV Novembre, T:
071 33214.
€€€ **Sot'Aj Archi**. In front of the port,
small very refined restaurant specialising in fish dishes. Don't be afraid to
order the red Rosso Conero with your
fish, they go very well together. Closed
Sun. 93 Via Marconi, T: 071 202441.
€€ **Gino**. Very well prepared food,
prize-winning dishes; eat outside in the
square in summer. Closed Sun. 26
Piazza Rosselli, T: 071 43310.
€€ **Osteria Teatro Strabacco**. Near
Piazza Roma and the port, rub shoulders
with celebrities at this informal tavern
for tasty snacks or a wide assortment of

more satisfying traditional dishes. Great
fun in summer when you can eat out in
the street. Amazing wine list. Closed
Mon. 2 Via Oberdan, T: 071 56748.
€€ **Traiano**. ■ Perfect local tradition,
fish soup Ancona-style, squid with
peas, mixed fried fish. Closed Wed. 6/a
Via XXIX Settembre, T: 071 205540.
€€ **La Barca sul Tetto**. Near the customs house in the port, almost submerged by trucks and cranes, an unmis-
takeable blue and white pre-fab building with red window frames—and one
of the best places in Ancona for fish. No
tablecloths, no frills; excellent home-
made desserts and local wines. Closed
Tues. Banchina da Chio, T: 071 55198.
€€–€ **La Cantineta**. No-fuss restaurant dear to the hearts of the people of
Ancona; close to the entrance to the
port, very fresh fish and generous portions. *Stoccafisso all'Anconetana* (dried
cod) and *brodetto all'Anconetana* (the
local fish soup, made with 13 different
kinds of fish from the Adriatic) are
served every day. Finish off with a cup
of *turchetto*, a mixture of coffee, rum
and sugar. Booking advisable even at
lunchtime. The *stoccafisso* is not easy to
prepare, every year there is a competition among the city restaurants for a
coveted diploma, awarded to the best.
The taste for dried cod goes back to the
days when ships from Ancona went
trading in the North Sea. Closed Mon.
1/c Via Gramsci, T: 071 201107.
Falconara Marittima
€€€ **Villa Amalia**. Romantic Art
Nouveau building with veranda, classic
dishes; superb *passatelli* in fish broth;
they also make delicious apple cake,
served warm with cinnamon ice cream.
Closed Tues, Sun evening in winter. 4

Via degli Spagnoli, T: 071 9160550.
€€ **L'Arnia del Cuciniere**. Delicious *antipasti*, seafood salad; try the soft rum ice cream with amaretto sauce. Choose Verdicchio dei Castelli di Jesi from the Bravi cellars. 9 Via della Repubblica, T: 071 9160055.
€ **Ortica Pub**. Very good value for money at this pub, where you can drink a glass of beer or wine accompanied by nettles cooked in many different ways, or more traditional dishes if you prefer. Closed Sun. 9 Via Repubblica, T: 071 9160055.
Marcelli di Numana
€€€ **Il Saraghino**. Elegant restaurant serving delicious, imaginative dishes. Closed Mon. 209 Via Litoranea, T: 071 7391596.
Numana
€€€ **Costarella**. Very refined cuisine, beautifully served (lots of steps to get there). Closed Nov–Mar. 35 Via IV Novembre, T: 071 7360297.
€€ **Eugenio**. A simple kiosk on the beach, for delightful lunches; try the seafood salad. Closed Mon. 5 Via Litoranea, T: 071 9330026
€€ **Il Saraghino**. Small restaurant on the beach, attentive service, delightful *antipasto*. Closed Nov–Feb. 209 Via Litoranea, T: 071 7391596.
Portonovo
€€€–€ **Clandestino Susci Bar**. ■ Memorable sushi, Italian-style, as invented by Moreno Cedroni. Late evening, rum and Cuban cigars. Closed Oct–Apr. On the beach, T: 071 801422.
€€€ **Il Fortino Napoleonico**. Fish dishes served in beautiful surroundings; prize-winning chef. Closed Mon in winter. 166 Via Poggio, T: 071 801450.
€€ **Il Laghetto**. In a lovely position,

this little restaurant offers superb antipasto of fish and vegetables, spaghetti or local home-made tagliatelle, grilled or fried fish, accompanied by local wines. Contrada Portonovo (on the beach), T: 071 801183, closed winter.
€€ **Mafalda**. Delightful little restaurant, delicious simple cooking. Closed Wed. Just inland from Portonovo at Poggio, T: 071 2139024.
€€ **Osteria del Poggio**. Opened more than 100 years ago, legendary tavern, cosy open fireplaces in winter, soup is on the menu year round. Delightful variations on the theme of fish, vegetables, pasta or meat, accompanied by local wines. They often organise musical evenings in summer. Closed Wed. 149 Frazione Poggio, T: 071 2139018.
Sirolo
€€€ **Le Azalee del Conero**. Not easy to find, the restaurant is a chalet in a pinewood just outside the town. Absolutely marvellous fish, imaginatively presented. Closed Mon. 1 Via Molinella, T: 071 9331874.
€€ **Il Grottino**. Very central, lots of atmosphere, original dishes and good wine list. Closed midday Tues and Thur. 9 Via Ospedale, T: 071 9331218.
Torrette
€€ **Carloni**. This restaurant has its own fishing boat; excellent *brodetto all'anconetana*, or *raviolini di pesce*; choose Rosso Conero to accompany your fish. Closed Mon, except in Aug. 247 Via Flaminia, T: 071 888239.

CAFÉS & PASTRY SHOPS

Ancona
Alla Tazza d'Oro. One of the oldest coffee houses in the city; superb espres-

so. Closed Sun. 134 Corso Garibaldi.
Bottega del Caffè. Family run, courteous service, excellent coffee, roasted on the premises. Closed Sun. 122 Corso Garibaldi.
Caffè Giuliani. Traditional old coffee house, great for morning cappuccino or Sunday brunch. Closed Sat. 3 Corso Garibaldi.
Cremeria Rosa. ■ Excellent ice cream, also fantastic fruit salads. 61 Corso Mazzini. Closed Sun.
Liberty. Elegant Art Nouveau cocktail bar. 7 Via del Traffico.
Falconara Marittima
Caffè Bedetti. Home-made nougat, ice cream, cakes and biscuits. Closed Mon. 560 Via Flaminia.
Numana
Bar Morelli. ■ Café specialising in home-made ice cream, try the delicious dessert *taglio al caffè*. Also rooms to rent. 5 Via Flaminia.
Sirolo
Caffè Centrale. Home-made ice cream, and cocktails in the evening. Closed Wed. 8 Corso Italia.

FESTIVALS & EVENTS

Ancona Feast of St Cyriacus, 1–4 May; Ancona Jazz Nov–July; Info from Spaziomusica, T: 071 2074239.
Camerano *Festa del Rosso Conero* is held in Sept with festivities to celebrate the grape harvest.
Numana Feast of Christ the King, a solemn procession accompanies the Crucifix from the parish church, Santuario del Crocifisso, to the port, last Sun in Nov.
Offagna *Feste Medievali*, the whole village becomes a medieval setting for

music and dancing, plays, exhibitions and contests, not to be missed; Info: T: 339 1604215 or Pro Loco, 17 Piazza del Maniero, T: 071 7107552, www.festemedievali.it. July.
Polverigi International Festival of Theatre, Music and Dance; Info: T: 071 9090007, www.inteatro.it. July.
Sirolo Feast of St Nicholas of Bari, 9 May; in summer there are plays and music in the open air at the *Teatro alle Cave*.

LOCAL SPECIALITIES

Ancona
Bontà delle Marche, 96 Corso Mazzini, T: 071 53985, sells wines, olive oil, cheeses and hams, including the rare smoked salami. **Enoteca Mimotti**, 42 Via Grazie, T: 071 2802359, has a vast selection of wines, olive oil, honey and cheeses. **Franca Angeloni**, at 18 Piazza del Plebiscito (in front of La Moretta restaurant), is a shop where linen, hemp and cotton are woven on the spot. **Grosi Gioielli**, 5 Via Orefici, T: 071 202324, is the place for handmade jewellery, also antique pieces. **La Stilografica**, 55 Corso Garibaldi, T: 071 203377, sells unbelievably beautiful fountain pens. **Re Formaggio**, 10 Piazza Kennedy, T: 071 201771, for olive oil, wine, cheese, ham, salami, honey and sweets from the Marche.
Montacuto di Ancona (Conero Park) Alessandro Moroder, 112 Via Montacuto, T: 071 898232, for DOC Rosso Conero wine.
Portonovo
Azienda Agricola Amelia Guglielmi, 131 Frazione Poggio, T: 071 801161, for essential oil of lavender.

JESI & THE ESINO VALLEY

Situated on a low hill overlooking the Esino river, is Jesi (97m, population 40,000). The inhabitants say deprecatingly, 'It's too cold in winter, and too hot in summer', but they are secretly proud of their ancient ochre-coloured town, with its intact walls, towers and bastions; its opera house, art gallery, elegant cafés and genial goldsmiths; its eight libraries, and some of the best-stocked bookshops in the region. Not only bookworms, however, they have excellent sports facilities too, including a fencing academy which has produced Olympic champions. Add to this the fact that they live in the birthplace of the Holy Roman Emperor Frederick II of Hohenstaufen, and the pride of the people of Jesi is understandable.

HISTORY OF JESI

The origin of ancient *Aesis* is lost in legend: some say it was founded by Umbrians, led by a king who had a lion on his banner, his personal totem. The settlement certainly became an important Roman colony from 247 BC. Conquered and destroyed, first by the Goths and then by the Lombards, in 756 it was donated to the Church, then taken by Charlemagne, and donated to the Church again in 999, finally becoming an independent commune in the 12th century. Jesi flourished under the Swabians, because Frederick II (*see box opposite*) was born in the city; it supported the Ghibelline cause until 1305, when it returned to the Church. The following two hundred years saw the city alternating between pope and emperor; fighting first Fabriano, then Ancona, then Fabriano again; besieged and attacked many times; passing from the Malatesta to Braccio da Montone, from the Sforza to the Malatesta once more; until 1512 when it was attacked and despoiled by the duke of Urbino, Francesco Maria della Rovere, who was fighting the Church. Rebuilt, in 1586 the city was accorded the status of semi-independent government, headed by a prelate chosen by the pope; commerce and industry flourished; silk and ropes from Jesi were exported far and wide. The *Respublica Aesina* came to an end in 1797, when Napoleon's troops entered the walls.

Jesi was one of the first cities in Italy to introduce the printing press; in 1472 Federico de' Conti from Verona printed the first edition of Dante's *Divine Comedy*. Its farms produce wine (the famous Verdicchio), fruit and vegetables. Local industries manufacture sugar, farm machinery, clothing, woollen cloth and food products. Gold and jewellery from Jesi are renowned.

EXPLORING JESI

The walls are particularly impressive when seen from Via Garibaldi, where there are houses built on top of them, and you can still see the corbels. About 1500m long, they are the old Roman fortifications, strengthened in the 14th century, and then again in 1488 by Baccio Pontelli. From Porta Garibaldi, the steep Via del Fortino leads to the central Piazza Federico II, corresponding to the Roman forum, with an ugly obelisk-fountain in the middle, on the spot where Frederick II was born.

STUPOR MUNDI

'The wonder of the world' is what his contemporaries called Frederick II of Hohenstaufen, for his many skills, ranging from languages (he could speak six), mathematics, astronomy, astrology, music, literature (he was the founder of the 'Sicilian School' which flourished at his court in Palermo; the first writers to use the Italian language in literature), the building of castles, hunting (his fundamental text on falconry, *De arti venandi cum avibus*, is still in the Vatican Library), to the fine arts of diplomacy. He was born quite by chance in Jesi, on 26th December 1194, because his mother, Constance de Hauteville, was travelling from Milan to Sicily to join her husband. She chose to give birth in the main square, under a canopy, so that the matrons of Jesi could witness the fact that the baby was really hers; gossip and speculation were rife; there was even a prophecy that the Antichrist was about to be born. Nine years earlier, Constance, as the last Norman princess of Sicily, had been brought out of a cloistered convent in order to marry the unpleasant, dissolute Henry IV of Swabia, eleven years her junior. Now she was 40, and this was her first child. Henry and Constance died soon after, so Frederick was brought up in Palermo, running free through the streets of the city, undoubtedly acquiring many of those accomplishments which would later stand him in good stead. Last of the medieval monarchs, first of the modern rulers, Frederick spent all his life trying to unite the Holy Roman Empire to the rich Kingdom of Sicily: unfortunately for him, the Papal States stood—both literally and metaphorically—between him and success. A colourful and fascinating figure in the history of Europe, defying the pope, even excommunicated, yet leader of the most successful and least bloody Crusade; the founder of modern diplomacy, and the first to draw up laws protecting the rights of women, and for the protection of wildlife; his body lies in the cathedral of Palermo.

Medieval streets and stepped alleys enter the square, with its elegant Baroque palaces. On the northern side are Palazzo Balleani, with balconies supported by caryatids, and the Neoclassical façade of the **duomo** (13th and 18th centuries), dedicated to St

Septimius, the patron saint and first bishop of the city (4th century); the bell-tower on the left is an 18th-century imitation of the one in Loreto by Vanvitelli. The striking interior is Latin-cross in form, and decorated with many works of art. The two 13th-century red marble lions supporting the holy water stoups were made for the original church. The first south chapel is the baptistery; Pergolesi was baptised in this font.

To the left of the cathedral, Via delle Terme leads down to Porta Bersaglieri, and public gardens under the walls, where the people of Jesi have carefully hidden away (by the beautiful Montirozzi tower), the bronze statue, **monument to Frederick II of Hohenstaufen** (1994); not everyone likes it.

Close to the cathedral is the **ex-church of San Floriano** (12th century), where every year in May representatives of the 16 castles around Jesi had to bring their banner (*pallio*) as a token of submission. The interior of the dome (18th century) was frescoed in 1851 by the local artist Luigi Mancini; since 2002 the church has been used as a theatre, Teatro Studio (*T: 0731 56572*). Next to the church is the 18th-century Franciscan convent, which houses the **Museo Archeologico** (*open 16 June–15 Sept 10–1 & 5–11; 16 Sept–15 June 10–1 & 4–7; closed Mon; T: 0731 56572*), a series of exhibits documenting the period from prehistory to the Roman domination. Many of the statues and marble heads were found in 1784 during excavations in this old convent (and in 1968 the remains of the Roman theatre were also identified nearby). In front is Palazzo Ripanti (18th century), with the **Museo Diocesano di Arte Sacra** (*open 1 July–30 Sept Tues, Thur and Fri 6–11; 1 Oct–30 June Tues and Sat, 10–11; Thur 4.30–7.30; T: 0731 56625*), a collection of paintings, sculptures and devotional objects from churches and convents of the area, including works by Ercole Ramazzani and Claudio Ridolfi.

Via Pergolesi

From Piazza Federico II Via Pergolesi leads southwest through Piazzetta Ghislieri, where Pergolesi was born, to Piazza Colocci and the imposing, rosy-brown Palazzo della Signoria (1498; Francesco di Giorgio Martini), which houses the prestigious **Biblioteca Planettiana** (*open 1 July–31 Aug 9–1; 1 Sept–30 June 9–1 & 3–7, Sat mornings only; closed Sun and holidays; T: 0731 538345/6*), founded in 1860, with 100,000 volumes, incunabula, letters and manuscripts. The city archives, some of which date back to the 12th century, are kept in the same building. This beautiful Renaissance palace, with the emblem of the city, a large rampant lion, in an ornate frame on the façade, has a tower completed in 1661, under which were the city dungeons. The clock was added in the 18th century. Just to the left of the central door are the official measurements for tradespeople.

Opposite is **Palazzo Colocci** (*T: 0731 208334 to request visit*), home of a noble family, preserved as a museum. By taking Costa Baldassini down from Piazza Colocci, to Piazza Franciolini, then Via Valle northeast, at no. 3 you will find Palazzo Pianetti Vecchio, an interesting palace, once a convent, now housing the **S.A.S.—Studio per le Arti Tipografiche** (*open July–Sept Wed–Sat 9–11 & 4–7; T: 0731 64272*), a museum dedicated to the art of printing, with two of the original city presses. Next door is the delightful little Baroque church of San Bernardo, once the private chapel of the Pianetti family. Close by is another lovely Baroque church, dedicated to St Peter the Apostle, approached by a double stairway, and with two little bell-towers on the façade.

Continuing south along Via Pergolesi, passing some remarkable Renaissance door-ways, on the right is Piazza dell'Indipendenza, with the 16th-century town hall in front of it. The smaller square on the left is Piazza Spontini, with the elegant Palazzo Ricci-Manganelli (16th century), decorated with a diamond-cut stone façade, and interesting windows. The double arches of the **Arco del Magistrato**, the ancient city gate, mark the point where the medieval town finishes, and the Renaissance exten-sion, called *Terravecchia*, begins. The spacious Piazza della Repubblica is dominated by the façade of the opera house, **Teatro Pergolesi** (*open 9–12.30 & 5–7.30; T: 0731 538355, www.teatropergolesi.org*), one of the most important theatres in Italy, built in 1798. Inside the theatre is a gallery dedicated to Pergolesi and Spontini (*open 10–1; closed Sun; Tues and Thur also 3.30–6.30; T: 0731 202944 or 0731 215643; www.fon-dazionepergolesispontini.com*), with memorabilia concerning the two musicians.

PERGOLESI & SPONTINI

Giovanni Battista Pergolesi (1710–36) crammed all his musical genius into ten short years. At sixteen he went to Naples to study, and showed enormous aptitude for improvisation on the violin. Here he composed his comic opera *La serva padrona*. He died of TB aged only 26. His *Stabat Mater* (1730), one of the most enduringly popular settings of the text, was described by Bellini as 'a divine poem of grief'. **Gaspare Spontini** (1774–1851), described by Riccardo Muti as a 'European genius', was of a sickly disposition. He was unable to take his vows as a priest, and dedicated the rest of his life to music. In Paris, under the patron-age of the Empress Josephine, he became celebrated for his melodramatic operas, most famous among them *La Vestale* and *Ferdinand Cortez*. He also spent 22 years in Berlin, where only the patronage of the court kept him in business as he was disliked by the public and the press. Berlioz was a great admirer.

Pinacoteca Civica

Two streets lead out of Piazza della Repubblica: **Corso Matteotti**, always crowded, with its elegant shops (and bookshops), and the narrow Via XV Settembre, with the long façade (more than 100 windows) of Palazzo Pianetti (18th century), a sumptu-ous town-house, now the **Pinacoteca Civica** (*open 16 June–15 Sept 10–1 & 5–11; 16 Sept–15 June 10–1 & 4–7; holidays 10–1 & 5–8; closed Mon; T: 0731 538342/3*). On the first floor, a 70m-long gallery decorated with Rococo stuccoes and pink and blue fres-coes offers views over the delightful Italian-style garden on one side, and access to the salons, with ceilings depicting the *Stories of Aeneas* (1786) on the other. The memo-rable and lovingly displayed collection includes a series of five paintings by **Lorenzo Lotto**: two panels of a triptych showing the *Annunciation* (1526; notice the almost mirrored images of St Francis and St Clare, founders of the mendicant orders of the Franciscans and Poor Clares, in the upper panel), with a recoiling Madonna dressed in red, a colour which gives her earthy substance, in contrast to the diaphanous blue garment of the Angel (the central panel was stolen by Napoleon); a sad *Madonna of the Roses* (1526), reluctant to relinquish her Son, even to Joseph and Jerome; a Giorgionesque-style *Deposition* (1512); a drastically over-cleaned *Visitation* (1531), and the plucky little Lucy of the *Story of St Lucy* panel (1532), with her homely yellow dress and practical cotton mules, defying the Roman governor and accepting her martyrdom—certainly this painting alone would be worth a journey to the Marche to see. The museum also houses the historical collections of the city, and paintings by masters such as Pietro Paolo Agabiti and Pomarancio.

Outside the city

Just northwest of the old walls, on a little hill is the church of **San Marco**, said to have been given to St Francis of Assisi by the Benedictine monks. Perhaps built on a preceding structure in the 12th century, it was used as a barracks by Napoleon, and rebuilt in Gothic style in 1854. The interior, with a central nave and two side aisles, has a striking cross-beam vault, painted with gold stars on a deep blue background; in the main apse is a magnificent 13th-century fresco of the *Crucifixion* by the Giotto School of Rimini, with more 13th-century frescoes to the right. Another ancient church is between Jesi and the river, outside Porta Valle: the church of **Santa Maria del Piano** formed part of a Benedictine monastery, probably founded in the early Middle Ages. It is possible to see the excavations under the church, where a beautiful 9th-century stone sarcophagus was found, decorated with scenes of fighting animals. Along the river east of the city is a nature reserve, the **Oasi Ripabianca** (*open 15 Sept–15 May Sun 10 & 3; Thur, Sat 3 for guided tours only; T: 0733 232076*), protecting the largest heronry in the region, with a colony of 50 pairs of night herons.

THE ESINO VALLEY

The River Esino, the ancient *Aesis*, springs from Mount Cafaggio, at 1275m above sea level, and flows for 90km to its mouth, just south of Rocca Priora, passing by Esanatoglia and Matelica, before heading north to pick up a few tributaries, then northeast to go through the Gola della Rossa gorge. The lower course of the river has created a wide and extremely fertile alluvial valley, known as the Vallesina, well-watered and colourful, renowned for the production of DOC Verdicchio wines. Close to the mouth of the river is **Rocca Priora** (*gardens open to the public daily; T: 071 9198970*), the fortress built by Jesi to defend its boundary with Ancona, in 1194. Rebuilt in the 18th century, it still has strong walls and towers, and a fine portal; in the courtyard is a small chapel designed by Vanvitelli.

Further north is the friendly little resort of Marina di Montemarciano, with a wide gravel beach, under the hilltop town of **Montemarciano**, once a castle, said to have been populated by a colony from Dalmatia on the orders of the duke of Urbino, now an industrious community of farmers and clothes manufacturers. Possibly this was a Roman station for changing horses; in fact, nearby at Mandracchio are the ruins of a 15th-century inn and stables built by the Malatesta on a Roman structure. The castle was totally destroyed in 1578 because it was a bandit stronghold, but the town was soon rebuilt; in the centre is the pearly-coloured collegiate church of San Pietro Apostolo (18th century), well-proportioned and elegant, with twin bell-towers provided with clocks. Inside there are several paintings by local artists dating from the 16th–17th centuries.

Between the coast and Jesi

Chiaravalle developed in the 16th century around one of the three abbeys founded in Italy by the Cistercian monks of Clairvaux, hence the name. A boost was given to the economy in 1759, when tobacco manufacturing was introduced; even today Chiaravalle grows and processes most of Italy's tobacco. On the spacious, central Piazza Garibaldi stands the abbey of Chiaravalle, Santa Maria in Castagnola, consecrated in 1172. The brick façade has a 17th-century portico and a simple portal in the middle, surmounted by a large rose-window; the tympanum on the top was added much later. The sides are also simple, with buttresses, and a small bell-tower. The

St Lucy defying her persecutors: panel painting by Lorenzo Lotto (1532).

interior is Latin-cross in form, with a central nave and two side aisles, divided by 12 brick pilasters; there are ornate Baroque altars in the two transepts. For many centuries the abbey was an important seat of learning in central Italy. At no. 10 Piazza Mazzini is the house where Maria Montessori was born. Montessori (1870–1952) was the first woman in Italy to obtain a university degree in medicine. The house is now a library and documentation centre on this sensitive and innovative teacher.

Monte San Vito, west of Chiaravalle, has always been famous for its olive oil. Inhabited since Neolithic times, the town became a defensive fortress for Jesi in the Middle Ages, before passing under the control of Ancona. The old centre, which is round, was built incorporating the ruins of the castle. On the top, in Piazza San Pietro, is the landmark of the town: the imposing collegiate church of San Pietro Apostolo (1753), unfinished, with a beautiful single-nave interior, surmounted by a dome, decorated with stuccoes. Over the main altar is the *Martyrdom and Triumph of St Vitus* by the Roman artist Pietro Labruzzi (1777), while in the south transept is a canvas by Filippo Bellini (a descendant of Giovanni) of the *Madonna of Succour* (16th century). Behind the church is the town hall, occupying Palazzo Malatesta (15th–16th centuries), built on the entrance to the old fortress, which had a drawbridge; the faded brick façade, on the other side, is very photogenic. On show inside are some paintings by Lorenzo Daretti (18th century), with fine perspective views. The Teatro Comunale La Fortuna (1758 and 1927), in Via Marconi, close to the castle, occupies an old oil press, while at no. 15 Via Gramsci is another press dating back to 1688.

Closer to Jesi is **Monsano**, a little medieval fortress-town, also famous for olive oil, which became one of Jesi's castles in the 14th century. Nowadays, besides oil, the inhabitants make mattresses. The rectangular castle, with three corner-towers, is still impressive, and offers views over the vineyards and olive groves to the Esino. At the foot of the castle is Piazza Mazzini, the town centre, with the parish church of San Pietro Apostolo, with a 17th-century painting of the *Madonna with Sts Peter, Paul and Gregory* by Claudio Ridolfi or Antonino Sarti on the main altar.

Opposite Jesi, south of the Esino, is **Santa Maria La Nuova**, on top of a hill (249m); its walls go back to the 16th century, and three of the original four towers are still standing. In the church of Sant'Antonio, the 18th-century organ is said to be one of Gaetano Callido's finest. Callido was born near Padua in 1727. He served as apprentice in the workshop of Pietro Nacchini, in Istria, and went on to be one of the finest and most celebrated organ makers in all Italy. He lived for 30 years in Corinaldo, where his daughter entered a cloistered nunnery.

The Esino valley beyond Jesi

On the north bank of the Esino stands **Moie**, in what was once a swampy area, drained for farming by the Benedictines in the 10th century. At the entrance to the town, on the left, is the Benedictine abbey church of Santa Maria delle Moie (12th century), a lovely Romanesque stone building. The interior is a Greek cross, with three small naves separated by four pilasters, and a cross-beam roof; there are three semicircular apses, and smaller apses on the sides, corresponding to the arms of the cross.

Countryside near Montecarotto.

On the crest between the Misa and the Esino valleys is the little town of **Montecarotto**, once a castle of Jesi, with formidable medieval walls, redesigned in 1509. Most of the inhabitants are farmers, who produce Verdicchio wine; there are also industries for the manufacture of shoes and farm machinery. In the central Piazza della Vittoria are two towers, one round and the other polygonal, still connected by the passageway for the sentries. Close by, at no 5 Piazza del Teatro, is the opera house, Teatro Comunale (*T: 0731 89495*), from 1875, with an elegant rose-coloured façade with a portico, which also houses the **Museum of Mail Art** (*T: 0731 89495 to request visit*), a collection of art which can be sent by post: drawings, CDs, small sculptures, including works by Pericle Fazzini, Umberto Mastroianni, and Orfeo Tamburi, born in Jesi, but best known for his Parisian skylines. In the highest part of the town is the simple brick façade of the 18th-century church of the Collegiata, built on a preceding church which took the place of the castle ruins in the 15th century. The interior is a single nave, with many paintings by local artists over the side altars, in the presbytery, and in the crypt; the organ is by Callido. In front of this church is that of San Francesco (1612), with an organ (1749) by Pietro Nacchini, Callido's master.

Castelplanio, surrounded by neat, well-tended vineyards, stands on a hill close to the Esino. One of Jesi's 16 castles, it was originally a fortress for the nearby Benedictine abbey of the Frondigliosi (now completely rebuilt and used as a hostel), and is in fact called *Castello* by the inhabitants. Taken by Francesco Sforza in 1433, it was attacked on behalf of the pope by Niccolò Piccinino ten years later, and completely destroyed. The inhabitants rebuilt the castle, strengthened the fortifications, and declared allegiance to Jesi, following the destiny of that city until the 19th century. Palazzo Fossa Mancini (*open 10–13.30; closed Sun and holidays; T: 0731 81340*), the home of one of the local aristocratic families, is now an interesting museum, giving an idea of the lifestyle of the count in the 18th century.

South of the river

On the south bank of the river is the attractive, unspoilt little town of **Castelbellino**, famous for its wine, with a collection of archaeological finds from local sites, and paintings by the Flemish artist Ernst van Schayck, at the Museo Comunale (*open 10–1 Mon–Fri; 10–11 Sat; T: 0731 702429*) in the town hall, on the central Piazza San Marco. Close by is the tiny opera house of Castelbellino, still in use, Teatro Beniamino Gigli (*T: 0731 7788211*). The castle of Castelbellino was a place of refuge for Ghibellines escaping from Jesi.

Monte Roberto is very picturesque, with 15th-century walls and towers. In the tiny main square is the little church of San Silvestro, with beautiful 18th-century carved wooden choir-stalls. The abbey of Sant'Apollinare, just under the town, is said to be one of the first founded by the Benedictines along the Esino, in the 9th century. The plain façade, with austere lines and a high portal, is superb. The fresco in the apse, dated 1508, is thought to be by little-known local artist Andrea da Jesi. Roman remains have been found under the church, perhaps relating to the city of *Planina*. Nearby an 8th-century BC Picene necropolis has been located.

Another castle of Jesi was **Maiolati Spontini**, where the people are so proud of their composer (*see p. 39*) that they added the surname Spontini to the name of the town in 1939. At no. 15 Via Spontini, in the house where the musician died, is the **Museo Spontiniano** (*open Apr, June, Sept and Dec Sat 3–7, Sun 10.30–12.30 & 3–7; July, Aug Tues–Fri 5–8, Sat, Sun 9–11; Mon closed; other times call to request visit; T: 0731 704451*), an interesting series of rooms still furnished as he last saw them, with his musical instruments, the family portraits, costumes from some of his operas, documents and other memorabilia; the visit is accompanied by the notes of *Li puntigli de le donne*, his first work, presented in Rome in 1796. Spontini was embalmed and buried in the church of San Giovanni nearby—the medallion on the tomb was made by Antonio Canova—but his heart was given to his wife. Maiolati was one of the strongholds of the Fraticelli heretical sect (*see opposite*), so the castle was destroyed by the pope in 1428.

San Paolo di Jesi, south of Monte Roberto, a small (pop. 900), ancient farming community producing Verdicchio wine, has an unusual tradition: in the first week of December, the two poorest girls in town are chosen to receive a small sum of money as a dowry, thanks to the last will and testament of Don Anton Jacomo Agabiti, who died in 1702. The townsfolk celebrate with little cakes called *cavallucci*, filled with *sapa*, concentrated must. In the parish church, over the main altar, is a canvas of the *Madonna with Christ Child and Saints*, by Pomarancio, signed and dated 1620. A recent initiative is the creation of a laboratory for the extraction of essential oils from wild plants, to be used for herbal medicines and cosmetics. A pleasant walk through the vineyards (c. 2km) leads southeast of San Paolo to the ruins of the medieval castle of Follonica.

On a hill between the Esino and the Musone, south of San Paolo di Jesi, is **Staffolo**, shaped like a stirrup, in a wonderfully panoramic position. Like so many of the other towns close by, its history is a long series of attacks, sieges and destructions, with relatively few periods of peace. A particularly heavy blow was the 1591 plague, when Staffolo lost more than half of its inhabitants. It is possible to walk all the way around the perfectly-preserved medieval walls (c. 700m), from which two gates give access to the centre: Porta Venezia to the north, and Porta San Martino to the south. On the main street, Via XX Settembre, is the 13th-century church of Sant'Egidio, with the beautiful original doorway; the interior has been completely rebuilt. This church was used as a hospital during the 1591 plague; recently, during repairs, some votive frescoes were found, going back to that time. Over the third south altar is an interesting polyptych (15th century) of the *Madonna with Saints* by the 'Maestro di Staffolo', an unknown follower of Gentile da Fabriano. Almost next to it is the 13th-century church of San Francesco, with an elegant single-nave interior; the organ is by Gaetano Callido, signed, dated (1769) and numbered (op. 51). The people of Staffolo are wine farmers, renowned for Verdicchio (*see box overleaf*). At the town hall is the **Museo del Vino** (*open Sat 3–7; 1 July–31 Aug 5–8, Sat 9–11; closed Mon T: 0731 771040*) dedicated to the subject.

Just outside the town is the sanctuary church of **Santa Maria della Castellaretta** (1571), built by the inhabitants to celebrate their safe return from the Battle of Lepanto; the interior is spectacular Baroque, with a lovely inlaid stone floor.

Cupramontana

Southeast of Jesi, on a beautiful green and fertile hill (505m), stands **Cupramontana**, on the site of a 5th-century BC temple to the Picene fertility goddess Cupra, known as *Bona* by the Romans. This is the most important centre of the Marche for the production of Verdicchio, white wine perhaps of Etruscan origin.

Probably a Roman city, all trace of it was lost after its destruction in the 6th century, except for a few stones in the nearby castle of Poggio Cupra (the castle church is said to be one of the places where the Holy Grail might be hidden). The town was rebuilt in the Middle Ages, and known as *Massaccio* until 1861, when it reverted to its old name. By 1100 it was one of the most important fortress-towns gravitating around Jesi, and was attacked many times; in 1355 Cardinal Albornoz (*see p. 7*) brought it under the wing of the Church, strengthened the fortifications, and excavated a secret passage between the convent of Santa Caterina, outside the walls, and the castle, to guarantee an escape route for the nuns in case of enemy attack or bandit raids. In the 15th-century Massaccio was one of the centres (the others were Mergo and Maiolati) of a religious sect called the Fraticelli, who advocated a rule of total poverty, even stricter than that of the Franciscans, and set themselves up in opposition to the pope (they elected their own). Most of the Fraticelli were burnt alive by the Inquisition, after 'spontaneous confessions', in 1449. In 1798, after a tenacious resistance to the attacks of the French troops, the town was taken and ravaged. The weekly market, still held every Monday in Piazza Cavour, was authorized by Pope Pius V in 1570. Cupramontana was so important in the 19th century for the production of millstones, which were exported all over Italy, that in 1866 the Esino Valley was preferred over the Potenza when a new railway line was planned: hence the Foligno–Jesi–Falconara Marittima line.

VERDICCHIO

Praised by Pliny and by Varro, 'the most learned of all the Romans', and reputedly the favourite drink of Alaric the Goth, Verdicchio was first grown by the Etruscans, and passed into history on the banqueting tables of Charlemagne, the Malatesta, the Montefeltro dukes, the Sforza and the della Rovere. The Verdicchio grape is particular to the Marche, more specifically to the Esino valley near Jesi, and to the vineyards around Matelica. The breezy climate of the Esino valley keeps the air free from disease, and allows the vines to flourish. Classic Verdicchio is the wine known as Castelli di Jesi: strict rules mean that 85% of the fruit used must be from the Verdicchio grape, the rest can be made up of other native varieties. Verdicchio dei Castelli di Jesi comes in a number of categories: *Spumante* (sparkling), *Passito* (made from grapes that have been carefully dried on straw, turning them into raisins, and lending a sweetness to the wine), *Classico* (minimum 11.5% alcohol), *Superiore* (minimum 12%) and *Riserva* (minimum 12.5%, and must have been aged for 2 years, with 6 months in the bottle). A light, straw-coloured wine with a delicate fruity perfume, the best Verdicchio always presents a hint of bitter almond on the palate, preventing the wine from being bland, and giving it a nice bite. It is an excellent accompaniment to salads, cold meats and fish.

The central square of Cupramontana is the sinuous Piazza Cavour, with the 18th-century town hall. By passing through the arch under the clock, you reach Via Sauro, leading up to the castle, the oldest part of town. On the left is the collegiate church of San Leonardo (1151 and 1760), with a graceful façade adorned with statues, corresponding to the first church built within the castle walls. Inside, over the first south altar, is a painting of the *Circumcision*, a masterpiece by Jesi-born Antonino Sarti (1615). The second south altar is lavish Baroque (1792); over it is an early 16th-century panel painting of the *Madonna Enthroned*, known as '*Madonna della Colonna*', by Andrea da Jesi. Over the main altar is a gilded wood carving by Andrea Scoccianti (1681). So famous was Scoccianti for his carvings with leaves and flowers, that he was often called the 'Raphael of Leaves'. The walnut choir-stalls, pulpit, and magistrate's bench were made by craftsmen from Pergola.

Piazza Cavour also gives access to Via Ferranti, and the church of San Lorenzo (1787; Mattia Capponi), a refined example of Neoclassical architecture, listed as a national monument. The stucco decorations in the elegant, single-nave interior were never completed. From here you can walk round to the east side of the castle, where in Corso Cavour you will find Palazzo Leoni (18th century), seat of the **Museo Internazionale dell'Etichetta** (*T: 0731 780199 to request visit; closed Mon*), a unique collection of over 90,000 wine labels, some of great historical interest.

PRACTICAL INFORMATION

GETTING AROUND

• **By train:** Jesi station (T: 0731 58297) is on the Rome–Fabriano–Falconara Marittima–Ancona line. Some towns of the Esino Valley can be reached from the stations of Montecarotto-Castelbellino (T: 0731 703272), Castelplanio–Cupramontana, Serra San Quirico, or Chiaravalle (T: 071 43933).
• **By bus:** Jesi central bus station is at 4 Via Valle, T: 0731 4864.
Jesi city buses are run by CIPA, Via Novella, T: 0731 4335.
Services to and from Macerata, Montecarotto, Ostra, Filottrano, Chiaravalle, Falconara and Ancona are run by Autolinee Crognaletti, T: 0731 204965, www.autolineecrognaletti.it
Services connecting the towns of the Esino Valley, also Chiaravalle, Falconara and Ancona are run by SACSA, T: 0731 56536.

INFORMATION OFFICES

A useful website for the region is www.misaesinofrasassi.it
Cupramontana Municipio, 1 Via Sauro, T: 0731 786833, www.provincia.ancona.it/comuni/cupramontana/default.htm; Pro Loco Pro Cupra, 12 Viale Vittoria, T: 0731 780660; Tourist Information Bureau (summer only), 3 Piazza Cavour, T: 0731 789746, www.cadnet.marche.it/cupramontana
Jesi IAT, Piazza della Repubblica, T: 0731 59788, www.comune.jesi.an.it; Associazione Turistica Pro Jesi, T: 0731 59788.

HOTELS

Jesi
€€€€ **Federico II**. Luxurious hotel out of town, indoor pool, gym, restaurant, car park. 100 Via Ancona, T: 0731 211079, www.hotelfederico2.it
€€€ **Mariani**. Close to the old town centre, a quiet and comfortable hotel, well run, in an old palace. Restaurant and garage next door. 10 Via Orfanotrofio, T: 0731 207286, www.hotelmariani.com
Castelplanio
€ **Hostaria della Posta**. ■ Small hotel with very good restaurant. 6 Via Carrozze Vaccili, Borgo Loreto, T: 0731

813528, locandadellaposta@libero.it

Maiolati Spontini

€ **Spontini**. Small hotel with good restaurant close to Spontini's house; the owner is a mine of information about the musician. 33 Via Spontini, T: 0731 703650.

Marina di Montemarciano

€€ **La Marinella**. Small inn, very good restaurant. 1 Piazza Magellano, T: 071 9198401.

Staffolo

€€ **Belvedere**. Small and friendly, with a restaurant. 1/3 Via Re di Puglia, T: 0731 779261.

FARM ACCOMMODATION

Cupramontana

Colonnara. ▪ Farm renowned for high-quality wines (the white *Tufico* is delicious) and olive oil. Accommodation is in an ancient convent. 8 Via Romita, T: 0731 789979, www.colonnara.it

La Distesa. Organises courses on wine and olive oil; mountain bikes available. English, French and Spanish spoken. 28 Via Romita, T: 0731 781230, www.ladistesa.it;

Montecarotto

Parva Domus. Lovely apartments to rent on a farm using 'low environmental impact' methods. Pool and bowls; English spoken. 13 Sobborgo Fornaci, T: 0731 89690;

Rosora

Croce del Moro. Panoramic position for this farm producing *Verdicchio di Jesi* wine, olive oil, wheat and berry fruits. Good cooking and good value for money. 5 Via Tassanare, Croce del Moro, T: 0731 812112, www.crocedelmoro.it

RESTAURANTS

Castelbellino

€€ **Tamburo Battente**. Simple friendly restaurant on the main square, for local dishes and *Verdicchio*. Evenings only; closed Tues. 10 Piazza San Marco, T: 0731 704083.

Chiaravalle

€€ **Enoteca Essentia**. Wine bar at lunchtime, restaurant in the evening; nice subdued music. Closed Thur. 27 Via Carducci, T: 071 94126.

Cupramontana

€ **Anita**. An ancient tavern still called *La Moretta* by the local people, exactly the same for about 50 years. Nothing fancy, only traditional food, served with a flask of Verdicchio. Closed Tues. 7 Via Filzi, T: 0731 780311.

€ **Antiche Fonti della Romita**. Out of town, a 12th-century convent transformed into restaurant, on a hilltop near the town. Tasty *antipasto*, followed by home-made pasta and roast or stewed meat, accompanied by wines from the Colonnara vineyards. Closed Wed. 8 Via Romita, T: 0731 789979.

Jesi

€€€ **Hostaria Santa Lucia**. Famous for fish; imaginative chef. Booking is essential as it's very popular. Closed Mon and Sun evening, Tues–Sat lunchtime. 2/b Via Marche, T: 0731 64409.

€€ **Antonietta**. Small cosy restaurant run by a family, with traditional home cooking. Closed Sun and Aug. 19 Via Garibaldi, T: 0731 207173.

€€ **Galeazzi**. ▪ Ask Mario for his famous gnocchi, then try his *fritto misto all'italiana*, mixed fried titbits of vegetables, fruit and cheese, incredibly light and crunchy. Local wines. Closed Mon. 5 Via Mura Occidentali, T: 0731 57944.

€ **Forno Ercoli**. A crowded tavern, you probably won't be able to sit down. Excellent cheese, salami and local wines, ideal for a quick meal at any time of day. Closed Mon. 8 Piazza Nova, T: 0731 56960.

€ **Trattoria della Fortuna**. Good value for money at this restaurant, which prepares excellent fresh egg pasta, grilled meats, accompanied by a flask of Verdicchio dei Castelli di Jesi. Pizzeria in the evening. Closed Sun. 1 Via Arco del Soccorso, T: 0731 59903.

Maiolati Spontini

€ **Maresciallo**. Family-run restaurant with a cosy atmosphere. Closed Sun. 1 Piazza Santa Maria, T: 0731 701964.

Marina di Montemarciano

€€€ **Rose**. Elegant restaurant offering traditional fare. Also has a pool. Closed Mon. 1 Via delle Querce, T: 071 9198127.

€€ **Lì Marina**. Excellent gnocchi, grilled fish, local wines; with a car park. 24 Via Pergolesi, T: 071 9198105.

Montecarotto

€€€ **Le Busche**. ■ Famous country restaurant, inventive blends of meat, fish and vegetables. Closed Mon and Sun evenings. 2 Contrada Busche, T: 0731 89172.

CAFÉS PASTRY SHOPS & SNACK BARS

Jesi

Caffè Bardi. ■ Elegant coffee bar, renowned for the cheese pizzas they make at Easter time, the meringues, the nougat, and the delicious ice cream. Closed Mon. 27 Corso Matteotti.

Caffè del Teatro. Near the opera house; a nice place to read the newspapers. 10 Piazza Repubblica.

Caffè Saccaria. Aromatic coffee roasted on the premises—you can buy some to take home. 24 Corso Matteotti.

Snoopy Bar. Excellent ice cream. 19 Corso Matteotti.

Montecarotto

Bar Centrale. Friendly coffee bar for espresso and local gossip. 8 Piazza del Teatro.

FESTIVALS & EVENTS

Castelplanio *Palio del Paese della Mongolfiera*, painted paper hot-air balloons are flown, cheese exhibition and cheese-tossing contest, 2nd weekend of June.

Chiaravalle Feast of St Bernard, 20 Aug–20 Sept.

Cupramontana *Sagra dell'Uva*, one of the oldest celebrations of the kind in Italy, festivities and parades for the grape harvest; Info: Comitato Sagra dell'Uva, 30 Piazza Cavour, T: 0731 789746, 1st weekend in Oct.

Jesi *Palio di San Floriano*, jousting and crossbow contests going back to 1227. Info: Palio di San Floriano, 6 Via A. da Jesi, T: 0731 56160. 1st week in May. Feast of St Septimius, with traditional fair, 22–25 Sept. Pergolesi Spontini Festival, concerts in Jesi and nearby towns; Info: T: 0731 226446, www.fondazionepergolesispontini.com, Sept. Opera and ballet season at the Pergolesi Theatre is Sept–Oct.

Maiolati Spontini *Fiera di Sant'Anna*, traditional summer fair; Info: Pro Loco, 1 Largo Pastori, T: 0731 702972, last week in July.

Monte San Vito *Sagra del Castagnolo*,

mid-Lent festivities, during which sausages are launched by parachute from the upper windows, and the *Apertura dell'Orcio*, solemn 'opening of the jar', tasting the new oil, March–April (Lent). *Festa d'Autunno*, autumn fair with local gastronomy, using the famous oil, Nov.

San Paolo di Jesi *La Cavata delle Zitelle*, two 'spinsters' are presented with their dowry, 1st week in Dec.

LOCAL SPECIALITIES

Castelbellino
Azienda Vinicola Umani Ronchi, in Via Montale, is renowned for Verdicchio Classico. **Casa del Pane Cingolani**, 128 Via Pantiere, for local sourdough bread.

Castelplanio
Fazi Battaglia, 117 Via Roma, has a long-standing reputation for Verdicchio dei Castelli di Jesi DOC wine. **Panificio Otello**, at 1 Via Sabbatucci, bakes delicious bread, cakes and biscuits.

Cupramontana
Dino Dottori, 20 Corso Leopardi, has local wines; let Dino advise you; ask for his under-the-counter homemade cherry wine called *Brio*, rather like port.

Jesi
Enoteca Regionale, at 5 Via Conti, is a show-case shop for more than 500 wines of the Marche, including the 12 DOC varieties. Open June–Sept 6–11; Oct–May, 5–9; closed Wed. **Il Cioccolato Bruco**, 70 Via Gallodoro, is a prizewinning locally-made chocolate, flavoured with aniseed, cinnamon, chilli or rum-vanilla, and chocolate-covered *lonza di fico*. **Qirat**, 1/a Via Pergolesi, for very beautiful, original jewellery; you will find many similar shops along this street, once called Via degli Orefici, street of the goldsmiths.

Maiolati Spontini
Pasticceria Piccioni, 20 Via Vallati, for excellent fig sweetmeats *lonzetta di fichi*.

Moie
Vittorio Piccioni, 20 Via Vallati, has excellent *lonzetta di fichi* and other traditional sweets.

San Paolo di Jesi
Cimarelli, 17 Via Coste, for honey; **Radicioni**, at 16 Via Piana, has delicious bread year round, and in winter, *cavallucci* biscuits (*see p. 44*).

FABRIANO & ITS TERRITORY

Fabriano (pop. 30,000) stands in a wide valley on the banks of the Giano stream, a tributary of the Esino, encircled by the eastern slopes of the Apennines, in an area prone to earthquakes. The compact medieval city of worn, milk chocolate-coloured brick is flanked by the new districts and the important industrial zone, which now covers a large part of the valley. The town has a businesslike atmosphere, due to a centuries-old tradition of manufacturing and trading. It is the most important centre in Italy for the manufacture of paper, for which it has long been renowned. Terribly stricken by the earthquake of 26th September 1997, rebuilding and restoration are almost complete, and the old city centre is beginning to acquire allure again.

HISTORY OF FABRIANO

The valley was inhabited in ancient times by Picenes, who had commercial ties with the Etruscan centres of Umbria; but the name derives from *Faberianus*, 'the estate of Faberius', a Roman patrician. The town developed between the 5th–8th centuries, when it became a place of refuge from the Barbarian invasions. In 1165 it was an independent commune, with two walled castles, an aristocracy which collaborated with the corporations of craftsmen and artists, its own statutes and statesmen. A series of fortunate wars and intelligent trade agreements led to the extension of its territory, an increase of its military power, and considerable prosperity through industry (paper, leather, wool and iron) and commerce. The Chiavelli family, of German stock, came to power in the late 14th century, and during their time the city reached its highest levels of power and wealth. But on 26th May 1435, all the men of the family were murdered by conspirators; during the consequent chaos Fabriano was taken by Francesco Sforza, who held it until 1444, when it passed to the pope. Many years of struggles ensued as the town tried to recapture its independence. A peace treaty was signed by Leo X in 1534; in 1728 Fabriano was declared a city and assigned a bishop. In 1795 the city was sacked by the Napoleonic troops under General Monnier.

The manufacture of paper is still the mainstay of the economy, supplemented by the industries of domestic appliances (Ariston, Merloni Elettrodomestici), food-processing (salami), clothes and building materials.

EXPLORING FABRIANO

NB: Many of the buildings described in the text may still be closed for repairs after the 1997 earthquake, and the works of art may still be at the Deposito Attrezzato delle Opere d'Arte (open 10–12.30 & 3–7; closed Mon; Via Fontanelle; T: 0732 629359; www.comune. fabriano.an.it/deposito), the old Miliani paper factory, where over 700 paintings and statues were brought from the ruined churches and palaces; they have been studied, cleaned and restored, and are gradually returning to their original settings as repairs are completed.

Piazza del Comune and San Biagio

The spectacular, triangular central square, Piazza del Comune, is dominated by the majestic grey stone Palazzo del Podestà (1255), with a large Gothic archway leading through to Corso Repubblica, once the street of the craftsmen. In front of the palace is the Fontana Sturinalto (1285). On the right, occupying the northeast side of the square, is the **Palazzo Comunale**, built in the 14th century as the court of the Chiavelli family, now the town hall; it is joined to the beautiful 17th-century Loggiato San Francesco, with 19 graceful arches, some of which were once part of the vanished church of San Francesco. The courtyard of the town hall gives access to the gorgeous opera house, **Teatro Gentile** (*T: 0732 709259*) dating from 1869, with 600 seats, and perfect acoustics, renowned for its beautiful interior and painted safety curtain.

On the same square are the 16th-century bishop's palace and 17th-century clock tower. Taking the tiny Via Verdi northeast, by the theatre, you reach Piazza Manin and the church of **San Biagio e San Romualdo**, an elegant Baroque structure built in 1741 to replace the 13th-century original, destroyed by earthquake; the stucco decoration in the interior and the paintings are admirable. The organ was made by Gaetano Callido in 1791. In the crypt under the altar is the body of St Romuald. The son of a duke, Romuald was born in Ravenna in the 9th century. As a young man, he took part in a family feud during which his father killed one of his relatives, an episode which shook Romuald deeply. Although innocent, he retired as a penitent to a Benedictine monastery. After a series of visions of St Apollinaire he decided to become a monk himself, but found the behaviour of his brethren too lax. Instead he travelled around as a wandering priest, founding hermitages and small monastic communities. Emperor Otto III tried to persuade him to settle down as an abbot, but his strict adherence to the rule of St Benedict made him unpopular with the monks. He took to the road again, sometimes with like-minded companions, sometimes alone. In 1012 Count Maldolo of Arezzo gave him a piece of land on the Apennines at Camaldoli, where he founded his most famous monastery, renowned for the severity with which the monks applied the Benedictine rule to their daily lives, and which was to give the name to his new Order. After his death in 1027, his body was stolen a few times by over-zealous monks and taken to various convents, until the 15th century when it was brought to San Biagio, the church of the Camaldoli in Fabriano, where it still lies. The cloister (16th century) is superb, with a portico of a series of brick arches supported by marble columns, repeated on a smaller scale in the airy loggia above it.

Piazza Giovanni Paolo II and district

Adjacent to Piazza del Comune is Piazza Giovanni Paolo II, which occupies the site of one of the two castle (Castelnuovo), with the **Duomo di San Venanzio** (1046 and

17th century; Muzio Oddi). The imposing brick façade is punctuated by three grey stone portals, preceded by a stairway, revealing its Romanesque origin in the polygonal apse. The interior is a single nave, with several highly ornate chapels. In the fourth north chapel is a *Crucifixion* by the follower of Caravaggio Orazio Gentileschi (1620); the same artist carried out the frescoes. Close to the apse are two small chambers, all that remains of 14th-century chapels. The one on the right is decorated with frescoes by Allegretto Nuzi (1365) illustrating the *Life and Martyrdom of St Lawrence*.

Allegretto Nuzi (1315–73)
Nuzi was born and died in Fabriano, and is a supreme example of an artist of the International Gothic style. He is thought to have served his apprenticeship in Florence, with Bernardo Daddi, hence the similarity which some scholars have noted between the two artists' work. On his return to the Marche, he never left again, living and working here for the rest of his life, and coming under the marked influence of Giotto and of the Sienese schools. His best works are of two types: those with a distinct narrative quality (for example, his frescoes of St Lawrence in the Duomo di San Venanzio); and the minutely executed, devotional altarpieces, such as that pictured here. His works are particularly well represented in Fabriano, in the duomo, the Pinacoteca and San Domenico, for which he produced his first signed and dated work, the *Maestà* of 1345. He was buried in the church of San Nicolò.

Gold-ground altarpiece of the *Madonna* by Allegretto Nuzi, native painter of Fabriano. The town preserves many of his works: this one is in the Galleria Nazionale delle Marche in Urbino.

To the right of the duomo is an imposing 19th-century fountain, but dominating the square is the **Ospedale di Santa Maria del Buon Gesù**, founded in 1456 by St James of the Marches as a church and hospital combined, with a magnificent red-brick portico of five arches, each surmounted by a double-light window. The little church is the only one spared by the 1997 earthquake; over the altar is an interesting painting, commissioned by St James of the Marches from an unknown artist, showing the Madonna kneeling in front of the Child Jesus, who is offering the city of Fabriano to the Holy Father (1460). The saint in the bottom left corner is Bernardino of Siena, under whom St James had studied theology. The painting is particularly venerated; in the past, when it was taken in procession through the streets, people would fight to have the honour of carrying it, to the point that the bishop had to stipulate that only the Franciscan friars (to whose order St James belonged) could accompany the Madonna on her outings. The complex houses, in five galleries, the **Pinacoteca Civica Bruno Molajoli** (the works are temporarily at the Museo della Carta; *see below*), an important collection of medieval art from the 13th–16th centuries, including paintings by Allegretto Nuzi, Francescuccio di Cecco Ghissi, Antonio da Fabriano, Venanzio da Camerino and Piergentile da Matelica.

By taking Via Leopardi from Piazza Umberto, you reach the quiet, shady Piazza Fabi Altini, with the large church of **San Benedetto** (1244 and 1590), restored in the 18th century. The interior is Baroque, but the square apse was frescoed by Simone de Magistris with *Stories of St Sylvester*; the wooden choir-stalls, where all the men of the Chiavelli family were murdered in 1435, come from the cathedral.

On leaving the church and turning right, at the bottom of the square is a ramp leading down to the **Oratorio del Gonfalone** (*T: 0732 625067, IAT, to request visit*), built in 1636. Though not very spectacular from the outside, it has a beautiful Baroque interior, a carved and gilded wooden ceiling, and a lovely *Annunciation* by Antonio Viviani (on the main altar, in a frame carved by the famous Scipione da Matelica, one of the finest craftsmen of his time).

San Domenico and the Museo della Carta

Via Balbo leads to Piazza Quintino Sella, with a fountain in the middle. On the left, the polygonal apse of the church of **San Domenico** (sometimes known as Santa Lucia) dominates the square. It is a magnificent Gothic construction in brick, built in the late 14th century; the façade was never completed, but along the sides and the apse are a series of blind arcades and little aedicules, which were originally frescoed. The lovely side portal, also in brick, is now blocked; over it is a rose-window. The bell-tower was increased in height in the 15th century. The vast, luminous interior has a single nave, with lavish Baroque stuccoes, gilded carved wood, rich altars, and fine paintings; notice over the third south altar, a panel painting by Francescuccio di Cecco Ghissi of the *Madonna of the Milk* (1359), and the canvas of the *Miracle of St Vincent Ferrer* over the third north altar. The magnificent organ is also Baroque. To the right of the presbytery is the sacristy, with a cross-beam roof and frescoes on the walls by Allegretto Nuzi and his atelier. In the **Cappella di Sant'Orsola** are many more frescoes by Allegretto.

To the right of the church, in Largo Fratelli Spacca, is the old Dominican convent, now the **Museo della Carta e della Filigrana** (*open 1 Apr–30 Sept 10–12 & 4–7; 1 Oct–31 Mar 10–12 & 2–5; 10–6, Sun and holidays; closed Mon; T: 0732 709297; www.museodellacarta.com*), a very interesting and instructive display of the methods of making paper through the centuries, with an excellent bookshop.

PAPER

The manufacture of paper in Fabriano, which goes back to the 12th century, is the oldest in Italy. In the 15th century there were 40 workshops, making about 250 tons of paper a year. In 1780 their paper, because of its excellent quality, was chosen for making bank notes, not only for Italian currency, but by many other countries as well; Euro notes are made and printed here today. Paper was almost certainly invented by the Chinese in the early 2nd century ad, and was brought to Europe by the Arabs in the 9th century, when flourishing paper factories had long been active in Baghdad and Damascus; rags of cotton, linen and hemp were used as the basic material. But it was the craftsmen of Fabriano who invented a method to stop the paper going mouldy, by coating the sheets with a thin layer of glue obtained from boiled-down beef bones and tannery by-products. They were also the first to invent the watermark, which gradually became an artform in its own right. And it was an enterprising man from Fabriano, Pietro Miliani, who convinced the authorities to choose paper from his town for making bank notes; in 1782 he opened his own company, which was one of the first to produce fine quality tissue paper, and the first to make the famous 'Fabriano' artists' sketch books, on an industrial scale.

The northern districts

From Piazza Quintino Sella, Via Gioberti (once Corso Grande, the street of the aristocracy; many of the houses reveal their 14th-century origin) leads northeast. After 200m, on the left, is the Rococo church of the **Sacro Cuore** (1710), with a splendid interior surmounted by a dome; the refined decoration and the carvings are outstanding.

Again from Piazza Quintino Sella, Via Chiesa leads north to the old city walls, overlooking the River Giano. Beyond is the Borgo San Nicolò, a district of workers who used water from the river to carry out their various occupations. At Piazza Garibaldi, the elegant **Portico dei Vasari** (1364), the portico of the potters, gives an idea of the wealth and power of the workers' corporations; the fresco is by the Allegretto Nuzi atelier. In the heart of the old quarter (follow Via Fratte to Piazza Cairoli, then turn left), is the imposing, ancient church and convent of **San Nicolò** (12th and 17th centuries), with a triple-arched loggia high up on the façade. In the single-nave interior are some wonderful paintings: in the second south chapel is a *St John the Baptist* by Andrea Sacchi, master of the Marche-born Carlo Maratta, and whose finest work (in

Rome) has a Marche-related theme: *The Vision of St Romuald*. In the third south chapel is a marvellous *St Michael Defeating Lucifer* by Guercino. The transept chapel was decorated by the local 17th-century artist Giuseppe Giulianelli. On the altar is the *Death of St Anne* by Giacinto Brandi; on the right-hand wall is the *Virgin in Glory with Four Saints and the Donor* by Filippo Bellini. The frescoes in the apse were carried out in 1690, and badly restored in 1830. In the chapel to the left of the presbytery are two paintings of *St Nicholas*, by the Neapolitan artist Mattia Preti. To the right of the church is the 17th-century cloister, all in brick, with a portico and a loggia above it. The artist Allegretto Nuzi (*see p. 53*) was buried in this church, but the tomb is lost.

The Castelvecchio district

From Piazza del Comune, Via Gentile da Fabriano leads to Via Santa Caterina and a fascinating medieval district on the hill of Castelvecchio, the second castle of the city. On the corner with Via Santa Caterina is the church of **Sant'Onofrio** (1407 and 1727; *if closed the sacristan lives at no. 5*), with an oval interior; the chapel on the right has 14 steps (some containing fragments of the Scala Santa in Rome, the holy stairs said to be those in Pilate's house, trodden by Christ after his condemnation), which were surmounted by an impressive 14th-century Crucifix, probably the work of German woodcarvers, now over the main altar. The figure on the Cross is definitely that of a corpse; the tormented body is almost disintegrating. The Crucifix was originally made for the church of St Francis, now no longer standing. Continuing up the steep, narrow street, on the right is the church of **Santa Caterina** (14th century), built by the Benedictines; the convent is now an old people's home (*ask to see the tranquil 15th-century cloister*). The interior of the church has a single nave and side chapels, richly decorated with paintings and frescoes; over the main altar is an arresting 16th-century painted wooden Crucifix, and in the first north chapel is a copy of the Turin Shroud, made in 1646.

On the northern limit of the old town, in Via Marconi, is the church of **Sant'Agostino** (13th century), built for Count Gualtiero Chiavelli; it was several times destroyed and rebuilt, even becoming a military barracks in 1913. The finely-carved side portal, with its two little lions perched on either side, is certainly worth the walk. The single-nave interior is decorated in the Baroque style, with stuccoes and carved wooden choir-stalls; from the choir it is possible to reach (*ask the priest or sacristan*) two Gothic chapels, part of the original building, decorated with superb 14th-century frescoes by the Giotto School of Rimini. The cloister gives access to the Oratorio dei Beati Becchetti, a chapel decorated by Lorenzo Salimbeni (*see p. 79*) with a monochrome fresco.

ENVIRONS OF FABRIANO

Cerreto and Albacina

Cerreto d'Esi, east of Fabriano, stands along the old road between the Esino and the Potenza rivers, in a strategic position. Roman soldiers digging trenches for fortifications found an underground temple dedicated to the goddess Ceres: hence the name (though some scholars say the name derives from *cerrus*, oak tree). The street plan in the centre is typically medieval (or of Roman camps), consisting of five narrow parallel streets from northwest to southeast, intersected by one street going through the middle, northeast to southwest. These occupy the area of the ancient castle. In the south is a round tower, 25m high, the Torre di Belisario, sometimes called *Torre Maestra*, which is leaning like the tower of Pisa. It looks rather like the Byzantine bell-towers of Ravenna. Belisarius, the Byzantine-Roman general of the 6th century, was in fact employed here by Justinian in his campaign against the Goths, but the tower was probably built in the 8th century (some scholars say the 12th). The construction technique is extremely interesting: although on the outside it is round, inside it is square.

North of Cerreto, near Mt San Vicino, is Borgo Tufico, once the Roman centre of *Tuficum*. From here a short road leads to **Albacina**, a little village on the western slopes of Monte Maltempo, probably built by the survivors of the destruction of Tuficum. The castle looks forbidding enough, and the houses are still protected by stretches of the ancient walls. In the Romano-Gothic parish church (*open 11–1*) is a collection of carved epigraphs from the old city, and a beautiful 15th-century triptych of the *Madonna and Christ Child with Sts Venantius and Marianus*, by the Maestro di Staffolo. Outside, in a niche, is a fresco of the *Madonna with Saints*, by an artist from Perugia, Orlando Merlini, signed and dated 1501.

From Albacina a steep, panoramic road climbs up to Poggio San Romualdo (936m), and the **abbey of Val di Castro** (*ask nearby for key, or T: 0732 22334, Claudia Crocetti*), founded in 936 by St Romuald (*see p. 52*), who died here in 1027. The abbey was suppressed in the 15th century, but you can still see the defensive tower, part of the fortifications, the 13th-century church with an older crypt underneath, and traces of frescoes, the chapter house, the refectory, and the lovely little 14th-century cloister.

THE ROSSA-FRASASSI REGION

GOLA DELLA ROSSA-FRASASSI REGIONAL PARK

Visitor centre: Località La Cuna, San Vittore, Genga, T: 0732 90093.
Founded in 1997, and extending over 9,167 hectares, the park protects a unique environment of limestone mountains, forests, streams, and caves, together with ancient roads, castles, bridges, churches and villages. Breathtakingly beautiful, and rich in wildlife, it is the realm of the golden eagle, goshawk, lanner falcon, peregrine falcon, red kite (recently reintroduced), owls, blue rock thrush, dipper, kingfisher, shrikes, nuthatch, wryneck; numerous mammals, including many species of bat, the wolf, edible dormouse and porcupine (symbol of the park). Flora include the *Moehringia papulosa*, a tiny plant which clings to the rockfaces of the gorge, or the *Ephedra major*, a relic from the Tertiary period.

Genga

Genga, in the heart of the Rossa-Frasassi Park, is a perfectly intact, tiny medieval town (pop. 2,000), set in the darkly forested hills. Its 11th-century castle was the seat of the counts of Genga. Entering the town through the old gate is a quiet square with the parish church of Santa Maria Assunta (1630). The little street in front leads to Piazza San Clemente, and the ex-church of San Clemente, built in the 11th century, now the Museo del Castello (T: 0732 973048), the civic museum, with two works by Antonio da Fabriano (15th century), who was born in Fabriano. There is also a triptych of the *Madonna with Sts Clement and John the Baptist*, signed and dated 1474, together with other paintings, a 15th-century Crucifix, some terracottas by Pietro Paolo Agabiti, and a white marble statue of the *Madonna with Christ Child* from the Valadier chapel in the Frasassi Gorge, perhaps made by the great Neoclassical sculptor Antonio Canova.

The caves

The deep valleys in the park, Gola della Rossa, Gola di Frasassi, and Valle Scappuccia, have always been popular with cave explorers because of the hundreds of fascinating caverns. In one of them, known as the **Grotta del Santuario** in the Frasassi Gorge, Pope Leo XII built the little octagonal chapel, with a bronze roof, of **Santa Maria Infrasaxa** (1828; Giuseppe Valadier); at Christmas time the inhabitants of Genga mount a *tableau vivant* of the Nativity here. The best-known caves are the **Grotte di Frasassi** (*closed 1 and 10–30 Jan, 4 and 25 Dec; T: 0732 90090, call day before for opening times which vary constantly. July–Aug also night visits; tours of caves are professionally guided, from June–Sept also in German, English, French. By previous booking, spelaeologists—min. 6 persons—can request a longer and more difficult exploration; c. 3 hours, the consortium will supply the gear*). The cave system is the most extensive in Europe (new cavities are frequently discovered), but at the time of writing their length is about 26km. In 1971 spelaeologists from Ancona, exploring a rockface, accidentally discovered the Great Cave of the Wind, and then the incredible Ancona Abyss. At 180m long, 120m wide and 200m high, this is one of the largest caves in the world, and could easily contain the Milan duomo. The Frasassi Caves are one of the most popular tourist destinations in the Marche. The tour (c. 1 hour) includes the most famous and spectacular caverns, underground lakes, stalactites, stalagmites and crystal formations; a glittering, magical world, absolutely not to be missed. (*NB: Bring a jacket; the temperature is maintained at 14°C, so as not to destroy the atmospheric conditions necessary to preserve the caves in their pristine state. Try to avoid summer weekends, and get there early.*)

The parking area in front of the caves is dominated on high by the castle of **Pierosara**, perhaps built by the Lombards. Extremely powerful in the 10th century, now only the ruins of the keep and the fortifications remain, but there are still people living in the village. At the foot of the hill, a Roman bridge protected by a Gothic tower crosses the River Sentino to the splendid, ivory-coloured stone church of **San Vittore**

The church of San Vittore alle Chiuse.

alle Chiuse (1007), the abbey of which once controlled more than 40 churches, besides castles and land in the territory of Arcevia, Fabriano, Genga and Sassoferrato. Alarmed that it was becoming too rich and influential, the pope suppressed the community in the early 15th century, and the buildings were used as farmhouses. The façade presents a small portal, with a strong, square bell-tower to the right of it, and a round tower with a spiral staircase inside, to the left. The interior is Greek-cross in layout, with five small apses, somewhat reminiscent of old Byzantine churches; four sturdy columns support the little cupola. Next to the church is the spa centre, while the old abbey now houses the **Museo Speleocarsico** (*T: 0732 97211*), a display of fossils and minerals from the area, including a fossilized ichthyosaurus, 150 million years old.

Serra San Quirico

In a strategic position on the route from Umbria to the coast, where the Esino emerges from the Gola della Rossa gorge, stands Serra San Quirico, surrounded by forests, famous for its walls with houses built on top of them, forming a series of covered streets called *copertelle*. Until quite recently, these were the streets used by the tradesmen and the craftsmen; severely damaged by the 1997 earthquake, many of them are still under repair. A Picene settlement later colonized by the Romans, the fortifications go back to the 10th century. Serra San Quirico has a long tradition for learning; in the 16th century there was a famous school of Greek. In the central Piazza della Libertà is a graceful fountain, in front of the town hall with a 13th-century clock tower. Opposite is the library and the city archives, with many 11th-century parchments, manuscripts and other historic documents. On the right of the square is a loggia offering views over the valley.

From the loggia, Via Mazzini leads to Via Marcellini; on the left is the church of Santa Lucia (13th–17th centuries), in a picturesque old district. The interior has a single nave with a lovely painted ceiling (1694), and a rich Baroque decoration, with gilded altars, stuccoes, many paintings and an elaborate 18th-century organ. The convent next to the church now houses the Cartoteca Storica Regionale delle Marche (*T: 0731 818214 to request visit*), a unique collection of maps of the region, from the 13th–19th centuries. In 1928 the 13th-century church of Santa Maria del Mercato was transformed into a tiny theatre, with the stage in the apse: it is still in regular use. In the highest part of the town, which was practically an impregnable citadel, is the Cassero, rebuilt in 1360, consisting of two towers and the house of the military commander. In the lower new town, Borgo Stazione, at the modern church of Santa Maria del Mercato, 4 Via Moro, is the Museo dei Fossili Don Giuseppe Mattiacci (*T: 0732 956231 or priest 339 3012867 to request visit*), a collection of fossils and minerals from the Esino Valley.

SASSOFERRATO & ENVIRONS

The town of Sassoferrato (pop. 7,100), is neatly divided into two parts: the modern town, known as *Borgo*, and the old centre, 2km above it, called *Castello*, dominated by the cube-like remains of the splendid old fortress. Earthquake repairs are under way, and the museums and churches should all be ready soon.

HISTORY OF SASSOFERRATO

The name derives from the Latin *saxum ferratum*, 'stone surrounded by iron'; it stands on a rocky crest, in an area rich in iron ore. Close by, at the confluence of the Sentino and Marena rivers, stood the Roman city of *Sentinum*, the place where the Romans in 295 BC achieved a momentous victory, known as the Battle of Sentinum, or Battle of the Nations, over the Gauls, the Etruscans and the Samnites; it was later (41 BC) destroyed on behalf of Octavian by Salvidienus Rufus, and rebuilt, when Octavian became Caesar Augustus, for his veterans. Sentinum was probably abandoned in the early Middle Ages, when the survivors of enemy attacks, pestilences and poverty built a new settlement on the top of the mountain, recorded from the 11th century, and the lower town in the 13th century. Control of the town passed from one aristocratic liege lord to another; Cardinal Albornoz, on behalf of the pope, built the castle in 1368. The last of the aristocratic tyrants, Luigi degli Atti, was killed in 1460; after that Sassoferrato became a free commune under the aegis of the Papal States, with its own statutes and coat-of-arms—a stone encircled by an iron band. The economy, based on potteries, stone quarries, bell-casting and the manufacture of nails, flourished. Nowadays the main activities, besides farming, are footwear, leather, clothing, paper, and bathroom fixtures.

The lower town

In the lower town of Borgo stands the 14th-century church of **Santa Maria del Ponte del Piano** (*T: 0732 959030, Don Giuliano, to request* visit), near the Roman bridge over the River Marena. Originally a vast chapel, built by Augustinian friars, it was frequently modified through the years; the bell-tower was added in 1597, and the façade, of brick and stone, was completed in the 17th century. The beautiful organ was installed in 1840. The single-nave interior is illuminated by a series of stained-glass windows on high, over the 12 side chapels. In the third south chapel is an early 16th-century *Madonna of Succour*; in the fourth are 17th-century stuccoes, a 15th-century wooden Crucifix, and two paintings of *Miracles of St Nicholas of Tolentino* by Giovanni Francesco Guerrieri (1614). In the fifth south chapel is a fine work by Ercole Ramazzani, the *Circumcision* (1589). The first north chapel has a panel painting by Pietro Paolo Agabiti of the *Nativity* (1511) and a badly preserved *Martyrdom of St Catherine* by Ercole Ramazzani. In the second is another panel painting by Agabiti of the *Madonna with Sts Catherine and John the Baptist*; in the fourth is a detached fresco of the *Madonna and Child* by a 14th-century Rimini master.

The upper town

On reaching the high town of Castello, in the central square, Piazza Matteotti, is the 14th-century Palazzo dei Priori, which houses the museums (*open 1 Sept–15 July 9–12, Tues and Thur also 4–6, Sun on request; 16 July–31 Aug 9–12 & 4–7 & 9–11, Sun 10–12 & 4–7 & 9–11; closed Mon; other times on request T: 0732 956230/1*). The **Pinacoteca e Sala Perottiana** display paintings (including some by Agabiti) and reliquaries from local churches, together with the old robes worn by the magistrates, and the **Museo Civico Archeologico Sentinate**, with a collection of sculptures, epigraphs, bronzes, mosaics and other objects, from the site of Sentinum. In the same square is the 15th-century home of Cardinal Oliva, Palazzo Oliva, with the **Biblioteca**, consisting of over 10,000 ancient volumes, incunabula, and precious documents.

By taking Vicolo Frasconi, in front of Palazzo dei Priori, and then Via Bentivoglio, you reach (on the left) the 13th-century **church and monastery of Santa Chiara**, where there are some paintings of the *Madonna* by the town's most celebrated native artist, Giovanni Battista Salvi, known as Il Sassoferrato (*see box*). There is also a *Nativity* by Antonio da Pesaro. Still further along, on the right, hidden away in the labyrinth of streets, is the collegiate church of **San Pietro**; a severe façade in white stone, preceded by a little stairway. Entrance is from the side door. The interior, a single nave with side chapels and a deep apse, has many interesting works of art, including a *Flight into Egypt* by Giovanni Contarini over the main door (*closed*), together with two works by Agabiti: a panel painting of *Christ giving the Keys to St Peter*, and a triptych of the *Madonna with Sts Catherine and Joseph*. In the last south chapel is a sculpture by Agabiti of *Baptism*, and over the altar in the third north chapel is a canvas by Claudio Ridolfi of the *Madonna with Christ Child and Sts Crispin and Francis*.

Giovanni Battista Salvi: 'Il Sassoferrato' (1609–85)

Though he was born in the Marche, and though he takes his name from his native town, Giovanni Battista Salvi did not remain long in the provinces. He went early to Rome, where he was apprenticed to Domenichino, and where he made his name. His oeuvre consists almost entirely of religious works (chiefly tender and sweet-faced Madonnas), all attractive and easy on the eye, and all with a serene, static quality that entirely rejects the charged emotion and swirling sensual exuberance of the Baroque. His palate is rich but never violent or unexpected, and his style soft—even sentimental—harking back to the High Renaissance, particularly to Raphael. Sassoferrato was a very fine draughtsman, and this is reflected in his classical exactitude of line and accuracy of depiction. His finest works are scattered in churches and museums worldwide, though the city where he was born does conserve a few, in Santa Chiara (*see above*). As well as religious pieces, Sassoferrato also executed a number of portraits (it is thought that he took a great many private commissions). A particularly fine self-portrait is in the Uffizi.

Going down along Corso Don Minzoni, you find a wide square dominated by the white stone church of **San Francesco**, of 1245–75 in Romanesque-Gothic style. The façade, preceded by an imposing stairway, has a simple portal surmounted by a rose window. The single-nave interior, with a wooden truss-beam ceiling, has a semicircular apse with two side chapels. Over the second south altar is a painting by Ercole Ramazzani of *St Francis and other Saints* (1589); over the third is a *Circumcision* by Guerrieri (1615). Over the high altar is a magnificent 14th-century painted Crucifix by Giuliano da Rimini, a follower of Giotto, thought to be one of the finest works of art in the region. Frescoes by local artists, dating from the 13th–15th centuries, can be seen on the walls.

The 13th-century Palazzo Montanari at 1 Via Montanari (*open same times as the other museums, T: 0732 956232*), built as a convent, later an orphanage, now houses the **Museo delle Arti e Tradizioni Popolari**, a collection of tools, instruments and equipment used by farmers and craftsmen of the area; and the **Galleria d'Arte Contemporanea**, with 3,000 works of art, one of the most important collections of modern art in the region, donated by the artists taking part in the annual exhibition, including Tamburi, Monachesi, Bartolini and Trubbiani.

Santa Croce and Roman Sentinum

Outside the town, c. 2km along the Genga–Arcevia road, surrounded by woods, stands the abbey of **Santa Croce dei Conti**, built in the 12th century by the Atti family, lords of Sassoferrato (the 'counts' of the abbey's name), for the Camaldoli monks of San Vittore, using materials from the Roman city of Sentinum; in its heyday it controlled about 50 churches and priories, but it was suppressed in the 15th century. The strong 14th-century bell-tower, still with its original bell, was probably also a watch-tower. The portal is also original, with four concentric arches supported by pilasters, with sculpted animals on the capitals; unfortunately it is hidden by two supporting walls built by the monks in the early 20th century. The interior is Greek-cross in form, with six small apses; it is a forest of marble and granite columns, some from Sentinum, with very interesting carved capitals. On the walls are many 14th-century frescoes, but the paintings belonging to the church, by Agabiti and Antonio da Pesaro, are in Urbino.

Near Sassoferrato (2km, Località Santa Lucia) is the archaeological park of **Sentinum** (*8–2, closed Sun and holidays; summer always open; T: 0732 9561*), with paved streets, ruined walls, and the remains of a Roman villa. Finds from the excavations are partly at the local archaeological museum, partly in Ancona, and partly in Munich.

ENVIRONS OF SASSOFERRATO

Serra Sant'Abbondio stands on the River Cesano, close to the border with Umbria, a spot inhabited since the Iron Age. The town was founded by the town of Gubbio in the 13th century, as an important checkpoint along the shortest—but most difficult— route from Umbria to the Adriatic. In 1384 the town became part of the Duchy of Urbino, and afterwards followed the destiny of that city. Two of the original four 13th-century gates are still standing, and the town retains its medieval aspect. Close by, on the banks of the Cesano, is the **Crypt of San Biagio**, built in the 4th century or 5th century, using material recuperated from a Roman temple: it is the oldest such crypt in the region, built at the time of the arrival of Christianity along the River Cesano.

On the eastern flank of Monte Catria, in a peaceful wooded valley, stands the isolated monastery known as the **Eremo di Santa Croce di Fonte Avellana** (*open 9–11 & 3–5; Sun and holidays 3–5; T: 0721 730118*), founded by St Romuald (*see p. 53*) in 980, and which gave hospitality to saints, bishops, and Dante Alighieri (1310). A total of 54 bishops, four cardinals, four popes and 60 saints came from this monastery; the community went through alternating periods of well-being and of decadence. It is still a functioning monastery, occupied by monks of the Camaldoli order. The convent buildings surround the white stone Romanesque-Gothic church, with its sturdy bell-tower (1482). Over the main altar is a famous, much-revered wooden Crucifix (1567).

To the right of the church is the chapel of St Peter Damian, who spent some time here in 1035. Still further to the right is the entrance to the hermitage, and the room dedicated to St Peter Damian, with antique 16th–17th-century furniture. Then comes the scriptorium, a luminous room designed to use natural light to advantage; it is also a solar clock, a meridian and a calendar, the rays of the sun arriving on different points of the floor and the walls, indicating times for prayers, equinoxes and solstices. In front is the Biblioteca Dante Alighieri, with more than 10,000 volumes, including rare editions of the 16th and 17th centuries.

Close by is a little cloister, with strong arches, some Romanesque and some Gothic. From the cloister you reach the oldest part of the convent; notice the little openings through which the food was passed to the monks in their cells. Ask the monks to point out the spot on the road to Pinacciano, c. 300m from the convent, where a very unusual echo repeats words of more than one syllable, or even short sentences, just once.

Further north is **Frontone**, at the foot of a small, strangely shaped castle (*open 10–12.30; winter Sat and Sun only; T: 0721 786302*), thought to be an excellent example of 11th-century military architecture. In 1530 Francesco Maria della Rovere, Duke of Urbino (*see p. 313*), made this the seat of Giammaria della Porta from Modena, naming him count. Splendid scenery surrounds the village, with the dramatic outline of Mt Catria dominating the view.

PRACTICAL INFORMATION

GETTING AROUND

• **By train**: Fabriano (T: 0732 3294 or 0732 22281), Genga-Terme, San Vittore and Serra San Quirico stations are on the Rome–Fabriano–Falconara Marittima line; from Fabriano another line reaches Sassoferrato and Pergola.

• **By bus**: Fabriano city buses and services to Genga (Frasassi Caves) leave from Piazzale Matteotti.
Autolinee Binni, T: 0732 629592/4, runs services to Camerino, Esanatoglia, Matelica, San Severino, Macerata, Porto Recanati and Ancona.
CONTRAM, T: 0737 634011 or 0737 632402, operates services to Cerreto d'Esi, Camerino, Pioraco, Visso and Pievetorina.
Autolinee Vitali, T: 0721 862515, www.vitaliautolinee.it, runs services to Pesaro, Fano, Arcevia, Sassoferrato, Pergola and Ancona.

INFORMATION OFFICES

A good source of information for this area is: Comunità Montana dell'Esino-Frasassi, 268 Via Dante, Fabriano, T: 0732 6951, www.cadnet.marche.it/cm, and a useful website is www.misaesinofrasassi.it
There are information offices at:
Cerreto d'Esi Municipio, 5 Piazza Lippera, T: 0732 670722, www.provincia.ancona.it/comuni/cerretodesi/default.htm.
Fabriano IAT, 70 Corso della Repubblica, T: 0732 625067; Municipio, Piazza del Comune, T: 0732 709238 or 0732 709319, www.comune.fabriano.an.it; Ufficio Cultura, T: 0732 709223 or 0732 709232.
Genga Tourist Information Bureau, 2 Largo Leone XII, T: 0732 973039 or 0732 973001; Municipio, 4 Via Roma, T: 0732 973014, www.provincia.ancona.it/comuni/genga; Ufficio Consorzio Grotte di Frasassi, T: 0732/ 97211, www.frasassi.com
Sassoferrato Tourist Information Bureau, 3 Piazza Matteotti, T: 0732 956231; Municipio, 5 Piazza Matteotti, T: 0732 956205, www.cadnet.marche.it/sassoferrato, www.comune.sassoferrato.an.it
Serra San Quirico Municipio, 1 Piazza Libertà, T: 0731 818214, www.provincia.ancona.it/comuni/SerraSanQuirico/default.htm; Tourist Information Bureau, 5 Piazza Marconi, T: 0731 880079; Pro Loco, 14 Piazza Libertà, T: 0731/86750; Parco Regionale Gola della Rossa e di Frasassi, headquarters: Complesso Santa Lucia, 4 Via Marcellini, T: 0731 86122, www.cadnet.marche.it/park_rossa; www.parcogolarossa.it

HOTELS

Fabriano
€€€€ **Hotel Relais Marchese del Grillo**. Small, exclusive hotel with a renowned restaurant, in the villa of an eccentric marquis made famous in a film by Alberto Sordi. Garden and car park. 73 Frazione Rocchetta Bassa, T: 0732 625690, www.marchesedelgrillo.com
€€€ **Borgo Antico**. Very comfortable small family-run hotel, with an indoor

pool, and a garden, but no restaurant. 32/a Frazione Borgo Tufico, T: 0732 678409, www.pinetahotel.com

Frontone

€ Locanda del Castello. Comfortable accommodation in an old inn near the castle, renowned for the *crescia* they prepare at weekends—you can eat it to your heart's content. 5 Piazza della Rocca, T: 0721 790661.

Genga

€€€ Hotel Frasassi. Convenient position in the park, with a restaurant. 33 Via Marconi, T: 0732 905003, www.hotelfrasassi.com

€€€ Hotel Le Grotte. Smart new hotel near caves; restaurant, garden, splendid views. Frasassi, T: 0732 973035, www.hotellegrotte.it

€ La Quercia. Country inn, with a good restaurant. 29 Boano di Colcello, T: 0732 972025.

Sassoferrato

€€€€ Relais degli Scalzi. Delightful central hotel with a good restaurant. 3 Piazza Mazzini, T: 0732 970820.

Serra San Quirico

€ Le Copertelle. ■ Rooms in a 14th-century building over an excellent restaurant. 3/a via Leopardi, T: 0731 86691.

FARM ACCOMMODATION

Fabriano

Gocce di Camarzano. Beautiful 16th-century farmhouse, near woodland; sheep and farm animals, cereals and vegetables; wonderful food and local wines. 70 Località Moscano, T: 0732 628172.

Il Casale. In a convenient position close to the SS76, an 11th-century farm hamlet with its own church, offering comfortable accommodation and organic food. 2 Via della Chiesa, Località Campodiegoli, T: 0732 723830 or 333 2906738, www.fabrianoedintorni.it/ilcasale

La Casa di Campagna. Farm raising sheep, also fruit and vegetables. A good centre for trekking. 32 Località Bassano, T: 0732 5720.

La Ginestra. Farm producing wheat, sunflowers and honey, also a museum of farming—Museo della Civiltà Contadina. Campers welcome. 145 Via Serraloggia, T: 0732 24013.

Frontone

Azienda del Catria. Comfortable cabins (at 1500m) provided by a logging company in the heart of the forest; pony-trekking and rambling. Open May–Oct. 90 Via Fonte Avellana, T: 0721 786158.

Sassoferrato

Il Miroccolo. Cosy, comfortable rooms in the little houses of an ancient farming hamlet; good restaurant, organic methods are used to produce wine, honey, hams and salami. Pool with sauna, archery, sculpture courses, English spoken. 1 Località Monte, T: 0732 974510, www.ilmiroccolo.it

Serra San Quirico

Chiaraluce. The farm, close to town, is famous for high quality olive oil; apartments to rent. Closed winter. 2 Via Pergolesi, T: 0731 86003.

La Tana del Lele. Farm where poultry and rabbits are raised, and olive oil, cereals, fruit, forage, timber grown. Home cooking with wine from the farm, pool, volleyball, table-tennis. Closed winter. 1 Località Madonna delle Stelle, T: 0731 86737.

Serra Sant'Abbondio

La Loggia. Small farm (guests can help) surrounded by forest, close to Fonte

Avellana monastery, pigs and boar are raised. 11 Via Fonte Avellana, T: 0721 730497.

MONASTERY ACCOMMODATION

Sassoferato
Convento La Pace. 1 via La Pace, T: 0732 9334 1–2.30 or 8–9.30 (padre Francesco).
Ostello San Biagio in Caprile. Benedictine monastery-farm, founded in 1390 in wooded countryside, where the monks raised goats and sheep. The beautiful stone buildings have recently been restored, and are now used as a hostel (Spartan accommodation). 91/b Frazione Campodonico, T: 0732 259455. Summer only.

EATING OUT

Borgo Tufico (Fabriano)
€€ La Fonte del Papa. Immensely popular restaurant not far from Fabriano, try the *pappardelle al cinghiale* (large flat noodles with wild boar sauce), accompanied by a bottle of Lacrima di Morro d'Alba from their own vineyards. Booking essential. Closed Mon evening and Wed. 4 Frazione Borgo Tufico, T: 0732 677161.
Cerreto d'Esi
€ Zeroincondotta. Run by enthusiastic and competent young people; a pleasant experience. Closed Mon and Sat midday. 22 Via Roma, T: 0732 678687.
Fabriano
€€€ Marchese del Grillo. Elegant, well-known restaurant offering beautifully prepared traditional dishes; very good wine list. Closed Sun evening & Mon. 73 Via Rocchetta, T: 0732 627958.

€€ La Vecchia Cartiera. This restaurant was once a paper factory. Interesting pasta dishes, followed by rabbit, boar, or crayfish from the river. Closed Mon. 76 Strada Statale, T: 0732 72167.
Frontone
€ Amabile. Small, family-run restaurant near the castle. Roasted and grilled meats, including rabbit, boar and venison; home-made pasta; *crescia* with cheese and ham; local wine. Closed Tues. 2 Via Leopardi, T: 0721 790710.
Genga
€€ Il Parco. Excellent restaurant, also rooms, walking distance from caves. Try *pincinelle al ragù*, the local spaghetti made from bread dough, served with meat sauce;. Very courteous management. 6 Via Marconi (in front of Genga railway station), T: 0732 90267.
€€ La Cantina. Sustaining food and wines, 100m from the caves. Closed Mon in winter. 1 Località San Vittore Terme, T: 0732 90330.
€ Da Maria. Just above the village, away from the hordes of tourists at Frasassi, a welcoming restaurant specialising in roast and grilled meat, and many different kinds of fungi. Well chosen wine list. Closed Thur. 66 Località Pierosara, T: 0732 90014.
Sassoferrato
€ Hostaria della Rocca. ■ Cosy in winter, with an open fireplace; in summer you eat outside, pasta or polenta, meat or fish, crayfish from the river are superb. Local wines. Also pizzeria in the evening. Closed Wed. 3 Via Cardinale Albornoz, T: 0732 95444.
€ Le Due Sorelle. Home cooking, using the best local ingredients; cakes and tarts for dessert. Closed Mon,

Jan–Feb. 18 Monterosso Stazione, T: 0732 974021.

Serra San Quirico

€€ La Pianella. ■ About 2km from Serra San Quirico, a country restaurant serving the simplest possible local food; absolutely delicious. Much use is made of fresh ricotta, pit-matured cheese, ham and country herbs. Try the wild strawberry mousse for dessert. Local wines. Good value for money. Closed Mon. 31 Via Gramsci, Località La Pianella, T: 0731 880054.

€€ Le Copertelle. The building is 14th century, the cuisine traditional; try the crayfish from the river, sometimes made into a spicy soup. Also serves delicious, sinful desserts. Closed Tues. 3 Via Leopardi, T: 0731 86691.

CAFÉS & PASTRY SHOPS

Fabriano

Bar Centrale. Coffee, tasty snacks and pastries. Piazza del Comune,

Caffè Ideal. Besides coffee, there is hot chocolate (many kinds), teas and herbal infusions. 32 Piazza del Comune.

Caffè Storelli. Historic café founded 100 years ago, home-made ice cream. 55 Corso Repubblica.

Sassoferrato

Fiori. For your coffee break, also home-made ice cream. 11 Piazza Matteotti.

FESTIVALS & EVENTS

Cerreto d'Esi Traditional fair, 6 Aug. *Festa dell'Uva*, festival to celebrate the grape harvest, last Sun in Sept.

Fabriano *Palio di San Giovanni Battista*, a series of competitions and traditional fairs, based on those of the 14th century;

Info: Ente Palio di San Giovanni Battista, 35 Via Balbo, T: 0732 626848. 24 June.

Genga *Presepio Vivente*: the Nativity scene is enacted by the people in the spectacular Sanctuary Cave at Frasassi; Info: Associazione Amici del Presepio, 1 Piazza San Clemente, T: 0732 973019 or 335 5972607. Christmas period.

Sassoferrato Feast of St Hugh, concert, procession and fireworks; 26 July; *Rassegna d'Arte G.B.Salvi e Piccola Europa*, celebrations held since 1951, exhibiting paintings, sculptures, graphics and artistic publications; Info: Municipio, 3 Piazza Matteotti, T: 0732 956230. July–Aug.

Serra Sant'Abbondio Procession of the Passion of Christ, Palm Sun; *Palio della Rocca*, competitions, games, dancing and eating, medieval style, 2nd week in Sept.

LOCAL SPECIALITIES

This part of the region is known for delicious salami, made by completely removing the fat from the pork before preparing the sausage, then adding tiny cubes of the best quality lard, before leaving it to mature for up to six months. The result is a fine-grain salami, dark red in colour, with a characteristic firm consistency, much sought-after by connoisseurs. In Fabriano **Bilei**, 7 Via Cialdini, is a historic grocery store which stocks it, as does **Sabatini**, 5 Piazza Miliani, where they will also make sandwiches (*panini*) for you on the spot. **Bartolini Carta**, 7 Palazzo del Podestà, for hand-made paper. **Lotti**, on 62 Corso Repubblica (founded 1735), stocks books and high-quality paper of many kinds.

CAMERINO, MATELICA & SAN SEVERINO MARCHE

These three ancient cities are deep in the southwest part of the region, close to the Sibylline Mountains. Almost perfectly equidistant, they form a triangle; and although similar in many ways, each has its own personality: Camerino has a tradition of learning and culture; Matelica is down-to-earth and friendly, with superb and unusual museums; San Severino Marche boasts the highest tower and the oldest church clock in the region, and is also a place to admire the skilful workmanship and design flair of Italian goldsmiths. It was the birthplace of the painters Lorenzo and Jacopo Salimbeni.

CAMERINO

The university town of Camerino (pop. 6,800) extends along a crest, protected by ancient fortifications. Damage caused by the 1997 earthquake has been the occasion for much reconstruction and renovation; the consequent bandbox-new appearance of the old town may be disconcerting for those romantics who prefer to see their history flaking off the walls together with the plaster. The town boasts a botanical garden, and the museums and well-stocked shops are a delight. The town is built of local rusty grey-coloured sandstone tuff; at sunset, the city turns to gold.

HISTORY OF CAMERINO

From its solitary, strategic vantage point in the hills, inhabited since the Neolithic period, Camerino has always dominated the surrounding area, a role enhanced by the castles which were built on the hilltops in the Middle Ages—it could signal to about 60 of them, by day or night, using smoke, flags, torches and drumbeats. Often mentioned in ancient texts, the city was able to forge an alliance with the Romans on the basis of absolute equality—*aequus foedus*. Over the course of the centuries it became one of the foremost political and cultural centres in Italy; its *marca*, or march, founded by Charlemagne, extended from the Apennines to the Adriatic. Further prestige came in the early 14th century, when the *Studiosus Camerinensus* was formed (declared a University in 1727); the teachers were often illustrious men of learning, such as Cino da Pistoia (1321), and the city was renowned for its artists—the so-called Camerino School. Under the da Varano family, from the 14th–16th centuries, the economy was particularly strong; trade and manufacturing gave rise to the creation of a Jewish ghetto, and besides wool, silk and leather, paper was also made in nearby Pioraco.

EXPLORING CAMERINO

NB: It is easy to park below the town; elevators then take you right into the centre.

In the southwest of the town is the **Rocca**, a fortress built by Cesare Borgia in 1503; from here there is a good view over the Sibylline Mountains. The moat has been filled in, and is now Piazza della Vittoria. Close by is one of the medieval city gates, Porta Malatesta, rebuilt during the Renaissance. Leading north from the square is the old main street, once called the *Arengo*, now, changing names along the way, it is Via Pieragostini, then Via Lilli, and then Corso Vittorio Emanuele. Notice on the left, in Piazza Umberto, the Baroque church of **Santa Maria in Via** (1639). Inside is a 13th-century panel painting of the *Madonna with Christ Child*, said to have been brought from Smyrna (modern Izmir) by the Crusaders.

Approaching the city centre, the aristocratic palaces become more frequent. At the end of Corso Vittorio Emanuele, on the left, is the Municipio, once the bishop's palace, heavily restored in the 19th century. The courtyard gives access to the splendid 19th-century opera house, **Teatro Filippo Marchetti** (*T: 0737 630854*), dedicated to the local composer Filippo Marchetti, a contemporary of Verdi. Scenes from his opera *Ruy Blas* decorate the ceiling in the auditorium. A Roman bath-suite was discovered under the building during restorations.

The city centre

Heart of the city is Piazza Cavour, elegant in its 16th-century lines, with a bronze statue of Pope Sixtus V (1587), by the local sculptor Tiburzio Vergelli, in the centre. To the north is the solid-looking **duomo** (1832), a reconstruction of the preceding Romanesque church, destroyed by the 1799 earthquake. The interior, with a central nave and two side aisles punctuated by columns and pilasters, is reminiscent of Vanvitelli's work. In the chapel to the right of the presbytery is a 15th-century local wooden statue of the *Madonna of Mercy*, while in the corresponding chapel to the left is a good copy of an *Annunciation* by Guercino. The crypt contains some fragments of the preceding church and two stone tombs: a 6th-century sarcophagus from Ravenna, and the Gothic-style tomb of St Ansovino (14th century). The tomb is interesting for the menagerie of strange animals cavorting around the base; above them are scenes from the life of the saint, who was bishop of Camerino in the 9th century; above these is the stone coffin, surrounded by protective figures. Surmounting the whole sculpture is the *Madonna* under a magnificent triple arch.

To the west is the Archbishop's Palace (1580), with a graceful portico. On the first floor is the **Diocesan Museum** (*T: 0737 630400; phone to book visit*), with works of art from local churches. Highlights include a 15th-century triptych by Girolamo di Giovanni, an exponent of the Camerino School whose eloquent paintings reflect his formative years in Padua, and his admiration for Piero della Francesca, Mantegna, and Filippo Lippi. There is also a large *Madonna in Glory and St Philip* by Tiepolo (1740). Long forgotten, it was identified by chance in 1960, in the church of San Filippo.

The east side of the square is dominated by the **Palazzo Ducale** (14th–15th centuries), home of the da Varano dukes, now seat of the university. There is a fine library, the Biblioteca Valentiniana, with a large collection of books and manuscripts preserved in a series of beautiful rooms. The typical Renaissance courtyard with its portico gives access to the various parts of the building, including the Tourist Office, the *Sala degli Sposi*, with 15th-century frescoes, and the terraces. At the foot of the high walls of the palace is the Botanical Garden of the University, at 2 Viale Oberdan (*open 9–1 & 3–5; Sat 9–1; Sun closed; T: 0737 633444*).

Around San Domenico

Continuing north, and going downhill, you reach Piazza Costanti with the enormous convent of San Domenico, now the property of the University, which has restored the buildings to house the city museums. Built in the 14th century, the convent passed through various hands until 1860, when true degradation set in—the two churches and the other monastic buildings became barracks, schools, offices and even the tram station. In the north wing of the convent is the **Pinacoteca e Museo Girolamo di Giovanni** (*open Apr–Sept 10–1 & 4–7; Oct–Mar 10–1 & 3–6; closed Mon; T: 0737 402310*), with archaeological displays, including a 2nd-century Roman mosaic floor found in the city centre, coins, bronzes and pottery. Particularly important is the collection of paintings, some of them by Girolamo di Giovanni (*see previous page*), including the *Madonna of Mercy* or *Tedico Banner* (signed and dated 1463) and a delightful fresco of the *Madonna with Christ Child and Angels, St Sebastian and St Catherine of Alexandria*. There are also 35 sculptures by the local contemporary artist Bruno Bartoccini (1910–2001), and the collections of the University Museum of Natural Science.

East of San Domenico is the church of **San Venanzio**, destroyed by the 1799 earthquake and rebuilt in 1875. It retains the beautiful 14th-century Gothic portal and part of the portico which once surrounded the building. The vast, luminous interior, damaged by the 1997 earthquake, contains many works of art; the cupola is impressive, as are the two monumental Baroque organs. In the presbytery, the carved walnut choir-stalls (18th century) come from the ex-church of San Francesco; the large wooden Crucifix (16th century) was locally made. The church is dedicated to St Venantius, a local martyr whose piety under torture was legendary. Seeing that persecuting him was exhausting his aggressors, he is said to have struck a rock from which a spring miraculously flowed to quench their thirst (*see below*).

The Spring of St Venantius

A walk north from San Domenico, along Via Venanzi (c. 400m), leads to the church of the Madonna delle Carceri (left), a high eight-sided brick building (16th century). Inside is an interesting fresco of the *Madonna with the Christ Child*, older than the church itself, because it was once a wayside tabernacle. Continuing along the road, keeping left at the first crossroads, you reach the 13th-century church of Sant'Anastasio and the Spring of St Venantius, said to have been created miraculously by the saint to provide water for his thirsty persecutors. From here there is a good view of Camerino, on high.

ENVIRONS OF CAMERINO

About 4km east of the city is the **Convento di Renacavata**, a modest building of 1531 with a small museum (*T: 0737 644480 to request visit if closed*) of religious articles and objects used by in the past by the Capuchin friars. On the high altar of the church is a 16th-century majolica of the *Madonna Enthroned with Sts Francis and Agnes*, thought to be by Mattia della Robbia, himself a Capuchin friar. North of the Capuchin convent is the delightful Romanesque church of San Gregorio Magno in Dinazzano, which can be reached by a narrow road of about 2km. There are some interesting sculptures in the interior, including a painted wooden Crucifix (16th century), a white marble statue of St James (15th century), a 14th-century shrine of carved wood, and a lovely 15th-century *Madonna of Mercy* with two groups of sufferers under her cloak.

Rocca da Varano and the south

A road leads southeast from the city to the dramatically situated **Rocca da Varano** castle (*open 25 Apr–2 June Sun 4–7; July, Sept, Oct Sat–Sun 4–7; Aug every day except Mon 10.30–12.30 & 3.30–7.30; T: 0733 232527, www.roccavarano.it*), dominating the surrounding hills, and probably built in the early 13th century. The picturesque ruins, animated by a colony of garrulous jackdaws, are now frequently used for concerts and exhibitions. Continuing south towards Polverina, after about 2km there is a turning left for the lovely 11th-century church of **San Giusto** (*open Sun 8.30–1 & 3–7*), surrounded by the houses of San Maroto, a tiny village of only 15 inhabitants. Circular, there are four little rounded chapels jutting out from the wall. Next to the church is the bell-tower, probably part of a castle which has since disappeared; some researchers say not a castle, but a hunting lodge of Charlemagne. The interior, with its low dome, is particularly impressive.

Southwest of Camerino is **Serravalle di Chienti**, almost on the border with Umbria. Surrounded by wooded hills, at the point where the Chienti enters a narrow gorge, it was formerly of great military importance, and a meeting-point for merchants. In the 13th century a hostel for pilgrims was built here, and the da Varano dukes of Camerino erected several formidable castles. Serravalle owes its greatest fame to the fossils of the Pleistocene period (now in the museums of Camerino and Ancona) found in the nearby hills, proving the contemporary presence of tropical fauna such as the hippopotamus, the sabre-toothed tiger, the rhinoceros and the elephant, with cold-climate animals including bear, deer and bison. The town was the epicentre of the September 1997 earthquake, which did so much damage, both here and in Umbria; it is ironically referred to as *Zio Terry*—Uncle Earthquake.

Pioraco and the west

At beautiful little Pioraco, summer resort of the da Varano family, there are paper factories which still use the energy of the Potenza falls, as in 1360 when the first ones

View over Camerino, with its green, rolling hills.

were built. The village itself is much older; it was probably a station along the Roman *Via Prolaquense*. In the main square, Piazza Leopardi, is the 14th-century church of San Francesco; over the second north altar is a wooden statue group of the *Crucifixion with the Madonna and St John*, donated by the paper manufacturers in the 17th century. The convent, with its attractive cloister, now houses the Paper and Filigree Museum (*open 10–12.30; closed Sun; T: 0737 42485*) and a little museum of fossils and fungi (*open July–Sept 11–12.30; Sun and holidays 11–12.30 & 5–7; T: 0737 42203*).

On the slopes of Monte Primo, just over 3km southeast of Pioraco, is the delightful hamlet of **Seppio**. In the parish church, *la Parrocchiale*, is a well-preserved *Madonna of the Tears* (1466) by Giovanni Boccati. Boccati was a cultivated man, both painter and musician, and is the most famous exponent of the Camerino School, although he lived and worked mainly in Perugia, and was influenced by the Siena painters and by Piero della Francesca. His style is original and pleasing, and provided inspiration for a much greater Marche-born artist: Raphael.

MATELICA

Matelica (pop. 10,100) stands on a spur dominating the point where the River Braccano joins the Esino. The town, built of rose-coloured brick, is a busy industrial centre, well known for its production of excellent DOC wine, Verdicchio di Matelica.

HISTORY OF MATELICA

Matelica, of ancient origin, was *Matilica*, a Roman *municipium*, and the seat of a bishopric in the 5th century. Later it was devastated by the Lombards. A commune in 1160, it apparently sympathised with the Guelphs, pro-pope; for this reason, in 1175, it was destroyed on behalf of the Swabians by Christian, the fearsome archbishop of Mainz. Matelica rose again, reaching such a strong position among the papal allies, that in 1340 it had a democratic constitution; the pope, however, gave Matelica to the Ottoni family, who ruled as despots, causing the collapse of the economy. In 1578 it passed under the direct rule of the Papal States and became exceedingly wealthy—there were 8,000 inhabitants and 90 churches. It has a strong manufacturing tradition, particularly famous in the past for woollen cloth.

Piazza Mattei and the cattedrale

The central Piazza Mattei is surrounded by aristocratic palaces. In the middle is an eight-sided fountain (1587) with four marine divinities; walking round the fountain seven times anticlockwise is said to grant a wish—though local people say whoever does it is *patentatu da mattu*, certified insane. On one side of the square is the elegant Loggia degli Ottoni (1511) and the Palazzo Pretorio (1270) with the clock tower

(1175). In front is the Baroque **Chiesa del Suffragio**, with an attractive elliptical interior; in the chapel to the right is a 17th-century painting of the *Crucifixion* by Salvatore Rosa. On the other side of the square is Palazzo Ottoni (1452) which houses the **Pinacoteca Comunale Raffaele Fidanza** (*open July–Sept 11–1 & 4–7; March–June mornings only; closed Tues; T: 0737 781830*), an interesting collection of works by the local 19th-century artist Fidanza, together with medieval and Renaissance pottery.

By following the main street, Corso Vittorio Emanuele, north, you reach the **cattedrale** (Santa Maria Assunta), completely rebuilt in the 18th and 19th centuries, with an unusual façade incorporating the 15th-century bell tower. The beautiful interior, a central nave with two side aisles and a dome, was returned to its original Renaissance form in 1928. Over the altar in the south transept is a polychrome terracotta *Deposition*, perhaps the work of a German artist. In the presbytery is a 17th-century carved wooden choir, with unusual caryatids.

Museo Piersanti

At no. 11 Via Umberto is the **Museo Piersanti** (*open Mar–Oct 10–12 & 5–7, closed Mon; Oct–Mar Sat and Sun only 10–12 & 4–6; T: 0737 84445*) a collection once belonging to Monsignor Venanzio Filippo Piersanti (1688–1761), an extraordinary, refined personality who was Master of Ceremonies and personal secretary to no fewer than six popes; an *éminence grise* with an obvious eye for beautiful things. The collection has been enriched through the years by members of the family and later by the city of Matelica. There is a particularly impressive panel painting of the *Crucifixion* by Antonio da Fabriano, signed and dated 1452, and considered to be his masterpiece, though so few of his works survive. The loincloth is of a type woven in Perugia in the Middle Ages, and still produced today in Matelica. The many other paintings include works by Vittore Crivelli, Francesco di Gentile, Lorenzo d'Alessandro (who was born in San Severino Marche in the 15th century) and Arcangelo di Cola (born in Camerino and active in the early 15th century); there is a majestic 12th-century painted wooden Crucifix from the church of Sant'Eutizio, considered one of the most important examples of Romanesque art in the Marche. The rooms of the palace still retain the original furnishings, and a vast assortment of ivories, miniatures, porcelain, natural curiosities, tapestries and religious objects—following the fashion of the day, it was a *Wunderkammer*.

Opposite the museum is the 19th-century opera house, **Teatro Piermarini** (*T: 0737 85088*), designed by Giuseppe Piermarini of Foligno, who also designed La Scala in Milan. A recent archaeological survey under the theatre has brought to light both a Picene hut and a Roman bath-house. Not far from here, in Piazza Lorenzo Valerio, is the church of Sant'Agostino (14th century), with a richly decorated Romanesque portal.

Piazza San Francesco

In Piazza San Francesco the 13th-century church of **San Francesco** has a Romanesque doorway, but the elegant interior is 17th century, with some particularly important paintings—Carlo Crivelli painted the altarpiece for this church, the lovely *Madonna of the Swallow*, now in the National Gallery, London. In the first south chapel, by the entrance, is a canvas of *Purgatory* by Ercole Ramazzani (1586); the same artist carried out the two paintings in the fifth south chapel, *Immaculate Conception* and *Ascension*. In the second south chapel is a precious composition by Marco Palmezzano, signed and dated 1501, and still in its original frame, of the *Madonna enthroned with Sts Francis and Catherine of Alexandria*. It is thought that Caterina Sforza, the 'female warrior' who struggled against Cesare Borgia and his nepotistic father, was the model for the Madonna. In the fourth south chapel is a triptych of the *Madonna with Saints* by Francesco di Gentile. Over the third north altar is an *Epiphany* by Simone de Magistris; in the first north chapel, is a panel painting by Simone Cantarini (17th century) of the *Madonna with Saints*. In the presbytery are fragments of a large fresco by Allegretto Nuzi (1350). More frescoes, some by the de Magistris brothers, are in the cloister corridors and in the little Cappella della Passione, which opens onto the cloister, and is not to be missed (*ask the friars for the keys*).

In the same square, the magnificent painted salons of Palazzo Finaguerra house the **Museo Archeologico** (*open Tues–Fri 4.30–6.30; Sat, Sun and holidays 10.30–12.30 & 4.30–6; T: 0737 781830*), a stupendous collection of finds relating to recent excavations in the city centre, including the contents of four Picene tombs: one is that of a little girl, another that of a warrior, with a fearsome helmet. A room is dedicated to the white marble sphere found near Palazzo Pretorio, called the *Globo di Matelica*.

THE STONE ASTROLABE

In 1985, during works of consolidation under the foundations of Palazzo Pretorio, a mysterious white marble sphere was found, 30cm in diameter and weighing 35kg. The marble is of a type found at Aphrodisias in Turkey. The globe is divided into two hemispheres, with a series of small regular holes with signs near them, and ancient Greek inscriptions. Experts have found that the words refer to the Zodiac, and that if pins are placed in the holes, the sphere functions as a kind of calendar, giving information about the movement of the constellations, solstices and equinoxes, when the object is observed in sunlight. A similar globe, now in the museum of Nafplion in Greece, was found at Mycenae in 1939. It is thought that the Matelica globe was purposely designed for this place, and would not function properly elsewhere. If it really does go back to the 4th century BC, as some experts believe, whole new realms of conjecture open up. Just what high levels of civilisation did Matelica achieve, so very long ago?

AROUND MATELICA

A country road leads northeast of Matelica to the village of **Poggetto** (c. 10km), then a stiff climb up a path will take you to the lowering ruins of the Ottoni family fortress,

Rocca degli Ottoni, or *Roccaccia*, on the slopes of Mt San Vicino. Probably built in the 10th century, its underground dungeons were notorious. Stories abound, telling of treachery, murders, and a hidden treasure protected by two huge snakes, which can only be eliminated by a magic spell. Even the birds are silent here; the atmosphere is forbidding; but the walk up is very panoramic.

Less than 2km east of the centre of Matelica is the village of **Braccano**, with brightly-painted house fronts; these works of art have recently been provided by artists from the academies of the Brera (Milan), Urbino and Macerata, a successful initiative which attracts many photographers.

Esanatoglia

West of Matelica is the small town of Esanatoglia, under Monte Corsegna, overlooking the San Pietro Valley and the River Esino. Esanatoglia was once known as *Sant'Anatolia*. After fighting a war for independence against Matelica in 1201, it was taken by the Visconti family in 1351, followed by a certain prosperity; during that period many churches were decorated with works of art by Diotallevi di Angeluccio. The town has numerous medieval houses with three doors—one for day-to-day use, one for the entrance of bridal couples (life), and one for the exit of coffins (death). On the edge of the town is a little 14th-century church, the **Madonna di Fontebianco**, the church of the cemetery. Inside is a fresco of the *Crucifixion* by Diotallevi di Angeluccio, who was born here, dated 1366. On the main street, Corso Vittorio Emanuele, is the 13th-century Palazzo del Pretorio, with Gothic arches; close by is the church of **San Martino** (11th century), which houses an impressive wooden Crucifix (13th century) carved from a walnut tree. In the sacristy of the church of **Santa Maria** is a painting of the *Crucifixion* by Simone and Giovanni Francesco de Magistris (1565).

Continuing along, passing under an archway, on the main street, which rises steeply up with steps, is a 13th-century public fountain. This is followed by a little square with trees, where on the right is the Romanesque **Pieve di Sant'Anatolia**, with a charming 13th-century portal, and an ancient bell-tower with a Roman epigraph forming part of the base. Local industries provide mineral water, liqueurs and leather.

A beautiful walk follows the San Pietro Valley to the source of the Esino (c. 7km, 3hrs there and back), between Mt Costa (914m) on the right, and Mt Corsegno (998m) on the left. The upper part of the valley is a nature reserve.

SAN SEVERINO MARCHE

San Severino Marche (pop. 13,300) is formed of two distinct parts: Castello, high on the Montenero hill, and Borgo at its foot, founded in the 13th century to make life easier for traders and manufacturers. The old Romanesque cathedral, Duomo Vecchio, is in the upper part, while the ample, elliptical Piazza del Popolo, the main square, is down below. That this has always been a relatively wealthy city can easily be seen: the solid 16th-century palaces, the Baroque churches, the elegant 19th-cen-

tury houses and the rich collections in the museums bear witness to a past (and present) of bountiful farms and profitable industry, including leather, building materials,
food processing and chemicals.

Always a traditional enemy of Camerino, San Severino Marche was a stronghold of
the Picenes and of the Romans, as witnessed by the imposing ruins of *Septempeda*
close to the town, and a place of many busy industries. In the 14th–15th centuries it
assumed an important place in European art, thanks to the Salimbeni brothers. Even
today the town has an aristocratic, medieval atmosphere which offsets the bustling
trade of the centre and the prosperous suburbs.

Piazza del Popolo and the Pinacoteca

The subdued ochre stucco and brick of the palaces around Piazza del Popolo and the
comfortable porticoes give it a relaxed, welcoming air. It was once the market place
and is always thronged with people. There are enticing shop windows, especially
those of the jewellers, who display elegant and unusual locally-made jewellery with
pearls, coral, turquoise, gold and silver. To the south, at no. 45, is the town hall, built
in 1764, housing a collection of paintings and sculptures by contemporary local
artists, the **Galleria d'Arte Moderna** (*T: 0733 6411 to request visit*). Among the palaces
is that of Servanzi Collio (16th century), and the Palazzo dei Governatori (16th century) with a clock tower designed by locally-born Ireneo Aleandri (19th century).
Next to it is the church of **Santa Maria della Misericordia** (14th century, rebuilt
17th). Inside are some frescoes by Lorenzo Salimbeni (*see box opposite*), signed and
dated 1404. After the porticoes on the south of the square is the opera house, Teatro
Feronia (*open 9–1 & 4–8; T: 0733 641296*) of 1827 by Ireneo Aleandri. The **Duomo
Nuovo** (*open 8.15–12 & 4–7*), dedicated to St Augustine, still has a Gothic portal
(1473) in brick, but little remains of the original 13th-century building, restored
many times through the centuries. In the interior (1827) is a canvas by Pomarancio,
Noli me tangere, over the third south altar, and many other works by local artists,
including a painted wooden Crucifix (1420) in the sacristy.

Palazzo Tacchi-Venturi, at 39 Via Salimbeni, was built in the 15th century incorporating a 10th-century tower. It houses the **Pinacoteca Tacchi Venturi** (*open 9–1;
closed Mon; T: 0733 638095*), with an admirable display of the works of the local brothers Lorenzo and Jacopo Salimbeni. There is also a *Madonna of Humility* by Allegretto
Nuzi; a large polyptych by Paolo Veneziano; another magnificent one, with many
saints, by Vittore Crivelli; and a masterpiece by Pinturicchio, a panel painting of the
Madonna of Peace.

San Lorenzo in Doliolo

Leaving the square by taking Via Salimbeni, on the left is a medieval quarter with the
ancient church of San Lorenzo in Doliolo. According to tradition, it was founded by
Basilian monks in the 6th century on the site of a pagan temple to the goddess
Feronia, but the present church goes back to the 12th century and has been modified
several times. Typical of San Severino is the 14th-century bell-tower, which forms the

façade, and with its double-lancet windows is similar to that of the Duomo Vecchio (*see p. 80 below*). The interior is simple and harmonious: a single nave with a series of brick columns, and a raised presbytery at the far end, under which is the crypt, with frescoes by the Salimbeni brothers. To the left of the high altar is a beautiful wooden Crucifix (14th century), particularly venerated by the local people because it is thought to be miraculous; it comes from the old abbey church of Sant'Eustacchio in Domora (9th century), now in ruins. Notice the 1572 baptismal font.

Lorenzo and Jacopo Salimbeni
(fl. early 15th century)
The Salimbeni brothers were born in San Severino Marche sometime in the late 14th century. Little or nothing is known of their lives: all we have comes down to us from their surviving works, which are superb local examples of the International Gothic, certainly on a par with the work of the style's most famous exponent, Gentile da Fabriano, even though the brothers are virtually unknown outside the Marche. The International Gothic, whose compass stretched across France, the Netherlands, Bohemia and northern and central Italy, is characterised by a poised elegance, still and static, but without the rigidity of the true Gothic. There is also a mingling of strong design with loving attention to detail, often of birds, animals and flowers. The natural and the stylized come together in images which are redolent of medieval courtliness. The best works by the Salimbeni that can still be seen in the Marche are in their native San Severino, in Urbino and in San Ginesio.

St Lucy, by the Salimbeni.

Castello

Up on the hill (343m) is Castello, the old city, founded by the survivors of Septempeda when it was destroyed by Totila in 545; their bishop Severinus had recently died and the people were unwilling to leave him, so they put his body on an ox cart and let fate decide where their new town would be. The oxen stopped high on Mount Montenera, so this is where the city was built. After passing through the 14th-century **Porta delle Sette Cannelle** (fountain with seven spouts), the old city centre is reached, offering splendid views over the old houses and the surrounding hills. On the right is the clock tower (at 40m, the highest medieval tower in the region), slightly leaning; this was the first in the Marche to have a clock installed, at the beginning of the 14th century.

The **Duomo Vecchio** stands on the left; perhaps 10th century, certainly remodelled in 1061, and again through the years. The 14th-century façade with its small rose window is a fine setting for the elegant portal, surmounted by an aedicule; the bell-tower, with large double-lancet windows, is the model for the others of San Severino. The interior was transformed in the 18th century; there is a beautiful 15th-century choir, and there are Salimbeni frescoes in the chapel under the bell-tower. Damaged in the 1997 earthquake, the cathedral may be closed temporarily for repairs. The body of the bishop-saint Severinus (*see above*), still intact, is on view in the chapel behind the building.

To the left of the old cathedral is the 15th-century cloister. The convent now houses the **Museo Archeologico Giuseppe Moretti** (*open 10–1& 4–8; Oct–June weekends only; closed Mon; T: 0733 638095*), with well-displayed prehistoric pottery and weapons, Roman epigraphs and funeral stones from Septempeda, and 6th-century BC objects from Picene graves. Giuseppe Moretti was born in San Severino Marche in 1876 and was well known for his Etruscan discoveries.

AROUND SAN SEVERINO MARCHE

By taking the SS 361 Macerata road, after 1km you reach the church known as **Santa Maria della Pieve** (13th century), which still has its Romanesque apse with unusual fin-shaped buttresses. Inside there are votive frescoes (*enquire at the town hall; T: 0733 638414, for permission to see them*). Near the church, down by the river, are the ruins of **Septempeda** (*to visit, enquire at the Museo Archeologico; see above*), with 2nd-century BC walls and the remains of the baths.

A short distance along the SS 502 road for Cingoli, c. 2km out of town, is the magnificent Renaissance sanctuary church of **Santa Maria del Glorioso** (1519), with a beautiful octagonal cupola; the solemn interior houses a terracotta image of the *Pietà* said to have wept tears in the 15th century.

Rocca d'Ajello

At 6km from the ancient crossroads town of Castelraimondo, in the locality known as Mergnano, stands Rocca d'Ajello, an impressive da Varano fortress built in 1260. Although private property, the castle has recently been restored and opened to the public (*open April–Nov: Mon–Fri T: 06 8541382; Sat–Sun T: 0737 644309 or 0737 644342, to request visit*). The courtyard with its well-head is notable, as is the Hall of Arms with a vaulted ceiling made of blocks of sandstone. There is a lovely Italian-style garden with turreted walls.

PRACTICAL INFORMATION

GETTING AROUND

• **By train**: Castelraimondo, Matelica and San Severino Marche stations are on the Civitanova–Fabriano line.
• **By bus**: Camerino, Castelraimondo, San Severino Marche, Esanatoglia and Matelica are connected by bus and can also be reached from Fabriano, Macerata, Recanati, Porto Recanati, Loreto and Ancona (CONTRAM, T: 0737 634011; Binni Autolinee, T: 0732 629592/4).

INFORMATION OFFICES

Camerino, Matelica, San Severino Marche, Esanatoglia, Castelraimondo and Pioraco form part of the association STL Terre dell'Infinito (T: 0733 843569, www.terredellinfinito.it), providing information and a tourist discount card, *infinito card*.
Camerino IAT Pro Camerino, 19 Piazza Cavour, T: 0737 632534; Tourist Information Bureau, Via Pieragostini, T: 0737 634725, www.camerino.sinp.net; Comunità Montana di Camerino, Via Venanzio Varano, T: 0737 61751, www.comcamerino.sinp.net
Esanatoglia Municipio, 1 Piazza Leopardi, T: 0737 889132, www.esanatoglia.sinp.net; Pro Loco, T: 0737 889149.
Matelica Municipio, 1 Piazza Mattei, T: 0737 781811, www.comune.matelica.mc.it; IAT Associazione Pro Matelica, 3 Piazza Mattei, T: 0737 85671.
Pioraco Municipio, 1 Largo Leopardi, T: 0737 42142, www.pioraco.sinp.net;
Pro Loco, 7 largo Leopardi, T: 0737 42715.
San Severino Marche Municipio, 45 Piazza del Popolo, T: 0733 6411, www.sanseverino.sinp.net; IAT, 43 Piazza del Popolo, T: 0733 638414, www.sanseverinoturismo.it

HOTELS

Camerino
€€€ **I Duchi**. Large 19th-century hotel with a good restaurant. 72 Via Favorino, T: 0737 630440, www.hoteliduchi.it
€€€ **Il Cavaliere**. Near Lake Polverina, with a restaurant. 33 Via Mariani, T: 0737 630125, www.hotelilcavaliere.com
€€ **Del Sole**. Tiny hotel with garden, tennis, and restaurant; close to Lake Polverina. 59 Via Mariani, T: 0737 46115.
€€ **Roma**. In a central position, with a restaurant and car park. 6 Piazza Garibaldi, T: 0737 630125.
Matelica
€€€ **Massi**. Very comfortable, with a restaurant, vegetarian food on request, and a car park. 8 Via Merloni, T: 0737 85470.
Pioraco
€€€ **Il Giardino**. Small, comfortable hotel with a good restaurant, also a garden and car park. 7 Viale della Vittoria, T: 0733 42591.
San Severino Marche
€€€€ **Servanzi Confidati**. A 17th-century aristocratic palace, very comfortable, with a good restaurant; car park. 13–15 Via Battisti, T: 0733

633551, www.hotels.it
€€€ Due Torri. ■ Comfortable family-run hotel at Castello, in the old city, with a good restaurant; very peaceful. 21 Via San Francesco, T: 0733 645419, www.duetorri.it

BED & BREAKFAST

Camerino
Poggio Maria. Lovely old building in the countryside. English, French and Spanish spoken. Open summer only. 5 contrada Agnano, T: 0737 644318.

Esanatoglia
Konka. ■ Isolated old cottage, homemade bread and cakes baked in a stone ovenl lovely peaceful position. 170 Località Conca, T: 0737 881481, konka12@libero.it

COUNTRY HOUSES

Camerino
Palazzetto Giochi, At Casale di Morro, 5km from Camerino. No children in this 16th-century villa; exclusive and expensive. Call Marche Segrete, T: 0736 818621, info@marchesegrete.com or T: 347 3336460.

San Severino Marche
Villa Berta Polo Club Piceno. Accommodation in a Renaissance villa with riding school, cookery or restoration courses; good restaurant. SS361 for Macerata, T: 0733 636350, villaberta@sanseverinoturismo.it

FARM ACCOMMODATION

Camerino
La Cavallina. Very good local dishes at this farm specialising in organic pro-

duce, in the Chienti valley near Lake Polverina, 10km from Camerino. Closed Dec. 13 Via Mariani, località Polverina, T: 0737 46173, www.lacavallina.it

Castelraimondo
Il Giardino degli Ulivi. Medieval atmosphere in ancient restored hamlet, organic food; mountain bikes available. 54 Via Crucianelli, Castel Sant'Angelo, T: 0737 642121.

Matelica
Locanda San Rocco. An 18th-century farmhouse between Matelica and San Severino Marche with delightful rooms. English, Spanish and Portuguese spoken. Bicycles available. Closed Easter, July and Sept. 2 Località Collaiello, Gagliole, T: 0737 641900.

Muccia
Col di Giove. Small farm with a justly famous restaurant; you won't want to go home! 8 Località Col di Giove, T: 0737 646291, www.coldigiove.it

San Severino Marche
Casal Villanova Country House. A comfortable old farmhouse, with delicious food. Località Pitino, T: 0733 636127.
Locanda dei Comacini. Comfortable rooms and a good restaurant; the farm produces olive oil and vegetables. 2 Via San Francesco, T: 0733 639691.

RESTAURANTS

Camerino
€€€–€€ Osteria dell'Arte. Delicious home-made food, high standard, good wines; member of the Slow Food chain. There is an inexpensive set menu at lunchtime. Closed Fri. 7 Via Arco della Luna, T: 0737 633558.

€€ **Ponti**. Small, simple restaurant serving tasty traditional dishes. Closed Mon. Via Tre Ponti, T: 0737 644539.

Esanatoglia

€€ **La Cantinella**. Classic dishes, including fish and crayfish from the river. Closed Thur. 9 Corso Italia, T: 0737 889585.

Matelica

€€ **Il Camino**. Elegant restaurant in an old farmhouse, with open fireplaces and veranda. Closed Mon. 593 Località Piannè, T: 0737 786095.

€€ **La Taverna della Torre**. Delicious local dishes, try grilled lamb with truffles; also wine bar and pizzeria. Closed Tues. 3 Via Leopardi, T: 0737 786063.

€ **Anna**. Simple, inexpensive meals. Closed Sat. 16/18 Via Pergolesi, T: 0737 786074.

Pioraco

€ **Trattoria Degli Amici**. Pasta dishes, including delicious lasagne; friendly atmosphere. 3 Piazza Matteotti, T: 0737 42130.

San Severino Marche

€€ **La Mia Cucina**. For traditional fare. Closed Tues. 5 Via Indivini Pacifico, T: 0733 638313.

€ **Alle Antiche Mura**. Tasty and inviting local dishes, including lasagne and pigeon. Closed Sun. 34 Via Gorgonero, T: 0733 638746.

CAFÉS PASTRY SHOPS & SNACK BARS

Camerino

Bar Centrale. Delicious pastries, hot chocolate, and home-made ice cream. Piazza Cavour.

Diana. Comfortable café, serving home-made ice cream. 55 Corso Vittorio Emanuele.

Pizzeria Re. Excellent pizza and snacks. 27 Via Camillo Lili, T: 0737 637133.

Rosa Blu, For locally-roasted coffee. 13 Piazza dei Costanti.

Matelica

Al Teatro. Traditional coffee shop, wine bar and restaurant. Closed Wed. 17 Via Umberto.

FESTIVALS & EVENTS

Camerino Feast of St Venantius, 18 May. *Corsa alla Spada*, historical evocations of the 15th century, including jousts and an exciting race to reach a sword, run on foot through the city streets; Info: Palazzo Ducale, Piazza Cavour, T: 0737 630512, www. corsaallaspada.com, May. International Music Festival, T: 0737 636041, www.gmicamerino.it, July–Aug. *Festa del Torrone*, the city streets are crowded with vendors of nougat, prepared according to the traditional recipe, mid-Dec.

Castelraimondo *Infiorata*, pictures and designs are created with flower petals along the streets, June (Corpus Christi).

Matelica *Matilica Municipium Romanum*, 1st-century Roman costume pageant, concluding with a chariot race. The chariots, from Cinecittà, were used for the film *Ben Hur*, end Aug–early Sept. Feast of St Adrian, 16–17 Sept.

Pioraco Festival of the Paper Manufacturers, 14 Sept.

San Severino Marche *Palio dei Castelli*, 15th-century fun and games, including archery contests and races; Info: Associazione Palio dei Castelli, 14 Largo Croce Verde, T: 0733 634322, www.paliodeicastelli.org, June. Feast of

St Severinus, June. San Severino Blues music festival, Aug.

Camerino
Francucci, at 17 Via Conti di San Maroto, for the famous local nougat. **Montanari**, at Via XX Settembre, is an old-fashioned grocer's for local cheeses and salami.
Matelica
Artelaio, Vicolo Cuoio, and 11 Corso Umberto (Piersanti Museum), for hand-woven cloth. **Cantina sociale Matelica e Cerreto d'Esi Belisario**, 12 Viale Merloni, has local wines.
Muccia
Distilleria Varnelli is the best-known distillery of the region for *mistrà*, liqueur flavoured with *Pimpinella anisum*, and Amaro Sibilla bitters.
San Severino Marche
Allegretto Galliano, Via Garibaldi, is the oldest bakery in town, selling marvellous bread. **ATO**, 56 Via Salimbeni, sells country produce and Cagnore olive oil, excellent quality. **L'Idea e la Forma**, 95 Piazza del Popolo, has distinctive jewellery made by the owner.

CINGOLI & THE
CENTRAL HIGHLANDS

The lovely town of Cingoli (pop. 10,100) stands on a natural terrace, high on the eastern side of the mountain of the same name. The surrounding countryside is rich in contrasting colours, a delight (and a challenge) for artists and photographers. Still enclosed by its ancient walls, Cingoli has a serene atmosphere and many Renaissance palaces and medieval churches to admire, although most of them have been altered through the years. Sadly, it is suffering from a dwindling population. Because of its high position, catching the sun from all sides, it is one of the last towns to get dark in the evening, which has given rise to a popular local proverb: *Ancora non è notte a Cingoli*! (In Cingoli it isn't yet night), meaning it's never too late. Apparently, this goes back to the Romans—*nondum cinguleis nox venit atra jugis*. The panorama from Cingoli over the woods and farms from the Conero promontory to the Sibyllines, said to encompass the entire Marche region and beyond, is so famous that the city is called *il balcone delle Marche*.

View from Cingoli: the 'balcony of the Marche'.

A walk around the city walls from the outside (c. 1500m), if possible in the early morning to avoid haze, is very pleasant; by keeping your binoculars and a map of the region handy, you will be able to distinguish Fermo, Recanati, Osimo, Ancona, Jesi, Senigallia, Pesaro, the Sibylline Mountains, Mount Conero and the Adriatic, the Apennines as far as Gran Sasso, and the rivers Tenna, Chienti, Potenza, Musone, Esino and Metauro.

HISTORY OF CINGOLI

The foundation of the town is uncertain, but could go back to a Roman colony, which settled here in the 3rd century BC, and soon became of military importance. *Cingulum* was destroyed in the 5th century AD by the Goths. Rebuilt, it was annexed by the Lombards, and later became part of the see of the bishop of Osimo. For some time Cingoli declared itself an independent commune, but it suffered the fate of many such towns during the intestine fights between the noble families of the region; it was taken over by the Cima family in the 14th century, and eventually came under papal control. Thanks to this, a long period of peace from the 16th–18th centuries turned Cingoli into a centre of learning: arts and sciences flourished, and many beautiful palaces were built. It was well known for the skill of its stonemasons and in fact most of the houses are built of the local grey stone, called *scagliola*. Silk was also manufactured here until the 19th century.

Piazza Vittorio Emanuele II

Centre of the town is Piazza Vittorio Emanuele II, which occupies the area of the Roman acropolis. On one side of the square is the 16th-century **Cattedrale di Santa Maria Assunta**, with an unfinished façade of 1831 and an interior which was completely transformed in 1938. The frescoes are by the local artist Donatello Stefanucci (20th century). The three large polygonal apses are unusual; in the sacristy is a 14th-century panel painting by Antonio da Fabriano. On the opposite side of the square is the **Palazzo Municipale**, built in the 12th century on the foundations of a Roman structure and renovated in 1531. It is dominated by the Romanesque clock tower, still with the original stone quadrant of 1482. The town hall houses the **Archaeological Museum** (*open Mon–Wed 8.30–1.30; Thur–Sun and holidays 3–5; T: 0733 603399*) with material found in the area of Cingoli going back to prehistoric, Roman and medieval times. The short Via Cassaro leads from the square to the public library which also houses the **Pinacoteca Comunale Donatello Stefanucci** (*open 10.30–12.30; closed Sun; T: 0733 602877*), dedicated for the most part to works by Donatello Stefanucci, and paintings from the churches of Cingoli.

Via Foltrani and Lo Spineto

To the left of the cathedral is Via Foltrani, where there are many imposing Renaissance palaces built by the noble families of the town—notice especially nos 5, 6 and 9. The street widens into Piazzetta Mestica, with the 14th-century church of **San Domenico** (*call Biblioteca to request visit, T: 0733 602877*). The interior, designed by Arcangelo Vici in 1725, is a particularly fine example of local Baroque architecture. The magnificent painted wooden Crucifix was made for this church in the 16th century by an unknown artist, while the altarpiece, a painting of the *Madonna of the Rosary Enthroned with Saints* by Lorenzo Lotto, signed and dated 1539, has recently been restored. The scene is presented in a golden afternoon light, forming a symmetrical pyramid, surmounted by the Mysteries of the Rosary neatly arranged in three rows. The Madonna is leaning slightly to the left to present St Dominic with the Rosary; her movement is balanced by that of Baby Jesus, who appears about to throw Himself to the right into the arms of the goodly bishop St Esuperantius, who is trying to give Him a model of the city of Cingoli. A cherub in the foreground is offering a rose to St Catherine, who looks rather shocked, while on the left Mary Magdalene gazes out at the onlooker flirtatiously, through lowered eyelashes, dressed in the latest Venetian fashion with a very low-cut bodice and the bleached blonde hairstyle that was all the rage at the time.

By keeping to the right at the end of the street, while admiring the wonderful panorama to the left, you will reach the church of **San Benedetto** (rebuilt in the 17th century). Over the main altar is a *Deposition* by Annibale Carracci. From here Via Leoni leads into the oldest part of Cingoli, still very medieval in character, to Piazza Puccetti. The local people call this district **Lo Spineto**. In the square is the massive Palazzo Puccetti, one of the most important in the town, built in the 17th–18th centuries. From the left of the palace Via dello Spineto leads down to Porta Spineto, one of the old city gates; along the way, a little street gives a view to the left over another ancient district, called Polisena, where the workers lived—a fascinating labyrinth of alleys, stairways, little gardens and tiny houses. Beyond Porta Spineto is the round church of **Santa Caterina d'Alessandria** (13th century); inside are some beautiful carved and gilded screens. The large building beside it, now a hospital, was the castle of the Cima family that was transformed into a monastery in the 15th century.

Corso Garibaldi and district

From Piazza Vittorio Emanuele II Via Podestà, one of the most characteristic streets in the town, leads east to the church of **San Filippo Neri**, built in the 13th century on the site of the first cathedral. Although the building has been considerably modified through the years, the portal is still that of the 13th century, and the interior is opulent Baroque, with little side chapels decorated with stuccoes and frescoes.

Also leading out from the main square is Corso Garibaldi, the ancient Via Maggiore, with a whole series of magnificent palaces, most of them of the 16th–17th centuries. A short distance along, on the right, Via Cavour leads to the 14th-century church of **San Francesco**, with a beautiful high polygonal apse. The image of the saint carved over the main doorway is by the local sculptor Jacopo da Cingoli (13th century). A little further along is the celebrated **Balcone delle Marche**, one of the best viewpoints in the entire region. Mount Conero can be seen isolated in front of the sea in the distance.

On returning to Corso Garibaldi, on the right is an old fountain called *fonte del Maltempo*, 'bad weather fountain', because the water only flows after storms; it is said that whoever drinks the water will return to Cingoli. The relief on the fountain shows the city coat-of-arms: a deer under a yew tree. At no. 87 is Palazzo Castiglioni (*open Aug 10–12.30 & 5–7; other months on request; T: 0733 602531*), where Pope Pius VIII was born. The furniture is original and in good condition; there is also a restaurant and wine bar in the building. By keeping to the left at the end of the corso you will reach another of the city gates, **Porta Pia** (sometimes called Porta Piana), erected by Ireneo Aleandri in 1845 in honour of Pius VIII, and the little church of **San Nicolò** (13th century), with a Romanesque portal from the church of Sant'Esuperanzio; the carving was carried out by Jacopo da Cingoli.

Figure of Christ, a copy by Sebastiano del Piombo of the figure from his own *Flagellation*, in Rome.

Sant'Esuperanzio

From Porta Pia the road for the cemetery leads to Cingoli's most important church, **Sant'Esuperanzio** (c. 500m walk). Romano-Gothic, it was erected in the late 12th century by Benedictine monks from the monastery of Fonte Avellana to accommodate the tomb of Esuperantius (5th century), an African bishop who is patron saint of the city, . It is outside the city walls because this was the spot indicated by the saint before he died. He never set foot in the town during his lifetime, telling his followers Cingoli would be destroyed if he entered. Even today the processions in his honour stop at Porta Pia. The grey stone façade has a rose window and a Romanesque doorway carved by Jacopo da Cingoli in 1295 with charming simple sculptures: *St Esuperantius between Two Angels*, and the *Mystic Lamb with Symbols of the Evangelists*. The interior is stunning: a single nave, with six great arches to support the roof; it looks like an upturned boat. The presbytery (1278) is slightly higher than the main church and is approached by two little staircases. On the walls are votive frescoes, some of which are very deteriorated, going back to various historical periods. Notice between the fourth and fifth right-hand arches, the altar of the Sacrament with its lovely marble decoration and candelabra; the altar itself is supported by a 14th-century marble sarcophagus. Above it, in the niche, is a 14th-century wooden Crucifix, probably locally made, where Christ is seen with His arms not nailed to the cross. Headache sufferers still come to pray in front of this Crucifix, said to give miraculous relief. In the centre, stairs go down into the crypt, renovated in 1777, where the relics of St Esuperantius are kept. In the sacristy, shown on request, is a panel painting by Sebastiano del Piombo of the *Flagellation* (16th century). a late work, a copy made by Sebastiano himself of a detail of the famous painting in Rome, showing only the body of Christ.

THE CENTRAL HIGHLANDS

Around Cingoli

By taking the SS 502 from Cingoli towards San Severino Marche, after about 5km, park just before the tunnel and take the path to the left, to explore protected woodland where many yew trees grow, some of which are hundreds of years old. Timber from these trees was once used for making longbows; Cingoli was famous for them.

About 9km east of Cingoli, on the secondary Valcarecce road to Apiro, is the **Sidecar Museum** (*13 Via Valcarecce, T: 0733 602651, www.sidecar.it, phone before visit*) with a good restaurant next door (*closed Tues*). This surprising collection of motorbikes, sidecars and scooters includes a 1914 Frera, an Afrika Korps 1942 BMW and the Bohmerland, the world's longest sidecar.

West of Cingoli is a large and lovely artificial lake, called by the inhabitants either Lago di Cingoli or Lago di Castreccioni, formed by a dam on the River Musone. At Moscosi, on the west bank, archaeologists have brought to light traces of an Iron Age settlement. Continuing on the road towards Monte San Vicino, you pass the abandoned village of **Coldigioco**, now used in the summer as a geological observatory for students from Carleton College, Northfield, Minnesota. This area is one of the best in the world for studying the effects of the supposed fall of an asteroid into the Gulf of Mexico, about 75 million years ago, probable cause of the extinction of the dinosaurs.

Apiro

Apiro, on an airy hilltop, was considered a holy place by the primitive populations of the area. Nowadays it gets quite crowded in July and August, when city dwellers arrive to spend their summer holidays. In the evenings they go to local country restaurants to eat *crescia*, soft tasty bread studded with lard and cheese. In the central square is the town hall, once Palazzo dei Priori (1286), considerably modified through the years. Inside is a luminous polyptych by Allegretto Nuzi, signed and dated 1366, of the *Madonna with Child*, *Crucifix* and *Saints*, and two 15th-century frescoes from the church of San Francesco. Close by is the Baroque collegiate church of **Sant'Urbano** (17th century), with magnificent wood carvings in the interior, such as the choir stalls on either side of the main altar, the gilded frame over it, and the walnut pulpit (all by Andrea Scoccianti, 17th century), and the Callido organ (1771). In the bell-tower is the so-called *campanone*, an enormous bell with a very harmonious sound, made here on the spot in 1885, and weighing 1,885kg. In the same building is the city museum, the Raccolta di Arte Sacra Sant'Urbano (*T: 0733 611118 to request a visit*), has religious objects, embroidered robes and works of art from nearby churches, including some 17th-century paintings by Andrea Lilli, Valentin de Boulogne, and Jusepe de Ribera.

By taking the main street, Corso Vittorio Emanuele, immediately on the right is the church and convent of **San Francesco** (13th century), once called San Martino, where the council meetings used to be held. The Romano-Gothic portal is original; in the Baroque interior are many 15th-century frescoes.

The Abbey of Sant'Urbano

By taking the road which leads west from Apiro towards Domo, after c. 9km you will see a turning on the right indicating **Sant'Urbano**. In a fertile valley on the banks of the Esinante stream, this was once one of the most powerful abbeys in the Marche, with its own castle, and dominating in its turn other castles and religious communities. The abbey is first mentioned in a document of 1033, when the abbot stipulated a convention with his counterpart at San Vittore delle Chiuse; the tone is authoritative, as if Sant'Urbano were of long standing; it was in fact probably founded in about 980. Before long, it was controlling a vast area, and the abbot was chosen from the pope's closest allies. From here many monks were sent to create communities in the Esino Valley. The power of Sant'Urbano was intolerable to the town of Apiro, quarrels were frequent, until in 1219 the abbey was devastated, and the abbot, in exchange for protection, vowed allegiance to Jesi, promising the tenth part of the income from the abbey lands. Frequent raids from Apiro, in spite of Jesi's attempts to avoid them, made this a rather inconsistent payment. In 1442 Sant'Urbano had declined to the point of becoming part of the possessions of Val di Castro Abbey, near Cerreto d'Esi. In 1810 it was confiscated by the French, and sold to a wealthy family. First restored in 1923, it has now been acquired by the town council of Apiro for use as tourist accommodation and a meeting centre.

The present church goes back to the late 13th century, retaining its Romanesque form. The brick façade is simple, tall and narrow, with a worn stone portal; to the rear are three splendid apses, a large central one and two smaller ones on either side of it, decorated with little blind arches at the top. The superb interior has survived the centuries very well, with a central Gothic-style nave, and two Romanesque side-aisles. There is a large presbytery, which was used by the monks, and an interesting crypt, separated into three aisles by walls, with small openings in them; on the altar is a carved inscription dated 1140. The various capitals to be seen in the church are carved with scenes of hunting, mythical animals, fish, birds, fruit and leaves with symbolic significance, and geometric motifs.

Filottrano

Filottrano, about halfway between Cingoli and Osimo, is a remarkable place: with 3,003 families, it has over 1,000 registered businesses. Many of these are menswear tailors who supply Italy's rag trade.

The town itself is one of the oldest in the Marche; there was a settlement of Bronze Age Celts on this spot about 3,000 years ago, but the name Filottrano derives from *mons filiorum Optrani*, 'mount of the sons of Optranus', a legendary Lombard chieftain. Because of its fine strategic position, Filottrano was often besieged by the warring factions of the area, and there were frequent boundary disputes with Cingoli and Osimo. In 1815 a violent battle was fought here between Austrian and Italian troops, which saw victory for the Italians. In summer 1943 a desperate ten-day street battle between liberation forces and the Germans earned the population a silver medal for valour.

Filottrano is built entirely of brick. Via Leopardi is the ancient main street; halfway along is the unfinished 16th-century church of **San Francesco** (once known as San Rocco) with a beautiful stone portal on the left side. The luminous interior (*open mornings on request, T: 071 7121560*) in the Baroque style, has a lofty cupola and fine old columns. The confessionals are particularly well preserved, as is the pulpit and the elegant tiled floor. In the apse is a panel painting of the *Resurrection of Lazarus*, signed and dated 1543 by Pompeo Morganti, while over the third north altar is a copy, contemporary with the original, of Guido Reni's famous *St Michael slaying the Devil*.

In front of the church a little street leads to Piazza Mazzini, dominated by the Chiesa Nuova, dedicated to St Mary of the Angels (17th–18th century), with an elegant and unusual Borromini-style bell-tower. The bronze statue in this square represents *Optranus the Lombard*, legendary founder of the town. Leading out from the square is a tiny medieval street called Vicolo delle Mura Castellane, where parts of the fortifications and a polygonal defence tower can be seen. In the central Piazza Cavour is the distinguished **Palazzo Municipale** (16th century), inspired by Bramante, with a clock tower on the left. The town hall encloses the opera house (1812).

Close by, in Palazzo Beltrami-Luchetti, are two important private museums. The **Museo del Biroccio** (*phone to book visit, T: 348 5226262*) is a collection of the famous painted farm carts, in four rooms.

THE BIROCCIO OF THE MARCHE

Sturdy and heavy, yet brightly painted, this two-wheeled cart was designed to be drawn by teams of oxen. It was used for farm work, but also for the transport of goods and people. Until quite recently a bride with her dowry would reach her new home on one of them, accompanied by musicians and dancers. Thought to be of Etruscan origin, a *biroccio* was always made of elm, with parts in walnut, oak and acacia. The painted designs vary from province to province; flowers predominate in Macerata and Ascoli Piceno, while '*pupi*', or human figures, are always seen on the Ancona carts, and countryside scenes on those of Pesaro. Every element has a symbolic meaning: the ear of wheat for wealth, the dog for loyalty, the swallow for love. Present on every cart is the reassuring figure of St Anthony Abbot, patron saint of farmers.

On the upper floor is the **Museo Giacomo Costantino Beltrami** (*same hours as above*), with many interesting maps and souvenirs of American tribes gathered here by Beltrami, the famous explorer. Born in 1779 at Bergamo, Beltrami was sent to Filottrano as a servant of the Napoleonic government. On the fall of Napoleon he was forced into exile and carried out several explorations; in 1823 he was the first to discover the source of the Mississippi. He died in 1855, in this house.

Appignano and Treia

Founded in the 13th century, **Appignano** has many skilled craftsmen and a thriving furniture industry; beautiful pottery and wicker or wooden furniture are made. The tiny town centre still has a medieval atmosphere. Close to the western wall is the parish church, San Giovanni Battista, originally built in the 11th century, with a Gothic bell-tower and a lavish Baroque interior with stuccoes and statues. In the chapel on the right is a canvas by Ernst van Schayck of *St Catherine*, while the organ is dated 1753.

Treia, southwest of Appignano, has a dramatic skyline of ancient walls, towers and palaces, and a particularly photogenic old centre. The summer festival here is very exciting, and includes a competition of *pallone al bracciale* (*see p. 103*). In the Middle Ages the town was known as *Montecchio*, reverting to the original Roman name of *Trea*, hence Treia, in 1790, when Pope Pius VI declared it a city. The centre is Piazza della Repubblica, which opens onto a superb view over the surrounding countryside. The central part of the balustrade is occupied by a bronze monument of Pope Pius (1785). On the square is the Municipio (16th–17th centuries), with a portico, seat of the Archaeological Museum (*open 10.30–1 by previous arrangement only; T: 0733 215117*), containing material coming from Roman Trea and the surroundings. Opposite the church of San Filippo Neri (18th century) is the attractive seat of the Accademia Georgica (*open Tues and Thur 4.30–7.30; Sat 9–12; T: 0733 215056*), by Giuseppe Valadier. Past members include Alessandro Volta, inventor of the electric battery.

Via Lanzi leads down to the Cattedrale, of which only the 12th-century bell-tower survives of the original building, which was reconstructed in the 18th century. Inside, on the pilaster next to the chapel on the left, is a bust of Pope Sixtus V thought to be by Giambologna. The main altar is constructed entirely of pieces of marble brought from Roman Trea. In the crypt is a panel painting of the *Assumption of the Virgin* by Vincenzo Pagani.

A short distance from Treia, on the Chiesanuova–Cingoli road, stands the **Santuario del Santissimo Crocifisso**, built in the early 20th century on the site of an ancient church. Inside, over the second south altar is a fresco of St Sebastian (16th century) of the Umbrian school, while on the main altar is a locally-made and much-revered wooden Crucifix (15th century), with a face that seems to change expression when viewed from the sides and the front. At the foot of the Crucifix is a model of Treia. This was the site of ancient Trea, and in fact there are numerous fragments of Roman sculpture included in the wall of the bell tower, along the perimeter wall, and inside the entrance to the convent.

South of the Potenza river

Perched on a rocky crest between the valleys of the Potenza and Chienti rivers, about 12km west of Macerata, is **Pollenza**. Founded in the Middle Ages with the name of *Monte Milone*, it was given the present name in 1862 because close by stood an important Roman settlement called *Pollentia*. Nowadays Pollenza has an important furniture industry which supplies local and overseas requests for *faux* antique pieces; many of the inhabitants are well known throughout Italy for their knowledge of antiques and their skill at restoring them.

The town centre is still partly surrounded by the old walls. Along Via Roma, the main street, is the church of San Giuseppe with a magnificent 16th-century doorway. Via Roma leads to the central Piazza della Libertà, where an old Roman altar is now used as the monument to the fallen soldiers of the town. Here is the exquisite Teatro Comunale Giuseppe Verdi (*open 8–1; T: 0733 548716*) by Ireneo Aleandri, his last work (1883). Continuing along Via Roma, on the right is the church of San Francesco e Sant'Antonio da Padova, rebuilt in 1932; the Gothic portal (1377) belongs to the original church.

The church of **Santa Maria Assunta di Rambona** (*open Mon–Fri 4–7.30; Sat and Sun 10–12 & 3–7, or by previous arrangement; T: 0733 216696*) stands about 4km from Pollenza, on a hillside overlooking the River Potenza. Built in sandstone, it was founded in the 8th century by the Lombard Queen Ageltrude on the site of a Roman temple to the fertility goddess Bona, called *Ara Bonae*; the name later became *Arambona* and then *Rambona*. The queen had dedicated her church to St Flavian, but in the 12th century the building was completely rebuilt, using the original stone and fragments of the Roman temple, and dedicated to the Madonna. The façade is no longer the original, but the three apses are still intact. Inside, the church presents a central nave with two side aisles; there are traces of 16th-century frescoes in the central apse. The crypt is magnificent, with 14 ancient columns complete with fascinating Romanesque capitals; the 15th-century frescoes in the central apse are of the school of Lorenzo Salimbeni.

It is said that **Montecassiano** was founded by refugees after the destruction of nearby *Helvia Ricina* (*see p. 103*). The town, a farming community, consists of a series of concentric streets, connected by steep alleys and stairways. At the entrance to the town is the oratory of San Nicolò (13th century), with a series of well-preserved 15th-century frescoes in the interior. This church has one of the oldest bells in the region, dated 1382. Close by is the turreted, photogenic Porta Santa Croce, which gives access to the stepped Via Nazario Sauro, leading to the main square, Piazza Leopardi, with the Municipio, once Palazzo dei Priori (15th century), and a particularly beautiful portico. Left of the town hall are an archway and more stairs, leading to the Gothic-style church of the Assunta, built in the 15th century to replace an earlier church erected in 1136 by the monks of the Santa Croce al Chienti abbey. The terracotta façade has a splendid rose window. Inside, over the first south altar, is a large enamelled terracotta altarpiece by Mattia della Robbia (1527) of the *Madonna with Child and Saints*, while in the left aisle is a panel painting by Giacomo da Recanati (15th century) of the *Madonna with Four Saints*.

PRACTICAL INFORMATION

GETTING AROUND

• **By bus**: Autolinee Crognaletti, T: 0733 602352, www.autolineecrognaletti.it; Autolinee Farabollini, T: 0733 215270; CONEROBUS, T: 071 2802092, www.conerobus.it; CONTRAM, T: 0733 230906 run services from Ancona to Macerata, Cingoli, Filottrano, Pollenza, Treia, Monte San Giusto, Jesi, Osimo, Civitanova Alta, Civitanova Marche and Corridonia.

INFORMATION OFFICES

Apiro, Appignano, Cingoli, Montecassiano, Pollenza and Treia form part of the association STL Terre dell'Infinito (T: 0733 843569, www.terredellinfinito.it), supplying information and the tourist discount card 'Infinito Card'.

Apiro Tourist Information Bureau, 6 Corso Vittorio Emanuele, T: 0733 613048, www.apiro.sinp.net

Cingoli ATC Pro Loco, Piazza Vittorio Emanuele II, T: 0733 602444; IAT, 17 Via Ferri, T: 0733 601913, www.cingoli.info

Filottrano Pro Loco, 96 Via dell'Industria, T: 071 7222364; Tourist Information Bureau, Municipio, T: 071 7220134, www.comune.filottrano.an.it

HOTELS

Appignano

€€€ **Villa Verdefiore**. Small, modern, and very comfortable; no restaurant. 37 Via Verdefiore, T: 0733 570035, www.villaverdefiore.it

Cingoli

€€€ **Antica Taverna della Selva**. Tiny inn with a very good restaurant; car park. 1 Via Cicerone, T: 0733 617119, www.tavernaallaselva.it

€€€ **Diana**. Built on the old city walls, with a restaurant. 21 Via Cavour, T: 0733 602313, www.hoteldianacingoli.it

€€€ **La Pineta**. In a quiet position, with an excellent restaurant and pizzeria. 135 Contrada Villa Pozzo, T: 0733 602547.

€€€ **Miramonti**. Comfortable rooms, garden and tennis court, near the lake. 31 Via dei Cerquatti, T: 0733 604027, www.hotelmiramonticingoli.it

€€€ **Tetto delle Marche**. With a good restaurant; panoramic views. 47 Via Cristianopoli, T: 0733 602882.

€€€ **Villa Ugolini**. Stay in a beautifully-restored manor house 4km from Cingoli; no restaurant. 30 Via Sant'Anastasio, T: 0733 604692, www.villaugolini.it

Filottrano

€€€ **Sette Colli**. ■ Newly renovated, with a very good restaurant; a short way from the centre. Via Gemme, T: 071 7220104, www.settecolli.it

€ **Americano**. Central position with a restaurant. 83 Corso del Popolo, T: 071 7220159.

Montecassiano

€€€€ **Villa Quiete**. An elegant country villa with a renowned restaurant. Vallecascia di Montecassiano, T: 0733 599559, www.gestire2000.com

Pollenza

€€€ **Parco**. Comfortable with a good restaurant and garden. 41 Via Dante,

T: 0733 549347.

Treia

€€€ **Grimaldi**. Central with a restaurant. 9 Corso Italia Libera, T: 733 215725, hotelgrimaldi@libero.it

€€ **Dina**. Friendly atmosphere with a restaurant; car park. 13 Via Bibiano, T: 0733 216566.

BED & BREAKFAST

Cingoli

Ferrarese della Rovere. A beautiful old aristocratic home; English and French spoken. Meals on request. Closed winter. 7 Via Cicerone, T: 0733 617113.

Il Palazzo. Apartment in an historic palace. English spoken. 8 Via Foltrani, T: 06 5672157, alemaria@iol.it

Palazzo Castiglioni. An historic palace in an excellent position. English spoken. 87 Corso Garibaldi, T: 0733 602531, castiglio@libero.it

FARM ACCOMMODATION

Apiro

Santa Maria del Gallo. A good base for trekking, bikes for hire, guests can help on farm (olive oil, chestnuts). English spoken. 17 Via Santa Maria, T: 0733 18105, www.santamariadelgallo.it

Appignano

Casale Petunia. An old restored cottage surrounded by sunflower fields; art courses on request. Open May–Sept. 13 Contrada Carreggiano, T: 049 8802365, alesspucci@tiscali.it

Cingoli

Gli Ulivi. An old farmhouse close to Cingoli. Closed Jan–Mar. 41 Via Capovilla, Frazione Torre, T: 0733 603361, www.gli-ulivi.it

La Corte sul Lago. On the lake of Cingoli (nice views), this farm produces wine and truffles, children welcome. There are lakeside activities and bowls. Closed Jan. 33 Villa Moscosi, T: 0733 612067, www.lacortesullago.it

Pollenza

La Sgaruina. Small farm close to Pollenza, friendly atmosphere, and excellent simple food. 15 Località Santa Lucia, T: 0733 549107.

Treia

Catignano. A delightful old farmhouse; nature walks nearby, lake, bowls, bicycles. Guests can help on the farm which produces olive oil and DOC white wine. 6 Contrada Vallonica, T: 0733 541570.

Fontechiara. Olive groves and orchards surround the farm, which raises bees, horses, pigs and goats; birdwatching, cycling and photography courses. 19 Contrada Paterno, Santa Maria di Paterno, T: 0733 216797; www.fontechiara.de

Il Villino. Quiet, comfortable farm with horses; very good restaurant. 29 Contrada San Carlo, T: 0733 215414, www.villino.it

La Fattoria di Paolo. ■ Helpful owners, an excellent choice (though no restaurant). Contrada Carreggiano, T: 0733 240937.

COUNTRY HOUSES

Cingoli

Badia San Vittore. A really beautiful old villa. 7 Via Cicerone, San Vittore di Cingoli, T: 0733 617113.

RESTAURANTS

Appignano

€ **Lord Byron**. ■ Friendly tavern, delicious food; try the home-made ravioli, or the *tagliata*, a marvellous beefy salad. Closed Tues. Via San Giovanni Battista, T: 0733 579385.

Cingoli

€€ **La Taverna di Ro'**. ■ Lunch here on the veranda is worth the journey to Cingoli. Give him a couple of days' notice, and Rossano will prepare sumptuous gastronomic delights for you, but the regular menu will not disappoint; exceptional *calcioni* (pasta) and gnocchi. Good local wines. Closed Wed. 13 Via della Portella, T: 0733 604713.

Filottrano

€€ **Saint Patrick**. Welcoming restaurant serving delicious local dishes, generous servings. Closed Mon. 32 Via Veneto, T: 071 7222560.

€€ **Sette Colli**. ■ Just outside town, smart restaurant with attentive service. Closed Tues. 1 Via Gemme, T: 071 7220104.

CAFÉS, PASTRY SHOPS & WINE BARS

Cingoli

Balcone delle Marche. Enjoy an aperitif or a cappuccino accompanied by excellent local confectionery while feasting your eyes on the magnificent view. 12 Via Balcone delle Marche.

Caffè dei Tigli. Home-made ice cream and yoghurt, just outside Porta Pia. 1–5 Via Borgo Paolo Danti.

La Cantina del Palazzo. Picturesque wine bar and restaurant in the basement of Palazzo Castiglioni. 87 Corso Garibaldi.

Filottrano

Bar Walli. An historic coffee-shop built on the site of the ancient Porta Romana. Piazza Mazzini.

FESTIVALS & EVENTS

Apiro Feast of St Urban; Info: T: 0733 611131, 25 May. *Infiorata di Corpus Domini*, the streets are decorated with flower petals, June. Folklore Festival, the inhabitants wear traditional 1800s dress, 10–15 Aug.

Appignano Traditional Spring Fair, last Sun in April. Feast of St John the Baptist, 24 June.

Cingoli Feast of St Esuperantius, 3rd Sun in July. *Cingoli 1848* is the occasion for everybody to dress up in 19th-century clothes and watch a game of *pallone al bracciale* (*see p. 103*); Info: Associazione Cingoli 1848, 5 Via Capo di Rio Piccolo, T: 0733 602091, 2nd week in Aug.

Filottrano Feast of St Michael Archangel, 8 May. *La Contesa dello Stivale*, reconstruction of an episode in the 1466 war between Filottrano and Osimo; Info: Società dello Stivale, 1 Via Buozzi, T: 071 7220968, 1st Sunday in Aug.

Montecassiano Feast of St Joseph, 19 March.

Pollenza Feast of St John the Baptist, 24 June. Exhibition of Antiques, Handicrafts and Restoration Techniques, July.

Treia *Disfida del Bracciale*, one of the most prestigious events of the region: the evocation of a legendary 19th-century match of *pallone al bracciale* (*see p. 103*); Info: Ente Disfida, T: 0733 218703, www.treia.sinp.net, 1st Sun in Aug. Feast of St Patrick, 24–25 Aug.

Apiro
Emilio Silenzi, at 2 Via Pelleoni, sells typical pastries, such as *cavallucci* biscuits, and a long cake called *serpe*, the snake.

Appignano
Ceramica Taruschio, at 3 Via Galileo, specialises in splendid pottery in traditional colours and designs, made using modern techniques. **Fratelli Testa**, 33 Borgo Santa Croce, is now the only remaining atelier for hand-made pottery.

Cingoli
Pamira, 71 Corso Garibaldi, has beautiful knitted garments. There's also a factory outlet by the lake at Moscosi di Cingoli, T: 0733 612101.

Filottrano
Oleificio Paoloni e Mazzieri, 36 Via Mattei, is a good place for olive oil.

MACERATA

This dignified city of hazelnut-coloured mellow brick (pop. 43,000), set in the heart of the rolling farmlands of central Marche, is the seat of one of Italy's oldest universities, has one of the finest libraries in the country, and boasts an unusual open-air theatre. Built on a crest between the valleys of the Potenza to the north and the Chienti to the south, the steep old centre, with its intricate web of narrow streets, is still almost completely surrounded by the 16th-century walls.

HISTORY OF MACERATA

The name Macerata probably derives from *macerie*, 'rubble', because the medieval city was almost entirely constructed using material coming from the ruins of the Roman *Helvia Ricina*, 3km away in the locality now called Villa Potenza. Helvia Ricina was originally founded by the Umbri about 3,000 years ago, in a position dominating a series of important trade routes. The town flourished until the decline of the Roman empire, when it was devastated by the Visigoths in 408, after which the site was abandoned, and Macerata was built.

In 1138 the town broke away from the diocese of Fermo and became an independent commune. During the struggles between Guelphs and Ghibellines Macerata sided first with one and then with the other, eventually deciding to join forces with the Guelphs (the papal faction) while jealously maintaining her independence and statutes, the earliest of which goes back to 1268. A prestigious law school was founded in 1290 and became the nucleus of the university. Pope John XXII declared Macerata a city in 1320, assigning a bishop, but in spite of this, powerful families of the area exerted their dominion over the territory, first the Mulucci (1326–55), followed by the da Varano (1385) and Francesco Sforza (1433). In 1455 the city came under the influence of the Church again when it was made the seat of the Legation of the March, the papal diplomatic representation in the region.

Macerata was bombarded and pillaged by the French in 1799, who occupied it again in 1808. In 1849 the city played a leading role in the Republican movement. During the First World War, more medals were awarded to soldiers from Macerata than to those of any other Italian province. Fierce bombing raids in April 1944 meant that the city had to be extensively rebuilt; new housing went up outside the city walls, leaving the old centre repaired and intact.

The town centre

Right in the middle is Piazza della Libertà, dominated on the west side by the portico of the **Palazzo dei Priori**, now the town hall, built in the 17th century and restored in 1820. In the courtyard is a collection of archaeological fragments from the Roman city of *Helvia Ricina* (*see p. 103*). To the right of the building, on Corso Matteotti, is the graceful Tuscan-style Loggia dei Mercanti (1505). On the north side of the square is the 16th-century **Palazzo della Prefettura**, once the residence of the papal legates. The marble doorway is of 1509 and traces of arches reveal the existence of a preceding 14th-century construction. Opposite is the clock tower or *Torre Maggiore*, commenced in 1485 and completed in 1653 (there is a good view over the rooftops from the top). The church of San Paolo (1655) occupies the east side of the square; the doorway in the centre is now the entrance to the University, which has several faculties and about 13,000 students. The steps going down to the right of the clock tower lead to the unusual church of **Santa Maria della Porta**, of which the lower part is Romanesque (10th century) and the upper Gothic, with a particularly beautiful 13th-century brick doorway.

Corso della Repubblica, one of the main streets of the city, leads from Piazza della Libertà to Piazza Vittorio Veneto. About halfway along, on the left, is the Baroque church of **San Filippo** (1732). There are two little bell-towers on either side of the façade, which was never completed. The interior is elliptical in shape, luminous and very effective, with stucco decoration and fine red marble. The paintings include one of *St Philip Neri in Glory* (1738) over the high altar. The sacristy is impressive, with 18th-century Baroque woodwork in walnut, and a canvas showing the *Tears of St Paul*, by an unknown 18th-century artist.

The elegant Corso Matteotti, with more interesting buildings, leads west from Piazza della Libertà. At no. 33 is **Palazzo Mozzi**, also known as the 'Palace of the Diamonds' for the characteristic cut of the decorative stonework on the façade; it is one of the best examples of 16th-century architecture in the city. At no. 41 is Palazzo Rotelli (1570), a dignified construction thought to be the work of Pellegrino Tibaldi.

Piazza Vittorio Veneto

The lovely collegiate church of **San Giovanni** dominates Piazza Vittorio Veneto, with the enormous Collegio dei Gesuiti next to it. The Jesuits, very influential in Macerata, built the complex in the 17th century, but the church façade was added only in 1854. The imposing interior has six side chapels, three on each side, and a deep presbytery. In the second chapel on the left is a painted wooden Crucifix (15th century) which has been set onto a panel painting (16th century; Vincenzo Pagani or Cola dell'Amatrice) showing the *Sts Mary on Calvary* and a city, perhaps Macerata, in the background. The painting over the high altar, showing *St Julian with Sts John the Baptist and John the Evangelist*, is the work of the Sicilian artist Gaetano Sortino (1774), while the 18th-century organ comes from the Venetian firm of Callido. The college now houses the civic museums and libraries, but it is planned to move the museums to Palazzo Buonaccorsi (*see below*), and the college will become the seat of the Academy of Art. The **Pinacoteca Comunale** (*open Tues–Sat 9–1 & 4–7.30; Sun 9–1; Mon afternoons only; T: 0733 256361*), is divided into two sections, the first dedicated to works by artists from Umbria and the Marche from the 14th–19th centuries, including Giacomo da Recanati, Sassoferrato, Simone Cantarini, Federico Barocci and Carlo Maratta. Taking pride of place in the collection is a luminous but fragmentary *Madonna with the Christ Child* (1470) by Carlo Crivelli. Originally a part of a polyptych, it is thought that the *Pietà* now in the Fogg Art Museum of Cambridge, Massachusetts, was part of the same work. The second section of the gallery is dedicated to contemporary art, with works by Bruno Cassinari, Emilio Vedova, Domenico Cantatore, Luigi Spazzapan and Ivo Pannaggi.

The **Museo Civico** (*open as Pinactoeca, above*) contains archaeological finds from Helvia Ricina, and documents, photographs and objects illustrating the history and traditions of the city. There is also a **Museo delle Carrozze** (carriage museum; *closed Mon*) in the basement, with an interesting collection of vehicles, including an 'ambulance', a tiny children's cart which was pulled by goats, a painted farm cart or *biroccio*, and some carriages donated by the aristocratic families of Macerata.

On the first floor is the magnificent Biblioteca Comunale, one of the finest in the region, comprising a public consultation section, and the historic **Mozzi Borgetti Library** (*open Mon–Fri 9–1 & 3–7; Sat and July–Aug mornings only; T: 0733 256360*) of which the Jesuit collection forms the nucleus. The beautiful rooms are the perfect setting for 300,000 rare manuscripts, incunabula, maps and medieval statutes. There is a reading room on the rooftop called the *Specola* (*open Mon, Wed, Fri 3.30–6.30*), a long gallery with views over the city on one side, and as far as the Sibyllines on the other.

A JESUIT IN THE FORBIDDEN CITY

Father Matteo Ricci was born in Macerata in 1522. After studying with the Jesuits, he became a missionary and travelled the world before settling in China, where he was known as Li Madou. He overcame the initial hostility of the people by dressing as a Buddhist priest and always showing respect for local traditions. He soon became a court adviser, founded a mission and several churches, carried out many conversions, and drew up maps of the world for the emperor. He was the first to translate the Bible into Chinese, and the first to compose a Chinese-Italian dictionary. When he died, Emperor Wan Li proclaimed national mourning, erected a monument to him, and officially recognised Christianity. Father Matteo is the only foreigner to be buried within the walls of the Forbidden City, and the Astronomical Observatory of Beijing is named after him.

Galleria d'Arte Contemporanea

Leading northwest from Piazza Vittorio Veneto is Via Domenico Ricci; at no. 1 is the 17th-century Palazzo Ricci, which houses the Galleria d'Arte Contemporanea (*open March–Dec Sat and Sun 10–1 & 4–8; July–Aug every day except Mon; T: 0733 261484, www.fondazionemacerata.it*), examples of 20th-century Italian art assembled by a local bank, the ex-Cassa di Risparmio della Provincia di Macerata. The collection was started in 1975 when the bank intervened to save the painting *Treno in corsa (Racing Train)*, by the local Futurist painter Ivo Pannaggi, from being sold abroad; there are now more than 400 paintings and sculptures, including works by Fontana, Morandi, de Chirico, Depero, Monachesi, Licini and Manzù. The beautifully-restored rooms, furnished with local antiques, constitute a strange but effective setting for the art, probably one of the finest collections of its kind in Italy.

Via Don Minzoni

On returning to Piazza Libertà, Via Don Minzoni leads eastwards down to the duomo passing handsome 18th-century palaces, now used as departments of the University, and the old grain market, the Loggia del Grano. On the right, at no. 11, is **Palazzo Compagnoni Marefoschi** (1771) with a particularly fine doorway surmounted by a balcony. In 1772 Charles Stuart, Bonnie Prince Charlie, married the Countess of Albany in this house. At no. 24 is **Palazzo Buonaccorsi** (1705), now the seat of the Academy of Arts and of the Accademia dei Catenati, an institution founded in 1574 'to incite and encourage the youth of Macerata to escape the torpor of idleness and aim for praise and honour'. Symbol of the academy is a golden chain extending from heaven to earth. At first the members published literary works, but a plague of locusts in 1840 convinced them to extend their studies to agricultural subjects as well. The academy is still active and organises prestigious international meetings on various themes. The palace has several refined details, for example the lobby is paved in oak to reduce the noise from carriages passing through from the street to the courtyard. Some of the rooms are decorated with frescoes and paintings on one theme; particularly famous is the gorgeous Rococo 'Salon of the *Aeneid*' (1707). After sacking the city in 1799, the French commander Pontavice decided to live here: the doors still bear the signs of the vicious blows he rained upon them with his sabre, when he was in a bad mood. The building is set to become the seat of the civic museums, while the Academy of Arts will take over the old Jesuit college.

Via Don Minzoni continues down to Piazza San Vincenzo Strambi, of which the **duomo**, dedicated to St Julian, occupies the east side. Building started in the 15th century (the bell-tower is of 1478) and continued from 1771–90 by Cosimo Morelli, it was never finished. In the bright, spacious interior, with a large central nave and two side aisles, attention is drawn to the magnificent fresco in the apse, of the *Assumption of the Virgin* (1930), and, beneath it, the panel painting of *St Julian begs the Madonna to save Macerata from the Plague* (Christopher Unterberger; 1786). The organ, by Gaetano Callido (1790), is one of the largest he ever made. In the north transept is the Chapel of the Sacrament, with two beautiful stucco angels made by Gioacchino Varlé in 1790. Under the altar is a piece of linen stained with blood which dripped from the host during Mass, on 25th April 1356. The south transept houses the altar dedicated to St Michael, with a 17th-century mosaic altarpiece. Some of the finest works of art are in the **Sagrestia dei Canonici** (*open 3–6, but it is often closed*), where there is an outstanding panel painting by Vincenzo Pagani (16th century) of

The *Assumption*: fresco by Francesco Mancini (1737).

the *Madonna and Child with Sts Julian and Anthony of Padua*, with the tiny figures of the donors kneeling between the two saints, and a river—the Potenza?—winding its way to the sea in the background; a splendid triptych by Allegretto Nuzi (1369) of the *Madonna between St Julian and St Anthony Abbot*, still in its original frame, and two canvases by Giovanni Baglione (1600): *Crucifixion of St Peter* and the *Resurrection of Tabitha*.

Left of the cathedral, dominating the square with its curved façade, is the sanctuary church of the **Madonna della Misericordia**, built in 1736 on the site of a votive chapel and enlarged in the late 19th century. It is the smallest basilica in the world and a national monument. The façade is unfortunately spoilt because partly contained within the front of a modern building, but the oval interior by Luigi Vanvitelli, although small, is dazzling: richly-decorated with stuccoes, precious marbles, paintings and wrought-iron work. The bronze doors are by Carlo Cantalamessa (1952), while the beautiful ceiling frescoes showing scenes from the life of the Madonna, gentle figures rendered with marvellous soft pastel colours, are by Francesco Mancini (1737). In the presbytery are two large 18th-century canvases of the *Immaculate Conception* and the *Nativity of Mary*, while a finely wrought, gilded bronze iconostasis protects the revered late 15th-century *Madonna of Mercy*, by three anonymous artists.

The Sferisterio

Certainly the most unusual building in Macerata is in Piazza Nazario Sauro, in the southeast corner of the town. The Sferisterio (*open 10.30–11 & 5–8; holidays, booking necessary; T: 0733 230735; www.macerataopera.org*), is a vast arena built in 1820–29 for a popular ball game, *pallone al bracciale* (*see box*). Semi-elliptical, and capable of accommodating 7,000 spectators, it was designed by Ireneo Aleandri, inspired by Palladian models. When the game for which it was built lost favour, it was used for jousts and circuses until the early 1920s, when operas and concerts began to be organised in the summer. Thanks to the perfect acoustics, these are still very popular. Nowadays seats are arranged for 1,800, while the stage—which is 90m wide—is the largest in Europe and has accommodated a performance of *Aida* with real elephants.

PALLONE AL BRACCIALE

One of the most ancient ball games in Europe, and one of the most exciting, *pallone al bracciale* goes back to Roman times, although some experts believe it to be a typical Spartan pastime. Two teams consisting of three players try to keep a leather ball (like a small football), weighing 350g, from touching the ground by bouncing it off a wall; they can make contact with the ball only with a heavy, spiky wooden arm guard, the *bracciale*, always made of sorb-apple wood and usually worn on the right arm. Very fast, the game can be quite violent. It was immensely popular in central Italy during the Renaissance, and again in the 19th century, but it has not been able to resist competition from football and is now seldom played, except in Treia (where an annual festival is dedicated to the game), Montelupone, and a few towns in Tuscany. A national championship is still held annually.

Walks on the city outskirts

A walk along the avenues which surround the old centre, Viale Giacomo Leopardi, Viale Pantaleoni, Viale Trieste and Viale Puccinotti, affords interesting details of the ancient walls, the bastions and the old gates, and lovely views over the modern town, the countryside and the Sibylline Mountains. At the end of Viale Giacomo Leopardi is Porta Duomo, and the perfect arches of what was an enormous public fountain, the Fonte Maggiore (1326). The western door, Porta Romana, was pulled down in 1857 and replaced with a formidable wrought-iron gate, the work of a local blacksmith; this is why the local people call it *i cancelli*—the gates. Another interesting walk leads from Porta Picena, in the southeast corner, along Corso Cairoli and Via Pancalducci to the 16th-century church of **Santa Maria delle Vergini**, 2km away. Architecturally it was inspired by Bramante, with an elegant eight-sided dome. In the interior are well-preserved stuccoes and frescoes dating from the 16th–18th-centuries and a painting by Tintoretto of the *Epiphany* (1587). Hanging from the roof on the left is a stuffed crocodile, about which there are many tales. Possibly brought back from the Holy Land by a crusader, it is said to have run rampant through the countryside, until it was killed by a peasant with his pitchfork after it had run off with his child.

The ruins of Helvia Ricina

At Villa Potenza, 3km from Macerata, the remains of *Helvia Ricina* with the vast Roman amphitheatre built by Trajan in the 2nd century AD can be seen (*visits by previous arrangement only, T: 0733 492937, but it is visible from outside the fence*), together with some architectural fragments found in the nearby River Potenza, where they had been used to strengthen the banks.

PRACTICAL INFORMATION

GETTING AROUND

• **By train**: the railway station in Macerata (unmanned) is a short distance from the city centre. Connections with Civitanova Marche, Ancona, and other major towns in Italy.
• **By bus**: Autolinee Binni, T: 0732 629592/4, runs services to San Severino Marche, Camerino, Matelica, Fabriano, Porto Recanati and Ancona.
Autolinee Crognaletti, T: 0731 204965, www.autolineecrognaletti.it, has services to Jesi, Ostra, Serra de' Conti, Montecarotto, Chiaravalle, Falconara and Ancona.
Autolinee Farabollini, T: 0733 215270, www.farabollini.it; CONTRAM, T: 0733 230906; STEAT, T: 800 630715, www.steat.it, runs services to Fermo.

INFORMATION OFFICES

Macerata forms part of the association STL Terre dell'Infinito (T: 0733 843569, www.terredellinfinito.it), providing information and a tourist discount card, 'Infinito Card'. IAT, 12 Piazza della Libertà, T: 0733 234807, www.comune.macerata.it

HOTELS

€€€€ **Claudiani**. ■ Comfortable city-centre hotel, an ancient palace. No restaurant, garage. 8 Vicolo Ulissi, T: 0733 261400, www.hotelclaudiani.it
€€€ **I Colli**. Recently built outside the walls; offers good service. Car park. 149 Via Roma, T: 0733 367063.
€€ **Arena**. ■ Hidden away behind the arena, simple but very comfortable, an excellent choice. 16 Vicolo Sferisterio, T: 0733 230931.
€€ **Lauri**. Particularly suitable for long stays. 6 Via Lauri, T: 0733 232376, www.gestionihotels.it

FARM ACCOMMODATION

Azienda Lucangeli. Apartments in a lovely old farmhouse 6km from Macerata; the farm produces excellent wines. 27 Contrada Valle, T: 0733 270072.
Floriani di Villamagna. Close to Villa Potenza and wooded countryside. The farm produces olive oil; guests can help. 3 Contrada Montanello, T: 0733 492267, www.florianicompagnoni.it

COUNTRY HOUSE

Le Case. ■ Restored hamlet, offering luxurious accommodation, fully-equipped fitness centre with sauna, inviting indoor pool, very well cared-for restaurant and wine cellar, vegetarian food on request, young and enthusiastic staff; about 5km from town. 16/17 Via Mozzavinci, Frazione Consalvi, T: 0733 231897, www.countryhouselecase.it

RESTAURANTS

€€ **Da Rosa**. Offers good local cooking, including *pistacoppi farciti* (stuffed pigeons) and *vincisgrassi* (special local lasagne); don't miss the (authentic) strudel. Good wine cellar. Closed Sun. 17 Via Armaroli, T: 0733 260124.
€€ **Da Secondo**. Closed Mon. Elegant

and tasteful rooms, full of atmosphere, this is a favourite with musicians and opera singers; watch out for Montserrat Caballé or Katia Ricciarelli. Good food, but presentation can be slapdash. 28 Via Pescheria Vecchia, T: 0733 260912.
€€ **Da Silvano**. Silvano offers excellent grills and pizza cooked on an open fire; friendly. Closed Mon. 15 Piaggia della Torre, T: 0733 260216.
€€ **Osteria dei Fiori**. ■ You will love this tiny trattoria, run by three dedicated and imaginative young people; specialises in typical Macerata delights, such as *panzanella al ciauscolo* (soft bread with salami) and *coniglio in porchetta* (rabbit); absolutely superb desserts; only local DOC wines served. Closed Sun in winter. 61 Via Lauro Rossi, T: 0733 260142.

CAFÉS, ICE CREAM & SNACK BARS

Caffè Venanzetti. Old-fashioned coffee house; favourite meeting place for university students, great for aperitifs; home-made chocolates. Closed Mon. 21 Via Gramsci (Galleria Scipione).
Il Ghiotto Mariotto. Home-made ice cream, innovative hot chocolate. Piazza Mazzini.
Pierino. Memorable aperitifs and atmosphere. 5 Piazza Cesare Battisti.
Laboratorio del Grano. Fabio and Lucia bake an amazing assortment of bread, cakes and biscuits; ideal for snacks. 40 Via Santa Maria della Porta.

FESTIVALS & EVENTS

Open-air Opera Festival at the Sferisterio; T: 0733 230735, www.macerataopera.org, in July and Aug. Feast of St Julian, 31 Aug. Procession of the *Canestrelle* to the sanctuary of the Madonna della Misericordia. Participants wear 1447 dress and carry baskets containing offerings of wheat for the Madonna, a tradition dating back to the ancient cult of Cybele, 1st Sun in Sept.

LOCAL SPECIALITIES

Macerata is renowned for its production of *ciauscolo* (traditional soft salami), biscuits and bread. **Cioccolateria Marangoni**, at 159 Via Cavour, is where the Marangoni family has been making chocolate by hand for many years; delicious pralines, also fresh fruit and nuts covered with chocolate, unusual chocolate with herbs. **La Tela**, 6 Vicolo Vecchio, here Patrizia Ginesi and Maria Giovanna Varagona weave linen by hand, using Renaissance techniques and patterns; their boutique is now recognised as a city museum. Go to **Pizzi e Ricami**, 36 Via dei Velini, for Franca Ercoli's fine hand-made lace and embroidery. **Ruffini Sandra**, 5 Corso della Repubblica, for cakes, biscuits and liqueurs.

TOLENTINO & ITS TERRITORY

Standing on the left bank of the Chienti, against a background of green hills, the ancient, largely unspoilt city of Tolentino (pop. 19,000) still has some fortifications in place. One of Italy's great mystic saints, San Nicola da Tolentino, lived and died here; the city has been an important destination for pilgrims ever since.

HISTORY OF TOLENTINO

Tolentino occupies a strategic position in the heart of the Marche, where the two rivers Chienti and Potenza flow closest together. Inhabited since the earliest times, it was a settlement of the Picenes and became the Roman *Tolentinum*, of which little trace remains. It played a vital role in the 10th century, assisting pilgrims and providing supplies for the monastic communities of the area—Santa Maria a Piè' di Chienti, Santa Maria Rambona, San Claudio al Chienti, Santa Croce al Chienti and Santa Maria di Chiaravalle di Fiastra. In 1170 it became an independent commune; this led to centuries of struggles with San Severino and Camerino. In the 13th century Tolentino became the seat of the pope's most important representative in the region, and many churches and convents were built. Craftsmanship flourished at the same time, thanks to a dam on the Chienti which brought abundant water to the western side of town, where leather workers, brick-makers, millers and wool manufacturers were plying their trade. Development continued even after the da Varano family of Camerino took control, in the name of the pope, in the 14th century. New hospitals, fortresses and a new set of walls were completed in the 15th century.

Important events in Tolentino history include the infamous treaty of 1797, when Napoleon forced Pope Pius VI to hand over lands, works of art and cash indemnities; the battle of 1815, when the Austrians defeated Napoleon's brother-in-law Joachim Murat (whom Napoleon had created King of Naples); and the arrival of the railway in 1888, which brought in its wake comfortable communications, but also regrettable demolitions of some ancient city structures. Today Tolentino flourishes, thanks to its leather industries—this is where you will find, among many others, the Nazareno Gabrielli company (founded 1907) and the Frau furniture factory (founded 1912). In contrast with many other similar centres, the population is increasing steadily.

Piazza Libertà and district

Centre of the city is Piazza Libertà, animated and elegant, surrounded by buildings the colour of warm toffee. On the north side is the unusual 16th-century **clock tower** (the bell-tower of the church of San Francesco) with five quadrants: the top one indicates the phases of the moon, the second shows the hours for the principal prayers, the third gives the time, the fourth the days of the month and the week. Lastly, only just visible, is a small solar meridian, which was used to adjust the other dials. In Tolentino they are very proud of their clock; other people in the region are a little envious of it, going so far as to call the inhabitants *'mezze facce di Tolentini'* (the people of Tolentino have only half a face) because the upper dial was stuck for years on the half-moon phase.

To the west is the town hall with its portico, a 19th-century reconstruction of the 14th-century original, and facing it is Palazzo Sangallo, on the second floor of which is the **Museo della Caricatura Luigi Mari** (*open 10–1 & 3–6.30; closed Mon T: 0733 969797*), a collection of 3,000 drawings, paintings, statuettes and puppets from all over the world, dating from the Stone Age to the present day, including works donated by the artists taking part in the biennial caricature and humour in art festival (*see p. 126*); there is also a specialist library of humour, and a vast collection of comic magazines and newspapers, both Italian and foreign.

Leading north out of Piazza Libertà is Via Filelfo; immediately on the left is the high polygonal apse of the church of **San Francesco** (13th century). Inside, through a little door in the right apse, is a chapel with 14th-century frescoes. The church faces onto the harmonious Piazza Mauruzi. Closing the square to the west is the little Romanesque ex-**church of the Carità** with its characteristic 16th-century dome, and lovely rose window. Close to San Francesco, at 20 Via della Pace, is **Palazzo Parisani Bezzi**, where the historic Treaty of Tolentino was signed on 19th February 1797 between the representatives of Pope Pius VI and Napoleon Bonaparte. It was a sad day for the pope: he was forced to renounce his treaty with Austria and to hand over Avignon, Venosino, the legations of Bologna, Ferrara, Ravenna and Forlì, together with an enormous sum of money and many precious works of art. The palace now houses the **Museo Napoleonico** (*temporarily closed; T: 0733 969797*), with the original furnishings and documents illustrating the dramatic sequences of the signing of the treaty.

Basilica di San Nicola

Via San Nicola, probably the old *cardo maximus*, leads south from Piazza Libertà through a picturesque medieval district to the 13th-century Porta del Ponte and the River Chienti. A short way along, the street widens in front of the **Basilica di San Nicola** (*open 9.30–12 & 4–7; T: 0733 976311; www.sannicoladatolentino.it*), where Nicholas of Tolentino, hermit, healer and great preacher (*see box on p. 111*), lived for 30 years. The church, originally dedicated to St Augustine and belonging to the Austin Fathers, is 13th century, but was remodelled in the 14th century and also a century later when the magnificent late Gothic portal of 1432, by Nanni di Bartolo, surmounted by St George and the Dragon (*pictured overleaf*), was added. The doorway was commissioned by the local soldier-of-fortune Nicolò Mauruzi, as a token of devotion to St Nicholas; he wanted St George to appear on the portal because he was the patron saint of soldiers-of-fortune. Maurizi chose Nanni di Bartolo of Florence, known as *il Rosso*, the Redhead, because he was a friend.

Nicolò Mauruzi: *Il Tolentino (1365–1435)*

Nicolò Mauruzi, valiant soldier-of-fortune, was born in Tolentino in 1365; the name of his home town became the nickname by which he was always known. His father, Giovanni, was a mercenary; Nicolò grew up among the soldiers, and at the age of 20 he joined the troops of Pandolfo Malatesta. He soon reached a position of command, and his troops loved him—his chroniclers report that he was 'good-looking, thin, lively, very brave and very agile; he knew every secret of the fortifications, and could always break a siege'. He fought for Francesco Maria Visconti of Milan, for Pope Martin V and for Queen Joan of Naples; then in 1425 he was hired by Florence to fight the Visconti, obtaining such brilliant results that in 1433 he was named captain-general. The following year, during another battle against Visconti, he fell from his horse and was unable to get up, owing to the weight of his armour; inevitably he was taken prisoner. The great powers of the day—the pope, the Republics of Venice and Florence, the Gonzaga of Mantua, the Este and many other cities and families—interceded on his behalf, but in vain. He died on 27th March 1435 when he fell into a mountain crevasse during a transfer from one prison to another. Many historians believe he was thrown there on the orders of Visconti, to whom he had become an embarrassment.

Although he never married, he had several children to whom he left an immense fortune, together with strict instructions (his will still survives) never to betray the cause of Florence. Visconti respected his last wish and returned his body to Tolentino, where his heart was walled up inside the basilica for which he had provided the splendid portal three years before.

The elegant façade in travertine marble with the star of St Nicholas was completed in the 18th century. The interior has a single nave, with side chapels, a polygonal apse, and an astonishing coffered ceiling of carved and gilded wood, with portraits of saints, completed in 1628. In the first chapel on the right is a canvas by Guercino of *St Anne with the Angel*, while the large canvases on the high altar, representing the *Amputation of the Holy Arms* and the *Madonna Appears for St Nicholas*, are the work of the local artist Giovan Battista Foschi (1628).

At the end of the church on the right is the entrance to the famous **Cappellone di San Nicola**, of which the walls and ceiling are entirely covered with a magnificent series of frescoes, carried out in the first years of the 14th century by Pietro da Rimini and his collaborators, known collectively as the Giotto School of Rimini, resulting in the most important expression of 14th-century painting in the Marche. On a background of sombre blue, a series of beautifully-portrayed figures dressed in colourful robes, tell us with graceful gestures and expressive faces the stories of the Madonna, of

St George and the Dragon by Nanni di Bartolo on the church of San Nicola da Tolentino.

Jesus and of St Nicholas; here and there groups of smaller figures kneeling in prayer represent the donors, who contributed to the cost of the work. In the vault above are the *Four Doctors of the Church with the Evangelists*, working hard at their studies, surrounded by books, using enviably lovely writing desks. From the altar clockwise, they are *St Ambrose and St Mark*, recognisable by his symbol the lion, followed by *St Augustine and St John* (eagle), *St Gregory and St Luke* (bull), and *St Jerome and St Matthew* (angel). The large lunettes are dedicated to *Stories of the Madonna*; unfortunately somewhat damaged in places. Around the walls, the upper series shows *Stories of the Life of Christ*, full of impressive detail: notice the bearded priest listening to the Child Jesus in the temple; his turban is of a typical pattern in medieval central Italy, still woven in Matelica, northwest of Tolentino; or the accurately-depicted wine jars in the scene of the *Wedding at Cana*, and the fine linen tablecloths, contrasting with the simple food on the tables. The lower paintings are dedicated to the life of St Nicholas and some of his miracles, particularly interesting for the tantalizing glimpses of the towns, and the dress of the people. The entire work is dominated by the *Crucifixion*, showing a beautiful Mary Magdalene embracing the foot of the Cross, between a dignified, pathetic Madonna and a weeping St John. The stone sarcophagus (1474) in the centre, made to replace the original wooden one, was never used for Nicholas's body, which had been hastily buried for fear of over-enthusiastic relic seekers, while the painted wooden effigy on top (15th century), is by a follower of Donatello.

From the Cappellone it is possible to reach the peaceful **cloister** (14th and 17th centuries), with a well in the centre, and an attractive loggia on one side. A small doorway leads into the saint's **oratory**, a tiny room decorated with frescoes, where it is thought Nicholas lived for 30 years, and where he died. Back in the church, you will find the richly decorated **Chapel of the Holy Arms** (*Cappella delle Santissime Braccia*); just outside the entrance is a tiny cell, the so-called 'prison of St Nicholas', and to the right of this, high up, is a niche in the wall covered with a coat-of-arms which holds the heart of Nicolò Mauruzi (*see previous page*). Behind the altar in the chapel is the wrought-iron coffer (1484) where Nicholas's mutilated arms were kept for centuries, and carried in procession through the streets of Tolentino. The statues of the *Virtues*, the cupids and the angels, which look as if they are carved from white marble, are in fact made of plaster of which the composition was kept a secret, the work of Giambattista Latini (19th century). The two paintings on the walls were offered by two Italian marine republics, Venice and Genoa, and represent miracles performed by Nicholas to save the cities. On the left is the *Extinguishing of a Fire in the Doge's Palace* by Matthias Stomer (1650), while that on the right shows *Nicholas Ends the Plague in Genoa* by Giovanni Carboncino (1677).

Leading off to the right from the Chapel of the Holy Arms is a doorway to a wide staircase down to the **crypt**, completed in 1932, where the body of the saint (and his arms) repose in a silver urn. On coming up from the crypt, you will find the access to the Basilica Museums, comprising the **Museo delle Ceramiche**, the magnificent collection of porcelain and ceramics offered to the city of Tolentino in 1933 by Cardinal Giovanni Tacci, on condition it be kept perpetually in the basilica; the

Museo dell'Opera, which includes paintings by Simone de Magistris and Vittore Crivelli, and a charming wooden *Nativity* (14th century) formed of three figures—the Madonna, St Joseph and the Child; and the **Museo degli Ex Voto**, a very interesting assortment of paintings and carvings, covering the period from the 15th–19th centuries, expressing gratitude for the intercession of the saint.

ST NICHOLAS OF TOLENTINO

Born in 1245 at Sant'Angelo in Pontano near San Ginesio, Nicholas joined the Augustinian order before being ordained as a priest at Cingoli in 1269, and from that moment wandered around the Marche, living a simple existence as a hermit and preacher. In spite of his austerity, he was a kind and good-humoured person. In 1275 he settled in Tolentino, where he stayed until his death on 10th September 1305. People travelled long distances to listen to his sermons, or to invoke his intercession for the sick or dying; at his canonization (1446) more than 300 miracles were reported, including some resurrections. In paintings or sculptures, he is recognisable by the star on his chest or just above his head; it appeared a few months before he died, following him during the night when he went to pray, and was seen by many witnesses. Forty years after his death, a German pilgrim opened his coffin in order to remove part of the body to take home as a relic. He cut off the arms, which started to bleed copiously; the man fled in horror, dropping them on the way. For centuries the cloths used to soak up the blood, and the arms themselves, were carried in procession in an iron chest through Tolentino, and many times the blood flowed miraculously, as if the mutilation had just taken place. To frustrate relic seekers, the rest of the body had been hastily buried in a location lost to memory, until it was discovered under the oratory of the church in 1926, and finally laid to rest in the crypt together with the arms. It was Nicholas who instructed his followers to pray for the souls in Purgatory, now a regular practice in the Catholic rite; he is invoked against injustice and natural disasters, and protects young mothers and infants. In 1400 Pope Boniface IX conceded the plenary indulgence to all those who visited his tomb, thus encouraging the pilgrimage to Tolentino, which became an organised event in many communities.

San Catervo and the Ponte del Diavolo

Leading east from Piazza Libertà is Corso Garibaldi (the ex-*decumanus maximus*), the main street. It leads to the **Cattedrale di San Catervo**, dedicated to St Catervius, patron saint of Tolentino. The church goes back to the 8th century, but was completely rebuilt in Neoclassical style in 1830. The low façade has a series of columns and a large pediment; all that remains of the preceding building are the bell-tower (which was also used for signalling) and the side portal. The spacious Latin-cross interior, with a central nave and two side aisles, has a wide transept. Over the side door is a 15th-century choir of inlaid panels, and in the first chapel to the left is a precious 14th-century painted wooden Crucifix. To the right of the presbytery is the so-called 'prison of Catervius' with Roman frescoes, and a carved lunette showing *Christ with the Archangels Michael and Gabriel and Sts Peter and Paul* (9th century), while left of the presbytery is the chapel of St Catervius, divided into two parts, the first covered by an octagonal dome (1882), and the second well-preserved Gothic (15th century). Around the sides are twelve early 15th-century choir stalls brought here from another church. Behind the altar, supported by four lions from the old church, is the magnificent carved stone **sarcophagus of Sts Catervius and Septimia** (4th century), containing the bodies of the saints together with their son Bassus. Little is known about these saints, possibly patrician Christians (Catervius was governor of the city) martyred under Diocletian. The bas-relief on the front shows the *Good Shepherd with Sts Peter and Paul*; that on the right shows the *Children burning in the Furnace*; on the left, *Epiphany*; and behind, in a medallion, are Catervius and Septimia themselves.

If continuing to San Ginesio or Civitanova Marche, you will cross the Chienti on the **Ponte del Diavolo** (Devil's Bridge), built in 1276 in one night, according to legend, by the Devil in person. The constructor had been delayed in the work and was unable to fulfil his contract; he made a deal, promising Satan the first soul to cross the bridge—Nicholas of Tolentino sent a dog over, and all was well; but it is said that the dog could be heard howling in misery for many centuries afterwards.

ENVIRONS OF TOLENTINO

The territory around Tolentino is mountainous and very beautiful; the thickly wooded slopes take on a blue hue in early morning, the reason why the poet Giacomo Leopardi called them the *Monti Azzurri*. The River Chienti flows through the valley—once marshy and unhealthy, until the Cistercian monks drained the land for farming. Besides wine, the delicious condensed wine called *vi'cotto piceno* is produced here, and rare olive oil called *olio della coroncina*, bright green in colour, with a slightly bitter flavour, ideal for *bruschette*.

Close to Tolentino, easily visible from the highway, the impressive, isolated, square **Castello della Rancia** (*T: 0733 901365*) was originally built as a fortified grain-store (*grancia* in old Italian) by the monks of Fiastra Abbey, at the end of the 12th century. In 1357 Rodolfo, of the da Varano family of Camerino, transformed it into a castle, part of their complex defensive system. Rancia was often the scene of fierce battles, including that won by the Austrians against Murat, Napoleon's brother-in-law, on 3rd May 1815. Some say that the bodies of many of Murat's soldiers were simply thrown into the water-cistern in the centre of the courtyard.

Serrapetrona

The picturesque medieval village of Serrapetrona, west of Tolentino, was built around an 11th-century castle which soon became part of the da Varano domain, to which it belonged until the Unification of Italy (1861). Built of stone and brick, in tones rang-

View of the village of Serrapetrona.

ing from golden brown through to cream and pale beige, it is still perfectly intact, a handful of houses nestling into the soft wooded hills. In the *chiesa parrocchiale* is a remarkable painted wooden Crucifix (13th century), and in the apse, an outstandingly beautiful polyptych by Lorenzo d'Alessandro (15th century) in the original, well-preserved gilded frame, showing the *Madonna with Christ Child and Sts Sebastian, Francis, Peter and James*; in the upper part is *Christ supported by Angels and Sts Bonadventure, John the Baptist, Michael and Catherine of Alexandria*; the lower part shows Apostles and Saints. There are also some frescoes, including one (1340) attributed to the Giotto School of Rimini, showing the *Resurrection of Christ*.

Serrapetrona is famed for its Vernaccia. Only 47 hectares of hillside vineyards are dedicated to the production of this very special sparkling red wine, which is available in three versions, sweet, dry and *passito*, this last obtained from specially dried grapes. According to Dante, this was the wine preferred above all others by Pope Nicholas IV: when he died of indigestion in 1285, it was probably after having drunk too much of it, together with a dish of eels from Lake Bolsena. Boccaccio frequently mentions *vernaccia*, but he was probably referring to the more widely known type from Liguria. The Serrapetrona vines, however, are native; their presence can be traced back to ancient times. The resulting wine is one of the proudest products of the Marche.

Belforte del Chienti

Perched on a ridge dominating the Chienti valley, still surrounded by its 14th-century walls, Belforte del Chienti is a farming community with a peaceful atmosphere and a pleasant climate. It is best explored on foot.

The steep and narrow medieval streets lead to the central church of Sant'Eustachio, where one of the most important paintings of the region can be seen: the **polyptych by Giovanni Boccati** of the *Madonna with Saints*, signed and dated 1468. (*Ask in the square for Angelo Diberi, who has the key, and allow yourself plenty of time for viewing this work of art.*) The polyptych, which is the largest in Europe and perhaps in the world (measuring 4.83m by 3.25m), consists of 35 paintings set into a magnificent, intricate gilded frame, thought to come from San Severino Marche, where the craftsmen were renowned for this kind of workmanship. Although painted during the Renaissance, it is Gothic in style, and it was commissioned as an altarpiece for this very church, by a certain Taliano di Lippo da Belforte. A series of dignified saints with gentle faces, painted on a gold background, surround the wondrous central panel. The Madonna is seated on a carved dais (on the front of the dais is the signature of the artist), with her feet on an Oriental rug. Little more than a child herself, she is gazing bemusedly at the gurgling Child on her lap, who is being playfully teased by two cherubs, one of whom is offering Him a goldfinch to kiss, and the other is apparently about to tickle His feet. Beautifully portrayed angel musicians (it is known that Giovanni Boccati played the lute), seraphim and two guardian angels crowd around the Madonna, as if jostling for space; the cherubs lifting the curtains above her look very mischievous. The Madonna is wearing a red silk brocade tunic and a magnificent deep blue velvet cloak, embroidered with gold acanthus leaves. Symbolism abounds: the goldfinch represents the human soul; the eight-sided dais refers to resurrection and eternity; red and blue are the colours signifying the divine and the human nature of Christ and the Virgin; the acanthus, a frequent element in pagan temples, came to assume some of the characteristics of the Madonna for early Christians; the coral around the neck of Jesus represents the blood of the Passion. Certainly a once-seen-never-forgotten work of art, it is thought to have provided inspiration for Raphael. High on the list of the masterpieces that Napoleon was anxious to take home to Paris in 1797, after the notorious Tolentino treaty (*see p. 107*), the priest was able to save it by dismantling all the various elements and hiding them in the roof, between the tiles and the ceiling.

In the same church is a 16th-century painted wooden statue of St Sebastian, brought here from the nearby church of the same name (*now closed*), and a delightful little Byzantine icon called the *Madonna contro le Tempeste*, which is only shown once every three years, or in times of grave danger from storms.

Caldarola

Not far from the artificial lake of Pievefavera is Caldarola, noted as the birthplace of a great family of artists, the de Magistris, who were active here between the 16th and

Detail of Giovanni Boccati's *Madonna and Saints* polyptych (1468).

17th centuries. In the long central square, Piazza Vittorio Emanuele, is the town hall, once the sumptuous town house of the Pallotta family. Of Sicilian origin, the family was particularly influential both in the history of the town, and of the Vatican—no fewer than four cardinals were Pallottas: unfortunately they are not all remembered for their piety. On view inside is the **Stanza del Paradiso**, entirely frescoed by Simone de Magistris towards the end of the 16th century. Probably reflecting the worldly tastes of the cardinal who commissioned the work, the imaginative paintings cover the walls (and even the ceiling) with a series of *trompe l'oeil* windows, each with a different view of Paradise; scenes of mythology and hunting, gentle people strolling through meadows, lakes with little islands covered with trees, recalling Chinese art. Cherubs, grotesque masks, floral garlands, fruit, flowers, vegetables and animals punctuate the designs, creating a charming—if somewhat overwhelming—overall effect. Other rooms in the palace, also decorated by Simone, show the festive greetings of the population when Pope Clement VIII visited Caldarola. The palace also houses the Civic Museum with the **Pinacoteca della Resistenza** (*open Thur, Sat, Sun 10–12.30 & 5–7; T: 0733 905529*), a collection of paintings with the Resistance movement of the Second World War as a theme, including works by Aligi Sassu and Renato Guttuso.

Next to the town hall is the elegant façade of the collegiate church of **San Martino**: over the main altar is a canvas by Simone de Magistris showing St Martin. In front of San Martino, preceded by a double stairway, is the church of **Madonna del Monte** (1781). Inside is a splendid panel painting of the *Madonna and Child, Eight Saints, Worshippers and the Donors*, by Lorenzo d'Alessandro, signed and dated 1491, with a particularly beautiful Madonna accepting the town of Caldarola under her protection. Nearby, in Via Pallotta, is the tiny, lovely **Teatro Comunale** (*T: 0733 905529*) of 1906, in perfect condition: it has only 291 seats.

Via de Magistris leads up to the picturesque **Castello Pallotta** (*open summer Tues and Fri afternoon 10–12 & 3–6.30; winter Tues and Fri afternoon 10–12 & 2.30–5.30; T: 0733 905242*), now the museum of Caldarola, with the original furniture (including the bathtub, carved from one block of marble) and collections of weapons and carriages. The castle, which is surrounded by wooded gardens, was probably built in 875 as a defensive structure; it was attacked, destroyed and rebuilt many times in the course of the centuries, passing to the Pallotta family in 1450, who transformed it into their summer residence.

SAN GINESIO & ENVIRONS

Enticing when it comes into sight, San Ginesio (pop. 3,800) does not disappoint on closer inspection. Proudly forming part of the Italian association of beautiful villages (www.borghitalia.it), it offers spectacular views over the Gran Sasso d'Italia park, and also the Sibylline Mountains park, of which it forms part. The defensive walls, built between the 14th and 15th centuries, are particularly impressive: the battlements, bulwarks and towers are still in excellent condition.

Founded in the 6th century, San Ginesio declared itself an independent commune in the 13th century, thanks to the prestige and wealth brought by the passage of pilgrims to or from Rome, Loreto, San Michele di Gargano and Jerusalem; but this was the cause of much strife. In 1230 there was a fierce struggle between the people and the nobles, followed by a long series of wars with Ascoli, Tolentino, Belforte, Matelica and Fermo. The town was then taken by Percival Doria on behalf of King Manfred (the son of Frederick II), who ruled with an iron fist. In spite of his tyranny, San Ginesio prospered, until it was taken a century later by the da Varano dukes of Camerino. These latter behaved so badly that the citizens requested the protection of the Church, and San Ginesio in the 16th century became part of the Papal States. It has been renowned for its schools since 1295, when the first one was opened

The Madonna of Mercy by Pietro Alemanno (1485), in the church of the Collegiata of San Ginesio.

Central San Ginesio

The main approach to the city is through Porta Picena (13th century), surmounted by battlements. Immediately on the right is the **Ospedale di San Paolo** (13th century), sometimes called *Ospedale dei Pellegrini*, one of several pilgrim hospitals that were erected here. The fame of the place spread rapidly, when many miraculous recoveries were reported. Built of ochre stone, the façade presents a portico surmounted by a loggia, both with a series of eight columns.

The town centre is **Piazza Gentili**, with a bronze statue of 1908 of Alberico Gentili (1551–1611), who taught at Oxford University and is considered the founder of the science of international law. The building with the portico is the delightful Neoclassical opera house, Teatro Giacomo Leopardi (1877). Taking pride of place in the square is the very unusual **Collegiata**, a Romanesque church with a late Gothic façade, probably the work of German craftsmen. The richly-decorated portal and the exceptional terracotta ornamentation at the top are by the otherwise unknown Enrico Alemanno (Henry the German), dated 1421. It is rather mysterious, because there is nothing like it elsewhere in the Marche, though similar examples are found in the Netherlands, Germany and Flanders. The interior has a central nave and two side aisles, divided by pilasters of different types. The chapels are all on the south side, while the apse is square. In the third chapel are three excellent canvases by Simone de Magistris (1588), the *Last Supper* and *Christ falls under the Cross* in the vestibule, and the *Crucifixion* over the altar. In the apse is an old fresco of the *Crucifixion* (Giotto School of Rimini) behind the altar, while on the left is a lovely panel painting by Pietro Alemanno, signed and dated 1485, of the *Madonna of Mercy*. Inside the main altar is the body of the patron saint, Lucius Ginesius (284–305), actor and mimic dear to the Emperor Diocletian for his mocking parodies of Christians. When Lucius converted, he was beheaded. Under the presbytery is the crypt, known as the *oratorio di San Biagio*, decorated with frescoes by Lorenzo Salimbeni (1406).

Behind the Collegiata, at 14 Via Merelle, is the ex-church of San Sebastiano, which now houses the **Museo Civico Scipione Gentili** (*open 9–12 & 3–4.30; Sat 3.30–4.30; T: 0733 656022*), with an archaeological section and a collection of paintings by Simone de Magistris, Vincenzo Pagani, Stefano Folchetti and others, and an anonymous 15th-century portrayal of the battle of 1377 between San Ginesio and Fermo, of great historical interest. The modern art collection, with works by local artists, is on show at the town hall (*open as above*), situated in the convent next to the church of San Francesco, near the central square. The highest part of the town is called Colle Ascarano, now the public gardens—the view from here over the surrounding countryside is exceptional.

Macchie and the *Omphalos*

On the SS 78 between San Ginesio and Urbisaglia is the tiny village of Macchie, a few houses surrounding one of the many Romanesque churches in the region—Santa Maria di Macchie, built in the 11th century as part of a Benedictine abbey. The crypt (12th century) is a forest of little columns, of which two, from *Urbs Salvia* (modern Urbisaglia), are of marble. The capitals are extremely interesting; one, which has been upturned to adapt it to its new use, is an *omphalos* (from the Greek for belly-button or navel), a carved stone pertaining to the cult of Apollo. In many places in the world certain stones are thought to have magic properties, or to exert magnetic attraction. They are the centres of the cosmos, points of origin of the creation of the universe. One of them is at Machu Picchu, in Peru; there was another in Rome (the stone has vanished, but the Eternal City is still thought to exert strong exoteric magnetism); a very famous one is the Rock in Jerusalem, sacred to Jews, Christians and Muslims alike; yet another is Stonehenge. For the Greeks the *omphalos* was above all the sacred stone in the temple of Apollo at Delphi, marking the spot where two eagles, loosed from the ends of the earth by Zeus, met. The stone (now in the Delphi museum) is about the size of a section of column, with a rounded top covered with a network of carvings. Delphi was thought to be the exact centre of the earth, the meeting-point between dark and light, the subterranean and the upper worlds. It could therefore favour the revelations of the oracle. Sometimes similar stones were placed in the temples dedicated to Apollo, and were venerated as symbolic of his wisdom. That such a stone should have found its way into a Christian church is not unusual; finely-carved stones were instantly recycled by medieval church builders.

Urbisaglia

In ancient times the town of Urbisaglia was an important settlement controlling the point where the road from Fermo to San Severino Marche crosses that from Macerata to Ascoli Piceno. The walls, which still partially surround the town, were built using stones from the ruins of the Roman *Urbs Salvia*, destroyed by Alaric the Goth in 410. In the central Piazza Garibaldi is a formidable castle (13th–15th centuries) called the Rocca (*open 15 June–15 Sept 10–12 & 4.30–7.30; 16 Sept–14 June 10–12 & 3–6 Sat and Sun only; T: 0733 506566*), complete with four impregnable towers and the keep.

Close to the castle is the **Collegiata di San Lorenzo** (18th century), eight-sided, where over the first south altar is a triptych by Stefano Folchetti of *The Wedding of St Catherine and Sts Peter and Lawrence*, signed and dated 1507. In Traversa Piccinini is the **Museo Archeologico** (*open Mon, Tues, Wed, Sun and holidays 8.30–1.30; Thur, Fri and Sat 8.30–7.30, ask here to visit the archaeological park if closed T: 0733 50107*) with an informative collection of finds from Urbs Salvia, including marble statues from the theatre and monumental inscriptions from the amphitheatre, giving a good idea of what the ancient city was like, and also generally on Roman times in the Marche.

Just northeast of the town, on the SS 78 to Macerata, is a group of houses called Maestà. Close to a Roman wall is the little **Chiesetta di Maestà** (15th century; *ask nearby for key*), interesting for the interior, a single nave with truss-beam roof, and the series of votive frescoes which almost entirely cover the walls. Some of them are particularly fine, for example on the right-hand side in a niche, a *Pietà* by Stefano Folchetti. It was a local custom to pray for delivery from the plague and other epidemics in this church, and to commission a painting as thanksgiving when the prayers were answered.

One of the entrances to the **archaeological park of Urbs Salvia** (*open 1 Mar–15 June and 16 Sept–31 Oct Sat 3–6, Sun and holidays 10–1 & 3–6; 16 June–15 Sept every day 10–1 & 3–7; 1 Nov–28 Feb Sat 3–4.30, Sun and holidays 10–1 & 3–4.30; T: 0733 506566*), which covers about 40 hectares, is close to the church. The amphitheatre was built outside the walls in AD 80, on the orders of Flavius Silva Nonius Bassus. It is a beautiful setting, crowned by shady oaks. Not far away, a sacred area has been brought to light, dedicated to the goddess Salus Augusta, with a covered passage showing conspicuous traces of frescoes in the third Pompeian style (painted architectural elements with human and animal figures). By following a track which leads back towards Urbisaglia, you reach the theatre. This, thought to go back to AD 23, is the most important archaeological monument in the Marche region, and one of the finest Roman theatres in Italy. Judging by the size, and by the quantity of statues, inscriptions and decorative carvings recovered by the archaeologists (now in the

Archaeological Museum), it must have been imposing and richly ornate; a providential landslide, which must have occurred soon after its construction, preserved it for posterity.

Santa Maria di Chiaravalle di Fiastra

For centuries an old signpost announced: *'O tu che passi per la via, rallegrati che vicina è l'abbazia'* (Rejoice o wayfarer, the abbey is near), and in fact, continuing along the SS 78 for Macerata, the Cistercian abbey of Santa Maria di Chiaravalle di Fiastra soon comes into sight, in what is now one of the most interesting protected areas of the region (*open 15 June–15 Sept 10–1 & 3–7; 16 Sept–14 June Sat, Sun and holidays 10–1 & 3–6; T: 0733 202942*).

Founded by Cistercian monks from Chiaravalle Abbey in Milan in 1142, on the site of a preceding Benedictine convent between the Fiastra and Chienti rivers, it became one of the most powerful and influential religious communities of central Italy. For their church and monastery, the monks used material from Urbs Salvia (notice the Roman columns in the refectory); they drained the marshy, unhealthy land, built roads and bridges, mills, oil presses and wineries, and inaugurated three centuries of intense social, economic and cultural activity, all documented in a series of 3,194 parchments called the *carte fiastrensi*, kept in the State Archives in Rome. Devastated by Braccio da Montone in 1422, the abbey lost its splendour, becoming something of an encumbrance which was passed from one cardinal to another, until it was acquired by the Bandini family of Camerino in 1773, who put things to rights. The last heir, Sigismondo, left the entire property to a foundation in his name when he died in 1918. Known as the *Fondazione Giustiniani-Bandini*, it still pursues agricultural research. The reserve was instituted in 1984.

It is particularly interesting to visit the farmland, created so painstakingly by the monks, and still perfectly functional: the *Selva*, or forest, now one of the few surviving examples of autochthonous woodland in central Marche; the River Fiastra; the Museo Naturalistico, with its helpful displays on local wildlife, and the Museo della Civiltà Contadina, with a collection of tools and other equipment used by the farmer-monks.

Built during the period of transition between Romanesque and Gothic, with some typically Cistercian features, the red brick church of the abbey, Santa Maria Annunziata, has a simple façade preceded by a narthex. The spacious interior has a single nave with truss-beam roof, and two side aisles, divided by four-lobed pilasters formed of half columns, characteristic of the churches of this Order. Many frescoes still survive, notably those of the square-sided apse, showing the *Crucifixion with Sts Benedict and Bernard*, dated 1473, by a follower of Giovanni Boccati; the altar stone comes from a Roman temple. Also typical of the Cistercians is the large square monastery (where the monks have now returned) next to the church, built around an enormous cloister (15th century). From the cloister it is possible to reach the chapter house and the refectory, the roof of which is supported by seven Roman columns with beautiful capitals and bases, brought here from Urbs Salvia. In the little bell-tower is a bronze bell made in 1492.

SANTA MARIA DI CHIARAVALLE DI FIASTRA

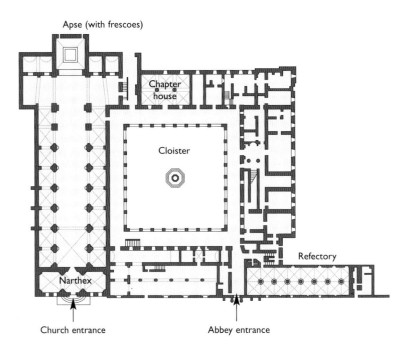

Loro Piceno and Monte San Martino

The farming community of **Loro Piceno** was once known as *Castrum Lauri*. The inhabitants can now legally sell their most famous product, condensed wine called *vi' cotto piceno*, once officially prohibited and only obtainable under the counter. There are also several textile industries which provide employment, but the population is steadily dwindling. In the town centre is an old castle called Castello Brunforte, built by the Normans in the 13th century. Later restored and used as a monastery, it now houses a museum dedicated to the two world wars, the Museo delle Due Guerre Mondiali (*open July every day except Mon; Aug every day; Sept–June Sat, Sun and holidays 10.30–12.30 & 3.30–7.30, other days on request; T: 0733 656890*) a unique and richly representative collection.

From Loro Piceno a road leads south to Sant'Angelo in Pontano, birthplace of St Nicholas of Tolentino, and then to **Penna San Giovanni**, with small industries which produce woollen cloth and kitchen crockery. In the central Piazza del Teatro is one of the smallest opera houses (90 seats) in the region—Teatro Flora (1780; *T: 0733 669119*). It is also a rare example of a theatre built entirely of wood. The views from the ruins of the fortress in the highest part of the town are splendid.

The same road crosses the Tennacola and then goes up the mountain on the other side, to **Monte San Martino**, in a very panoramic position on a thickly forested hill, with a sheer drop down to the Tenna below. The town is said to have been founded by the Franks in the 9th century. Silkworms are raised, and silk cloth is woven by the young people of the village. A walk along the walls, which are still largely intact, leads to the Belvedere with splendid views, and to the church of San Martino, which has two remarkable 15th-century paintings: a polyptych of the *Madonna and Child with Saints* by Carlo and Vittore Crivelli (notice the slender hands, with long tapered fingers, of the saints, and the elaborate ringlets of their hair), and a triptych by Vittore Crivelli of the same subject.

Mogliano

Mogliano is an attractive little town on a ridge between the Cremone and Ete Morto rivers. It is of ancient origin, once inhabited by the Picenes, later a Roman settlement, then the property of the abbey of Farfa, near Rieti. Not far from the town is the industrial area; many people here are expert in working bamboo, vimine and straw—you will be tempted to renew the furniture in your conservatory. Other craftsmen make leather and woollen goods. The old centre is very spick-and-span, and easy to explore on foot. The main street, Via Roma, leads through colourful old buildings, passing on the left the imposing church of **San Gregorio Magno**, preceded by a Baroque double staircase. Over the main altar is a splendid panel painting by Durante Nobili, who was a follower of Lorenzo Lotto, showing the *Immaculate Virgin with Four Saints*. Further along is the central square, Piazza Garibaldi, and the mother church, **Santa Maria Assunta**, with a high, unfinished 18th-century façade. Over the main altar is a masterpiece by Lorenzo Lotto, a large panel painting signed and dated 1548, of the *Assumption of the Madonna with Sts John the Baptist, Anthony of Padua, Mary Magdalene and Joseph*, at last reassembled in its original frame, which was removed in 1720 and taken to another church. This painting is similar to the one Lorenzo painted two years later for the church of San Francesco alle Scale in Ancona (*see p. 19*), on the same subject; it has a melancholy air to it, and subdued colours. Nearing 70, he was probably going through a difficult period; perhaps lonely, certainly still smarting for the scathing criticism he had just received from the influential Pietro Aretino, who had called him 'outdated'; as a fervent Catholic he was maybe depressed by the continuing strife between Catholics and Protestants. The theme here, in fact, would appear to be a Counter-Reformation invitation to reconsider the Sacraments: the desperately pleading figures in the foreground show from the left *John the Baptist* (Baptism), *Anthony of Padua* (Confirmation), *Mary Magdalene* (Last Rites), and *Joseph* (Matrimony). These figures are isolated by a high wall from the city (Mogliano?) which can just be seen behind it, while the Madonna, ascending to Paradise on a white cloud, appears indifferent to their pleas.

To the right of the church is the narrow façade of the **Oratory of St Mary** (1420), now the clock tower, with a lovely portal in brick, terracotta and stone. The painting in the lunette represents the *Pietà with Sts Roch and Sebastian*. These two saints were frequently invoked in times of pestilence, and in fact the little church was built after several years of plague. On the opposite side of the square is the opera house, Teatro Apollo (1837; *T: 0733 559822 to request visit*). Continuing along to the eastern gate, Porta da Piedi (15th century), which is Gothic in style and particularly photogenic, a picturesque brick stairway called the *Immattonata* leads down to the church and convent of **Santa Colomba**, probably the oldest in the town, founded before the 11th century. In 1215 the Benedictines dedicated the church to St Francis, during a journey he was making through the area; in 1361, during troubled times, the convent was abandoned by his friars who took refuge in the castle. In 1548 they returned, rebuilt the convent and repaired the church. The convent is now the old people's home of Mogliano; on request the courteous staff will show you the delightful cloister, decorated with 17th-century frescoes, and the interior of the church. The impressive coffered ceiling, with portraits of saints, is the work of a local artist, Giovanni Battista Fabiani (1750). Over the main altar is a very beautiful panel painting by Durante Nobili of the *Madonna and Christ Child with Sts Joseph, Colomba, John the Baptist, Francis of Assisi and Benedict*, signed and dated 1554, interesting for the finely rendered 16th-century costumes and the expressive faces of the characters in the scene. The magnificent 18th-century walnut woodwork of the choir and the confessionals is by craftsmen from Montappone.

PRACTICAL INFORMATION

GETTING THERE

• **By train**: Tolentino and Urbisaglia are on the Civitanova- Fabriano–Rome line.
• **By bus**: CONTRAM, T: 0733 230906 has services from Belforte del Chienti, Caldarola, Mogliano and Tolentino to Camerino, Macerata, Loreto, Recanati and Ancona.
SASP, T: 0733 663137, 0733 663358 or 0733 663247 has services to San Ginesio and Urbisaglia from Macerata, Amandola, Sarnano, Comunanza, Fermo and Ancona.
ASSM, T: 0733 95601, has services from Tolentino to Serrapetrona.

INFORMATION OFFICES

The townships have a central organization called Comunità Montana dei Monti Azzurri (12 Via Piave, San Ginesio, T: 0733 202942, www.montiazzurri.it).
Loro Piceno and Mogliano adhere to the association STL Terre dell'Infinito (T: 0733 843569, www.terredellinfinito.it), providing information and a tourist discount card, 'Infinito Card'.
Other tourist offices for the area are at: **Abbadia di Fiastra** IAT, T: 0733 202942, www.meridianasrl.it; Fiastra Abbey Wildlife Reserve, T: 0733 201049.
Belforte del Chienti Tourist

Information Bureau, T: 0733 951010,
www.belforte.sinp.net
Caldarola Municipio, 16 Via
Piandassalto, T: 0733 905529, www.
caldarola.sinp.net; Tourist Information
Bureau, 1 Viale Umberto, T: 0733
905529.
Mogliano Municipio, 54 Via Roma, T:
0733 559840, www.mogliano-mc.
sinp.net; Pro Loco, 2 Via Leopardi, T:
0733 559840; www.promogliano.it
San Ginesio Municipio, 35 Via
Capostello, T: 0733 656022,
www.sanginesio.sinp.net; IAT, Piazza
Gentili, T: 0733 656014; Casa del
Parco, Località San Liberato, T: 0733
694404; Tourist Information Bureau, T:
0733 656072, www.sanginesio.com
Serrapetrona Pro Loco, 18 Via
Leopardi, T: 0733 908321,
www.comune.serrapetrona.mc.it
Tolentino Municipio, 3 Piazza Libertà,
T: 0733 9011, www.comune.
tolentino.mc.it; IAT and Pro Loco, 19
Piazza della Libertà, T: 0733 972937.
Urbisaglia Municipio, 45 Corso
Giannelli, T: 0733 512626, www.
urbisaglia.sinp.net; Pro Loco, 9 Via
Sacrario, T: 0733 506566,
www.urbisaglia.com

HOTELS

Belforte del Chienti
€€ **Belvedere**. Comfortable hotel, with
a garden; vegetarian food on request. 21
Via Santa Lucia, T: 0733 906153.
Caldarola
€€€ **Tesoro**. Small, modern hotel with
a good restaurant; well situated in the
outskirts of town. Via Matteotti,
T: 0733 905830.
€€ **Da Sandro**. Small and friendly,

with a good restaurant and pizzeria. 16
Piazza XXIV Maggio, T: 0733 905325.
Penna San Giovanni
€€ **Vecchi Sapori**. An inn, with excel-
lent restaurant. Viale B.Giovanni,
T: 0733 699030.
San Ginesio
€€€ **Centrale**. In a central position,
with a restaurant. 10–12 Piazza Gentile,
T: 0733 656832. Closed Thurs.
Serrapetrona
€€€ **Ferranti**. Comfortable, and with
a good restaurant. 60 Via Nazionale,
T: 0733 905493.
Tolentino
€€€€ **Holiday**. With a good restau-
rant, pool and garage. 90 Viale Buozzi,
T: 0733 967400.
€€ **Milano**. In a central position, with
a restaurant. 13–15 Via Roma, T: 0733
973014.
Urbisaglia
€€€ **La Maestà**. Comfortable hotel in
panoramic position. Contrada Maestà,
T: 0733 506495.
€ **Della Cacciagione**. An inn with a
delightful restaurant. 20 Via della
Rocca, T: 0733 50134.

BED & BREAKFAST

Urbisaglia
Villa d'Aria. A beautiful 17th-century
farmhouse within Abbadia di Fiastra
reserve boundaries. English, French and
Spanish spoken. 30 Contrada Abbadia di
Fiastra, T: 0733 30677, www.bbmarche.it

FARM ACCOMMODATION

Caldarola
Il Frutteto. Quite a discovery, this little
farm serves delicious, simple local dish-

es. Contrada Acquevive, T: 0733 905317.

L'Eremo. Comfortable farm with good restaurant, close to Pievefavera lake, surrounded by woods. 3 Frazione Bistocco, T: 0733 905595.

Loro Piceno

Al Castelluccio. Beautiful 18th-century farmhouse in lovely position; maize, sunflowers, sugarbeet, pigs and poultry; they make their own *vi' cotto*. Località Borgo San Lorenzo, Contrada Appezzana, T: 0733 510001.

San Ginesio

Il Casolare. Small, solid farmhouse at 835m; good food. 44 Via Vallimestre, T: 0733 656688 or 0733 656289.

La Cioppa. Comfortable accommodation in a lovely house 4km from San Ginesio. Garden, pool, Turkish bath, tennis and archery. 2 Contrada Gualduccio, T: 0733 694265, www.lacioppa.com

Sambuco. Has panoramic views over Sibylline Mountains; poultry (ducks), olive oil, cereals, fruit. Open Apr–Oct. 29 Contrada Necciano, T: 0733 656392.

Silvia. Apartments, very close to town; free dinner Sat evenings July–Aug, with food produced on the farm: pigeons, poultry, cereals, fruit and wine. Panoramic views. 86 Contrada Santa Croce, T: 0733 656315.

Serrapetrona

Caravanserraglio. A restored cottage with panoramic views; horse-riding, pottery and cookery courses. They will pick you up from Tolentino. 10 Contrada Colli, T: 0733 908284, www.caravanserraglio.com

Urbisaglia

La Fontana. Within the Abbadia di

Fiastra reserve boundaries; with a good restaurant and plenty of sports facilities. 8 Località La Selva, T: 0733 514002.

MONASTERY ACCOMMODATION

Abbadia di Fiastra

A few rooms are available at the abbey, for men only, who wish to take part in the monastic community for a few days; let the abbot know well ahead. For information and bookings, T: 0733 202190.

RESTAURANTS

Caldarola

€€ **Il Picciolo di Rame**. ■ Booking is essential for this amazing old tavern in the fortified township of Vestignano, near Caldarola. Very, very exciting food. Castello di Vestignano, T: 348 3316588.

€ **Da Sandro**. A family-run inn serving traditional dishes: try *frittura mista maceratese*, mixed fried veal, chicken, vegetables and confectioner's custard. Local wines. Closed Mon. 16 Piazza XXIV Maggio, T: 0733 905183.

Colmurano

€ **Peccato di Gola**. Restaurant and pizzeria—superb pizza. 3 Piazza Umberto, T: 0733 508345.

Loro Piceno

€€ **Al Girarrosto**. Specialising in spit-roasted food, this charming restaurant occupies the wine cellar of a 17th-century Franciscan monastery. Closed Wed. 3 Via Ridolfi, T: 0733 509119.

Monte San Martino

€€ **Priori**. A family-run restaurant offering interesting local dishes. Closed Thur. Piazza XX Settembre, T: 0733 660209.

San Ginesio

€ **Paracallà**. Delicious local dishes. 14 Via Zaccagnini, T: 0733 656256.

Serrapetrona

€€ **Cantinella**. Excellent grills, snacks with ham and salami. Closed Tues. 3 Piazza Santa Maria, T: 0733 908112.

€€ **Hostaria dei Borgia**. ■ A very old inn; Maurizio, Sandro and Stefania prepare their own hams and salami; innovative and imaginative dishes. A wide selection of local cheeses, served with home-made jams or honey; leave room for the fantastic desserts. Good local wines. Closed Mon and Tues in winter, Mon in summer, Aug open every day. 3 Via Camerano, Borgiano, T: 0733 905131.

Tolentino

€€ **Holiday**. A well-chosen menu of ancient traditional dishes, local wines. 90 Viale Buozzi, T: 0733 967400.

€ **Da Santina**. Good simple food, robust servings; try grilled vegetables or *pasta al forno*. Closed Mon. 14 Via Beato Tommaso.

€ **La Locanda**. Pizzas baked in wood oven (evenings); good pasta lunchtime. 3 Via San Salvatore, T: 0733 966295.

CAFÉS & PASTRY SHOPS

Colmurano

Melody. Coffee bar, home-made ice cream, and sandwiches. Piazza Umberto.

Mogliano

Bar degli Amici. A friendly bar close to the bus stop, ideal for coffee and snacks. 7–8 Piazzale Diaz.

San Ginesio

Caffè Centrale. Serves excellent home-made ice cream. Piazza Gentili.

Tolentino

Bar Zazzaretta. Historic central bar for people-watching. Piazza Libertà.

Pasticceria La Mimosa. ■ Famous pastry shop: try *crostata frangipane* or *torta di pere e Vernaccia di Serrapetrona*. Closed Tues. 69 Viale Vittorio Veneto, T: 0733 969950.

FESTIVALS & EVENTS

Caldarola *Giostra delle Castella*, everyone dresses up in 16th-century clothes for jousting, archery and races; Info: Pro Loco, 7 Via Pallotta, T: 338 9664649, 1st and 2nd Sun in Aug. Feast of St Martin, roast chestnuts and fireworks, 11 Nov.

Colmurano *Artistrada*, artists of all genres create and perform in the medieval centre; Info: 0733 508489, July. Vintage Motorbike Parade; Info: Municipio T: 0733 508287, Aug.

Mogliano Procession of the Passion through the streets, Good Friday. Feast of the Patron Saint's Birthday (John the Baptist), end June–early July. *Mogliano 1744*, a series of celebrations during which the whole town plunges back into the 18th century; Info: Municipio, 54 Via Roma, T: 0733 559840, www.promogliano.it, end June–early July.

Penna San Giovanni Carnival, with fancy-dress parades and allegorical floats; Info: Municipio, T: 0733 699003, Feb.

San Ginesio *Palio*, in a perfect medieval setting, two exciting horse races; Info: Associazione Tradizioni Sanginesine, 46 Piazza Gentili, T: 0733 656022, www.sanginesio.it, 13 and 15 Aug. Feast of St Ginesius, 25 Aug.

Tolentino Rancia Castle, Tolentino 815

evokes the famous battle; Info: Associazione Tolentino 815, 2 Via Nazionale, T: 0733 960778, 1st Sun in May. *Biennale internazionale di umorismo nell'arte*, caricatures, films and other humour in art; Info: www. biennaleumorismo.org, July–Oct, odd years. *Dono dei Ceri a San Nicola*, when the city corporations donate elaborate wax candles and a banner to their saint; 15th-century costumes, races, archery contests and a tug-of-war; Info: Pro Loco, end Aug–early Sept. *Sul Ponte del Diavolo*, craftsmen demonstrate their skill; folk dancing, archery and a joust on the Devil's Bridge; Info: Associazione Ponte del Diavolo, 7 Via Ributino, T: 0733 972782, end Aug–mid Sept. Feast of St Nicholas, particularly heartfelt; Info: T: 0733 966210, 10 September and 3rd Sun in Sept.

Urbisaglia Feast of St George, 23 April. Classical drama season at the Roman Amphitheatre in July–Aug; Info: T: 0733 512626.

LOCAL SPECIALITIES

Caldarola

Adolfo Pieroni, 9 Via San Lorenzo, for Olio Massimo, superb *olio della coroncina* olive oil. **Carducci**, 24 Viale Aldo Moro, has a wide assortment of home-made biscuits. **Giuliano Annavini**, Via Buscalferri, this biscuit factory also sells to the public, wonderful local pastries.

Loro Piceno

Along the main street many shops sell

vi'cotto; next to the church of San Francesco there is an interesting exhibition explaining its manufacture. For many years considered illegal (like poteen), because it cannot be classified as wine, in 2000 it obtained recognition as a traditional local product.

Mogliano

Articles made of straw and wicker are the speciality here. Good places to buy them include **Claudio Nardi**, Zona Industriale San Pietro; **Giuseppe Parigiani**, at 2 Contrada Trataiata; **Pacifico Bartolacci**, 2 Via Castello.

Serrapetrona

Alberto Quacquarini, 1 Contrada Colli, produces and sells the DOC wines *Vernaccia di Serrapetrona*. **Azienda Claudi**, 13 Piazza Maria, is another good source. **Massimo Serboni**, 6 Frazione Borgiano, produces and sells *olio della coroncina*.

Tolentino

Ales Pelletterie, 9 Via Tobagi, is one of the best-known places for hand-made leather articles; discount prices. At **Ambrosia**, 72 Via Flaminia, buy your delicious pasta straight from the manufacturer; guaranteed locally-grown durum wheat. **Laipe**, 2 Via Tobagi, for hand-made leather goods. **Multifirme**, 14 Viale della Repubblica, is an outlet for Nazareno Gabrielli clothes and leather goods. **Tre Mori**, 27 Via Santa Lucia, T: 0733 969955, is a charming shop selling sweets made on the premises: Easter eggs, nougat, local honey, and freshly roasted coffee beans.

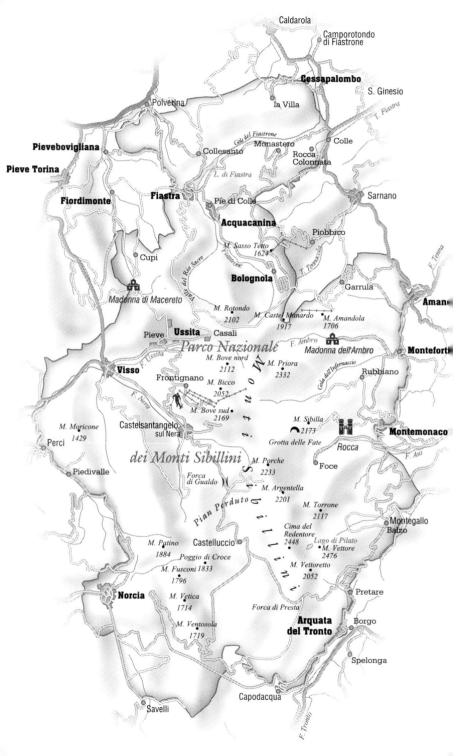

THE SIBYLLINE MOUNTAINS

This stretch of the Apennines, the watershed between the Tyrrhenian Sea and the Adriatic, is now one of Italy's most beautiful and interesting national parks, where the mountains and valleys, scattered with numerous small medieval communities, illustrate the centuries-old, often precarious existence of the inhabitants in an extremely fragile environment and in perfect ecological balance. The park, which protects one of the most important mountain systems of Europe, is situated partly in the Marche region and partly in Umbria. At least 20 of the mountains are more than 2000m high. With a series of limestone peaks and deep ravines, lush forests and alpine meadows, gullies, waterfalls and rushing streams, it is a natural paradise, which also holds a fascinating, age-old air of mystery. There is something here to interest everyone: botanists, climbers and skiers, birdwatchers, free-flyers, artists and photographers, and some well-signposted trails provide itineraries for ramblers, trekkers and mountain bikers. The institution of protective measures has brought a certain degree of prosperity, and besides wildlife, several varieties of orchard fruits (notably the *mela rosa* apple, so called not for the colour, which is green and red, but for its aroma of roses) and farm animals (such as the *sopravvissana* sheep) have been preserved from extinction and their production much intensified. Demand for the tasty Castelluccio lentils, or the local truffles, is now worldwide.

HISTORY OF THE MOUNTAINS

Inhabited since the Neolithic era, these mountains offered refuge to the Sabines, the Umbrians and the Picenes; at the same time, they constituted a barrier between east and west; they were a source of timber, resin and furs; a place to pasture flocks and herds in security on lush upland meadows, for the production of formidable cheeses, while the woods supplied forage for pigs, resulting in excellent hams, salami and sausage. People thought of the Sibyllines as the dwelling place of witches, demons, necromancers and fairies, and in particular, of the Sibyl, a wise woman who lived in a cave close to the summit of Mount Vettore, and who could sometimes be persuaded to give a hint about the future. Some say she was the Sibyl of Cumae, condemned to live chained up in the cave till Judgement Day. Lake Pilato, according to legend the final resting-place of Pilate, was thought to be infested with devils. Among the writers who were inspired by these stories and who came to explore for themselves, were Andrea da Barberino (15th century), who composed a poem called *Guerin Moschino*, and Antoine de la Sale (1420), with his *Paradis de la Reine Sibylle*.

The foresters who supplied wood for shipbuilding often became seamen themselves; the inhabitants of the village of Spelonga, near Arquata del Tronto, built a ship to fight in the Battle of Lepanto against the Turks (1571); they still keep their trophy, a Turkish silk banner, in the church of St Agatha, and they still build a complete ship every third year in the square and ceremoniously burn it.

In the latter part of the 16th century, the *Prefettura della Montagna*, controlled by the papacy, was created to combat the brigands infesting the road between Umbria and the Marche, who had their headquarters in the Kingdom of Naples. Troops were used to keep the numbers of the bandits down. However, during the two French occupations between the 18th and 19th centuries, the phenomenon got worse, because common criminals were using politics and religion to justify their actions; some became heroes in the popular imagination. In spite of the danger, scientists from all over Europe carried out important work in the Sibyllines, such as botanists Luigi Anguillara (1560) and Johann Winther (1624), and astronomer Christopher Maire (1753).

After the Second World War the mountains were gradually abandoned, as people moved to the cities to find work. Then skiing became fashionable and a possible source of wealth: roads and sports facilities were rapidly built, ski-runs constructed and rivers diverted. Plans for a National Park were dismissed until in 1968 two climbers from Ascoli Piceno, Maurizio Calibani and William Scalabroni, pointed out that the Strada della Sibilla, the new road over the mountains, was a permanent scar on the landscape, visible from an enormous distance. The park was finally created in 1993, protecting 70,000 hectares of this lovely part of central Italy.

Visso

A handful of neat, pastel-coloured houses grouped around three lovely old churches; fortifications, gates and towers still intact; traditions and gastronomy proudly maintained: this little community is delightfully coherent with its past, but at the same time Visso has a rather worldly air, deriving probably from its strategic position on the main route from Umbria to the Marche. It has seen many centuries of travellers. Standing at the confluence of the Ussita and Nera rivers, at the foot of Mount Bove, it controls now, as it always has, the most important route over the Apennines from Rome and Terni, and one of the best-known approaches to the upper mountains. It was therefore often contested between Camerino, Spoleto and the Papal States. Visso houses the offices of the Sibylline Mountains National Park, and is the natural point of entry when arriving from Camerino or Umbria.

Heart of the little town (one of Italy's 'beautiful villages') is Piazza Martiri Vissani. The collegiate church of **Santa Maria** dominates the square, with its 14th-century portal, above which is a striking *Annunciation* by the local artist Paolo da Visso (1444). In front of the beautiful 14th-century wooden door are two worn stone Romanesque lions. You may find that the priest's plump and purring ginger cat will act as your guide to the interior. There are some frescoes of the 14th–15th centuries; those in the apse have a particularly successful chromatic effect. The large effigy of St Christopher has only recently been brought to light. In front on entering, up some steps, is the Romanesque Cappella del Battistero with sculptures from the original 12th-century church, including two very unusual carved stone coffins. With two naves, this was the nucleus of the Romanesque church.

Left of the collegiate church is the simple 14th-century church of Sant'Agostino, now the city art gallery and museum, **Pinacoteca Civica** (*T: 0737 95200*), with many paintings and sculptures, including the delightful 15th-century wooden *Madonna di Macereto*. On the opposite bank of the Ussita river is a little square with the interesting Gothic church of San Francesco (15th century), with a horizontally-styled façade some times seen in Abruzzo—a wide Gothic portal surmounted by a graceful rose window.

Environs of Visso

Near Visso the Nera river forms the **Gola del Nera**, a beautiful gorge surrounded by woods of oak and beech, animated by the sudden flight of the sparrowhawk and the dipper. From Visso another road goes up (c. 5km) to the lazily straggling, picturesque houses which form the village of **Ussita**, really a collection of twelve hamlets, of which one is Frontignano (1400m), famous for skiing.

The Fiastra road leads north from Visso to the magnificent, isolated sanctuary church of the **Madonna di Macereto** at 998m. Built in 1528–38 using the local limestone, eight-sided in Bramante style, the interior encloses a 14th-century oratory of the Madonna. The wooden image inside is a copy of the original, said to be miraculous, which is now in the museum of Visso. The architect was Giovanni Battista da Lugano, who fell from the scaffolding during the construction and was buried under the church. Next to the church is the so-called *Palazzo delle Guaite* (1583). The long arcade to the left of the buildings was used in the 16th century for important markets and fairs, where the local people could trade their produce. There are spectacular views of Mount Bove (2112m). From the sanctuary there is a pleasant walk to the hamlet of Cupi (986m); from here the road continues down to Fiastra.

PARCO NAZIONALE DEI MONTI SIBILLINI

Park office: 55 Piazza Capuzzi, Visso, T: 0737 95262, www.sibillini.net
At the heart of the mountain system are Mount Vettore (2476m), which is the highest peak; Cima del Redentore (2448m); Pizzo del Diavolo (2410m) and Cima del Lago (2422m), which form an amphitheatre enclosing Lake Pilato (1940m), the only glacier lake of the Apennines. The icy waters of this lake are home to a little red shrimp called *Chirocephalus marchesoni*, found here and nowhere else in the world. Pizzo del Diavolo slopes steeply down to the three upland plateaux of Castelluccio: Pian Grande, Pian Piccolo, Pian Perduto, famous for the spectacular, colourful blossoming of the wildflowers in June and July: swathes of red poppies, blue cornflowers, yellow mustard, and white lentils and narcissus. On Pian Perduto is a small lake called Stagno Rosso, which turns red periodically due to the presence of a tiny organism called *Euglena sanguinea*. More than 50 different varieties of wild orchid can be found, including *Dactylorhyza sambucina*, *Orchis mascula* and *Gymnadenia conopsea*. In the area of Madonna di Macereto varieties of *Ophrys* orchid are especially abundant. There are also some endemic species of flowers limited to the central Apennines, such as the *Viola magellensis* and the *Saxifraga italica*. This is the southernmost point for finding alpine plants such as the *Ranunculus alpestris*, the *Campanula alpestris*, and a rare local form of the edelweiss, *Leontopodium nivale*, and the dwarf willow. There are two very rare glacier plants, *Carex buxbaumii* and *Carex distica*, and a rare fern, *Ophioglossum pinnatum*.

Wolf packs are concentrated in the heights above Castelluccio, while there are so many wild boar that they constitute a problem—more than 4,000, according to a recent count. The lynx, once extinct, was reintroduced by an animal lover in the 1990s and the population is thought to be quite strong. Wildcats are frequent, and their number is increasing. The brown Marsican bear makes sporadic visits to the woods of Arquata del Tronto, but it is not officially considered to be a resident species of the park. It is planned to reintroduce the chamois and the fallow deer, while the recently introduced roe deer is doing well.

Interesting birds include the short-toed lark, *Calandrella cinerea*, which nests on the plateaux of Castelluccio at a height of 1452m, while its normal maximum in Italy is 850m. In June and July its song fills the air, creating an intoxicating combination with the colours and the scents of the flowers. At the end of summer, the pallid harrier preys on the flocks of migrating birds, and it is planned to reintroduce the majestic Lammergeyer vulture.

Sarnano

An excellent base for exploring the park is Sarnano, on the right bank of the Tennacola. When arriving from Macerata, Tolentino, or San Severino Marche, the road leads by Caldarola to this russet-coloured town with the ancient centre perched on a steep hill, and the new residential area at its foot. Sarnano is a perfect example of a brick-built, fortified medieval city; it is also a well-known and much appreciated spa centre.

From the central Piazza Perfetti, Corso Garibaldi leads up to the *borgo medioevale*, which still has three gates; going through Porta Brunforte, you reach Via Leopardi. Immediately on the right is the town hall with the city museums and the library (*open summer 5–8; winter 4–7; T: 0733 658126*). The **Pinacoteca** includes a *Last Supper* by Giovanni Andrea de Magistris; a *Crucifixion* by Stefano Folchetti, signed and dated 1513; several panel paintings by Vincenzo Pagani; another panel painting by Vittore Crivelli, and a *Madonna and Child* attributed to Niccolò Alunno. There is an interesting **Hammer Museum** (*same hours as above*), with more than 500 hammers from all over the world, a display of weapons, and the **Museo dell'Avifauna**, a collection of more than 600 stuffed birds, some of which are now extinct, from the area of central Italy. Next to the town hall is the 14th-century church of San Francesco, with an interesting Gothic portal on the left side, and blind Romanesque windows.

Continuing up the steep, stepped Via Piazza Alta, you reach the quiet main square, where all the most important buildings of the city (signposted) are grouped: the Palazzo del Popolo with the clock tower, the Palazzo dei Priori, the Palazzetto del Podestà and the tiny opera house, Teatro della Vittoria (*T: 0733 659923*), of 1834, dedicated to the tenor Mario del Monaco.

Dominating the square is the *chiesa madre*, **Santa Maria Assunta**, consecrated in 1280. The façade is adorned with a rich Gothic doorway, while the Romanesque bell-tower is of 1396. The interior, with one nave and a truss-beam roof, has been heavily restored. Immediately on the right, in a Gothic niche, is a fresco by Lorenzo d'Alessandro (1483) portraying the *Madonna and Child with Angel Musicians and Saints*, while in the last chapel on the right is a 16th-century wooden Crucifix. In the presbytery, on the left, is a wooden banner with the *Annunciation* and the *Crucifixion* by Girolamo di Giovanni, a panel painting of the *Madonna of Mercy*, signed and dated 1494 by Pietro Alemanno, and elements of a polyptych by Niccolò Alunno. The wooden 15th-century crib figures come from the Tyrol. The crypt has four naves and more frescoes by Pietro Alemanno. Right in front of the church is a mysterious, ancient white marble **menhir**, vaguely egg-shaped, with a basin hollowed out in the top. About one and a half metres high, its original purpose is unknown; there are conjectures that it was a tombstone, a sacrificial altar, or (by filling the basin with water to reflect the stars) an astronomical observatory. The priest has planted his geraniums in it for now.

From Sarnano a spectacular road leads up to the mountains of Sassotetto and the Maddalena, then through woods of oak and beech to Piobbico, the splendid Fiastrone Valley and Bolognola (22km). There are many trails for walkers in this area, of various degrees of difficulty, offering marvellous views and the different aspects of nature in the Sibyllines. **Bolognola** is the smallest town in the Marche (pop. 180), and also the highest (1070m). It is said to have been founded by Ghibellines forced to flee from Bologna in the 13th century.

Amandola

South of Sarnano is Amandola, founded in the 13th century, once famous for the textile industries which made it one of the most populous cities in the region, with 14,000 inhabitants, and now a popular summer holiday resort. Its name derives from *mandorlo*, almond tree, because an enormous one survived for centuries in the middle of the town, and is now shown on the coat-of-arms. From the central Piazza Risorgimento, with the Gothic Porta San Giacomo, destroyed and rebuilt in the 19th century and now the clock tower, wide steps go down to the 14th-century church of **Sant'Agostino** or *Beato Antonio*, much altered in 1759 and in the early 20th century, with a graceful 15th-century Venetian-Gothic portal. This church is the sanctuary of the Blessed Anthony, patron saint of Amandola, whose body can be seen behind the high altar. To the right of the church is the 15th-century cloister.

From the square, Via dell'Indipendenza and then Via dello Statuto lead, steep and winding, up to the oldest part of the town. After a level stretch of road, on the right is the church of **San Francesco**, founded in the 13th century but rebuilt in the 14th and completely restored in 1660. The luminous 18th-century interior has one nave; over the altar is an impressive 13th-century wooden Crucifix brought here from the old ruined Benedictine abbey of Santi Vincenzo e Anastasio. A little Gothic doorway to the right of the presbytery leads to the base of the bell-tower, where 15th-century frescoes are visible. To the right of the church is the **Oratory of the Rosary**, with a massive Baroque wooden altar framing 15 medallions with the *Mysteries of the Rosary* and a central panel with the *Madonna of the Milk*, attributed to local 15th-century artists. The cloister of the church now houses the **Museo della Civiltà Contadina** (*open summer 10–12.30 & 4.30–6.30; winter on request; T: 0736 848037*), a collection of tools and articles used by the local farmers, and the **Fossil Museum** (*open summer 9–1 & 4–7.30*). A steep climb up Via Roma, in front of the church, leads to **Piazza Umberto**, a panoramic square with public gardens, and the squat *Torrione*, the only remaining tower of the castle built here by the pope's representative in 1368. Just before reaching the square you will find a place where the road widens, Largo Leopardi, and the little opera house, **Teatro La Fenice** (1731 and 1920), with 160 seats, still in regular use.

About 7km northeast of the town, along the SS 210, is the Benedictine **Abbazia dei Santi Rufino e Vitale**, in the Tenna valley with its deep gorges and wonderful mountain views. The abbey was built of white limestone in the 6th century, during the lifetime of St Benedict, but was completely restructured in Romanesque form in the 13th century. The sturdy bell-tower, with its wide lancet windows, is unusual; it was also a watch-tower. The church interior, with a central nave and two side aisles, divided by columns, has a raised presbytery with two frescoes of the *Madonna with Christ Child*—the one on the right is 15th century, while that on the left is 14th century. The

Typical Sibylline landscape, with the fields and meadows of Castelluccio.

ancient crypt, originally a cave, has columns with cube-shaped capitals, and a stone casket containing the body of St Rufino, invoked against hernia; on his feast day, 19th August, sufferers crawl through the space underneath in order to find relief.

Montefortino

The picturesque little stone and brick town of Montefortino clings to a steep, wooded hillside; there are still many 16th-century tower-houses, once a protection against bandits and raiders, which give it a characteristic skyline; from a distance it looks like Brueghel's *Tower of Babel*. In the 16th-century Palazzo Leopardi is an important art gallery, the **Pinacoteca Civica Fortunato Duranti** (*T: 0736 859491 for opening times; closed Mon*), a collection of paintings and statues donated to the town by a local artist in 1842, including significant 15th–18th-century works, such as a *Madonna* by Perugino, three panel paintings by Pietro Alemanno, parts of a polyptych thought to be his masterpiece, and a lovely *Madonna with Christ Child* by Francesco Botticini. The top floor of the building is dedicated to the **Diocese Museum**, with works of art coming from Montefortino itself and the surrounding villages, including a very impressive painted wooden *Madonna and Child* (14th century), and paintings by Simone de Magistris and Giuseppe Ghezzi.

In the main square, Piazza Umberto, is a private collection of stuffed local birds which can be seen on request, the **Raccolta dell'Avifauna delle Marche** (*T: 0736 859122*). On the northwest side of the town, close to the top of the hill, is the 14th-century church of **Sant'Agostino** which still shows many traces of a preceding Romanesque church. In the interior are some wooden choir-stalls, carved in the Gothic style in the 15th century. Surmounting Montefortino is the 13th-century church of San Francesco.

A pleasant, level road follows the River Ambro for c. 7km to the sanctuary church of the **Madonna dell'Ambro**, in the heart of the Sibyllines, founded in 1073 to celebrate a miracle of the Madonna: many pilgrims still come here in May and September, often on foot. The present church was built between the 16th–17th centuries, in a beautiful position in a narrow cleft between two rock faces, and is now cared for by Capuchin friars. The interior has a single nave, and six side chapels; in the apse is the Chapel of the Apparition, with a 16th-century painted stone statue of the Madonna, a copy of the original, stolen in 1562. Over the second right-hand altar is an ancient painted leather banner, decorated with carved and gilded wood, while the frescoes, showing the Sibyls and episodes from the life of the Virgin, were painted by Martino Bonfini, an artist from Montalto delle Marche, in 1610–12. Some of the texts held by the Sibyls are said to contain ciphered information, useful to alchemists.

The **Gola dell'Infernaccio**, a wild, magnificent gorge formed by the River Tenna, is c. 15km from Montefortino. It is reached from the Madonna dell'Ambro road, by turning left towards Rubbiano just before the bridge over the Tenna. Situated between the Sibilla and the Priora mountains, it is almost 4km long; in the first stretch it is not more than 2 or 3m wide, but it opens up further along, and passes through ancient beeches, before narrowing again between sheer rock faces, until reaching a lake surrounded by woods and numerous springs. A further climb of c. 2 hours leads to the source of the Tenna, at 1178m.

Montemonaco

The road which leads south from Amandola to Arquata del Tronto (c. 40km) is tortuous but very scenic. One of the most attractive communities along the route, said to have been founded by Benedictine monks in the 6th century, is Montemonaco, where the panorama stretches from the sea to the mountains of Abruzzo. High up in the town, near ruined castle walls, are two ancient churches, next to one another: San Biagio (15th century), and San Benedetto, probably much older, with a portal dated 1546.

Montemonaco stands on **Monte Sibilla**; it is the ideal departure point for further exploration of this mythical mountain (2175m), with a strange rounded peak surrounded by a necklace of enormous pink rocks: the view from the top (c. 5 hours on foot) is breathtaking. The cave close to the summit said to have been the dwelling of the sybil-priestess is not accessible, due to rock falls.

Another possible excursion from Montemonaco leads to **Lago Pilato**, a glacier lake at 1949m, which periodically colours red due to the presence of a shrimp. This fact has given rise to local legends about Pilate and his bloodstained hands. Now rather reduced in size after a long series of dry summers, it is usually about 500m long and 15m deep in winter. Just south of Montemonaco there is a crossroads; the turning to the west follows the course of the River Aso to the tiny village of Foce. From here there is a trail to the lake and also to Mt Vettore (2476m), the highest peak of the Sibyllines and of the Marche region.

Montegallo and Arquata del Tronto

Another excellent base for excursions to Mt Vettore is **Montegallo**, a collection of 27 hamlets. The civic administration is at Balzo (886m), where the 17th-century parish church of San Bernardino has an ancient, richly-decorated portal, and inside, six monolithic sandstone tuff columns. Montegallo owes its origin to a castle dedicated to Santa Maria in Lapide, built in the 8th century to protect the 'grain road', the path over the eastern slopes of Mt Vettore followed by the reapers travelling between Umbria, the Marche and Lazio, through the Galluccio Pass and the meadows of Castelluccio.

The ruins of the old church of Santa Maria in Lapide are still visible in Valle del Rio, and give an impressive idea of the original dimensions. The high transept is still standing, and the 9th-century crypt is in good condition. On Mt Torrone, at 1159m, facing Mt Vettore, stands the starkly simple, ancient church of Santa Maria in Pantano (sometimes called Santa Maria delle Sibille), which goes back to the early Middle Ages. In the interior, over the high altar is an interesting aedicule decorated with sandstone carvings. The 17th-century frescoes show scenes from the New Testament, Prophets and five of the Sibyls. In the Montegallo area you will often see marguerites, or twelve-pointed stars, carved over the doorways; a Templar sign.

From Montegallo to Arquata del Tronto the road is spectacular, cut into the hillside, with breathtaking views over the valleys. Just before arriving at **Arquata del Tronto** (777m), the 13th-century Rocca (*open summer 10.30–12.30 & 4–6; winter 3–5; T: 0736 809122*), a fairytale castle, comes into view, as if protecting the town at its foot. According to legend, it was built by King John II of Naples (13th century) as a suitable setting for his anything but clandestine love affairs. In the 15th century it became the favourite home of Queen Joan II of Anjou, after she was crowned by Pope Martin V.

In Roman times, Arquata was an important mansion on the Via Salaria, a strategic point between Lazio, Abruzzo, the Marche and Umbria. The town has the distinction of being included in two national parks, that of the Sibyllines and that of the Gran Sasso and Monti della Laga, most of which is in Abruzzo; the two parks are divided by the River Tronto. In the pocket-handkerchief-sized main square, Piazza Umberto, is the clock tower, with a 16th-century bell.

The surrounding villages are well worth a visit. At **Spelonga**, in the parish church of Sant'Agata, there are well-preserved 15th-century frescoes. **Capodacqua** has the delightful 16th-century church of the Madonna del Sole, octagonal, with naïve votive frescoes, and a beautiful rose window over one of the two entrances, and symbols of the sun and the moon. At **Borgo**, in the church of San Salvatore is a particularly impressive 13th-century Romanesque wooden Crucifix, painted at a later time, while in the church of San Francesco there are some splendid wood carvings carried out in the 16th and 17th centuries: the altars, the ceiling, the pulpit, the choir and the confessionals. A mysterious replica of the Turin Shroud is kept in the church, a faithful 17th-century reproduction made, it is said, simply by placing a piece of linen on top of the original; it is seldom shown in public. The church of San Silvestro at **Colle** stands isolated over a sheer drop; inside there are some beautiful 16th-century frescoes.

PRACTICAL INFORMATION

GETTING AROUND

• **By bus**: The following companies run services in the area: Cameli Tours, from Ascoli Piceno (T: 0736 259091); CONTRAM, from Camerino (T: 0737 634011) or Macerata (T: 0733 230906); Mazzuca, from Ascoli Piceno (T: 0736 402267) to Montefortino (T: 0736 859305) or Montemonaco (T: 0736 856114); START, from Ascoli Piceno (T: 800 443040 & 0736 263053); STEAT, from Fermo (T: 0734 623866 or 800 630715, www.steat.it).

INFORMATION OFFICES

A central organisation of the towns and villages of the area is Terre di Parchi e di Incanti, 14 Via Piave, San Ginesio, T: 0733 656890, www.sibiliniturismo.it A useful website for Amandola, Montefortino, Montemonaco, Montegallo and Arquata del Tronto is www.galpiceno.it
Amandola: IAT, 9 Via XX Settembre, T: 0736 848706; Pro Loco, Piazza Risorgimento, T: 0736 847439 (summer only); Casa del Parco, 73 Via Indipendenza, T: 0736 848480, www.montisibillini.it
Arquata del Tronto Municipio, T: 0736 809122; Casa del Parco, 2 Via del Mattatoio, T: 0736 809600.
Montefortino Casa del Parco, 8 Via Roma, T: 0736 859414.
Montegallo Casa del Parco, Frazione Balzo, 14 Via Annibal Caro, T: 0736 806606.
Montemonaco Pro Loco, Piazza

Risorgimento, T: 0736 856411, www.montefortino.com; Casa del Parco, Via Roma, T: 0736 856462.
Sarnano Municipio, 1 Via Leopardi, T: 0733 659911, www.sarnano.sinp.net; IAT, 1 Largo Ricciardi, T: 0733 657144, www.sarnano.com
Visso Municipio, 1 Largo Antinori, T: 0737 95421, www.visso.sinp.net; Tourist Information Bureau (summer only), Piazza Martiri Vissani, T: 0737 9239; Casa del Parco, 55 Piazza Capuzzi, T: 0737 95262; Parco Nazionale dei Monti Sibillini, Largo Antinori, T: 0737 972711, www.sibillini.net

HOTELS

Arquata del Tronto
€€€ **Camartina**. Small and very comfortable; excellent restaurant. 8/c Frazione Camartina, T: 0736 809261, camartina@libero.it
€€€ **Regina Giovanna**. Has a good restaurant. Borgo di Arquata del Tronto, T: 0736 809148.
Castelsantangelo sul Nera
€ **La Baita**. A very simple mountain inn; good food. Località Monte Prata, T: 0737 821167.
Montefortino
€€ **Ambro**. A comfortable mountain inn, with memorable food, near the sanctuary. Santuario Madonna dell'Ambro, T: 0736 859170.
Montegallo
€€ **Vettore**. In a lovely position; open summer only. Località Balzo, T: 0736 806116.
Montemonaco
€€€ **Guerrin Meschino**. Very small

but comfortable; with a restaurant.
Frazione Rocca, T: 0736 856356.

Sarnano

€€€€ **Montanaria**. A comfortable
hotel with restaurant, vegetarian on
request, garden, tennis, pool and
garage. Open summer only. Località
Marinella, T: 0733 658422,
www.montanaria.it

€€€ **Terme**. Has an excellent restaurant. 82 Piazza Libertà, T: 0733 657166.

€€ **La Villa**. Comfortable, with a
restaurant, garden and garage. Viale
Rimembranza, T: 0733 657218.

Visso

€€€ **Tre Monti**. No restaurant but a
good base for excursions. Via Valcanuta,
Borgo Sant'Antonio, T: 0737 95427.

BED & BREAKFAST

Bolognola

B&B di Cristina e Laura. English and
French spoken; home-made cakes for
breakfast. 1 Via dei Sibillini, T: 0737
520136, b-bgarden@libero.it

Montefortino

Tabart Inn. A charming old building.
Open May–Oct. 24 Via Papiri, T: 0736
859054, www.tabart-inn.com

Tenuta Rossi Brunori Pierluigi. ■
Delicious meals available in this luxurious 18th-century villa with lovely garden and pool. Cookery courses available; English and French spoken. 6
Frazione Pretattoni, T: 0736 859167,
www.tenutarossibrunori.it

FARM ACCOMMODATION

Amandola

San Lorenzo. ■ A 19th-century farm
in a panoramic position; wonderful

food and pleasant atmosphere. 3 Via
San Lorenzo, T: 0736 847535.

Tenuta Le Piane. A restored 18th-cen-
tury farming hamlet inside the national
park. 21 Località Villa Piane, T: 0736
847641, marcosel@tin.it

Montefortino

La Terra del Vento. Homely brick
farmhouse, comfortable accommodation, and good food. Località Colle
Turano, T: 0736 844607,
nik10@interfree.it

Montemonaco

Cittadella dei Sibillini. ■ Lovely stone
farmhouse, panoramic position, surrounded by woods; horses raised. Has a
renowned restaurant. T: 0736 856361,
www.cittadelladeisibillini.it

Pievebovigliana

Terre della Sibilla. In the heart of the
forest, old restored stone houses, with
an orchard with ancient varieties of
fruit. Excellent restaurant. Ideal base for
trekking on foot, horseback, or mountain bike; there are also botany courses,
birdwatching, drawing and basketry.
English spoken. Località Peschiera, T:
0733 263285, ilgelso.bio@libero.it

RESTAURANTS

Amandola

€€ **Da Stefano alle Scalette**. Friendly
restaurant and pizzeria. 31 Piazza
Risorgimento, T: 0736 847915.

Arquata del Tronto

€ **Al Kapriol**. Informal atmosphere,
excellent pasta, grilled meats and home-
made desserts. Also rooms to rent.
Closed Mon. 4 Forca Canapine, T: 0736
808119.

€ **Camartina**. Grilled meats, trout,
fungi and truffles. Choose *zuppa inglese*

(trifle) for dessert. Closed Mon. 8/c Frazione Camartina, T: 0736 809261.

Castelsantangelo sul Nera

€€ L'Erborista. ■ A delightful country restaurant midway between Castelluccio di Norcia and Castelsantangelo, once a pharmacy. The grandfather was a renowned herbalist, an activity no longer possible under park laws, so his descendants now exercise their skill in the kitchen, using herbs and wild vegetables. Very good lentils, grills, local wines. Closed Thur in winter. 55 Via San Martino, Gualdo, T: 0737 98134.

Fiastra

€ Agli Alti Pascoli. The food is fantastic at this farm, where they prepare their own hams and salami; also home-produced wines and jams made with wild fruits. Meals are cooked in a wood-burning oven. Closed Tues, open weekends only in winter. 10 Contrada Sant'Ilario, T: 0737 52588.

Sarnano

€€ Il Girarrosto. Famous for risotto; meats are grilled on an open fire; good wine cellar. Closed Tues. 82 Piazza Libertà, T: 0733 657166.

Visso

€€ La Filanda. Also pizzeria in summer; good pasta dishes. Closed Wed. 4 Via Pontelato, T: 0737 972027.

€ Richetta. Marvellous trattoria very popular with locals, generous servings. Closed Mon. 7 Piazza Garibaldi, T: 0737 9339.

CAFÉS & PASTRY SHOPS

Amandola

Gran Caffè Belli. ■ A classic coffee house serving excellent pastries and ice cream, many kinds of tea and hot chocolate. Closed Thur. 13/15 Piazza Risorgimento.

Pievebovigliana

Il Gelato. Home-made ice cream. 2 Via Fornace.

FESTIVALS & EVENTS

Amandola *Carnevale di Amandola*, parades and fancy-dress on Thur, Sun and Tues of Carnival, funeral of King Carnival on Shrove Tuesday. *Infiorata di Corpus Domini*, the streets are covered with designs made with flower petals, June. Feast of the Beato Antonio, an Austin monk invoked for good crops and rain; for his feast day baskets of wheat, the *canestrelle*, are taken to the church of Sant'Agostino; Info: T: 0736 848037, last weekend in Aug. International Theatre Festival involving the whole town; Info: T: 0736 848698, Sept. *Diamanti a Tavola*, white truffle fair, 1st weekend in Nov.

Arquata del Tronto *La Discesa delle Fate*, at the nearby village of Pretare, festival to commemorate the marriage of the shepherds and the fairies, origin of the inhabitants of the Sibyllines, 16 Aug every third year (2006, 2009). *Alla Corte della Regina*, medieval pageant and banquet, 19 Aug. Feast of the Holy Saviour, last Sun in Aug.

Castelluccio *La Fiorita*, ancient festivity to celebrate the flowering of the meadows, mid-June.

Montefortino Festival of the Real Truffle, Feb. Feast of the Holy Crucifix: people singing hymns form a procession to bring the *canestrelle*, offerings of wheat and flowers, to the sanctuary church of Madonna dell'Ambro; Info: T:

0736 859115; first Sun in Sept.
Montegallo Feast of St Bernardino, 1st
Sun in Aug.
Sarnano Exhibition of Crafts and
Antiques, May–June. *Palio del Serafino*,
the coat-of-arms of the town comprises
a seraph, chosen for Sarnano by St
Francis in person; the Palio celebrates
the choice with a series of contests,
Aug.
Ussita Feast of St Mary, 15 Aug.
Visso Feast of St John the Baptist, 24
June. *Torneo delle Guaite*, a series of
contests evoking 13th-century Visso,
between five *guaite* or districts; Info:
Associazione Torneo delle Guaite, Borgo
San Giovanni, T: 0737 9363, end July–
early Aug.

Montemonaco
Bottega della Cuccagna, Via San
Lorenzo, is good for local hams, salami,
cheeses and lentils.
Pievebovigliana
Cecilia Pallotta, 8 Via Colle del Fiano,
is a farm producing ancient varieties of
fruit, including *limoncella, rosa gentile*
and *rosa San Pietro* apples; also chest-
nut-blossom honey and salami.
Ussita
Calvà Fabiana, in Piazza Cavallari, is a
fascinating shop for objects in wood.
Visso
Ser Faustini Bernardo, 5 Via
Castelsantangelo, has lovely wood carv-
ings. **Vissana Salumi**, Via Battisti, is the
best place for local hams and salami.

ASCOLI PICENO

One of Italy's loveliest cities, and capital of the province, Ascoli Piceno (pop. 53,000) lies in the extreme south of the region, close to the border with Abruzzo, where the Castellano stream joins the River Tronto. Small enough to be friendly, yet large enough to be almost intimidating for its beauty, the place is imbued with history and tradition. Skilled craftsmen excel in the most varied fields—making Stradivarius-quality violins, for example, or wrought-iron gates; beautifully decorated ceramics, or tasty cheeses cured in walnut-leaf wrappings. Travertine marble was used to build the old city's houses, churches, palaces, fountains and pavements; the swirling milky-white colour of the stone, combined with the burnt sugar tones of the rooftops and the steeples, makes Ascoli look like a luscious concoction of *crème brûlée*, set into the fresh green bowl of the surrounding hills. The fortunate inhabitants have at their disposal two sublimely beautiful squares, two theatres and three concert halls, plus an array of museums, libraries, art galleries and churches (17 of which are Romanesque). They are only minutes away from the Sibylline Mountains, or the sandy beaches of the Palm Riviera.

The Ponte di Solestà in Ascoli Piceno.

HISTORY OF ASCOLI PICENO

The strategic position at the confluence of two rivers, and the easy passage from the mountains to the sea, made this from the 9th century BC the most important centre of the Picenes. In 286 BC it was captured by the Romans, together with all the surrounding Picene territory, and named *Asculum*. In 91 BC the people rebelled against Rome, causing the Social War, which ended in 89 BC with the destruction of the city. It soon rose again, however, and became one of the most important markets of central Italy. In 578 it was taken by the Lombards and became part of the Duchy of Spoleto; then in 774 the city was donated to the Church. During the 9th century Asculum was attacked twice by the Muslims. In 1185 the city declared itself an independent commune; this was followed by a long period of financial prosperity and artistic vitality, which lasted throughout the Renaissance. In the Middle Ages Ascoli was called *città turrita*—city of towers—because there were 200 of them, some even 40m high, though in 1242 Frederick II of Hohenstaufen destroyed 91. About 70 towers can still be traced in the fabric of the town, many of them in good condition. In 1799 Ascoli was invaded by the French, reverting to the Papal States in 1815. With the Unification of Italy in 1861, Ascoli Piceno became a provincial capital. Ascoli was one of the first Italian cities to have a printing press (1477), and the manufacture of paper (now only newsprint and packaging) was encouraged by the pope. It is also important for agriculture, and many people are employed by local industries, producing for example stone for building, electric cables and chemicals. The city was awarded the gold medal for valour for the Resistance in the Second World War.

EXPLORING ASCOLI PICENO

The city is not visible from a great distance; you come across it suddenly, after a fold in the hills. Breathtaking, with a skyline positively bristling with towers, steeples and spires, Ascoli Piceno exceeds every expectation. A curiosity: the secondary streets of the town are called *rua* instead of *via*, deriving from the Latin *ruga*, meaning 'wrinkle' or 'channel'.

Piazza Arringo

Piazza Arringo (or Arengo) stands where once there was the Roman forum, and throughout the Middle Ages it was the place for public meetings, hence the name, which translates as 'harangue'. It is still the cultural centre of the city, and houses the principal museums, the town hall, the Bishop's Palace and the cathedral, in buildings of various styles and epochs. The twin fountains (19th century), with sea horses and dolphins, make it a welcoming place, especially in summer.

To the east stands the austere **Duomo di Sant'Emidio** with an unfinished façade (1529 by Cola dell'Amatrice. It is dedicated to St Emygdius of Triers, martyred in 303, first bishop and patron saint of the city; his remains are kept in a Roman sarcophagus in the very ornate crypt. Invoked against earthquakes, because when he arrived in town a tremendous shock caused all the pagan temples to fall down, he was behead-ed for having converted Polisia, the daughter of the Roman governor. It is said he picked up his head and walked to the Christian graveyard on the outskirts of town, where he dug his own grave.

The church was first built in the 4th century, on the Roman basilica of the forum, and was frequently modified. For example, the crypt was added in the 11th century togeth-er with the bell-tower on the right, which was finished in 1592, while that on the left was left incomplete, but most of the construction is 15th century. The side wall to the left shows four superb Gothic double-light windows and a Renaissance portal. The Latin-cross interior has a nave and aisles of equal height and width in the late Gothic style, separated by octagonal pilasters and high, slightly pointed arches. The presbytery and the transept are raised, and surmounted by the octagonal cupola. Above the main entrance is the choir with a fine organ, the work of the local brothers Vincenzo and Giovanni Paci (19th century). The impressive frescoes which adorn the vaults, with episodes of the life of St Emygdius, are by Cesare Mariani (1884–94), while over the central altar is a lovely neo-Gothic ciborium made by Giuseppe Sacconi in 1895. Opening off the south aisle is the Chapel of the Sacrament (1798); the altarpiece is thought to be Carlo Crivelli's most important work, the **polyptych of St Emygdius**, or the *Madonna Enthroned with Christ Child and Saints* (1473), in a beautiful Gothic frame made in the artist's own workshop. Notice the slender, tapering fingers of the saints, the expressive faces and the characteristic Crivelli fruits and vegetables above the Madonna, each with a different symbolic meaning. This arresting painting, more than any other work of art in the city, has always strongly influenced the people: for example, the cos-tumes worn during the annual jousting contests are based on those seen in the polyp-tych. On the altar is a precious tabernacle (16th century) in gilded and painted wood, attributed by some to Cola dell'Amatrice, while the front panel of the altar is a 13th-cen-tury silver representation of scenes from the life of Christ.

To the left of the cathedral, in an isolated position, stands the interesting and unusual **Baptistery** (4th century, rebuilt 12th century), an octagonal construction on a square base, with a loggia on the top with three arches on each side, except for the rear which has four, and a round dome. The symbolism of the numbers is deliberate; three for the Trinity, four for humanity, eight for resurrection and eternity which can be achieved through baptism, and a circular dome representing perfection. Traces of the original baptismal pool can be seen inside, together with the more recent font, which stands on a 14th-century spiral column. It is thought that the building was originally the Temple of Mars.

Central panel of Carlo Crivelli's famous polyptych of St Emygdius (1473).

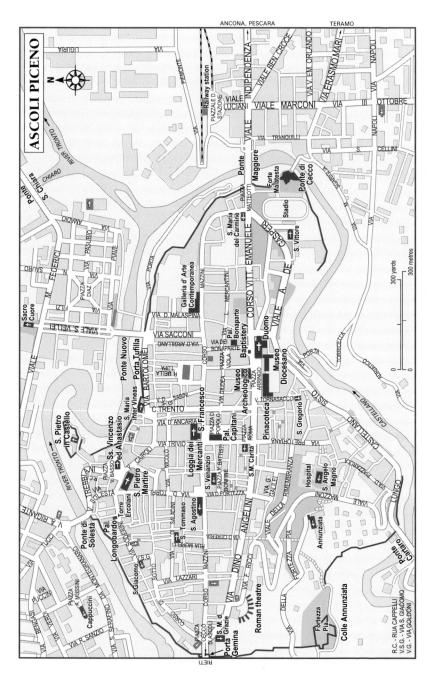

ASCOLI PICENO

R.C. - RUA CAPPELLI
V.S.G. - VIA S. GIACOMO
V.G. - VIA S. GOLDONI

Museums on Piazza Arringo

Close to the cathedral stands the Palazzo dell'Episcopio, the Bishop's Palace, consisting of three different constructions built between the 15th and 18th centuries, housing the **Museo Diocesano** (*open Feb–Sept daily 10–7; winter Mon–Fri 9–1, Sat and Sun 9–1 & 3.30–7.30; guided tours also in English and Japanese every day except Mon 9.30–12.30; T: 0736 252883*), a rich collection of sacred art coming from churches and monasteries of the area. The paintings include works by Carlo Crivelli, Cola dell'Amatrice, Pietro Alemanno and Ludovico Trasi; there are also many sculptures in wood and stone, and 13th-century frescoes detached from ruined churches. In 1547 Marcello Fogolino, a gifted local artist, completely frescoed one of the salons on the first floor, illustrating the life of Moses together with allegorical figures. The ground floor of the palace contains the 50,000 volumes of the Diocesan Library and the church archives.

Next to the Bishop's Palace and close to the fountains is the long façade of the **Palazzo Comunale** or Palazzo dell'Arengo, decorated with carved stone caryatids and telamones, and with a porticoed entrance; seat of the magnificent **Pinacoteca Civica** (*open 9–1 & 3–7; T: 0736 298213*) where one of the most important collections of paintings and sculptures in the region is displayed on two floors, in a series of splendid galleries. One of the most interesting rooms is the 'Sala del Piviale', on the first floor, where paintings by Carlo Crivelli and his follower Pietro Alemanno have been arranged together with the astonishing *piviale*, the cope of Pope Nicholas IV.

THE POPE'S COPE

When Girolamo da Lisciano became Pope Nicholas IV in 1288, he gave this precious embroidered robe to the cathedral of his native city. It is thought to have been made in England between 1266–68, and consists of a series of roundels representing saints, popes, Doctors of the Church, the Crucifixion and the Madonna with the Child, worked with coloured silk and gold threads on thick, heavy silk, still in excellent condition. Tiny semi-precious stones and seed pearls form the outlines. The robe was originally encrusted with larger precious stones and pearls, which were removed and sold to pay for the construction of the Chapel of the Sacrament in the cathedral in 1798. In 1902 the cope was stolen, and reappeared two years later, in an exhibition held at London's South Kensington Museum (now the Victoria and Albert) as a loan from the American millionaire J. Pierpont Morgan, who had bought it in Paris. The cope was recognised, and Morgan was obliged to return it to the Italian authorities. At last, in 1907, the cope was displayed in this gallery, where it has been ever since.

The Pinacoteca also houses the **Raccolta Pasqualini**, a collection of musical instruments and the tools and equipment necessary for their manufacture.

Opposite is the dignified 17th-century façade of Palazzo Panichi, now the **Museo Archeologico** (*open 8.30–7.30, closed Mon; T: 0736 253562*). The collections are exhibited on three floors, with objects dating from the Palaeolithic, Neolithic, Bronze and Iron Ages with the Picene culture, through the Roman domination to the arrival of the Lombards, all recently rearranged and shown to great advantage together with some Roman mosaics. We discover that the Picenes, 3,000 years ago, liked elaborate bronze pectorals, often shaped like ships, with seashell pendants, or large bronze pins imported from Bosnia. Chieftains were sometimes buried with their chariots, warrior-like ones for the men and daintier ones for their wives, while Roman women were usually buried with their bronze beauty-cases, the men with their wine cups and their breastplates. One of the most interesting exhibits is a funerary stele from Castignano with an inscription in the Picene language, written in the boustrophedon manner (where each line was meant to be read in a different direction), containing the warning of a son not to violate the tomb of his parents. Some of the objects—gold and amber jewellery, ornamental plaques and fibulae—come from the nearby Lombard necropolis of Castel Trosino, discovered by chance in 1893, with over 200 tombs of the 6th–7th centuries AD, many of them intact. Unfortunately, most of the material was sent to Rome for examination and was never returned; it has since been displayed there at the Museo dell'Alto Medioevo, but the collection will soon be rehoused in a new Lombard museum at Forte Malatesta in Ascoli Piceno.

Piazza del Popolo

From Piazza Arringo, Via Cino del Duca leads to Piazza del Popolo. This square, the second 'drawing room' of the people, owes its present aspect to renovations carried out in the early 16th century, when all the shopkeepers were obliged to contribute to the construction of the arcade according to the dimensions of their own shopfronts—this is why the harmonious arches surrounding most of the square are of many different widths. The west side is dominated by the **Palazzo dei Capitani** (*open 9–1 & 4–7.30, closed Sun; T: 0736 244985*), a real history book of the city, once the residence of the Captain of the People. First built in the 13th century, the palace was modified by Cola dell'Amatrice after 1520, and further modified many times after that. The tower, however, is still the original 13th-century one, and the massive portal with the monument to Pope Paul III is of 1549, with a wide arch on either side. The impressive façade includes a clock, added in 1543, and four statues representing the Virtues (1549), a token of the city's gratitude to Cardinal Alessandro Farnese, who as papal legate had obtained several concessions for Ascoli from his uncle, Pope Paul III. The courtyard is Renaissance in style, with a portico surmounted by a loggia. The building was seat of the commune from 1400 to 1564, then the residence of the governors and the papal legates. To the left of the Palazzo dei Capitani is one of the historic cafés of Italy, the Caffè Meletti, founded in 1907 and famous for its *anisetta* liqueur, made on the premises.

On the north side, the soaring Gothic lines of the church of **San Francesco** make a perfect backdrop to the square. Construction of the church, which began in the 12th century, was not completed until some 300 years later, so the lower five metres of the building are Romanesque, while the upper part is Gothic. The beautiful Venetian-style main portal, on Via del Trivio, is framed by elaborate, delicate carvings and by slender columns, five on each side, which are all very worn at the same height. In fact, when struck sharply with the palm of the hand they each emit a different musical note, and few can resist the temptation to make a little music before going into church. Over the side door, on the square, is the **monument to Pope Julius II**, a member of the influential della Rovere family (*see p. 313*). The rear of the church is particularly scenographic; the magnificent apses appear to be nine instead of seven. The large stone phallus perched up on the balustrade of the second bell-tower is no optical illusion; for the ancient Romans the large phallus was a symbol of fertility and happiness.

The interior, restored to its original aspect in the 19th century, has a central nave with two side aisles. On the left on entering is a Crucifix (15th century) brought here from Palazzo dei Capitani when it miraculously survived the fire of 1535. In the sacristy are some interesting paintings, including a panel painting by Cola dell'Amatrice of *Sts Anthony of Padua, Francis of Assisi, Bonaventure, James of the Marches and Dominic.*

Left of the façade is the main cloister, built by architects from Lombardy in the 16th century, and now used as a daily market for fruit and vegetables. It is sometimes possible to visit the second cloister (14th century), now encapsulated in a modern building. Close to the church is the Loggia dei Mercanti, erected by Cola dell'Amatrice for the influential Wool Corporation in the 16th century. The building represents better than any other the commercial power of the city, and still preserves the official measurements for bricks and tiles.

Santi Vincenzo e Anastastio and San Pietro Martire

A short walk north along Via del Trivio, once the *cardo maximus*, and then along Via Cairoli, leads to a particularly interesting and picturesque part of the city, with many of the old towers now incorporated into the more recent buildings, or transformed into bell-towers, like that of the church of St Peter Martyr. At the top of Via del Trivio, on the right, is the ex-church of San Francesco da Paola (19th century), now an auditorium, which uses another ex-church as foyer, San Giovanni—once used by the Templars. The church of **Santi Vincenzo e Anastasio** in Piazza Ventidio Basso, is an 11th-century Romanesque construction, amplified in 1389. The façade is divided into 64 rectangles which probably once framed fresco paintings; even the statues over the doorway (the Madonna with Sts Vincent and Anastasius) were originally painted. Over the doorway is a long inscription, dated 1036, from the original church. The interior has a central nave, pertaining to the old church, with two side aisles. Under the building is the 6th-century crypt, with recently restored frescoes.

Opposite is the large church of **San Pietro Martire** (St Peter Martyr; late 13th–early 14th centuries), the left side portal is by Cola dell'Amatrice (1523). The lovely interior, full of golden light, has eight Baroque altars made by a local family, the Giosafatti, in 1674. That of the *Madonna of the Rosary* (fourth on the south) is very imposing, with different kinds of marble, gilded stucco, and two statues representing *Humility* and *Purity*. There are many paintings in this church by Ludovico Trasi (1634–94), a gifted local artist who studied in Rome with Andrea Sacchi. In the cloister is an interesting fresco with the Guzmán family tree (St Dominic, for whose cause St Peter Martyr was the first to suffer death, was from the Guzmán family).

Solestà and across the Tronto

From San Pietro Martire the attractive street called Via Solestà, with towers and medieval houses, leads north to Porta Solestà (1230) and the **Ponte di Solestà**, built in the early days of the Roman Empire, when Augustus decided to improve communications with this important city. The remarkable bridge is 62m long, 6.5m wide, 25m high, with a central span of 21m over the Tronto. It is hollow inside, and it is sometimes possible to visit the interior (*ask at the Tourist Office*). The bridge and the gate are particularly photogenic. There is a beautiful walk along the river, by the city walls, on old cobblestone streets, with enticing glimpses of little houses and gardens. You can go as far as the little church of San Pietro in Castello, site of an ancient castle, which dominates a curve of the river. The local people call this walk '*rrete li mierghe*', behind the battlements. On the other side of the bridge is Borgo Solestà, once the industrial area for the manufacture of wool, silk and leather. Some blacksmiths still work here.

Following Via Berardo Tucci, you reach the **Tempietto di Sant'Emidio Rosso**, a tiny red octagonal church built in 1623 over an ancient chapel containing the stone where St Emygdius was beheaded. Also in this district is the church of San Serafino di Montegranaro and **Convent of the Cappuccini**, founded in the Middle Ages and completely restructured in 1771. It was a Capuchin friar, Giovanni da Teramo, who set up a printing press here in 1477 and printed the first book to be published in Ascoli, *Le Storie di Sant'Isidoro*, and then the city statutes in 1496.

Via de' Soderini and district

Via de' Soderini, one of the most characterful streets, with many medieval and Renaissance houses, leads west from Piazza Ventidio Basso to **Palazzetto Longobardo** on the right (now a youth hostel). The tower (called *Torre Ercolani*) was erected in the 11th–12th century together with its palace, and is the best preserved example of its kind in the city. It narrows slightly towards the top, is 35m high, and detached from the dwelling next door as an earthquake precaution. The equilateral triangle over the door has several possible explanations. Was it an extra architectural measure against earthquakes? Is it a reference to the Trinity? Does it have something to do with the Templars? Or was it simply copied from Roman funerary stones, many of which had similar triangles at the top? Other triangles like this can be seen over the door to the Baptistery in Piazza Arringo, and on several other towers of Ascoli.

A little further along, on the left in a tiny square called Largo della Fortuna, is the church of **San Giacomo** (13th–14th centuries), with a fresco of saints over the main door, and a small rose window. Recent restorations have revealed the original colours of the wooden statuettes (13th century) over the side door. Near the church, at 3 Via San Giacomo, is the **Museo-Biblioteca Francesco Marcucci** (*July 3–7.30; other days phone to request visit; T: 0736 259952*), a fascinating 18th-century library and collection of objects relating to the 250-year history of the Conceptionist convent, occupying the home of the founder, Monsignor Marcucci. Don't miss the lovely little private chapel. Further along, Via de' Soderini becomes Via Annibal Caro, with several interesting 16th-century houses. Over the doorway to no. 54 is the inscription '*non senza fatica*', not without fatigue, one of many similar examples going back to a period when it was fashionable to have a witty or religious motto or proverb over your front door. Another, on Palazzo dei Capitani, says '*difficile piacere multis*', it is difficult to please many. There are more than 100 of these inscriptions around the town.

Near the river

Close to the Tronto is the small Romanesque church of **Santa Maria inter Vineas**, so called because once surrounded by a vineyard. Recently restored, it was built in the 12th century to replace an older church thought to go back to the 5th century. The simple interior, with a central nave and two side aisles, has frescoes of the 13th–15th centuries. The 15th-century fresco at the end of the right-hand nave, once on the outside wall, is called *Madonna dell'Impiccato*, Madonna of the Hanged Man, because it is said she leaned her head from the wall when an innocent person was being led by to the gallows. The wooden Crucifix (16th century) on the main altar is also particularly venerated. By the door is a funerary monument of 1482, attributed to Pietro Alemanno. The majestic, isolated bell-tower was once a watch-tower.

Further ahead is one of the city gates, **Porta Tufilla** (1553), and the bridge known as **Ponte Nuovo** (1911). Many craftsmen have their workshops in this quarter; such as Sergio Baiocchi (at Lungotronto Bartolomei), a stonemason expert in working travertine marble; and Piero Castelli (also at Lungotronto Bartolomei), who makes violins and other musical instruments.

THE VIOLINS OF ASCOLI

According to legend, many years ago a travelling Hungarian musician fell off his horse and broke his violin near Ascoli, and a young farm hand, Giuseppe Odoardi, who had a musical ear, offered to repair it for him. Before returning the instrument, the boy traced its outline on the barn door, and from that moment dedicated his spare time to experimenting with the construction of stringed instruments. His first efforts were only passable, but the young man persevered, thus starting a strong local tradition in the field, now carried on by Piero Castelli, son of Cesare (recently deceased at the age of 91, working until the day he died), who was declared the world's finest maker of stringed instruments. Each violin takes about two months to make, using two kinds of wood, maple and fir, seasoned for 20 years. Then 40 coats of varnish (one a day), and two years' rest before the instrument can be played. A good Castelli violin is not cheap, but one day it will be as highly prized as a Stradivarius.

Piazza Sant'Agostino and its neighbourhood

Right in the centre of the city, the beautiful **Piazza Sant'Agostino** is dominated by the 12th-century twin towers on Via delle Torri, one of which leans noticeably. To the north is the graceful neo-Gothic facade of Palazzo Merli (1929), while to the west is the church of **Sant'Agostino** (12th century, successively rebuilt). The simple rectangular façade is enriched by a splendid portal (1547), like the side door of the cathedral. The interior has a central nave and two side aisles; the altars are the work of the Giosafatti family. Among the many paintings, over the second south altar, behind a grille, is a lovely panel painting by Francescuccio di Cecco Ghissi of Fabriano (14th century) known as the *Madonna of Peace*, which is thought to have miraculously restored peace among the citizens in certain difficult moments of history. The July jousts are carried out in her honour. There are some more 16th–17th-century paintings in the sacristy. The Augustine convent now houses an auditorium, halls for exhibitions, the Biblioteca Comunale with more than 200,000 volumes and precious manuscripts, and the **Galleria d'Arte Contemporanea** (*open 9–1& 4–7; closed Mon; T: 0736 248662*), dedicated to the abstract painter Osvaldo Licini, who was born at nearby Monte Vidon Corrado. The fine collection includes many works by this artist, who lived in Paris for a while, and frequented the circles of Picasso and Modigliani. Other important contemporary Italian artists represented here include Severini, Fontana, Vedova and Capogrossi. Leading north from the square is the picturesque **Via delle Torri**, along which some of the most beautiful houses of the city can be seen; a short way up, on the left, is the Teatro dei Filarmonici of 1832 (*information from the Tourist Office*), an acoustically perfect theatre.

By taking Via Dari, just east of Piazza Sant'Agostino, you reach Piazza Bonfine and the church of **San Venanzio**, built in the 12th century on the site of a pagan temple, with a perfectly preserved civic tower transformed into bell-tower. The Baroque interior, in Greek-cross form, is by Giuseppe Giosafatti, as is the elaborate high altar. Recent restoration has revealed a 13th-century fresco of the *Madonna of Childbirth*.

Corso Mazzini and the west

Corso Mazzini was once the main street of Roman *Asculum*. At no. 39 is the **Museo di Storia Naturale Antonio Orsini** (*open Mon, Wed and Fri 9–2, Tues and Thur 3–6; T: 0736 277540*), where you can see the collections of this dedicated naturalist, still displayed in his original 19th-century showcases: shells, rocks, fossils and plants, his famous meadow viper, letters and scientific instruments. A little further along the corso, also on the left, is the Baroque church of Santa Maria del Buon Consiglio (18th century; Lazzaro Giosafatti), with a lavish interior, followed by the ex-church of Sant'Andrea (13th century), where some ancient frescoes have recently been brought to light.

Corso Mazzini leads to **Porta Gemina**, which was built in the 1st century BC to span the Via Salaria, the Roman salt road which led from the coast to Rome. You can still see traces of the 3rd–2nd-century BC fortifications. On the square dedicated to Cecco d'Ascoli—because this is where his house once stood—is the little church of **Santa**

Maria delle Grazie (*open for Mass Sun mornings, but the sacristan lives next door and will open for you*), also known as Santissimo Crocifisso dell'Icona, which owes its present form to Lorenzo Giosafatti (1780). Inside, in the first north chapel over a fine altar, also by Giosafatti, is a painted 16th-century wooden Crucifix of Venetian origin, said to be miraculous. The interior of the church was decorated in 1924. Over the main altar is a detached fresco by Pietro Alemanno of the *Madonna with Christ Child*, known as the *Icona*.

Tucked away close by at the foot of the Colle dell'Annunziata hill, along Via Ricci, are the ruins of the **Roman theatre** of Asculum, built towards the end of the 1st century BC and modified in the 2nd century AD. Unfortunately, the theatre has been systematically pillaged through the centuries as a source of building material, and not much of what remains has been brought to light yet by the archaeologists, so there is little to see, although excavations are in progress. It was here that the hated magistrate Servilius, who had been sent from Rome, was assassinated in 91 BC, sparking the Social War (*see p. 143*). The theatre was inside the city walls, close to the *decumanus maximus* (part of the Via Salaria), and was quite large; the diameter was 98m.

Rua Morelli is a narrow little turning off Corso Mazzini, on the right if you are coming west from Piazza Sant'Agostino. After the arch is the old church of **San Tommaso**, built in 1064 using material from the Roman amphitheatre, which stood in front. The façade is modern, but the bell-tower, unfinished, is still the original. At the top is the oldest church bell in Ascoli, dated 1286. Inside the church (*open for Mass on Sun mornings*), with a central nave and two side aisles, are some remarkable works of art. On the second column on the left is a very well-preserved fresco of the *Madonna of the Milk* (14th century; Maestro di Offida), while on the main altar is a precious 16th-century tabernacle in gilded wood, and a group of sculptures representing the *Madonna with St Thomas and St John the Baptist*, by the Giosafatti family. There is a beautiful little cloister, too.

By passing through Porta Gemina and continuing along the Via Salaria, you reach the banks of the Tronto and the simple church of **Santa Maria delle Donne**, smooth blocks of travertine, built in 1232 for the Poor Clares, and one of the first Franciscan foundations in Ascoli. The interior is simple, effective architecture, with a high presbytery supported by a wide arch, and reached by a curving staircase on the left.

The eastern city

In the eastern part of the city, **Piazza Matteotti** is an important road junction; it stands at one extremity of the lovely Ponte Maggiore over the River Castellano. On the corner with Corso Vittorio Emanuele is the church of **Santa Maria del Carmine** (1663), with a fine façade and rich interior by the Giosafatti family. The bronze statue in the square (1919) represents Cecco d'Ascoli (1269–1327; *see box overleaf*).

North of here, at no. 224 Corso Mazzini, is **Palazzo Malaspina** (late 16th century), consisting of three 14th-century houses and a tower, with a severe, slightly curving façade surmounted by an unusual loggia with stone 'tree trunks' instead of columns; in the courtyard is a decorative 16th-century fountain. A little further along, on the corner with Via Sacconi, next to an abandoned church, is the **Fontana dei Cani**, so-called because the marble animals shown drinking the water, worn smooth by the centuries, look like dogs; apparently they were originally lions.

Cecco d'Ascoli (1269–1327)

Francesco Simili, doctor, philosopher, poet, mathematician and astrologer, was born in Ascoli Piceno in 1269. Known as Cecco d'Ascoli, he was the eternal rival of Dante, and never as famous (though today many critics consider him to be Dante's equal). Bologna University requested his services as teacher of medicine in 1324, but he was punished by the Inquisition for his flippant attitude towards the Church, and all his books of astrology were confiscated. Soon reinstated on the insistence of his students, his fame spread, and Charles, duke of Calabria, appointed him court doctor in 1326. When consulted by the duke about his two-year-old daughter's future, Cecco bluntly replied that she would turn out a whore; it was this that probably brought about his ruin. Denounced to the Inquisition for having written heretical works, he was burnt at the stake in 1327. Defiant to the end, enveloped in flames, he shouted 'I said it, I taught it, I believe it!' His followers were able to save many of his books, in spite of the orders of the Inquisition to destroy them. The duke's little daughter grew up to become Queen of Naples, the notorious 'Giovanna la Pazza' or 'Crazy Joan' (1343–81). Excommunicated for her unseemly behaviour, she had four husbands and an untold number of lovers, and was eventually strangled to death.

A short distance to the south is the **Forte Malatesta** (1349), built during the long war with Fermo and used until recently as a prison. It is planned to house a new museum on the Lombards here soon. Close by is a rebuilt Roman bridge called Ponte di Cecco, said to have been built in one night by the ubiquitous Cecco, but certainly once part of the Via Salaria; both this bridge and Ponte Maggiore were destroyed by the Germans in 1944. In the vicinity is the extremely simple, stark Romanesque church of **San Vittore** (966), with a lovely rose window and a low bell-tower, probably unfinished. The interior has frescoes of the 13th–14th centuries, though some have been detached and are now in the Museo Diocesano (*see p. 147 above*). Under the sacristy is a crypt, accessible from outside, with a series of early 15th-century frescoes of the life of St Eustace.

The south

On Piazza Roma, by the War Memorial (1927), is the elegant façade of the church of **Santa Maria della Carità**, also called *Chiesa della Scopa*, 'Church of the Broom', because once used by the Confraternità dei Disciplinati, or *Battuti dalla Scopa*, penitents who used to beat one another with brooms. The building was finished in the 17th century to a design by Cola dell'Amatrice. The interior is superb Baroque, with lavish stucco and many paintings and statues. The frescoes on the vaults represent stories of the Old Testament. The side altars, made by craftsmen from Lombardy, are contained in niches surmounted by beautiful shell-shaped canopies.

The steep Via Pretoriana leads from Piazza Roma through the medieval district of Piazzarola, up to the Colle Annunziata. A left turn leads to a characteristic medieval square and the church of **San Gregorio** (3rd century, rebuilt 13th century), which was a Roman temple, perhaps dedicated to Isis, transformed into a Christian church. Many traces remain of the original construction, visible both from outside and from the interior, which corresponds to the cella, and is in *opus reticulatum*. One of the 13th-century frescoes inside shows *St Francis preaching to the Birds*, thought to be the earliest-known representation of the episode.

Turning left from Via Pretoriana on Via Barro, you reach the present-day hospital, which was once a convent; it encloses the Romanesque church of **Sant'Angelo Magno** (rebuilt 1292). This was the church of particularly influential Benedictines who had come here from Lombardy. Under the roof (unfortunately not visible) are some perfectly preserved 12th-century frescoes, the oldest in the city, with portraits of the Prophets. In 1461 the church and convent were taken over by the Olivetan Benedictines, who over the next 300 years were to transform the church into the impressive treasure-chest of art that it is today. The interior has a central nave and two side aisles, divided by four pilasters and two columns with Byzantine capitals, while the presbytery is raised to accommodate the sloping nature of the site, and has three apses. There are eight beautifully carved wooden side altars. The vaults and the walls are entirely covered with 18th-century frescoes—there are *Stories of Angels* on the walls, *Sibyls* on the central vault, and the *Fall of Lucifer* on the central arch—and canvases by some of the finest local artists of the time. The sacristy (15th century) is a large room with a Gothic ceiling and a well-head in the centre; over the altar is a canvas of *Jesus consigning the Keys to St Peter*.

Colle dell'Annunziata is a favoured spot for pleasant walks from the city. On the top (600m), surrounded by pines and cypresses, are the ruins of the **Fortezza Pia**, a castle built on the orders of Pope Pius IV in 1560, on a point dominating the River Castellano, and where ancient ruins testify to the presence of a defensive structure of the Picenes. The portal is still intact, the interior is destroyed. The fresh air makes the hill a good place for hospitals; in fact the convent of the Annunziata, now the Department of Architecture of the University of Camerino, was a famous hospital in the Middle Ages. The 14th-century cloisters are impressive. In the ex-refectory is a large fresco by Cola dell'Amatrice (1519) of *Christ going up to Calvary*.

Outskirts of the city

South of the city, on the far side of the Castellano, is the **Cartiera Papale**, rebuilt in 1512 by Pope Julius II on the site of medieval paper factories, which used the hydraulic energy of the river to work the machinery. Paper was made here until the end of the First World War; now the beautiful Renaissance buildings are used as a cultural centre.

The cave-church of Sant'Emidio alle Grotte.

The characteristic little Baroque church of **Sant'Emidio alle Grotte** is to the north of the city, c. 30min walk from Ponte Nuovo. This hill of tufa, with several caves, was the early Christian necropolis. After a terrible earthquake spared Ascoli in 1703, it was decided to build the church as an ex-voto, and Giuseppe Giosafatti was chosen to carry out the project; it is thought to be his masterpiece.

AROUND ASCOLI

South of the town, dominating the River Castellano from a strategic natural rampart, is **Castel Trosino** (418m) a village surrounded by woods of oak and beech. In the centre of the town is a medieval house called *Casa della Regina*, said by some to be the dwelling of a Lombard queen, by others that of Manfred, son of Frederick II of Hohenstaufen. An important Lombard necropolis was discovered accidentally near here in the 19th century.

North of town **Monte Ascensione** rises abruptly to a height of 1103m. It has always been considered a sacred mountain; the ancient population considered it the home of the goddess Esu. Early Christians believed that Polisia, the Roman governor's daughter baptised by St Emygdius, and for whose conversion he suffered martyrdom, found refuge in a cave here. Since the Middle Ages it has been dedicated to the Madonna, and in May pilgrims accompany the statue of the Madonna from the little village church of Polesio to another church on the top of the mountain. Around the base of the mountain you will see many *calanchi*, small parallel gullies and ravines caused by the topsoil being washed away from the underlying clay deposits, creating a landscape of 'elephant's feet'.

PRACTICAL INFORMATION

GETTING AROUND

• **By train**: Porto d'Ascoli is on the main Bologna–Ancona–Pescara line.
• **By bus**: Autolinee START, T: 0736 342243, www.startspa.it, runs services to Civitanova Marche, San Benedetto del Tronto, Fermo, the Sibylline Mountains and Rome.

INFORMATION OFFICES

Visitors' Centre, Municipio, Piazza Arringo, T: 0736 298204; Associazione Turistica, 54/A Via Salaria, T: 0736 801291. Many of the smaller churches mentioned in the text are normally closed to the public, they can be visited during the summer, Christmas and Easter 4.30–7.30 except Mon; Info: Cooperativa Pulchra, 16 Via Vidacilio, T: 0736 256417.

HOTELS

€€€€ **Hotel Palazzo Guiderocchi**. In the heart of the old city, a beautiful aristocratic *palazzo*, carefully restored. Comfortable rooms, good restaurant with selected wine cellar, however they skimped a little on the bathrooms. 3 Via Battisti, T: 0736 244011, info@palazzoguiderocchi.com
€€€€ **Marche**. Simple hotel in new town, with a restaurant. 34 Via Kennedy, T: 0736 45475.
€€€ **Pennile**. Modern structure, good value for money, restaurant, garage, garden, in new town. Via Spalvieri, T: 0736 41645, www.hotelpennile.com
€€€ **Roxi Miravalle**. Hotel with restaurant, pool and tennis. Via Pianoro San Marco, T: 0736 351100.
€ **Pensione Cantina dell'Arte**. Rather spartan, but a charming little place with a restaurant, in the heart of the old city. 8 Rua della Lupa, T: 0736 255620.

FARM ACCOMMODATION

Conca d'Oro Villa Cicchi. ■ A farm producing organic food, while the farmhouse is a carefully restored aristocratic villa, open summer only. Very pleasant, and their Rosso Piceno wine is absolutely superb. 137 Via Salaria Superiore, Abbazia di Rosara, T: 0736 252272, www.villacicchi.it
Il Castagneto. A small farm, in a hillside position with good food. Via Colle San Marco, T: 0736 351097.
Castel Trosino
Le Sorgenti. Lovely spot near the lake, home cooking, open year round. 155 Frazione Lago di Castel Trosino, T: 0736 263725
Roccafluvione
La Locanda della Civetta. This is a tiny, ancient inn; the ideal place for a quiet country holiday. Open May–Oct only. 1 Via Caserine, T: 0736 365135.

RESTAURANTS

€€€ **Gallo d'Oro**. Historic restaurant close to the Baptistery, family-run, with local specialities. Closed Sun, Christmas–New Year and Aug. 13 Corso Vittorio Emanuele, T: 0736 253520.
€€€ **Il Boccon Di Vino**. Hidden away in an alley; serves fabulous *antipasto*. 29

Via d'Argillano, T: 0736 6262168.
Closed Tues.

€€€ **Le Scuderie**. Refined restaurant
in the elegant setting of Palazzo
Malaspina. Meat is grilled in the enormous open fireplace. 226 Corso
Mazzini, T: 0736 263535.

€€ **C'era una Volta**. Friendly restaurant offering traditional dishes. Try the
stuffed gnocchi with asparagus or the
mixed grill. Closed Tues. Via dell'Arco
della Luna, T: 0736 261780.

€€ **La Locandiera**. Famous for traditional fare such as the fried stuffed
olives, or mixed fried vegetables. Very
courteous staff. 2 Via Goldoni, T: 0736
262509. Closed Sun evening and Mon.

€€ **Laliva**. Children are particularly
welcome here; excellent simple traditional dishes, well presented, delicious
desserts. Closed Tues evening and all
day Wed. 13 Piazza della Viola, T: 0736
259358.

€ **Bella Napoli**. For the best pizza in
Ascoli Piceno. Closed Thur. Piazza della
Viola, T: 0736 257030.

CAFÉS & PASTRY SHOPS

Caffè Meletti. ■ Incredible old coffee
house; they produce a famous liqueur
called *anisetta*. If you order it *con la
mosca*, with the fly, you will find some
coffee beans in the bottom of the glass.
Closed Mon in winter. Piazza del
Popolo.

Centrale. Just the place for breakfast,
or for cocktails, or for after-dinner
lounging over liqueurs. Closed Tues. 9

Piazza del Popolo.

Da Sestili. Founded more than a century ago, still with original furnishings.
175 Corso Mazzini. Closed Mon.

FESTIVALS & EVENTS

Throughout the summer concerts, ballets and plays are presented in the city
squares, and there are traditional markets all year. *Giostra della Quintana*,
spectacular jousts in 14th-century costume; competition between the six *ses-
tieri*, or city districts; Info: Ente
Quintana, 8 Piazza Arringo, T: 0736
298223, www.comune.ap.it, July–Aug.
Feast of St Emygdius, magnificent firework displays conclude the festivities,
26 July–5 Aug.

LOCAL SPECIALITIES

Cordivani, at 1 Rua Cappelli, is one of
the finest creative ceramic artisans in
the city, the showrooms are worth a
visit in their own right. **Enoteca
Gastronomia Migliori**, 2 Piazza
Arringo, has a vast array of local foods
and wines, including the tender local
olives. **Lazzarotti**, 3 Via de' Soderini,
has lovely ceramics in very unusual
designs, **Liuteria Castelli**, 7
Lungotronto Bartolomeo, is where Piero
Castelli makes fine violins and other
musical instruments. **Ottaviani**, 26 Via
Mazzini, sells cakes, pastries and the
traditional sticky sweetmeat made with
figs, *torrone di fichi*.

THE TRONTO VALLEY
& PALM RIVIERA

From its source in Abruzzo, the Tronto flows for 115km first through the Sibyllines, then through Acquasanta Terme before reaching Ascoli Piceno where it meets the Castellano, then under the hilltop towns of Appignano del Tronto, Castignano, Offida and Acquaviva Picena, entering the sea at Porto d'Ascoli. This was the route chosen by the Romans for the Via Salaria, the important road which brought salt to the Eternal City, described by Edward Lear in 1846 as, 'the loveliest of all the Roman roads, for the awe-inspiring scenery through which it was constructed by those marvellous people'.

THE TRONTO VALLEY

Acquasante Terme and environs

Acquasanta Terme, known to the Romans as *Vicus ad Acquas*, was an important stop on the Via Salaria, a place where infirm soldiers could use the thermal mineral waters for various therapies. It is really a group of 54 villages; in Acquasanta itself, only 350 people live. It is a popular spa even today, allowing for a healthful holiday in a lovely peaceful spot; it is also a good base for walking, as a large part of its territory is included in the Monti della Laga and Gran Sasso National Park. Many of the tiny surrounding hamlets, all 53 of which are worth exploring, can also be reached on foot. One of them, Gaglierto (on the road to Umito), was completely abandoned in 1955 when all the inhabitants went to Canada to seek their fortune. The main street, Corso Schiavi, is lined with old pastel-coloured houses with crumbling plaster, and little shops, many offering the famous truffles and wild fungi in the autumn, while in spring and summer swifts and house martins whirl around the rooftops, and in winter there is often snow. The theatre of Acquasanta Terme, at 12 Piazza XX Settembre, called 'Casa del Combattenti' (*T: 0736 801262*), is unusual because Fascist-style, completed in 1932. Very small, it has just 141 seats.

The strange castle known as **Castel di Luco**, just east of Acquasanta Terme, is almost perfectly circular. It was built in the 12th century on a large mass of travertine, used by the ancient inhabitants for rituals to ensure the coming of spring—*lux, lucis*, light. The castle was reconstructed in the 14th century, and resists time very well, picturesque with the ancient houses (which offer comfortable accommodation) around its foot. Continuing along the Via Salaria towards Ascoli Piceno, you reach Taverna Piccinini, a Roman station for changing horses.

After Ascoli Piceno, the river banks are lined with industries and farming communities. Just after the city, south of the river are Folignano and Maltignano, originally built as bulwarks to protect Ascoli from the Kingdom of Naples to the south. At **Castel Folignano**, in the church of Santa Maria delle Grazie, is a triptych by Pietro Alemanno of the *Madonna with Saints*; baby Jesus is precariously balanced on her lap.

Above the river

Leaving the highway here (Marino del Tronto) and driving north, by Monte dell'Ascensione, you pass through the attractive little village of Ripaberarda before reaching **Castignano**, a pyramid-shaped town surrounded by *calanchi*, often damaged by landslides and earthquakes, said to have been one of the headquarters of the Templars in the Marche, who inaugurated a hospital which functioned until the 18th century. Legend says there is a Templar cemetery nearby, where hundreds of the knights were buried face down, in full armour, awaiting the call to fight. There are several small industries for the manufacture of food products, bricks and shoes; many of the women are expert lace-makers. The inhabitants are renowned for their stubbornness, and every year they give a trophy—*il Coppo d'Oro*, the Golden Roof-tile—to the most tenacious among their number. At the summit of the tiny, ancient city centre is Piazza San Pietro, with the church of San Pietro Apostolo (11th–14th centuries), which has a terracotta portal surmounted by a rose window with a mysterious carved head in the middle, said to represent Christ. There are lovely views from this point. In the interior is a 16th-century painted wooden statue of St Peter, a carved wooden choir, locally made in 1440, and an interesting, but fragmentary, 15th-century fresco of the *Last Judgement*, which almost completely covers the south wall. In the crypt, which is reached from an outside door to the right of the church, are frescoes by Vittore Crivelli and the atelier of Cola dell'Amatrice, discovered in 1955 during repairs; also a painted terracotta *Our Lady of Sorrow* (15th century), probably brought here from northern Italy. The church also houses the local section of the Sistine Museums of the Picene Area, the **Museo di Arte Sacra** (*open evenings July–Sept 6–8 & 9.30–11.30; T: 0735 594960*), a collection of religious objects from the churches in the town, including a glittering, bejewelled gold and silver reliquary of the Holy Cross (13th–15th centuries), from the workshop of Pietro Vannini. Another interesting church is that of Santa Maria al Borgo or *Chiesa dei Templari* (14th century; but probably much older), in Via Margherita, with the remains of a Templar symbol over the portal—the Greek letter *tau*. The ruined building next to the church is all that remains of their hospital. Under the town is a complex series of channels connecting the wells and the water cisterns, now partly collapsed due to earthquake damage. Many houses also had cellars, kept cool with snow, where silk cocoons were kept to prevent them from opening up too soon. Castignano also boasts a ghost, an unhappy lady called Sora Pia, who can sometimes be seen floating down Via Roma, from her home at Palazzo de Sgrilli, towards Piazza Umberto. She died in 1930, and since then her house has been closed up; now the local council plans to restore it, so perhaps Sora Pia will find peace at last.

Built, according to legend, by a Roman family after the Social War (*see p. 143*), **Appignano del Tronto** was an important stronghold of Ascoli during the Middle Ages and the wars with Fermo. It was destroyed several times, but always rebuilt, because of its strategic position on a tributary of the Tronto. In the course of time it became a place of refuge for exiles from Ascoli. Most of the inhabitants are farmers (this area is renowned for wine and olive oil), and the women are expert lace-makers.

KNIGHTS TEMPLAR

Ancient carvings on old churches, especially Maltese crosses; local place names; the memory of long-gone hospitals and leper colonies; legends of knights buried face down (a sign of humility), ready to spring up and fight when called: all these things indicate a widespread presence of the Templars in the Marche, where they probably protected pilgrims journeying between the various holy shrines, Rome, San Michele di Gargano, and Jerusalem. They also owned hostels in various towns, such as Castignano, Montedinove and Offida, where they could stay when they themselves were going to embark for the Holy Land, from Ancona or Otranto.

Founded in 1119 in Jerusalem, and called the Templars because their first house was close to the Temple of Solomon, they were soldier-monks whose story follows that of the Crusades, during which more than 7,000 of them were killed. When the Christians were forced to leave the Holy Land, they settled first in Cyprus and from there throughout Europe, increasing their wealth and power with the acquisition of lands and castles, and through the banking activity (which they probably invented) which they carried out on behalf of kings and princes. By the early 14th century there was no love lost between the Templars and the sovereigns of Europe, especially Philip the Fair of France, who was in their debt for an enormous sum. Unable to repay, he decided to eliminate them. After torturing and killing many on the accusation of heresy, he succeeded in convincing Pope Clement V to suppress the order and confiscate all its property. This was 1311. After that, there was no mercy, until in 1314 the last Grand Master, James de Molay, was slowly burnt alive after atrocious torture, cursing Philip and Clement as he went: both king and pontiff died less than a year later. The Templars took their secrets with them—if they really had any. Conjectures about their mysterious activities abound, especially after a fire in Cyprus destroyed their archives. Were they Freemasons? Alchemists? Worshippers of a secret, obscene divinity? Or simply the medieval equivalent of an international police force?

In the southeast corner of the medieval centre, at the foot of Via Roma, the main street, is the church of San Michele Arcangelo, built by masons from Lombardy in the 15th century and repaired in the early 20th. Over the main altar is a panel painting by Vincenzo Pagani of the *Madonna*, signed and dated 1539. Continuing along Via Roma, you reach Piazza Umberto, the main square, with the lovely 15th-century Palazzo Comunale and the church of San Giovanni Battista (14th century), with an imposing Gothic façade and Renaissance-style portal, with a rose window above it; there are two similar doors on the sides, and a 14th-century bell-tower at the back. The interior has a central nave with two side aisles, divided by polygonal pilasters and Romanesque arches. On the south wall is a panel painting by Simone de Magistris of the *Pentecost*, signed and dated 1589.

OFFIDA & ENVIRONS

Offida (pop. 5,400), with its old ivory houses and churches, the colour of the local lace, or the colour of the surrounding wheatfields just after harvest, stands on a crest between the valleys of the Tesino and the Tronto. The most important centre in Italy for the production of hand-made lace, most of the women and many of the men are expert in this craft, learning when little more than toddlers; you can see them inside half-closed doorways, or sitting out in the street, adroitly tumbling the tiny spindles (sometimes as many as 300) on the round pillows which serve as the support. You will also see people making simple, comfortable kitchen chairs. Many of the inhabitants are farmers, famous for their wines, and there is also an industrial area (furniture, building materials) in the new town, at the foot of the old. The name of the town could derive from the Greek *ophys*, snake, because a huge golden serpent is said to live in a cave deep below the main street.

In the northeast corner of the old city, at the foot of the castle (15th century; Baccio Pontelli), is a wide panoramic square, **Piazzale delle Merlettaie**, with a bronze monument showing three generations of lace-makers (1983). From here Corso Serpente Aureo leads southwest; one of the little streets to the left leads to the **Museo Aldo Sergiacomi** (*to visit, enquire at the Tourist Office*), the studio of a local sculptor (1912–94), restored by his widow and opened as a museum, with nine rooms arranged exactly the way Sergiacomi wished, with sketches, casts and photographs of the beautiful marble statues he created here.

Lace-tatting in Offida.

Piazza del Popolo

Following the corso, you reach the central Piazza del Popolo, unusual because triangular, with what is surely the most beautiful town hall in the Marche region, the **Palazzo Comunale** (12th–13th centuries), built of pale blond brick, with a high portico surmounted by a loggia and decorative blind arches, and a stunning 14th-century clock tower. The building incorporates the opera house, Teatro Serpente Aureo (*T: 0736 88938*) of 1820, with a splendid vault painted by the local artist Alcide Allevi (1831–93). On the west side of the square is the church of the **Collegiata** (18th century), with a harmonious square façade completed in the 19th century, surmounted by a high dome. The vast interior is richly decorated with stuccoes. Under the high altar is the body of St Leonard, the patron saint of Offida, who came here as an abbot from Noblat in France. In the crypt is a grotto dedicated to the Madonna of Lourdes.

After the square, the corso becomes Via Roma. A short way along, on the left (no. 17), is Palazzo de Castellotti, seat of the **Civic Museum** (*open summer daily 10–12.30 & 4–8; winter Sat and Sun 10–12.30 & 3–7; T: 0736 888609*), with finds made by the local archaeologist Guglielmo Allevi, including many Picene objects in bronze and iron; a well-preserved bronze *situla* with dolphin design, and fragments from the Roman temple to the snake divinity Ophys. The pillow lace section shows examples of the local craft from the 15th century on. The showcases are renewed every six months, in order to give all the townsfolk a chance to show their skills. On the walls of this room are two important panel paintings: *St Lucy* (1490; Pietro Alemanno) and *Three Kingdoms* (1589; Simone de Magistris). The small Art Gallery displays 16 portraits of notables from Offida by Vincenzo Milione (18th century). Lastly, the Local Traditions section illustrates the daily life of farmers, labourers, vintners, weavers, carters and cooks, in a series of displays cleverly arranged in the old rooms of the palace.

Santa Maria della Rocca

Certainly the most important building in Offida is at the far end of Via Roma, just outside the town. The Gothic church of Santa Maria della Rocca (*open summer daily 10–12.30 and 4–8; winter Sat and Sun 10–12.30 & 3–7; T: 0736 888609*) was constructed in 1330 on a bluff where the Lombards had built a castle between the 6th–9th centuries; the remains of it can still be seen in the crypt. The original 11th-century church was much smaller, but when the abbot of Farfa donated the body of St Leonard to Offida at the end of the 13th century, it was decided to create a more suitable resting-place for him. The result is a splendid monument; the pale, warm brick glows against the sky, while the solemn lines of the apses punctuate the superb architecture. The interior is very simple: a single nave, decorated with Baroque stuccoes (1734), and a cross-beam roof. Fragmentary traces of 13th- and 14th-century frescoes can be seen. The beautiful carved portal to the crypt is in the centre of the main apse, approached from outside by a wide, graceful staircase. The crypt occupies the same area as the upper church and is divided into different spaces by small columns. The walls were once entirely covered with frescoes, many by the Maestro di Offida in 1365. Abundant traces of them can still be seen in the chapels of St Lucy and St Catherine of Alexandria. The attached monastery was demolished in 1798 when the new collegiate church was built in the town centre. The building became the property of the local council at the end of the 19th century.

TOWARDS THE COAST

Southeast of Offida, looking down onto the Tronto, are three small towns, all easily reached from the highway, and all with wonderfully unspoilt city centres. **Spinetoli** was once an important Roman settlement, built on the hill sacred to a Picene divinity of the fields, the goddess Tellure. Later an important medieval fortress was built on the hilltop, but it was destroyed by Francesco Sforza in 1425.

Monsampolo del Tronto is a farming community inhabited since prehistory, then refounded in the early Middle Ages by the Benedictines, with a fascinating atmosphere. It is possible to walk on the medieval walls and in secret passages under them (signposted *Percorsi ipogei*). Just outside the walls, in Piazza Marconi, is the interesting Civic Museum and Biblioteca Comunale Tomistica di Sant'Alessio (*open Easter and summer, phone to request visit; T: 0735 704116*), with a collection of ancient books, prints and manuscripts, housed in the convent of San Francesco, with a lovely 17th-century cloister; there is also an archaeological collection with a restoration laboratory.

THE VILLAGE OF DRIED FIGS

Monsampolo del Tronto has always been famous for its 'lonzino' of dried figs; soft and sweet, the tradition goes back to the Romans. In AD 65, the writer Columella describes the technique for making it, in *De ficis siccandis*; noting how advisable it is to wash one's feet before 'treading' the dried figs in the vats. Figs grow easily here; the problem is that they all ripen together in September, so drying them on trays in the sun was a good way of avoiding waste. When they were of the correct consistency, they were pressed with herbs and spices, sometimes with walnuts or almonds, rolled into a kind of sausage, then wrapped in fig leaves and tied with cord; they could be stored in a cool place for months. This was a very nourishing food; a couple of thick slices of 'lonzino' with some good bread and maybe a piece of cheese, was a lunch for schoolchildren, or for those working in the fields. Fortunately, the tradition has not died, you will find this unusual product in many places in the region, and nowadays adventurous confectioners offer new varieties, with chocolate or other flavourings. The best of all, however, is still that from Monsampolo.

Monteprandone is a friendly town, perched on a panoramic hilltop and surrounded by luxuriant vineyards; many new homes have been built at the foot of the hill, where there is an important industrial area (furniture, packaging, machine tools). Birthplace

Farmstead and cornfields in the Tronto Valley, near Offida.

of St James of the Marches (*see p. 54*), his house in the medieval Via Roma is now a museum: Libreria San Giacomo della Marca (*T: 0735 71091, Servizio Cultura, to request visit*) with his collection of 60 codices, on vellum and on paper, including some written by the saint himself. There were originally almost 200 of these documents, but through the years many have been stolen as relics; all of the surviving ones have been restored. On the hillside is the Museo del Santuario di San Giacomo della Marca, housed next to the church of Santa Maria delle Grazie (*open July–Sept 4–8; T: 0735 594960*), with some of the personal belongings of the saint, while in the church are some interesting paintings by Vincenzo Pagani and Cesare Peruzzi.

Acquaviva Picena

On the hill close to San Benedetto del Tronto is the picturesque Acquaviva Picena, a quiet town probably founded by Charlemagne, dominated by its superb Rocca degli Acquaviva d'Atri (c. 10th century, then 14th–15th centuries; Baccio Pontelli), a castle in very good condition, and which also houses the Museum of Ancient Weapons (*open June–Sept 10.30–12.30 & 4–7; Oct–May Sat, Sun and holidays 10.30–12.30 & 3–5; T: 0735 764407*). This was the seat of the powerful dukes of Acquaviva, who played an important role in the medieval history of the Marche, especially after 1234, when Forasteria, the daughter of Duke Rinaldo Acquaviva, married Rinaldo di Brunforte, lord of Mogliano and a close ally of Frederick of Hohenstaufen. The sumptuous wedding, later blessed with seven children, became legendary and is still recorded every year with a series of celebrations which involve all the inhabitants of Acquaviva. Most of the inhabitants are farmers (they produce the marvellous DOC wines Rosso Piceno and Rosso Piceno Superiore), but through the years they have developed an aptitude for making straw baskets called *pagliarole*, and even the fishing nets for San Benedetto del Tronto. In Via del Cavaliere you will find a small museum-workshop dedicated to the craft, called Fili di Paglia.

THE PALM RIVIERA

The stretch of coastline between Cupra Marittima and San Benedetto del Tronto is known as the *Riviera delle Palme*, for the elegant promenades fringed with palms and tamarisks that characterise the resorts. Sandy beaches, crowds of fashionable fun-lovers and families on holiday, good restaurants serving fish or pizza are all to be found here. At the same time the coastal centres are only minutes away from the unspoilt interior, with its intact farmland and tiny medieval cities, such as the splendid towns of Ripatransone or Cossignano, with a totally contrasting, peaceful atmosphere.

Cupra Marittima

Cupra Marittima has 2km of clean white sands. Not given to excesses, it has a peaceful atmosphere, lots of trees and flowers, and an affectionate clientèle of holidaymakers who return year after year.

This was the religious centre of Picenes, who worshipped the goddess Cupra, an Etruscan divinity called *Bona* by the Romans, in a temple on Colle Morganti. Important in Roman times, when it was known as *Iulia Cuprensis*, it was destroyed in 554 and again in the 9th century, then rebuilt, first with the name *Castrum Maranum*, then *Marano*, assuming its present name in 1862. More than 400 Picene tombs of the Iron Age have been found in the area, many containing chariots, weapons, jewellery, ornaments and pottery.

In the centre of the modern resort is Piazza Libertà with a fountain and a fine clock tower, dominated on high by the collegiate **church of San Basso** (1887), which is reached by a double stairway. In the interior is a triptych by Vittore Crivelli of the *Madonna with Christ Child and Sts Sebastian and Bassus*, while in the sacristy is a memorable enamel from Limoges (13th century) of *St Michael striking the Devil*. The vault paintings were carried out in the 1930s by a local artist.

From the collegiate or from the main street, it is an easy walk (c. 600m) through pines to **Cupra Alta** or Marano (112m), the picturesque old centre, still surrounded by defensive walls complete with towers, erected in the 15th century by Francesco Sforza (*see p. 179*). At no. 5 Via del Castello is Palazzo Cipolletti, housing the **Museo Archeologico del Territorio** (*open summer Tues–Sun 5–7 & 9–11; winter Fri–Sun and holidays 3–7; T: 0735 778561*), with a selection of some of the interesting finds from the Picene necropolis; other items are at the museums of Ancona and Ascoli Piceno.

The highest point of the town is the church of Santa Maria in Castello, with a rectangular façade and Romanesque portal. Continuing up through towers and villas, you reach the mountaintop with pine trees and the ruins of the medieval castle.

Just north of Cupra is the **Archaeological Park of Cupra Maritima** (*open summer Mon–Sat 6–8; winter Mon–Sat 9–12; T: 328 4166406*), where the conspicuous remains of the Roman township can be seen, surrounded by olive trees; there is a nymphaeum with frescoes.

Grottammare

South of Cupra Marittima is the bustling, fashionable little resort of Grottammare, with a splendid beach extending as far as San Benedetto del Tronto. Franz Liszt sometimes spent his holidays here, and Queen Christina of Sweden once visited. The climate is particularly mild; in fact orange trees flourish on the hillsides, and nurseries for the production of plants and flowers are an important part of the local economy. Along the seafront (Lungomare della Repubblica) are many charming Art Nouveau villas. One of the most attractive of them, the Kursaal, houses the MIC, or Museo dell'Illustrazione Comica (*open Fri, Sat, Sun 3.30–7.30; T: 0735 736483*), a collection of the cartoons participating in the yearly exhibitions dedicated to humour in art.

The old centre on top of the hill, called Monte Castello, was founded in the 11th century and was often strongly contested between Ascoli and Fermo. The Museo Sistino di Grottammare (*open July–Sept evenings 6–8 & 9.30–11.30*) is housed in the church of San Giovanni Battista, in the lovely little Piazza Peretti in the upper city; the collection includes two panel paintings by Vittore Crivelli. A large orange tree once embellished the square, thus giving the name to the recently restored 18th-century opera house, Teatro dell'Arancio, now used only for exhibitions. Close by is the ancient church of Sant'Agostino (of which half of the bell-tower was demolished as punishment for the congregation having voiced support for Martin Luther), with a fresco of the *Madonna of Mercy* by Vincenzo Pagani dated 1577; and the church of Santa Lucia (1597), built by Camilla Peretti in memory of her brother Pope Sixtus V. The beautiful organ, used in summer for concerts, is from the Fedeli workshop (1751). From here it is a steep walk up to the ruins of the 14th-century castle.

Another walk leads south from Grottammare, c. 1km, to the Romanesque **abbey church of San Martino** (9th–10th centuries), believed to be built on the site of the Temple of Cupra, and containing an epigraph in which Emperor Hadrian records his restoration of the temple. Nearby is a large circular Roman water cistern, known as the *Bagno della Regina*, or Queen's Pool.

Ripatransone

From Grottammare a beautiful panoramic road leads to the ancient walled city of Ripatransone, in a breathtaking position between the Menocchia and the Tesino valleys, inhabited since prehistoric times, gaining importance in the 9th century when the bishop of Fermo entrusted it to the Transone family (hence the name). It was besieged and destroyed several times, before becoming, in 1205, the first free rural commune of Italy. Francesco Sforza burnt it down in 1442, but when his soldiers returned in 1445 they were repelled. The Spanish sacked the town in 1515, but when they tried to repeat their exploit in 1521, they were routed by a courageous woman, Bianca de Tharolis, who heroically rallied the inhabitants. In 1571 the pope declared it a city, and assigned a bishop. During the 18th century religious communities and cultural institutions flourished. Popular as a summer resort, the little town, almost entirely built of honey-coloured brick, is well cared-for and the streets still have a medieval atmosphere.

The main street, Corso Vittorio Emanuele, passes through the town from west to east. When you reach Piazza Condivi, where Michelangelo's biographer lived, you will see the narrow Via Ghislieri on the left, which leads to the **cattedrale** (1597), dedicated to the two saints Gregory and Margaret. The façade was completed in 1842, and the bell-tower was erected in 1902. The lovely interior has many works of art by the contemporary local painter Michelangelo Bedini. In the first south chapel is a precious painted wooden Crucifix (16th century), the gift of Pope Pius V, while in the south transept is a painting of St Charles Borromeo (1623) thought to be by Guercino. To the left of the main chapel, a copper door gives access to the richly ornate Santuario della Madonna di San Giovanni, patron saint of Ripatransone. The miraculous 17th-century painting of the *Madonna* is by Sebastiano Sebastiani. The fine organ is from the famous Callido workshop.

Continuing up the corso, you reach the Episcopio, the bishop's palace, and the ancient Augustine convent, now seat of the Curia. In the central Piazza XX Settembre is the imposing **Palazzo del Podestà** (1304; enlarged 19th century), with a portico. The building incorporates the Opera House (*T: 0735 99329*) of 1843, dedicated to the local poet Luigi Mercantini, who wrote the Italian national anthem. In front is the 17th-century town hall, which houses the **Museo Archeologico** (*open 9.30–12.30 & 3.30–7.30; T: 0735 99329*) with objects illustrating local history, from prehistory through the Roman civilisation and the Middle Ages. Close to the Archaeological Museum is the Vicolo Stretto (signposted), the narrowest street in Italy, only 43cm wide.

After passing through Piazza Donna Bianca de Tharolis, on the main street (Corso Vittorio Emanuele) is the finest of the civic buildings of Ripatransone, Palazzo Bonomi-Gera (17th century), donated to the city together with his private collection by the local philanthropist and sculptor Uno Gera (1890–1982). Here is the **Pinacoteca Civica** (*open 9.30–12.30 & 3.30–7.30; T: 0735 99329*) displaying many paintings, etchings, ceramics, porcelain and furniture, including works by Vittore Crivelli, Vincenzo Pagani, James Stark, James Webb, and Annigoni. There is also a cast gallery with plaster sculptures by Uno Gera.

Behind Palazzo Bonomi-Gera, in Via Annibal Caro, is the church of **San Filippo** (1680–1722) with an elegant interior consisting of a single nave and side chapels, surmounted by a superb dome; there are several sculptures by Uno Gera. The crypt houses the **Museo della Civiltà Contadina ed Artigiana** (*open holiday afternoons, other days by appointment T: 0735 9378*), a collection of tools, equipment and curiosities illustrating the lives of the local peasants and artisans in the 19th century.

Cossignano

Surrounded by really spectacular *calanchi*, Cossignano stands defiant and strong on its hilltop, still protected by its ancient walls. This was once a possession of the abbey of Farfa, but during the wars between Ascoli and Fermo it was a stronghold of fundamental importance, and passed from one city to the other, until becoming an independent commune in the 15th century. Recent studies suggest that the town was founded by the Picenes, who built a temple to Mars and venerated the magpie (*see p. 10*); for many years Cossignano was known as *Castello di Marte*. In the tiny main square, Piazza Umberto, is the church of Santa Maria Assunta (18th century) and the ancient town hall, with a slender 15th-century bell-tower. The tubular bell inside was cast in 1303. In Via Verdi, a little street just below the square, is the 12th-century **Chiesetta dell'Annunciata**, with damaged frescoes by Cola dell'Amatrice and Vincenzo Pagani, and a small museum with objects found locally. The Gothic east gate, called Porta San Giorgio (14th century), is complete with tower; St George is the patron saint of Cossignano.

San Benedetto del Tronto

Probably founded in the early Middle Ages on the site of a Roman settlement called *Truentum*, San Benedetto del Tronto (pop. 45,000) formed part of the bishopric of Fermo, but its possession was strongly contested by Ascoli Piceno, causing many wars. In 1478 the population was decimated by an epidemic and the survivors abandoned the area, which was repopulated later by immigrants from Romagna and the northern Marche. Now it is both an elegant seaside resort and one of the most important fishing ports of the Adriatic, with a busy fish market (worth a visit at dawn to see the auction), boat-building yards, and industries for processing fish. There is a long sandy beach, with an impressive promenade flanked by more than 7,000 palms, oleanders, tamarisks and pines.

The modern town lies at the foot of the ancient centre on the hilltop, around the 14th-century Torre dei Gualtieri, probably all that remains of a medieval castle. Close to the tower, in Palazzo Radicioni, is the **Museo Catani** (*open evenings July–Sept 6–8 & 9.30–11.30; T: 0735 594960*), with a collection of religious objects from local churches. Perched on the top of the hill is the church of San Benedetto Martire, rebuilt in the 18th century on the site of an early Christian church.

At the foot of the hill, on the other side of Corso Mazzini, is Piazza Nardone with the **Cattedrale** (19th century), dedicated to the Madonna of the Marina. Inside are several Baroque altars, retrieved from ruined churches. The beautiful painting in the apse, imaginative and colourful, is by Ugolino da Belluno, an artist-priest born in 1919, skilled in mosaics and frescoes. At the northern end of the promenade, after the lighthouse, is a large yachting harbour, the fishing port, and the fish market.

Next to the fish market, at no. 28 Piazza del Pescatore, is the **Museo Ittico Augusto Capriotti** (*open summer 9–1 & 4–9; winter 9–12 & 4–6.30; closed Mon and holidays; T: 0735 588850*), a collection of 6,500 fish to be found in the Adriatic Sea, while the other civic museums are nearby in Viale de Gasperi: the **Antiquarium Truentinum** and the **Museum of the Amphorae** (*open 9–12 & 3–6; closed Sun in winter, stays open later in summer; T: 0735 592177*) display archaeological finds, some coming from shipwrecks. The same building houses the **Museo della Pesca e della Civiltà Marinara**, a vivid description of fishing methods and techniques, and the lives of the people who dedicate their energies to this important part of the local economy. The central Viale Secondo Moretti is a pedestrian area; part of it, called Isola dell'Arte, boasts contemporary sculptures by, among others, the American Mark Kostabi, Ugo Nespolo and the local artist Paolo Consorti.

PRACTICAL INFORMATION

GETTING AROUND

• **By train**: Porto d'Ascoli is on the main Bologna–Ancona–Pescara line; from here trains go to Ascoli Piceno. The Palm Riviera towns of San Benedetto del Tronto, Cupra Marittima and Grottammare are all on the main Bologna–Ancona–Pescara line.
• **By bus**: Autolinee START, 29 Via Mamiani, Porto d'Ascoli, T: 0735 75981, www.startspa.it, runs services connecting all the towns of the Tronto Valley. They also run services from San Benedetto del Tronto to Ascoli Piceno, Acquasanta Terme, Acquaviva Picena, Civitanova Marche, Offida, Cossignano and Ripatransone. Autolinee STEAT, T: 0735 592186, run services to Fermo, Civitanova Marche and Porto d'Ascoli; Fratelli Massi, 3 Frazione San Martino, Acquasanta Terme, T: 0736 402154, this company connects many of the villages of Acquasanta Terme.

INFORMATION OFFICES

A website on the towns of the Tronto Valley is www.parcopiceno.com.

Another is www.galpiceno.it. A detailed website for the Palm Riviera is www.rivieradellepalme.com
Acquasanta Terme Tourist Information Bureau, Municipio, T: 0736 801262, www.acquasanta.it
Cupra Marittima IAT, 11 Piazza Libertà, T: 0735 779193, www.cupramarittima.org; Tourist Information Bureau, T: 0735 776731; ACOT, 4 Via Garibaldi, T: 0735 777800, www.assoturcupra.it; IDREA, Piazza Possenti, T: 0735 778622, www.cupramarittima.net
Grottammare IAT, 6 Piazza Fazzini (upper city), T: 0735 631087; Associazione Operatori Turistici, 24 Via Pascoli, T: 0735 583166.
Offida Tourist Information Bureau, 79 Corso Serpente Aureo, T: 0736 889381, www.comune.offida.ap.it
Ripatransone IAT, 12 Piazza XX Settembre, T: 0735 99329.
San Benedetto del Tronto IAT, 5 Via Tamerici, T: 0735 592237, www.sanbenedettodeltronto.it, www.comune.san-benedetto-del-tronto.ap.it; Ufficio Beni Culturali Diocesano, 16 Via Forte, T: 0735 594960,

www.museisistini.it, for the Sistine Museums of the Picene Area.

HOTELS

Acquasanta Terme

€€€ **Grande Albergo Italia**. This rather forbidding-looking, but comfortable, hotel forms part of the spa centre. 59 Via del Bagno, T: 0736 801269.

€€€ **Il Passo**. An excellent choice, small, comfortable, with a very good restaurant. Also has a fitness centre. 9 Piazza Terme, T: 0736 801099.

€€€ **Le Terme**. A comfortable hotel with a good restaurant. 20 Piazza Terme, T: 0736 801263.

€€ **Roma**. Quaint little hotel near the spa, with a restaurant. 5 Corso Schiavi, T: 0736 801325.

Acquaviva Picena

€€€ **Abbadetta**. A very comfortable hotel, with pool, garden, tennis and restaurant, but it does stand out like a sore thumb on the landscape. 36 Via Abbadetta, T: 0735 764041, www.abbadetta.it

€€€ **Duca degli Acquaviva**. In a countryside position, with a garden and a good restaurant. 21 Contrada San Vincenzo, T: 0735 764045.

€€€ **O'Viv**. Pretty little hotel in town centre, with a garden and restaurant; attentive service. 43 Via Marziale, T: 0735 764649.

€€ **La Perla**. Hotel with a good restaurant and a private beach. 68 Via Nazario Sauro, T: 0735 777162, hotel.laperla@tin.it.

€€€ **Hotel Villa Picena**. A small hotel in a convenient position, comfortable rooms, restaurant. 66 Via Salaria, T: 07356 892460, www.villapicena.it

Cupra Marittima

€€€ **Anita**. A nice little hotel with private beach and a garage. 127SS Adriatica Nord, T: 0735 778155, www.hotelanita.it

€€ **Castello**. ■ Situated in the delightful medieval town (Marano) on the hilltop, this peaceful little hotel (closed winter) has a good restaurant. 67 Via Castello, T: 0735 778463, www.cupramarittima.com/castello

Folignano

€€€€ **Villa Pigna**. In an elegant Art Nouveau villa, with a good restaurant. T: 0736 491868.

€€€ **Roma**. This hotel offers every amenity, right in front of the beach. 16 Lungomare de Gasperi, T: 0735 631145, www.hotelromagrottammare.com

€€ **Lo Squalo**. Small family-run hotel with restaurant. Comfortable rooms, bikes rented, short walk from beach; a good choice. 67 Via Marconi, T: 0735 736131, www.hotellosqualo.it

Offida

€€ **Caroline**. Hotel with restaurant. 7 Via Mazzini, T: 0736 880811.

Ripatransone

€€€ **Il Tuo Corbezzolo**. With a garden and restaurant; situated out of town. 25 Via Sant'Egidio, T: 0735 9476, www.iltuocorbezzolo.com

€€€ **Romano**. Hotel with garden, restaurant and car park. 30 Via Fonte Abeceto, T: 0735 9421, www.hotelromano.it

San Benedetto del Tronto

€€€€ **Haus Charlotte**. Clean, comfortable and excellent service. Private beach and pool. 10 Via Giannini Milli, T: 0735 81874, www.hotelhauscharlotte.it

€€€€ **Regent**. Charming little hotel, very central position, garage, no restau-

rant. 31 Viale Gramsci, T: 0735
582720, www.hotelregent.it
€€€ **Pineta**. In a quiet position surrounded by trees, close to the beach.
Has a restaurant with vegetarian meals
on request, and garage; a good choice.
103 Via dei Mille, T: 0735 659875,
www.hotel-pineta.it
€€€ **Rivamare**. An attractive building
on the beach, with a particularly good
restaurant. 13 Via San Giacomo, T:
0735 751177, www.hotelrivamare.it
€€ **Meublé La Playa**. No restaurant
but excellent value for money. Open
May–Oct, 25/a Via Cola di Rienzo, T:
0735 659957.
Spinetoli
€€€ **Country Club**. With restaurant
and garage, this hotel is about 2km
from Spinetoli. Via I Maggio, T: 0736
899428, countryclub@interbusiness.it

BED & BREAKFAST

Castignano
Maria Giovanna Recchi.
Accommodation in an 18th-century villa
at the foot of Monte dell'Ascensione. 3
Contrada Fabbrica, T: 0736 821746.
Cossignano
Palazzo Fassitelli. An historic palace in
main square. 5–6 Piazza Umberto,
T: 0735 98173.
Monteprandone
Villa San Giuseppe. Beautiful old villa
with a lovely garden. 38 Contrada Colle
Sant'Angelo, T: 348 3346566,
entoma@tin.it
Offida
Mary. On the lovely main street.
English and French spoken, 5 Corso
Serpente Aureo, T: 071 2863190.
San Benedetto del Tronto

A useful website with information on
B&B accommodation in San Benedetto
and surroundings is www.
unmarediaccoglienza.com
Alfred Chatelain. In an historic building
in the centre. English, French and
Spanish spoken. 58 Via XX Settembre, T:
0735 588694, sciarramassimo@libero.it

FARM ACCOMMODATION

Acquasanta Terme
Il Roccolo. An imposing stone farm-
house within park boundaries, good
restaurant. Open March–Nov. Località
Pomaro, T: 0736 801251.
Castignano
Fiorenire. A well-organised farm with
vineyards, olive grove and orchard; ten-
nis and horse-riding. 9 Contrada Filette,
T: 0736 821606, www.fiorenire.it
Cupra Marittima
La Castelletta. An attractive farmhouse
on the hillside; excellent food. 17
Contrada Sant'Andrea, T: 0735 779088.
Oasi degli Angeli. Ideal for families
with young children, a comfortable farm
not far from Cupra. Very good cuisine.
Closed Oct. 50 Contrada Sant'Egidio,
T: 0735 778569, kurni@jumpy.it
Grottammare
A casa da Angelo. On the hill behind
Grottammare, an old converted cottage,
with excellent food. 26 Contrada San
Giacomo, T: 0735 631730.
Offida
Azienda Agrobiologica Aurora. At
10km from Offida, this large farm pro-
duces wine, olive oil and cereals, organ-
ically. Interesting. 98 Via Ciafone, T:
0736 810007, www.viniaurora.it
Rosa dei Venti. Close to town, the
restaurant serves traditional local dishes;

gym. 261/a Via Tesino, T: 0736 889201.

Ripaberarda di Castignano

Piane di Enea. In lovely countryside near Castignano, a farm producing wine. Guests can help on farm. English, French and German spoken. 4 Via Piane, T: 0736 823190.

Ripatransone

C'era una Volta. ■ Lovely old house in isolated, panoramic position (hard to find). The farm produces olive oil and wine, and offers horse-riding. Marvellous breakfasts. 34 Contrada San Gregorio, T: 0735 98150, sambugu@interfree.it

MONASTERY ACCOMMODATION

Acquasanta Terme

Monastero Valledacqua. Open to all who seek the silence and the spirituality of a sojourn with the Benedictine monks; their monastery was founded in 970. T: 0736/801078, www.valledacqua.it

COUNTRY HOUSES

Acquaviva Picena

La Solagna. Perfect for families with young children, with a relaxed atmosphere. In a strategic position 9km from the sea; has an internet point. English and Russian spoken. 3 Contrada Casarica, T: 0735 764413, lasolagna@hotmail.com

Castel di Lama

Borgo Storico Seghetti Panichi. Exclusive accommodation in lovely aristocratic 18th-century villa. Gardens, pool, courses in Italian, history of art, applied arts, music and local cuisine. Very good food and wines. English spoken. 1 Via San Pancrazio, T: 0736

812552, www.seghettipanichi.it

Ripatransone

I Calanchi. Very comfortable and exclusive. 1 Contrada Verrame, Località San Savino, T: 0735 90244, www.i-calanchi.com

La Cascina dei Ciliegi. A comfortable and friendly place. 4 Via Pianacciole, Località San Savino, T: 0735 90606, cascinadeiciliegi@libero.it

RESTAURANTS

Acquasanta Terme

€ **Castel di Luco**. The special dish here is roast lamb; mushrooms are good too. Closed Mon. By the castle, T: 0736 802319.

€ **Il Passo**. Simple, well-prepared dishes, often with wild fungi and truffles, booking always necessary. Closed Mon and Christmas. 9 Piazza Terme, T: 0736 802755.

Acquaviva Picena

€€ **Il Grillo**. Large restaurant often used for banquets. The chef prepares interesting fish dishes: try the gnocchi with seafood. Excellent local wines. 29 Via Colle in Su, T: 0735 583285.

Appignano del Tronto

€€ **Santa Lucia**. Very pleasant meals in the garden, good *vincisgrassi*, try the salt cod (*baccalà*) with sultanas. Closed Mon and Nov. 192 Via Valle Chifenti, T: 0736 817177.

Grottammare

€€€ **Lacchè**. Very good fish dishes, try *I fagioli di Franca*, a soup of beans and fish. Good wines. Closed Mon. 1–3 Via Procida, T: 0735 582728.

€€€ **Osteria dell'Arancio**. ■ Amazing wine cellars with a good assortment French wines. Innovative food and very pleasant atmosphere. Open evenings only. Closed Wed. Piazza Peretti (upper city), T: 0735 631059.

€€€ **Tropical**. Beautiful terrace; good fish dishes and splendid desserts, excellent local wines and liqueurs. Closed Sun evening and Mon, Christmas. 59 Lungomare de Gasperi, T: 0735 581000.

€€ **Il Grillo**. Heavenly fried fish or *guazzetto dell'Adriatico* fish soup; local wines. 57 Lungomare de Gasperi, T: 0735 581103.

€€ **Ristorante Borgo Antico**. Beautiful little restaurant in an old wine press; fabulous ravioli, gnocchi and *crespelle* (crêpes), fish soups, roast pork; good local wines. Closed Tues in winter. 1 Via Santa Lucia (upper city), T: 0735 634357.

€€ **Stella Marina**. Friendly beach restaurant, well known for the sea food *antipasto*; they also rent loungers and sunshades on the beach. 16 Via Colombo, T: 0735 633610. Closed Mon.

Offida

€€ **Rosa dei Venti**. This country restaurant doesn't look much from outside, but the food is delicious and there is a friendly atmosphere. Closed Tues. 261 Via Tesino, T: 0736 889201.

€ **Osteria Ophis**. Simple food consisting of perfect ingredients, well prepared; ask for the traditional *chichiripieno*, tasty and explosive soft bread pie, containing anchovies, tuna, capers and chilli pepper. Closed Tues. 54/c Corso Serpente Aureo, T: 0736 889920.

Porto d'Ascoli

€€ **Osteria Caserma Guelfa**. This interesting restaurant is housed in what was once the pope's customs office. Closed Mon. 5 Via Caserma Guelfa, T: 0735 753900.

€€ **Pescatore**. Very good mixed fried fish and local wines. Closed Mon. 27 Viale Trieste, T: 0735 83782.

Ripatransone

€ **La Petrella**. Out of town, *crespelle* substitute bread here if you like; the home-made egg pasta with an array of dressings is delicious, accompanied by the best local wines, Rosso Piceno, Rosso Piceno Superiore and Falerio dei Colli; fantastic atmosphere. Closed Wed. 54 Contrada Petrella, T: 0735 9345.

€ **Trattoria Rosati**. Everything is home made, including the bread and the pasta. Closed Mon and Tues. 27 Corso Vittorio Emanuele, T: 0735 9345.

San Benedetto del Tronto

€€€ **Messer Chichibio**. Pleasant restaurant close to the port, excellent fish and *antipasti*. 5 Via Tiepolo. Closed Mon.

€€€ **Ristorantino da Vittorio**. Restaurant with a garden, famous for its fish dishes and excellent pasta. Closed Mon. 31 Via Liberazione, T: 0735 84489.

€€ **L'Anghiù**. Very good seafood *antipasto*, try their home-made *tagliatelle allo Scoglio*; local wines. 3 Via Doria, T: 0735 591222.

€€ **Papillon**. The best place for the local fish soup *brodetto alla sambenedettese*, but call the day before as it is specially made. 158 Via Nazario Sauro, T: 0735 751902.

€€ **Trattoria Cognigni**. Appetizing dishes, all home-made, including the pasta, bread and desserts. Closed Wed. Via Val Tiberina, T: 0735 751341.

€ **Il Grottino**. Family-run restaurant near the port, informal, good simple dishes; also rooms for rent. Closed Mon. 107 Viale Cristoforo Colombo, T: 0735 585160.

Offida

Caffè del Corso. Traditional coffee bar on the main street; the typical aniseed-flavoured biscuits are called *funghetti*. 77 Corso Serpente Aureo.

Ripatransone

Aldo Nucci Pasticceria. Try the local speciality, *crostata di ricotta* (ricotta tart). 30 Corso Vittorio Emanuele.

Bar Sammagno. The ideal place for a coffee break; home-made ice cream; they sell stamps as well. 9 Piazza XX Settembre.

Campanelli. Bread and cakes baked on the premises, excellent ricotta tart. 28 Via Garibaldi.

San Benedetto del Tronto

Caffè Florian. ■ '20s atmosphere in this comfortable coffee bar, with tea room and restaurant; in summer, live music Fri and Sat evenings. Closed Mon. 74 Viale Secondo Moretti.

Four Roses. Even the bread for the sandwiches is home made, in this well-run coffee bar. Closed Wed. 44 Via de Gasperi.

Gran Caffè Sciarra. Founded in 1862, a good choice for breakfast or lunch. Open Sun, but closed Wed in winter. 31/a Viale Moretti.

Acquasanta Terme

The thermal springs consist of a pool of sulphurous water, which gushes constantly at a temperature of 38.6°C, only 30m above the River Tronto, in an extremely beautiful setting. A short distance from the pool is a grotto with steam and very hot gases, used as a sauna. Mud and massage therapy are available at the spa centre. The treatment is particularly effective for arthritis, arthrosis, rheumatism, sciatica, fractures, and skin diseases. Spa centre, 59 Via del Bagno, T: 0736 801268; open May–Nov.

Acquasanta Terme Particularly colourful costumes are worn for Carnival in the villages of Pozza and Umito, called the Zanni; probably of Lombard origin, February. Feast of Autumn to celebrate the good things from the forests: fungi, truffles, chestnuts; Info: T: 0736 801291, 3rd Sun in Oct. At nearby Quintodecimo, *Presepio*, a series of 30 Christmas cribs, involving the whole village, Dec–Jan.

Acquaviva Picena *Acquaviva nei fumetti*, comics and caricatures, each year dedicated to a different theme, on show in the old city centre; Info: T: 0735 633410, July. *Sponsalia*, a banquet, medieval music and dancing, spectacular games, to enact the 1234 marriage between Forasteria of Acquaviva and Rinaldo of Brunforte (*see p. 165*); Info: Associazione Palio del Duca, 7 Via San Rocco, T: 0735 764115, www.paliodelduca.com, Aug. Feast of St Nicholas, 6 Dec.

Castignano *Li Moccoli*, or Death of Carnival, a mock funeral procession followed by bonfire. Info T: 0736 821432, Shrove Tuesday. *Templaria*, medieval fun and games in honour of the Templars; Info: T: 0736 822060, 16 Aug.

Cupra Marittima Feast of St Bassus, much banqueting with fish, great firework displays, Easter Monday and Aug. *C'era una volta il pane*, celebrations for bread organized by local baker Settimio Bassotti, many times Italian and European champion, 25 May–5 June. Classical drama and music at the Roman Forum in summer; Info and programmes from **MuseiOn**, T: 0735 776723, www.comune.cupra-marittima.ap.it

Grottammare *Sagra giubilare*, since 1755, plenary indulgence for Catholics, a privilege granted by a pope on finding refuge here, when surprised by a storm, held on 1 July only when it falls on a Sun. Feast of St Paternian, 10 July. Concerts at the church of Santa Lucia (upper city), July–Aug. *Baci dal Mare*, operetta performances at the Public Gardens, 1–10 Aug.

Offida *Corrida e morte del Carnevale*, including a mock bullfight and racing through the streets, ancient Carnival traditions of Offida; Info from the town hall, T: 0736 6889381, Feb. Feast of the Holy Cross, 3 May.

Ripatransone *Il Cavallo di Fuoco*, magnificent fireworks: a wooden horse is gradually set ablaze, a 17th-century tradition, 1st Sunday after Easter. Feast of St Mary Magdalene, 3rd Sun in July.

San Benedetto del Tronto Feast of St Benedict, last Sun in May. *Madonna della Marina*, festivity of the fishermen, last Sun in July.

LOCAL SPECIALITIES

Acquaviva Picena
Cantina dei Colli, at 35–37 Via Boreale, sells DOC wines (Rosso Piceno Superiore). **Forno Volpiani**, in Via Castello, is a good bakery.

Appignano del Tronto
Allevi, at 1 Vicolo del Passo, has fresh

crunchy bread and biscuits. **Oleificio Stipa Felice**, 72 Viale delle Rimembranze, for the excellent local olive oil.

Cupra Marittima
Oasi degli Angeli Azienda Agricola, 50 Contrada Sant'Egidio, this farm produces small quantities of exceptional wines; try their Kurni IGT Rosso.

Grottammare
Vini Carminucci, 39 Via San Leonardo, open since 1928 for local wines, especially the DOC Falerio dei Colli Ascolani.

Monsampolo del Tronto
Catalini, 27 Corso Vittorio Emanuele, for *panetti*, traditional sticky sweets made of figs. **Ottaviano Redi**, 26 Via Mazzini, for delicious home-made fig sweetmeats, on sale only in winter.

Offida
CO.AR.ME, Via Roma (near museum), is an outlet for the local lace-makers' association. **Enoteca Regionale**, at 75 Via Garibaldi, in the ex-convent of San Francesco, is a representative selection of local DOC wines and other typical products. **Il Gioiello**, at 60 Corso Serpente Aureo, and **Rita Pierantozzi**, 10 Piazza del Popolo, are both good places for hand-made lace.

Ripatransone
Egidio Amurri, Piazza Condivi, for miniature pottery. **Achille Cardarelli**, 37 Corso Vittorio Emanuele, makes delicious salami and *ciabuscolo*. **Ines Cataldi**, Piazza Matteotti, sells wood carvings. **La Fontursia Azienda Agricola**, 1 Contrada Fontursia, www.lafontursia.it, for DOC wines straight from the vineyard, especially good Rosso Piceno.

FERMO & ITS TERRITORY

Fermo (pop. 36,000), provincial capital, is a quiet town with strong traditions, perched on a hill only a stone's throw from the sea. It has a splendid main square, and an unusual cathedral surrounded by gardens, built on the summit. This is a particularly fertile part of the region, lovely in early spring when the fruit trees are in blossom—the peach orchards are renowned. Fermo is surrounded by dozens of small hilltop towns, most of which were originally its castles. Communication with them was possible by day or night, as messages were transmitted by drumbeats, flags or lighted torches.

EXPLORING FERMO

Piazza del Popolo

Piazza del Popolo, city centre since Roman times, a lovely square with high porticoes, is the favourite meeting-place of the people. A colourful market is held here every Thursday morning, and in July and August it becomes a popular antique market in the afternoon. In its present form it goes back to 1569. To the north are the **Palazzo dei Priori** (once the town hall) and the Palazzo degli Studi (once seat of the university), joined by a loggia. The Palazzo dei Priori was first built in the 14th century, then restructured and finally completed in 1525, with an attractive double staircase in the centre of the façade, surmounted by a bronze statue of Sixtus V (1590), token of gratitude of the population to Felice Peretti, who before becoming Pope Sixtus V had been their archbishop and had obtained many privileges for the university. The building now houses the **Pinacoteca Civica** (*open summer 10–1 & 3.30–7.30; winter 9.30–1 & 3.30–7; closed Mon; T: 0734 217140*), with a rich collection of paintings, including a glowing, nocturnal *Adoration of the Shepherds* by Rubens (1608), a polyptych by Andrea da Bologna, and eight panel paintings from a polyptych by Jacobello del Fiore with *Stories of St Lucy*. There are also some 15th century Flemish tapestries, and the so-called *Marguttu*, the mannequin used as the jousting target for many centuries.

Left of Palazzo dei Priori is the warm apricot-coloured, Baroque-style **Palazzo degli Studi** (16th–17th centuries), with a 16th-century statue of the Virgin above the portal, which houses the important Biblioteca (*open Mon–Fri 8–2 & 3–7; Sat 8–2; closed Sun; T: 0734 217140, entrance from 2 Via Bon Conte*). The library boasts some rarities, such as a 14th-century prayer book, a first edition of Petrarch's *Triumphs*, a 15th-century herbarium and a large wooden globe (1712). Part of the collection was donated by a local man, Romolo Spezioli (1642–1723), who had been Queen Christina of Sweden's physician; still more volumes were donated by Cardinal Decio Azzolino Junior, her personal counsellor.

An old Roman building nearby in Largo Calzecchi Onesti houses the **Museo Archeologico** (*to request a visit T: 0734 217140*), with an interesting collection of Roman and Etruscan funerary urns, and swords, buckles and vases of the Picene period.

HISTORY OF FERMO

The strategic hill called *Sabulo* was a Picene stronghold from the 9th century BC. Taken by the Romans in 268 BC, a large group of perhaps 5,000 settlers arrived four years later to found *Firmum Picenum*. The city was further enlarged when space was assigned to veteran legionaries in 42 BC, and soon a theatre and huge water-storage cisterns were built. In 526 the Lombard queen Amalasunta chose the city as her dwelling. In the 7th century, as part of the Duchy of Spoleto, Fermo controlled a large area, and in 825 a prestigious school was established by the Lombard emperor Lothair I. In the 14th century it became a university, functioning until 1826. The city became the seat of a powerful bishopric in the 9th century, and several religious communities came to Fermo to open monasteries and build new churches. By the early 10th century Fermo was capital of the vast *Marca Fermana*, with a convenient harbour close by (now Porto San Giorgio). In 1176 Christian, Archbishop of Mainz, took the city on behalf of Frederick Barbarossa; his troops sacked and burnt it, but Fermo soon rose again, rebelled against the emperor, and became an independent commune in 1199. In the 13th century Fermo was made part of the March of Ancona, but if anything this only increased its wealth and influence. The harbour was fortified to protect it from pirates, and soon, as the most populous city in the march, it was controlling 80 castles. City dignitaries created alliances with as many influential communes as they could, but the most significant of these was the one signed in 1275 with Venice; it became a firm friendship, and besides guaranteeing a constant supply of wheat for the Venetians, it opened up new worlds for Fermo (and interesting new markets in the east). Venetian artists were welcomed with open arms, explaining the arrival of painters like Jacobello di Bonomo, Jacobello del Fiore, and the Crivelli brothers, Carlo and Vittore. Ancona, however, was decidedly jealous of the relationship, and broke off its friendly ties with Fermo.

The most important statesman to lead Fermo was the *condottiere* Francesco Sforza, employed by the Pope Eugenius IV in the service of his league of Venice and Florence against the Milanese Visconti. Francesco turned Fermo into an extremely beautiful, well-run Renaissance city. In 1549 the city council decided to turn over Fermo to the papacy, 'for the common weal' (Sixtus V was a local man and had obtained many privileges for the city). The strong ties with Milan were broken, and Fermo entered a quieter phase.

In the 18th and 19th centuries, Fermo was high on the list of places for travellers planning to embark on a Grand Tour. A humiliating decision came in 1861, when with the Unification of Italy, Ascoli Piceno acquired the status of provincial capital, and was given control over Fermo and all its surrounding townships. Today Fermo has regained its status of provincial capital, and is ready to take its old place in the civic organisation of the region.

The Roman cisterns and San Domenico

East of Piazza del Popolo, accessible from Via Paccarone, is the stepped alley called Via degli Aceti; at no. 1 is the entrance to the underground **Cisterne Romane** (*for guided tour T: 0734 217140*), 30 enormous water-storage cisterns, perfectly efficient, built between AD 40 and 60. Each one measures 9m by 6m, and is 6m high; six of them are still in use by the municipal water board.

Southeast of Piazza del Popolo, in Largo Maranesi, is the Romano-Gothic church of **San Domenico**, built in 1233 and successively transformed. The portal (1455) in the centre of the plain brick façade is remarkable, and so is the semicircular apse, with its arches and pilasters, and the bell-tower, repaired in 1733. The interior is one vast nave, with beautiful modern stained-glass windows, and an imposing high altar (1422), consisting of a large slab of travertine marble supported by 13 little columns; behind the altar is a particularly fine wooden choir, carved and inlaid by Giovanni da Montelparo in 1448, surmounted by the organ (Callido; 1803).

Francesco Sforza (1401–66)

Born of humble origins in 1401, Francesco Sforza was a soldier all his life, and all-time rival of the ferocious *condottiere* Braccio da Montone. A persevering man, he succeeded in fulfilling his greatest ambition: securing the Duchy of Milan for himself and his descendants. His father Muzio was an intelligent mercenary, famous for his great strength, from which derives his nickname *Sforza*. Francesco inherited both his astuteness and his strength, and fought for various lords, but when Pope Eugenius IV sent him to take Fermo on his behalf in 1434, against his enemy the Visconti of Milan, Francesco was probably already nurturing personal sympathies for the Visconti. The admiration was mutual: Duke Visconti liked him enough to give him his daughter in marriage (he had to have her first marriage annulled in order to achieve this). On the death of Visconti in 1447, Francesco struggled to consolidate the duchy (which the inhabitants in the meantime had proclaimed the Republic of Milan); he was forced to besiege the city for eight months. The hungry citizens capitulated at last on 22nd March 1450, and Francesco was proclaimed Duke Francesco I Sforza; he governed well for 16 years, founding a dynasty which ruled for more than a century.

Duomo della Madonna

From Piazza del Popolo, Via Mazzini leads steeply up to Piazzale del Girfalco (often called *Il Girone*), with its public gardens and the cathedral. A short way up, on the left at no. 8, is the opera house of Fermo: Teatro dell'Aquila of 1790 (*T: 0734 217140 and ticket office 0734 284295*), one of the largest historical theatres of the region, with more than 1,000 seats, and almost perfect acoustics.

The magnificent **Duomo della Madonna** (1227; Maestro Giorgio da Como), surrounded by cedars of Lebanon and other beautiful trees, some of which are centuries old, was built on what was once the acropolis of the Picene and the Roman cities. It was Frederick II of Hohenstaufen who commissioned the work, to make amends for the havoc wreaked by his grandfather Barbarossa in 1176. The white stone was brought from Istria by his Sicilian fleet. A Christian basilica had been erected here in the 5th century, but in the early Middle Ages the whole of the top of the hill was occupied by a citadel (destroyed by the citizens in 1446) and the basilica was replaced by a larger church in the days of Charlemagne (8th century), of which only the portal survives. Further modifications were carried out through the years, culminating in a massive restructuring completed by Cosimo Morelli in the 18th century.

The exterior
The bell-tower, partly original, is enormous, and stands out on the skyline for miles around; it occupies almost half of the façade. Notice the lovely rose window (1348), and above all the portal, surmounted by a niche with a bronze group of the *Madonna and Angels* (1758). The carvings around the door, in local stone, representing the Tree of Life with birds, animals (notice the lobster with a snake writhing in its claw), people and demons, are particularly fine. The architrave, with a series of accurately carved figures, is thought by some scholars to be an early work by Nicola Pisano. The figures could represent Christ with the twelve Apostles, or Frederick with his *magna curia*, or even with 12 poets of the Sicilian school of literature; all the figures, in fact, are holding rolls of parchment. Part of the right side of the building is original, with a Romanesque portal surmounted by a 14th-century *Pietà*; to the right of it is an inscription dated 1227 giving the name and birthplace of the constructor. The rest of the building is 18th-century, brick, with large semicircular windows and a polygonal apse. On the roof of the apse is a small marble column with a wrought-iron weather cock, replacing the original one in bronze, now in the town library after being struck by lightning in 1912.

The interior
Entering from the front, to the right of the entrance in the atrium is a beautiful funerary monument to Giovanni Visconti da Oleggio (1366), while to the left, through a Gothic arch, is the base of the bell-tower with 14th-century frescoes.

The interior is spacious and solemn, with a central nave and two side aisles, divided by pilasters, crowned by a succession of arches, vaults and false cupolas, decorated by Pio Panfili; along the sides are many statues and paintings, including a very rare 11th-century **Greek Byzantine icon** over the fourth south altar. In between the steps leading up to the presbytery can be seen the mosaic floor of the Palaeochristian basilica (5th century), discovered in 1934. The perimeter of the ancient church is shown by a strip of red marble. In the apse is a sculpture of the *Madonna* (Gioacchino Varlè, 18th century). The **Chapel of the Sacrament** in the north aisle has a canvas of the *Circumcision* by Andrea Boscoli, and a beautiful bronze tabernacle (1571), like a little Doric temple, with an elaborate support. Also in this aisle is the entrance to the sacristy. It is sometimes possible to visit the crypt, and even the **Sotterraneo** (*ask the sacristan*), where there are some interesting archaeological finds, and many traces of the preceding churches.

Around the duomo

Next to the cathedral is the splendid **Museo Diocesano** (*to request visit T: 0734 229350*), occupying an old oratory and the rooms of the confraternity, and displaying a selection of works of art from the cathedral and local churches, including silverware, ancient Missals, paintings by Crivelli, Barocci, Maratta, Pomarancio and Hayez, and priestly robes—pride of place is given to the exceptional **chasuble of St Thomas à Becket**, possibly the oldest piece of embroidery in Europe (authenticated by the University of London), worked in gold thread on silk, with medallions,

Detail of the chasuble of St Thomas à Becket.

quotations from the Koran, and an inscription in Arabic saying it was made in Almeria (Mariyya) in the year 510 of the *Hegira* (corresponding to 1116). St Thomas gave this precious robe to his old friend Presbitero, who had studied with him at Bologna University, when he was made Bishop of Fermo.

Almost in front of the bell-tower is Via del Teatro Antico, which leads down through the sparse ruins of the **Roman theatre**, probably built in the 1st century, and hence to Largo Matteotti (which borders the old Jewish quarter), the 13th-century **Torre Matteucci** belonging to a glorious family of soldiers-of-fortune, generals and governors, and the **Monte di Pietà** (14th century), with a remarkable Gothic portal; a pawn shop founded by the Church in order to fight the problem of usury.

Corso Cavour

Corso Cavour is flanked by a number of aristocratic palaces and beautiful churches. At no. 68 is Palazzo Paccarone (16th century), solid and elegant, now the seat of the Conservatory of Music. In front is the unfinished church of San Filippo (1607), with a large convent, now the Law Courts. In front of the 14th-century Palazzo Fogliani, with splendid windows, is the 12th-century church of **Santo Zenone**; the enigmatic carvings above the portal are extremely interesting, and so are the rose window and the bell-tower, both of 1222.

By taking Via Lattanzio Firmiano, to the left of the church, you will immediately see on the right the church of **San Pietro**, built by the monks of Farfa in 1251, and modified several times afterwards; the side portal is Romanesque, with carvings above it of St Peter and ten Saints.

In Largo Valentini, at the far end of Corso Cavour, is the church of **Sant'Agostino** (13th century, modified in the 14th century and in 1738), a large church with a simple façade. The stunning Latin-cross interior has a vast series of brilliant frescoes on the walls and in the chapels, dating from the 13th–15th centuries. In the north transept is the Cappella della Santa Spina, where a thorn from the crown of Christ, stolen from the town of Sant'Elpidio a Mare in 1377 and never returned, is kept in a lovely enamelled Gothic reliquary. The painting on the altar, *Crown of Thorns*, is by the Venetian artist Giovanni Trini (late 16th century). Notice the beautiful wrought-iron lamp, made in 1892. More frescoes can be seen in the Oratory of Santa Monica, next to the south transept, and reached from the square. The oratory was originally built in 1425, and dedicated to St John the Baptist; the paintings relate episodes from his life. To the left of the façade of St Augustine is the ex-convent (1772), which now houses one of the most important technical colleges in central Italy, also the first of its kind to be founded in the country (1861), the Istituto Tecnico Industriale Montani.

San Francesco and the Villa Vitali

The Franciscans, a mendicant order of friars who relied on alms for survival and who swore an oath of poverty, preferred to build their churches and convents well outside the city walls, but close enough to maintain contact with the citizens. Fermo's church of **San Francesco d'Assisi** (1240), at the far end of Via Perpenti, is a perfect example of this. The building was completed in the 15th century, but the present façade was added in the 18th century, and the portal is of 1604. The sides have long lancet windows alternating with sturdy pilasters, surmounted by blind arches; the high, polygonal apse also has lancet windows and pilasters. To the left is the 1425 bell-tower, with double-lancet windows, blind arches, and majolica decorations. The interior is divided into a central nave and two side aisles by six tall, slender brick columns which support the vault; the apse, seen from inside, is lovely. At the far end of the south aisle, a large Gothic arch gives access to the Cappella del Sacramento; on the right is a magnificent funerary monument to Lodovico Euffreducci (Andrea Sansovino; 1527), erected by his mother, Celanzia degli Oddi. On the altar is a 17th-century canvas of the *Madonna with Child and Six Saints*. Next to the chapel are some well-preserved 15th-century frescoes; in the north aisle there are some more, while the series in the apse chapel are by Giuliano da Rimini (14th century).

Beyond San Francesco, in Viale Trento, just outside the walls, is the 19th-century Villa Vitali, surrounded by wooded public gardens. The villa houses two museums, the **Museo Polare Silvio Zavatti** (*to request visit T: 0734 217140 at weekends or 0734 226166, www.museopolare.it*), unique in Italy, with numerous books, maps, native sculptures, artefacts and objects documenting the many Polar expeditions carried out by the explorer Professor Zavatti, and the **Museo di Scienze Naturali Tommaso Salvadori** (*telephone as above*), with a collection of 500 stuffed birds, some extremely rare, donated by the heirs of the 19th-century ornithologist Tommaso Salvadori Paleotti, together with interesting old photographic equipment, fossils, and the famous meteorite of Fermo, found here on 25th September 1996, and weighing over 10kg.

Capodarco

Northeast of Fermo, along the road to Lido di Fermo, is the picturesque fortress-town of **Capodarco**, in a panoramic position. In the church of Santa Maria is a polyptych by Vittore Crivelli of the *Madonna with Saints*. Nearby is the ancient Benedictine priory of **San Marco alle Paludi**, a hospital and leper colony in the Middle Ages, which, according to recent studies, could have been founded in the late 3rd–early 4th century, by the first bishop of Fermo, Alessandro.

THE COAST OF FERMO

A series of resorts along the coast, not big enough to be overwhelming, allows visitors to make the most of the beaches, some sandy, some shingle, provided with good restaurants and comfortable accommodation

Porto Sant'Elpidio and Porto San Giorgio

Nowadays **Porto Sant'Elpidio** bases its economy on the manufacture of footwear, especially ladies' shoes; there is a certain degree of prosperity, and unemployment figures are low. Tourism, however, is also important, and many visitors come for the wide gravelly beach and the cool, refreshing pinewood that runs parallel to it. In the old centre there are still many characteristic and colourful fishermen's houses, and a 14th-century clock tower, originally a watch-tower built to keep the pirates—who infested the Mediterranean—at bay. In the crypt of the modern church of Santa Maria Annunziata is a large Christmas crib, a great visitor attraction. There are several aristocratic villas in this area, one of them, the 18th-century **Villa Barrucchello** (*gardens open 9–sunset, side entrance; T: 0734 908249*), has spectacular Italian-style gardens, with many rare trees, including cedars of Lebanon and unusual palms. On the seafront are many little Art Nouveau houses with gardens, well maintained.

Continuing south along the coast, through the array of holiday camps, hotels and summer apartments forming the small communities known as Marina Faleriense, Tre Archi, Casabianca and Lido di Fermo, which only come to life in the summer, you reach **Porto San Giorgio**, site of a defensive castle in the Middle Ages, now a busy and prosperous resort, with important harbours, for fishing and for yachts. In summer an open-air antiques fair is held on Tuesdays. The long, wide beach, awarded the EU Blue Banner, is sandy, and the promenade is shaded with palm trees. Some historians believe the town was founded by Venetian fishermen in the Middle Ages; it was however mentioned by Pliny, who called it *Castellum Firmanum*. Surrounded by flower gardens is the Rocca Tiepolo, built in 1267 by the governor Lorenzo Tiepolo (who would later become Doge of Venice), when Fermo was at the height of its splendour and political importance. Near the castle, in Piazza San Giorgio, is a lovely Art Nouveau fountain, the Fontana della Democrazia (1897), with two-tailed mermaids. In front is the 18th-century church of San Giorgio, with a vast, luminous interior and a fairly good copy of a Carlo Crivelli polyptych.

Close by is the Neoclassical **Villa Bonaparte** (Ireneo Aleandri; 1826), built for Prince Jerome Bonaparte, brother of Napoleon, during his exile from France; you can glimpse the lovely gardens.

Torre di Palme and Pedaso

South of Porto San Giorgio are the little family resorts of Santa Maria a Mare and Marina Palmense, then the charming fortress-town of **Torre di Palme**. Although small (pop. 300), it is quite unspoilt, and one of the best examples of medieval towns in the region. The buildings are of stone, and there are flowers everywhere. Entering the main square, with an old fountain and marvellous views, to the left is the church of San Giovanni (10th century), with traces of 15th-century frescoes inside. Also on the left is the Palazzo Municipale (10th century), followed by the parish church of Sant'Agostino of the 12th century (*open Sat and Sun 6pm–8pm; Mon–Fri 8am for Mass*). Inside is a large polyptych by Vittore Crivelli, stolen in 1972, recuperated (minus three panels), restored in Urbino and now finally returned to the church for which it was painted.

Almost at the far end of the street, on the right, is the church of Santa Maria a Mare (12th century), a simple building of brick and stone, with a sturdy bell-tower (once a watch-tower), and a Gothic chapel next door, dedicated to St Roch. The interior has a central nave with two side aisles, and a raised presbytery preceded by three Gothic arches. The marvellous frescoes, Byzantine in style, go back to the 14th century. Next to the church, in a little garden, is a well-head once used for christenings.

From Torre di Palme, a pleasant walk leads to the protected woodland of **Cugnolo**, down through the narrow valley called Fosso di San Filippo, with beautiful glimpses of Torre. The vegetation is mainly Mediterranean maquis, with centuries-old oak trees.

Pedaso is a quiet resort close to the mouth of the River Aso, renowned for the shell-fish gathered by the local fishermen, especially mussels. Farming is also important, including peas, beans, peaches and apricots. From here the SS 483 follows the course of the Aso as far as Amandola, a lovely drive.

THE TENNA VALLEY

The River Tenna, 62km long, has its source in the Sibylline Mountains, at a height of 1178m on Monte Porche. After the spectacular gorge called Gola dell'Infernaccio, it flows northeast through a wide, pleasant and colourful valley. In prehistoric times this was an important route from the Adriatic to the Sibyllines.

Sant'Elpidio a Mare

In spite of its name (*a Mare*: on sea), the busy and prosperous town of Sant'Elpidio a Mare, probably founded in the early Middle Ages, is about 5km from the sea, on a crest between the Ete and the Tenna rivers. The flourishing economy, here as in the nearby villages, is based on the manufacture of footwear, which is exported all over the world; even Boccaccio, in the *Decameron* (written in 1350), describes the inhabitants as being masters of the art of shoemaking. Dominating the central Piazzale Guglielmo Marconi is the sturdy and uncompromising Palazzo Mannarini, which houses the **Museo della Calzatura** (*to request a visit T: 0734 8196371*), illustrating the history of footwear through the centuries (a local proverb says: *Shoes are just as important as your bed, because when you're not in one, you're in the others*). There is also an interesting collection of shoes belonging to famous people.

From here it is easy to reach the medieval town centre, still perfectly intact, and the main street, Corso Baccio. A short way along on the left is the harmonious façade of the **Teatro Cicconi** (*T: 0734 859110*) by Ireneo Aleandri, built in 1862 but unfortunately completely dismantled inside in 1952, when it was transformed into a cinema. At no. 31, in what was once a convent, is the **Pinacoteca Civica Vittore Crivelli** (*open summer 5–7, closed Mon; winter Sat and Sun 4–7; T: 0734 859279*), where you will find a famous 18-panel polyptych showing the *Coronation of the Virgin and Saints*, and a triptych of the *Visitation*, painted by Vittore Crivelli.

In the main square, Piazza Matteotti, is the **Torre Gerosolimitana** (14th century), a watch-tower 28m high, built by the Knights of Jerusalem. In the lunette over the door is a 9th-century carving of *Christus Triumphans*, brought here from the abbey of Santa Croce al Chienti (*see below*). In the 17th century the tower was provided with a clock, and later with bells. It is possible to climb up inside (*ask at the Tourist Office for keys*), quite an experience, but definitely not recommended for the claustrophobic.

To the left of the tower is the church of the **Collegiata** (14th century, rebuilt in 1639). The interior has a central nave and two side aisles separated by pilasters. On the high altar is an 18th-century panel painting of the *Madonna with Patron Saints*; behind the altar is a very fine **Roman sarcophagus** (4th century) made of Greek marble, with a complex carving of a lion hunt. In the north transept is a canvas by Palma Giovane of the *Crucifixion with Saints*, while in the south transept is a large altar to the Madonna with statues (1702). Over the first north altar is an 18th-century wooden Crucifix. The painting of *Our Lady of Carmel* is by Pomarancio, and the 17th-century organ was rebuilt by Callido in 1765.

Right of the Collegiata is the basilica of **Maria della Misericordia** (16th century), with a single nave decorated with stuccoes, lovely frescoes by Andrea Boscoli (1603), and an impressive canvas by Andrea Lilli (1602) showing the *Embarking of St Martha*, reminiscent of Caravaggio. The two 18th-century organs have an extremely fine sound; concerts are given here in the summer. That on the right is by Nacchini of Venice, and the one on the left by his follower, Callido. Notice the 16th-century carved oak door of this church, still in perfect condition. On the other side of the square is the attractive classical façade of the town hall (17th century; Pellegrino Tibaldi, 19th century; Ireneo Aleandri). A walk around the city walls, with the seven old gates, is interesting; the views from the west stretch from Fermo to the Sibyllines.

Basilica of Santa Croce al Chienti

Down by the Chienti, near Casette d'Ete, is the ruined Basilica Imperiale di Santa Croce, urgently in need of repair, and yet once the most richly endowed abbey in the valley. The local people are deeply concerned about this neglected treasure, and an association has been founded to drum up support (*www.associazionesantacroce.it*).

In the strategic spot where the River Ete Morto joins the Chienti and controls an important route inland from the sea, the Romans built a defensive settlement. Later, with the arrival of Benedictine monks, a small abbey was set up in the same place. It could have been Charlemagne who built the abbey, assuring the prestige of imperial support; it was however consecrated on 14th September 886, in the presence of Charlemagne's grandson, Charles III, and the bishop of Fermo. According to the many documents kept in the historical archives of Sant'Elpidio a Mare and in Rome, this abbey became one of the wealthiest and the most powerful of the region, and enjoyed the protection of emperors and popes. The year 1291 was a turning point for Santa Croce. After a long period of struggles among the religious orders, the last abbot, Filippo, was excommunicated for refusing to collaborate with the Cistercians, and fled from the monastery. The abbey lands reverted to the bishop of Fermo. In 1790 Bishop Andrea Minnucci transformed the abbey with the monastery buildings, a small city in its own right, into a farm, almost completely destroying what had been one of the most admirable religious foundations along the Chienti. Now only the battered abbey survives, clinging defiantly to the last shreds of its dignity, humiliated by the old cow sheds and chicken houses, the weeds and the brambles, and the ugly mesh fence which surround it.

WESTWARDS UP THE VALLEY

Montegranaro and environs

A small, panoramic town west of Sant'Elpidio a Mare, **Montegranaro**, of ancient origin and with a strong economy based on the production of high quality footwear (600 manufacturers, 6,000 employees, 70% of the production is exported), has an exceptional series of 13th- and 14th-century frescoes, in the crypt of Sant'Ugo next to the church of Santi Filippo e Giacomo, in Via Sant'Ugo. It is thought that the crypt was once a Roman temple to Ceres. Nearby Monte Urano also concentrates on footwear; the industries there produce 150,000 pairs a day. Torre San Patrizio and Rapagnano are shoe towns too; so is Magliano del Tenna, which has the highest pro-capita income of the provinces of Fermo and Ascoli Piceno. There are more luxury cars registered here than anywhere else in Italy.

Closer to the River Ete Morto is **Monte San Pietrangeli**, once a castle of Fermo; traces of the fortifications can still be seen. On the main street, Via Roma, is the old 19th-century opera house (now a cinema, Sala Europa), which incorporates a Romanesque tower with Gothic decorations. On the summit of the hill is the collegiate church of San Pietro (or San Lorenzo) of 1798 by Giuseppe Valadier, an imposing building with Neoclassical columns in the front, and a beautiful interior, decorated by Luigi Fontana. On the opposite side of the little town, in Piazzale Leopardi, is the Baroque church of San Francesco d'Assisi, with a spacious interior and one nave. Behind the main altar is a 15th-century polyptych by an unknown local artist, showing the *Madonna with the Child and Saints.*

Montegiorgio

Montegiorgio, founded by the Farfa monks in the 11th century, was frequently engaged in wars with Fermo. The town trades butcher's meat from the local farmers, much of which is sent to Rome, and there are small industries producing metal trimmings for shoes, belts and handbags, kitchen equipment, and wire for the electrical appliance manufacturers of Fabriano. Local craftsmen are particularly skilled in making carved and gilded picture frames. The attractive town, built of hazelnut-coloured brick, is triangular, with three gates. Entering through Porta Santa Maria, and taking Via Passari and then Corso Italia, you reach the central Piazza Matteotti, from which steps lead up on

The skilful hands of master shoemaker Basilio Testella of Montegranaro, at work on a pair of boots.

the right to Piazza Ungheria, like a terrace. Here are the remains of the 14th-century church of Sant'Agostino, consisting of a richly decorated marble portal.

Piazzale XX Settembre is dominated by the large Romanesque church of **San Francesco d'Assisi** (*may be closed for earthquake repair*), with an elegant 14th-century portal. The church goes back to the 11th century, when it formed the nucleus of the Benedictine community, and was dedicated to St Mary the Great. The sides and the apse have terracotta decorations. The interior, a single nave, was altered in the 19th century. At the back of the church, on the left, is the entrance to the Gothic **Cappella Farfense**, with marvellous, but fragmentary, frescoes on the walls and the vault portraying the *Legend of the Cross*, in the style of Ottaviano Nelli (c. 1450), and *Stories of the Madonna*, by another 15th-century artist. One scene shows the *Queen of Sheba riding to meet King Solomon*; it is worth the journey to Montegiorgio to see this lady alone, with her sensible straw hat and an anticipatory grin on her face, nonchalantly wading her horse through what appears to be a river in full spate. Even her dog appears unwilling to follow her. To the right of the church is the town hall, rebuilt after an earthquake; inside, you can see part of the surviving entrance hall, and the monumental staircase (1780). In the civic archives are some interesting 13th-century parchments. The panorama from the square is extraordinary, embracing Mt Conero and the sea, the Sibyllines and Gran Sasso. By taking the stairs down between the church and the town hall, you reach Via Garibaldi and then Via Cavour; following it to the right, you will see on the left the church of **Sant'Andrea**; inside, on the main altar, is a wonderful panel painting of the *Madonna feeding the Child Jesus* by Francescuccio di Cecco Ghissi, signed and dated 1373.

Massa Fermana

Monte Vidon Corrado, birthplace of Osvaldo Licini, the abstract painter; Montappone, surrounded by wheatfields; and Massa Fermana, 13km further north, are all places where making straw hats is a fine art (nowadays they also make hats of felt and cloth), and whose products are exported all over the world, including to China. The people have been working with straw here for centuries; the quality is superb. **Montappone** has a museum dedicated to the history of this activity, the Museo del Cappello in Via VIII Marzo (*to request a visit T: 0734 761140*). On the top of the hill, in the old town, is the church of Santa Maria in Castello, with a canvas by Pomarancio of the *Madonna and Child with Saints* on the main altar.

   Massa Fermana was originally the castle of the Brunforte family. Entering the old centre you will see on the left the magnificent 14th-century Porta Sant'Antonio, one of the best preserved in the region; surmounted by a tower, and with two double loggias, one on each side. Continuing up along Via Garibaldi, you will find the parish church of San Lorenzo, where on the main altar is the first painting Carlo Crivelli carried out in the Marche, a polyptych of the *Madonna enthroned with Child Jesus and Sts Francis, Sylvester, Laurence and John the Baptist*; above these, three panels of the original five, depicting *Christ in the Tomb, the Virgin Annunciate and Gabriel*, signed and dated 1468. In the chapel to the right of the presbytery, on the left-hand wall, is a panel painting by Vittore Crivelli of the *Madonna with the Child and Angels, Sts Lawrence, Francis, Rufino and Sylvester, Monks and Worshippers*, and in the sacristy, a canvas by Sebastiano Ghezzi from Comunanza of the *Madonna with Saints* (17th century). At the top of the street is Piazza Garibaldi and the town hall, seat of the Pinacoteca (*to request a visit T: 0734 760127*), with a collection of paintings by Vincenzo Pagani, Simone de Magistris, Durante Nobili, and others.

SERVIGLIANO & SOUTH OF THE TENNA

In a region with such a medieval character, it comes as quite a surprise to find a truly Baroque town like Servigliano. The old town, founded in the 11th century and now known as *Paese Vecchio*, started to collapse in 1750 because built on unsafe land. Pope Clement XIV ordered it to be rebuilt on a safer site. Finished in 1772, it was renamed *Castel Clementino* in his honour, until 1866 when it took the name of Servigliano. The architect Virginio Bracci planned a modern, quadrangular centre, with three gates, straight streets of houses, and three squares, one of which with the town hall and the mother church, the **Collegiata di San Marco**, with 18th-century paintings by the local brothers Andrea and Filippo Ricci. The town has now spread considerably beyond the original quadrangle. For Corpus Christi in June, the streets are decorated with patterns made of flower petals. Servigliano was used as a concentration camp from 1916 during the First World War for Austrian and German prisoners, then from 1940–43 for Anglo-Americans; between 1943 and 1944 hundreds of Jews were interned here, most of whom ended up at Auschwitz. After the war the camp was used for refugees; now it has been transformed into playing-fields and a venue for sports events.

Belmonte Piceno and Falerone

Belmonte Piceno was an important Picene settlement, much frequented by merchants; the 300 tombs of a nearby necropolis have yielded hundreds of objects (now mostly in the Archaeological Museum of Ancona) attesting this. It also seems that there were specialised workshops here for making objects and jewellery of amber, brought here from the Baltic. Just outside the city walls, surrounded by oaks, is the little church of **San Simone**, once known as *Santa Maria in Muris*, of which the façade is a medieval watch-tower, and parts of the walls are Roman; the church itself is thought to be Romanesque. Still further south, the 11th-century battlements of Monsampietro Morico and its twin castle of Sant'Elpidio Morico can be seen from a long distance; it is said they were built by Malugero Melo as a wedding gift for his wife, Morica, when they married in 1061.

Below Belmonte Piceno, in a point where the valley widens and wheat is grown, the Romans suffered a crushing defeat at the hands of the Picenes in 90 BC, but they got their revenge by founding on the same spot, in 31 BC, *Faleria*, or *Falerio Picenus*, a lavish city destined for the veterans of the battle of Anzio, and provided with a theatre, an amphitheatre, baths, villas, and imposing tombs. These are now protected as an **Archaeological Park** (*open April–June and Oct Sat, Sun and holidays 10–12 & 4–6; July and Sept Fri–Sun and holidays 10–12 & 5–7; Aug Mon–Sun 10–12 & 5–7; winter on request; T: 333 6564215*). At some point in its history the city was abandoned; in fact Falerone was moved up to its present hilltop position for security during the Middle Ages. In 1777 Pope Pius VI organized the first archaeological investigations of the old site, and the theatre was brought to light, together with countless works of art, which went to the Vatican Galleries and many other museums (a fine statue of Venus is in the Louvre). An interesting collection of the remaining finds is displayed in Piazza Libertà, at the **Museo Archeologico Antiquarium** (*open as Archaeological Park; T: 0734 719813*).

Close by is the church of **San Fortunato** (13th–14th centuries). The single-nave interior is rather plain; however, over the third north altar is a panel painting by Vittore Crivelli (1479) of the *Madonna and Child with Two Angels*.

THE ASO VALLEY

The River Aso, 75km long, flows from its source at 950m on Mount Porche in the eastern Sibyllines, forming one of the most beautiful valleys in the region, with mountains on either side, studded with tiny castle-cities, and the river flowing through forests, vineyards, wheatfields and orchards of apricots and peaches. An ancient route from the Sibyllines to the coast, it is particularly lovely in early spring, when all the fruit trees are in blossom. After Comunanza (*see p. 197*), where there is a reservoir, the volume of the river diminishes considerably; the water is used for irrigation.

Campofilone and Massignano

From Pedaso two roads follow the Aso valley, one on either side of the river, passing through the orchards which are characteristic of this area. High up on the right is Lapedona, while on the left is **Campofilone**, renowned for its production of thread-like, rich egg noodles, called *maccheroncini di Campofilone*. The town, which is very picturesque, with three magnificent 14th-century gates, gradually formed in the Middle Ages, around a Benedictine abbey dedicated to St Bartholomew, known to be already flourishing in 1066. At first it was called *Campus Fulloni*, the place of the fuller. It is thought that there was a Roman villa or mansion here, a resting-place on the road from Cupra to Fermo, because many stones with Roman carvings were used to build the abbey; the abbey possibly continued the tradition of offering hospitality to travellers. The enormous church still dominates the town, but it was completely rebuilt in the 19th century, after earthquake damage. The interior, with a central nave and two side aisles, was frescoed by Luigi Fontana (1899). In the central Piazza Umberto is the new town hall (the old one was also destroyed by an earthquake), and the attractive façade, with a brick portico surmounted by a terrace, of the Teatro Comunale (1928). Here too, was one of the castles of Fermo, of which only a section of wall and a tower, called the *Torrione*, remains.

Massignano, a strategic fortress in the 12th century, occupies a hill where several Roman villas have been discovered. Fermo and Ascoli Piceno squabbled over it for centuries, until 1532 when the town came under the control of the pope, finding peace at last. The old centre, with its pale honey-coloured buildings, has a town hall which was once a convent. The bell-tower is now the clock tower and over the clock is a sundial. In front is the mother church, dedicated to St James (1785), with a panel painting of the *Madonna with the Child and two Angels* by Vittore Crivelli, and a parish museum next door (*to request a visit T: 0735 72112*), with paintings, crucifixes, robes and other religious articles from local churches.

Montefiore dell'Aso

Rose-coloured Montefiore dell'Aso, one of Italy's 'beautiful villages', stands on a steep crest (411m) between the valleys of the Aso and the Menocchia; its castle was contended frequently between Ascoli and Fermo, until they signed a peace treaty there in 1421. It is thought to be the site of *Mons Floris*, sacred to the cult of the goddess Flora, in pre-Roman times. The old centre still has long stretches of defensive walls, with the gates and six towers. From Belvedere de Carolis, with wonderful views from the Sibyllines to the sea, the steep Via Cavour leads to the central Piazza della Repubblica and the collegiate church of **Santa Lucia** (rebuilt 1850). Inside, there are many canvases by Luigi Fontana, and over the first north altar, a polyptych by Carlo Crivelli, consisting of six panels (in the course of the years it has lost two), thought to be among his finest works. The painting is in an unhappy position, just behind the door, so it is difficult to view properly (with the light on it is even worse); probably binoculars would be useful. It was in fact originally painted in 1474 as the altarpiece for the nearby church of St Francis of Assisi. The lower panels show St Mary Magdalene, St Peter, and St Catherine of Alexandria; above them are Sts Louis of Toulouse, Clare and James of the Marches, all painted in glowing colours on a dusky gold background.

Following the street to the left you reach the high apse, with a door of the original church, decorated with Romanesque bas-reliefs. To the left, occupying the old convent of St Francis, is the **Sala Adolfo de Carolis** (*T: 0734 938103*), a collection of more than a hundred of his works, and the **Sala Domenico Cantatore** (*telephone as above*), with paintings by this honorary citizen. The church of **San Francesco d'Assisi** (13th century) was modified in the 17th century, so the entrance is now through a portal in the polygonal apse. On entering, a door on the right leads to stairs to the upper part of the apse, with a wonderful series of 14th-century frescoes (Maestro di Offida), very well preserved. Inside the church, to the right, is the tomb of Adolfo de Carolis.

West of Montefiore

Four kilometres west of Montefiore, at a crossroads, is the church of **Santa Maria della Fede**, built in the 15th century to celebrate the peace treaty between Ascoli and Fermo, testified by the two clasped hands painted over the altar. On the south side of the Aso is the panoramic castle-town of **Carassai**, famous for its production of hams, salami, sausage, cakes and biscuits; some craftsmen still make traditional pottery, and there are several goldsmiths who make attractive jewellery. The town is in two parts: Castello Vecchio, with narrow, winding alleys, and Castello Nuovo, built in the 15th century, with defensive walls. West of the town, c. 4km, is the perfectly preserved **Rocca di Monte Varmine** (10th century, rebuilt 14th century), with photogenic sandstone walls, swallowtail crenellations, and one of the oldest firearms in existence, the *bombardella manesca* (1341). Close to the river are the ruins of the 11th-century abbey of Sant'Angelo in Piano.

NORTH OF THE ASO

On the north side of the Aso, Lapedona has a beautiful painted wooden ceiling in the church of San Niccolò. **Moresco**, one of Italy's 'beautiful villages', is a castle-township with only three streets, a population of under 1,000, and a tiny triangular square in front of the keep, with a 16th-century Gothic portico. The origins of the castle are uncertain, but the small community enjoyed considerable prosperity in the 16th century, when several churches were built (outside the walls, for lack of space), and well-known artists were commissioned to decorate them. Between 1869 and 1910, Moresco was classified as a suburb of nearby Monterubbiano, but now it is an independent municipality. The little town is dominated by its beautiful towers, the soaring, crenellated *Torre Eptagonale* (12th century), which can be climbed up inside to see the panorama, and the square clock tower (13th century). In the town hall council chamber is a well-preserved panel painting by Vincenzo Pagani of the *Madonna and Child with Saints*, while just outside the walls below the town, at the church of Santa Maria dell'Olmo, is a tabernacle, frescoed by the same artist.

Monterubbiano

Just above Moresco is Monterubbiano, a beautiful village, of ancient origin—signs of Palaeolithic and Neolithic habitation and a Picene necropolis have been found—which became a Roman city in 268 BC, and was destroyed by the Goths in the 5th century. In the Middle Ages it was rebuilt and named *Urbiano*; its strategic importance was such that in 1443 Francesco Sforza (*see p. 179*) ordered the construction of the walls, called *Mura Castellane*, a rare example of military architecture. Austere buildings of ancient russet brick flank quiet, cobbled streets; here and there strange carved stones inserted into the walls, with stars, lions, bulls and faces, set you guessing about their meaning. On the central square, Piazza Calzecchi Onesti, is the 15th-century town hall which houses the **Museo Civico e Pinacoteca** (*to request a visit T: 0734 2599890*), a small museum and art gallery, with finds from the archaeological excavations, coins, a beautiful 15th-century coffer, paintings by followers of Pietro Alemanno, and the city coat-of-arms. In front of the town hall is the elegant 16th-century Palazzo Calzecchi Onesti, with Renaissance windows on the first floor. Also in the square is the collegiate church of **Santa Maria dei Letterati**, rebuilt in the 19th century; the original floor is still visible underneath the new one. The spacious interior, with a single nave, has a painting of the *Madonna* by Vincenzo Pagani in the apse; the organ is by Callido. The carved wooden choir stalls are by the gifted craftsman Alessio Donati of Offida (1778), while in the left-hand chapel are some paintings by Lattanzio and Vincenzo Pagani; more works by these artists are in the sacristy.

Continuing along Corso Italia, you reach the church of **Sant'Agostino** (where six panels of a polyptych by Stefano da Verona can be seen on the altar), and then the church of **San Michele Arcangelo** (14th century), with an uncommon façade formed of a single, splendid Gothic arch. Notice a carved stone on the outside wall of this church; apparently a lion and an eagle on top, with the head of a bull underneath. Also on Corso Italia is the Romanesque church of Sts John the Baptist and John the Evangelist, with 14th–15th-century frescoes.

By taking Via Piave from Corso Italia, you reach the ex-church of **Santi Flaviano e Biagio**, now a carpenter's workshop (admire this clever craftsman at work; he will let you view the interior). A carved stone high on the outside wall would appear to be half of a sarcophagus, with a vivid portrayal of an animal with a many-pointed star on its side, under a cross (possibly a Templar symbol). More of these stars can be seen carved over the doorways at Montegallo, in the Sibyllines; according to local scholars, they were a conventional sign used by the knights (*see p. 161*).

THE UPPER ASO VALLEY

One of the most interesting old city gates in the region can be seen at the entrance to **Petritoli**, now a farming community, founded in the 10th century by the monastery of Farfa. The gate consists of three Gothic arches between two cylindrical towers. Passing through the gate, on the left is an old convent which incorporates the church of Sant'Andrea, with a lovely 18th-century interior, full of stuccoes and rich ornamentation. In the high part of the town is Piazza del Castello, with the isolated, 17th-century clock tower, with a square base, hexagonal middle part, and a cylindrical top. On the far side of town, in Via del Teatro, is the 19th-century opera house, Teatro dell'Iride (*T: 0734 658141*), with a striking crimson and ivory interior.

Beyond Petritoli is **Monte Giberto**, a Picene settlement that became one of the castles of Fermo, with formidable walls and four towers. The town centre, built of ivory-coloured brick, is particularly handsome. Near the entrance to the town is the sanctuary church of Santa Maria delle Grazie (1750), with a lovely façade, Baroque stuccoes in the interior, and many paintings by local artists. On the main altar is a marble statue from Pisa of the *Madonna and Child* (14th century). Continuing up the street, you find Piazza della Vittoria with the church of San Giovanni, with the belfry on top of one of the surviving defensive towers, and no fewer than three organs inside, by Callido, Morettini and Paci.

Northeast of Monte Giberto (c. 8km) is the Romanesque church of **Santa Maria Mater Domini**, sometimes called San Marco (*ask for keys nearby*), a Benedictine monastery church of the 6th–7th centuries, rebuilt in 1154, modified in the 15th century, and finally restored in 1924. The magnificent façade has two portals and a massive bell-tower, probably once a watch-tower. The sides have decorative blind arches, while the great round apse has two smaller apses, one on each side. The interior has a central nave and two side aisles, divided by pilasters and columns; there are traces of 15th-century frescoes, and in the central apse, 13th-century frescoes of *Christ the Judge* and episodes from *Genesis*.

At **Montottone** craftsmen still produce pottery, copper and wrought-iron work; at the entrance to the town is the attractive church of Madonna delle Grazie, built of old hazelnut-coloured brick. On a nearby hilltop is the church and convent of San Francesco d'Assisi, consecrated in 1360. The Romanesque portal, in white Istrian marble, is the original. The lovely interior is decorated with gilded stucco work carried out in 1763. Notice the ancient wooden beams overhead, frescoed in the 15th century with hunting scenes, and a detached fresco of *St Francis* by Pietro da Rimini (1333), the only dated work of his in the Marche, which comes from the church of San Nicolò in Jesi. On the high altar is a canvas of the *Crucifixion* by Carlo Maratta. On leaving the convent, you reach the centre of the beautiful little town, a medieval castle surrounded by walls, with a high tower, through Porta Marina.

Montalto delle Marche

Although standing on a spot used by prehistoric populations, which later became a Picene settlement, then a refugee camp founded by Ascoli in 548 for the victims of the wars between Goths and Byzantines, the harmonious, elegant centre of Montalto delle Marche is the result of the vision Pope Sixtus V had for his home town, which in 1586, with the help of the architect Pompeo Floriani, he wanted to rebuild and transform into a dream city, stopping at nothing to do so. He also wanted it to be a 'cushion' between Ascoli and Fermo, who were always at loggerheads. He did not live long enough to achieve all his aims, but he certainly made a difference to the aspect of the centre. Today Montalto is a farming community. At the entrance to the town is the fanciful bronze monument to Sixtus V (1980; Pericle Fazzini), after which is Piazza Sisto V, with the War Memorial and the Cattedrale dell'Assunta (1586, modified 19th century). The façade is imposing, with a portico and a polygonal bell-tower. The graceful interior has a central nave and two side aisles, frescoed by Luigi Fontana with scenes from the *Poem of Mary*. In front of the cathedral is the Seminary (1825), housing the Museo Sistino Vescovile (*open summer 3.30–7.30; winter on request T: 0735 594960*), an important collection of religious articles and robes, including the famous reliquary the pope donated to his city, a magnificent enamel work by a Flemish master (early 15th century), while the base and the back were made by an Italian craftsman perhaps a century later.

A BANQUET FOR THE CARDINAL

When in 1574 Monsignor Felice Peretti, who would later become Pope Sixtus V, paid a visit to the town of Montalto delle Marche, where he had lived for so long, the townsfolk decided to celebrate with a banquet, the like of which had never been seen before. According to local records, agents were sent to the coast to buy the finest fish; they also bought two calves, two sheep, three goats, two lambs, 50 pigeons, hundreds of eggs and plenty of flour for the tagliatelle, bacon and meat for the sauces, 51 pounds of sheep's milk cheese, 32 chickens, four hams, cabbages, lettuces and green vegetables; spices including cinnamon, saffron and cloves; chick peas and lentils, together with an unspecified number of barrels of wine. Now that's quite a shopping list!

To the right of the cathedral is Corso Vittorio Emanuele, which leads up through the 15th-century Porta Patrizia to the central Piazza Umberto, with a marble bust representing the architect Giuseppe Sacconi. Born here in 1854, Sacconi is best known for his enormous monument to Vittorio Emanuele II in Rome, irreverently nicknamed 'Mussolini's typewriter'. The old bishop's palace, with the clock tower, now houses the Civic Library, with many precious old volumes, and the City Archives at no. 2 Via Volta (*to request a visit T: 0736 828507*). The handsome 16th-century town hall houses the Pinacoteca Civica (*open summer 3.30–7.30; winter on request T: 0736 828015*), with some drawings by Licini, an ethnographic collection and a collection of archae-ological finds (*same opening times as above*). Walking around Montalto delle Marche in summer is particularly pleasant because of the hundreds of sweetly-scented lime trees planted along the streets. The picturesque weekly market is held on Wednesdays.

Montedinove and Montelparo

A strange little town, almost perfectly circular, with a venerable air of aloofness, Montedinove could be the ancient *Novana* mentioned by Pliny, although some histo-rians say it was founded in the 6th century by the Lombards. Now a farming com-munity, it is still surrounded by impressive, high medieval walls, and many of the old brick buildings in the centre go back to the 15th century; there are also clues here and there indicating the presence of the Knights Templar; it was one of their strongholds. Just outside the town is the sanctuary **church of St Thomas à Becket**, still an impor-tant destination for pilgrimages today. The interior, with one nave, has side altars and a decorated ceiling of the 16th century, and canvases of the same period, by unknown artists. On the last north altar is the much venerated statue of St Thomas à Becket, which is said to have miraculous properties. The saint is said to be particularly effec-tive in curing bone disorders: around the statue are several tokens, crutches and cal-lipers left as ex-votos. The narrow Via Umberto leads up into the centre, where you will see the church of **Santa Maria de Cellis**, built on top of the old Templar church of the Crucifix; outside on the left wall is a beautiful Gothic portal of the original church. Over the main altar is a splendid carved wooden Crucifix (14th century)

At **Montelparo**, the enormous ex-Augustine convent in the central Piazza Marconi has been put to good use: the upper floors have been transformed into a very comfort-able hostel, while the ground floor houses the Mostra degli Artigiani su Ruote (*open sum-mer 9–1 & 4–6; winter on request; T: 0734 780099*), a unique and varied collection of bicycles, carts, hand-carts and trolleys, used by local artisans to go from one farmhouse or village to the next: literally taking their workshops with them, they mended shoes and umbrellas, sharpened knives and scissors, fixed faulty stoves, and many other things besides. Also in the square is the town hall, which incorporates a large cylindri-cal tower, part of the 14th-century fortifications, in ivory-coloured brick. Steep, narrow streets lead to the top of the hill, and the parish church of San Michele Arcangelo (15th century), with fine portals, and a cusped bell-tower. The interior, with a single nave, is still the original structure, and both here and in the crypt are many traces of 15th-cen-tury frescoes. Montelparo was founded by the Lombard chieftain Eliasdoe in the 8th century, and its fortifications were built soon afterwards. The people in this town like to eat *polenta*, maize flour cooked slowly in water until soft and thick, then dressed with various sauces. A common dish in the north, it is less usual here.

Monteleone and Santa Vittoria

Monteleone di Fermo is a strange, triangular-shaped little castle-town, with a long narrow main square, Piazza Umberto, and the parish church of San Marone, rebuilt in the 16th century on the ancient original. The church of San Giovanni Battista has a beautiful 11th-century hexagonal bell-tower, once part of the fortifications. Just outside the town is the 11th-century church of the Misericordia (sometimes called Crocifisso), a simple Romanesque structure in stone and brick, with a large 16th-century fresco.

Santa Vittoria in Matenano was one of the most important castles of Fermo because of its dominating position, and also an important Benedictine centre; the Matenano hill was the first place of refuge of the monks of Farfa, when their convent near Rieti was destroyed by the Saracens in 898. In 934 the monks brought here the relics of the Sabine martyr St Victoria, who died during the persecution of Decius (3rd century). Soon the monastic affairs of the entire area were being run from this convent, and during the 15th century an artistic school was formed under the guidance of Fra' Marino Angeli, which had considerable influence on other artists of the time. Fra' Marino was a monk from the rich and influential Abbey of Farfa. His order called in the finest artists to decorate their churches. As he was a talented artist, he was probably given occasion to study with some of the best-known painters of his day, perhaps Jacobello del Fiore in Fermo, for example. Although he is considered an exponent of the so-called International Gothic school, his work is unique: he saw other artists' paintings, but he didn't copy them.

At the entrance to the town is Piazza della Repubblica, shaded with trees; from here Corso Matteotti leads through the 14th-century tower of the abbot Odorisio, by aristocratic palaces, to the 16th-century church of Sant'Agostino, with a bright interior formed of a single nave, with 18th-century decorations. Via Roma leads to the high part of the town, and the 18th-century collegiate church of Santa Vittoria; in the crypt is the 15th-century urn containing the bones of the saint. To the right of the church, on a little wooded hill, is the so-called *Cappellone* (*priest or sacristan has keys*), with a stunning series of 15th-century frescoes by Fra' Marino Angeli and his collaborators.

Force and Comunanza

Force is perched on a panoramic mountain, dominating the surrounding valleys. It was founded by the Farfa monks, who probably also introduced the art of working copper and iron, still practised by the inhabitants. This proud community soon declared its independence, even fighting a war with Ascoli in the 13th century to defend it; Sixtus V, however, took away the privilege. In 1804 another pope, Pius VII, sent a bishop and pronounced Force a city. Because of this, in 1849 the people gave refuge to the pope's representative, the hot-headed patriot Felice Orsini (sentenced to life imprisonment by the pope in 1834 for his activities, he had been pardoned and given an important post; in 1858 he was guillotined after throwing some bombs at Napoleon III, who was unhurt) and was besieged by brigands and Austrian troops; after allowing Orsini to escape, the town surrendered. Entering the town along Via San Francesco, you will see the church of San Francesco, rebuilt in 1882 to replace the ruined Romanesque church; the bell-tower, although modified, is the original one. The street climbs steeply between old house fronts in mellow brick, to reach the highest point in the town, Piazza Vittorio Emanuele, with the brick 18th-century town hall and lovely clock tower. Also in this square is the 16th-century priory, with arches and loggias, and the 17th-century church of San Paolo, replacing the Romanesque original, of which you can still see the apse. In the sacristy of the church are some panel paintings by Simone de Magistris.

The sizeable crossroads community of **Comunanza**, on the River Aso, was inhabited by the Romans, who built elaborate baths. Later, however, refugees from Ascoli, fleeing the barbarian invasions, arrived in the 5th century and called the place *Comunali di Ascoli*; hence the present name. In the town centre, at the church of Santa Caterina, is the local branch of the Sistine Museums of the Picene Area, the Museo di Arte Sacra (*open summer 10.30–12.30 & 5–7; winter on request; T: 0735 594960*) with religious articles, and some 17th-century canvases by Amorosi and the Ghezzi brothers, local artists. The economy is based on the production of electrical appliances, mechanical engineering, clothes, wood and copper. The artificial Lago di Gerosa, 3km from town, is a popular destination in the summer for fishing. On the banks of the lake is the ancient church of **San Giorgio all'Isola**, built in the 9th century to assist pilgrims and shepherds, on what was an extremely important route through the Sibyllines. On the original Romanesque apse you can still see some extraordinary 12th-century frescoes.

Montefalcone and Smerillo

The castle-town of **Montefalcone Appennino**, a popular summer-holiday destination, stands at 757m on the edge of a sheer cliff overlooking over the River Aso. Many fossils have been found in this rock formation. The streets are particularly attractive, because the façades of the houses, in stucco, have been decorated with various colourful designs. The town grew around the 13th-century Rocca, the castle, now in ruins; around the church of San Pietro, with a Gothic façade and a Romanesque bell-tower; and also close to the church of St Michael the Archangel, the patron saint. Palazzo Felici, in Largo Felici, houses, in a series of beautiful rooms with painted ceilings, the museums of Montefalcone: the Museo Pietro Alemanno (*to request a visit T: 0734 79136*), with an interesting historical collection; and the Museo dei Fossili (*to request a visit T: 0734 79194*), with a display of fossils found here and abroad. From Palazzo Felici a path leads along the edge of the cliff, allowing breathtaking views over the Aso valley.

A short distance from Montefalcone Appennino is **Smerillo**, a castle built to defend Santa Vittoria in Matenano. In the high part of the town is the Romanesque church of Santa Caterina. The museums are housed at no. 11 Via Nobili: the Museo di Fossili e Minerali (*to request a visit T: 0734 79423*), with local minerals and fossils, and the Pinacoteca di Arte Contemporanea e dei Bambini (*as above*), with an unusual collection of children's paintings. From Smerillo a path leads to a cleft in the sandstone cliff called the *Fessa*, a narrow passage through the rockfaces, full of fossils of the Pleiocene era. Nearby is protected woodland called the Bosco di Smerillo.

PRACTICAL INFORMATION

• **By train**: The mainline station for Fermo is at Porto San Giorgio (T: 0734 678114), bus connections every 30mins to the town centre. The main line Bologna–Ancona–Pescara connects all the localities.

• **By bus**: Autolinee STEAT, T: 800 630715, www.steat.it, runs services to and from Macerata, Civitanova Marche, Porto d'Ascoli, Porto San Giorgio, Morrovalle, Amandola, Sant'Elpidio a Mare, Naples and Rome (www.roma-marchelinee.it), and also from Fermo to the coastal towns and the Aso Valley. Autolinee Piergallini, T: 0734 59127, connects Fermo to Porto San Giorgio, Lapedona and Monterubbiano, and some towns of the Aso Valley. Autoservizi Portesi, T: 0734 962031, runs services connecting Montegiorgio with many towns along the Tenna, and also with Santa Vittoria in Matenano.

Fermo IAT, 6 Piazza del Popolo, T: 0734 228738, www.fermo.net, www.culturafermo.amhost.it; Tourist Information Bureau, Municipio, 4 Via Mazzini, T: 0734 2841. www.fermo.org
Aso Valley 19 towns and villages of the Aso Valley form an association called Valdaso, T: 0734 917016, www.associazionevaldaso.it. Among recent initiatives, a series of ancient roads and paths have been repaired and signposted, enabling ramblers, trekkers, riders and cyclists to explore the countryside with its castles and country churches, and the off-the-beaten-track villages. Another useful association is Gal Piceno Leader, 2 Piazza IV Novembre, Comunanza, T: 0736 845813, www.galpiceno.it
Comunanza Piazza IV Novembre, T: 0736 84381.
Montalto delle Marche 12 Piazza Umberto, T: 0736 828015.
Montefalcone Appennino 27 Via San Pietro, T: 0734 79111.
Montefiore dell'Aso 2 Piazza della Repubblica, T: 0734 938103, www.comune.montefioredellaso.ap.it
Montegiorgio 1 Via Roma, T: 0734 961934.
Monterubbiano Via Trento e Trieste, T: 0734 59875.
Moresco 15 Piazza Castello, T: 0734 259983, www.comunemoresco.com
Porto San Giorgio IAT, 5 Via Oberdan, T: 0734/678461; Tourist Information Bureau, Municipio, 4 Via Veneto, T: 0734 6801, www.comune.porto-san-giorgio.ap.it
Porto Sant'Elpidio IAT, Piazzale Virgilio, T: 0734 998705, summer only; Pro Loco, 17 Piazza Garibaldi, T: 0734 9081, www.comune.porto-sant-elpidio.ap.it
Sant'Elpidio a Mare Tourist Information Bureau, 35 Corso Baccio, T: 0734 810008; Municipio, 8 Piazza Matteotti, T: 0734 8196371, www.santelpidioamare.it
Santa Vittoria in Matenano Corso Matteotti 13, T: 0734 780111.
Tenna Valley A useful website for the area is www.galpiceno.it

HOTELS

Fermo
€€€ **Astoria**. In a central position, with a restaurant. 8 Viale Vittorio Veneto, T: 0734 228601, www.hotelastoriafermo.it

€€€ **Casina delle Rose**. Close to the cathedral, the hotel looks out onto the public gardens. Bright restaurant. 16 Piazzale Girfalco, T: 0734 228932.

Casabianca di Fermo
€€€€ **Royal**. Modern, comfortable, with many amenities, close to the beach. 3 Piazza Piccolomini, T: 0734 642244.

Force
€€ **La Vecchia Posta**. A charming inn with a good restaurant, right in the centre of tiny little Force. 10 Piazza Marconi, T: 0736 373255.

Montalto delle Marche
€€€ **Pinella**. Comfortable, well-run establishment, good position in the old city. 1 Via Peretti, T: 0736 829251.

Montappone
€€ **San Giorgio**. Simple little hotel, with a restaurant. 37 Borgo XX Settembre, T: 0734 760460.

Montedinove
€€ **Novano**. Comfortable, with garden and restaurant. 1 Via Del Duca, T: 0736 829159.

Montelparo
€€€ **La Ginestra**. Good place for a relaxing holiday, countryside location, pool, tennis, minigolf, open fireplace in the dining room. Contrada Costa, T: 0734 780449, www.laginestra.it

Monterubbiano
€€€ **Degli Sforza**. Charming small hotel with restaurant, in a central position. 8 Corso Italia, T: 0734 59822.

€€ **Pazzi**. ■ This small hotel has a famous restaurant; an excellent choice. 16 Via Laurenzi, T: 0734 59163.

€ **Da Checco**. An inn, with a very good restaurant. 5 Via Porta Marina, T: 0734 59170.

Montottone
€ **I Daini**. Simple inn, close to old centre, meals on request made with local organic produce. 11 Piazza Cigola, T: 0734 775466, idaini@micso.net

Pedaso
€€€€ **Relais Villa Ricci**. ■ Handsome old villa with lovely garden. 19 Via Marconi, T: 0734 917113, www.relaisvillaricci.it

€€€ **Hotel Valdaso**. Family-run establishment with a good restaurant; garage. Valdaso, T: 0734 931349.

€€€ **San Marino**. Small hotel with a good restaurant. 2 Via San Marino, T: 0734 931241.

€€ **Verde**. Open summer only; simple, with restaurant. 24 Via Matteotti, T: 0734 933250.

Petritoli
€ **Roma**. Comfortable hotel, with garden and restaurant. 10 Via Sant'Antonio, T: 0734 658146, www.albergoroma.it

Porto San Giorgio
€€€€ **David Palace**. Modern hotel with a good restaurant and garage, on the seafront. 503 Lungomare Gramsci Sud, T: 0734 676848, www.hoteldavidpalace.it

€€€€ **Il Caminetto**. Very comfortable, with a garage and private beach. 363–365 Viale Gramsci, T: 0734 675558, www.hotelcaminetto.it

€€€ **Anni Verdi**. Small, simple hotel, no restaurant; garage. 83–85 Via

Nazario Sauro, T: 0734 675176,
www.hotelcaminetto.it

€€€ **Tritone**. Comfortable place, with a restaurant, private beach and garden with pool. 36 Via San Martino, T: 0734 677104, www.hotel-tritone.it

€€€ **Victoria**. Comfortable little hotel, but no restaurant. 240 Viale della Vittoria, T: 0734 674033, www.hotelvictoria.net

€€ **La Veranda**. In a quiet, central position, with a restaurant and garage. 5 Via Martiri di Cefalonia, T: 0734 674706.

€ **Vera**. Open summer only, with a restaurant and private beach. 3 Via Donizetti, T: 0734 674811.

Porto Sant'Elpidio

€€€€ **Holiday**. A comfortable hotel with lots of amenities. Via Trieste, T: 0734 9071, www.holiday.centroturistico.it

€€€ **Hotel Pineta**. Comfortable, but no restaurant, garage. 191 Via Trieste, T: 0734 900259.

€€ **Belvedere**. Well-run establishment, with restaurant, near Villa Barrucchello. 1 Via Belvedere, T: 0734 991712.

Rapagnano

€ **Il Vecchio Mulino**. Simple inn, with wine bar and restaurant. 22 Via Tenna, T: 0734 510939.

€ **San Giovanni Battista**. Country restaurant near Rapagnano, with comfortable rooms, very friendly owners. 2 Via da Campogrande, T: 09734 510613.

Santa Vittoria in Matenano

€€€ **Farfense**. ■ Small, central hotel with garden and restaurant, in a beautifully-restored old building. 41 Corso Matteotti, T: 0734 780171, hotel.farfense@libero.it

BED & BREAKFAST

Campofilone

Dal Capo. Countryside location, very comfortable. English spoken. 3 Via Marina, T: 0734 932288, www.dalcapo.it

Montedinove

Il Fienile. Beautiful country house in panoramic position, farm produce. 1 Contrada Valle, T: 0736 828276, il.fienile@katamail.com

Montefiore dell'Aso

La Villa. In a peaceful position; a good centre for cyclists and ramblers. Summer only. 112 Via Menocchia, T: 0734 938419.

Montelparo

Casa Giulia. Medieval building. Open summer only. 14 Via Castello, T: 335 6865527.

La Golosa. Hospitality in the home of an enthusiastic young farmer; you can buy his products. 24 Via Coste, T: 0734 780030, www.lagolosacm.it

Monterubbiano

Acquaticci. In the city centre. Summer only. English and French spoken. 4 Via Annibal Caro, T: 0734 59694.

Vento di Rose. Beautiful flower garden; great for ramblers. Open Apr–Sept. 7 Via Canniccio, T: 0734 59226, ventodirose@libero.it

Torre di Palme

Villa degli Aranci. A villa close to the sea, surrounded by Mediterranean maquis vegetation. English spoken. 14 Contrada Cugnolo, T: 0734 632401.

COUNTRY HOUSE

Massignano

Chiaraluce. ■ A very good choice, the

house is close to the sea and to several little towns such as Massignano, Montefiore and Campofilone. English, Spanish and French spoken; internet point; English breakfast and delicious meals on request. Helpful owners. 34 Contrada Fonte Trufo, T: 0735 72376, www.countryhouseonline.it

FARM ACCOMMODATION

Fermo
Il Picchio. In a hillside position, apartments to rent 6km from Fermo and 4km from the beach of Porto San Giorgio. Sea views, the farm produces wine and fruit. 110 contrada Camera, T: 0734 936202.
Il Piccolo Bosco. This comfortable farm produces olive oil; wonderful food. 7 Via San Biagio, T: 0734 621752.
Levandara. 5km from Fermo, a friendly farm producing vegetables, olive oil and cattle; restaurant serving lovely food accompanied by their own wines, Rosso Piceno and Bianco Falerio. Also horse-riding available. 9 Contrada Levandara, T: 0734 59666.
Lapedona
Casa Vecchia. 10km from Lapedona, the farm produces olive oil, fruit and vegetables; comfortable old farmhouse. 11 Contrada Valdaso, T: 0734 933159, www.casavecchia.it
Il Rustico. Tidy little farm 4km from Lapedona producing wine. You will love the food. 3 Via Madonna Bruna, T: 0734 936252.
Santa Elisabetta. Beautiful, large old farmhouse, in olive groves, close to sea, 3km from Lapedona. Breakfast only served. 6 Contrada Santa Elisabetta, T: 0734 936202,

agriturismosantaelisabett@tin.it
Montefiore dell'Aso
Il Rocchetto. A well-organised farm with plenty of things to do: fishing, trekking, cookery courses on request. English, French and German spoken. 63 Via Aso, T: 0734 939129, ilrocchetto@libero.it
La Campana. Large, well-run farm producing wool, cheese, wine, oil and vegetables. Very comfortable accommodation, excellent food. 39 Contrada Menocchia, T: 0734 939012, www.lacampana.it
Monterubbiano
Agriturismo Crosta. Large farmhouse 2km from Monterubbiano; pool, bowls, and a good restaurant. Località Valdaso, T: 0734 59169, agcrosta@tin.it
Monte San Pietrangeli
Fonte Carella. Old farmhouse in a panoramic position, with a good restaurant and pool. Interesting walks in the vicinity, horse-riding and cycling. 4–6 Via Carella, T: 0734 960387, fontecarella@tin.it
Moresco
La Meridiana. Beautiful farm, good centre for cyclists and trekkers. 8 Contrada Forti, T: 0734 223881.
Ortezzano
Vecchio Gelso. Surrounded by fruit orchards, with views over the Aso, very comfortable accommodation and renowned cuisine; pool and horse-riding for children. English spoken. 11 Contrada Casali, T: 0734 779348, www.vecchiogelso.com
Santa Vittoria in Matenano
Matenano. 17th-century farmhouse in the hills, producing fruit; good spot for trekkers. 7 Via del Monastero, T: 0734 255212.

Servigliano
Cascina degli Ulivi. Delightful old farm producing wine and olive oil, excellent food, in lovely countryside. Has a pool, also birdwatching, archery. English spoken. 4 Contrada Commenda, T: 0734 710235.

RESTAURANTS

Fermo
€€ **L'Enoteca Bar e Vino**. This friendly wine bar and restaurant was an old church. Excellent salami and cheeses, including sheep's milk cheese from Cartoceto cured in walnut leaves. Rabbit or chicken, prepared in various ways, or fish; local wines. Closed Mon. 2 Via Mazzini, T: 0734 228667.
€ **Da Orsolina**. Fantastic little restaurant specialising in pasta dishes, including the famous *vincisgrassi*; in summer you eat on the veranda. Closed Sun. 5 Piazza Dante, T: 0734 225563.
Campofilone
€ **Le Cinque Ragazze**. The place to try the exquisite local *maccheroncini*. Closed Tues. Via XXV Aprile (the road to Pedaso), T: 0734 932405.
Comunanza
€€ **Da Roverino**. Exceptionally good restaurant close to the river. Closed Sun. 10 Via Ascoli, T: 0736 844242.
€ **Osteria della Posta**. Very good local dishes. 10 Località Croce di Casale, T: 0736 858113.
Lapedona
€€ **La Storiella**. Countryside restaurant serving local dishes with good wines; call first because they often organise receptions, etc. They also have beautiful rooms to rent, with sea view. Closed Tues. 53 Contrada Madonna

Manù, T: 0734 936373.
Magliano di Tenna
€ **Osteria dell'Arco**. Simple friendly tavern, serving delicious food, strictly organic, no GMOs. Open evenings only, closed Thur. Piazza Gramsci, T: 0734 631630.
Montalto delle Marche
€€ **Il Banchetto del Conte**. In the central square, well-prepared local dishes, excellent wine list. Piazza Sisto V, T: 339 4508082.
Montegiorgio
€ **Il Grottino**. Tavern for a quick plate of tasty spaghetti, or very inviting *bruschette*. 5 Via Ospedale Diotallevi, T: 0734 962447.
Montedinove
€ **Chamade**. Try the home-made *agnolotti* with ricotta and spinach, or the tripe, or grilled lamb; also pizza in the evenings. Closed Wed. 55 Via Umberto, T: 0736 829001.
Montefalcone Appennino
€€ **Da Quintilia Mercuri**. ■ A prize-winning restaurant so tiny you think you are in someone's parlour; excellent traditional dishes, booking essential. Lunches only. Closed Wed. 9 Via Corradini, T: 0734 79158.
Monterubbiano
€€ **Da Checco**. Home-made bread and pasta, robust servings made using the freshest ingredients. Closed Mon. 1 Via Porta Marina, T: 0734 59170.
Moresco
€€ **Castello**. Right in front of the old castle; famous for fish dishes. Closed Tues. 25 Via Angelini, T: 0734 59143.
Petritoli
€ **Osteria de le Cornacchie**. ■ Eating here, possibly out in the alley, is a pleasant experience; tasty food includ-

ing broad beans, tripe, snails, home-made gnocchi, marvellous polenta in winter with pork chops and sausages, good Rosso Piceno wine; booking essential. Open evenings only. Closed Tues (not in summer). 10 Via del Forno, T: 0734 658707.

Sant'Elpidio a Mare
€€ **Hostaria dei Ponti Oscuri**. Local hams and cheeses, pasta dishes, roast and grilled meat. Closed Wed. Via Ponti Oscuri, T: 0734 810014.

Pedaso
€€ **La Locanda del Faro**. Situated in what was the old prison, new management has given a touch of liveliness to traditional dishes; good value for money. Closed Wed. 3 Via Colombo, T: 0734 933174.

€€ **Perotti**. Traditional family-run restaurant serving very good fish and pasta. Shellfish from Pedaso are said to be the finest in the region. 3 Via Bramante d'Urbino, T: 0734 931887. Closed Mon.

Porto San Giorgio
€€€ **Damiani e Rossi**. Home-made salami and delicious cheeses, excellent risotto and polenta, good desserts, extensive wine list, Italian liqueurs. Closed Mon, Tues and Jan, always open in summer. 2 Via Misericordia, T: 0734 674401.

€€ **Pino & Camillo**. This is the place for fresh fish, served alone, or imaginatively with vegetables, or as soup; the wine to choose is Bianchello del Metauro DOC. Always open from Apr–Oct, winter open weekends only. 173 Lungomare Gramsci, T: 0734 678744.

€€ **Skipper's**. 429 Via Gramsci Sud, T: 0734 679005. Situated in an old boathouse, good fish dishes. Closed Wed in winter.

Porto Sant'Elpidio
€€€–€ **Il Baccaro**. New restaurant near the station, offering downstairs wine bar and snacks, rare cheeses including some cured in walnut leaves, served with honey or jam; ham and salami. Upstairs delightful restaurant, marvellous desserts, good wine cellar. Closed Wed. 41 Via San Francesco d'Assisi, T: 0734 903436.

€€ **Fante di Coppe**. Only a few dishes are offered each day, reflecting what the cook finds at the market; simplicity is the keynote. The *stoccafisso* (dried cod) is particularly good, so are the desserts, especially the *crema pasticcera*. 36 Via Mameli, T: 328 6186300. Closed Mon and Tues.

€€ **Papillon**. On the seafront. Fish is the speciality, superb seafood *antipasto*. Closed Mon. Viale Trieste, T: 0734 900203.

€€ **San Crispino**. Friendly atmosphere, good pasta dishes and fish. 31 Via Solferino, T: 0734 900219.

Torre di Palme
€€ **Il Galeone**. This tiny restaurant, once the local inn, is too small to stay open in winter—you have to eat on the terrace, with its breathtaking view. Fish dishes are good, served with local wines. Closed from Oct–Mar and Mon, always open July–Aug. 10 Via Piave, T: 0734 53631.

Servigliano
€ **Re Leone**. Simple restaurant, good pizza. 2 Via Togliatti, T: 0734 750959.

CAFÉS, PASTRY SHOPS & ICE CREAM

Fermo
Caffè Alimento. Busy, popular café; try the home-made ice cream, or their

unique cake 'torta tartaruga'. 56 Piazza del Popolo.

Porto San Giorgio
Gelateria Matilda. exceptional ice cream. 129 Viale Cavallotti.

Massignano
Bar Mai a Letto. The place to see and be seen; very friendly. Piazza Garibaldi,

Montegranaro
Pasticceria Pan di Zucchero. Local sweets and pastries. 4 Piazza Mazzini, T: 0734 893649.

Sant'Elpidio a Mare
Bar Centrale. For morning coffee or afternoon tea, with delicious cakes and biscuits. Piazza Matteotti.

FESTIVALS & EVENTS

Campofilone Feast of St Bartholomew, with a traditional night fair, 24 Aug.
Fermo Feast of the Holy Thorn, a procession takes place in the afternoon from the church of Sant'Agostino, with this precious relic stolen by the troops of Fermo from Sant'Elpidio a Mare in 1377, Good Friday. Cavalcata dell'Assunta, for this occasion more than 1,000 people dress in 15th-century costume; the Palio, which goes back to 1182, is contended by stalwarts representing ten districts or contrade; Info: Cavalcata dell'Assunta, 32 Corso Cavour, T: 0734 225924, www.cavalcatadellassunta.it, 15 Aug.
Force Exhibition of copper and wrought-iron work, July–Aug.
Falerone Drama at the Roman theatre, July–Aug. La Contesa della 'Nzegna, traditional dances and contests probably of pagan origin, in honour of St Fortunatus, including a parade of old farm carts called birocci, Aug.
Magliano di Tenna La Trebbiatura, his-

torical threshing demonstrations, 2nd Sun in July.
Massignano Sagra delle Frittelle, pancakes are fried in enormous pans, and distributed to everyone, 14 Aug.
Montalto delle Marche Notte dei Folletti e delle Streghe, the town assumes a fairy-tale atmosphere, people dress up as witches, elves, etc, 14 Aug.
Montappone Lavorazione della Paglia, celebrations in honour of straw handicrafts, and Straw Hat Festival; Info: T: 0734 760426, www.ilcappellodi-paglia.it), late July or early Aug.
Montedinove Feast of St Thomas à Becket. 1st Sun in June.
Montefiore dell'Aso Feast of St Lucy, 13 Dec.
Montegiorgio Raccantando, festival of street story-tellers and singers, 1–15 July.
Monterubbiano Armata di Pentecoste Sciò la Pica and Giostra dell'Anello, particularly evocative celebrations for the legendary arrival of the Picenes, guided by a magpie, followed by parades in Renaissance costumes and a joust; Info: Pro Loco, Via Pagani, T: 333 4999372, Whitsun. Feast of St Nicholas, 6–10 Sept.
Ortezzano Festa del Vino, a festival to celebrate the grape harvest, with folk dancing and traditional parades, mid-Sept.
Petritoli Festa delle Cove, Harvest Festival, with the canestrelle, offerings of wheat to the Madonna, and enormous haystacks artistically arranged on the beautiful oxcarts called birocci, and a barrel-organ contest, 2nd Sun in July.
Ponzano di Fermo Da Castello a Comune Libero-1570, four days of celebrations in 16th-century costumes, with

a banquet, pageant, and a barrel-rolling contest, last weekend in July.

Porto San Giorgio Feast of St George, 23 April. Festival of the Sea, fried fish for everyone, cooked in a pan 5m wide and a handle 8m long; the day ends with spectacular fireworks; Info: Municipio, T: 0734 6801, 3rd Sun in July.

Porto Sant'Elpidio Feast of St Crispin, patron saint of shoemakers, 25 Oct.

Sant'Elpidio a Mare *La Città Medioevo*, traditional games and shows, all in sumptuous 15th-century costumes; to make the setting more authentic, all cars, bicycles, road signs etc, are removed from the old centre, 3rd week in July. *Contesa del Secchio*: in the Middle Ages, the results of this competition disputed between four city districts gave the right of precedence in drawing water from the only civic well; Info: Ente Manifestazioni Storiche Contesa del Secchio, 10 Piazza Matteotti, T: 0734 858218, www.contesadelsecchio.it, 2nd Sun in Aug. Organ concerts at the church of Santa Maria della Misericordia, Aug.

Servigliano *Corpus Domini*, the streets are decorated with designs made of flower petals, June. *Torneo Cavalleresco di Castel Clementino*, with pageants and jousting, to celebrate a donation of the abbot of Farfa in 1450; Info: Ente Torneo Castel Clementino, 1 Piazza Roma, T: 0734 750583, www.torneocavalleresco.it, Aug.

LOCAL SPECIALITIES

Fermo

The industrious population of this province supplies 70% of the entire national production of footwear, and 90% of the hats. **Pasticceria Gallucci**, 93 Via Salette, the Gallucci family offer a vast assortment of prize-winning confectionery, from traditional cakes and biscuits, to many types of chocolate, nougat and desserts. In August you will find the *dolce del Palio*, a special aniseed-flavoured cake made in honour of the jousts.

Belmonte Piceno

Fontegranne, 11 Via Castellarso Ete, buy your cheese on the farm.

Campofilone

La Campofilone, 41 Via XX Settembre, sells delicious egg noodles, unique to this town. **Spinosi**, 23 Via XXV Aprile, is another dependable name for the world-famous *maccheroncini*, angels' hair noodles; they supply the Savoy Hotel and Harrod's in London, and the Petrus restaurant in Hong Kong.

Falerone

Dino Zamponi, at Viale Resistenza, for the local olive oil, from the *piantone* variety.

Massa Fermana

Try **Panetteria Cosimi**, 18 Via Roma, for crunchy bread and typical local products.

Montappone

Cappeldoc, Via VIII Marzo, has fine quality straw hats, produced here and in Massa Fermana. **Complit**, 2/b Via San Giorgio, is another straw hat manufacturer, as is **N.T.S.**, 9/a Via Spazzi.

Montedinove

Cantine Pezzoli, 30 Borgo San Tommaso, is the place for local wines.

Montegiberto

Quinto Tommasini, 3 Via La Madonna, a factory outlet for knitwear.

Montegranaro

Blue Star, 207 Via Fermana Sud, for

famous men's shoes—a factory outlet.
Chiappini, 14 Via Zoli, another factory outlet.

Monte Urano

Donna Serena, 1 Via Montegrappa, T: 0734 842393. Factory outlet for comfortable footwear for women.

Montelparo

La Golosa, 24 Via Coste, is where you can buy cheese of various kinds, prepared on the farm, including sheep's milk cheese cured in walnut leaves, which give an indescribable flavour.

Monte Vidon Combatte

Passamonti, 12 Via Leopardi, for naturally-cured salami, ham and *ciauscolo*.

Montottone

Mario Bozzi, 10 Via degli Orti, is good for local pottery.

Porto San Giorgio

Claudia e Gabriele, Piazza del Mercato, for cheese and salami.

Sant'Elpidio a Mare

Caves Shoe Factory, 21 Via Celeste, factory outlet for ladies' shoes for special occasions. **Tod's**, Via Filippo della Valle, contrada Brancadoro, is a factory outlet for top-quality footwear; clothes too. **Forneria Totò**, 1 Piazza Marconi, sells fragrant bread and biscuits, local sweets and delicious home-made chocolate. At Christmas time they make a very ancient, simple cake called *frustingo*, said to go back to the Picenes; the Romans (who loved it) called it *panis picentinus*.

CIVITANOVA MARCHE & THE LOWER CHIENTI VALLEY

The River Chienti springs near Colfiorito, in the Sibylline Mountains, entering the sea just south of Civitanova Marche, after flowing through the heart of the Picene lands. The lower valley was particularly swampy, and was reclaimed for agriculture by Benedictine farmer-monks. In the early Middle Ages, the area was inhabited by French-speaking people, of northern stock. Civitanova Marche (pop. 38,000), with long sandy beaches, fishing and yachting harbours, and important footwear industries, is an ideal base for touring in the area. It was either the ancient *Cluana*, founded by the Picenes in the 8th century BC, then refounded by the Romans, or *Novana*, mentioned by Pliny. For many years it was known simply as *Portocivitanova*, a coastal appendage of the hilltop city of Civitanova Alta close by, but now the positions are reversed and this is the more important of the two; Civitanova Alta (pop. 4,400) has even lost its town council. The busy port, with its colourful fishing boats, is particularly interesting in the early morning and the late afternoon; the Art Nouveau-style fish market is not to be missed. Along the sea front, to the south of it, there are many attractive Art Nouveau houses and gardens.

Civitanova Marche

In the centre of the town is the large Piazza XX Settembre, of which the eastern part forms the public gardens; the west side of the square is occupied by the imposing town hall. To the rear of the building, in Via Buozzi, is the modern **Teatro Rossini** (*T: 0733 812936*). Via Buozzi becomes Via Cecchetti, and a turning on the right leads to the modern-looking sanctuary church of **San Marone**, probably founded in the 11th century, but almost completely rebuilt in 1890. Of the original building, a little window can be seen on the right side, and in the interior, near the entrance wall, some fragments of capitals. Inside is the large stone which forms the sarcophagus of St Maron, who was martyred in the year 100, beheaded (his right as a Roman citizen), for having converted people to Christianity. Between the church and the railway line archaeological investigations have partially brought to light the remains of the ancient city.

The main street of Civitanova Marche is the spacious and animated Corso Umberto, lined with shops with sleek window displays (recently voted the best along the Adriatic coast). Locally-made clothes, shoes, furniture and jewellery take pride of place. In the afternoon (especially on Sunday), this is the favoured stretch for the *passeggiata*, when what appears to be the entire population comes to stroll, chat with acquaintances, see and be seen. The affection they feel for their town is almost tangible.

On the hillside between Civitanova Marche and Civitanova Alta, at Contrada Asola, is an unusual museum, the **Museo Storico del Trotto** (*open Mon–Fri 9–12 & 4–6, or request visit; T: 0733 893000*), where posters, old sulkies, photographs, trophies and other memorabilia have been lovingly collected by Captain Ermanno Mori, a lover of trotting races—he still has some beautiful horses in his stables.

Civitanova Alta

Civitanova Alta, on a hill close to the sea, was built in the Middle Ages as a place of refuge by people coming from the coast, victims of the Goths. The 15th-century walls, however, were added by citizens from Como who were living there at the time. A cypress tree grows spontaneously right on top of one of the two old gates, Porta Marina. The beautiful little **Teatro Annibal Caro>** (*T: 0733 892101*), of 1872, at no. 2 Corso Annibal Caro, is dedicated to a local man of letters.

Centre of the town is Piazza Libertà, with the churches of San Paolo, San Francesco and the ex-town hall, an elegant 16th-century palazzo with an airy portico and a double staircase, which houses the **Galleria di Arte Moderna Marco Moretti** (*open Tues–Fri 9–12.30; Sat also 4–8; T: 0733 891019*). Besides works by the local artist Moretti, the collection includes paintings by Ligabue, Manzù, Carrà, Tamburi and Morandi. A walk through the town is a pleasant experience; many of the picturesque little streets and alleys are stepped, sometimes offering views over the surrounding countryside to the coast. Particularly fine olive oil, called *olio della cilestra*, is produced by a limited number of local farms.

THE LOWER CHIENTI VALLEY

Santa Maria a piè di Chienti

About 8km from Civitanova Marche, on the SS 485 Tolentino road, at Montecosaro Scalo, is an interesting abbey church which played an important part in local history (*open 8–8; no visits during Mass*). According to legend, Santa Maria a Piè di Chienti ('at the foot of Chienti') was founded by Charlemagne to celebrate a victory over the Saracens which had taken place nearby. The church was perhaps built a century later, in the 9th century, but the first written mention of it is dated 936. Attached to the church was a small monastic community, a dependency of the important abbey of Farfa, near Rieti. The monks drained the marshy land to cultivate it. Using the water from the drainage channels and also from the Chienti, they activated watermills and filled a series of moats, which together with high dykes, protected the community from attack. When Berengarius surrendered to the Holy Roman Emperor Otto I in 964 it is thought that his son, Guido, was offered refuge here by the monks. The antipope Calixtus also came here to escape Otto, but he was captured and thrown down the well with a stone round his neck. Three days later he emerged alive, so Otto let him go. By the 11th century this monastery was one of the most important Farfa possessions, and probably a stop for pilgrims on their way to Rome, San Michele in Gargano and Jerusalem. The present church goes back to 1125. On two levels, built entirely of brick, the façade is quite plain, but the rounded lower apses jut out in the northern style, surmounted by the apse of the upper church, which was added in the 15th century. Further embellishments were added in the 16th century, when the church was at the centre of an important yearly market which attracted merchants from all central Italy and even from Dalmatia. In 1477 Pope Sixtus IV donated the church, with the monastery and its possessions, to the hospital of Camerino, which had just been built by Giulio Cesare da Varano—from that moment Santa Maria a Piè di Chienti was controlled by that powerful family.

The interior is atmospheric, with its volumes and light and arches—the windows are of alabaster. The first part of the central nave is open to the roof; halfway along it becomes a low presbytery, culminating in three chapels in the apses, while the upper church consists of another presbytery and the area reserved for the monks. The luminous frescoes, dominated by Christ in a mandorla, are dated 1447. The wooden Crucifix, which can be seen immediately on entering, in the centre, is 15th century, as are the terracotta statuettes of the Virgin Annunciate and the Angel.

The interior of Santa Maria a piè di Chienti, with its characteristic dim, yellowish light, caused by the window panes of alabaster.

Montecosaro and Morrovalle

From the church of Santa Maria a piè di Chienti the road goes up to **Montecosaro**, with three towers punctuating the skyline. The little town was a fortified castle in the Middle Ages, and had frequent boundary disputes with Civitanova. There are still traces of the 14th-century walls. Just outside the walls is the eight-sided church of San Rocco (outside the walls because it was used as a hospital during plague outbreaks). Inside, over the high altar, is a fresco by Pomarancio of the *Madonna and Child with Sts Roch and Sebastian*, two saints often invoked against contagion. In the main square is the church of the Collegiata, with a 13th-century wooden Crucifix, and the 18th-century church of Sant'Agostino. Superb *ciabuscolo* (the spelling adds a 'b' in this area) sausage is made here, also cheeses aged in caves or in *fosse*, underground pits.

On a nearby hilltop is the town of **Morrovalle**, said to have been founded by Charlemagne. The inhabitants claim theirs to be one of the loveliest villages in Italy; it has always been appreciated by artists and poets, and the centre, Piazza Libertà, is very attractive, with its 14th-century clock tower, the 18th-century town hall with portico, and the aristocratic 14th-century Palazzo Lazzarini. Fine DOC wine is produced in this area, including the white Colli Maceratesi and the red Rosso Piceno and Rosso Piceno Superiore.

CHIENTI-LA-CHAPELLE?

Do you imagine Charlemagne's fabulous palace to have been built at Aachen (Aix-la-Chapelle), in Germany? Did the emperor really dream of creating a new Rome in those northern climes? And is the gorgeous Palatine Chapel at Aachen truly the one designed by the Charlemagne himself? If you believe it to be so, you may be among the many victims of a hoax. Professor Giovanni Carnevale is a sane, erudite, extremely convincing person; a priest, and retired teacher. For many years, he has been accumulating evidence to support his theory; by now he has quite a following (including German, Italian and French historians), and a website (www.carolingi.org). His thesis is the following: Charlemagne (742–814) built his palace in the Chienti valley; his new Rome was here (Corridonia still has a church dedicated to St Peter); the Palatine Chapel was the church of San Claudio (*see below*), and this is where he was buried. Even the Imperial Throne in Aachen, used for centuries to crown kings and emperors, is probably the imperial seat from the Roman theatre of Urbisaglia. In the early Middle Ages, modern France was still known as Gaul; 'France' was along the Chienti, where everyone spoke French. The switch to Aachen was organised by Frederick Barbarossa in 1176. Charlemagne had been declared a saint, possession of his body would legitimise Barbarossa's position as Holy Roman Emperor, a position which was disputed by the French. Frederick accordingly had the body exhumed and taken to Germany, before the French could get their clutches on it to give weight to their own imperial claims. All traces of the Chienti 'Rome', 'Aquisgrana', 'Palatine Chapel', etc, were deliberately erased from memory, and re-created in Germany. If you research the subject you will come upon a number of incongruities in the official Charlemagne story; for example, one of his biographers, Einhard, talks about 'frequent earthquakes' and 'abundant cultivation of melons' as being characteristic of Charlemagne's new Rome: the description fits the bill for the Chienti, certainly not for Aachen.

San Claudio al Chienti

By continuing along the old SS 485 Tolentino road, San Claudio al Chienti (*no visits during Mass*) is a turning on the right, about 18km from Civitanova Marche. Certainly an unusual and arresting church, the construction is on two levels, giving an impression of sturdiness and symmetry, quite unlike any other building in the region; architects say it could be the work of Abd Allah ibn Sulaym, who designed the uncannily similar palace of Khirbet al Mafjar, near Jericho, in 746. This was the site of Roman *Pausulae*, mentioned by Pliny and Frontinus. Seat of a bishop in the 5th century, it was totally destroyed by Goths or by Lombards a century later. The church was built on the ruins of the old city in the 8th century, but it was restructured in the 11th century, and finally restored in 1925. Two cylindrical bell-towers stand on either side of the façade, with a wide Romanesque portal. The interior is square, luminous, with four pilasters, and 15th-century frescoes in the central apse, representing St Claudius and St Roch. Two little spiral staircases in the towers, or a wide stairway outside, lead to the terrace, which gives access to the upper church, provided with an immense doorway; this second portal is particularly beautiful and well preserved.

CORRIDONIA & ENVIRONS

Immediately recognisable from a distance because of the three bell-towers which stand out on the skyline is Corridonia (pop. 12,800), overlooking the River Chienti. It has the distinction of being the only town in the world to be named after a trade unionist—local man Filippo Corridoni, who died a hero's death in the 1915 Battle of the Carso. The population chose the name Corridonia in 1931; before that, the town had been known as Mont'Olmo until 1851, when it took the name of Pausula in memory of the nearby Roman city of *Pausulae*. A particularly industrious place, with furniture and footwear manufacturers, it dates back to 1115 when its castle was built. In 1306 and 1317 it was the seat of the Parliament of the Marches. Francesco Sforza completely destroyed it in 1433, but the people rebuilt their town.

Via Cavour

Halfway along the main street, at 54 Via Cavour, is the 19th-century Neoclassical church of **Santi Pietro, Paolo e Donato**, designed by Giuseppe Valadier. The interior has a single nave and two side aisles, which curve to form a transept, surmounted by a cupola. There are two painted wooden Crucifixes, one behind the first pilaster on the right (16th century) and the other on the fourth north altar (15th century). The paintings of the cupola, the central vault and the triptych in the apse were carried out by Silvio Galimberti of Rome (1939–41). In the sacristy are 13 statuettes of Christ and the Apostles made in the 18th century. Next door is the beautiful opera house, Teatro Giovanbattista Velluti. The priest's house next door houses the important **Pinacoteca** (*phone to request visit, T: 0733 431832*) of Corridonia, with paintings of the 14th–16th centuries, including a *Madonna with Christ Child* by Carlo Crivelli, *Our Lady of Carmel* by Pomarancio, and a *Madonna of Humility*, panel painting by Andrea da Bologna, signed and dated 1372.

Continuing along Via Cavour, and turning right into Via Roma, is a house (no. 1) with 14th-century windows. Not far away, opening off Piazza del Popolo, is Piazza

Corridoni, where at no. 8 is the **Collezione Filippo Corridoni** (*open 7.30–1.30; T: 0733 433225*), with photographs, documents and other information on the life of Filippo Corridoni. The statue (1936) of Corridoni in the square was made of bronze from captured Austrian cannons. The handsome church facing onto the square is that of **San Francesco** (10th–14th centuries), with a striking slender 15th-century bell-tower decorated with brickwork and majolica. The interior was restored in the 18th century and has lavish stucco decoration. Between the first and second north altars is a local 16th-century painting of the *Redeemer in Glory and the Madonna with Saints*, while in the sacristy are some notable works by Giovanni Andrea de Magistris (16th century). By taking Via Matteotti from the piazza, Via Lanzi will be reached, where more works by this artist can be seen in the church of **Sant'Agostino**. The interior is decorated with a monochrome design of cherubs representing the *Four Seasons*.

Monte San Giusto

At 236m, Monte San Giusto enjoys a panoramic position facing the sea. The town's economy is based on its flourishing footwear industries. The historic city centre is well preserved, especially the Palazzo Municipale, which was finished in 1513. The elegant façade has a high frieze and large windows terminate at the top with a pointed arch. The little 14th-century church of **Santa Maria Telusiano** (*open 7.30–12.30 & 4.30–6.30; if closed ask in side alley for key*), in Via Tolomei, has one of Lorenzo Lotto's finest and most impressive works, a large painting of the *Crucifixion* (1529–34), over the altar, still in its magnificent original frame. One of the masterpieces of the Italian Renaissance, Lorenzo probably painted most of it in Venice, completing the work in Monte San Giusto when he added the portrait of the donor, Bishop Niccolò Bonafede, shown as a monk in the bottom left-hand corner. The dramatic scene is enacted on three distinct levels: in the foreground, the sorrow of the Mourners; in the middle, the cynical, jeering Soldiers, with the exception of Longinus, on horseback, who stretches out his arms to Jesus, as if begging forgiveness; at the top, the Crosses, against a lowering black sky. Power and movement are given to the scene by the diagonal position of the forest of lances and the outstretched arms. The dark, bearded man in the middle, at the foot of the Cross, gazing out defiantly at the onlooker, is perhaps the artist himself.

SOUTH OF THE POTENZA

Potenza Picena

North of Civitanova Marche is the busy resort of Porto Potenza Picena, with long sandy beaches, the coastal appendage of Potenza Picena, a honey-coloured town still surrounded by medieval walls, on a strategic hilltop close to the River Potenza. Built by refugees from the destroyed Roman town of *Potentia* on the coast, it was sacked by

Crucifixion by Lorenzo Lotto (1529–34).

Emperor Henry V in 1116, and rebuilt 12 years later by the bishop of Fermo, who renamed it *Montesanto*. In 1862 the people chose the name of Potenza Picena. Once famous for the production of fine quality damask and brocades of silk and wool (still made by the nuns), nowadays the economy is based on farming (wines, peas, beans) and industries producing construction materials and toys.

In the central Piazza Matteotti, with its charming fountain, is the largely rebuilt, turreted 14th-century Palazzo del Podestà, and to the right is the handsome **Municipio** (1750), which incorporates the opera house, Teatro Bruno Mugellini (*T: 0733 679260*) of 1863. In the Council Chamber (*visible on request*) is an interesting panel painting of the *Madonna with Angels and Saints*, dated 1506, still in its original frame, by an anonymous follower of the Crivelli brothers. Close to the town hall is the church of **San Tommaso**, with lavish Baroque altars and carved wooden choir stalls, next to the monastery of St Clare, founded in 1180. The imposing palaces in the square belonged (or still belong) to the wealthy and aristocratic landowners of the area, such as Mazzagalli, Carradori, Buonaccorsi and Marefoschi. Between Potenza Picena and Porto Potenza Picena is an aristocratic villa with beautiful 18th-century Italian-style gardens and lovely views, **Villa Buonaccorsi** (*open summer 9–1 & 3–7, gardens only; T: 0733 688189*). To reach the villa from Porto Potenza Picena, follow the signs for Monte Canepino. The writer Georgina Masson described it as 'one of the most fascinating and least known of all Italian gardens'.

The beautiful gardens of the Villa Buonaccorsi.

Montelupone

Further inland, 10km from the sea, is Montelupone, an attractive little town of medieval aspect, surrounded by impressive 15th-century walls complete with towers. It is one of Italy's 'beautiful villages'. Archaeologists have found traces here of a Picene settlement of the 6th century BC. Later, some important Roman families built villas on the hill, and later still it became an important Lombard stronghold. The castle on the summit was built in the 12th century. In the central square, Piazza del Comune, is the lovely 14th-century **Palazzo del Podestà**, with an impressively high clock tower. On the first floor of the palazzo is the Pinacoteca Civica, with an archaeological collection, frescoes and paintings, especially by local artists. Also in the square is the **Palazzo Comunale**, with the lovely little opera house, Teatro Nicola degli Angeli (*T: 0733 226421; www.nicoladegliangeli.it*) by Ireneo Aleandri (1894), with 192 seats. It is named after a local 16th-century poet. The same building houses a small collection of tools and apparatus used by craftsmen and artisans, arranged in replicas of the workshops.

Almost opposite the opera house is the 18th-century church of **Santa Chiara**, with beautiful inlaid doors and a vaulted ceiling carved and painted by Gioacchino Varlè; the altarpiece is a rare canvas by Onofrio Gabrieli (1616–1705) from Messina, who had fled Sicily for his pro-French sympathies in 1674, and was making a brief stay in Ancona. By proceeding southeast from Piazza del Comune, you reach Piazzale Cairoli and the church of **San Francesco d'Assisi**, originally built in 1251. Inside are some unusual 18th-century statues in stucco by the Flemish artist Pierre Lejeune, and an 18th-century organ by Nacchini of Venice. The impressive wooden choir is 18th century. From the square, Via Roma leads to Viale Cola, and the church of the **Collegiata** (18th century), where many works of art from other churches in the area have been collected, including two 16th-century canvases by Antonio da Faenza; notice especially the lovely *Madonna of the Milk* (1525). The game of *pallone al bracciale* is still popular in this town; the arena is near Porta Ulpiana.

The Abbey of San Firmano

Just north of the town, on the banks of the River Potenza, is the ancient abbey church of San Firmano, the only remaining trace of an important Benedictine abbey founded in the 10th century, when the monks arrived here to drain and reclaim the land for farming. The church was rebuilt in the 13th century, but the portal, with an arresting portrayal of the *Crucifixion*, Byzantine style, belongs to the original building. The interior is divided into a central nave and two side aisles by a series of pilasters; the presbytery is raised, with three semicircular apses. In the sacristy is a 14th-century wooden Crucifix, while the beautiful crypt, with many columns, houses an enamelled terracotta by Ambrogio della Robbia, signed and dated 1526.

PRACTICAL INFORMATION

GETTING AROUND

• **By train**: Civitanova Marche railway station (T: 0733 812907) is on the main Bologna–Pescara line. There is also a line for Macerata, Tolentino and Fabriano.
• **By bus**: Civitanova Marche is well connected to Macerata, Camerino, Ancona, Cingoli, Jesi and Osimo with services run by CONTRAM, T: 0733 230906 and Farabollini, T: 0733 215270. A good local bus service (ATAC, T: 0733 890107) connects Civitanova Marche to Civitanova Alta, also to Fontespina, the industrial areas, and Santa Maria Apparente. There are many stops in town, for example at the railway station and Piazza XX Settembre.

INFORMATION OFFICES

Montecosaro, Montelupone, Morrovalle and Potenza Picena form part of the association STL Terre dell'Infinito (T: 0733 843569, www.terredellinfinito.it), providing information and a tourist discount card, 'Infinito Card'.
Civitanova Marche IAT, 193 Corso Umberto, T: 0733 813967; Tourist Information Bureau, Piazza XX Settembre, T: 0733 822213, www.comune.civitanova.mc.it
Corridonia 8 Piazza Corridoni, T: 0733 43225.
Montecosaro 4 Via Gatti, T: 0733 560711.
Montelupone 2 Via Alighieri, T: 0733 226419, www.comune.montelupone.mc.it

Monte San Giusto Piazza Aldo Moro, T: 0733 839006.
Morrovalle 10 Via Vittorio Emanuele, T: 0733 222913, www.morrovalle.sinp.net
Potenza Picena Tourist Information Bureau, 49 Viale Regina Margherita, T: 0733 688299.

HOTELS

Civitanova Marche
€€€€ **Chiaraluna**. ■ Delightful small modern hotel, ideal position between the beach and the city centre; no restaurant. 37 Via del Grappa, T: 0733 817451, www.hotelchiaraluna.it
€€€€ **Miramare**. Central, comfortable hotel with a good restaurant and garden. 1 Viale Matteotti, T: 0733 811511, www.miramarecivitanova.it
€€€€ **Palace**. Comfortable new hotel with garage. No restaurant. Opposite the railway station. 6 Piazza Rosselli, T: 0733 810464, www.timropa.com
€€€ **Aquamarina**. A small, comfortable family-run hotel; a good choice. 47 Viale Matteotti, T: 0733 810810, www.hotelaquamarina.it
€€ **Il Gabbiano**. On the seafront, with a famous restaurant, rooms available summer only. 256 Viale IV Novembre, T: 0733 70113.
Corridonia
€€€€ **Grassetti**. Large, comfortable hotel, with restaurant and garage. 1 Via Murri, T: 0733 292822, www.grassetti.it
€€€ **San Claudio**. ■ Charming new hotel occupying part of the bishop's palace of San Claudio al Chienti. 14 Frazione San Claudio, T: 0733 288144.
€€ **Apollo** 17. Small hotel with atten-

tive service; central position, restaurant serving vegetarian food on request. 2 Via Liguria, T: 0733 203250.

Montecosaro
€€€ **Luma**. Charming and very comfortable; excellent restaurant, tennis, and car parking. 3 Via Cavour, T: 0733 229466, www.laluma.it

Montelupone
€€€ **Hotel Moretti**. Simple structure with good restaurant, garden, and car park. 4/a Via Fermi, T: 0733 226060, hr-moretti@libero.it

Porto Potenza Picena
€€€ **Gallo**. Near the station, comfortable rooms, and a good restaurant. 14 Piazza Stazione, T: 0733 688218, ristoranteVIIcielo@virgilio.it
€€ **Lido**. Small and comfortable, with a restaurant. 131 Via Dante Alighieri, T: 0733 880142, lido.hotel@tiscali.it

BED & BREAKFAST

Civitanova Alta
Nobile Palazzo del 1789. A restored ancient palace. English spoken. 34 Via Oberdan, T: 0733 814609, mauro.giganti@tin it

Civitanova Marche
La Piazzetta. Small home of a friendly family; home-made cakes for breakfast. Very central. 26 Via Pola, T: 339 7355832, bebcerquetti@hotmail.com
La Villetta di Giò. Friendly owner, generous breakfasts. 34 Via James Cook (Fontespina), T: 0733/816144, www.lavillettadigio.com
Sammarone. An hospitable place, with a garden; bicycles available. 9 Via Guerrazzi, T: 0733 771104, www.bb-sammarone.it

FARM ACCOMMODATION

Civitanova Marche
Agriturismo Campolungo. 2km from Civitanova Marche, an old cottage transformed into mini-apartments in a panoramic position. The farm produces the famous olive oil called *la cilestra*. English spoken. Open summer only. 30 Contrada Migliarino, T: 0733 709504.

Morrovalle
Il Casale. Very comfortable; organic food, and a pool; guests can help on the farm. English and Spanish spoken. 125 Via Campomaggio, Trodica, T: 0733 865931, www.ilcasale.org

Potenza Picena
Sogno d'Estate. Comfortable apartments in a modern farmhouse, the farm produces olive oil, hams and salami, wine, 2km from the sea. 27/a Contrada San Girio, T: 0733 870099, www.sognodestate.com

COUNTRY HOUSES

Morrovalle
Villa San Nicolino. Very panoramic position. English and French spoken. 2 Via Fonte Murata, T: 0733 564653, vvicoli@tin.it, sannicolino@tin.it

Potenza Picena
Cipolla d'Oro. Old 19th-century farmhouse, very good food; pool. English spoken. 33 Contrada San Girio, T: 0733 676424.

MONASTERY ACCOMMODATION

Porto Potenza Picena
Foresteria Suore Addolorata. 11 Via Regina Margherita, T: 0733 688126; Aug only.

RESTAURANTS

Civitanova Alta

€€ **Trattoria Assunta**. ■ Try the simple, superb *insalata Assunta*. Evenings also pizzeria. Closed Wed. 4 Piazza XXV Luglio, T: 0733 892848.

Civitanova Marche

€€€ **Da Enzo**. Good reputation, especially for pasta and fish dishes. Closed Mon. 213 Corso Dalmazia, T: 0733 814877.

€€€ **Miramare**. Perfect service, refined atmosphere. Closed Sun. 1 Viale Matteotti, T: 0733 818065.

€€ **Baia Papaia**. Excellent, prize-winning fish. 28 Via Pola, T: 0733 784277, Closed Mon and 20–30 Aug.

€€ **Le Due Sorelle**. Simple dishes, made using the freshest possible ingredients. Closed Sun in winter, Sun evening in summer. 636 Via Cristoforo Colombo (Fontespina), T: 0733 70126.

€€ **Lo Monte**. Excellent fish, good value for money. Closed Mon. 36 Via Cagni (Fontespina), T: 0733 70194.

€€ **Vai Mo'**. Near the Arena Barcaccia where many ballets are presented in summer, this is one of the best places in town to eat fish, evenings also pizza. Closed Mon. 2 Via Menotti, T: 0733 816830.

€ **L'Oasi**. ■ Very good fish dishes, casual family atmosphere; in summer this is also a bathing establishment. Closed Tues. 14 Lungomare Piermanni, T: 0733 816396.

€ **Osteria della Mal'Ora**. Friendly rustic tavern, delicious food, good wine. Closed Wed. 1 Via Trieste, T: 0733 774122.

Corridonia

€€ **Da Silvia**. Charming homely restaurant serving traditional food. Closed Wed. 38 Via Crocifisso, T: 0733 292028.

Montecosaro

€€ **Osteria Moonlight**. ■ Tucked away by a bottle factory, a fantastic little trattoria serving excellent food and wine; conversation with the owner Antonio is good, too. Closed Sun lunchtime. 19 Via Piave, Montecosaro Scalo (lower city), T: 0733 564890.

Monte San Giusto

€ **C'era una volta**. ■ Simple restaurant serving pizza in the evenings, pasta, polenta or thick soup at lunchtime, carefully prepared and served; small but well-chosen wine list. Closed Sun. 66 Via Purità, T: 0733 53145.

€ **Ristorante San Filippo**. Self-service at lunchtime, pizza in the evening, tasty, simple dishes, excellent value for money (it was discovered by lorry drivers and the word has gone around). Closed Wed evening. 11 Via Chienti, Villa San Filippo, T: 0733 530471.

Morrovalle

€€ **Al Solito Posto**. Good pasta dishes and local wines. Closed Mon evening and all day Tues. 7 Via Oberdan, T: 0733 222086.

Porto Potenza Picena

€€€ **Il Pontino**. Well-prepared fish dishes, with generous use of vegetables, a lot of care is dedicated to the desserts, good choice of local wines. Closed Mon evening and all day Tues. 13 Via IV Novembre, T: 0733 688638.

€€ **Nettuno**. Inventive cook prepares interesting and tasty dishes with fish and vegetables; also bathing establishment in summer. Closed Mon. Via Sottopassaggio Stazione, T: 0733 880714.

€ **Da Giovanni**. Very good pizza. 14 Piazza Matteotti, T: 0733 671200.

CAFÉS & SANDWICH BARS

Civitanova Alta
Bar Cerolini. Old-fashioned café for people-watching and conversation. Piazza Libertà.
Civitanova Marche
Caffè Aurora. Historic café on the main square; just right for reading the morning papers. 31–32 Piazza XX Settembre.
Vecchio Caffè Maretto. Elegant, fashionable old coffee house, delicious breakfast pastries. Closed Tues. Piazza XX Settembre.
Potenza Picena
Bar del Teatro. ■ Popular for morning coffee. 27 Piazza Matteotti.

FESTIVALS & EVENTS

Civitanova Alta *Lo Vattajò*, evocation of an ancient battle, medieval costumes, parades and games, fireworks, end July.
Civitanova Marche *Civitanova Danza*, contemporary ballet; Info: www.teatridicivitanova.com, all year. Feast of St Maron, protector of seamen, 18 Aug.
Corridonia Feast of Sts Peter, Paul and Donatus, 28–29 June. *Contesa della Margutta*, evokes a moment in 15th-century history, with pageants and jousting on horseback; Info: Associazione Contesa della Margutta, 46 Via Rampa Procaccini, T: 0733 433663, www.contesadellamargutta.it, early Sept.
Montecosaro Feast of St Lawrence, 9–10 Aug. *Contesa dei Cento Ducati*, archery competitions and jousting; Info: Associazione Contesa dei Cento Ducati, 56 Località San Giacomo, T: 0733 229001, 1st weekend in Aug.
Monte San Giusto Feast of the Madonna, 8 Sept.

Morrovalle Feast of St Bartholomew, 14–24 Aug.
Potenza Picena *Festa del Grappolo d'Oro*, parades and banquets to celebrate the grape harvest, Sept.

LOCAL SPECIALITIES

Civitanova Alta
Frantoio Natali, 70 Strada del Pincio, is renowned for stone-ground olive oil, including the variety *la cilestra*.
Civitanova Marche
Busatti. 53 Viale Vittorio Veneto, for hand-woven fabrics in wool, linen, cotton and hemp. **Cioccolateria Antica Nursia**, 1 Corso Umberto, for handmade chocolates, confectionery and liqueurs. **Fornarina**, 30 Via Einaudi, is a factory outlet for famous shoes and boots in the industrial area of Santa Maria Apparente. **Montanari**, 100 Via Elena, sells freshly-baked bread, cakes and biscuits, absolutely second to none.
Montecosaro
Tre Torri, 50 Via Monte della Giustizia, for excellent local ham, salami, *ciabuscolo* and cheeses.
Monte San Giusto
Blackstone, 10 Via Martin Luther King, makes and sells these world-famous shoes.
Morrovalle
Fratelli Capinera, 16 Contrada Crocette, has fine DOC wines from the local hills. **Romagnoli Calzature**, 10–14 Via Goldoni, is a factory outlet for beautiful shoes.
Potenza Picena
La Bottega dei Damaschi, Via Umberto, for hand-woven cloth in the tradition of the nuns at the convent of the Addolorata.

LORETO, RECANATI & OSIMO

Among gentle hills once covered with mulberry orchards (planted on the orders of Pope Sixtus V, to create a silk industry for the region; the industry died out in the 20th century), are some of the most interesting towns in the Marche.

LORETO

Loreto (pop. 11,300), where the house of the Madonna arrived from Nazareth (*see opposite*), is one of the most important Roman Catholic shrines in the world, receiving many thousands of pilgrims a year. In Europe, only Lourdes attracts more, but the little Italian town can claim a much longer history, having received streams of visitors since the end of the 13th century. A long tradition of hospitality has left the town perfectly equipped with accommodation, restaurants, and shops selling religious articles and souvenirs. Loreto is twinned with the important pilgrim destinations of Altoetting in Bavaria and Czestochowa in Poland.

HISTORY OF LORETO

In the late 13th century Palestine was conquered definitively by the Muslims, and Christians were obliged to leave the country, taking with them whatever relics they could. In 1291 the house where Jesus had lived with Mary and Joseph, scene of the Annunciation, disappeared from Nazareth, and after a mysterious interval of three years, reappeared on 10th December 1294 in a clump of laurels (*laureto*—loreto) near Recanati, apparently transported there by angels. It is now believed that the house had been dismantled and shipped to Dalmatia by the Crusaders, with the help of the powerful Byzantine family of the Angeli (angels). In September 1294 Princess Ithamar Angeli married Prince Philip, son of Charles II of Naples, and the house formed part of her dowry. The acting pope, Bishop Salvus of Recanati, ordered the ship transporting the stones to land at Porto Recanati, and had the house reconstructed within his territory, as a matter of prestige (and probably because he wanted to keep a close eye on it). Recent scientific tests prove that the stones really do come from Nazareth, and correspond perfectly to the remaining part of the house which is still there, partially carved into the rock. In 1962 five crosses of red cloth, like those worn by the Crusaders, were found buried under one of the walls, and also two Byzantine coins minted at the time of Ithamar's marriage.

A church was built around the house, which through the centuries became more and more magnificent; successive popes summoned the finest artists, craftsmen and architects to work on the building, especially after 1469, when Pope Paul II granted a plenary indulgence to all those who went there on pilgrimage, and decided to give the church the characteristics of a fortress, to protect it from pirate attacks. Lodges and a hospital were provided for the pilgrims, and later an aqueduct was built, bringing water into the heart of town, and providing drinking fountains along the access roads. Pope Sixtus V took particular interest in the sanctuary of Loreto, completing the fortifications, providing a bishop, and declaring the town a city in 1586, thus raising it above Recanati. He dreamed in fact of Loreto, Recanati and Porto Recanati becoming one ideal city, called *Felix Civitas Lauretana*, extending from the hills to the sea, but he died before realising his project.

In 1797 Napoleon arrived, hoping to take the priceless works of art to Paris—but Pope Pius VI had taken most of them to Rome, hidden in wine barrels; the French soldiers requisitioned everything that was left. Besides wheat and maize, they took 94kg of gold, 17 quintals of silver, all the remaining paintings and carvings, even the Bohemian crystal wine glasses and the ancient cedarwood statue of the Madonna—the only object he returned, in 1801 (it was destroyed by fire in 1921). A gang of thieves succeeded in stealing precious artworks and votive offerings in 1974; their identity is still unknown, and the loot was never recovered.

The Santa Casa and its church

Church open April–Sept 6.30–8; Oct–Mar 6.45–7; closed for lunch 12.30–2.30 all year; T: 071 970104. Santa Casa open 10.30–1.30 & 2.30–4.30; Apr–Sept until 6.30.

The main street of Loreto is Corso Boccalini, which leads to the monumental Piazza della Madonna, dominated by the great fortress-church, and animated with countless pilgrims, and noisy jackdaws. In the centre of the square is a splendid Baroque fountain (1614), with bronze eagles, dragons and mermen riding dolphins. To the east of the piazza is the white marble façade (1571) of the **sanctuary church of the Santa Casa**, with the 76m-high bell-tower by Luigi Vanvitelli (1755) to the left. The beautiful octagonal dome of 1499 by Giuliano da Sangallo, visible from a great distance, is the third largest in Italy, with a diameter of 22m, and was completed in only nine months; the gilded copper statue of the Madonna on the top was added in 1894. Poised on the steps leading to the church is the dignified bronze monument to Sixtus V **(1)**, looking as if his chair-lift has broken down. It is worth walking all the way around the church first, to see at the rear the massive brick apses (Baccio Pontelli), complete with the passage for patrolling sentries at the top. The three bronze doors in the front were made for the 1600 Jubilee. The interior of the building is Latin-cross in form, 93m long and 60m wide, with a central nave and two ample side aisles, divided by 12 pilasters and Gothic arches, designed to accommodate large numbers of worshippers.

The Santa Casa

Under the dome is the Holy House itself **(2)**, protected by an intricately carved marble screen, one of the highest expressions of 16th-century art in Italy, designed by Bramante in 1509 and completed by the finest artists of the day. Two grooves have been worn into the floor around the screen, by pilgrims going around it on their knees. Every part of the somewhat overwhelming interior of the basilica is decorated with frescoes, carved marble, rich altars, bronze sculptures; many of the paintings over the altars have been replaced by mosaics, carried out in the Vatican studios. Surrounded by so much magnificence, the simple little house of Nazareth, with its stones blackened by centuries of candle smoke, looks very humble. On the altar inside the house is the statue of the *Madonna with the Child Jesus* (1922) a copy made to replace the Byzantine original, lost in a fire the previous year.

The sacristies

Some of the most beautiful works of art are in three of the little circular chapels in the four corners of the transept, dedicated to the Evangelists and corresponding to the four round towers of the original fortification of the church. To the southwest is the so-called **Sacristy of St Mark (3)**, frescoed by Melozzo da Forlì from 1477–80, with some splendid angels and Prophets in the vault, and on the side walls, *Jesus Entering Jerusalem*, interesting for the tidy countryside. Unfortunately Melozzo never completed his project; however, the part he did finish is a masterpiece of 15th-century art. To the southeast is the **Sacristy of St John (4)**, decorated in 1479 by Luca Signorelli, it is thought with the assistance of Perugino, with angel musicians in the vault, and on

SANCTUARY CHURCH
OF THE SANTA CASA

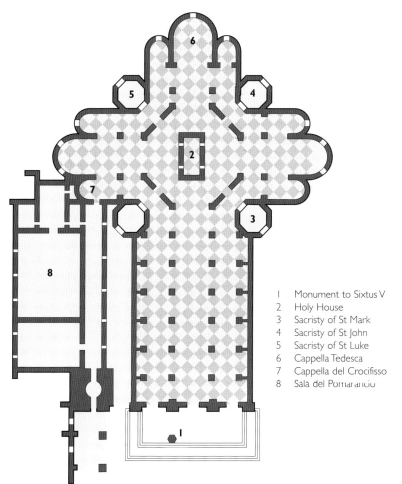

1 Monument to Sixtus V
2 Holy House
3 Sacristy of St Mark
4 Sacristy of St John
5 Sacristy of St Luke
6 Cappella Tedesca
7 Cappella del Crocifisso
8 Sala del Pomarancio

the walls—marvellously understated and almost modern-looking—the *Conversion of Saul*, *Incredulity of St Thomas*, and ten Apostles. The northwest tower, the **Sacristy of St Luke (5)**, has a terracotta image of St Luke the Evangelist in the lunette, by Benedetto da Maiano; inside are some beautiful inlaid wooden cupboards, made in Florence in 1516 to designs by Benedetto da Maiano and Andrea Sansovino. Don't miss the central chapel in the apse, called **Cappella Tedesca (6)**: the lovely neo-

Gothic frescoes (1892–1908) were carried out by Ludovico Seitz, on the theme of the life of Mary. In the **Cappella del Crocifisso (7)** is a beautiful wooden Crucifix made by the Sicilian friar Innocenzo da Petralia, in 1637.

Sala del Pomarancio

This room (*open 7–12 & 3.30–5.30*), once the Treasury **(8)**, is reached by taking the door to the left from the north transept. It is decorated with exquisite Mannerist-style frescoes by Pomarancio (1605–10), with ten stories of the life of the Madonna, six Prophets, and six Sibyls. The Crucifix on the altar is also by Pomarancio. The wooden cupboards in this room contain votive offerings to the sanctuary.

PILGRIMS TO LORETO

Among past visitors to the Holy House have been Christopher Columbus (by proxy in 1493); Bartolomeo Colleoni, soldier-of-fortune (1475); Don John of Austria, the victor of Lepanto (1576); four Japanese aristocrats (1585), whose visit was pronounced at the time to be a triumph for the Church; Michel de Montaigne; Galileo (1618); Descartes (1619), who arrived on foot from Venice; Queen Christina of Sweden (1655); James Stuart the Old Pretender and his consort Maria Clementina (1727); Casanova; the poet Vittorio Alfieri (1768), who did not like it; Wolfgang Amadeus Mozart (1770), who did, played the organ and purchased souvenirs for his mother; Stendhal; Silvio Pellico; Mussolini; Ezra Pound; and Pope John XXIII, who for his pilgrimage in 1962 was the first pope to exit the Vatican since the Unification of Italy.

The Museo-Pinacoteca

The north and west sides of the square are taken up by the L-shaped **Palazzo Apostolico**, which was originally intended to continue to the south as well. It has a majestic portico surmounted by a loggia. Many artists were engaged in this project, from Bramante (1509) to Sangallo the Younger, Vanvitelli, and others. The palace, once used as lodgings for the monks, houses the sanctuary archives, and on the upper floor, the **Museo-Pinacoteca** (*open 9–1 & 4–7; closed Mon, 31 Mar, 1 April and 15 Aug; T: 071 977759*), consisting principally of the rich donations made to the sanctuary through the centuries, in 28 beautiful galleries. The paintings include works by Giandomenico Tiepolo, Parmigianino, Palma Giovane; part of a polyptych by Giovanni Angelo da Camerino, *St John the Baptist*, and nine works by Lorenzo Lotto, who spent the last years of his life in Loreto, poor and ill. These magnificent canvases represent his maturity, the conclusion of his search for an indefinable truth through religion. Unforgettable is the *Struggle between the Archangels Michael and Lucifer*, where the two angels divide the canvas diagonally, as if reflected in a mirror, their movement underlined by Michael's sword and Lucifer's newly-forming tail; between them the torch of knowledge, broken by pride. A recent donation, *Fame defeats Time*, again uses the mirror-image device. The influence of Giorgione is clear in the *Baptism of Christ*, with the stormy sky forming the background; in *Christ and the Adulteress*, dramatic and explicit, our attention is caught by the woman's beauty and the apparent detachment of Christ—on the right, a man in a red hat with his finger on his lips (probably a self-portrait of Lorenzo) warns us to make no comment. The *Presentation at the Temple*, almost Impressionistic, is Lotto's last work, and full of symbolic meaning; notice, for example, the human feet of the altar, an allusion to the sacrifice of Christ, while the three priests behind the altar represent the three ages of religion—the Old Testament, Judaism, and Christianity. The upper part of the painting, showing the Temple of Solomon, is in fact the interior of the Sanctuary of Loreto. The collections also include ten 17th-century Flemish tapestries, worked to designs by Raphael, of which four are usually on view. There is also a silver Crucifix by Giambologna; antique furniture, and a marvellous array of 500 ceramic vases and pharmacy jars, some of which were donated by the Duke of Urbino in the 16th century.

Other sights in Loreto

On leaving the museum, a passage leads out of the square, through the west side of the palace, to Piazza Papa Giovanni XXIII and the unfinished bronze monument to that pope (1967). From this point there are magnificent views over the countryside, from the mountains to the sea. Via Sisto V leads down to the post office and the enormous round bastion (1519) built to the orders of Pope Leo X, worried about Turkish incursions.

Southeast of the bastion is Piazza dei Galli (or Piazza Leopardi), with a portico built in the 18th century to protect pilgrims who arrived too late at night to enter the city. The Baroque fountain is enlivened by boisterous bronze cockerels (1616). In front of the fountain is Porta Romana (1590; Pompeo Floriani), and, a little further ahead, the brick town hall and the main street, Corso Boccalini. On the other (east) side of the Sanctuary of the Holy House is the public garden of Piazzale Lotto, and Porta Marina (17th century), decorated with honey bees, symbol of the Barberini family and of Pope Urban VIII. Passing through Porta Marina and crossing the road, you can see the War Cemetery on the hillside below, with 1,100 graves of Polish soldiers killed in the Second World War between Rimini and Pescara.

RECANATI

Golden-brown Recanati (pop. 20,000), built along a winding crest, with an intricate web of narrow streets, is imbued with the spirit of Giacomo Leopardi, the lonely, introvert poet who took the Italian language soaring to dizzy heights. It is a shrine for lovers of literature, crowded for much of the year with poetry lovers; but also for fans of *bel canto*, because the great tenor Beniamino Gigli was born here too.

HISTORY OF RECANATI

Mentioned for the first time in 1139 in official documents, the town's history before that date is uncertain. Often forced to defend its boundaries from the attacks of Osimo, peace came only in 1202, when an agreement was reached between the cities of the Marche, putting an end—albeit temporarily—to the struggles between Guelphs and Ghibellines. Frederick II of Hohenstaufen granted several privileges in 1229, including the construction of a harbour (Porto Recanati). Ungratefully, in 1240 Recanati took sides with Pope Gregory IX when he was squabbling with Frederick; in return the pontiff sent a bishop, proclaimed the town a city, and allowed the people to mint their own coinage. It was a moment of great prosperity; trade was carried out by Jewish merchants, and many immigrants arrived from Albania to farm the land. Changing sides yet again, Recanati became an ally of Frederick's son Manfred, and was caught up once more in the Guelph-Ghibelline disputes; the pope took away the bishop and severely punished the people in 1322, but Cardinal Albornoz returned them their city status in 1357, and Pope Gregory XII even chose Recanati as his place of retirement when he was forced to abdicate in favour of Benedict XIII in 1415.

Yet another pope, Martin V, instituted a fair, held every year from August to October, which attracted merchants from near and far, becoming even more important than that of Ancona. The main street became a huge market-place (240 stalls were registered in 1485), where locally-made pottery, woollen cloth, bone combs and shoes were exchanged for luxury goods from abroad, at special low tariffs. The ever-increasing movement of pilgrims to Loreto, and the construction of the magnificent basilica there, added enormously to the wealth of Recanati and attracted artists (like Lorenzo Lotto), craftsmen and intellectuals, until the balance of power shifted away from Recanati in favour of the burgeoning religious centre of Loreto itself. The trade fair and the port declined never to regain their ancient prestige.

Nowadays the economy is based on farming, but there are some industries of standing which produce exciting kitchen ware (Guzzini), toys and games (Clementoni), and silver tableware (Ottaviani).

Central Recanati

Centre of the town is Piazza Leopardi, animated and elegant, with the large town hall (1898), in front of which is the bronze **monument to Giacomo Leopardi** (1898). To the south is the picturesque 12th-century tower called **Torre del Borgo**, 36m high, with a clock dating back to 1562. The swallowtail battlements are typical of Ghibelline towers. On the left side is the carving by Andrea Sansovino of the coat-of-arms of Recanati, a lion rampant. You will also find the official measurements for the tradesmen, and a 17th-century bronze relief of the *Transporting of the Holy House of Loreto*.

Opposite the town hall is the **Museo Gigli** (*open 10–1 & 3–6; closed Mon; T: 071 7570410*), with a reconstruction of the tenor's dressing-room, many of his costumes, and other memorabilia relating to his long and successful career (he died in 1957); his piano is in the Aula Magna of the town hall. Next to the Gigli Museum is the church of **San Domenico** (11th–14th centuries), with a beautiful carved marble doorway (1481). Inside, over the second north altar, is a detached fresco by Lorenzo Lotto (1515), showing *St Vincent Ferrer in Glory*.

The cattedrale and the west

Going west along the main street, Corso Persiani then Via Falleroni, where signs of the old market porticoes can still be seen, you reach the **cattedrale** (14th century), dedicated to St Flavian, of which only the side and the apse are visible, due to 19th-century rebuilding which incorporated the façade into the bishop's palace. The interior has a magnificent wooden ceiling, carved, painted and gilded in 1620. From a door in the right aisle of the vestibule you reach a courtyard with the **Palazzo Vescovile** and the old papal prison (32 witches were imprisoned and tortured here by the Inquisition, before being burnt at the stake), and the impressive **Museo Diocesano** (*open 15 June–15 Sept 9.30–12 & 3.30–7; 16 Oct–14 June 9–12 & 4.30–7.30; T: 071 981022 summer and 071 982194 winter*), with a collection of magnificent paintings by Mantegna, Giacomo da Recanati, Guercino, Guglielmo da Venezia, and Sassoferrato. There are also Etruscan and Roman vases and bronzes, and a striking 12th-century wooden Crucifix.

Via Falleroni continues along to **Villa Colloredo-Mels** (12th–18th centuries), with a large park incorporating part of the old Jewish Cemetery (now a nature reserve with botanical gardens and a butterfly garden), which houses the **Pinacoteca Comunale** (*open Tues–Fri 9–12 & 3–7, Sat, Sun 9–1 & 3–8; closed Mon T: 071 7570410*), one of the most important galleries in the region, with a display of works by contemporary artists, and a precious collection of paintings by Lorenzo Lotto. These include the first commission he carried out in the Marche, the polyptych for the church of San Domenico in 1508, and perhaps his best-known work, the *Annunciation* (?1527; *pictured overleaf*), showing Mary strangely twisting her body as she turns to us for support, while God sternly marks her out as chosen, disrupting her orderly existence forever. Her startled tortoiseshell cat runs away from the Angel (who casts a shadow, and looks frightened enough himself).

At the end of Via Falleroni is the so-called **Casa del Boia** (house of the executioner) at no. 62, with a 14th-century façade.

Teatro Persiani and the east

By going east from Piazza Leopardi along Via Cavour, you will see on the right the splendid opera house, **Teatro Persiani** (1840) famous for its perfect acoustics and said to be the best of all the Italian theatres. Continuing along Via Calcagni, on the left is the imposing 18th-century Palazzo Roberti (no. 19), and further along on the right, the 13th century church of **Sant'Agostino**, with decorations in terracotta and a

fine marble doorway. The interior was redesigned in the 18th century, with a series of beautiful marble altars surmounted by paintings, including works by Pomarancio, Fanelli, and Damiani. From the cloister you can see the bell-tower, decapitated by lightning, which inspired Leopardi's *Il passero solitario* ('The Lonely Sparrow'). The convent houses the **Museo d'Arte Contemporanea** (*open Sat and Sun 4–8; T: 071 7570410*) a small collection of works by modern artists, particularly local people who emigrated in the 19th century, such as Lorenzo Gigli (a relative of Beniamino), who became famous in Argentina.

By keeping to the left of the church and then turning right in Via Roma, you reach the **church of San Vito** (11th century), rebuilt by Vanvitelli after the 1741 earthquake, using bricks of different colours to give a decorative effect. Next to the south aisle is an oratory with a canvas by Pomarancio of the *Presentation at the Temple*, where Leopardi as a boy used to read his sermons (deeply religious, he wrote sermons from childhood).

Palazzo Leopardi and the south

Via Roma continues through the old town to Via Leopardi and Piazza Sabato del Villaggio, where the poet used to live, at Palazzo Leopardi (17th century), which houses his library at **Casa Leopardi** (*open summer 9–12 & 3–6; winter 9–12 & 3–5; T: 071 7573380*), 14 Via Leopardi, consisting of 20,000 books, documents and manuscripts, and the Centro Nazionale di Studi Leopardiani (*open summer 9–12 & 4.30–7.30; winter 9–12 & 4.30–6.30; closed Sun and Sat afternoon; T: 071 7570604*), with an interesting museum describing his life and times. Born in Recanati, Leopardi (1798–1837) died in Naples during a cholera epidemic, and was probably buried in a communal grave; his tomb, recently opened, was found to contain only a shoe. The 16th-century church of Santa Maria in Montemorello, to the east, was used by the family, and Giacomo was christened there on 30th June 1798. Behind Palazzo Leopardi is the summit of Monte Tabor, now called Colle dell'Infinito after one of the poet's most famous works, *The Infinite*, written when he was only 21. Steps give access to a pleasant walk along the hill, offering beautiful views. There is an old monastery here, now used by an international organisation dedicated to poetry and culture, the Centro Mondiale della Poesia e della Cultura Giacomo Leopardi (*T: 071 980292, www.leopardi.it*).

ENVIRONS OF RECANATI

A short distance from Recanati, on a hilltop at Montarice on the way down to Porto Recanati, is the fabulous villa (*unfortunately not open to the public*) Beniamino Gigli (1890–1957) built for himself at the height of his career, in the 1920s. The architect was Florestano di Fausto, a friend of Gigli's brother, and already well known for his

The Annunciation (?1527), one of the most famous and original works of Lorenzo Lotto.

work. The superb white Art Nouveau-style house is surrounded by a large park; there are 60 rooms and 20 bathrooms, one of which is opulently Pompeian, with a pool in the middle. The furniture and all the wooden fittings were supplied by Ducrot of Palermo (the top company of the time, and widely exported), while the interior decoration was the work of Adolfo de Carolis of Montefiore dell'Aso, who was inspired by the Pre-Raphaelites. On the top of the villa is a glass tower surmounted by statues, with a winter garden. West of the villa is a large fountain with bronze mermaids, shown in the act of interrupting their song, because enchanted by the voice of Gigli.

Porto Recanati

Porto Recanati, close to the mouth of the River Potenza, was founded in the 13th century by Frederick II of Hohenstaufen as the harbour of Recanati. It is now a fishing harbour and bathing resort, renowned for its fish soup, enriched by the addition of local wild saffron. It is thought that Hannibal camped on this spot (with his surviving elephants) after his victory over the Romans at Lake Trasimene in 217 BC. The wide beach of golden sands and fine shingle (EU Blue Banner) terminates to the north in the lovely green headland of Monte Conero (*see p. 25*). Its clean and tidy streets are dominated by the imposing castle (1229), built to protect this stretch of coast from pirate attacks, and which now houses the **Pinacoteca Comunale Attilio Moroni** (*open summer only 4–7.30; T: 071 7591283*), with works by Rosso Fiorentino, Antonio Canova, Elisabetta Sirani, Salvatore Rosa and Jusepe Ribera (Lo Spagnoletto), together with an important collection of 19th-century Italian paintings. The courtyard of the castle, dedicated to the tenor Beniamino Gigli, is used in the summer as an auditorium. From the 11th-century church of Santa Maria in Potenza (now a private home), on the south bank of the Potenza, there is a signposted track (the old pilgrims' route) up to Loreto, affording a memorable walk (c. 4km). Close by are the remains of the Roman city of *Potentia* (*open July–Aug Mon and Fri only 2–8*), mentioned by Livy, where archaeological excavations are still in progress.

Montefano

As you approach Montefano, on the road west from Recanati, you see the stunning Castello Montefiore, built at the end of the 13th century by the people of Recanati to protect their territory from Osimo. Badly damaged during the Second World War, it has now been perfectly restored. The high tower (40m) of the keep is a landmark for miles around.

Montefano itself is a small, quiet farming community on a hilltop. It was the birthplace of Marcello Cervini, who as Marcellus II, reigned for 22 days in 1555, one of the shortest pontificates on record. Palazzo Carradori, an aristocratic 17th-century palace on Via della Vittoria, the main street, has been transformed into an elegant hotel. Opposite is the 19th-century Palazzo Municipale, which incorporates the delightful little opera house, Teatro Rondinella, inspired by the Fenice in Venice, but with only 150 seats. There are lovely views from the public gardens on the north side of the town.

OSIMO

Osimo (pop. 29,000), built of warm brown terracotta, is a town of noble aspect, with harmonious streets and piazzas, surrounded by a maze of steep, narrow alleys. One of the oldest and most mysterious cities of the Marche, its people are often jokingly called *senza testa*, 'the headless ones', by the other inhabitants of the region, because of the decapitated marble statues at the town hall. The city has a strong musical tradition, and every year holds an important competition for concert pianists.

HISTORY OF OSIMO

Founded in the 7th century BC by Greeks and Sicels (who had already established themselves on the coast at Ancona and Numana), on a hilltop once inhabited by the Picenes, it became an important Roman city called *Auximum*, indispensable protection for the port of Ancona, and bitterly fought over in 539 during the war against the Goths, when it was besieged for seven months before capitulating out of hunger. A long stretch of the wall erected in 175 BC is still visible, while the main street, Corso Mazzini, probably represents the Roman *cardus*, and Via Lionetta and Via Baccio Pontelli the *decumanus*. Numerous statues, inscriptions and sarcophagi have been found, indicating that Auximum was a particularly wealthy town. In 774 Charlemagne donated it to the Church. Hoping for independence, Osimo sided with Holy Roman Emperor Frederick Barbarossa in 1172 during the war with Ancona. The town became a free commune in the early 12th century; its statutes are the oldest and best preserved of the region. Osimo controlled Cingoli, Filottrano, Montefano, Appignano, Staffolo, Castelfidardo, Montecassiano and Santa Maria Nova, together with numerous castles and country estates. The 14th and 15th centuries were troubled times. Osimo was forcibly taken over by various warlords, until in 1487 it was returned to the Church. This led to a period of great prosperity, during which many beautiful churches and aristocratic palaces were built. The economy today is based on farming and textile industries.

Palazzo Municipale and San Giuseppe di Copertino

The main entrance to the city was originally through the northern gate, Porta San Giacomo, still protected by a massive tower. Via Baccio Pontelli leads to the main square, and the imposing **Palazzo Municipale**, built between the 16th and the 18th centuries; the façade was designed by Pompeo Floriani. In the atrium are 12 headless marble statues found on the site of the Roman forum, and an interesting collection of epigraphs and sculptures. Next to the town hall is the 13th-century clock tower, with Guelph battlements, and the official measurements for tradesmen, while opposite is an elegant palace, **Palazzo Balleani-Baldeschi** (16th century), said to be haunted by the ghost of a woman who had been walled in alive; the hauntings stopped when a tiny window in Via Sacramento was opened from the outside, revealing a small space with a skeleton in it, since when the window has always remained open. Next to it is a charming neo-Gothic palace, also belonging to the Balleani-Baldeschi family.

By going east through Piazza Boccolino you reach the 13th-century sanctuary church of **San Giuseppe di Copertino** (St Joseph of Cupertino), with a high, austere brick façade; the interior is Latin-cross in form with a dome, gradually transformed between the 16th and 18th centuries. Over the second north altar is a large, splendidly proportioned panel painting by Antonio Solario (1503) of the *Madonna and Christ Child with Saints*, with the donor, Captain Boccolino Guzzoni of Osimo. This same church is visible in the background, behind the throne of the Madonna. In the transept are magnificent Baroque altars surmounted by 18th-century paintings, while in the modern crypt (1962) is the body of St Joseph of Cupertino; students still come to invoke his aid when preparing for exams, and he is frequently called on for protection by American pilots. The apartment where he spent his last years is now the **Museo San Giuseppe** (*open 7–12 & 3–7; T: 071 714523*).

'I CAN FLY, I CAN FLY, I CAN FLY!'

Giuseppe Desa was not a good scholar; as a child, a painful illness kept him in bed for years, and when he recovered, he was too old to go to school. He wanted to join the Church, and was accepted as a stable-boy by the Franciscans of the convent of La Grottella, later becoming a friar, and then ordained as a priest in 1628. He had studied hard every night, and always passed his exams, in spite of his reputation as a dunce. Saying Mass, however, was no easy thing for Father Joseph; he only had to pronounce the words 'Jesus Christ' or 'Madonna', to cry out in ecstasy and levitate to the ceiling. Once, he was walking in a grove with another friar, who uttered the word 'God': Joseph spent the rest of the morning perched in an olive tree. People flocked to see the flying priest, who became a decided embarrassment to his convent. In 1636 he was sent to Naples to be tried by the Inquisition. Instead of condemning him, however, the judges were convinced of his innocence when he levitated at their mentioning St Gregory, and it was decided to send him to a remote hermitage, in the hope that the fuss would die down. Of course it didn't. Wherever Father Joseph went, he was preceded by his fame, and crowds of people travelled long distances to see him. Only when he reached—in great secrecy—the convent of St Francis at Osimo, where a hidden apartment had been prepared for him, was he left in peace, and this is where he spent the last years of his life. Besides ecstasies and levitations, Joseph could communicate with animals (wild hares would often run into church and take refuge in his cassock, when the hunt was in progress), and predict the future. He is the patron saint of students, particularly those about to take exams.

Piazza Dante and the eastern districts

From Piazza del Comune, the main street, Corso Mazzini, leads east to Piazza Marconi and the opera house, Teatro La Nuova Fenice of 1894 (*T: 071 7231797*), and Piazza Dante, where there is a renowned old school, **Collegio Campana** (*open Tues–Sat 5–7; Sun 10–12.30 & 5–8; T: 071 714694*), now used as an auditorium, which also houses the important library, with 65,000 volumes, incunabula, and works in Latin and Greek; the civic archives, including the statutes and the famous *Libro Rosso*, documents regarding the city and which date back to the 11th and 12th centuries; and the **Civica Raccolta d'Arte**, a collection of paintings by Giacinto Brandi, Andrea da Bologna, Claudio Ridolfi and Piranesi; a magnificent polyptych by Antonio and Bartolomeo Vivarini (1464) of the *Coronation of Mary* with Sts Anthony of Padua, Peter, Francis and Louis, and above, Sts Catherine of Alexandria, John the Baptist, Jerome and Clare, together with an archaeological collection of objects found locally.

Corso Mazzini becomes Via Matteotti, leading to the eastern gate, Porta San Marco, and the church of **San Marco**, with a high bell-tower, and a lovely Baroque interior. Over the first altar on the left is a fresco attributed to Arcangelo di Cola of the *Madonna with Christ Child and Sts Dominic and Peter Martyr*, while in the apse is a canvas by Guercino of the *Madonna of the Rosary with St Dominic and St Catherine*.

The duomo and the west

From Piazza del Comune, the steep Via dell'Antica Rocca leads up by the ruins of the old 15th-century castle on the right, to the beautiful white stone duomo (8th century, rebuilt 12th–14th centuries), dedicated to St Leopardo, who in the 5th century was the first bishop of Osimo. This is the highest point of the town, where a Roman temple to Aesculapius and Hygieia once stood. The cathedral faces into the courtyard of the Bishop's Palace, while the stupendous left side, on the square, has a wide stairway surmounted by a Romanesque portico, with three wide decorated arches over two richly ornamented portals. The high transept has a fragmentary rose window, decorated with carvings of animals in high relief, while the apse, which is lower than the transept, has three small lancet windows, also decorated with interesting carvings. You will need your binoculars to admire these vigorous sculptures. The spacious interior is Latin-cross in form, with a central nave and two side aisles, a raised presbytery, and a beautiful mosaic floor. The 12th-century wooden Crucifix, of which the body is covered with flesh-coloured linen, is said to be miraculous, and a procession is organised in its honour on 2nd July. Under the transept is the lovely 12th-century crypt, with 16 columns from Roman buildings, and various sarcophagi; notice that of San Leopardo (4th century), and in the centre, the tomb of Diocletian, Florence and companions (4th century), early Christian martyrs. On the front is a dramatic hunting scene, while on the lid are scenes from the Old and the New Testaments.

To the right of the cathedral, next to the Bishop's Palace, is the 12th century **Baptistery**, or church of San Giovanni (*ask at the Museo Diocesano for key*), with a lovely interior and 15th-century wooden ceiling, painted by Antonio Sarti of Jesi in 1629, while the impressive bronze font in the centre is the work of the Jacometti brothers (1627). In the cloister is the **Museo Diocesano** (*open 1 July–18 Sept 10–12 & 4–7, Aug also 9pm–11pm Wed and Fri; winter Sat 4–7, Sun 10–12 & 4–7, other days phone to request a visit T: 071 7231808*), with a collection arranged in 15 rooms, giving the complete history of Christianity in Osimo through works of art brought here from churches.

By coming down from the cathedral to the west, you reach the spectacular public gardens, laid out in 1925 on reclaimed vegetable plots. By using a map and binoculars, on a clear day you can see a very long way: from San Marino to Mt Catria, Mt San Vicino, the Sibyllines and the Adriatic, the Gran Sasso, and many towns.

The Fonte Magna

Via di Fonte Magna follows the northern walls, built in the 13th century; the big square blocks of tuff, however, are part of the Roman fortifications of the 3rd–2nd centuries BC. About halfway along is a monumental Roman fountain, the Fonte Magna.

CASTELFIDARDO

Castelfidardo (pop. 17,000), a long winding town on a crest, with a picturesque, 18th-century atmosphere, is remembered for a historic battle fought here on 18th September 1860, between Piedmont forces and the Papal States. The defeat of the pope, Pius IX, signed the passage of the Marche and Umbria to the area controlled by King Vittorio Emanuele II, a definitive step in the Unification of Italy. At the entrance to the town, on the left, a cypress-lined avenue leads to the enormous bronze **monument to the Battle of Castelfidardo** (1912; Vito Pardo), showing the Piedmont soldiers attacking, led by a six-metre General Cialdini on horseback. The monument is surrounded by a park of conifers.

Close by, in Palazzo Ciriaco Mordini in Via Mazzini, is the **Museo del Risorgimento** (*open 1 Mar–31 Dec 8–8; T: 071 7206592*), with documents and relics illustrating the battle. The local economy is based on the peaceful production of musical instruments; accordions and concertinas have been produced on an industrial scale here since the 19th century, and about 30 businesses are still active, exporting throughout the world, especially to South America. The accordion was the chosen instrument of Italians emigrating to the New World between 1895–1910, and is considered a symbol of emigration. In the central Piazza della Repubblica is the 15th-century Municipio, which houses the interesting **Museo Internazionale della Fisarmonica** (*open 10–12 & 4–6; closed Sun and holiday afternoons; T: 071 7808288*), a collection of more than 150 instruments, illustrating their evolution and manufacture through the years, since 1863 when the first one was made by Paolo Soprani (though the Chinese made them first, about 3,000 years ago).

PRACTICAL INFORMATION

GETTING THERE

• **By train**: Loreto (071 978668) and Porto Recanati- Recanati (T: 071 9799162) railway stations are on the main Milano-Bologna-Pescara line, so is Osimo (T: 071 781195), the best station for Castelfidardo; the best station for Montefano is Macerata (16km), on the Fabriano-Civitanova Marche line.
• **By bus**: from Ancona: CONERO BUS, T: 071/2802092, www.conerobus.it; from Macerata: Autolinee Farabollini, T: 0733 215270, www.farabollini.it; Autolinee Reni, T: 071 8046504, services to Marcelli and Numana (summer only), Sirolo, Camerano and Ancona; Autolinee Binni, T: 0732 629592-4, services to Ancona, Macerata, Camerino, San Severino Marche, Matelica, and Fabriano.
• **By road**: If going to Osimo, park in the large Maxiparcheggio (T: 071 7132727, open 7am–9pm, signposted), there is a lift from the parking area to the centre.

INFORMATION OFFICES

A useful website for this area is www.conero.it
Loreto, Recanati, Porto Recanati and Montefano form part of an association called STL Terre dell'Infinito (T: 0733 843569, www.terredellinfinito.it), providing information and the 'Infinito Card', which allows discounts in many museums, theatres, shops, hotels, farms, B&Bs etc.
Loreto: IAT, 3 Via Solari, T: 071 970276, iat.loreto@regione.marche.it;

Tourist Information Bureau, Municipio, Corso Boccalini, T: 071 750561, www.comune.loreto.an.it;
Pro Loco 'Felix Civitas Lauretana', 67 Corso Boccalini, T: 071 977748;
Guided tours of the Sanctuary: T: 071/970104, www.santuarioloreto.it
Osimo: Piazza Boccolino, T: 071 7249282; Municipio, 1 Piazza del Comune, T: 071 7249247, www.comune.osimo.an.it.
Porto Recanati: IAT, 111 Corso Matteotti, T: 071 9799084, www.portorecanatiturismo.it;
Tourist Information Bureau, Municipio, 230 Corso Matteotti, T: 071 759971, www.comune.porto-recanati.mc.it;
Pro Loco, Piazza Fratelli Brancondi, T: 071 7591872.
Recanati: IAT, 31 Piazza Leopardi, T: 071 981471, iat.recanati@regione.marche.it;
Tourist Information Bureau, Municipio, 26 Via Leopardi, T: 071 7587218 or 071 75871, www.comune.recanati.mc.it;
Pro Loco, T: 071 982244, www.giacomoleopardi.it.

HOTELS

Castelfidardo
€€€€ **Parco**. Smart and comfortable, central, restaurant. 2 Via Donizetti, T: 071 7821605, www.hotelparco.net
€ **La Ginestra**. Simple, friendly restaurant with rooms; central, a good choice. 5 Via Ventiquattro Maggio, T: 071 78617.
Loreto
€€€€ **Villa Tetlameya**. ■ Lovely old villa just outside town, with car park

and excellent restaurant, run by the same family since 1785. Extremely helpful owner. 187 Via Villa Costantina, T: 071 977476, www.loretoitaly.com
€€€ **La Vecchia Fattoria**. Small hotel at the foot of the hill, with good restaurant, car park. 19 Via Manzoni, T: 071 978976.
€€€ **Pellegrino e Pace**. Welcoming little hotel in the square, garage. Piazza della Madonna, T: 071 977106, www.pellegrinoepace.it
€€ **Giardinetto**. On the old bastions, 100m from the church, hotel opened in 1894; garden, car park and restaurant. 10 Corso Boccalini, T: 071 977135, www.hotelgiardinetto.it
€ **Sorelle Francescane**. Small hotel run by nuns, restaurant, good value for money. 26 Via Marconi, T: 071 970306

Montefano
€€€€ **Palazzo Carradori**. ■ Elegant rooms in a beautifully restored 17th-century palace, very exclusive, wonderful restaurant; a pleasant experience; summer courses are organised in cookery, Italian and photography. 7 Via della Vittoria, T: 0733 850498, www.palazzocarradori.it

Osimo
€€€ **La Ruota dei Pavoni**. Comfortable hotel 4km from the centre, car park, no restaurant, but there is a good one next door. 64 Via Ancona, T: 071 7109100.
€ **Bartolini**. Good value for money, garden, car park, restaurant, near centre. 25 Via Cristoforo Colombo, T: 071 717161.

Porto Recanati
€€€ **Bianchi Nicola**. Small comfortable hotel on seafront, open summer only, good restaurant. 38 Piazza

Brancondi, T: 071 9799016.
€€€ **Il Brigantino**. On the sea front between Porto Recanati and Numana, just below Loreto, renowned hotel recently refurbished, comfortable rooms and good restaurant. 10–12 Viale Scarfiotti, T: 071 976684, www.brigantinohotel.it

Recanati
€€€€ **La Cantina di Palazzo Bello**. Comfortable rooms, restaurant, in 18th-century villa. 7 Contrada Sant'Agostino, T: 071 7573333, www.palazzobello.com
€€€ **La Ginestra**. In old centre, restaurant and car park. 2 Via Calcagni, T: 071 980355.
€€ **Emilio**. Small hotel with restaurant and car park. 6 Via Belvedere, T: 071 981291.

BED & BREAKFAST

Loreto
Dimora Maghelli. Apartment in historic building, English spoken, comfortable rooms. 16 Via Brancondi, T: 071 7500366, www.amicidiloreto.it

Recanati
Palazzo dalla Casapiccola. Aristocratic palace on hillside, English French Spanish spoken, exclusive. 2 Via Piazzola Gioberti, T: 071 7574818.

FARM ACCOMMODATION

Montefano
Azienda Agricola Eredi Sinistrario. ■ Although officially at Recanati, the farm is on a crest near Montefano, offering lovely views over a vast area of the region; comfortable apartments, pool, fishing in the lake, good centre for ram-

blers and trekkers. No restaurant, but Montefano is close by. Contrada Bagnolo, Recanati, T: 0721 4770246, www.aziendagricola.com

Recanati
Il Gelso. The farm is on the crest between the Musone and Potenza rivers; organic production of cereals, pulses, fruit and medicinal herbs; donkeys and poultry are raised; the farmers are keen nature lovers. 46 Contrada Santa Croce, T: 071 987002, ilgelso.bio@libero.it

COUNTRY HOUSE

Montefano
Locanda Cantalupo. Countryside inn, excellent restaurant. 7 Via Fossa Lupara, T: 0733 850572, locandacantalupo@hotmail.com

MONASTERY ACCOMMODATION

Loreto
Casa Accoglienza Malati e Pellegrini. 1 Piazza della Madonna, T: 071 9747208 or 071 977195.
Istituto Suore Gesù Redentore. 121 Via Bramante, T: 071 970284.
Villa Pio XII. 94 Via Marconi, T: 071 976714.

ROOMS & APARTMENTS TO RENT

Recanati
Il Telaio. Lovely apartments in an old house immortalised by Leopardi, opposite his house; short-term rental available. 5 Piazza Sabato del Villaggio, T: 071 7573380, iltelaio@giacomoleopardi.it

RESTAURANTS

Loreto
€€€ Andreina. Fanciful preparations to please the eye and the palate, well cooked and served, good wine list. 14 Via Buffolareccia, T: 071 970124, closed Tues.
€€€ Zi' Nenè. ■ Romantic restaurant, local dishes well prepared and served; good wine cellar, in summer excellent value-for-money menus. 187 Via Villa Costantina, T: 071 978863 or 071 977476, closed Mon.
€€ Garibaldi. ■ Delicious, simple food, robust servings, also pizza in the evening, good fish, English-style puddings to send delightful shivers up your spine. Rather slow service. 2 Via Vanvitelli, T: 071 977690, closed Mon.
€ Antica Pizzeria del Corso. Very good pizza. 74 Corso Boccalini, T: 071 970682.

Montefano
€€€ Palazzo Carradori. Here tradition is respected, with an innovative touch, in a beautiful setting. Excellent wine list. 7 Via della Vittoria, T: 0733 850498.
€ Dolly. Homely, satisfying dishes, excellent pizza. Via Montefiore, T: 0733 852535, closed Tues.

Porto Recanati
€€€ Dario. Excellent fish dishes, attentive service and good wines, carefully superintended by the affable Dario and family. 9 Via Scossicci, closed Mon, Sun evening in winter, T: 071 976675.
€€€ Torcoletto. Chef Beatrice prepares local dishes with her personal slant; interesting desserts, extensive wine list. 47 Via Scarfiotti, T: 071 7590196, closed Mon.

€€ **Fatatis**. Try the local fish soup with saffron; a meal in itself. 2 Via Vespucci, Lido Scossicci, T: 071 9799366, closed Mon and Christmas period, open every day in summer.

€€ **L'Aragosta**. Try the ravioli with chick peas and cherry tomatoes, the amazing light-as-a-feather mixed fried fish and vegetables, the lemon sorbet with rose petals. Local wines. Car park. Viale Scarfiotti, Lido Scossicci, T: 071 976683.

€€ **L'Uomo del Brodetto**. This restaurant specialises in the local *brodetto*, fish soup with saffron, always available and really worth the journey. Drink Verdicchio from the flask, you won't need anything else. Book first, because the large dining room is often used for banquets. 15 Via Garibaldi, T: 071 759981, closed Mon.

CAFÉS, PASTRY SHOPS & ICE CREAM

Loreto
Pasticceria Picchio. Absolutely delicious cakes and pastries, also pizza, buffet lunches. 1 Via Don Rampolla (at the foot of the hill), closed Mon.
Osimo
Caffè del Corso. Excellent home-made pastries and ice cream, also wine cellar. 2 Piazza Gallo, closed Mon.
Porto Recanati
Deep Blu Caffè. Fashionable bar for morning coffee and newspapers, afternoon tea, or evening cocktails with live music. Piazza del Borgo, Parco delle Rimembranze, T: 071 7592339.
Pasticceria Adriatica. Have your breakfast where the fishermen go. Maura opens at dawn. 263 Corso Matteotti.

FESTIVALS & EVENTS

Loreto: Feast of the Madonna of Loreto, also the patron saint of airmen and astronauts, 8 Sept. *Traslazione della Santa Casa*, or *La Venuta*, thousands of pilgrims from all over Italy arrive for this celebration, dating back at least to the 15th century, of the transportation of the Holy House from Nazareth to Loreto; you will see many people reaching the church barefoot, or on their knees; bonfires are lit to light up the path for the angels who are said to have carried the house here. Even today the cinders are carefully collected, superstitious people think they are a powerful talisman against the Evil Eye; Info: IAT, 3 Via Solari, T: 071 970276; night of 9–10 Dec.

Osimo: International Ballet Festival, July. *Festa del Covo*, as an offering to the Madonna, an enormous symbolic sculpture made of ears of wheat is borne by tractor to the Sanctuary of the Madonna at Campocavallo, followed by young people in traditional costume, first Sun in Aug. *Pianisti d'Italia*, competition for concert pianists, Sept. Feast of St Joseph of Cupertino, with processions, a cycle race, concerts and fireworks, 16–18 Sept.

Porto Recanati: *Processione del Cristo Morto*, a coffin bearing the statue of the dead Christ is carried in procession by barefoot fishermen, Good Friday. *Festa del Mare*, fishermen carry the painting of the *Madonna of Succour* in a solemn procession; it is said the picture was found in a net together with the fish, 2nd Sun in July; *Festival del Cinema Muto*, dedicated to silent movies, 2nd Sun in July. *Estate in*

Musica, concerts, shows and films at the 'Beniamino Gigli' Arena, June–Aug. Feast of St John, with parades in traditional dress and competitions among the seven city districts, Aug.
Recanati: Poetry and music on the 'Colle dell'Infinito', summer evenings.

LOCAL SPECIALITIES

Castelfidardo
Dino Baffetti, 51 Via Raffaello Sanzio, makes and sells accordions and concertinas. **Beniamino Bagiolacchi**, 14 Via Garibaldi, makes belts and straps for accordions.
Loreto
Cioccolateria Antica Nursia, 17 Corso Boccalini, for hand-made chocolates, confectionery and liqueurs.
Dolciaria Loretana, Via Rampolla di Napoli, prize-winning confectionery.
Gastronomia Pasqualini, 46 Piazza Kennedy, for cheeses, salami, fresh pasta.
Montefano
Oleificio Gabrielloni, Via Montefiore, Recanati, manufacturers of high quality stone-ground olive oil.
Osimo
Pasticceria Lombardi, 141 Via Cristoforo Colombo, closed Thurs afternoon, delicious local pastries and sweets.
Porto Recanati
In autumn the bakers prepare *pane noci-ato,* by adding parmesan and pecorino cheese, walnuts, black pepper and currants to the dough before baking—delicious eaten as a snack together with a glass of wine.
Recanati
Alessandro Lorenzetti, 51 Via Giunta, makes and sells briar pipes, a family tradition.
Antica Bottega Amanuense, Via Villa Colloredo, www.malleus.it, a beautiful medieval scriptorium where the mastercraftsman Malleus, who studied with the legendary Michael Harvey, writes and illuminates by hand documents, diplomas and invitations, using paper specially made for him in Fabriano, and carves texts on stones.
Clementoni, Zona Industriale Fontenoce, open Tues, Fri, Sat 4–7.30; factory outlet of this manufacturer of toys and games, famous for jigsaw puzzles.
Guzzini Outlet, 31 Via Le Grazie, open Tues and Fri 5.30–8, Sat 4.30–8; factory outlet for elegant and practical kitchen ware.
Paolo Notturni, 8 Via dell'Ospedale, makes accordions and concertinas by hand.
Sartoria Latini, 50 Via Roma, downstairs Lucia Latini makes beautiful clothes and accessories using leather; upstairs is the domain of her father, one of the most acclaimed made-to-measure tailors in Italy.

SENIGALLIA & ENVIRONS

Senigallia (pop. 41,500) is a sprawling, overgrown town, with an elegant city centre, a long tradition of trade fairs (in 1760 the playwright Carlo Goldoni wrote a musical play called *La Fiera di Senigallia*), and 13km of fine, white, velvety sand beaches, the *spiaggia di velluto*, awarded the EU Blue Banner. Emblematic of the resort is its Art Nouveau pier, known as the *Rotonda sul Mare*.

HISTORY OF SENIGALLIA

Sena Gallica was founded in the 4th century BC by Senonic Gauls; in 289 BC it became the first Roman colony on the Adriatic. In 207 BC, on the nearby hills of Scapezzano and Montedoro, the Roman legions tackled the Carthaginians, camped on the opposite bank of the Cesano, defeating them and killing their general, Hasdrubal, near the Metauro. Destroyed by Alaric in 400, Senigallia soon rose again to become a member of the Maritime Pentapolis (*see p. 13*).

During the Middle Ages it was sometimes independent, sometimes subject to the Church; sometimes Guelph, more often Ghibelline; sometimes ally, sometimes bitter enemy, of Osimo, Fano, Jesi and Ancona. The town became known for an important fair, the *Fiera della Maddalena*, held every year in July and August, which attracted hundreds of merchants from home and abroad; the fair reached its maximum splendour in the 17th–18th centuries, when customs tariffs were abolished, and games and entertainment were organized for those who came to trade wheat, spices, timber and manufactured goods. Many important nations had consulates in the town, and a large Jewish quarter developed (some of which can still be seen; in Via Commercianti there is a synagogue).

On the death of Francesco Maria II della Rovere, last duke of Urbino, in 1631, Senigallia went to the Church; as a consequence, new trading partners appeared, including Venice. With the Unification of Italy, in 1861, Senigallia lost the right to cancel customs duties, and was unable to reverse a general decline. In 1854, however, the first bathing establishment was opened, and by 1930 tourism had become the mainstay of the economy. Today Senigallia is one of the foremost bathing resorts of the Adriatic coast.

EXPLORING SENIGALLIA

Piazza del Duca

Heart of the city is the massive, compact **Rocca Roveresca** (*open 8.30–7.30; T: 071 63258*) of 1480 (Baccio Pontelli and Luciano Laurana), in the central Piazza del Duca, close to the railway station. The castle incorporates preceding defensive structures going back to Roman times. In front of the entrance is an 11th-century square tower built of blocks of limestone, which was surrounded by the 14th-century Albornoz fort, and later by that of Sigismondo Pandolfo Malatesta. Besides functioning as a castle, the building has also been used as a training college for soldiers, a prison, a hospital and an orphanage. Nowadays it is used for exhibitions and cultural events.

In the square is the pink marble **Fontana delle Anatre** (1599), surrounded by four bronze lions, off-centre because the square was used for military exercises and parades. The fountain was erected by Francesco Maria II della Rovere to celebrate his draining of the nearby marshes, hence eliminating the problem of malaria. *Anatre* means 'ducks'; the local people, however, call it *la Fontana delle Oche*—geese. To the left is the **Palazzetto Baviera** (*open 8.30–12.30 & 3.30–6; closed Sat, Sun and holidays; T: 071 6629266*), first built in the 14th century and modified a century later. Five rooms of the interior were decorated with a magnificent sequence of stuccoes by Federico Brandani in 1560, illustrating episodes from the *Iliad*, *Genesis*, the history of Rome and the Labours of Hercules.

In front of the castle is the **Palazzo del Duca** of the 16th century, (Girolamo Genga), built by Guidubaldo II della Rovere as official residence for his court; his son Francesco Maria II, last of the dynasty, enlarged the building, thus spoiling its symmetry. Just north of the castle is the magnificent Neoclassical market-place, **Foro Annonario** (1831), with 30 brick Doric columns, still used in the mornings for the food market, and on Thursdays for the weekly market.

To the right of the market is the colourful, photogenic canal-port, while to the left are the **Portici Ercolani**, a long sequence of porticoes along the River Misa, designed by Cardinal Giuseppe Ercolani in 1745 for the annual trade fair. The first building along houses the **Biblioteca Antonelliana** (*open 8.30–7; Sat 8.30–12.30; closed Sun and holidays; T: 071 6629302*), a prestigious collection of books, manuscripts and prints. At the end of the portico is Corso 2 Giugno, popular for strolling and window-shopping.

Piazza Roma and district

The severe Palazzo del Governo (17th century; Muzio Oddi) stands in **Piazza Roma**, a favourite meeting-place; on the right side of the façade is a fountain with a statue of Neptune, called *il monc' in Piazza*—the mutilated man in the square—by the locals, because his arms are missing. Some authorities believe it to be the work of Giambologna, others say it is Roman. By going through the central portico of the palace, you reach the 16th-century **Palazzo Mastai** (*open 9–12 & 4–6; closed Sun and holidays; T: 071 60649*), birthplace of Giovanni Maria Mastai Ferretti, who became Pope Pius IX, the first pope to be photographed, and the last to hold temporal power, before the Papal States and then Rome were absorbed into the new Kingdom of Italy. The house is now a museum with memorabilia of the pope, in rooms still containing the original furnishings and paintings.

Close by, in Via Gherardi, is the **Chiesa della Croce**, designed by the duke's architect Muzio Oddi and consecrated in 1608. The exterior, in rose-coloured brick, is simple, elegant Renaissance style, but the sumptuous interior is Baroque, a single nave with six side altars, glittering with gilded stucco, precious marbles, paintings and statues, with a carved and painted wooden coffered ceiling, and an organ made by Callido in 1775. Over the altar is a dazzlingly lovely *Burial of Christ* (1582; Federico Barocci), with the Palazzo Ducale of Urbino in the background—Barocci was born in Urbino.

San Martino and district

By taking Via Mastai south as far as Via Marchetti and then turning right, you reach the little Baroque church of **San Martino** (1740), with a simple interior, a central nave and two side aisles. Over the second south altar is a canvas of the *Madonna with Jesus and St Anne* by Guercino (1643); in the apse is a large canvas of *St Martin Giving his Cloak to the Beggar*, and over the third north altar a canvas of the *Madonna with Child and Saints* by Palma Giovane (1580).

Close by, in Via Battisti, is the opera house, **Teatro La Fenice** (*T: 071 7929509*), originally of 1838, but completely rebuilt after its destruction by earthquake in 1930. Great composers such as Verdi, Mascagni and Leoncavallo conducted their own works here, and all the most admired singers performed. In 1989, during the reconstruction, a large portion of the Roman city was brought to light—**Area Archeologica La Fenice** (*entrance from Via Leopardi, to request a visit; T: 071 6629266*), with the crossing between a *cardo* and a *decumanus*, little shops, the first of which was a *thermopolium*, selling hot cooked food and drinks (Roman fast food), and a luxurious dwelling opening onto the *cardo*. One hundred and thirty medieval tombs were also found, one of which has been left in place.

Close by again, at no. 84 Via Pisacane, is the **Museo Comunale di Arte Moderna e dell'Informazione** (*open 8.30–12.30 and Tues–Fri also 3.45–7; closed Sun, Mon and holidays; T: 071 60424*), a collection of works by contemporary artists, including many photographs by Mario Giacomelli, particularly clever in revealing the personality of his subjects; notice the young priests dancing around in the seminary of Senigallia.

The duomo

The cathedral of Senigallia is in Piazza Garibaldi (also frequently called Piazza Duomo), still harmonious and elegant, in spite of the damage caused by the 1930 earthquake. Consecrated in 1790, and probably the fifth cathedral the city has had, it is rather austere, with a vast Latin-cross interior, and nave and aisles separated by pilasters. In the south transept is a panel painting of the *Madonna with the Christ Child*, signed and dated 1578 by Ercole Ramazzani. In the baptist chapel is another work by this artist, dated 1575, the *Crucifixion between the Madonna and St George*. Pope Pius IX was christened in the font. In the chapter house is an interesting 6th-century monolithic sarcophagus, said to have held the body of St Gaudentius until 1520, when it was stolen by the inhabitants of nearby Ostra (and never returned).

The bishop's palace, Palazzo Episcopio, with its opulently decorated salons, now houses the **Pinacoteca Diocesana di Arte Sacra** (*open 10–12 & 4–6; closed Sun and holidays; T: 071 60498*), a rich collection of paintings and religious objects from local churches, covering the period from the 16th–19th centuries. Among the works of art is a wonderful, swirling black and gold *Madonna of the Rosary* (Federico Barocci; 1588–92).

Santa Maria delle Grazie

On the hill behind the city (c. 2km along the road for the cemetery) is the convent of Santa Maria delle Grazie (1491, Baccio Pontelli; completed 1684), built by Giovanni della Rovere who had promised a church and convent to the Madonna and St Francis if he had a son—Francesco Maria was born on 25th March 1490. The frescoes in the lunettes of the cloisters, painted in 1598, illustrate the life and miracles of St Francis, while the altarpiece in the apse of the church is a splendid *Virgin Enthroned with Saints*, by Perugino (1498). The famous painting by Piero della Francesca known as *Madonna di Senigallia* was removed from this church in 1915 because of the war—it is still in Urbino. The elegant cloisters now house the **Museo della Mezzadria** (*open 8.30–12; closed Mon; T: 071 7923127*), an interesting collection of farm implements and documents illustrating the history of farming in the region, particularly from the point of view of the share-croppers, *mezzadri*, widely employed in local agriculture in the 18th–19th centuries.

THE CESANO VALLEY

The Cesano River, 55km long, has its source on Monte Catria, 1000m above sea level. Its fertile valley produces onions and spelt, called *farro* in Italy, a cereal grown since ancient times and now becoming increasingly popular for its nutritional qualities

Castles of Senigallia

From the Cesano a little road winds up to **Monterado** (161m), **Castelcolonna** (125m) and **Ripe** (314m), three defensive castles of Senigallia, all of ancient foundation, and all now farming communities (forage, sugarbeet, tomatoes and wine) with a common history of war and strife, and continual change-of-hand from one powerful family to another. Castelcolonna has particularly beautiful 13th-century walls, in the form of a ship, and is renowned for olive oil; Ripe has a stunning castle, now used as the town hall, and fosters artisans—it is known as *il paese dei mestieri*, the village of crafts.

Corinaldo

A little further inland is Corinaldo, one of the best-preserved towns in the region, and one of Italy's beautiful villages. The name derives from *Cor in Altum* ('Heart on High'): on a hilltop (203m), it is almost perfectly symmetrical, and heart-shaped, divided in two by the long stairway called the *Piaggia*, and surrounded by magnificent fortifications; it is still possible to walk along the top of them, for almost their entire length. It was thanks to its walls, in 1517, that the town successfully repulsed an attack by

Francesco Maria della Rovere. Only Ascoli was able to do the same, in the whole region, and as a token of his appreciation, Pope Leo X declared Corinaldo a city—this status was endorsed by Pius VI in 1786.

Entering the town through Porta Santa Maria del Mercato (or *Porta di Sotto*), built in 1366, you find the 109 steps of the *Piaggia* leading up to a central garden, called the *Terreno*, with holm-oaks and aristocratic palaces; on the steps is a well called ***Pozzo della Polenta***, said to have provided polenta instead of water during the della Rovere siege. Close to the *Terreno* is the sanctuary church of Santa Maria Goretti (*open 8–12 & 3–8; T: 071 67123*), of 1717, originally dedicated to St Augustine, with a splendid Callido organ in the choir. The narrow, stepped Via del Sagrato leads south to the main street, Via del Corso, and the **Palazzo Comunale** (18th century), with a panoramic portico.

Continuing west, you reach Porta Nuova and the beautiful little opera house, **Teatro Goldoni** (*T: 071 679047, Associazione Pro Corinaldo*), of 1864; from here, Via del Teatro leads to the ex-Benedictine convent, which houses the **Civica Raccolta d'Arte Claudio Ridolfi** (*open April, May, June, Sept, Oct 10–12.30 & 3–7; July–Aug 10–12.30 & 4–7.30 & 8.30–10.30; other months Sat, Sun and holidays only 10–12.30 & 2.30–6; T: 071 679047*), a collection of paintings including works by the Venetian artist Ridolfi (1570–1644), often called 'Il Veronese' after his birthplace, Verona. In the first years of the 17th century Ridolfi was invited to the court of Urbino by Barocci. It was there that he met the Augustine priest Bartolomeo Orlandi, who was from Corinaldo, and with whom he formed a life-long friendship. Ridolfi even bought a house in Corinaldo, while maintaining another at Verona. He helped to strengthen the bond between Veneto and the Marche, and thanks to his friendship with the priest, he was flooded with commissions to paint for churches. This was the era of the Counter-Reformation, when the Catholic Church was striving to attract the faithful to lavish churches where you could feast your eyes on sumptuous art and sculpture, and witness the mystery of the Holy Sacraments in an almost theatrical setting. The museum also has an interesting collection of 17th-century wooden reliquaries, brought back from Sicily by Orlandi, and other religious articles from local churches. Close by is the **church of the Addolorata**, with a lavish Baroque interior, a Callido organ over the door, and a crypt dedicated to St Maria Goretti, and the little church of the **Suffragio**, a medieval tower converted into a church in 1637. Over the main altar in the elliptical interior is a painting of the *Madonna and Child in Glory* by Claudio Ridolfi.

Via del Cassero leads along the old walls to the bastion called the ***Sperone***, by the great military architect Francesco di Giorgio Martini. In front is a stepped alley, Vicolo del '400, which descends into the medieval quarter of the city. Behind the *Sperone* is the 18th-century church of **San Francesco** (unfinished), with three paintings by Claudio Ridolfi in the vast, single-nave interior.'

Mondavio

Mondavio stands on a panoramic hill (280m) overlooking the Cesano valley. The old centre is still surrounded by the medieval walls, and dominated by the astonishing castle that you find on entering the town, the Rocca (1492; Francesco di Giorgio Martini), which houses the Museo di Rievocazione Storica e Armeria (*open 9–12 & 3–7; T: 0721 97102*), a display of costumes and weapons from the 15th–18th centuries. In Piazza Matteotti, the main square, is the Palazzo Municipale, where a painting of the *Madonna with Christ Child* by Carlo da Camerino can be seen on request. The Museo Civico (*open 9–12 & 3–7; T: 0721 97102*), housed in the cloister of the convent of San Francesco, has paintings by Federico Barocci.

THE MISA VALLEY & ENVIRONS

Ostra

The River Misa, once known as the *Sena*, flows for 40km from the hill of San Donnino near Arcevia (where it is called *Acquasanta*) through some of the finest vineyards of the Marche before reaching the sea. South of the Misa, overlooking it and still surrounded by its medieval walls complete with nine towers, is Ostra, a serene place built of honey-coloured brick. It was known as *Montalboddo* until 1881, when the inhabitants decided on the present name, after bitter disputes with Montenovo (now Ostra Vetere); both claimed origin from the Roman city of *Ostra* in the valley. *Monte Boddo* is first mentioned in a document dated 1194, as a *comune*. It passed from one noble family to another, suffering considerably for the various wars fought in or around its territory, until Pope Pius VI pronounced it a city in 1790, assigning it a bishop. Nowadays most of the inhabitants work in the nearby furniture factories, or in small ateliers where they make furniture by hand, to order.

In the older, upper part of the town, is Piazza dei Martiri, with the 15th-century clock tower, the symbol of the city, and the magnificent town hall which incorporates the opera house Teatro La Vittoria (*T: 071 7980606*) of 1867, and the church of **San Francesco** (14th century, restructured several times), with the original bell-tower. The interior is a single nave, with chapels on the right, and the presbytery of the original building. In the third chapel, Baroque in character, is a painting of the *Martyrdom of St Gaudentius* and frescoes by Filippo Bellini (1594). The body of Gaudentius, stolen in 1520 from Senigallia, is in the altar, while in the presbytery, on the south wall, is a canvas of the *Madonna with St John the Baptist and St Matthew* by Ercole Ramazzani; further paintings by Ramazzani can be seen over the altars on the north wall.

The old convent of this church, at no. 10 Via Gramsci, now houses the **Pinacoteca Comunale** (*open Tues 4–6.30; Sat 9.30–12.30; other days on request; closed 1–17 Aug, T: 071 7980606*), with paintings and items from local churches. Corso Mazzini, the main street, leads down to the attractive Piazza Santa Croce, passing by some remarkable aristocratic palaces, and, on the left, the 14th-century church of the Crocifisso, with a lovely truss-beam roof. Close to the entrance to the town is the dignified pink brick sanctuary church of the **Madonna della Rosa** (18th century), built over a preceding chapel dedicated to a miraculous event; inside are numerous interesting ex-votos, including two Turkish flags.

Belvedere Ostrense and the eastern valley

Just south of Ostra is **Belvedere Ostrense**, also founded by the inhabitants of ancient Ostra. The economy is based on the production of olive oil; fertile soil, careful cultivation, harvesting by hand and processing the same day, are all elements contributing to its success. Patron saint of the little town is Rufus, martyred in Roman times; he is said to have been a *tabellarius*, or messenger, which is why he is the patron saint of postmen, and why, at no. 3 Via Vannini, you will find the Museo Internazionale dell'Immagine Postale (*to request a visit T: 0731 617003*), dedicated to the history and evolution of postal services throughout the world, with a section devoted to the 'ideal postage stamp', and a library with many books on the subject, including postal legislation from nation to nation. The relics of St Rufus are kept in the church of San Pietro (magnificent Neoclassical façade, but the church is of medieval origin), in the square in front of the old castle. In the sanctuary church of the Madonna del Sole is a much-revered, detached fresco by Andrea di Bartolo, of the *Madonna del Sole* (1471), said to be miraculous, and now kept over the main altar.

Nearby **San Marcello** was founded by Benedictine monks in the 10th century. Because of its strategic position, it became an important castle contended between Senigallia and Jesi. In 1213 it passed to Jesi, and was repopulated with settlers from that town in 1234. It was completely destroyed in the 14th century, and rebuilt in 1429. Harmonious and colourful, it is now famous for excellent wine (including the DOC Lacrima di Morro d'Alba) and olive oil. In Via Rossetti, close to the old southern gate called Porta di Mezzogiorno, is one of the smallest opera houses in the region, the exquisite Teatro Primo Ferrari (1870).

The road continues to **Morro d'Alba**, on the border between the territories of Senigallia and Jesi, and famous for its DOC Lacrima di Morro d'Alba wine, of which the production is small because limited to very few vineyards. The small historic centre, consisting of the old 13th-century castle (built on a base apparently representing a pentacle), with a square in front, is still surrounded by walls, with a passageway along the top. Under the walls are many caves and tunnels, carved into the rock, once used for defence and for storing merchandise. At no. 48 Via Morganti is a small museum, Utensilia (*open Sat 3–7; Sun 10.30–12.30 & 3–7; April and July–Aug 5–8; closed Mon; T: 0731 63824*), dedicated to all the handiwork carried out by the inhabitants in the not-too-distant past, and the various materials they used—wood, vegetable fibres, leather, stone and metal.

Serra de' Conte and across the river

From the Misa valley a panoramic road leads to **Serra de' Conti**, an interesting medieval town with a very large historic centre, still surrounded by its old walls, complete with ten towers and a fortified gate, and with a bustling economy based on the production of shoes, clothes and metallic components. It has an unusual museum at the town hall, at no. 6 Via Marconi, dedicated to the nearby convent of Santa Maria Maddalena, built on the old walls in Piazza Leopardi, the Museo delle Arti Monastiche Le Stanze del Tempo Sospeso (*open Sat 3–7; Sun 10.30–12.30 & 3–7; April, July and Aug*

5–8; closed Mon; T: 0731 871711), illustrating the life of the Poor Clare nuns. You can buy the famous *spumette*, meringues made by the nuns. At the end of the main street stands the isolated, 13th-century church of Santa Maria di Abbatissis, where the tomb and a beautiful 15th-century panel painting of the Beato Geraldo, who died in 1367, can be seen in his chapel at the end of the north aisle; behind the altar is the stone he used for a bed, where suffering people still climb today to invoke the miraculous cures he sometimes concedes.

Ostra Vetere, once known as *Montenovo*, is on a hill between the Misa and its main tributary, the Nevola. The inhabitants chose the present name in 1882, after much discussion with the town of Montalboddo, now Ostra; both communities claimed origin from the ancient Roman city of *Ostra*, the sparse ruins of which can be seen down by the Misa, close to the SS 360. Local farms provide excellent wines and olive oil. Dominated by the dome and the bell-tower of the church of Santa Maria di Piazza, the town consists of a series of terraces joined by stepped streets.

Picturesque **Barbara**, on a crest overlooking the Misa, was founded after the destruction of the Roman city of *Suasa*. The old city, called Castello, occupies the high part of the town, while the more recent Borgo and Castellaro are on the slope facing the sea. Castello still has its old walls, with the 13th-century bastion and the old gate. In the church of Santa Barbara is an interesting portrait of the Madonna, painted on a millstone. In the Castellaro part of town there are many tunnels and underground caves, carved into the sandstone tufa; they were originally shelters and secret passages to the castle, used in case of enemy attacks; now many of them have been turned into storage chambers or restaurants. This area is well known for the production of good wines: Esino, Verdicchio dei Castelli di Jesi, and Rosso Piceno. There are also textile mills providing the cloth for many of the region's fashion houses. The River Nevola, which flows nearby, offers pleasant rambles; near the boundary with Ostra Vetere it forms waterfalls.

THE UPPER CESANO

Castelleone di Suasa, the much-loved home of Livia della Rovere, last Duchess of Urbino, is a stunningly pretty little town near the Cesano, with narrow streets of tiny ancient houses, grouped around the medieval castle. Besides Rosso Piceno and Verdicchio dei Castelli di Jesi, local farmers produce the mellow Rosso Suasano wine, and particularly flavoursome onions. The mosaics, frescoes, and other finds from the site of the Roman city of *Suasa Senonum*, founded in 232 BC and destroyed by Alaric in 409, can be seen at the Museo Archeologico A. Casagrande (*open as archaeological park; T: 071 966524*), housed in the imposing Palazzo Compiani della Rovere at no. 7 Via Ospedale. The excavations at Pian Volpello are now protected in an **Archaeological Park** (*open April–June and Sept–Dec Sat, Sun and holidays 3.30–7.30; July–Aug Tues–Fri 4–8, Sat 3.30–7.30, Sun 10.30–12.30 & 3.30–7.30; closed Jan–March; T: 071 966524*). Archaeologists have brought to light a large 1st-century amphitheatre, a forum with shops and porticoes, and a magnificent private home, the *Domus Coiedii*, which had mosaic floors and Pompeian-style wall paintings.

Not far from Castelleone di Suasa is **San Lorenzo in Campo**, a farming community known for good quality onions and spelt, founded as a Benedictine monastery between the 7th and 9th centuries, using stones and other material from the Roman city. The monastery enjoyed considerable prestige; one of its abbots, Giuliano della Rovere, became Pope Julius II. Now the mellow brick Palazzo della Rovere in Via Mazzini houses the interesting Museo Archeologico del Territorio di Suasa (*open as archaeological park; T: 0721 76825*), a collection of objects found at the site of Suasa and in the necropolis. On the façade, above the della Rovere coat-of-arms, is a clock giving the hours for prayers. In the same palace is the tiny, charming 19th-century opera house, Teatro Tiberini (*T: 071 776479, Pro Loco*), still in regular use, dedicated to the local tenor Mario Tiberini, a favourite of Giuseppe Verdi. A new museum has been opened in Via Leopardi, Museo delle Terre Marchigiane (*open Sat–Sun 10–12.30 & 4–7.30; T: 0721 776904, www.museoterremarchigiane.it*), with a collection of tools and utensils used until recently by local craftsmen. In the highest part of the town, where the castle used to stand, is a little square affectionately known as the *padella* (frying-pan), with some remarkable 16th-century palaces around it. If you like walking, a few kilometres will bring you to the medieval castles of Montalfoglio and San Vito sul Cesano, very photogenic, and offering lovely views over the valley.

Among the hills between the Metauro and the Cesano rivers stands beautiful, pink brick **Fratte Rosa**, famous for its production of unusual pottery, glazed a bluey-black colour called *melanzana* ('aubergine') by a secret procedure known only to the craftsmen of this village. When a baby is born here, the proud parents decorate the entire house front with flowers, balloons, papier-mâché storks, and a banner saying 'welcome', with the name of the newcomer. It is peaceful enough now, but in the Middle Ages Fratte Rosa (once known as *Castrum Fractarum*), was of considerable strategic importance, and was fought over by many powerful families. From the 9th–13th centuries it was the centre of a city-state called *Ravignana*, controlled by the monks of Ravenna, who felt the need for a foothold in the area. A short distance from the town they built the convent of Santa Vittoria (1216), now the seat of the **Museo delle Terracotte** (*to request a visit T: 0721 777506*), an interesting display of the local production, with a research laboratory; some say the convent was founded by St Francis in person.

PERGOLA

Pergola (pop. 6,800), known as the city of 100 churches, is the long-time rival of nearby Cagli; in the centre many Gothic doorways and medieval tower-houses can be seen, and a noticeable change of atmosphere distinguishes the three city districts, that of the *Vasai* (potters), of the *Tintori* (dyers), and the *Conciatori* (tanners).

HISTORY OF PERGOLA

Founded by the town of Gubbio in 1228, on the site of ancient *Pertia* (Roman tombs have been located at the railway station), at the strategic confluence of the Cinisco and the Cesano, in order to favour trade between Umbria and the Adriatic, Pergola soon blossomed, and was renowned for the skill of its artisans and the beauty of its architecture. In the mid-14th century it was taken by the Malatesta of Rimini, but this was contested by the Church. Cardinal Albornoz was sent to occupy the city, which was returned to the control of Gubbio, but not for long—in 1445 Francesco Sforza ravaged the city and destroyed the walls. Pergola was then taken by Federico da Montefeltro, and later by Cesare Borgia, who in 1502 strangled the 82-year-old Giulio da Varano of Camerino and his children in the castle: Camerino was then presented to Giovanni Borgia, Cesare's brother. The shocked population threatened rebellion. Back under the control of the Montefeltro family, it followed the destiny of Urbino, until it was ceded to the Church in 1631, and declared a city by Pope Benedict XIV in 1752. Pergola was awarded the gold medal for valour during the movement for the Unification of Italy. Famous in the Middle Ages for its woollen cloth and leather, the economy is supported today by the manufacture of garments, furniture, ovens, and machine tools. The dialect and the traditions of the people are still noticeably Umbrian in character.

Sights of the old town

In Via Don Minzoni stands the **duomo**, built in 1258, but completely restructured in the 19th century. The bell-tower is original. The side aisles have altars of gilded wood; the presbytery is particularly deep. Via Don Minzoni becomes Corso Matteotti, and enters the oldest part of town. On the right is the lovely old church of Sant'Andrea, with a high medieval tower; on the left, the imposing 18th-century town hall with a high portico. In Via San Francesco is the charmingly asymmetrical Gothic church of **San Francesco** (13th century), with a single-nave interior dominated by the 16th-century dome. The 17th-century building opposite, once the Monte di Pietà pawn-shop, now houses the opera house, **Teatro Angel dal Foco** (*T: 0721 734943*), of 1758, with an unusual U-shaped interior.

By taking Via XX Settembre and crossing the Cesano, you reach what was once the dyers' quarter: on the corner with Via de Amicis is their church, **Santa Maria delle Tinte** ('St Mary of the Colours'), an ancient church surmounted by a Renaissance-style octagonal cupola, and a small belfry on the façade. The interior is Greek-cross in form, with opulent Baroque stuccoes and statues.

Museo dei Bronzi Dorati

At the point where the main street of the town, Viale Dante, becomes Viale Gramsci, is a little square called Largo San Giacomo, with the ex-church of San Giacomo (13th century). In the Baroque interior, on the left, is a fresco of the *Crucifixion* by Lorenzo d'Alessandro; the magnificent wooden main altar is surmounted by a 15th-century polyptych. The cloister of the church has been transformed into one of the best-run museums of the region: the **Museo dei Bronzi Dorati e della Città di Pergola** (*open 2 Jan–30 June and 1 Sept–31 Dec 9.30–12.30 & 3.30–7.30; 1 July–31 Aug daily 9.30–1 & 4–8; closed Mon, T: 0721 734090, www.bronzidorati.com*), with a well-displayed collection of paintings, etchings (mostly by the local contemporary artist Walter Valentini), sculptures, coins minted in the city of Pergola, and the famous group of statues known as the *Bronzi di Pergola*. There is also a bookshop.

THE PERGOLA BRONZES

Found by chance in 1946 near Cartoceto di Pergola, the group of life-size statues, partly fragmentary, is formed of two men on horseback and two ladies, in gilded bronze. They are unique; when similar bronzes were casually found in the past, they were immediately melted down for the value of the metal. Made by the lost-wax method, using bronze containing a high proportion of lead, they were covered with gold leaf, and therefore certainly represent members of a high-ranking family; a recent theory suggests they are Cicero, his wife Terentia, his brother Quintus and his sister-in-law Pomponia (second half of the 1st century BC). The artist was probably from Sentinum (Sassoferrato), where there was an atelier for the manufacture of bronze. As there is no trace of them having ever been fixed to a base, it is thought they were stolen by bandits when they were being transported from Sentinum to an unknown destination, and hastily broken up and hidden—the spot, of no particular archaeological context, was close to a busy road connecting the Metauro valley to the Chienti and the Tronto. After being restored, they were shown at the Archaeological Museum of Ancona, but there was an earthquake in 1972 and they were sent to Florence for restoration, while repairs were carried out at the museum. The people of Pergola asked to have the statues for an exhibition, and then refused to return them, even walling up the door of the showroom in their determination to keep them. The beautiful new museum was prepared at San Giacomo, with a special controlled-climate room for the statues, and since then Ancona has had to make do with copies, originally intended for Pergola.

ARCEVIA & ITS CASTLES

Arcevia (pop. 5,800), on the top of Mount Cischiano (535m), has a startlingly beautiful skyline, rising above wooded hills and valleys, where memories of the Knights Templar abound. Duchess Livia della Rovere used to spend the summer in her elegant little palace at no. 104 Corso Mazzini, close to the church of San Medardo (patron saint of Arcevia), which she founded in 1634.

HISTORY OF ARCEVIA

At the height of its splendour in the 17th century, Arcevia commanded 40 castles and protected numerous farming communities, resisting attacks and sieges with aplomb, thanks to its superb position and magnificent fortifications. Key stronghold of the Sforza family and later of the popes, even the formidable Malatesta, or astute *condottieri* like Pietri Navarro or Agnolo della Pergola, were unable to dent its defences. Known as *Rocca Contrada* until 1816, Arcevia was probably founded by Senonic Gauls, but the area was certainly inhabited constantly since the Palaeolithic era. At Conelle, between Ripalta and Piticchio, there is a prehistoric defensive trench which has yielded useful information about the successive periods of habitation. Declared a city in 1266, Rocca Contrada became a centre where art and culture flourished, along with important industries producing pottery and iron. The town took an active part in the 19th-century Unification movement; in 1944 many civilians were killed by retreating Germans on Monte Sant'Angelo. Nowadays the population is sadly diminishing, but Arcevia is a popular destination for summer holidays, and there are footwear and textile industries, as well as a company manufacturing heaters and radiators.

San Medardo and district

Entering the city through the impressive Porta Santa Lucia you find the main street, Corso Mazzini, which proceeds all the way through to the public gardens on the other side of town, neatly dividing the city in half. Soon, on the right, is the imposing brick collegiate church of **San Medardo** (rebuilt 1634), which was never finished, though the interior contains many important works of art. Spacious and high, Latin-cross in form, surmounted by a dome, with lavish chapels on both sides, the altarpiece in the apse is a polyptych by Luca Signorelli, signed and dated 1507, of the *Eternal Father, Madonna with Christ Child and Saints*, with stories of the Nativity on the predella, and 14 Saints on either side, surrounded by the original splendid gilded frame. Another painting by Signorelli, a spectacular *Baptism of Christ*, is over the baptismal font. Also in the apse is a magnificent Gothic choir, carved and inlaid in 1490, but unfortunately never completed. On the left-hand wall of the presbytery is a painting of the *Last Judgement* by Ercole Ramazzani (1597), inspired by Michelangelo. Ramazzani also

View of Arcevia, on its hilltop.

painted the *Souls in Purgatory* in the second south chapel, and *St Adrian and St Catherine of Siena* in the second north chapel; the majolica *Crucifix* in this chapel is by Mattia della Robbia. In the first north chapel is a marvellous panel painting, still in its original frame, of the *Madonna with Christ Child and Sts Anne, Joseph, Joachim and the Eternal Father*, dated 1529 and signed Piergentile da Matelica and Venanzio da Camerino. The altarpiece in the north transept is a precious majolica panel of the *Virgin of the Miracles*, made by Giovanni della Robbia in 1513.

On the opposite side of the street to San Medardo is the imposing church of **San Francesco** (13th century), with a fine Romanesque portal, and a sturdy bell-tower. The convent next door, which was visited at least once by St Bernardino of Siena, St Charles Borromeo and Pope Sixtus V, has a beautiful 15th-century cloister, now housing the **Museo Archeologico Statale** (*open 8.30–1.30; T: 0731 9622*), a large collection of objects found locally, dating from the Palaeolithic to Roman times. Pottery, weapons and armour, jewellery and imported Etruscan bronzes are the highlights of the collection. A short deviation to the right after leaving the museum, will take you down to Largo Cesari and the church of **Santa Maria**, belonging to the convent of St Clare next door (*ring and the nuns will open the church for you if closed*). Inside, at the end of the south aisle, is a striking panel painting of the *Madonna of Succour* (15th or 16th century, artist unknown), showing a sweet-faced, but determined Madonna, defending some suffering people (including a weeping, frightened child) with a heavy club. Tiny cherubim look on approvingly. The altars in the north aisle are particularly ornate; at the end is a majolica *Annunciation* by Mattia della Robbia (1528).

Piazza Garibaldi and the public garden

In the central Piazza Garibaldi is the beautiful medieval **Palazzo del Podestà** (now used as the town hall), with the 36m clock tower next to it; both were built in the 13th century, when Rocca Contrada became an independent commune. Close by is Palazzo Pianetti (16th century), with a fine portal and a beautiful interior. On the opposite side of the corso is another elegant palace, **Palazzo dei Priori** (14th century), now used as the Pro Loco office, and the charming opera house, **Teatro Misa** (1845), unusual for its circular interior. Next to the palace is the octagonal church of **Sant'Agata** (18th century), once part of the Benedictine monastery. The colourful, elegant interior is a triumph of lavish altars, paintings, frescoes and stuccoes; over the main altar is a notable painting by Claudio Ridolfi (*see p. 244*) of the *Coronation of the Virgin* (17th century).

Continuing along Corso Mazzini, on the left is the ex-church of San Giovanni entro le Mura, now the **Biblioteca Comunale**, with a collection of old books and manuscripts. At the far end of the corso a set of steps leads up to the War Memorial (1923); on the right is the entrance to the lovely public garden, **Giardino Leopardi**, full of pine trees and shady avenues. In the highest part of the town, it surrounds the ruins of the ancient castle.

CASTLES OF ARCEVIA

Of the many fortresses once controlled by Arcevia, nine are still inhabited, and fascinating to visit; it is possible to see them all in one day, though better to linger. **Avacelli** stands on the top of a steep hill, c. 6 km southeast of Arcevia; it was built in the early 13th century, on the border between the Byzantine Pentapolis and the Lombard Duchy of Spoleto. The little church is dedicated to St Lawrence; inside are some well-preserved frescoes and wooden statues. The altarpiece is an interesting painting on terracotta, the work of Pietro Paolo Agabiti (16th century). At the foot of the hill, in protected woodland, stands the 11th-century church of Sant'Ansovino (*closed*), the only Romanesque church in the area, with a Templar cross over the portal.

The castle of **Castiglioni**, c. 6 km east of Arcevia, was captured by Rocca Contrada (modern Arcevia) in the 13th century, but often tried to regain its independence—always in vain. In the early 15th century it was attacked and ravaged by the ruthless *condottiere* Braccio da Montone. The medieval walls are impressive, complete with two fortified gates. The church is dedicated to St Agatha; inside is a 15th-century wooden Crucifix, and one of Ercole Ramazzani's best works, a *Madonna del Rosario* (1589).

Caudino, c. 10 km northwest of Arcevia, is a small medieval fortress with only a single inhabitant. In the centre, next to the ancient bell-tower, stands the church of St Stephen, with a beautiful 16th-century fresco of the *Madonna of Loreto*. **Loretello** and **Nidastore** (Nest of the Goshawk) stand on the crest between the River Cesano and the Fenella stream, c. 10km from Arcevia. They are among the most glamorous castles in the region, with walls and towers still intact; Loretello has a spectacular portal with a ramp in front. Nidastore has been inhabited since prehistory.

Piticchio, c. 5km north of Arcevia, has the largest population of the fortress-towns and is also the best preserved; the people still cling to their traditions. **Montale**, about 3km from Piticchio, was also attacked by Braccio da Montone in the 15th century. The church is dedicated to St Sylvester, and was founded by monks of his order, who had a monastery close by. **Palazzo**, on the slopes of Mt Caudino, c. 5km northwest of Arcevia, is a small walled town clinging to the slopes of the mountain. Senigallia and Fossombrone squabbled over it for years, until it was taken by Rocca Contrada. In the church of St Anne, near the castle, are some frescoes by Piergentile da Matelica and Venanzio da Camerino. The Vici family, illustrious architects, were originally from Palazzo. **San Pietro** is a tiny castle not far from Loretello, with some fine stone buildings, on a spot of great strategic importance for Rocca Contrada. Close to the walls is the Sanctuary of the Madonna of Monte Vago, the church for which Piergentile da Matelica and Venanzio da Camerino painted the brilliantly coloured Madonna, now in the church of San Medardo in Arcevia (*see p. 252 above*).

PRACTICAL INFORMATION

GETTING AROUND

• **By train**: Senigallia station (T: 071 64313) is on the main Milan–Bologna–Pescara line. Pergola has its own line from Fabriano.
• **By bus**: The central bus station in Senigallia is at Via Montenero, T: 071 7925805.
Autolinee Reni, T: 071 8046504, www.paginegialle.it/reni-srl, runs services to Ancona, Numana, Fano, Pesaro, and beyond, June–Sept only.
Autolinee Bucci, T: 071 7922737, has services connecting the valley towns with Senigallia, Falconara, Jesi and Ancona, also services between Arcevia and its castles.
Autolinee Vitali, T: 0721 862515, www.autolineevitali.191.it, runs services to Fano, Pesaro, Ancona, Chiaravalle, Jesi, Fabriano, Pergola, Arcevia and Sassoferrato.

CONEROBUS, T: 071 2802092, www.conerobus.it, runs services to Jesi, Chiaravalle, Falconara and Ancona.

INFORMATION OFFICES

Senigallia This town, together with Gubbio, Pesaro, Novafeltria and Urbino, forms part of the association 'La Terra del Duca', dedicated to the Montefeltro; inf: www.terradelduca.it. A useful website is www.misaesinofrasassi.it, while www.musinf-senigallia.it gives information on the city museums. IAT, 2 Piazzale Morandi, T: 071 7922725, www.senigalliaturismo.it; Ufficio Cultura, T: 071 6629348; Tourist Information Bureau, Municipio, 1 Piazza Garibaldi, T: 071 6629258, www.comune.senigallia.an.it
Arcevia 1 Piazza Garibaldi, T: 0731 981972, www.cadnet.marche.it/arcevia
Castelleone di Suasa Pro Loco, 9 Via

Ospedale, T: 071 966770, www.provincia.ancona.it/comuni/castelleonedisuasa; Consorzio città romana di Suasa, T: 071 966524.

Corinaldo Associazione Pro Corinaldo, 20 Via del Velluto, T: 071 679047; Tourist Information Bureau, Largo XVII Settembre, T: 071 679047, www.corinaldo.it; Municipio, Ufficio Turistico, 9 Via del Corso, T: 071 6793257, www.provincia.ancona.it/comuni/corinaldo

Misa and Cesano Valleys useful websites include www.misaesinofrasassi.it, www.valcesano.com, and www.cm-pergola.ps.it

Mondavio Pro Loco, 1 Corso Roma, T: 0721 977331, www.mondavioproloco.it; IAT, 11 Piazza Matteotti, T: 0721 97102.

Ostra Corso Mazzini, T: 071 7980606, www.comune.ostra.an.it

Pergola Pro Loco, 48 Via Don Minzoni, T: 0721 736469, www.prolocopergola.it; Comunità Montana Catria e Cesano, 9 Via Don Minzioni, T: 0721 735701, www.cm-pergola.ps.it

HOTELS

Senigallia

€€€€ **Duchi della Rovere**. Elegant, central hotel, with garden, rooftop pool, restaurant, and garage; bikes available. Children welcome. 3 Via Corridoni, T: 071 7927623, www.hotelduchidellarovere.it

€€€€ **Metropol**. Family-run establishment with restaurant, pool, private beach and car park. Closed winter. 11 Lungomare Da Vinci, T: 071 7925991, www.italiaabc.it/h/metropol

€€€ **Bel Sit**. Quiet position on hill behind the city. Panoramic, elegant hotel with restaurant, pool, tennis, private beach, children's playground and car park. 15 Via dei Cappuccini, Scapezzano, T: 071 660032, www.belsit.net

€€€ **Bice**. In the town centre, comfortable, with a good restaurant, private beach and garage. Run by the same family for more than 50 years. 105 Viale Leopardi, T: 071 65221, www.albergobice.it

€€€ **Cristallo**. Ideal position on the seafront, with a patio and roof-garden, private beach and good restaurant. Closed winter. 2 Lungomare Alighieri, T: 071 7925767, www.h.cristallo.it

€€€ **La Vela**. Horrible modern construction in a wonderful position on the port; private beach, restaurant and garage. 35 Piazzale Bixio, T: 071 7927444, www.senigallia.it

€€€ **Lory**. ■ Good value for money at this little hotel on the seafront at Marzocca, south of Senigallia. Children welcome, private beach, very good simple restaurant, garden and car park. 28 Lungomare Italia, Marzocca, T: 071 69042, www.hotellory.com

€€€ **Palace**. A good choice; central, close to the station, and children welcome. The restaurant closes in winter. 7 Piazza Libertà, T: 071 7926792, www.hotelpalace.net

€€€ **Regina**. ■ A quaint little hotel right on the beach, with restaurant. 5 Lungomare Alighieri, T: 071 7927400, www.albergoregina.it

€€€ **Villa Pina**. Delightful Art Nouveau building with shady garden, 100m from beach. Comfortable rooms, and a restaurant. Closed winter. 158 Via Podesti, T: 071 7926723, www.villapina.it

€€ **Mietta**. Small, central and close to beach; with a restaurant. 19 Via Panzini, T: 071 63886, albergomietta@libero.it

€€ **Panoramica**. Panoramic hillside position; restaurant, park, tennis and bowls. 10km from Senigallia. 40 Via Grottino, San Silvestro, T: 071 665010.

€€ **Patrizia**. Bright, central hotel, with private beach, and a good restaurant; car park. Unfortunately flanked by the railway and a cement works, but good value for money; praiseworthy management. 6 Via Sanzio, T: 071 64401, www.hotelpatrizia.com

€ **Primavera**. Attractive, tiny hotel on the seafront, with restaurant, and bikes available. Open all year. 136 Lungomare Mameli, T: 071 7929464.

Arcevia

€€€ **Alle Terrazze**. With a restaurant, garden, pool, and tennis. 24 Via Rocchi, T: 0731 9391.

€€€ **Park Hotel Arcevia**. Central, with a garden and restaurant. 5 Piazza Roma, T: 0731 97085, www.parkhotelarcevia.it.

Barbara

€€€ **La Chiocciola**. A small hotel with restaurant. 59 Via Fratelli Kennedy, T: 071 9674036.

Castelleone di Suasa

€€ **Bellocci**. Tiny, central hotel, with restaurant and garden. 7 Via Marconi, T: 071 966117.

Corinaldo

€€€ **Al Casolare**. A new hotel in the lower town; excellent restaurant. 6 Via Corinaldese, T: 071 7976389,

www.alcasolare.it

€€€ **Bellavista**. A small hotel with a good restaurant; car park. 9 Via dei Cappuccini, T: 071 67073.

€€ **I Tigli**. ■ A small hotel once a 17th-century monastery; central, with a renowned restaurant. 31 Via del Teatro, T: 071 7975849, www.imieiviaggi.com/itigli

Fratte Rosa

€ **Locanda della Ravignana**. A comfortable inn with garden and tennis. Via I Maggio, T: 071 777520.

Mondavio

€€€ **La Palomba**. Comfortable little hotel with restaurant and garden. 13 Via Gramsci, T: 0721 97105, www.lapalomba.it

€ **Ai Cappuccini**. Tiny rooms in a 16th-century convent; garden and restaurant. 6 Via Cappuccini, T: 0721 981250.

Ostra

€€€ **La Cantinella**. With a garden and restaurant. 5 Via Amendola, T: 071 68081.

Pergola

€€ **Le Sorgenti**. An old hotel c. 2km from town; comfortable with a restaurant and garage. 18 Via Molino del Signore, T: 0721 736015.

San Lorenzo in Campo

€€€ **Albergo Ristorante Giardino**. Small, modern hotel, children welcome, with a excellent restaurant. 4 Via Mattei, T: 0721 776803, www.hotelgiardino.it

San Marcello

€€€ **Morobello**. Just outside town, a modern, comfortable hotel with a renowned restaurant, garden, pool and garage. 27 Via Serra, T: 0731 267060, www.morobello.it;

Serra de' Conti
€€€ De' Conti. ■ Pleasant modern building with comfortable rooms, restaurant and garden; an excellent choice. 58 Via Santa Lucia, T: 0731 879913.

BED & BREAKFAST

Senigallia
Sergio Fraboni. Nice house with garden on the hill behind town. English, French and German spoken. 30 Via Grazie, Scapezzano. T: 071 6608097, www.senigalliabedandbreakfast.it
Monterado
Castello di Monterado. Comfortable rooms in this 18th-century villa, designed by Vanvitelli, with a beautiful garden. The same management offers apartments for short-term rental in the village of Monterado; good restaurants nearby. Località Monterado, T: 071 7958395, www.castellodimonterado.it

FARM ACCOMMODATION

Senigallia
Beatrice. Country house with restaurant, farm produces cereals and sugarbeet; within easy reach of the sea. The owners are wine experts. Bridge parties every Thur. 1 Via San Gaudenzio, Borgo Bicchia, T: 071 7926807.
Il Papavero. With a good restaurant, tennis, bowls, table tennis, cookery courses. Olive oil, wine, vegetables and fruit are produced. Campers welcome. 98 Via Arceviese, Località Bettolelle, T: 071 66405.
Arcevia
Le Betulle. Small farm, with horses, within boundaries of Gola della Rossa

wildlife park. 260 Frazione Avacelli, T: 0731 983086.
Corinaldo
Villino Campagnolo. Small farm producing wine, olive oil, vegetables and fruit. Comfortable simple rooms, good value. 4 Via Gasparini, T: 071 7975159.
Pergola
Alla Vecchia Quercia. Surrounded by woodland, with a pool and horses. 26 Via Montaiate, Località Valdarca, T: 0721 773085, www.vecchiaquercia.it
Calamello. A good position for touring; the farm produces apples and vegetables. Località Cartoceto di Pergola, T: 349 4032397, cavallinifiorenza@libero.it
Isola Verde. This comfortable farm raises cattle by organic methods; guests can help. Open Apr–Sept.121 Via San Luca, T: 0721 778891.
Merlino. A hillside farm run by young farmers, cereal and vegetable production; good cooking and comfortable rooms. 29 Località Mezzanotte, T: 0721 778222, www.agriturismomerlino.it
Serra de' Conti
La Giara. An old farm in a panoramic position producing wine and olive oil; comfortable accommodation. 18 Via San Paterniano, T: 0731 878090, lagiara@infinito.it

COUNTRY HOUSES

Senigallia
Antica Armonia. Comfortable house on a hill behind Senigallia, with a good restaurant; horse-riding. 67 Via Soccorso, Scapezzano, T: 071 660227.
Finis Africae. Very comfortable; restaurant; pool and tennis. 155 Strada Sant'Angelo, T: 071 662501,

www.finisafricae.it
L'Arca di Noe. Lovely house with pool and restaurant. 79 Via del Cavallo, T: 071 7931493, www.arcadinoecountryhouse.com
Locanda Strada della Marina. ■ With a good restaurant, pool and internet, 265 Strada della Marina, Scapezzano, T: 071 6608633, www. locandastradadellamarina.it

RESTAURANTS

Senigallia
The restaurants of Senigallia are said to be among the best in Italy.
€€€ **Al Cuoco di Bordo**. Pasta and fish, with a personal touch; no menu, the chef will tell you what he has prepared that day. Closed Wed and Nov. 4 Lungomare Alighieri, T: 071 7929661.
€€€ **Locanda Strada della Marina**. A hillside restaurant, with innovative dishes prepared by an enthusiastic young chef. Closed Tues. 265 Strada della Marina, Scapezzano, T: 071 6608633.
€€€ **Madonnina del Pescatore**. ■ This is one of Italy's most interesting restaurants, where the creative chef, Moreno Cedroni, proud of his first Michelin star, presents his wonderfully inventive and imaginative cuisine, using fish as it has never been used before. An absolutely unforgettable experience; it is worth coming all the way to the Marche just to eat here. *Semel in anno licet insanire*—it's all right to go crazy every now and again in the course of the year. Closed Mon and Nov. 11 Lungomare Italia, Marzocca, T: 071 698267.

€€€ **Marinero**. Classic restaurant serving good fried fish and home-made pasta, you can eat on the terrace overlooking the sea. Closed Tues. 56 Lungomare Italia, Marzocca, T: 071 698462.
€€€ **Riccardone's**. Excellent mixed fried fish and vegetables. Closed Tues. 69 Via Rieti, T: 071 64762.
€€€ **Uliassi**. Refined, romantic atmosphere, in elegant surroundings for classic fish dishes, good wine cellar—Marco Uliassi also has a Michelin star. Closed Mon. 6 Banchina di Levante, T: 071 65463.
€€ **Barone Rosso**. Nice atmosphere, well presented fish dishes. Closed Mon, Dec–Jan. 23 Via Rieti, T: 071 7926823.
€€ **Cucina Mariano**. If you don't like fish, this is the place for you. Mariano serves cheese with home-made jam or honey, excellent ham and salami, mushrooms, rabbit, duck, lamb, home-made bread. Very nice desserts. Closed Mon, open evenings only in summer. 25 Via Manni, T: 071 7926659.
€€ **Hostaria La Posta**. Homely little restaurant serving simple dishes, prepared with the freshest ingredients. On Fridays you will find *stoccafisso*, dried cod from the Lofoten Islands, immensely popular in Italy. Delicious. Wine from the flask is good. Closed Sun. 26 Via Cavour, T: 071 60810.
€€ **Il Gatto e la Volpe**. Simple dishes, well cooked, generous servings. Closed Tues. 168 Lungomare Mameli (near the port), T: 071 660533.
€€ **Osteria del Teatro**. Casual, friendly tavern for a glass of wine and simple, tasty food. Closed Wed, June. 70 Via Fratelli Bandiera, T: 071 60517.
€ **Il Pirata**. Excellent pasta with scampi

and fried fish, evenings also pizza. Closed Tues. 85 Via Del Cavallo, T: 071 63980.

€ **Macumba Club**. Good seafood salad, spaghetti with clams, grilled fresh fish, evenings also pizza. Value for money. Closed Tues and winter. Lungomare Alighieri, T: 071 7927000.

€ **Osteria da Adamo**. Simple restaurant specialising in robust pasta dishes and grilled meats. Closed Mon. 7 Via Grazie, T: 071 7923136.

€ **Self Service Bar Paola**. Self-service offering delightfully original dishes. Closed Sun. 22/a Via Giordano Bruno, T: 071 7922400.

Arcevia

€€ **Pinocchio**. ■ Cosy little tavern, especially in winter around the open fire; traditional dishes, friendly atmosphere. Closed Wed. 135 Via Ramazzani Vici, T: 0731 97288.

Belvedere Ostrense

€ **Taverna degli Archi**. Typical local dishes in a medieval grotto. Closed Mon. 26 Via Comune Vecchio, T: 0731 62986.

Castelleone di Suasa

€€ **Bellucci**. Family restaurant opened in 1880, famous for *vincisgrassi*, roast and grilled meat, delicious desserts. 11 Corso Marconi, T: 071 966117.

Corinaldo

€€ **Bellavista**. Satisfying food accompanied by local wines; truffles and fungi are often on the menu; on the hillside overlooking Corinaldo. Closed Tues. 9 Via dei Cappuccini, T: 071 67073.

€ **I Nove Tarocchi**. Good value for money, the simplest possible food. 8 Viale Dietro le Monache, T: 071 7976277.

€ **I Tigli**. ■ Restaurant in a 17th-century monastery serving delicious local dishes, very good *antipasto*. Closed Mon. 31 Via del Teatro, T: 071 7975849.

Marotta

€€€ **Da Ciacco**. Delightful little restaurant serving carefully prepared fish, simple and appetizing; the desserts are up to the standard; local wines. Car park. 102 Via Faà di Bruno, T: 0721 969512.

Mondavio

€ **La Palomba**. Try *tacconi allo sgagg*, the local pasta with a sauce of crushed broad beans; you may find goose or boar, fungi and truffles in season. Closed Mon in winter. 13 Via Gramsci, T: 0721 97105.

Morro D'Alba

€€ **Dal Mago**. In the town centre, family restaurant with a long tradition for simple, tasty food. Closed Wed. 16 Via Morganti, T: 0731 63039.

Pergola

€ **Osteria Il Cantuccio**. Specialises in *crescia*, typical soft bread, with many accompaniments; local wines. Closed Thur. 5 Via Cavallotti, T: 0721 736495.

€ **Ostaria La Pergola**. Local cuisine in an old restored inn, very good wine list, but ask for Vernaccia Rossa di Pergola. Closed Tues. 4 Via de Gasperi, T: 0721 734297.

San Lorenzo in Campo

€€ **Giardino**. ■ Very interesting food, superbly cooked and presented, with well-chosen wines. Closed Sun evening and Mon. 4 Via Enrico Mattei, T: 0721 776803.

Serra de' Conti

€ **La Bona Usanza**. Simple, delicious, old-fashioned local dishes. Closed Sun evening, Mon midday and Christmas. 58 Via Santa Lucia, T: 0731 879913.

CAFÉS & BARS

Senigallia
Caffè Portici. ■ Delicious pastries, coffee roasted on the premises, outside tables in the nicest little corner of Senigallia—what more do you need? Closed Mon. 63–64 Via Portici Ercolani.
Da Cesare. Elegant coffee bar, delicious light meals. Closed Tues and winter. 13 Lungomare Dante Alighieri.
La Meridiana. Coffee bar, ice cream, tasty snacks, also the traditional cake to take home, *Dolce Pio IX*, approved by the Vatican. Closed Tues in winter. 16 Piazza Roma.
Les Chattes. Imaginative sandwich bar. Closed Sun. 26 Via Marchetti.
Saltatappo. For a small sum you can drink a glass of wine accompanied by tasty bites of the local hams, salami, *ciauscolo*, *bruschette*, olives or biscuits. Closed Mon. 70 Portici Ercolani.
Arcevia
Bar Centrale. Good coffee, home-made pastries and ice cream. 14 Piazza Garibaldi.
Barbara
Antica Gelateria Raissa. ■ Delicious home-made ice cream, pastries and snacks. 12 Corso Vittorio Emanuele.
Ostra
Caffè del Teatro. Also cabaret and piano bar. Piazza dei Martiri.
Pergola
Bel Bon. ■ Popular ice cream parlour, ask for the famous *moretto di Pergola*, chocolate and hazelnut ice cream cone

covered with dark chocolate. Corso Matteotti.

FESTIVALS & EVENTS

Senigallia Feast of St Paulinus, 4 May. Summer Jamboree, top bands for this festival dedicated to American '40s and '50s swing; Info: www. summerjamboree.com, Aug. Traditional St Augustine Fair, exhibition and sale of food products; Info: T: 071 6629258, 28–30 Aug. *Pane Nostrum*, a celebration of bread, from the Marche and all over the world; Info: T: 071 6629258, www.panenostrum.com, Sept.
Arcevia Feast of St Medardus, with traditional fair, fireworks, 8 June. Plays, films, and concerts are presented in the open air at Arcevia and in the surrounding castles. *Festa dell'Uva*, pageant to celebrate the grape harvest, with exhibitions, gastronomy, parades of floats; the tradition goes back to the 14th century, Sept.
Barbara Feast of St Barbara, procession and fireworks, 4 Dec.
Belvedere Ostrense *Vecchi Sapori d'Autunno*, events involving all the restaurants and taverns of Belvedere, presenting typical autumn dishes, 3rd weekend in Nov. Feast of St Rufus, large gathering of postmen from all over Italy, who recognise Rufus as their patron saint, 28 Nov.
Corinaldo *Contesa del Pozzo della Polenta*, commemorating Corinaldo's defeat of Francesco Maria della Rovere in 1517, with pageants, contests, flag-tossing and archery; Info: Associazione Pozzo della Polenta, 6 Largo XVII Settembre 1860, www.

pozzodellapolenta.it, 3rd Sun in July. *Corinaldo Jazz*, open-air music festival in the old centre, Aug. There are open-air plays, concerts and shows throughout the summer, in the square. Hallowe'en and the *Festa delle Streghe*, witches flit through the streets after sunset; there is a competition for the best-dressed witch; Info: Associazione Pro Corinaldo, and www.missstrega.it, 25–31 Oct.

Fratte Rosa Traditional July Fair, 2nd Sun in July. *Oh che bel castello*, a medieval atmosphere is created in the tiny streets, music, food prepared to ancient recipes, giving an idea of life in the castle, 14–15 Aug.

Mondavio *Caccia al Cinghiale*, a Renaissance banquet, archery contests, fireworks and other celebrations at the Rocca Roveresca castle, commemorating the arrival of Giovanni della Rovere after marrying Giovanna da Montefeltro; Info: Pro Loco, 1 Corso Roma, www.mondavioproloco.it, Aug.

Monterado *Sagra degli Sciughi*, the grape harvest is celebrated with a traditional delicacy: the '*sciughi*' are made with cornmeal and must, the grape juice, 1st weekend in Oct.

Morro D'Alba *Cantamaggio*, a series of celebrations (probably of pagan origin) terminating with the solemn burning of a tree in the little square, May.

Ostra *Mostra Nazionale dell'Antiquariato*, exhibition of antiques and crafts, Aug. Feast of St Gaudentius, followed by the traditional fair on the successive weekend, 14 Oct.

San Lorenzo in Campo Feast of St Lawrence, 11 Aug. *Mestieri e Mercanti—Palio della Rovere*, horse races, pageants, and an exhibition of handicrafts and produce, 1st week in Sept.

Serra de' Conti Feast of the Beato Geraldo, 16 Nov.

LOCAL SPECIALITIES

Senigallia

Anicò, 10 Piazza Saffi, Moreno Cedroni's shop for cured and smoked fish and gourmet sauces; you can also purchase straight from his workshop, Officina, 9 Lungomare Italia, Marzocca di Senigallia, T: 071 69152, or online www.madonninadelpescatore.it

Arcevia

At **Panificio Pagnani**, 1 Vicolo delle Carceri, the bread is so delicious you will probably find lots of people waiting to buy. Signor Pagnani also bakes biscuits and snacks (*calcioni*).

Barbara

Santa Barbara, 35 Borgo Mazzini, produces and sells good wines, such as Verdicchio Classico, Rosso Piceno spumante, and grappa.

Belvedere Ostrense

Luciano Landi, 16 Via Gavigliano, produces and sells the famous Lacrima di Morro d'Alba wine.

Fratte Rosa

Gaudenzi Terrecotte, 21 Via del Borgo, for local pottery, called *cocci*.

Morro d'Alba

Stefano Mancinelli, 62 Via Roma, excellent DOC Lacrima di Morro d'Alba wine, also olive oil.

Ostra

Pastificio Rossigni, at 104 Via Mazzini, for good quality pasta, made on the premises.

Ostra Vetere

Delizie dell'Orso, 2/m Via Crocifisso, sells traditional biscuits and the local speciality, *maiorchino* or *marocchino*, almond-flavoured sponge cake to eat with a glass of wine or ice cream.

Pergola

Corrado Tonelli, 66 Viale Dante, produces and sells *visner*, delicious cherry wine. Go to **Massaioli**, 11 Piazza Leopardi, for the red Vernaccia di Pergola wine, white Bianco Pergola, and *visciolata*, made with wild cherries.

Piticchio di Arcevia

Oleificio Rosa Mauro, 173 Via Piticchio, for the local stone-ground olive oil, one of the best in the region.

San Lorenzo in Campo

Aldo Bianchini, 55 Via Oberdan, sells delicious home-made sourdough bread. Try **La Mieleria di San Lorenzo**, 22 Via Oberdan, for organic honey from their own hives. **Macelleria Marianelli**, 151 Via Fratelli Rosselli, for home-made hams and salami from their own pigs. **Prodotti Biologici Gianfranco Bossi**, 1 Via Marconi, sells stone-ground wheat and maize flour, local chick peas, beans and lentils.

San Marcello

Maurizio Marconi, 23 Via Melano, produces and sells Lacrima di Morro d'Alba wine.

Serra de' Conti

Center Shopping Calzature, 1 Via Merli, for locally-made shoes. **La Bona Usanza**, at 60 Via Santa Lucia, for *lonza di fico*, the traditional sticky fig sweetmeat. **Maffeo**, 5 Via Famato, sells traditional sweets.

FANO, FOSSOMBRONE & THE LOWER METAURO VALLEY

The River Metauro, 83km long, which enters the Adriatic just south of Fano, is historically the most important in the Marche; in 207 BC the Carthaginian general Hasdrubal was defeated by the Romans in an epic battle near Serrungarina (trying to interpret the description given by Livy, other historians say near Fermignano, or Montemaggiore, or Orciano), in which Hasdrubal was decapitated, and 56,400 of his troops and their allies were killed, against 8,000 Roman dead; in 271 AD, Roman forces exterminated here a huge, rag-tag army of Germanic tribes. From Fossombrone the river is flanked by the Via Flaminia, coming from Rome via Scheggia near Gubbio, and continuing after Fano to Rimini; even today it is one of the key routes from central Italy to the northeast. Built by Gaius Flaminius in 220 AD, it was improved by Augustus and Vespasian, and several times again during the Middle Ages.

The town of Fossombrone, on the banks of the Metauro.

FANO

Fano (pop. 57,400) is an attractive seaside town with an important fishing harbour, a colourful old centre. It is a forward-looking place, and pleasant to visit at any time of the year. Nevertheless, stormy days in winter have a special atmosphere, when you can feel the sea spray on your face. The carnival festivities (the oldest in Italy), the *brodetto alla fanese* (fish soup), and the *moretta* (fishermen's coffee), are unique.

HISTORY OF FANO

The town is mentioned for the first time in *De bello civili*; when Julius Caesar occupied Pesaro and Ancona in 49 BC, he also occupied *Fanum*. After the Roman victory over the Carthaginians in 207 BC, a thanksgiving altar was erected on this spot, dedicated to *Fanum Fortunae*, the goddess of Fortune, and a community soon grew around the temple. The architect Vitruvius (1st century BC) erected a basilica on the Forum. Augustus brought a colony of settlers, developed the town and called it *Colonia Julia Fanestris*. The harbour soon became important for trade; larch timber was brought down the coast from the River Po, and stored here in the warehouses together with wine and oil from the southern Adriatic and the Ionian, ready to be taken to Rome along the Via Flaminia. Destroyed by the Goths during their war against Byzantium in 538, Fano struggled to recover, eventually joining Pesaro, Rimini, Senigallia and Ancona in an alliance called the Maritime Pentapolis, which was subject to Ravenna. Taken over by the Lombards and then by the Franks, it was donated to the pope by Charlemagne. In the 11th century, Fano declared herself an independent commune with allegiance to Venice. When Frederick Barbarossa attacked Ancona (1164 and 1174), Fano, as the ally of Ghibelline Venice, supported him. In gratitude Barbarossa granted several privileges. The late 12th century saw the rise of two opposing factions: the Guelph (pro-pope) del Cassero family, against the Ghibelline (pro-emperor) da Carignano clan. Malatestino Malatesta murdered the heirs of both families, and Pope Benedict XI took charge in 1304, appointing Malatestino as governor. In 1357 Cardinal Albornoz defeated the Malatesta and instituted the Parliament of the Marches at Fano. A constitution was drawn up, but Fano was given back to the Malatesta.

Despite its chequered history, Fano's periods of prosperity allowed it to mint its own coinage and found a university, which flourished until 1841. In 1501 Girolamo da Soncino opened a printing press; he was followed by others, and Fano became renowned for its production of books. The lovely beaches and picturesque canal-port brought tourism in the 19th century. The town suffered heavy damage in the First World War, when it was bombarded from the sea, and again in 1944, both from Allied bombs and during the German retreat, when all the towers and bell-towers were deliberately destroyed.

EXPLORING FANO

The main entrance to the old city is the **Arco d'Augusto**, built of sandstone and travertine marble in the year AD 9, as part of the improvements made to the town by the Emperor Augustus. The defensive walls were originally about 12m high (now the surviving stretches reach 8 or 9m). The large central opening was for carts, while the smaller ones on either side were for pedestrians. The monumental cornice was destroyed by Federico da Montefeltro during a siege in 1463, but you can see a large bas-relief reproduction of the gate on the façade of the ex-church of **San Michele**, to the right, where the stones were utilized. The lovely portal of this church was made in 1512. On the other side of the gate is the **Loggia di San Michele**, once a hospice for abandoned girls, with a portico and a pretty courtyard (1495)

The cattedrale

Via Arco d'Augusto corresponds to the *decumanus* of the Roman town, and is the favourite street for strolling and window-shopping. On the right is the Cattedrale di Santa Maria Assunta, built in the 12th century to replace the original 10th-century church, and much modified since then. The pale brick façade (1925) is effective in its simplicity, but sadly mutilated, with a marble portal surmounted by a sculpted Lamb and the Cross, above which is the frame of the rose window, now destroyed, and decorative loggias on either side. The bell-tower was one of those destroyed in 1944. Inside is a magnificent pulpit, supported by four stone lions, made in 1941 from Romanesque elements found in the cathedral; on the back of some of them are pagan designs, indicating they had been recycled at least once before, and that there was probably a Roman temple on or near this spot. Another example of this is in the second south chapel, where an ancient carving has been used for the **tomb of Bishop Vincenzo del Signore**; figures dance around a man playing the lyre, in an obviously pagan celebration. The third south chapel, the **Cappella Nolfi**, is richly decorated with frescoes illustrating episodes of the life of Christ and of the Virgin by Domenichino (1618), which cost a princely sum. The painting on the altar, of *Paradise and the Madonna*, is by Andrea Lilli (1606), and the sculpted busts of the Nolfi brothers on their monuments were added in 1612. In the chapel to the right of the presbytery is a canvas by Ludovico Carracci (1613) of the *Virgin in Glory with Saints*, while in the Baroque Chapel of the Sacrament, to the left of the main altar, is an 18th-century painting of *Jesus with the Sacrament*, and on the walls, two canvases of the Bologna school, representing the *Fall of the Manna* and the *Last Supper*.

Santa Maria Nuova

By taking Via Alavolini behind the cathedral, you reach the church of Santa Maria Nuova (*open 10–12 & 4–6*), or San Salvatore, in Via de Tonsis, a medieval church renewed in 1518 and again in 1708, with an attractive 16th-century portico in front of the magnificent portal (1498). The interior is a single nave, with side chapels and a deep presbytery, beautifully decorated with early 18th-century stuccoes. Some of the paintings are exceptional: over the third south altar is a **panel painting by Perugino** (1497) of the *Madonna with Christ Child and Sts Mary Magdalene, Paul, Peter, Francis and John the Baptist*, with an authoritative *Pietà* in the *cimasa*, where some scholars see the hand of Raphael (who was an apprentice in Perugino's atelier), also in the scenes depicted in the predella underneath. In the apse are finely-carved and inlaid wooden choir-stalls, with little *trompe l'oeil* cupboards, made by the master craftsmen Antonio and Andrea Barili of Siena (1484–89), sadly damaged with the destruction of the bell-tower in 1944, and arbitrarily repaired afterwards. The first north altar is surmounted by a panel painting of the *Visitation*, signed by Giovanni Santi (father of Raphael), while the second north altar has a memorable *Annunciation* by Perugino (1489).

Close by, between here and the Arco d'Augusto, in little Piazzetta Cleofilo, is what is reputedly one of the three churches built by the del Cassero family, who were Templars, on their return from Jerusalem, each housing a fragment of the Cross: the church of the Crocifisso, now the church of **Santa Maria del Suffragio**; rebuilt in 1593, when the Austin nuns came here from their old convent which had been destroyed. Unfortunately, the church is often closed, but it is sometimes used for exhibitions, and you can ask for the keys at the confraternity next door. Over the main altar is a fresco that the nuns brought with them, a *Crucifixion* (14th century; Giotto School of Rimini), which was framed with stucco in 1710. The rich decorations of the vault were carried out in 1692.

Central Fano

The city centre is **Piazza XX Settembre**, the traditional market place. The bronze **Fountain of Fortune** is the symbol of the city. This is a copy of the original, now in the nearby museum, showing Fortune as a young girl, therefore capricious, with her eyes closed, and ready to pull her veil over her face. On the south side of the square is the elegant Baroque façade in sandstone and brick, of the church of **San Silvestro** (rebuilt 1606), usually called *Madonna di Piazza* by the people, because of a venerated portrait of the *Madonna* over the main altar; this church was severely damaged in 1944. The magnificent terracotta façade of the Gothic **Palazzo del Podestà** (1299; also known as Palazzo della Ragione), dominates the north side of the square. Once the council chamber, Cardinal Albornoz convened here in 1357 the Parliament of the Marches. Just over the central arch is a Renaissance composition with statuettes of the *Three Patron Saints*, the central one, *St Paternian*, in stone, the other two, *St Fortunatus* and *St Eusebius*, in terracotta. This is now the opera house, **Teatro della Fortuna** (*T: 0721 800750*), of 1863, with 656 seats, one of the loveliest in the region. The ugly clock tower (1950) replaces the original, destroyed in 1944.

Next to the palace, on the eastern side of the square, is the Arco Borgia-Cybo, an imposing Renaissance portal, giving access to the Corte Malatestiana, a lovely courtyard over which face the **Case dei Malatesti** (1357 and 1930), once the homes of the powerful Malatesta family (*see box*), now seat of a bank. The bank has a small but well-chosen collection of paintings, the **Quadreria Fondazione Cassa di Risparmio di Fano** (*T: Laura Lippera, 339 5424237; www.fondazionecarifano.it*), which can be seen on request, including a *Wedding of the Virgin* by Guercino (1649), a panel painting of the *Madonna with Christ Child* by Giovanni Santi, 17 stunning still-lifes and portraits by Carlo Magini, and a display of coins minted in Fano.

'BAD HEADS': THE MALATESTA FAMILY

The powerful Malatesta family originated in Pennabilli, in the Montefeltro. In 1214, for reasons unknown, Giovanni Malatesta presented himself to the city of Rimini with a rope around his neck, his sword pointed towards his heart, to make redress for an offence. He was pardoned, and he and his nephew were given citizenship and other privileges, in exchange for their protection; they built the castle of Rimini. Traditionally Ghibelline, in 1248 Malatesta da Verucchio, described by Dante as the 'Old Mastiff', changed sides and became Guelph. The Ghibelline leaders were assassinated or exiled, and the Malatesta became absolute lords of Rimini, supported by the pope. The Old Mastiff died in 1312, over 100 years old, leaving three sons: Malatestino dell'Occhio ('of the Eye', because he squinted, Giovanni lo Sciancato ('the Cripple', because of his limp), and Paolo il Bello ('the Handsome'). The two latter brothers are the protagonists of the tragedy which took place in the castle of Gradara, the story of Paolo and Francesca (*see p. 294*). In the mid-14th century Malatesta Malatesti il Guastafamiglie, 'Ruiner of Families', invaded the Marche. Pope Innocent IV chose the energetic Spanish cardinal Egidio Albornoz to curb his ambitions. The Ruiner's grandson Carlo came to power in 1385, governing well and re-building the port. His illegitimate grandson Sigismondo became lord of Rimini at 16. Brilliant *condottiere*, diplomat, generous patron of the arts, but bad-tempered, his contrasting personality makes him one of the most interesting figures of his day. He fought for the pope against Federico da Montefeltro, but also for Alfonso of Aragon against Venice and Florence. When Alfonso failed to pay him, Sigismondo changed sides and fought for Florence instead. In 1456, on the death of his wife Polissena Sforza, he married his long-time mistress Isotta, who had already given him numerous children. This was the most splendid period of the Malatesta court; artists and intellectuals such as Piero della Francesca, Leon Battista Alberti, Agostino da Duccio and Matteo de' Pasti were all assiduous visitors. In 1459 Pius II, hostile to the Malatesta, was elected pope. He confiscated all Sigismondo's dominions, leaving him only Rimini. His son Roberto il Magnifico achieved reconciliation with Federico da Montefeltro, and married his daughter Isabetta. In 1481, on the battlefield on behalf of Venice, he gained a victory over a coalition of Milan, Florence and Naples, but he died while going to meet the pope, either of malaria or poison. Pandolfo il Pandolfaccio, 'Nasty Pandolfo', his son, was too ferocious even for the patient people of Rimini: with the help of Pope Clement VII they forced him into exile in 1528, never to return.

On the opposite side of the courtyard is the entrance to the **Museo Civico e Pinacoteca** (*open 9.30–12.30 & 4–7; 15 June–15 Sept also 9–11; closed Mon; T: 0721 887514*), housed in the 15th-century Palazzo Malatestiano. Under the portico is the famous 2nd-century mosaic known as *La pantera*, depicting a man (?Dionysus) riding a leopard. The archaeological collection displays objects found at local prehistoric and Iron Age sites, together with an important group of Roman statues, epigraphs and mosaics, including a marvellous *Neptune on his Chariot* (2nd or early 3rd century). The numismatic department has an exceptional collection of the Malatesta medals coined by Matteo de' Pasti (15th century), together with coins from the local mint. Among the numerous paintings is a triptych of the *Madonna and Child with St Michael and St Paul*, the famous polyptych of the *Madonna of the Rose with Christ Child and Saints*, by Michele Giambono (1420), a sumptuous *Guardian Angel* by Guercino, *David with the Head of Goliath* by Domenichino, and works by more recent artists such as Ettore Tito, Antonio Mancini, Gerolamo Induno, and others.

Palazzo Montevecchio (18th century) is the most luxurious of the aristocratic dwellings of Fano. The façade, on Via Montevecchio, is superb, and so are the atrium and the great stairway. Almost opposite, on Via Nolfi, is the **Torre di Sant'Elena**, a surviving medieval tower; originally a dwelling, later it was used as the bell-tower of the destroyed Templar church of Santa Croce, which had a hospital; now there is a modern convent on the spot. Close by is the russet-coloured **Palazzo Martinozzi** (1564), thought to be designed by Jacopo Sansovino, built by the noble Francesco Martinozzi on the ruins of the church of San Maurizio, of which traces can still be seen, especially on the north side, while the northeast corner corresponds to what was once a medieval tower. A descendant of the Martinozzi family, Maria Beatrice (Mary of Modena), married James II of England; the ghost of another Martinozzi is said to haunt the streets of Fano on certain dark and stormy nights, driving noisily along in his black carriage at great speed, and suddenly disappearing into a chasm at the foot of the Arco d'Augusto.

San Domenico to the Rocca

Via Arco d'Augusto crosses Corso Matteotti (the ancient *cardo*). In the angle of the two streets is the enormous brick church of **San Domenico** (13th century), still under repair after the damage caused by the bombing of the bell-tower in 1944, but occasionally open for exhibitions. This is where young Jacopo del Cassero was buried in 1298, murdered by Malatestino; an episode mentioned by Dante in his *Purgatory*. In the simple interior are some particularly delicate frescoes (14th, 15th and 16th centuries). It is hoped to return the original paintings of the church, at present in the Museo Civico, as soon as the repairs are complete.

By taking Via Vitruvio northeast from San Domenico, you reach the church of **Sant'Agostino**, originally Santa Lucia, rebuilt in 1265 for the Austin monks of St Nicholas of Tolentino, and said to be on the spot where the old Temple of Fortune once stood (*see p. 264 above*). Badly damaged by 1944 air raids, it is under repair and will probably become the Diocesan Museum. The Renaissance-style cloister survived the war, and still preserves its 17th-century frescoes in the lunettes. To the left of the steps in front of the church is the entrance to the ruins of a large Roman building, thought by some scholars to be the remains of the **Basilica of Vitruvius**, described in his *De Architectura*. Close by, in Via de Amicis, recent excavations have brought to light part of the 1st-century BC amphitheatre.

At the north end of Via Nolfi is Piazzale Malatesta, and the imposing remains of the **Rocca Malatestiana**, the fortress built by Sigismondo Malatesta in 1438, on preceding medieval and Roman constructions; this too, sadly destroyed by the retreating Germans in 1944. For many years this fortress was used as the prison of Fano. From here an interesting walk goes around the existing walls.

Via San Francesco d'Assisi

South of Piazza XX Settembre, in Via San Francesco d'Assisi, next to the town hall (once the convent of St Francis, and thought to be by Luigi Vanvitelli), are the **Arche Malatestiane** (Malatesta tombs), under the portico of the ex-church of San Francesco, brought here from the interior of the church in 1659. On the left is the elaborate tomb of Paola Bianca Malatesta (1398), the so-called 'great lady', first wife of Pandolfo III, whose lovely image can be seen on the lid, surmounted by statues, red marble arches, and a Crucifix, all Venetian workmanship. On the eastern wall is the tomb of Bonetto da Castelfranco, the personal doctor of the Malatesta, who died in 1434. The tombstone above it, in red marble, shows the Malatesta coat-of-arms, with a unicorn. On the opposite side of the 14th-century portal is the tomb of Pandolfo III Malatesta, commissioned by his son Sigismondo in 1460, at least 30 years after his father's death. During recent repairs, Pandolfo's mummified body was found to be still in this tomb.

At the end of Via San Francesco d'Assisi, on the opposite side of Via Nolfi, is the unfinished façade of the 17th-century church of **San Pietro in Valle** (*open 10–12 & 4–6*), strongly contrasting with the dazzling interior, a single nave with six side altars, richly decorated with gilded stucco, marble sculptures and paintings, and with a really exceptional dome. The frescoes on the vault and in the presbytery, together with some of the canvases and the stuccoes, were carried out in 1618. In the first north chapel is a particularly gentle *Annunciation* by Guido Reni (1621). Over the main altar is a large canvas representing *Christ giving the Keys to Peter*, by the local artist Carlo Magini, a good copy of the original by Guido Reni, stolen by Napoleon. To the right of it is a vibrant *Peter heals the Cripple* by Simone Cantarini; old Fano is visible behind the group of figures. To the left is *Peter Resuscitates Tabitha*, by Matteo Loves.

To the right of the church is Via Castracane. Opposite no. 4 is an ex-convent, now the **Biblioteca Federiciana** (*open 8.30–12.30 & 2–7; Sat 8.30–12.30; closed Sun; T: 0721 803415*), founded by Abbot Federici, a learned diplomat who spent many years at the court of Vienna. He left his collection of books to his city, on condition that the library be opened to the public for at least an hour each day. In the Sala dei Globi are two globes made for the abbot by the famous Venetian cosmographer Father Vincenzo Coronelli in 1689–92; one is of the world, the other of the skies. There is also an interesting navigation map (1504), showing the world as it was then known, including the coast of Brazil and the Indian peninsula.

Viale XII Settembre

Continuing south to the end of Via Nolfi, then east along Viale XII Settembre, you reach the railway station and the **Bastione del Sangallo**, the formidable bastion erected by the Sangallo brothers from 1532–52, to protect the city from pirate attacks; the marble coat-of-arms on the point is that of Pope Julius III, to celebrate the 1550 Holy Year. By going west along Viale XII Settembre and taking the second turning to the right, Via San Paterniano, you find the basilica of **San Paterniano** (16th century; Jacopo Sansovino), the patron saint of Fano; the elegant portal (1571) stands out on the plain façade, while the bell-tower is a faithful copy of the original, destroyed in 1944. In 1860 the convent next door became a barracks, but in 1922 it was returned to the Capuchin friars. The solemn interior is decorated with numerous works of art. The interior of the dome, frescoed with the *Glory of Paradise*, is by Giovanni Battista Ragazzini (1556), while the beautiful organ (1779) is the work of Callido. The bones of St Paterniano, bishop of the city, who died in 350 at the age of 96, are kept in the chapel to the right of the presbytery, in the original Roman sarcophagus. The cloister is particularly photogenic.

A walk leads southeast from the railway station, c. 3km, to the River Metauro and the little 14th-century church of **Santa Maria del Ponte**; inside is a small fresco of the *Madonna Feeding Child Jesus*, said to be miraculous. Probably painted in the 13th century in what was a roadside aedicule, the picture has been repeatedly restored. In a large lunette on the right wall of the presbytery is a 15th-century fresco of the *Last Supper*, showing Judas with a black halo. The man wearing a red cloak kneeling in front of the table, is thought to be Carlo Malatesta, who in 1399 led a pilgrimage here from Rimini.

AROUND FANO

South of Fano, on a popular stretch of sandy beach, are the small resorts of Torrette, Marotta, and Cesano, at the mouth of the river. Just inland from Marotta is the cross-road locality of **Cento Croci**, with the isolated little church of San Gervasio in Bulgaria, with an ancient crypt; inside is a fine 6th-century stone sarcophagus from Ravenna, with two carved peacocks, the symbol of immortality Two kilometres north of Cento Croci is **Mondolfo**, still partly surrounded by its medieval walls, and in a very panoramic position; the views from the belvedere at the top of the city are impressive. You will find many craftsmen hard at work in their little shops in the old centre; there are also small industries for the manufacture of accordions and concertinas, furniture, and clothes. *Pallone al bracciale* (*see p. 103*) has always been popular here, and is still regularly played; it forms the theme for the summer pageant. There is even a local summer version, played using a tambourine to bounce the ball, instead of the heavy wooden arm guard.

North of Mondolfo, on the crest between the Cesano and the Metauro rivers, surrounded by vineyards, stands **San Costanzo**, an attractive cattle-farming town, still protected by the walls erected by the Malatesta in the 14th–15th centuries. Steps lead into the old centre; close to the top is the little Teatro La Concordia (*T: 0721 950124*), of the 18th century, occupying an ancient tower. The elegant lemon-yellow town hall in Piazza Vittoria was once the palace of the Cassi counts; on request you can see the collection of paintings, Quadreria Comunale (*T: 0721 950158*) among which is a splendid canvas of the *Baptism of Constantine* by Terenzio Terenzi, known as 'Il Rondolino' (17th century). In the nearby Chiesa Collegiata (16th century) are a very old wooden Crucifix, and a *Nativity* by Ercole Ramazzani (1580) over the first south altar; the organ is by Callido.

North of the Metauro

Saltara is a busy and picturesque little town on the old Via Flaminia, with a long portico along the street where markets were held in the Middle Ages; the modern section, close to the railway line, is called Calcinelli. In the pastry-shops you will find the typical local biscuits called *berlingozzi*. The outlying 16th-century Villa del Balì houses the **Museo del Balì** (*open Sat 4–8; Sun 3–9.30; other days on request; T: 0721 892390; www.museodelbali.org*), an interactive planetarium and science centre. The villa was built around the old chapel of St Martin, probably a Templar base in the 12th century, by Bishop Negusanti of Fano, who used it as an astronomical observatory. On the spot once stood a Roman temple to Mars (Mars=Marte=Martin). Known as Villa San Martino for many years, it has been called Villa del Balì since 1677, when it was acquired by Count Marcolini, who was a '*balì*', a high office in a chivalrous order.

    Cartoceto has been famous since the 12th century for the excellent quality of its olive oil, perhaps the finest in the world, which bears the DOP—*Denominazione d'Origine Protetta*—label. The town also has industries manufacturing cardboard packaging, and produces pit-matured cheese. Originally a castle for the defence of Fano, it still has a delightfully medieval air, although some scholars believe it to be very ancient, founded in 207 BC by Carthaginian survivors of the Battle of the Metauro. Near the top of the hill are the ruins of the castle, built by Galeotto I Malatesta in 1351. In Piazzale Marconi, with lovely views over the olive groves, is the opera house, Teatro del Trionfo (1801), in what was once an oil press.

    A road leads out of Cartoceto back down towards the river, passing through the ochre-coloured, perfectly concentric **Serrungarina**, probably very ancient, but mentioned for the first time in a document of 1305. A Roman inscription, now in the Vatican library, states this to be the spot where Hasdrubal was killed in 207 BC. In the attractive little central square is a centuries-old lime tree, the town hall and the church, dedicated to St Anthony Abbot; over the main altar is a painting by Guerrieri (*see p. 274*) of *Sts Fortunatus, Anthony Abbot and Mary Magdalene*. The people of Serrungarina grow fruit: they are particularly proud of a pear called *pera Angelica*, juicy and with a delicious flavour; this is the only place in Italy where it is grown. On the river, at **Tavernelle**, archaeologists are excavating a Roman resting-place along the Via Flaminia; bird-watchers will spot ducks and herons, many of which nest here.

Montemaggiore al Metauro

Montemaggiore, on the south bank of the river, is an ancient castle, certainly founded before the 8th century, and bitterly contested between the Malatesta and the Montefeltro until it was appropriated by the Church in 1631. It is now famous throughout Italy for its production of chrysanthemums, which Roman Catholics take to the cemeteries for the Feast of the Dead (All Souls Day, 2nd November). Besides flowers, Montemaggiore is renowned for *Valmetauro* cheeses, and the DOC wine, Bianchello del Metauro. Some historians believe the battle between Romans and Carthaginians of 207 BC was fought here: in August 1944 Winston Churchill, together with generals Alexander and Leese, followed the progress of a much later battle over the nearby Gothic Line from this vantage point. At the entrance to the village, the little ex-church of the Madonna del Soccorso (17th century) now houses the **Museo Storico Ambientale del Fiume Metauro** (*to request a visit T: 0721 879343*), with an interesting collection of documents and photographs regarding the battle.

FOSSOMBRONE

The old centre of Fossombrone has a delightfully dilapidated air, as if it were on the point of crumbling away into the river; but its castles still cling doggedly to the heights, and a daring bridge, certainly the most beautiful in the region, soars majestically over the Metauro. The rich collections in the museums, galleries and libraries are the result of centuries of feverish collecting by local noble families—it was hard to beat Tiberio Sabbatelli: in the 16th century he possessed an Egyptian mummy.

HISTORY OF FOSSOMBRONE

The name derives from *Forum Sempronii*, a settlement founded in 133 BC by Senator Caius Sempronius Gracchus, when he came to check the application of his Agrarian Laws. The settlement became a flourishing city, but devastation by the Goths in the 6th century forced the population to take to the hills. Governed by Ravenna after the victory of Byzantium (555), it later formed part of a coalition of five towns with Urbino, Cagli, Gubbio and Jesi. Completely destroyed by the Lombards in the 8th century, it was rebuilt on the hill overlooking the modern town, and in 999 passed under the protection of the pope, and hence to various aristocratic families, including the d'Este and the Malatesta, until 1444, when it was sold to Federico da Montefeltro. A long period of prosperity began under his government, when arts and culture flourished, together with industries for the manufacture of silk, wool and paper. The silk was of excellent quality, and found markets in Paris and London. The main street (Corso Garibaldi) was at one time the largest market in Italy for silk cocoons. Guidubaldo da Montefeltro, Federico's son, lived permanently in Fossombrone, for the mild climate and fresh air. On his death the city went to the della Rovere family, who consolidated its prosperity and enlarged the town as far as the Metauro. In 1631 it passed to the Church together with the Duchy of Urbino. Nowadays the economy is based on the manufacture of furniture, electric water-pumps, barometers and garments.

EXPLORING FOSSOMBRONE

Corso Garibaldi

The main street of this charming, golden-brown-and-cream coloured town is the cobbled Corso Garibaldi (crowded on Monday for the weekly market), along which there are many old aristocratic palaces (also along the parallel Via Giganti) and comfortable porticoes. Starting from the east, on the left is the rather scruffy, unfinished exterior of the ex-church of **San Filippo**, built in 1613 (*open Jan–May and Oct–Dec Sat 3–6, Sun and holidays 10.30–12.30 & 3–6; June–Sept 10.30–12.30 & 4–7; closed Mon*), with a surprising, elegant single-nave Baroque interior; fine works of art and precious stuccoes in white and gold. Behind the main altar is a painting of the *Madonna in Glory with Saints* by Giovanni Francesco Guerrieri (*see box overleaf*); under the Madonna five local saints are offering her a model of the church, built by the people as thanksgiving for the birth of a son to the old Duke Francesco Maria II della Rovere—they taxed themselves to the hilt to pay for it. Guerrieri wanted 300 *scudi* for his Madonna, a colossal sum—but he got it. In the first north chapel is a 17th-century wooden Crucifix, while in the second is a panel painting of the *Madonna of Loreto* by Francesco Gessi, pupil of Guido Reni. In the first south chapel is a 17th-century canvas of the *Madonna and Child with Sts Charles Borromeo and Francis*; in the second is an impressive work by Claudio Ridolfi, the *Madonna with Christ Child and Sts John the Baptist and Jerome*. The third south chapel, of the Azzi family, has another two paintings by Guerrieri, *St Michael Archangel and the Trinity* (1624), and the splendid *St Barnabas in Prayer*. A lovely polychrome mosaic covers the floor. The church, which has exceptional acoustics, is used for concerts and exhibitions.

Also on the left of the street is the church of **Sant'Agostino** (14th–19th centuries; *closed at the time of writing*), completed in 1387. On the worn façade the coats-of-arms of the financiers—the chessboard of the Malatesta, together with the pestle and mortar of the *aromatarii*, spice traders—are still visible. On the 17th-century wooden door are the statues of St Augustine and his mother St Monica. The imposing interior is a single nave, with high columns. Over the main altar is a lovely painting by Federico Zuccari of the *Nativity* (1594); while over the second north altar is a canvas, signed and dated 1621, by Giovanni Francesco Guerrieri of the *Madonna with Sts Monica and Augustine*. The deep apse was added in the 18th century.

Almost opposite is the dilapidated 16th-century **Corte Rossa**, once residence of the della Rovere dukes, and connected by a little bridge to the **Corte Bassa**, built in the 15th century by Francesco di Giorgio Martini and Girolamo Genga (*to request a visit T: 0721 723240*) behind it, in Via Battisti; one palace was used during the day, the other during the night. The ceiling of the chapel of St Peter in Corte Bassa, decorated with 16th-century polychrome stuccoes, is absolutely spectacular.

From the cattedrale to the Rocca

In Piazza Mazzini, are the 15th-century Episcopio, the bishop's palace, and then the **cattedrale** (18th century). Dedicated to St Maurentius and his companion martyrs (all sculptors who had refused to carve images of pagan divinities for the Romans), the church was founded by Benedictine monks in the 11th century, and completely restructured by Cosimo Morelli; the façade is Neoclassical. The interior has a magnificent central nave and two side aisles, with opulent altars, made by the stonemasons of Sant'Ippolito. In the first north chapel is a 14th-century fresco of the *Madonna feeding the Child Jesus;* in the second is a painting by Simone Cantarini (1678) of the *Madonna with the Christ Child and Sts Peter and Paul,* and in the fourth is an old wooden Crucifix from the original church. The first south chapel has a remarkable 17th-century wooden statue of Christ, the third has two paintings by Guerrieri, of the *Madonna with the Christ Child and Sts Joseph and Francis* (1625) and *St Catherine* (1622). In the fourth south chapel is another painting by Guerrieri, of the *Madonna with the Christ Child and St Anne* (1627), and an impressive panel painting by Claudio Ridolfi (1629) of the *Madonna with Sts Anne and Hildebrand,* showing the town of Fossombrone. The meridian line in the transept, lit by the rays of the sun at midday, was traced by the local mathematician Count Sempronio Pace in 1800. The beautiful **Sagrestia dei Canonici**, with splendid carvings, is part of the old church. It is sometimes possible to visit the intriguing underground passages, the *sotterranei (ask the sacristan).* Behind the cathedral, in Via Passionei, are several medieval tower-houses.

Giovanni Francesco Guerrieri (1589–1657)

'Provincial' in the best sense of the word, Guerrieri travelled widely between 1610 and 1618, living in Rome, Sassoferrato and Fabriano, studying painting techniques and styles, before returning to his native Fossombrone—a quiet town perhaps, but where his art was much in demand: public, religious and private commissions kept him busy for the rest of his life. A perfect exponent of Counter-Reformation tendencies, his arresting paintings, with their tense, dramatic brushstrokes, reveal the influence of Caravaggio, but with a lighter touch. In Rome Guerrieri had befriended Orazio Gentileschi, a fervid follower of Caravaggio, who tempered that artist's stark realism with a softer approach; his influence on the younger artist from the Marche is clear. While in Rome Guerrieri collaborated on the decoration of Palazzo Borghese (a series of allegorical designs with symbolic significance), an experience which he enjoyed. His frequent still lifes, with vegetables, fruit, birds and flowers, indicate that he never lost his taste for realism. His daughter Camilla (b. 1628) also became a proficient artist.

In front of the cathedral, from Piazza Mazzini, Via Zanghi leads up to the 15th-century Corte Alta, Federico da Montefeltro's official residence in Fossombrone, now housing the **Museo Archeologico Vernarecci** and the **Pinacoteca Comunale** (*both open Jan–May and Oct–Dec Sat 3–6, Sun and holidays 10.30–12.30 & 3–6; June–Sept*

10.30–12.30 & 4–7; closed Sun), a collection of finds from ancient *Forum Sempronii*, but also from prehistoric and Picene sites. The pinacoteca has paintings from local churches, and pottery from Pesaro and Casteldurante (Urbania). Don't miss the lovely painted wooden ceilings.

From here a steep path leads up to the top of the hill (also reached by road, taking the long way round) and the **Rocca** (13th–15th centuries), from where there are marvellous views over the Metauro valley. The castle is an admirable example of the defensive architecture of Francesco di Giorgio Martini; it is said to be connected by a secret passage to the lower town. In the courtyard is the 18th-century church of Sant'Aldebrando, rebuilt on the ruins of the old cathedral.

Via Roma

After the cathedral the Corso, the ex-Via Flaminia, becomes Via Roma, in a very old part of the town, with cobbled streets and little houses painted blue, pink or yellow. On the right is the church of **Santa Lucia** (13th century), once the church of the shoemakers and cobblers; a 15th-century fresco of St Christopher has recently been discovered on the interior south wall. Close by is the lovely bridge over the Metauro, a reproduction of the original, built in 1780, destroyed in the Second World War. There are usually swans underneath it. Via Roma becomes Via Pergamino; on the right is Palazzo Cangi (16th century), which now houses the **Quadreria Cesarini** (*Jan–May and Oct–Dec Sat 3–6, Sun and holidays 10.30–12.30 & 3–6; June–Sept 10.30–12.30 & 4–7; closed Sun; T: 0721 714650*), a private collection of modern paintings, drawings,

Palazzo Cangi, home to the Quadreria Cesarini modern art collection.

etchings, sculptures and ceramics, mostly by the local artist Anselmo Bucci, but including works by Carnevali, Carrà, Morandi, Caffè, Severini, Tosi, Messina and many others, bequeathed to the city in 1977. The setting for the works of art is particularly interesting; a beautifully kept old palace with the family furniture, the home of a notary who loved contemporary figurative art.

Roman Fossombrone

The archaeological site of the Roman city of **Forum Sempronii** (*to request a visit T: 0721 716324*), lies a few kilometres away, at San Martino del Piano, on the Via Flaminia. Excavations have brought to light traces of the walls with a tower, and a bath-suite; the objects discovered can be seen in the Archaeological Museum in town (*see p. 274 above*).

AROUND FOSSOMBRONE

At San Lazzaro, 2km from the town, the Metauro has scoured a deep gorge and some enormous round depressions, the *Marmitte dei Giganti* (Giants' Saucepans), unique in central Italy.

At the foot of the Cesane hills, between the Metauro and the Foglia rivers, just north of Fossombrone, stands tiny **Isola del Piano**, a farming community surrounded by wheatfields, olive groves and vineyards; these farmers were among the first in Italy to practise organic farming methods, and to form an association for ecologically-sensitive agriculture. Throughout the long history of this little place, the inhabitants have often been forced to defend their homes against attack. In 1284 they were stormed by Rimini and their castle was burnt to the ground. In the ex-church of the Annunziata, now an auditorium, 15th–16th-century frescoes have been found, including one by Giovanni Santi, the father of Raphael (*see p. 296*).

Sant'Ippolito and environs

Near Fossombrone, in an area inhabited since the Neolithic era, stands the small centre of **Sant'Ippolito**, still surrounded by medieval walls, from which there is a magnificent panorama, and with the ruins of a crusty old castle, going back to the days when it was a defensive point for Fossombrone. Since the Middle Ages the inhabitants have been exploiting the nearby veins of blue and yellow sandstone and marble, becoming skilled stonemasons—their town is known as *il paese degli scalpellini*, the village of chisellers; in the 18th century they imported coloured marbles, brought up the valley by oxcart from Fano, to produce exquisite inlaid marble for export. Beautiful examples of their work can be seen all over the town, and in Via Raffaele is a museum dedicated to the subject, Museo dell'Arte degli Scalpellini (*to request a visit T: 0721 728144*).

From Sant'Ippolito a panoramic road leads to Barchi and to **Orciano di Pesaro**, on a hillside, a centre for markets and fairs for over a thousand years; a picturesque market is still held every Thursday. In the old town is the church of Santa Maria Nuova

(15th century; Baccio Pontelli), a lovely Renaissance construction, with a low rectangular façade in brick and a richly ornate portal, said to be designed by Raphael; the elegant square interior is surmounted by a dome and has three apses; that on the right is decorated with stuccoes by Federico Brandani. The bell-tower behind the church, built in 1348, is now the clock tower. The town was the birthplace of the sculptor Giò Pomodoro (1930–2003).

Five kilometres from Orciano is the picturesque castle of **Montebello**, built by Guidubaldo da Montefeltro; beautiful stucco decorations by Brandani survive in the interior. In the chapel of Sant'Anna, protector of women in childbirth, is a great bell: an ancient tradition says that husbands who can ring three strokes of the bell, using only their teeth, can save the lives of their wives and offspring during difficult births. In 1759, near Orciano, some elephant bones and a tusk were found; perhaps the remains of those used by the Carthaginians in the battle of 207 BC.

PRACTICAL INFORMATION

GETTING AROUND

• **By train**: Fano station (T: 0721 803627) is on the main Milan–Bologna–Pescara line; there is also a station at Marotta.
• **By bus**: Autolinee Baldelli, T: 0721 714963, www.baldelli.it, runs services connecting the towns along the Metauro Valley with the Cesano Valley and Pergola.
Autolinee Fratelli Bucci, T: 0721 32401, runs services to Montemaggiore al Metauro, Cartoceto, Serrungarina, Fossombrone, Senigallia, Ostra, Arcevia, Jesi, Falconara, Ancona.
Autolinee Vitali, T: 0721 862515, www.autolineevitali.191.it, has services to Pesaro, Chiaravalle, Jesi, Ancona, Pergola, Arcevia and Fabriano.
Autolinee Reni, T: 071 8046504, www.paginegialle.it/reni-srl; services to Pesaro, Senigallia, Ancona and Porto Recanati, June–Sept only.

INFORMATION OFFICES

A useful website for the area is www.lavalledelmetauro.it
Fano Tourist Information Bureau, Piazza XX Settembre, T: 0721 887523, www.comune.fano.ps.it, www.fano.it; IAT, 10 Via Battisti, T: 0721 803534, www.turismofano.com
Fossombrone IAT, Piazza Dante, T: 0721 716324; Pro Loco, T: 0721 723240, www.comune.fossombrone.ps.it; Comunità Montana del Metauro, Palazzo Sorbolonghi, 23 Via Roma, T: 0721 74291.
Montefelcino Municipio, Piazza Francesca da Rimini, T: 0721 743039, www.comune.montefelcino.ps.it; Pro Loco, T: 0721 729125.
Montemaggiore al Metauro Piazza Italia, T: 0721 895036, www.comune.montemaggiore.pu.it

HOTELS

Fano

€€€€ **Augustus**. Very pleasant hotel near Porta Giulia, with restaurant, gym and sauna. 2 Via Puccini, T: 0721 809781, www.hotelaugustus.it

€€€€ **Elisabeth Due**. Comfortable hotel in quiet position, with a restaurant. 2 Piazzale Amendola, T: 0721 823146, www.hotelelisabethdue.it

€€€ **Amelia**. Small hotel in central position, with restaurant; run by the same family for 50 years. 80 Viale Cairoli, T: 0721 824040, www.hotelamelia.it

€€€ **Continental**. Good value for money, with a garden, restaurant and water sports. 148 Viale Adriatico, T: 0721 800670, www.hotelcontinental-fano.it

€€€ **Corallo**. Small, modern hotel on seafront, with comfortable rooms, restaurant and internet point. 3 Via Leonardo da Vinci, T: 0721 804200, www.mobilia.it/corallo

€€€ **Cristallo**. Pleasant hotel, in a good position. 27 Viale Cesare Battisti, T: 0721 803282, www.hotelcristallo-fano.it

€€€ **Excelsior**. In a good position, with restaurant, garden and car park; children welcome. 57 Lungomare Simonetti, T: 0721 803558, www.hotelangela.it

€€€ **Marina**. Comfortable hotel in central position, good restaurant, garden, private beach and car park. Children welcome. 15 Viale Adriatico, T: 0721 803157, www.alexhotels.it

€€€ **Orfeo**. In a unique position on the main street, comfortable little hotel, with restaurant and pizzeria. 5 Corso Matteotti, T: 0721 803522.

Fossombrone

€€€ **Al Lago**. Comfortable hotel with garden, tennis, pool, restaurant and garage; children welcome. Near the Furlo Gorge. 79 Via Cattedrale, San Lazzaro, T: 0721 726129.

€€€ **Da Marco**. Small hotel with restaurant. 20 Via Giganti, T: 0721 714917.

€€€ **Mancinelli**. Essentially a restaurant, with comfortable rooms. 5 Piazza Petrucci, T: 0721/716550.

Marotta di Fano

€€€ **Spiaggia D'Oro**. On a particularly nice stretch of beach, comfortable, with a good restaurant. 54 Via Faà di Bruno, Marotta, T: 0721 96619, www.hotelspiaggiadoro.it

Saltara

€€€ **Metauro**. Small, modern, comfortable hotel with restaurant. 278 Via Flaminia, Calcinelli, T: 0721 891071, persio@interfree.it

Serrungarina

€€€ **Casa Oliva**. ■ Beautiful little hotel in a medieval village; excellent restaurant. 19 Via Castello, Bargni, T: 0721 891500, www.casaoliva.it

Torrette di Fano

€€€ **Casadei**. Well-run, with restaurant, private beach and lots of amenities. 53 Via Ammiraglio Cappellini, T: 0721 884661, www.hotelcasadei.it

€ **Edelweiss**. With a restaurant; good value for money. 27 Via Buonincontri, T: 0721 884535, www.hoteledelweiss.it

BED & BREAKFAST

Fano

Piergiorgio Mariani. Comfortable room in villa, private bathroom, meals available. English and French spoken. 12 Via

Martinetti, località Rosciano, T: 0721 864281.

Fossombrone

Mulino delle Ginestre. An historic water-mill. 13 Via delle Querce, T: 0721 714072, abucchi@libero.it

Sant'Ippolito

Il Pino. Comfortable accommodation with garden. 11 Via Serra, T: 328 6493768.

FARM ACCOMMODATION

Fano

Santa Cristina. The farm has vineyards and olive groves, raises rabbits and chickens; guests can help. Good home cooking. 2 Località Rosciano, T: 0721 862685.

Cartoceto

Locanda del Gelso. Farmhouse with comfortable rooms, marvellous food; they grow corn, fruit, olives and saffron. 12 Via Morola, T: 0721 877020.

Fossombrone

El Gatarel. Apartments in an 18th-century farmhouse with pool. The farm produces poultry, sugarbeet, wine and cereals. Closed winter. 10 Via Pantaneto, Isola di Fano, T: 0721 727189.

Isola del Piano

Alce Nero. This farm produces organic olive oil, cereals for pasta, and raises cattle; good food. 21 Via Valli, Località Montebello, T: 0721 7720221, www.alcenero.it

Montemaggiore al Metauro

La Carbonara. An organic farm producing olive oil and kiwi fruit; bikes available, art courses. Closed winter. 26 Via Carbonara, San Liberio, T: 0721 895028. **Villa Tombolina**. Luxurious villa-farmhouse, surrounded by vineyards,

orchards and olive groves, in a panoramic position; tennis and a pool. English, French, Russian and German spoken. Farm products on sale: if you want to indulge your sinful nostalgia for toast and dripping, buy some *goletta* to take home—don't tell your doctor. Località San Liberio, T: 0721 891918, www.villatombolina.it

Orciano di Pesaro

Azienda Agricola Montebello. B&B or self-catering flatlets in lovely farmhouse; they will help you plan your trekking. 13 Via Ville Fanti, T: 0721 287183, www.monsbelli.it

San Costanzo

Bartolacci. Large farm, with vineyards, olive groves, orchards, using organic methods. Good restaurant; also a pool and fishing in the lake. English and French spoken. 5 Via Breccione, Località Stacciola, T: 0721 930065, www.bartolacci.it

Serrungarina

Il Mandorlo. Apartments to rent on this conveniently situated farm producing olive oil, wine and fruit. 57 Via Tomba, T: 0721 891480.

COUNTRY HOUSES

Fano

Relais Villa Giulia. ■ Panoramic villa set in a luxuriant park, 3km from Fano railway station, built for Eugène de Beauharnais, Napoleon's stepson, now belonging to Count and Countess Passi. Bed and breakfast or self-catering accommodation. Via di Villa Giulia, Località San Biagio, T: 0721 823159, www.relaisvillagiulia.com

Fossombrone

Villa La Cerbara. A lovely villa, in a

hillside position; beautiful pool, garden, and a refined restaurant. 33 Strada San Pietro in Tambis, T: 0721 720292, www.lacerbara.it

Serrungarina

Villa Federici. Old building beautifully restored, with a restaurant. 4 Via Cartoceto, Bargni, T: 0721 891510, www.villafederici.it

MONASTERY ACCOMMODATION

Fano

Eremo di Monte Giove. 90 Via Montegiove, T: 0721 864603.

Marini Marina delle Suore Missionarie dell'Eucarestia. 51 Viale Gramsci, T: 0721 803593.

Saltara

Casa per ferie 'San Francesco'. Hotel run by nuns, for spiritual retreats. Via San Francesco, Località Borgaccio di Saltara, T: 0721 896287.

RESTAURANTS

Fano

€€€ **Casa Nolfi**. Imaginative dishes combining fish with vegetables, excellent wines. Closed Mon and Sun lunchtime. 59 Via Gasparoli, T: 0721 827066.

€€€ **Lisippo**. Elegant restaurant, well cooked and presented dishes, wide choice of local wines. 27/a Viale Adriatico, T: 0721 830204.

€€€ **Taverna dei Pescatori**. Simple setting close to the port, try the local fish soup, *brodetto alla fanese*, or a delicious dish with asparagus and prawns, *passatelli con asparagi e scampetti*. Closed Mon. 1 Piazzale Calafati, T: 0721 805364.

€€ **Da Maria Ponte Rosso**. ■ Tiny trattoria where Maria serves only the fish brought to her daily by a local fisherman. Always crowded, book at least the day before. Try her delicate fish soup called *passatelli con brodo di pesce*, or the tagliatelle with sole. Simple desserts, all home-made, sponge cake or jam tarts. Closed Sun in winter. 86 Via IV Novembre, T: 0721 808962.

€€ **Da Sandro il Pescatore**. Sandro's *brodetto alla fanese* is a meal in itself; local wines. Closed Mon. 110 Viale Adriatico, T: 0721 800273.

€€ **Il Bottigliere Enoteca**. Excellent wines and local dishes, in an attractive little corner of the old town. Closed Tues. 12–14 Via Bonaccorsi, T: 0721 822989.

€€ **La Perla**. On the seafront, homely atmosphere, excellent fish antipasto. Parking. Closed Mon. 60 Viale Adriatico, T: 0721 825631.

€€ **Nadia**. Family-run restaurant specializing in fish dishes with an unusual slant. Closed Mon. 25 Via del Bersaglio, T: 0721 806648.

€€ **Ristorantino Da Giulio**. ■ Giulio is a fantastic cook; try his fresh sardines baked in the oven, or the delicious, spicy *guazzetto* (fish soup without tomato), tasty pasta and risotto, grilled fish. The desserts are to die for; good local wines. Closed Tues. 100 Viale Adriatico, T: 0721 805680.

€€ **Quinta**. On the port, typical Fano recipes with fresh fish, local wines. Closed Sun. 42 Viale Adriatico, T: 0721 808043.

€ **Al Pesce Azzurro**. Self-service run by the fishermen, low fixed price for the whole meal, great fun. Closed Mon and Oct 1–Apr 30. 48 Viale Adriatico, T: 0721 803165.

Cartoceto

€€€ **Symposium Quattro Stagioni.** Reputedly one of Italy's best restaurants, it is a temple to fine cooking, and the pleasant sensations which accompany eating good food and drinking the right wines, in an elegant setting. An interesting, instructive, and delightful experience. Lucio Pompili presides over the kitchen. Closed Mon. 38 Via Cartoceto, T: 0721 898320.

€€€ **Osteria del Frantoio Trionfo.** Luminous, new tavern, where the famous local olive oil plays an important role in the kitchen; it is even used for making the chocolate cake. You can buy this excellent oil on the spot. Closed Mon. 5 Via San Martino, T: 0721 898286.

Fossombrone

€ **La Taverna del Falco.** Simple, welcoming tavern in old cellar, run by young people Via Vichi. Closed Mon, Tues evenings, T 0721 715396.

Isola del Piano

€ **Alce Nero.** Old-fashioned recipes, using the best quality ingredients from the local countryside. Closed Mon. 1 Via Montebello, T: 0721 720126.

Marotta di Fano

€€ **Alda.** Well cooked and presented fish. Closed Mon. 177 Via Faà di Bruno, T: 0721 967629.

€€ **Da Ciacco.** Traditional dishes with an innovative touch. Closed Mon. 102 Via Faà di Bruno, T: 0721 69512.

Montemaggiore al Metauro

€€€–€ **Locanda Borgo Antico.** Local sausage with olives, cheese and radicchio quiche, pasta made with chestnut flour, stuffed goose or fried lamb. Quite an experience. Closed Jan and Tues. 4 Via Panoramica, T: 0721 896553.

Saltara

€ **Sasà.** Luminous restaurant offering delightful local cuisine, good pasta dishes, roast meat, home-made desserts. Closed Wed and Thur evenings. 43/g Via Flaminia, Calcinelli, T: 0721 895690.

San Costanzo

€€€ **Rolando.** Eat in the garden if possible, at this welcoming restaurant specializing in meat dishes. Closed Wed. 123 Corso Matteotti, T: 0721 950990.

€€ **La Cerasa.** Delightful little restaurant, well run. Closed Wed. 1 Strada Piagge, T: 0721 935117.

Serrungarina

€€€ **Villa Federici.** In a 17th-century villa, restaurant serving memorable food accompanied by good local wines. Closed Mon and Tues lunchtime. 4 Via Cartoceto, Bargni, T: 0721 891510.

€€ **Da Luisa.** At the foot of the famous stairway, delicious local dishes: try the soft bread *crescia*, or the *passatelli in brodo*. Closed Jan–Feb. 8 Via Roma, T: 0721 896120.

CAFÉS, PASTRY SHOPS & ICE CREAM

Fano

Bar Giuliano. Serves excellent *moretta*, the fishermen's coffee. 270 Via Sauro.

Caffè Aurora. Good espresso or afternoon tea. 31–32 Piazza XX Settembre.

Caffè Berto. Favourite meeting-place for an aperitif. 41 Via Cavour.

Caffè Centrale. Morning coffee or hot chocolate. Closed Mon. 104 Corso Matteotti.

Caffè del Pasticciere. The place to go if you are hungry; enormous *cappuccini*, delicious pastries, very good *moretta*. Closed Wed. 8/a Via della Costituzione.

MORETTA

Invented by the fishermen to keep themselves awake on chilly winter days, this coffee drink is a stiff brew consisting of hot, sweet espresso, anisette liqueur, rum, brandy and lemon peel. It is extremely difficult to prepare, and not all of the coffee shops can make it properly. The proportions of the ingredients must be perfect, but the tricky part comes when they are poured into the glass—there should be three distinct layers: alcohol at the bottom, then coffee, then a frothy, amber-coloured topping. Better sit down before you try it!

FESTIVALS & EVENTS

Fano Carnival; Info: Ente Carnevalesca Fano, 7 Via Garibaldi, www.carnevaledifano.com, www.cartapesta.it, Feb. *Fanojazzbythesea*, jazz festival; Info: Ufficio Festival, T: 0721 820275, July. *Mostra-Mercato del Libro e della Stampa Antichi*, exhibition and sale of old books and prints along the streets of the centre; Info T: 0721 887514, July. *Disfida delle Zuppe di Pesce*, who makes the finest fish soup? A competition sees the cooks of the coastal towns of Italy preparing soup—the public votes for the best; Info: T: 0721 828310, www.confesercentipu.it, Sept. Open-air Antiques Market in the streets of the old centre, second weekend of every month. Open-air concerts and shows at the Corte Malatestiana in summer.

Cartoceto *Mostra-Mercato dell'Oliva e dell'Olio*, lectures, debates, a traditional market, visits to the oil presses, and typical gastronomy, all dedicated to olives and olive oil, Nov.

Fossombrone *Mostra-Mercato del Tartufo Bianchetto*, a day dedicated to the famous white truffles, 1st Sun in March. Concerts at the church of San Filippo, March–May. Jazz Festival in summer. *In Viaggio*, ethnic music and traditional dishes from various localities of the world, different every year; Info: Centro Aggregazione Roberta Capodogli, T: 0721 723244, www.comune.fossombrone.ps.it/inViaggio, June.

Mondolfo *La Cacciata*, competition between the four city districts in a series of *pallone al bracciale* games, all in 16th-century costumes, ending with a torchlit pageant, July.

Orciano di Pesaro Tris, Via Schiappe, T: 0721 981966, is a *balera* for the traditional Italian *liscio*, a cross between ballroom and country dancing, usually in the open air. *Mercato Antico di San Rocco*, traditional 19th-century handicraft market, 16–17 Aug.

Saltara *La Via Dolorosa*, Easter procession in medieval costume, Good Friday.

Sant'Ippolito *Scolpire in Piazza*, come and try chiselling, under the watchful eye of the local stonemasons; courses rom May–Sept; Info: T: 0721 728144, www.scalpellini.org, last week in July.

Serrungarina *Fiera della Pera Angelica*, a festival of the famous pears, last Sun in Aug.

LOCAL SPECIALITIES

Fano
Enoteca Drogheria Ricci, 67 Via Cavour, an old-fashioned grocery store offering wines, olive oil and many other things. **Pasticceria Guerrino**, 23 Via Togliatti, is good for excellent cakes and pastries, including seasonal biscuits, and the *cavalluccio*, a cake once made for children on special occasions, with marzipan, almonds, pine kernels and sultanas, in the shape of a horse; prize-winning confectioner.
Barchi
Furiassi, 24 Via San Bartolio, makes and sells terracotta casseroles in various shapes, for oven-cooking without fat.
Cartoceto
Frantoio Serafini, 2 Via San Michele, founded in 1465, prize-winning olive oil. **Gastronomia Beltrami**, 21–23 Via Umberto, old-fashioned grocery store, with an irresistible array of olive oils, cheeses, hams and salami, home-made jams and pasta.
Fossombrone
Pasticceria Rinci, Via Roma, traditional pastry shop, the oldest in Fossombrone.
Mondolfo
Idillio Ciuccoli, Via Vandali, craftsman who still makes the spiky wooden *bracciali*, the arm-guards for the exciting game of *pallone al bracciale* (*see p. 103*)

FANO CARNIVAL

Probably the oldest in Italy, the Fano Carnival can be traced back to 1347, when struggles between opposing factions in the town were resolved, at least once a year, by jousting. In 1450 Carnival was officially approved by statute, in the form of races between horses and donkeys, after which the winners were to throw honey-cakes at the crowd. Today the cakes are replaced by chocolates and sweets, thrown at the people from participants on floats, and returned with vigour. The event can feel like a real battle; so wear a hat, and take a bag to put the sweets in; some people use upturned umbrellas. The parades are magnificent; enormous *papier-mâché* satirical figures wobble dizzily around, accompanied by raucous music, dancing, and crowds of people in fancy dress. The enthusiasm is contagious. As the sun goes down, the lights of the *Luminaria*, the night parade, create a magical atmosphere; fireworks conclude the day. The people of Fano take their Carnival very seriously; a whole year is spent on planning the event, and the best entertainers are chosen to do the job. The particularly successful events of 2003 and 2004 were organised by Nobel prizewinner Dario Fo.

PESARO & THE NORTH MARCHE COAST

PESARO

Although some houses are painted yellow, orange or red, the predominating colour of Pesaro (pop. 90,000) is rose—just as it should be, because the rose is the emblem of this captivating city, appearing frequently as an architectural motif, and of course on the famous china.

HISTORY OF PESARO

Pisaurum was founded in 184 BC as a Roman colony on the Via Flaminia, at the mouth of the River Foglia, where the Picenes had a small settlement (probably a dependency of the then more important town of Novilara). The marshy area proved to be so unhealthy that more colonists had to be sent at regular intervals, and extensive drainage was necessary. The thick, sticky clay, however, was perfect for making bricks and tiles, and later it would prove to be the mainstay of the economy when the ceramics industry was introduced. The position, too, on the most important trade routes, was perfect, and Pesaro was fought over by Goths, Byzantines, Lombards and Franks, until it was donated to the Church by Charlemagne in 774. Between the 6th and 7th centuries Pesaro, together with Rimini, Fano, Senigallia and Ancona, had formed part of the Maritime Pentapolis, under the protection of Ravenna. An independent commune in the 12th century, in the 13th it was taken by the Malatesta of Rimini, then by the Sforza (who built the castle and the Palazzo Ducale), and then by the della Rovere. These last fostered the ceramics industry, erected a new set of walls, and built the canal-port at the mouth of the Foglia river. The city remained in their hands until 1631, when on the death of the last duke, it returned to the Papal States. Under della Rovere rule Pesaro became the administrative and cultural centre of the Duchy of Urbino, attracting artists of the quality of Titian, and great writers, such as Torquato Tasso. In June 1799 a rebellious band of patriots, consisting mainly of peasants, succeeded in taking the city from Napoleon's troops and holding it for a few months. In 1861 Pesaro became part of the Kingdom of Italy.

Today Pesaro is an important centre for the manufacture of furniture, especially for offices and kitchens (Scavolini, Berloni, Febal); for mattresses, glass (Fiam), and motorcycles (Benelli, Morbidelli). Tourists are attracted by the sandy beaches and the cosmopolitan atmosphere, and opera fans by the famous Rossini Opera Festival.

EXPLORING PESARO

Between the sea and the old city centre is a pleasant district with hotels, villas, gardens, shops and restaurants, focusing on **Piazzale Libertà**, with its round pool and the bronze sphere by Arnaldo Pomodoro (1998). Close by is the delightful Art Nouveau Hotel Vittoria (1907). The sea front (Viale Trieste) from here to the picturesque canal-port on the River Foglia is a favourite for strolling. At no. 9 Via Pola, in the heart of this district, one of the early 20th-century houses, Villa Molaroni, houses the **Museo del Mare** (*open Tues, Thur, Sat 5–8; T: 0721 387474*), a poignant collection of old figureheads and other equipment from long-since-gone ships, including objects recuperated from a sunken galleon. Also in this area, in Piazza Doria, is the seamen's church—**Santa Maria della Scala** (1320 and 1822), a Neoclassical façade surmounted with a clock and three statues from the original church. In front is the 18th-century statue of St Andrew, the patron saint of fishermen, and in the centre of the square is a white stone fountain with an obelisk, which once stood in the port.

The cattedrale

Viale della Repubblica, flanked by shady trees, which becomes Via Rossini and then Via Branca, corresponds to the main street of the Roman *Pisaurum*, and leads right through the centre, which is traffic-free and full of bicycles. On reaching Via Rossini, on the left is the cattedrale, a worn, honey-coloured building, with a simple Romanesque façade and two 12th-century stone lions on either side of the portal. In the 19th century, repairs to the floor brought to light two preceding mosaic floors, now partially visible thanks to an ingenious system of glass viewing panels and shifting blocks of mosaic. The artistic quality of both floors is exceptionally good, with imaginative designs rich in colour and symbolic allusion, carried out using tiny coloured marble tesserae. The upper section measures c. 600m square (some scholars think perhaps 900m square), was laid in the 6th century, and repairs were carried out until the 13th century, while the lower floor, c. 70cm beneath it, was that of a 4th-century Palaeochristian basilica, and is probably about the same size. Historians believe the first church was destroyed in 553 during the war between Goths and Byzantines, and rebuilt a few years later by Belisarius, the emperor Justinian's general, who simply packed down the rubble and laid the new floor on top. In the 13th century the church was rebuilt again, this time with a tiled floor. There are plans to remove both mosaics and place them in a purpose-built exhibition area.

   In the chapel to the right of the main altar is a 15th-century wooden Crucifix known as the Crocifisso di San Bernardo, while to the left of the main altar is a detached 15th-century fresco of the *Madonna with Saints*, recently attributed to Raphael—he would have been 15 when he painted it. In the vestibule of the Bishop's Palace, at no. 62 Via Rossini, is a stone sarcophagus found at the church of San Decenzio (in the cemetery), once the first cathedral of the city. The 7th-century sarcophagus has enigmatic carvings on all four sides, still not fully explained. The two figures on the front probably represent the two martyrs Terence and Decentius, respectively the patrons of the new and old cathedrals. On the back an exorcism is being carried out; on one of the sides is a snake eating its own tail (symbol of eternity), and on the other are two deer drinking from a vase.

Casa Rossini

At no. 34 Via Rossini is the house where the composer was born, Casa Rossini (*open Tues and Wed 9.30–12.30; Thur–Sun 9.30–12.30 & 4–7; July–Aug 9.30–12.30 & 5–8; Tues and Thur closes 11pm; closed Mon; T: 0721 387357*), a simple building where the Rossini family lived between 1790 and 1796, in two rooms on the first floor. Casa Rossini is now a museum, with various memorabilia, and a collection of prints representing some of the greatest 19th-century singers, depicted dressed as the characters they played. On the first floor are paintings, drawings, prints and caricatures of Rossini himself.

ROSSINI'S PHILOSOPHY

Rossini enjoyed life very much, especially good food, music and beautiful women. By the time he was 37, he had composed almost all of his operas, culminating with the masterpiece *William Tell*; he spent the remaining 39 years of his existence as a *bon viveur*, living in a luxurious villa at Passy (Paris), and organizing memorable parties for his friends, for which he often did the cooking himself. He said he cried only three times in his life: when his first opera was booed; when a roast turkey stuffed with truffles fell overboard during a boat trip; and when he first heard Paganini play. 'Other than doing nothing', he said, 'I know of no other more delightful occupation than eating. Eating the way you should, of course. The appetite is for the stomach what love is for the heart. An empty stomach is like a bassoon or a flute, in which discontent grumbles or envy whines. A full stomach, on the other hand, is the triangle of pleasure or the harpsichord of joy. As for love, I consider it the 'prima donna' par excellence, the soprano who sings in our brain, making us drunk with the sound, stealing our heart away. Eating and loving, singing and digesting—these are, in truth, the four acts of this comic opera we call life, which vanishes like the froth of a bottle of champagne. Whoever lets it escape without enjoying it, is crazy'. But was Rossini really so carefree? Recent biographies suggest that he suffered from well-concealed depression, because his inspirational vein dried up too soon…..

Next door, in Palazzo Gradari, is the elegant **Enoteca** (*T: 0721 64916; www. enotecacomunalerossini.com*), an opportunity for sampling local wines and foodstuffs. Opposite Rossini's house is the smart 18th-century **Palazzo Mazzolari Mosca** (Giannandrea Lazzarini), where the town council plans to open a new museum of industrial art, in accordance with the wishes of Vittoria Toschi Mosca, who bequeathed the palazzo to the city in 1877.

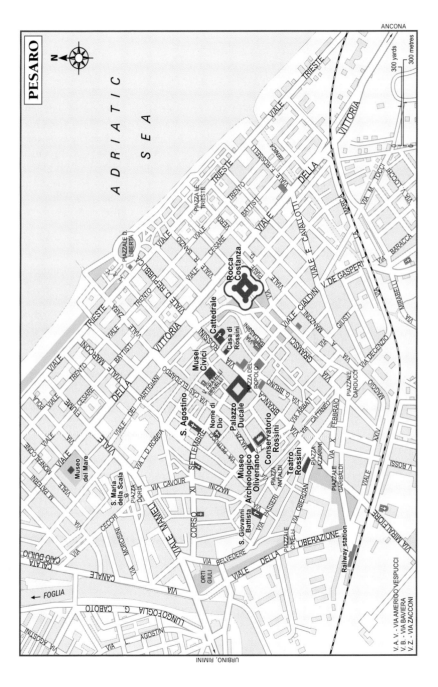

PESARO

ADRIATIC SEA

ANCONA

URBINO, RIMINI

V. A. V. - VIA AMERIGO VESPUCCI
V. B. - VIA BAVIERA
V. Z. - VIA ZACCONI

300 yards
300 metres

Musei Civici

Behind Palazzo Mazzolari Mosca is another beautiful palace belonging to the same lady (she was a member of one of the most influential aristocratic families of Pesaro), the 17th-century **Palazzo Toschi Mosca**, housing the Musei Civici (*open Tues and Wed 9.30–12.30; Thur–Sun 9.30–12.30 & 4–7; July–Aug 9.30–12.30 & 5–8; Tues and Thur closes 11pm; closed Mon; T: 0721 387541*), the Art Gallery and the Ceramics Museum. In the courtyard, you are confronted by Ferruccio Mengaroni's impressive *Medusa*. Mengaroni, a gifted ceramicist, produced the work for an art exhibition in Monza. Inspired by the famous painting by Caravaggio, he depicted himself as Medusa, with his face surrounded by horribly realistic snakes. It is said that the mirror he was using smashed without apparent cause. When the crate containing the work was about to be hoisted up to the first floor of the exhibition hall, the ropes broke, and Mengaroni, running to save it, was crushed under its weight. His body cushioned its fall, so the ghastly Medusa (the terror of school groups) is still perfectly intact. This was 13th May 1925. The bizarre accident is still the cause of endless comments about the dangers of messing around with such an unlucky lady.

The collection of paintings inside includes masterpieces by Paolo Veneziano, Jacobello del Fiore, Giovanni Antonio da Pesaro, Marco Zoppo, Guido Reni, Simone Cantarini, Vettor Romogni (fantastic *trompe l'oeil* paintings) and Christian Berentz (exquisite still lifes); all leading up to the magnificent panel painting by **Giovanni**

Detail of Giovanni Bellini's *Coronation of the Virgin* (1475).

Bellini, perhaps his greatest work, the *Pala di Pesaro* or *Crowning of the Virgin* (1475), brought here by sea from Venice, for the church of St Francis—a sign of the strong cultural relationship between the two cities under the Sforza. Depicting Christ crowning his Mother, on an ornate double throne (the castle seen on the back of the throne, certainly painted from life, has not yet been identified), with Sts Paul, Peter, Jerome and Francis of Assisi, the Holy Spirit and cherubim of different colours, the painting is contained within a frame consisting of smaller panels: Saints on either side, and stories of Saints at the bottom. The *cimasa*, or crowning panel on the top (only the frame remains), representing the *Embalming of Christ*, was taken by Napoleon and exhibited in the Louvre. Returned to the Papal States thanks to the intervention of Antonio Canova, it is now in the Vatican Gallery.

Leda and the Swan, from a plate made in Pesaro.

The **Ceramics Section** is one of the richest collections in Europe, tracing the history of the art, both in Pesaro and Casteldurante (Urbania) through the centuries. Casteldurante was renowned for love-cups known as 'beautiful women'. Gifts from a young man to his betrothed, they showed the face of a lady with a scroll giving her name and the word *bella*, beautiful; Pesaro acquired fame for richly-decorated, colourful majolica plaques and plates, and later for white china dishes, dinner and coffee services, decorated with floral motifs, especially pink roses (the symbol of the city), daisies, anemones and leafy tendrils. The museum has a well-stocked bookshop and library.

Piazza del Popolo and the Rocca

The central square, corresponding to the Roman forum, is Piazza del Popolo, with a riotous Baroque fountain (1685) in the middle, full of exuberant tritons and sea horses. On the northwest side is **Palazzo Ducale**, now seat of the prefecture (*to request a visit T: 0721 387393 or the Museum Service 0721 387474*). Most of the building goes back to the 14th century, but the elegant façade, with porticoes and battlements, and the magnificent **Salone Metaurense**, with its coffered ceiling, were added by Alessandro Sforza in 1465.

By taking Via San Francesco, opposite Palazzo Ducale, on the left is the 13th-century sanctuary church of **Santa Maria delle Grazie** (ex-San Francesco d'Assisi), with a red and white marble Gothic portal (1373) which lights up the scruffy brick façade.

In the Baroque interior, traces of 14th- and 15th-century frescoes are still visible on the front wall and on some of the arches. In the apse is a little marble temple housing the 16th-century panel painting of the *Madonna of the Graces*, said to be miraculous. In the south aisle is the lovely golden *Triptych of Montegranaro*, showing the *Madonna with St James and St Anthony Abbot*, by Jacobello del Fiore, signed and dated 1407. This painting, which disappeared in 1922, only to reappear on the market recently, was purchased by a private citizen and donated to this church, to which it rightfully belongs. In a room to the left of the main altar are more frescoes, and a painting of *St Ursula* by Palma Giovane.

The next turning on the left leads to Piazzale Matteotti and the **Rocca Costanza** (*to request a visit T: 0721 387474*), built for Costanzo Sforza (son of Alessandro) in 1480 by Luciano Laurana. The massive structure, which once housed the prison, is one of the earliest examples in the region of a castle designed for flat terrain.

Recent archaeological excavations in Piazzale Matteotti have brought to light a stretch of city street and some homes of wealthy Roman citizens (*for information T: 0721 387409*). Close by, in Via Gramsci, in Palazzo della Provincia, the building housing the offices of the provincial administration, is the **Galleria di Arte Contemporanea** (*to request a visit T: 0721 359311, www.spac.pu.it*), displaying part of the vast collection of paintings donated to, or acquired by, the administration since the Second World War, including works by Bucci, Caffè, Fiume, Mastroianni, Valentini and Schifano.

Sant'Agostino and the Nome di Dio

By taking the picturesque, colourful Corso XI Settembre from Piazza del Popolo, you will find on the right the 14th-century church of **Sant'Agostino**, with a splendid early 15th-century Venetian-Gothic portal, rich in detail, from the lions at the foot to the statues of saints in little aedicules on the sides. The single-nave interior was restored in 1776; over the second north altar is a canvas by Pomarancio showing a dramatic *St Nicholas of Tolentino Pleading on Behalf of the Souls in Purgatory*—the city in the background is Pesaro. On the third north altar is a painting by Simone Cantarini of *St Rita*. On the first south altar is a painting of the *Holy Family* by Gian Giacomo Pandolfi, and over the third south altar a lovely *Annunciation* by Palma Giovane. Over the main altar is a canvas by Pietro Tedeschi of the *Holy Trinity with the Virgin and Sts Lawrence and Augustine*. In the little chapel to the left of the presbytery is a large, impressive *Crucifixion* in stucco, by Federico Brandani. But the *pièce de resistance* in this church is the amazing 15th-century carved and inlaid wooden choir, full of interesting details—views of Pesaro, for example; you will recognize Palazzo Ducale and the church of San Giovanni, the Rocca Costanza and the castle of Gradara. The exquisite decoration is completed by two small carved dragons with human faces: they have been identified as Costanzo Sforza and Camilla of Aragon, who married in 1475.

Almost opposite the church is Via Petrucci, where on the left is the little church of the **Nome di Dio** (*open July–Aug Wed–Sat 5–8; T: 0721 67815*), of 1618, with a sumptuous, coherent Baroque interior, full of paintings by Pandolfi on the walls, and on the magnificent ceiling; coloured marble, and carved and gilded wooden frames. The beautiful organ is by Antonio Paci. Over the altar was a famous painting by Federico Barocci of the *Circumcision*, now substituted by a copy, because the original was stolen by Napoleon; it is now in the Louvre.

Museo Archeologico and district

Turn left at the bottom of Via Petrucci, to reach the **Museo Archeologico Oliveriano** at 97 Via Mazza (*open July–Aug Mon–Sat 4–7; Sept–June 9–12; T: 0721 33344, ask at Library first*), housed in the 17th-century Palazzo Almerici. Most of the archaeological collection was put together by Annibale degli Abbati Olivieri Giordani, an 18th-century intellectual, and includes many rare pieces: coins, statues, Etruscan bronzes and vases, found in excavations here in Pesaro and at the Picene necropolis of Novilara. The gem of the collection is the famous 7th-century BC tombstone from Novilara showing a sea battle fought between a Greek merchant vessel, helped by a Picene craft, and a pirate ship—pirate corpses are being thrown into the sea. On the first floor of the palace is the prestigious historical library of Pesaro, founded in the 18th century, the **Biblioteca Oliveriana** (*open Mon–Fri 9–1.30 & 2.30–7; Sat 9–1.30; closed 17 July–31 Aug; T: 0721 33344*). Like the archaeological collection, this too was donated by Olivieri Giordani in 1756. Since then, the contents of many private libraries, and books from suppressed religious orders, have been added. The collection contains one of the oldest geographical maps in the world, the Oliveriana World Map of 1508.

Opposite the building is the concave façade of the church of **Santa Maria Maddalena** (1744; Luigi Vanvitelli), once belonging to the Benedictine nuns, and replacing an older church, consecrated in 1325; their convent, already suppressed in 1861, was destroyed by bombs during the Second World War. The luminous interior is decorated with stucco relief and paintings by Giannandrea Lazzarini; it is normally closed, and used for exhibitions. Close by, in Via Fratelli Benelli, is another interesting church—the **Santissima Annunziata** (1356 and 18th century), once belonging to a confraternity which buried the poor and offered hospitality to pilgrims. The superb altarpiece, a work in white stucco showing the *Annunciation*, is by Giuseppe Mazza. The church has recently been acquired by a local bank, which will restore it and use it for cultural events.

Next to Palazzo Almerici, facing Piazza Olivieri, is the apricot-coloured **Conservatorio Rossini** (Giannandrea Lazzarini), the academy of music, opened in 1882 thanks to the legacy of Rossini, who left his estate to his city. Inside the building is a concert hall, Auditorium Pedrotti (1885), unfortunately badly restored in the past, but with particularly good acoustics, and in front of it is a graceful modern sculpture of a centaur, joyfully 'escaping'. To the left of the academy is the church of **San Giacomo** (*ring the doorbell loudly if closed; the priest—a charming person—is a little hard of hearing*). Despite the Neoclassical façade, it is one of the oldest parish churches of the city, first mentioned in 1062. Over the altar is a fresco, once on the outside of the old church, thought to be by Giovanni Santi—the *Madonna of the Palms*. Unfortunately it was over-restored in the 19th century, but you can still see the quality of the original work. On the north altar is a delightful canvas by Giovan Francesco Ferri (1736) of the *Virgin and St Anne*, which seems to be inspired by the other painting.

The western districts

On Piazza Lazzarini is the famous opera house, **Teatro Rossini** (*T: 0721 69359*) of 1816, inaugurated by Rossini himself in 1818, conducting his opera *The Thieving Magpie*. The interior and the acoustics are superb. To the right of the theatre is Via Passeri, where you will find on the right the unfinished—but strangely fascinating in its decadence—church of **San Giovanni Battista** (Girolamo and Bartolomeo Genga), once belonging to a Franciscan order; their old convent next door, at no. 177, has been transformed into the sleek public library. Most of the works of art originally painted for this church are in various museums of the world—Napoleon again—but the north transept is entirely decorated in lovely stucco relief, which he could not take away. In the corner of this transept is the interesting monument (1854) to the local writer and poet Giulio Perticari. It was in his honour, in 1827, that the **Orti Giuli** were created. These, at Via Belvedere, on the northern bastion close to Porta Rimini, are one of the oldest public gardens in Italy (*open Nov–Feb 8–6; Mon–Sat 8–4*). Typical of their period, they have shady walks, a folly and a fake temple. There is a meteorological observatory housing the **Museo Scientifico L. Guidi** (*to request a visit T: 0721 30677*), with an interesting collection of rare 19th-century and 20th-century scientific instruments.

Other sights of Pesaro

At no. 25 Via delle Scuole (turning of Via Sara Levi Nathan), is the **Sephardic synagogue** (*open July–Aug Tues–Fri 5–8*), built in the late 16th century, an interesting example of Jewish architecture in the region—the prayer room, on the first floor, has a high barrel vault, decorated with large rose motifs. This is now the only surviving synagogue in Pesaro.

In a district on the other side of the railway, close to the river, at no. 39 Via Fermo, is the **Museo Morbidelli** (*open Sat only 2–7; T: 0721 22346*), a nostalgic collection of over 250 motorcycles, dating from the early 20th century to 1980, when the company stopped production (they only make the engines now).

A short walk (c. 2km) west of the centre, on the old inland road to Gradara, leads to **Villa Caprile** (*open 15 June–15 Sept 3–7; other days on request; T: 0721 21440*), on Strada Caprile, with Italian-style gardens and fountains, built for Marquis Giovanni Mosca in 1640, and completed by Carlo Mosca in 1763. Famous visitors include Casanova; Caroline of Brunswick, Princess of Wales, who lived here for a time; Stendhal; and Giacomo Leopardi (*see p. 229*). The villa is now seat of the Institute of Agrarian Studies.

Novilara

South of Pesaro is the village of Novilara, surrounded by vineyards, with a long stretch of Roman aqueduct nearby. It was once an important Picene centre, more important than Pesaro itself (the necropolis just below the town can be visited on request; *T:*

0721 286114). In Via delle Scuole Nuove is a new museum dedicated to Picene and Roman finds, the **Centro di Documentazione Archeologica e Sentiero Santa Croce** (*to request a visit T: 0721 286114*), providing information on the health and the diet of the people buried in the necropolis, and a display of carved stone stelae, of great historical importance.

FROM PESARO TO GABBICE MARE

About 5km from Pesaro, along the panoramic road for Gabicce (near the lighthouse), is a sign indicating **Villa Imperiale** (*Via dei Cipressi, T: IAT 0721 69341 to enquire about visiting possibilities, the villa is a private home, usually Wed May–Sept*), a good example of a luxurious Renaissance summer residence, commenced in the 15th century for Alessandro Sforza, and completed by Girolamo Genga in 1530 for Francesco Maria I della Rovere and Eleonora Gonzaga. The beautiful pearly-pink, castle-like villa is surrounded by elegant gardens and pinewoods. The road continues to **Fiorenzuola di Focara**, a fortified township mentioned by Dante, perfectly preserved, dominated by a slender bell-tower on the edge of the cliff, then **Casteldimezzo**, with a 13th-century parish church housing a wooden Crucifix painted by Jacobello del Fiore, and stunning views over the coast, before arriving at Gabicce.

Between Villa Imperiale and the sea is Monte San Bartolo, forming a high cliff and a rocky coastline, which suddenly interrupt the long series of sandy beaches running practically from Trieste to the Gargano (with the exception of Mt Conero). Since 1994 the area has been protected as the **Parco Regionale Monte San Bartolo**, and includes olive groves, vineyards, wheat fields, and oak woods, to the edge of the cliff with its Mediterranean maquis, spectacular in springtime when the golden-yellow, scented broom contrasts against the deep blue of the sky and the sea. It is the perfect environment for animals such as badgers, porcupine and roe deer, but also for small mammals and birds; foxes can often be seen scavenging dead fish and seabirds on the rocky beaches. During autumn migration large numbers of starlings swoop down onto the olive groves, but the farmers are one step ahead of them in protecting their trees. The spring migration sees many birds of prey, including harriers, buzzards, and ospreys. Some peregrine falcons winter in the park. It is a good place for spotting sea birds; there are several gulls, including the Mediterranean, common, and slender-billed; cormorants, divers, grebes, and shearwaters.

Gabicce Mare is a small, practically perfect seaside resort, with a sandy beach, separated from Cattolica (in Emilia Romagna) by the River Tavollo. It has won many Blue Flags for the quality of its beaches. The town can trace its history back to the 10th century, when a small village grew up around the church of Sant'Ermete, in what is now Gabicce Monte on the slopes of Mt San Bartolo. Just offshore, and now submerged, are the ruins of the Roman port of *Valbruna*. The small size of Gabicce—and the fact that it is in a park—have saved it from being over exploited. The pleasant surroundings and the long tradition for hospitality create the ideal conditions for a carefree holiday.

Gradara

Gradara is a large, beautifully preserved, romantic castle, surrounded by olive trees hundreds of years old, the setting for one of the most tragic love stories ever told. One of Italy's 'beautiful villages', it is a golden brick masterpiece, in such good condition because (practically in ruins) it was purchased as a private dwelling in 1920 by a wealthy engineer, who dedicated the rest of his life to restoring it. On the death of his widow in 1983, Gradara was donated to the Italian government. The castle is particularly attractive when approached from the sea, and the beauty of the walls, with their 17 towers, can be fully appreciated. Sometimes, when there is a full moon, the ghost of a lady can be seen walking slowly along the battlements: people say it is Francesca da Polenta, murdered by her own husband (*see box*).

PAOLO & FRANCESCA

In 1275 Giovanni ('Gianciotto') Malatesta married the beautiful Francesca da Polenta daughter of Guido da Polenta, lord of Ravenna, by proxy, sending his handsome brother Paolo to sign the marriage contract. Poor Francesca was horrified to discover that she had married a very unpleasant and exceedingly ugly man. Gianciotto was sent to Pesaro as governor, and as he wasn't allowed to take Francesca with him, he closed her up in the fortress of Gradara, where the gallant Paolo kept her company, reading to her from romantic books. The two young people fell madly in love. One night Gianciotto returned to Gradara without warning, and caught them together—Paolo tried to escape, but his cloak caught on a nail (the guide will show you this), and the two lovers were stabbed to death by the outraged cuckold. The story has inspired many writers, poets, composers and painters, from Dante and Boccaccio to Byron and Ingres.

The castle was first built in 1150; in the 14th century the Malatesta enlarged it, surrounded it with a double defensive wall, and frescoed the salons, as an elegant venue for their guests. In 1464 it was taken by the Sforza, who gave it a Renaissance aspect, with an imposing stairway and a loggia. Lucrezia Borgia lived here for three of the five years of her marriage (1493–97) to Giovanni Sforza. In 1513 Francesco Maria della Rovere took Gradara, on behalf of the pope. On his death the castle reverted to the Papal States, and was practically abandoned. Ransacked by Napoleon's troops in the early 19th century, an earthquake in 1916 almost completely destroyed it.

Entrance to the town is through the only gate, Porta dell'Orologio, or *Porta Firau*—it is possible to walk along on top of the walls, for the entire length, from here (*open 9–1 & 2–7; also 8–midnight from 15 June–30 Sept; T: 0541 964115*), opening onto the steep main street, with medieval houses on either side. Another set of walls separates the township from the parish church of San Giovanni Battista (on the altar is a 15th-century wooden Crucifix), and the awesome **Rocca** (*open 8.30–7; late closing Sat from*

15 June–15 Sept; T: 0541 964181), with a series of rooms decorated with paintings and frescoes, and carefully furnished with antiques. Among the most interesting are Lucrezia Borgia's room and Francesca's room. From the walls there is a splendid view over the surrounding countryside and the promontory of Gabicce.

TAVULLIA & THE FOGLIA VALLEY

Tavullia (pop. 5,200), close to the border with Emilia Romagna (the nearby Tavollo stream is in fact the boundary), was once known as *Tomba di Pesaro*; Mussolini changed the name when he was invited for a visit; superstitious, he didn't like the idea of being sent to a tomb. Its strategic position was such that it was frequently contested between the Malatesta and Montefeltro. The castle of Tavullia, rebuilt by the della Rovere, was destroyed in the 19th century, and in September 1944 the town, being on the Gothic Line, was heavily bombed—this is in fact where the Allies were able to break through the German defences. Parts of the castle have now been restored, and you can walk along the walls, which offer lovely views over the countryside. The people are immensely proud of their world-famous motorcycling champion, Valentino Rossi; his impish face is everywhere.

From Tavullia the road winds down to the Foglia. On the far side of the river is **Montelabbate**. The name means 'Mount of the Abbot', and in fact the town stands at the foot of a hill where a castle was built in the 12th century by the monks of the nearby abbey of San Tommaso in Foglia (*see below*), as a safe residence for their abbot. The fertile land alongside the river attracted the interest of the aristocratic families of Pesaro, and the castle and its village were governed by various lords, until Napoleon took it in 1808. Now the attractive little town of golden-brown brick has an important industrial area for the production of furniture, but Montelabbate is famous above all for peaches; every year in July, there is a big festival for the peach harvest. The ruined castle on the top of the hill is very picturesque, with the keep and the prison still standing.

About 2km southwest of Montelabbate, on the road to Apsella, is the **Abbadia di San Tommaso in Foglia** (*to request a visit T: 0721 490706*), founded by Benedictine monks in 970 on the ruins of a pagan temple to the woodland god Sylvan. The abbey prospered, and soon became one of the most important in central Italy. Pope Clement II died here of malaria in 1047; in 1137 Holy Roman Emperor Lothair III used it as a military base. In the 15th century the institution gradually lost its importance, but now, after centuries of decline restored to its former dignity.

Mombaroccio

Mombaroccio is still surrounded by robust 15th-century walls; the town is said to have been built using the materials from five ruined castles in the area. Entering through the solidly rotund and reassuring Porta Maggiore (15th century), you reach Piazza Barocci and the palace of the della Rovere family, now the town hall, which houses an exhibition of locally-made lace and embroidery (*open 9–12 & 3–7; T: 0721 471156*), illustrating several different techniques; this was once a widespread skill in Mombaroccio, and is still a popular pastime. In the same square is the parish church of Santi Vito e Modesto (18th century), with some paintings of the Barocci school inside, and the 15th-century church of San Marco, with a stone lion over the portal. In the church is an 18th-century organ, and beautiful carved walnut choir-stalls. The convent of the church is now used as the civic museum, Museo della Civiltà Contadina (*open 9–12 & 3–7; T: 0721 471103*), with a lovingly displayed collection of tools and equipment used until recently by local farmers, and a rich collection of sacred art: paintings, furniture and other treasures from the churches of the area.

Along the road from Mombaroccio to Cartoceto is the hamlet of Passo, and a short road (c. 300m) leading to the wooded hill of the **convent of Beato Sante**, supposedly founded by St Francis of Assisi in 1223, and enlarged in the 14th century and again in the 16th, when the large cloister was added. On the first south altar is a wooden 16th-century Crucifix and a panel painting by Cola dell'Amatrice of the *Madonna with the Marys*. The chapel of the Blessed Sante is to the right of the presbytery; the mummified body of this Franciscan (1343–94), thought by many to be a saint, is kept inside the altar; he became a friar after involuntarily killing someone, and performed several miracles. He has been proclaimed protector of young children.

Colbordolo and Petriano

Colbordolo, an old town overlooking the River Foglia, was probably founded in the 12th century; its castle was frequently contested by the powerful families of the area, until it was taken by the troops of Federico da Montefeltro. The local economy is based on agriculture, and the area is rich in sulphur and kaolin. The old centre is entered through an arch under the clock tower. In the parish church of San Giovanni are several 17th-century paintings. In the centre (16 Via Roma) is the **Centro Culturale Giovanni Santi** (*to request a visit T: 0721 495171*), with paintings and various documents about Giovanni Santi, the father of Raphael.

Giovanni Santi (1440–94)

Giovanni's family moved to Urbino when he was ten, to escape the raids of the Malatesta on Colbordolo, border territory. A competent poet and painter, he was soon summoned to the court of Duke Federico da Montefeltro, who became his patron, but he left Urbino between 1474 and 1480, perhaps to work in Florence or Perugia, which would explain why he sent his young son Raphael to serve his apprenticeship with Perugino. In 1488 he organised the theatre performances and pageants for the wedding of Guidubaldo da Montefeltro and Elisabetta Gonzaga. He also wrote a long poem on the life and the accomplishments of Federico da Montefeltro. He recognised his son's talent when he was still a small child, and arranged for his artistic training, but he died when Raphael was only eleven.

Petriano, in the heart of the Pesaro hills, was for many centuries a defensive outpost for the city of Urbino; it also had a hospital for travellers, renowned in the 15th century, while the nearby Valzagona springs attracted the inhabitants of Urbino to spend a few days in the country occasionally, 'taking the waters'. Even Federico da Montefeltro is said to have benefited from the cure, while Raphael pronounced the waters to be 'miraculous'. Petriano still maintains its aspect of a medieval fortified village. The central church of San Martino (11th century) has a lovely cross-beam ceiling; on a side altar is an old painting of the *Madonna*, particularly venerated because it is said She offers protection against thunderbolts.

PRACTICAL INFORMATION

GETTING AROUND

• **By air**: Rimini Fellini (25km, T: 0541 715711, www.riminiairport.com), Ancona Falconara (45km, T: 071 28271, www.ancona-airport.com), and Forlì (60km, www.forliairport.com) airports serve this area and there are good train connections for Pesaro and Gabicce Mare.
• **By train**: Pesaro and Cattolica-Gabicce stations are on the main line, with good services to and from Milan, Rome, Bologna, Ancona, Civitanova Marche and San Benedetto del Tronto. In summer a miniature train connects Gabicce Monte with Gabicce Mare and Gradara.
• **By bus**: The central bus station in Pesaro is in Piazzale Matteotti, behind the Rocca Costanza; buses for Urbino leave from the railway station. AMIBUS, T: 0721 289145, www.amibus.it; and SOGET, T: 0721 371318) run express buses to and from Pesaro and Urbino (also Urbania and Apecchio), also in connection with trains (c. 55min Pesaro–Urbino); and

services to Gabicce Mare, Gradara and Cattolica; also services connecting the towns and the villages in the area of Pesaro.
Autolinee Fratelli Bucci, T: 0721 32401, runs services to Fano, Fossombrone, Urbino, Fermignano, Urbania, San Sepolcro.
Autolinee Reni, T: 071 8046504, www.paginegialle.it/reni-srl; runs services to Rimini, Fano, Senigallia, Ancona, Porto Recanati June–Sept only.
Autolinee Vitali, T: 0721 862515, www.vitaliautolinee.it, runs services to Fano, Senigallia, Chiaravalle, Ancona, Jesi, Pergola, Arcevia, Sassoferrato and Fabriano.
Pesaro city buses are run by Autolinee Capponi, Piazzale 1 Maggio, T: 0721 67980.
• **By sea**: Pesaro port (T: 0721 371258); there is a weekly ferry service to Croatia; summer daily excursions to Cattolica (T: 0721 407196).

INFORMATION OFFICES

Pesaro Useful websites for the area are:

www.turismo.pesarourbino.it,
www.altamarina.it
For information on the museums of
Pesaro: www.museicivicipesaro.it; IAT,
164 Viale Trieste, T: 0721 69341,
www.comune.pesaro.ps.it; Tourist
Information Bureau, 4 Via Mazzolari,
T: 800 563800,
www.turismo.pesarourbino.it. Pesaro,
together with Gubbio, Novafeltria,
Senigallia and Urbino, forms part of the
association La Terra del Duca, dedicated
to the Montefeltro; Info: www.
terradelduca.it
Gabicce Mare IAT, 41 Viale della
Vittoria, T: 0541 954424,
www.comune.gabicce-mare.ps.it,
www.gabiccemareturismo.com
Gradara Pro Loco, 1 Piazza V
Novembre, T: 0541 964115,
www.gradara.org; IAT, Via Zanvettori,
T: 0541 964560, summer only,
www.gradara.net
Mombaroccio Pro Loco, 37 Via Del
Monte, T: 0721 471103, www.
provincia.ps.it/comune.mombaroccio
Parco Naturale Monte San Bartolo,
40 Via Alighieri, T: 0721 371075, and
127 Viale Vittoria, T: 0721 371600,
www.parcosanbartolo.it
Tavullia Municipio and Pro Loco, 81
Via Roma, T: 0721 476116,
www.comuneditavullia.it

HOTELS

Pesaro

€€€€ **Savoy**. A well-run establishment, central, with pool and restaurant;
bikes available. 22 Viale della
Repubblica, T: 0721 67440,
www.viphotels.it
€€€ **Des Bains**. ■ Good position

close to sea and centre, private beach,
restaurant and garage. 221 Viale Trieste,
T: 0721 34957, www.innitalia.com
€€€ **Principe**. Comfortable, family-
run central hotel, with restaurant, good
breakfasts and car park. 180 Viale
Trieste, T: 0721 30222.
€€€ **Villa Serena**. 18th-century villa
of Count Pinto de Franca y Vargas, with
its own park, pool, luxurious accommodation, expensive and exclusive, the
choice of artists and musicians here for
the Rossini Festival. 6/3 Via San Nicola,
T: 0721 55211, www.villa-serena.it
€€ **Villa Cattani-Stuart**. 18th-century
villa with magnificent park; in a hillside
position overlooking Pesaro. 67 Via
Trebbiantica, T: 0721 55782,
www.villacattani.it
€€ **Vittoria**. Romantic Art Nouveau
building near the sea, with pool, restaurant, garden, gym and car park.
Previous guests range from Pirandello
to Sting. 2 Via Vespucci, T: 0721
34343, www.viphotels.it

Gabicce Mare

€€€€ **Posillipo**. ■ Charming old
hotel in an unbelievably panoramic
position on the hillside; comfortable
rooms, garden, pool, and excellent
restaurant. 1 Via dell'Orizzonte, Gabicce
Monte, T: 0541 953373, www.
hotelposillipo.com
€€€ **Lido**. Family-run, a good choice,
excellent value for money; situated on
the beach, with a restaurant. 6 Via Diaz,
T: 0541 954369,
www.gabiccemare.com/lido
€€€ **Marinella**. Comfortable, well-run
hotel, on the beach. 127 Via Vittorio
Veneto, T: 0541 954571,
www.gabiccemarevacanze.com
€€€ **Miramare**. Spacious and com-

fortable, with a large pool, on the beach. 163 Via Vittorio Veneto, T: 0541 950552.

€€€ **Sans Souci**. Recently rebuilt, on the beach, an excellent choice offering good value for money; garden, fitness centre, pool, bikes available, restaurant and car park. 9 Viale Mare, T: 0541 950164, www.parkhotels.it/sanssouci

€€ **Cavalluccio Marino**. A family-run hotel on the beach, central, with a nice restaurant. 111 Via Vittorio Veneto, T: 0541 950053, www.gabiccemare.com/cavalluccio

€€ **Da Nando**. Simple, comfortable accommodation, with restaurant; picturesque position on the canal-port. 44 Via del Porto, T: 0541 954572.

€€ **Maria**. Situated in the town centre. Children especially welcome; very good restaurant. 102 Via Cesare Battisti, T: 0541 954185.

€ **Everest Dependance**. Simple accommodation; no restaurant. 96 Via Panoramica, T: 0541 953434, www.hotel-everest.com

Gradara

€€€€ **Villa Matarazzo**. Luxurious, expensive accommodation in a beautiful country villa surrounded by a large park (you can imagine Tiberius being quite happy with it), close to the town of Gradara, and not far from the sea. Jogging track and pool in the park, also an excellent restaurant. 1 Via Farneto, località Fanano, T: 0541 964645, www.villamatarazzo.com

Petriano

€€€ **Da Ciacci**. Small and comfortable, with a good restaurant. 105 Via Roma, T: 0722 355030.

Spa Centre Terme di Raffaello. Baths and mud-massage for various disorders; the spa was used by Raphael and by Federico da Montefeltro. Open May–Nov. Via San Gianno, T: 0722 35111, www.termediraffaello.it

FARM ACCOMMODATION

Pesaro

Colle San Bartolo. In the heart of the Monte San Bartolo Park. Open all year. 2 Strada Bocca del Lupo, T: 0721 22756.

Gradara

Agricola della Serra. 3km from Gradara, the farm raises animals and grows fruit and vegetables, cereals, olives and vineyards, strictly organic; guests can help. Has a particularly good restaurant with home-made bread baked in the wood-fired oven; cosy rooms. English spoken. 8 Via Serra, Località Fanano, T: 0541 969856, www.agriturismogradara.it

COUNTRY HOUSE

Pesaro

Villa Torraccia. Old 12th-century watch-tower transformed in the 15th-century into a villa. Comfortable accommodation, with a garden; ask to see the huge *neviere*, cellars once packed with snow in winter, used to store silk-worm cocoons. Lots of stairs. 3 Strada Torraccia, T: 0721 21852, www.abitarelastoria.it

MONASTERY ACCOMMODATION

Pesaro

Casa Sacro Cuore. Full board is good value for money; open summer only. 20 Via Amendola, T: 0721 30178, coloniasacrocuore@libero.it

RESTAURANTS

Pesaro

€€€ **Alceo**. Elegant restaurant for formal meals, special occasions. Closed Mon and Sun evening. 101 Via Panoramica Ardizio, T: 0721 55875.

€€€ **Al Molo da Peppe**. Definitely for special occasions, the restaurant stands on stilts in the water, near the eastern pier; simple but beautifully prepared dishes, good choice of wines. Calata Caio Duilio, T: 0721 400395. Closed Mon.

€€€ **Il Castiglione**. ■ Elegant restaurant serving classic local cuisine accompanied by the best local wines and liqueurs; it occupies the fanciful Art Nouveau castle-workshop of Ferruccio Mengaroni. Closed Mon. 148 Viale Trento, T: 0721 64934.

€€€ **Lo Scudiero**. Good service, interesting dishes, wide choice of wines, in the stables of Palazzo Baldassini. Closed Sun. 2 Via Baldassini, T: 0721 64107.

€€ **Antica Osteria La Guercia**. Famous old tavern, traditional local fare, good value for money. Closed Sun. 33 Via Baviera (Piazza Ducale), T: 0721 33463.

€€ **Bristolino**. Modern restaurant with innovative touches to the local cuisine, generous servings. Closed Sun. 7 Piazzale della Libertà, T: 0721 31609.

€€ **C'era una volta**. Good home-made pasta and pizza. Closed Mon. 26 Via Cattaneo, T: 0721 30911.

€€ **Da Teresa**. Modern restaurant with beautiful views, interesting innovative dishes. Closed Sun evening and Mon. 118 Viale Trieste, T: 0721 30096.

€€ **Polo**. Beautifully presented meals, snacks and pizza. Closed Mon. 231 Viale Trieste, T: 0721 375902.

€ **Marisa**. Marisa makes delicious fish soup, a meal in itself, and lemon sorbet; excellent local wines. 73 Via Monfalcone, T: 0721 25330.

€ **Osteria di Pinocchio**. Typical little trattoria-wine bar; delicious simple food. Closed lunchtime Sat and Sun. 12 Piazza Antaldi, T: 0721 34771.

Casteldimezzo

€€ **Canonica**. Creative cooking, using the local ingredients, fish, cheese, vegetables; good wine list. In the Monte San Bartolo Park. Closed Mon. 20 Via Borgata di Casteldimezzo, T: 0721 209017.

Gabicce Mare

€€€ **La Cambusa**. On the picturesque harbour, delicious fish prepared in many different ways, evenings also pizza, nice desserts. Closed Mon. Via del Porto, T: 0541 954784.

€€€ **Posillipo**. Excellent food, well prepared and served by the courteous, professional staff, accompanied by the right wines, in lovely surroundings. Who could ask for anything more? 1 Via dell'Orizzonte, T: 0541 953373.

€€ **Osteria della Miseria**. Simple, tasty dishes, generous servings, good wine cellar. Closed Sun and Mon–Sat lunchtime. 2 Via dei Mandorli, Gabicce Monte, T: 0541 958308.

Gradara

€€–€ **Hostaria della Botte**. A tavern and a restaurant in the heart of the medieval town; snacks and a glass of wine, or a full meal—try the *ravioli di pasta al cioccolato ripieni di formaggi freschissimi e conditi con formaggio di fossa*, ravioli made with chocolate-flavoured pasta, filled with fresh cheeses, and served with pit-matured cheese.

Absolutely delicious. 11 Piazza V Novembre, T: 0541 964404. Closed Wed in winter.

€€ **La Nuova Gradarina**. 8 Strada della Romagna, T: 0541 964504. Large restaurant famous for fish; abundant seafood antipasti, mixed grill, local wines.

€€ **Paradiso**. Traditional dishes, pizza in the evening, at this inn which opened more than 100 years ago. Closed Wed. 42 Via Tanaro, T: 0541 964132.

Monteciccardo

€€ **Osteria il Conventino**. ■ A restaurant specialising in thick, delicious vegetable soups, and meat prepared in several ways; end up with one of the fantastic desserts, *millefoglie* perhaps, or yoghurt mousse with strawberry sauce, or fresh figs with cherry brandy ice cream and nut brittle. Good wine list. You can also buy local food products. Open Thur–Sun, evenings only. 1 Via Conventino, T: 0721 910588.

€ **Ristorante Walter**. If visiting in winter, ask for *pignataccia*, a tasty dish of mixed game, slowly cooked in an earthenware pot. Closed Tues. 11 Via Lubiana, Montegaudio, T: 0721 910147.

Novilara

€€ **Il Pergolato di Maria**. Charming restaurant near the castle, old fashioned; lovely meals under the pergola, famous for home-made pasta. Closed Tues in winter. 5 Piazzale Cadorna, T: 0721 287210.

CAFÉS, SNACK BARS & ICE CREAM

Pesaro
Alberini. Historic coffee bar, excellent

pastries and snacks. Closed Mon. 119 Corso XI Settembre.

Café de Paris. Elegant little coffee bar, also serves wines, cocktails and snacks; garden. 49 Via Cattaneo.

Casetta Vaccai. Said to be the oldest house in Pesaro, this café is a real institution. Closed Sun. 22 Via Mazzolari.

Germano. Just the place for afternoon tea and cakes, or hot chocolate. Closed Mon. 12 Piazzale Collenuccio.

Germano. Probably the best ice cream parlour in Pesaro, fantastic assortment of flavours, served with crunchy wafers and whipped cream, if you want to indulge… Closed Mon, open summer only. 9 Piazza Libertà.

Zanzibar. ■ Fashionable meeting-place for cocktails and aperitifs, also delicious snacks; try the *espresso con zabaglione*. Closed Sun. 4 Piazzale Moro.

Gabicce Mare
Caffetteria Reale. For morning coffee and newspaper browsing. 12 Via Cesare Battisti,

FESTIVALS & EVENTS

Pesaro *Mostra del Nuovo Cinema*, film festival dating back over 40 years; Info: T: 06 4456643, www.pesarofilmfest.it, end June–July. **ROF—Rossini Opera Festival**, one of the most prestigious musical events in Europe; Info: Rossini Opera Festival, Piazza Lazzarini, T: 0721 33141, www.rossinioperafestival.it, Aug.

Gabicce Mare International Bicycle Touring Week at the Sea; Info: Associazione Albergatori, Palazzo del Turismo, Viale della Vittoria, T: 0541 953600, www.gabiccemareturismo.com, Easter

Gradara *Gradara Ludens*, a festival dedicated to games and pastimes, for the young and the young at heart; Info: T: 0541 964142, www.gradaraludens.it, April–Sept.
Monteciccardo Ceremonial tasting of the new wine and opening of the cheese pits (Conventino Servi di Maria), Nov.

LOCAL SPECIALITIES

Pesaro
Bibi, 52 Viale Fiume, offers all the best wines of the Marche, and olive oil from Cartoceto, pasta from Campofilone and Osimo, and cherry wine. **Bottega d'Arte Sora**, 35 Via Rossini, is the place for family tradition for lovely majolica and ceramics, while **Molaroni**, 9 Via della Robbia, also has distinctive pottery. **Ser Jacopo dalla Gemma**, 136 Via Rossi, has hand-made pipes, of unusual design. **Fattoria Mancini**, 35 Strada dei Colli, in the Monte San Bartolo Park, is a farm producing some of the famous Colli Pesaresi wines; try their DOC Focara Pinot Nero.
Belvedere Fogliense
Francesco Bartolucci, Località Belvedere Fogliense, is a carpenter who makes beautiful wooden toys.
Gabicce Mare
M 2 A, 30 Via Cesare Battisti, sells delicious bread, cakes and biscuits.
Mombaroccio
Ricami, Piazza Barocci, this town has a centuries-old tradition for embroidery.
Monteciccardo
Frantoio Andrea Marcolini, 23 Via Arzilla, Villa Betti di Monteciccardo, sells stone-ground virgin olive oil.
Sant'Angelo in Lizzola
Torrefazione Foschi, 5 Via Arena, Montecchio, founded in 1929, Foschi is one of the oldest and best-known coffee manufacturers in Italy—they also deal in tea and other products. Buying straight from the factory is advantageous.

URBINO

Urbino (485m, population 16,000), known to the Romans as *Urvinum Metaurense*, is famous throughout the world as one of the principal centres of the Italian Renaissance. It has one of Italy's most interesting and well-preserved historical centres, considered an 'ideal city' by many. The colours are warm: rosy-red brick façades, with roofs of a deeper red, offset by the white marble details around the doorways and the windows.

NB: It is possible to buy a combined ticket for all Urbino's museums.

HISTORY OF URBINO

Probably inhabited since prehistory, there are few traces to be seen of that period, and little remains of the Roman city either, except perhaps for the street layout on the Poggio hill, where the duke's palace stands. The town was in fact destroyed during the war between the Goths and the Byzantines, and suffered considerably during the Lombard invasion. Reconstruction began in the 12th–13th century, when it passed to the Montefeltro family. The 14th century saw rebuilding on the other hill, called Monte, but the 15th century was the 'Golden Century' for Urbino, with the most impressive achievements in the fields of art and culture. Federico da Montefeltro summoned to his court the most illustrious and influential figures of the age, including architects like Luciano Laurana and Francesco di Giorgio Martini, and painters such as Piero della Francesca and Joos van Ghent. After founding the University in 1506, Guidubaldo, the last of the Montefeltro (one of the speakers in Castiglione's *Courtier*), died without heirs, and the city passed to their kinsmen the della Rovere. Francesco Maria della Rovere held Urbino until 1516, when he was driven out by Pope Leo X, who wanted the duchy for his Medici nephew. The della Rovere only returned after Pope Leo's death, and remained lords of the city until 1631, when Urbino passed to the papacy. In the 18th century, with the Albani family, some repairs and reconstruction were carried out, respecting the Renaissance aspect given to the town by Federico, but in 1797 Napoleon's troops occupied the city, including it in the Republic of Rome. After many years of quarrels over Urbino between France and the Papal States, in 1860 it was taken by General Cialdini of Piedmont, and a year later became part of the new Kingdom of Italy.

Well known in the past for its potteries (particularly in the 16th century), Urbino's economy is now based mainly on tourism, and on the presence of its University.

EXPLORING URBINO

The best approach to the walled city is from the enormous parking area called Borgo Mercatale, once the market (there is a convenient left-luggage office; *T: 0722 2196*; stairs and lifts). The magnificent ramp, designed by Francesco di Giorgio Martini, leads to Corso Garibaldi, passing by the opera house, Teatro Sanzio completed in 1853. From there you continue up to Piazza Rinascimento and the fairytale castle of Duca Federico, the **Palazzo Ducale** (*open 8.30–7.15, last tickets 6; Mon 8.30–2, last tickets 12.30; T: 0722 322625*), built in the 15th century by a number of architects: the Florentines Maso di Bartolomeo and Luca della Robbia, and Luciano Laurana, Francesco di Giorgio Martini and Girolamo Genga. Described as a 'city in the form of a palace', it is particularly impressive for the series of beautiful doorways and fireplaces; it now houses the principal museums of Urbino. The western façade, called the Facciata dei Torricini, with its two slender cusped towers and airy loggias, is perhaps the best-known image of the Marche region, and the emblem of the Italian Renaissance throughout the world. Laurana designed it to look towards Florence, seen as the cultural capital. In many places you will see the initials 'F.C.' and 'F.D.', indicating 'Federico Conte' and 'Federico Duca'.

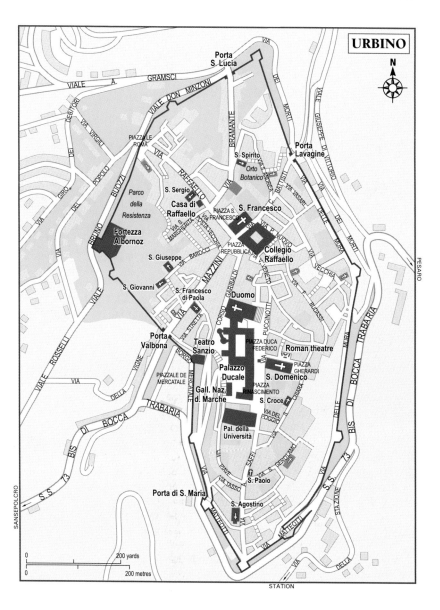

Opposite page: View of the city of Urbino, with the Palazzo Ducale and duomo.

Galleria Nazionale delle Marche

The vast Galleria Nazionale delle Marche, one of the most important art galleries in Italy, both for the number of works on display and for their excellent quality, is on the first floor, reached by Laurana's splendid staircase, in the apartments opening onto the loggia around the lovely golden-hued courtyard of honour, with its rigorous geometry.

Appartamento della Jole: Contains many sculptures. Some rooms were frescoed with figures of Warriors by Giovanni Boccati. Federico's room, *L'Alcova*, was decorated with tempera by Giovanni da Camerino; the furniture is 15th century.

Appartamento dei Melaranci: Contains 14th-century works, including a splendid polyptych by Giovanni Baronzio of the *Madonna and Christ Child with Saints and Stories of the Life of Christ* (1345), a painted Crucifix by the Maestro di Verucchio, and a *Madonna* by Allegretto Nuzi (*see p. 53*).

Appartamento degli Ospiti: Includes a room stuccoed by Federico Brandani, representing the emblems of the Montefeltro and della Rovere families; there are 15th-century wooden sculptures, a hoard found in Mondavio of 103 15th-century gold coins, and paintings by Carlo and Vittore Crivelli, Giovanni Bellini, and Alvise Vivarini.

Piero della Francesca: *Flagellation* (c. 1469).

GALLERIA NAZIONALE DELLE MARCHE
FIRST FLOOR

A Appartamento della Jole
B Appartamento dei Melaranci
C Appartamento degli Ospiti
D Appartamento del Duca Federico
    (Di): Studiolo
    (Dii): Camera da Letto del Duca
    (Diii): Sala degli Angeli
E Appartamento della Duchessa
F Sala del Trono

Luciano Laurana (attrib.): *View of an Ideal City* (15th century).

Appartamento del Duca Federico: The most precious works of art are housed here. In the **Sala delle Udienze**, with lavish decoration in carved and inlaid marble, where Federico held his audiences, is the famous *Flagellation* by Piero della Francesca, painted on poplar wood, where the refined perspective acquires an allegorical significance—the human figures, indifferent to the torture taking place behind them, seem less vital than the architectural lines of the city where the scene takes place. Also by Piero is the enigmatic *Senigallia Madonna*, where the solemn, colossal Christ Child appears to accept His future sacrifice, symbolised by the coral necklace around His throat, and the white rose in His left hand. Calm and silent, His mother supports Him as if she were an element of the architecture. The scene is imbued with impending tragedy; the only lighter touch is given by the basket of nappies on the shelf in the background.

Studiolo del Duca: The inlaid woodwork on the walls of this room **(Di)**, Federico's study, is by Baccio Pontelli, using designs by Botticelli, Bramante and Francesco di Giorgio Martini. Joos van Ghent painted the portraits of 28 *Illustrious Men* for this room; 14 of them, now in the Louvre, have been replaced by reproductions.

Camera da Letto del Duca: Federico's bedchamber **(Dii)** has the famous portrait of *Federico da Montefeltro with his son Guidubaldo* by Pedro Berruguete; and a panel painting of the *Madonna* from the atelier of Andrea del Verrocchio.

Sala degli Angeli: This room **(Diii)** some famous works, including the *Miracle of the Profaned Host* by Paolo Uccello, and the famous *View of the Ideal City*. Authorship is disputed between Luciano Laurana, Piero della Francesca, and Fra' Carnevale, though it is most usually attributed to Laurana. Apart from a couple of pigeons on the building on the right, no living creature is in sight, but the half-open door of the church in the centre seems to invite us to enter.

Appartamento della Duchessa: Devoted to 16th-century works, including *La Muta* (1507) by Raphael, one of his finest (and most enigmatic) paintings, dating to the period when he had returned from his stay in Florence. Also by Raphael is the earlier *St Catherine of Alexandria*. The magnetic portrait of *Christ Blessing* is by Bramantino. More splendid works are in the **Duchess's bedroom**, including the *Last Supper* and the *Resurrection* by Titian, the *Annunciation* by Vincenzo Pagani, and the Coxcie Tapestries (*see box overleaf*).

Sala del Trono: This imposing apartment, used by the duke as a setting for his parties, has another series of Flemish tapestries on the walls, the famous *Acts of the Apostles*, for which Raphael provided the designs.

LA MUTA

Considered a masterpiece of portraiture, the painting (oil on panel) reveals the influence of Leonardo da Vinci in the pose, the careful rendering of the simple dress and jewellery of the sitter, and above all her gentle personality. Little is known about the history of the painting, which appears for the first time in 1710 in a list of works belonging to the Uffizi in Florence. Sill less is known about the sitter, but nowadays many scholars believe her to be Giovanna Feltria della Rovere, daughter of Duke Federico da Montefeltro, who lost her husband in 1501. Analysis of the work shows that the original drawing was of a younger version of the lady, made at the start of Raphael's career; he painted her later with a slightly different attire, before completing the portrait probably in about 1507, ageing her features each time. Her recent widowhood would explain her sad expression of mute pain, and the name by which the picture is universally known.

Second floor

The second floor of the palace, known as the Appartamento Roveresco, was designed by Bartolomeo Genga for Guidubaldo II della Rovere. It is now the **Museo della Ceramica**. The first section is dedicated to paintings, especially by Federico Barocci and his school, while the second has a vast display of pottery, from Urbino and also from Siena, Deruta, Faenza and Castelli; the pieces on show are frequently changed. On the walls are fine prints and drawings.

Ground floor

On the ground floor, on the left-hand side of the courtyard, is the **Museo Archeologico Urbinate**, consisting mainly of two collections of stone inscriptions and sculptures: that of the local intellectual Raffaele Fabretti, and that of Cardinal Gianfrancesco Stoppani, both ardent 17th-century collectors. There are many pagan and Christian gravestones, and urns decorated in relief. The same courtyard gives access to the vast **Sotterranei**, the underground rooms which served as the stables, baths, kitchens and storerooms; one, the *neviera*, carefully packed with snow during the winter, was like an enormous refrigerator; while the baths were fully equipped with hot and cold water and drainage.

THE COXCIE TAPESTRIES

These beautiful wall-hangings were good to look at, and useful too, as they helped maintain the temperature of these stone rooms pleasant, cool in summer and warm in winter. Federico da Montefeltro commissioned the tapestries in Flanders, to designs by the Flemish artist and imitator of Raphael Michiel Coxcie. When the della Rovere family died out in 1631, the last member of the great line, Vittoria, went to Florence as the bride of Ferdinando de' Medici. She had the right to take with her the 'wardrobes', in other words the household goods and furniture; everything else was requisitioned by the pope. This explains why so many of the Urbino treasures are now either in the Vatican, or in the Louvre where Napoleon took them from the pope, or in Florence. But the tapestries never left Urbino in Vittoria's baggage train: someone hid them in a secret room, which was walled up and forgotten. During renovation work in 1868, the chamber was discovered, and the perfectly-preserved tapestries were listed as rightfully belonging to the contents of the palace, which was being turned into a museum.

The duomo and San Domenico

Next to the palace, in Piazza Federico, is the Giuseppe Valadier's Neoclassical **duomo** (*open 8–12 & 2.30–6.30*), of 1802, which replaces Federico's cathedral, destroyed by an earthquake in 1789. The interior has a central nave and two side aisles, and is surmounted by a dome; in the chapel to the right of the main altar, on the right-hand wall, is a painting of the *Madonna* by Carlo Maratta, on the opposite wall is the *Nativity of Mary* by Carlo Cignani. The painting of the *Madonna* over the main altar is by Christopher Unterberger. The only part of the building to survive the earthquake is the Chapel of the Sacrament, to the left; on the left-hand wall is a painting of the *Last Supper* by Federico Barocci.

To the right of the cathedral, at 2 Piazza Pascoli, is the **Museo Diocesano Gianfrancesco Albani** (*open 9–12 & 2.30–6; T: 0722 2850*), with a precious collection of 14th-century frescoes from the church of San Domenico, pottery from Casteldurante, a 14th-century bronze lectern from England, and paintings of the 14th–17th centuries. You can ask at the museum to see the crypt of the cathedral (sometimes called *Oratorio della Grotta; to request a visit T: 0722 2613*), where there is a lovely 16th-century marble *Pietà* by Giovanni dell'Opera.

Opposite the Palazzo Ducale, in Piazza Rinascimento, by the Egyptian obelisk brought here from Rome by Cardinal Albani in 1737, is the Gothic church of **San Domenico** (1365), with a double-ramp stairway leading to a simple brick façade, decorated with a stunning stone portal of 1451, by Maso di Bartolomeo, commissioned by Duke Federico. The terracotta lunette by Luca della Robbia is now in the palace gallery; the doorway is surmounted by a frieze of little arches and columns. The spacious interior is a single nave, with paintings of angels on either side of the central arch, and a magnificent canvas of the *Madonna with Sts Dominic and Catherine of Siena* by Giovanni Conca in the apse. To the left of the church is Via San Domenico, leading east to the remains of the **Roman theatre** which came to light in 1943. Behind San Domenico is the **Oratorio di San Gaetano** (*to request a visit T: 0722 2613*), a tiny chapel with an interesting fresco of the *Madonna with Saints* by Ottaviano Nelli (15th century) on the back wall.

At the bottom of the street is Piazza Gherardi, with **Palazzo Passionei** (*to request a visit T: 0722 305311*), a fine example of a 15th-century Renaissance palace in the style of Francesco di Giorgio Martini.

Via Santa Chiara and the south

By taking Via Santa Chiara from Piazza Gherardi, you reach the enormous monastery of Santa Chiara, probably built by Francesco di Giorgio Martini on the orders of Duke Federico (or perhaps his daughter Elisabetta), now used by the Institute for Artistic Industries. The round **church of Santa Chiara** was unfortunately spoilt in the early 19th century when it became the vestibule for the hospital; buried inside are Francesco Maria I della Rovere, duke of Urbino, his wife Eleonora Gonzaga, his son Cardinal Giulio and his niece Lavinia.

Opposite is the **Oratorio di Santa Croce** (*to request a visit T: 0722 2613*), with a Gothic portal on the side. The single-nave interior has a cross-beam roof decorated with stories of the Cross by Giorgio Picchi, a follower of Barocci (early 17th century), and magnificent stucco decoration by the master craftsman Pompilio Lanci in the Chapel of the Thorn to the right. On the south wall of the church is a fresco of St Sebastian, perhaps by Raphael's father Giovanni Santi, and a painting of *Christ at the Column* by Federico Zuccari. On the north wall is a fresco by Ottaviano Nelli of the *Madonna with Christ Child and Angels* (1432), while over the altar is a *Deposition* by Francesco Antonio Rondelli.

Via Santa Croce leads to Via Saffi. By going south you reach the convent and church of **Sant'Agostino** (consecrated in 1292), a huge brick construction with an elegant terracotta frieze. Although the interior was transformed in the 18th century, there are some remarkable works of art, including a fresco of the *Madonna* dated 1432 on the second south altar; paintings by Claudio Ridolfi and Timoteo Viti; and a meridian line on the floor, traced in 1550.

Piazza della Repubblica and the Casa di Raffaello

Piazza della Repubblica, with a graceful fountain, occupies the valley between the two hills of Urbino. On the northeast side is the 18th-century Collegio Raffaello, which houses the **Museo del Gabinetto di Fisica** (*open Mon–Fri 9–1; Wed and Thur also 3–6; closed Sat, Sun and holidays; T: 0722 2613*), a collection of scientific instruments dating from the 17th century to the present day. To the left of it is the portico of the 14th-century church of **San Francesco** (*open 7–12.30 & 3–7*), with some finely-carved marble arches in the interior. In the apse is the *Pardon of St Francis* by Federico Barocci (1581). The little square becomes a fruit and vegetable market in the morning.

From the church, Via Raffaello leads up to the **Casa Natale di Raffaello** (*open 9–1 & 3–5.30; Sun and holidays 10–1; T: 0722 320105*), Raphael's birthplace, where some of his early works can be seen, together with reproductions of his most famous paintings, and canvases by his father, Giovanni Santi, and by Timoteo Viti. The house itself is interesting for its typical architecture of the times. Next door is the oldest church in Urbino, **San Sergio** (5th and 15th centuries). Traces of a Roman swimming pool came to light during repairs to the floor. The paintings are by Claudio Ridolfi and Girolamo Cialdieri.

Via Bramante

Almost opposite Raphael's house is the picturesque Via Bramante: at no. 17 is Palazzo Albani, birthplace of Pope Clement XI (Giovanni Francesco Albani reigned 1700–21), now seat of the **Gipsoteca** (*closed Sun and public holidays; to request a visit T: 0722 320534*), a collection of plaster casts. From here, Via Scalette Santo Spirito leads to the **Orto Botanico** (*open 9–12.30 & 3.30–5; closed Sun and holidays, Thur and Sat afternoons; T: 0722 2428*), opened in 1806, with c. 5,000 plants, some of which rare and exotic, and the 16th-century church of **Santo Spirito**, with a beautiful portal. The rectangular interior has a lovely ceiling painted by Girolamo Cialdieri (1637) with the Prophets, the *Seven Gifts of the Holy Spirit*, and other stories; the same artist is probably responsible for the pictures along the walls of the Twelve Apostles, still in the original wooden frames, painted to look like marble. The painting over the main altar of the *Pentecost* is by Taddeo Zuccari. On the corner of the street is the statue of Pope Alexander VIII (1737), usually known as San Pietro Celestino, one of the patron saints of Urbino; the features were changed and the inscription was erased during the Napoleonic occupation, in an attempt to eradicate the memory of the pope.

Continuing along Via Bramante to Porta Santa Lucia, you pass some noteworthy houses (no. 56 was the home of the Genga family), to turn round and admire the view back along the street, with the cathedral in the background; to the left, along Viale Don Minzoni, you can admire the imposing 16th-century walls.

From Piazzale Roma into the old town

From Piazzale Roma there is a breathtaking view over the town, and surrounding countryside. Close by is the **Monument to Raphael** (1897), a sensitive sculpture in bronze and marble. The avenue, now Viale Buozzi (the weekly market is held here every Saturday morning), continues along by the **Parco della Resistenza** (*open 9–6*), public gardens where people often fly kites, to the ruins of the 16th-century Fortezza Albornoz.

By taking the steep and narrow steps of Via dei Maceri down from Piazzale Roma to Via Barocci (the artist Federico Barocci was born at no. 18), you will find the **Oratorio di San Giuseppe** (*open 10–12.30; weekdays also 3–5.30; T: 0722 350025*), a 16th–17th-century church formed of two chapels, in one of which is the famous stucco **Presepio** (Christmas crib) by Federico Brandani. On 6th January, if the day is clear, a ray of sunlight comes through the window and alights upon Baby Jesus. The oratory was built for the influential Company of St Joseph, which had many important members, including Francesco Maria I della Rovere and James Stuart, the Old Pretender.

Further along the street is the 14th-century **Oratorio di San Giovanni** (*open 10–12.30; weekdays also 3–5.30; T: 0722 350025*), entirely decorated with an amazing, true-to-life series of frescoes (1416) by Jacopo and Lorenzo Salimbeni (*see p. 79*), dedicated to the life of St John the Baptist; some authorities believe these to be among the best examples of the period to be seen in Italy; the fine details are incredible. The original wooden ceiling is also exceptional.

Turn right outside the church and take the alley called Via Scalette di San Giovanni, offering stupendous views over the Palazzo Ducale, down to Corso Mazzini: almost opposite is the 17th-century church of **San Francesco di Paola**, or Corpus Domini, built as an ex-voto by Francesco Maria II della Rovere, who wanted a son (his prayer was heard; the baby was Federico Ubaldo). The frescoes on the vault of the interior, of stories of the Saint, are the masterpiece of Antonio Viviani (1614).

THE DELLA ROVERE DUKES

The family, originally from Savona, gave two popes to the Church: Francesco, who ruled as Sixtus IV (1471–84), and Giuliano (Julius II, 1503–13). A nephew of Pope Sixtus, Giovanni, was made lord of Senigallia in 1474, where his government was much appreciated by his subjects. He married a daughter of Federico da Montefeltro, and his son Francesco Maria I della Rovere (1490–1538) inherited the duchy of Urbino when the Montefeltro family died out in 1508; in 1513 he was awarded the city of Pesaro by the Church for his services as *condottiere*. Guidubaldo II (1514–74), his son, was no soldier. Patron of the arts, he loved Pesaro and turned it into a sumptuous Renaissance court, while preferring to live in Fossombrone because of the finer climate. In 1534 he married the ten-year-old Giulia da Varano of Camerino, commissioning from Titian the famous painting known as the *Venus of Urbino* (now in the Uffizi); this same painting later inspired Edouard Manet's controversial *Olympe*, and even some works by Botero. Blatantly erotic, the chubby Venus is provocatively draped over an unmade bed, with a knowing grin and her gorgeous titian hair in disarray. The painting was hung in the little girl's boudoir, probably in the hope of awakening her senses before her husband died without an heir. Guidubaldo's son, Francesco Maria II (who was born 9 years later) preferred Urbania. After building a magnificent palace there, he took the intelligent Livia as his second wife, and, being of a studious turn of mind, hoped to pass the responsibilities of government to his young son Federico Ubaldo (1605–23), but the boy, after dutifully marrying and producing a daughter, died prematurely without a male heir. His father was forced therefore to resume his role as head of state. When he died in 1631, he was the last of the della Rovere dukes. In the Museo Civico of Urbania (*see p. 319*) there is a poignant portrait by Giovanni Francesco Guerrieri of a sad-faced Duchess Livia with her little granddaughter, Vittoria, last of the della Rovere, on her knee.

OUTSKIRTS OF URBINO

A pleasant walk (c. 2km) east of the city, towards the cemetery, leads to the interesting 15th-century church of **San Bernardino degli Zoccolanti** (*open 8–6*), thought to be the work of Francesco di Giorgio Martini or Bramante. In brick, it has a beautiful tall and narrow façade, decorated with bands in sandstone; the top of the bell-tower collapsed in the 1741 earthquake. The church is the mausoleum of the dukes of Montefeltro, commissioned by Federico himself; but his tomb, and that of his son Guidubaldo, are Baroque in style because they were made much later (17th century). The famous painting by Piero della Francesca of the *Madonna with Duke Federico in Adoration*, which hung over the main altar until 1810, is now in the Brera Gallery in Milan.

Close to Borgo Mercatale, in Via Stretta, is the old **Synagogue**, built in 1633 when the ghetto was instituted. The beautiful 15th-century *aron* (ark) is now in the Jewish Museum of New York, and has been replaced by a 19th-century one, equally lovely.

PRACTICAL INFORMATION

GETTING AROUND

• **By train**: The nearest station to Urbino is Pesaro (35km), on the Milan–Bologna–Ancona–Pescara line. There is an express bus service connects with most trains; journey takes 55 mins.
• **By bus**: The bus terminal is at Borgo Mercatale, with a useful left-luggage service 8–8.
AMI and SOGET (T: 0721 371318, www.amibus.it), runs services to Urbania, Apecchio, Pesaro and Fano. Autolinee Fratelli Bucci, T: 0721 32401, operates services to the Montefeltro towns, and daily services to Rome.
• **By road**: When arriving by car to spend the day, try to get here early: the car parks fill up surprisingly quickly, even in winter; besides the useful Borgo Mercatale car park, there is another good one on the opposite side of town,

outside Porta San Bartolo, a narrow passage leads to the gate.

INFORMATION OFFICES

A useful website to Urbino and the area is: www.montefeltrotour.it. The town forms part of the association La Terra del Duca, dedicated to the Montefeltro; www.terradelduca.it; IAT, 35 Via Puccinotti (Piazza Duca Federico), T: 0722 2613; Infopoint, Borgo Mercatale Car Park, entrance to Francesco di Giorgio Ramp, T: 0722 2613; Tourist Information Bureau, 1 Piazza Rinascimento, T: 0722 328568, www.comune.urbino.ps.it; Tour Guide Association Urbino Ducale, Borgo Mercatale Car Park, T: 0722 2196. Also Sistema Turistico Locale Urbino e il Montefeltro, 33 Via Puccinotti, T: 0722 320437, www.urbinoeilmontefeltro.it

HOTELS

€€€€ **Bonconte**. Beautiful hotel not far from Palazzo Ducale, with garden and restaurant. 28 Via delle Mura, T: 0722 2463, www.viphotels.it

€€€€ **San Domenico**. ■ Marvellous position in front of Palazzo Ducale for this luxurious hotel in what was an old convent; you have breakfast in the cloister. 3 Piazza Rinascimento, T: 0722 2626, www.viphotels.it

€€€ **Dei Duchi**. In new town.12 Via Dini, T: 0722 328226, www.viphotels.it

€€€ **Italia**. Very central, it is the oldest hotel in town, but no restaurant. 32 Corso Garibaldi, T: 0722 2701, www.albergo-italia-urbino.com

€€€ **La Meridiana**. Convenient position just out of town. Modern and comfortable, with a pool. 154 Via Calbiancone, T: 0722 320169, www.la-meridiana.com

€€€ **Raffaello**. Comfortable little hotel in the heart of the old city, with a shuttle-bus service to the car parks. 40 Via Santa Margherita, T: 0722 478.

€ **Locanda La Brombolona**. ■ In a tiny village c. 10km from Urbino, with views over the city, a delightful inn situated in an ex-church; the friendly atmosphere and the marvellous home cooking make it a good choice. 22 Via Sant'Andrea in Primicilio, Canavaccio, T: 0722 53501.

BED & BREAKFAST

B&B Ca' Il Governatore. In countryside surrounded by olive groves and orchards, 3km from Urbino. 171 Località Giardino della Galla, Pallino di Urbino, T: 0722 327060, www.ilgovernatore.it

B&B Ca' Marchigiano. Old country house. Theatrical activities. English, French and German spoken. 25 Via Monteavorio, Località Pieve di Cagna, T: 0722 345417.

Ca' Maggio B&B. Ancient country tower 10km from town. English and French spoken.107 Via Santa Maria di Pomonte, Canavaccio, T: 0722 53118, camaggiobb@yahoo.it

FARM ACCOMMODATION

Ca' Andreana. Delicious food at this farm using organic methods; sheep and goats are raised, vegetables and fruit are grown. Comfortable rooms; cookery courses, bikes available for hire. French and English spoken. 119 Via Gadana, T: 335 6767430, www.caandreana.it

La Corte della Miniera. ■ Old farm and sulphur mine, 8km from Urbino, with excellent restaurant. Open Feb–Nov. 74 Podere Pozzo Nuovo, Località Miniera, T: 0722 345322, cortedellaminiera@abanet.it

Dei Duchi. Hillside farm (guests can help), 4km from Urbino, producing wines. Good restaurant. English and French spoken. 7 Via Colonna, Località Trasanni di Urbino, T: 0722 320292, www.agriturismodeiduchi.it

RESTAURANTS

€€€ **Vecchia Urbino**. Elegant restaurant in a 16th-century palace. Vast array of local cheeses; traditional desserts (try the *bostrengo*), only organic, no GMO ingredients; amazing wine list. 3–5 Via Vasari, T: 0722 4447. Closed Tues.

€€ **Da Vanda**. An excellent place for sampling the traditional dishes of Urbino and the Montefeltro area; try the *piatto del Duca* (stewed boar), good value for money. Car parking. 6 Via Mari, Località Castelcavallino, T: 0722 349117. Closed Wed and Christmas.

€€ **L'Angolo Divino**. Small tavern serving interesting soups and unusual local dishes; good desserts and wine list. 14 Via Sant'Andrea, T: 0722 327559. Closed Sun evening and Mon.

€€ **Nenè**. Large, noisy, friendly restaurant, good food, vegetarian on request, excellent value for money, also rooms to rent. Closed Mon. 30 Via Crocicchia, T: 0722 2996 (c. 2km from centre; call to ask directions).

€ **Il Girarrosto**. A *rosticceria*, an Italian-style snack bar, on the picturesque square used as a vegetable market in the morning; where you can eat outside. Steaks, roast lamb, sausages, salads and cooked vegetables; you drink Bianchello from the flask. In winter take-away service only. Closed Sun evening and Mon midday in winter. 3 Piazza San Francesco, T: 0722 4445.

€ **Il Portico**. Interesting place for a salad or some *crescia*, with a glass of wine, this is a tavern-bookshop combined. Closed Mon. 7 Via Mazzini, T: 0722 2722.

CAFÉS PASTRY SHOPS & ICE CREAM

Caffè Basili. Popular with students, home-made ice cream, excellent coffee. Piazza della Repubblica.

Caffè Cartolari. Near the house of Raphael, with good coffee, also cakes, pastries, ice cream and snacks. 52 Via Raffaello. Closed Mon.

Caffè del Corso. Traditional old coffee house, serving good coffee, ice cream and snacks. 3 Corso Garibaldi.

Il Cortegiano. Pleasant central café, also serves excellent lunches. Closed Mon in winter. 13 Via Puccinotti, T: 0722 320307.

FESTIVALS & EVENTS

Urbino Antiquaria, antique market in Piazza San Francesco and Piazza Repubblica, 4th Sun every month.

Festival di Musica Antica, exhibition of instruments, concerts and courses in antique music; Info: Fondazione Italiana per la Musica Antica, 7 Via Col di Lana, 00195 Rome, T: 06 3210806, www.fima-online.org, July.

La Festa del Duca, celebrating various episodes in the history of the duchy and the good old days of Montefeltro and della Rovere, a tourney with jousting, lovely costumes and horses; Info: Associazione Rievocazioni Storiche, Palazzo del Collegio Raffaello, T: 0722 320855, www.comune.urbino.ps.it, 3rd Sun in Aug.

Festa dell'Aquilone, kites are flown from the Cesane hills; Info: AUDA, T: 0722 4874, 1st week in Sept.

LOCAL SPECIALITIES

Casa del Formaggio, 47 Via Mazzini, for the famous soft cheeses called *casciotte di Urbino*. **Enoteca Magia Ciarla**, 54 Via Raffaello, for specialities from all over the region—*casciotta di Urbino*, olive oil from Cartoceto, pasta from Campofilone, all DOP. **Maiolica di Urbino**, 27 Via Puccinotti, has a selection of locally-made majolica and ceramics. **Ordito**, at 89 Via Mazzini, offers rust-printed linens and cottons, hand-woven cloth, 18th-century techniques and designs.

Chocolate-brown brick Urbania (pop. 6,750) is surrounded on three sides by the Metauro, which literally washes the medieval walls, still in good condition, though the old centre was almost completely rebuilt after the destruction caused by bombing raids in 1944. This was the favourite city of Francesco Maria II della Rovere; he lived here, and this is where he died, in 1631. At his death, the duchy became extinct, and was taken over by the Papal States. He was not the only duke to appreciate the place; Federico da Montefeltro enjoyed the atmosphere too, and built a fast road between here and Urbino, enabling him to get from one to the other in only three hours, with a light carriage.

Originally the city stood on a nearby hill, and was called *Castel delle Ripe*. One day in 1227, when the inhabitants had gone to a fair at Sant'Angelo in Vado, it was destroyed by the Ghibellines of Urbino; the pope immediately ordered it to be rebuilt, closer to the river, by Cardinal Durante; from then on (1284) the town was known as *Casteldurante*, until 1636, when Pope Urban VIII sent a bishop and pronounced it to be the city of Urbania. During the Renaissance Casteldurante was one of the most prestigious centres in Italy for the production of pottery, of which the decoration was inspired by Raphael; the tradition is still alive and flourishing, providing a strong base for the economy, along with agriculture (cattle, pigs, chickens, horses), the manufacture of designer jeans, and the academies for foreign students.

Piazza San Cristoforo

Urbania still has a 13th-century system of streets and bridges. It is divided into four districts, among which there is considerable rivalry. Centre of the city is Piazza San Cristoforo, into which the main streets converge. In the middle is a column bearing a statue of St Christopher (1870); to one side is the famous opera house, **Teatro Bramante** (1857), and opposite is the elegant 17th-century Palazzo Brancaleoni Materozzi. Along Via Garibaldi, on the left, is the **oratorio del Corpus Domini** (14th century), decorated inside with frescoes of Prophets and Sibyls by Raffaellino del Colle. On the main altar is a 15th-century wooden statue of the *Dead Christ*. Further ahead, on the left, is the convent and church of **Santa Chiara** (13th century and 1626), with a particularly interesting single-nave interior, richly decorated; among the many works of art, on the main altar is a splendid panel painting by Girolamo Cialdieri di Bartolomeo (1629), said to be his masterpiece: the *Madonna and Child in Glory with Saints*. Over the north and south altars are paintings by Giovanni Francesco Guerrieri; along the side walls are the tombs of the Ubaldini family. The convent next door, the oldest building in Urbania, parts of which are carved into the rock and go back to the days of Charlemagne, has a Romanesque chapter-house and courtyard, and a main part designed by Girolamo Genga. It is now used as a school, and visits are not normally allowed.

By taking Via Roma from Piazza San Cristoforo, you will see on the right the **oratorio del Carmine** (15th century); over the altar is a fresco of the *Madonna*, thought to be by Giotto, and brought here from the castle when it was demolished in 1516. On the left is the public garden; further on, next to the hospital, is the church of the **Crocifisso**, inspired by Vanvitelli, rebuilt after 1944. In the single-nave interior, on the right, is the tomb (1631) of Francesco Maria II della Rovere, last duke of Urbino. In the right-hand chapel is a splendid canvas by Federico Barocci of the *Madonna of the Clouds*; it is thought he also painted the *Crucifixion* on the main altar.

Palazzo Ducale

One side of the impressive brick Palazzo Ducale faces onto Corso Vittorio Emanuele. The palace was built by the Brancaleoni family in the 13th century, and later modified by Francesco di Giorgio Martini and by Girolamo Genga. The most attractive façade looks out over the Metauro, with an airy loggia and two round towers; you get a good view of it from the Ponte del Riscatto bridge. This is where Federico da Montefeltro's celebrated library, over 15,000 precious books, was brought by Duke della Rovere in 1607—but not for long. The books were taken to Rome in 1667 by Pope Alexander VII, who wanted to recreate there the famous Library of Alexandria. The **Biblioteca Ducale** (*to request a visit T: 0722 313151*) has since recuperated something of its past splendour, with over 35,000 old volumes, parchments, incunabula and manuscripts. The palace also houses the **Museo Civico** (*open 10–12 & 3–6; closed Mon; T: 0722 317175*), entrance from Via Piccini, with a rich collection of paintings and frescoes, including works by Palma Giovane, Federico Barocci and Giovanni Francesco Guerrieri (don't miss his thought-provoking portrait of a court lady with a little girl, probably Livia della Rovere with her granddaughter Vittoria; an unhappy-looking lady, richly dressed and bejewelled, clutching the things she loves most to her ample bosom—the child and her spaniel). Also here are the Ubaldini family's collection of etchings and drawings, one of which is 12m long, and represents Emperor Charles V at Bologna with all his court; 16th–18th century maps; Mercator's globes (1541 and 1551), and a vast assortment of local pottery. In the basement is the museum of history of local agriculture. Behind the palace is the market place, where the weekly market is held on Thursday.

Piazza Libertà and district

At the end of Corso Vittorio Emanuele is Piazza Libertà, with the elegant 16th-century town hall, and the high unfinished clock tower. Close by is Via Urbano VIII, where on the right you will see the 15th-century bishop's palace (Francesco di Giorgio Martini), seat of the **Diocese Museum** (*to request a visit T: 0722 319555*), containing many art treasures from the churches of the city and the surroundings, including a picture gallery, a section dedicated to Casteldurante pottery, from the origins to the present day, an interesting Palaeochristian stone Crucifix, and 14th-century frescoes of the Fabriano school. The same street leads to Piazza Duomo, and the **cathedral**, surrounded by some rather anonymous post-war buildings, and dedicated to the patron

Giovanni Francesco Guerrieri: portrait of a noble lady, thought to be Livia della Rovere, and her grand-daughter Vittoria, last of the family line.

saint of the city, Christopher. Its present aspect is 18th century, but one of the bell-towers (the one behind) betrays the Romanesque origin of the construction. Inside, over the main altar, is a large painted wooden **Crucifix** by Pietro da Rimini (1320); the chapel to the left of the presbytery is beautifully decorated with stucco, while most of the carved stone work in the cathedral was carried out by craftsmen from Sant'Ippolito.

By taking Via Ugolini from Piazza Libertà you reach on the right the vast convent and church of **San Francesco** (13th century and 1762), a good example of local Baroque architecture, with a lovely Romanesque bell-tower (14th century); the peaceful cloister was built at the same time. Next to the convent is the **chiesa dei Morti** (*open 10–12 & 3–6; mid June–mid Sept 10–6; closed Mon; T: 0722 319841*), a little Romanesque church with a nice portal, famous for the rather macabre collection of mummies. They were found buried in front of the church, mysteriously preserved by a kind of mould, when in 1804 Napoleon ordered all the corpses in the cities to be moved to hygienic out-of-town cemeteries.

The Barco Ducale

A short distance from Urbania, along the road to Sant'Angelo, is the magnificent hunting-lodge of the dukes of Urbino, where the nobles arrived by boat along the river, the **Barco Ducale** (*open July–August only; T: 0722 317015*). The villa was designed by Francesco di Giorgio Martini and Girolamo Genga, while the church of San Giovanni Battista, designed by Vanvitelli, was added in the 18th century. Five kilometres north-west of Urbania is the fortress-town of **Peglio**, built by the Lombards, perfectly occupying the summit of a huge limestone rock. There are fantastic views from the top, over the surrounding countryside.

THE UPPER METAURO VALLEY

Sant'Angelo in Vado

Sant'Angelo in Vado stands in a strategic position on the River Metauro, where the Romans built a settlement called *Tiphernum Mataurense*, destroyed by the Goths in the 6th century. The survivors rebuilt their town, dedicating it to the Archangel Michael; 'in Vado' means a point where the river can be crossed by wading. The old town, built of worn stone and mellow milk-chocolate-coloured brick, is still intact, now flanked by a flourishing industrial area for the production of building materials and furniture. Local wine farmers produce the rare liqueur-like white wine called *Vinsanto*, so called because the grapes, gathered in September, are pressed in Holy Week, after having been hung to wither indoors; every family puts aside a cask of *Vinsanto* when a child is born, to be drunk on their wedding day. It is an important truffle centre, especially for the prized white *Tuber magnatum* (the name means 'tuber for wealthy people'). In October and November the old centre is crowded with people bargaining for 'white diamonds'; the truffle-hunters themselves can be seen sitting around in the coffee bars, showing off their finds—and their dogs.

Sant'Angelo was the fief of the Brancaleoni family, passing in 1437 to the Montefeltro, when Federico married Gentile Brancaleoni, his first wife, and later to the Papal States. In 1636 it was declared a city, sharing a bishop with Urbania. For many years it was the capital of the Massa Trabaria Forest (*see p. 322 below*).

At the entrance to the town (when coming from Urbania), at Pratello Santa Maria, just after the public gardens, is the plain 14th-century church of **Santa Maria dei Servi Extra Muros** (*may be closed for repairs; to request a visit T: 0722 81853*), a national monument, with a fine bell-tower. The interior has 13 beautiful 17th-century gilded and carved altars, each one the responsibility of one of the aristocratic families, surmounted by numerous exceptional works of art; over the altar to the left of the main door (*closed*) is a bronze bas-relief of the *Madonna in Glory*, an early work by Lorenzo Ghiberti, from which the angels were stolen a few years ago. Over the altar by the side door is a panel painting of the *Madonna and Child with Saints*, signed and dated 1543 by Raffaellino del Colle, while on the fourth north altar is a painting by Francesco Mancini, of the *Vision of St Philip Benizi*. In the apse are beautifully carved walnut choir-stalls. By the church is the **Museo Archeologico Tifernum Mataurense** (*open summer 9–1 & 3–7; winter on request; T: 0722 88455*), housing a collection of Roman epigraphs, statues, mosaics, coins and pottery sherds, found locally.

After crossing the Metauro, along Corso Garibaldi you will see several Renaissance palaces and old churches, and, at the far end, one of the old gates, Porta Albani. On the right, very elegant, is **Palazzo Grifoni Nardini Ridarelli** (15th century), decorated with stone bas-reliefs—notice the lion of St Mark, awarded to the soldier-of-fortune Matteo Grifoni for his services on behalf of the city of Venice. In front of this palace is the church of **Santa Caterina del Corso**, with a lovely Renaissance portal; inside, stuccoes tell the story of St Catherine. In this old part of town there are many tiny medieval streets where it is pleasant to lose one's way; on sunny days you will see old ladies sitting outside their door, sewing, or spinning wool; some houses have the 'door for the dead', only opened to allow the passage of a coffin, and then walled up again.

In the quiet, central Piazza Pio XXII is the ex-town hall, **Palazzo della Ragione** (14th century), with an attractive portico; the high bell-tower, affectionately called *El Campanon*, is the symbol of the city. Opposite is the **duomo**, rebuilt in the 18th century. On the main altar is a painting of *St Michael Archangel* by Francesco Mancini (1754); also in the apse is a painting of the *Three Kings* by Claudio Ridolfi, while close to the sacristy is *St John the Baptist*, a work by Guido Reni. Also in the cathedral is the Chapel of the Madonna del Pianto ('Lamentation'), erected in 1855 when there was a terrible epidemic of cholera; the painting of *Our Lady of the Tears* on the altar has recently been attributed to Gentile da Fabriano. Since 1838 the town hall is housed in **Palazzo Fagnani** (17th century), in Piazza Umberto, often called *Piazza del Papa* because of the statue of Pope Clement XIV (a local man) in the centre. In the council chamber, visible on request, is a fine work by Federico Zuccari, representing the *Artist's Family in Prayer with Saints*. Also in the square is the eight-sided church of San Filippo, and Palazzo Mercuri, which houses an interesting museum dedicated to the various crafts and trades which once flourished in Sant'Angelo, **I Vecchi Mestieri** (*open June–Oct 9–12 & 3–7; winter on request T: 0722 818536*), with the reconstructed shops of a carpenter, cooper, hatter, shoemaker, basket-maker, rope-maker, goldsmith, blacksmith, and rust-printer on cloth.

Mercatello sul Metauro

Mercatello sul Metauro was an Etruscan centre, which became one of the most important castles of the Massa Trabaria. Once known as *Pieve d'Ico*, 'the church of the icon', it assumed its present name in the 13th century, because of its flourishing markets; a characteristic market is still held every Saturday. In the central Piazza Garibaldi, said to be the loveliest in the region, is the **Collegiata**, once the Pieve di San Pietro d'Ico, a church that was already important in the 12th century. Inside is the famous old icon, *Madonna of the Graces* (11th century). Next to the church is the Museo della Collegiata (*to request a visit T: 0722 89114 or ask Pro Loco*), with religious items coming from this and the other churches of the town, dating from the 13th–17th centuries. In the heart of an intact medieval quarter, in Via Bencivenni, is the stunning 13th-century Romano-Gothic church of **San Francesco** (*to request a visit T: 0722 89114 or ask Pro Loco*), the art gallery of the town; binoculars are useful. The single-nave interior has a truss-beam roof and a square apse, approached by a late Gothic triumphal arch with two statues of Saints, illuminated by a large double-light window. On the beam is an unforgettably lovely wooden Crucifix, signed by Giovanni da Rimini (13th century), while on the main altar is a polyptych by Giovanni Baronzio (14th century) of the *Madonna and Christ with Saints*. To the right of the altar is a 13th-century panel painting of the *Madonna*; opposite is a 14th-century panel painting of the *Madonna with St Anthony* by Luca di Tommè. The frescoes on the vault of the apse, showing the Evangelists, are thought to be the work of Girolamo Genga, and on the north wall is a fresco of *St Clare* by Lorenzo Salimbeni. On the walls on either side of the entrance are two medallions by Benedetto da Maiano of Federico da Montefeltro and Ottaviano Ubaldini. The modern stained-glass panes in the church were inspired by that on the left side of the presbytery, showing St Francis, the only one to survive of the original windows. More priceless old masters are in the sacristy, including works by Giovanni Francesco Guerrieri, Claudio Ridolfi and Giorgio Picchi. A walk along the Meta, c. 3km northwest of Mercatello, leads to the romantic, beautifully preserved village of **Castello della Pieve**, where it is said that the decision to exile Dante from Florence was made, on 4th October 1301.

The Massa Trabaria

At the foot of the Alpe della Luna, where the Meta and the Auro rivers join forces to become the Metauro, and an ideal base for trekking in the fir forest (called *Massa Trabaria* by the Romans, and one of their most important sources of deal trunks, *trabes*, which were floated down the Tiber to Rome), is the small community of **Borgo Pace**, originally a castle built to defend the nearby Benedictine monastery dedicated to the Archangel Michael. At the Centro di Educazione Ambientale Aula Verde is the Museo del Carbonaio (*open 10–12 only; to request a visit T: 0722 816048*), a collection of photographs illustrating the activity of the charcoal burners of the forest. Through the centuries Borgo Pace has developed into a group of hamlets: **Lamoli** stands at the foot of the 9th-century Benedictine abbey of San Michele Arcangelo, built of lovely faded stone, still with the original apse; inside there is a single nave with two side aisles, and splendid 15th-century frescoes. Nearby is the Museo dei Colori Naturali Delio Bischi (*to request a visit T: 0722 80133*), where plant species used for the manufacture of natural colours are cultivated, and the essences extracted, to tint wool, paper and pottery. **Parchiule** is a delightful little collection of very ancient houses built of blocks of sandstone, surrounding the church of Santa Maria.

THE GOLA DEL FURLO & ENVIRONS

Just south of Urbino is the beautiful grey stone town of **Fermignano**, on the River Metauro, probably founded by the Romans, because of its key position on the river and on the road to Urbino. Some historians believe that the historic battle between the Romans and the Carthaginians in 207 BC, took place here. In the Middle Ages Fermignano had important paper industries, replaced more recently by pasta factories and textile mills for woollen cloth; there is a factory manufacturing jeans, and another for kitchen furniture (Veneto Cucine). Entering the city centre, you see the Roman three-arched bridge, and the medieval tower to protect it, over the Metauro, which forms a double waterfall. The wool mill, once a paper factory, near the tower, is a good example of industrial archaeology. The medieval heart of the town, surrounded by a curve of the river, with a labyrinth of tiny streets, is called *Pianello*. In the public gardens there is a bronze bust of Bramante (the inhabitants of Fermignano say he was born nearby, but the people of San Marino and those of Urbania make the same claim). Market day here, very colourful, is Friday. From Fermignano you can walk (c. 3km) up the wooded hill of Serra Alta (400m), for magnificent views over Urbino and the Apennines.

Gola del Furlo

Not far from Fermignano, just before joining the Metauro, the River Candigliano forms a gorge, now a wildlife reserve, **Riserva Naturale Gola del Furlo** (*Centro informazioni, 40 Via Flaminia, T: 0721 700041*), of which the symbol is a golden eagle flying over a chasm. It is spectacularly photogenic, and interesting both from the point of view of the wildlife (golden eagle, sparrow hawk, goshawk, peregrine falcon, lanner falcon, Montagu's harrier, pallid and alpine swifts, blue rock thrush, and chough—to mention only the birds) and for the tunnels built by the Romans to allow the passage of the Via Flaminia: the **Galleria del Furlo**, 38m long, just over 5m wide, and 6m high, was chiselled through the limestone by slaves for Vespasian, in AD 76–77. It has seen the passage of many kings, emperors and popes, with their carriages, cohorts and courtesans; many crucial battles; and, in 1502, Lucrezia Borgia, on her way to Ferrara. But the gorge gradually became infested with highwaymen and

The dramatic scenery of the Gola del Furlo.

bandits, and was extremely dangerous for travellers until the 19th century. Close to the opening of the main tunnel is a smaller one carved by the consul Flaminius in 217 BC. Although only 8m long, it is an impressive achievement, deeply scarred by the wheels of chariots and carts. Close to the gorge is a dam (*to request a visit T: 0736 293210, ENEL Green Power Marche*) for hydroelectricity, inaugurated in 1923, one of the oldest in Italy. A 14km trail, **Sentiero Energia e Natura** (*T: 071 2824481*), has been cleared by the ENEL from Gola del Furlo to the sea, so you can follow the Metauro to its mouth at Fano, on foot, on horseback, or by bicycle. If walking, it takes a whole day. A short distance along the Via Flaminia to Acqualagna, on the left, is the church of **San Vincenzo al Furlo**, part of an 8th-century abbey, remodelled in the 13th century. Close by is a little Roman bridge.

Acqualagna and environs

The Via Flaminia from the Furla Gorge to Piobbico follows the Candigliano, first on one side, then on the other, passing by castles and monasteries, and through another splendid gorge about 2km long, with spectacular outcrops of pink, red and white limestone. Just outside Acqualagna (c. 2km), at Petriccio, on the right, almost hidden by a house, is the old Gothic church of **Santa Maria**, preceded by a narthex, with well-preserved 14th-century frescoes over the portico; inside is a single nave with

Gothic arches. Modern-looking **Acqualagna** stands at the confluence of the Burano and Candigliano streams. The preceding Roman town of *Pitinum Mergens* is still unexplored. Acqualagna is the most important centre in Italy for the production and sale of truffles, which are available throughout the year; two-thirds of all the truffles in Italy come from here. One out of four inhabitants possesses a truffle-hunting licence; the local economy depends on the aromatic fungus. But Acqualagna is also famous for its stonemasons, who supply fireplaces and fitted kitchens, throughout Italy.

DIAMONDS FOR DINNER

Truffles certainly don't come cheap: in 2003 the price of white truffle, *Tuber magnatum pico*, reached €3,000 a kilo (in past years even €4,000 on occasion). In spite of the cost, they will always find a buyer, at least in Italy and France. The prized white truffle is harvested from October to December, followed by the excellent quality black truffle, *Tuber melanosporum*, until mid-March; then come the less aromatic *Tuber albidum*, and the black summer truffle, *Tuber aestivum*, found from May to December. Truffles are also found in Spain, France, China, Morocco and Tunisia, but the best come from Italy: perhaps 200 tons a year. Fortunately, you don't need very much truffle to impart a distinctive aroma and flavour. They are found in the woods, forming under the roots of certain trees. It is practically impossible to detect them by sight, so the hunters use animals to pick up the scent. Pigs, or rather sows (it is a sexually stimulating smell for them), are the best at finding truffles, but nowadays dogs are used, being much easier to manage. A good truffle dog is worth more than his weight in gold. Judging from what you see in Acqualagna, Sant'Agata Feltria, or Sant'Angelo al Vado, most of them are mongrels, but there is a particular breed, like a large woolly poodle, called *lagotto romagnolo*.

THE UMBRIAN BORDER

Piobbico

The mild climate and good spring water attract many holidaymakers to Piobbico, a beautiful stone town built in the 11th century on the ruins of a Roman settlement called *Publicum*, at the confluence of the Candigliano and Biscubio rivers. In the 12th century it was taken by the Brancaleoni family, who were able to extend their control over the whole Massa Trabaria forest. It took the Brancaleoni seven centuries to complete their luxurious residence dominating the town; they were continually modifying the structure, to adapt it to the times. In 1573, under the influence of the splendour of Urbino, they called on the famous architect Girolamo Genga and his son Bartolomeo, to give the castle a refined Renaissance touch; the result is a magnificent

Holy Family (1574) by Federico Barocci, the artist's favourite of his own works.

building with over 100 rooms, graceful staircases, ornate stone fireplaces, and stuccoes by Federico Brandani. An unusual feature is the timepiece in the clock tower, unique in Italy; the face behind (inside the tower) has the hands going round in an anticlockwise direction.

While the castle was being made beautiful, the town at its foot, which is entered by two gates, was also receiving attention; it is one of the most attractive places in the Montefeltro. The **Castello Brancaleoni** (*open Sun and holidays 10.30–1 & 3.30–6.30; other days on request 9–12 & 3.30–6.30; T: 0722 985444*) houses an interesting collection of 17th-century costumes and jewellery, found in a secret room in the castle by Countess Clorinda, in the early 19th century. She organised a 'dressing-up' party for her friends, but since then the clothes have been freshened up, repaired, and carefully looked after. Another collection displays palaeontological finds from Mt Nerone, including the fossilized remains of a bear, *Ursus spelaeus*, 350 thousand years old, and found by chance in a cave. The private chapel of the Brancaleoni, dedicated to St Charles Borromeo, and decorated with frescoes and stuccoes by Brandani (1575), can be reached from the courtyard. More stuccoes by Brandani can be seen in the church of **Santo Stefano** (18th century), with an unusual elliptical interior; but all eyes are drawn to the magnificent canvas by Federico Barocci, representing the *Holy Family*, resting under a cherry tree. It is a joyful scene, full of light and colour, and is a guache copy of an oil-on-canvas on the same subject, now in the Vatican. It was painted on the request of Count Antonio Brancaleoni in 1574. Barocci thought that this copy was his finest work.

Not famous for their good looks, but with a remarkable sense of humour, the people of Piobbico have founded the world-wide Club dei Brutti, 'ugly ones', awarding a prize each year to the most horrendous among their number. Founded in 1879, the club has 24,000 members at the time of writing. The sworn duty of each president is to find a husband for an unmarried lady of Piobbico every year. Hand-woven woollen rugs are still made, an ancient tradition; they were once coloured blue with woad, *Isatis tinctoria*, which was cultivated for the purpose. The inhabitants are fond of a particular thick polenta, called *polentone*.

Apecchio and environs

Surrounded by woods of pines and oaks, **Apecchio** was an Etruscan centre, taken over by the Romans; by the 11th century the religious community of San Martino was controlling 44 parishes, and numerous farms. It was the feud of the Ubaldini family until 1498, when the territory became part of the Duchy of Urbino; in 1752, on the extinction of the Ubaldini counts, it passed to the Papal States. Today there is not much to be seen of the medieval city, because of the 1781 earthquake: only the humpback bridge (14th century, said to be haunted) over the River Biscubio, once the entrance to the town, and the clock tower, which was the entrance to the castle. In the central Via XX Settembre is Palazzo Ubaldini, once the home of the counts, now the town hall. Only the courtyard, with its sandstone columns, survives of the original building. In the basement of the palace is the Museo dei Fossili Minerali (*open Mon–Fri 9–1 & 3–6; Sat and holidays 10–12.30 & 3–6.30; T: 0722 989004*), a fine collection of ammonites from nearby Mt Nerone. To the left of the palace is the church of the Santissimo Crocifisso, or San Martino, of which traces of the Romanesque structure can still be seen; it was built on top of a Roman temple. In the single-nave interior are two Romanesque stone lions from the church of Santa Maria Maggiore in Rome, a gift of Pope Clement IX to Count Ubaldini, on either side of the north altar. The little church of the Madonna della Vita, with 17th-century paintings inside, and a much venerated 15th-century Crucifix, was built over the ruins of the synagogue (Apecchio had an important Jewish community). At **Colombara**, outside town, is the largest globe in the world, 10m in diameter, made of wood by a local man. It can hold 600 people and is mentioned in the *Guinness Book of Records*. **Monte Nerone** (1525m) offers plenty of opportunities for excursions; in winter it is covered with snow, and the village of **Serravalle di Carda** (745m), on the southwest slope, becomes a ski resort—in summer it is a departure point for pony-trekkers and ramblers.

Cagli

Situated on the slopes of Mt Petrano, at the confluence of the Bosso and Burano streams, Cagli certainly goes back to pre-Roman times. It became a Roman town in 295 BC, and under the Byzantines, in the 5th century, its strategic importance along the Via Flaminia was such that it formed part of a pentapolis, or five-city alliance, together with Jesi, Fossombrone, Urbino and Gubbio. In the centre of this rather severe city of hazelnut-coloured stone is the sturdy, elliptical **Torrione** (*to request a visit T: 0721 780731*), which now houses a collection of modern sculptures by Italian and foreign artists, and is all that remains of the fortifications built by Francesco di

Giorgio Martini in 1481; a secret passage (which still exists) led from this tower to the castle up above. Close by, in Piazza del Teatro, is the lovely opera house, **Teatro Comunale** (1878); the same building, which is a 16th-century Renaissance palace, also houses the public library and the Conservatory of Music. Via Celli passes through the square; to the east is the massive 14th-century gate, Porta Massara, while to the west is Piazza San Francesco, with the imposing, stark façade of the Romano-Gothic church of San Francesco, with a beautiful 14th-century portal. The **Palazzo Pubblico**, now seat of the town hall and the civic museum, is south of the theatre, in Piazza Matteotti. It was also restructured by Francesco di Giorgio Martini, but it is of medieval origin. The attractive façade has a balcony in the centre with a niche containing a statue of the Madonna, and is surmounted by a small bell-tower, with an old clock. The **Museo Archeologico e della Via Flaminia** (*open June–Sept 10–12 & 4–7; Oct–Mar Sat & Sun 10–12 & 3–6; T: 0721 78071*) illustrates the role of the Roman road in the history of the city, and how it affected trade. Nearby, in Via Fonte del Duomo, is the **duomo** (13th century and 1790), with an interesting, imposing façade. Inside (left-hand chapel) you will find several luminous, colourful canvases by the local artist Gaetano Lapis (1706–76). Just outside the town, on the Via Flaminia, is a Roman bridge, the **Ponte Mallio**, 2,000 years old, and in very good condition. The weekly market (Wednesday), held in the narrow streets and squares around the Torrione, has a particular medieval flavour.

Cantiano and Monte Catria

Picturesque **Cantiano** stands at the confluence of the Bevano and the Burano streams, surrounded by mountains. Probably of very ancient origin, the town has strong medieval traditions, evoked at Easter with the *Turba*, a dramatic procession in which the whole population takes part (Cantiano forms part of *Europassion*, an association of European towns with particularly significant religious celebrations). The old centre is dominated by the ruins of the Torrione, a tower, part of a fortress built by Francesco di Giorgio Martini. In the central Via IV Novembre stands the Romanesque church of Sant'Agostino; the convent of which houses the civic museums, the Museo Geo-Territoriale (*open Sat–Sun 3–7; 1 Aug–15 Sept 4–8 & 9–11; T: Archeoclub 0721 788493 or Municipio 0721 88321*), a collection of local stone types and fossils, including the fossilized tracks of a small dinosaur, known affectionately as 'Ugo'. In the same building is the archaeological collection, with locally-found objects dating from the Palaeolithic to the Middle Ages, relating particularly to the Via Flaminia. A little further along the street, on the right, is the Collegiata di San Giovanni Battista (1631), with an unfinished façade. The vast single-nave interior has a beautiful Baroque altar in the south transept, and paintings by Ridolfi and Zuccari. In the Chapel of the Misericordia is a round painting known as the *Madonna of the Goldfinch*, recently attributed to Perugino, who painted it together with Pinturicchio. The street leads into the main square, Piazza Luceoli, with the town hall and the clock tower (the beautiful quadrant of the clock is the symbol of Cantiano). On the square is the church of San Nicolò, with a medieval bell-tower. Inside, over the first left-hand altar, is a

Crucifix of the Bellini school; in the apse is a painting of *St Nicholas* by Carlo Maratta; other paintings are said to be by Caravaggio and Gentile da Fabriano.

Picturesque little streets flanked by medieval houses, lead out from the square, such as Via Fiorucci, once the Jewish Ghetto. The inhabitants of Cantiano, farmers and foresters, raise horses, an activity which goes back to 1128, when they were taught the art by the monks of the Fonte Avellana monastery. This area is particularly famous for *amarene*, morello cherries, and for the delicious bread—Cantiano forms part of the *Associazione Nazionale Città del Pane*, a group of 21 Italian towns and villages where particular care is dedicated to the 'staff of life'. The district where the best bakers are found is Chiaserna.

A panoramic road leads (c. 15km) to **Monte Catria** (1701m), now a wildlife reserve, with wooded slopes carpeted with wildflowers in springtime, and home to the rare Orsini's, or meadow viper. Two cross-country trails, the Italia Trail and the Frassati Trail, pass over the mountain, both signposted.

PRACTICAL INFORMATION

GETTING THERE

• **By train**: The nearest railway station is Pesaro, with express bus connections from the station to Urbino, Urbania, Apecchio (AMIBUS, T: 0722 350738, www.amibus.it).
• **By bus**: AMIBUS (see above), operates services connecting Urbino, Urbania, Apecchio and Fermignano. Autolinee Bucci, T: 0721 32401, has services connecting Urbino, Urbania, Fermignano, Apecchio, Pesaro, Fano, Fossombrone and San Sepolcro.

INFORMATION OFFICES

Comunità Montana Catria e Nerone, Via Pianacce (Furla Gorge), T: 0721 700224, www.lamacina.it; information and free guided tours of the gorge.
Acqualagna Tourist Information Bureau, Piazza Mattei, T: 0721 796741,

www.acqualagna.com; **IAT**, Via Pianacce, 0721 700148;
Apecchio Tourist Information Bureau, 5 Via San Francesco, T: 0722 989004; IAT, 25 Via XX Settembre, T: 0722 99279, www.comune.apecchio.ps.it; Pro Loco Serravalle di Carda, Via Cagli, T: 0722 90140.
Cagli Pro Loco, 3 Via Leopardi, T: 0721 787457, www.comune.cagli.ps.it, www.cm-cagli.ps.it; Comunità Montana Catria e Nerone, 19 Via Alessandri, T: 0721 787752, www.cm-catrianerone.ps.it
Cantiano Pro Loco, 1 Piazza Luceoli, T: 0721 788902, www.comune. cantiano.pu.it; Mt Catria Forestry Commission (Foresta Regionale del Catria), T: 0721 788694.
Fermignano Pro Loco, 3 Corso Bramante, T: 0722 330523, www. proloco-fermignano.it; Riserva Regionale Gola del Furlo, Via Flaminia,

T: 0721 700041,
www.riservagoladelfurlo.it
Mercatello sul Metauro Municipio
and Pro Loco, 5 Piazza Garibaldi, T:
0722 89114, www.cm-urbania.ps.it/
comune.mercatello
Piobbico Municipio and Pro Loco, 2
Viale dei Caduti, T: 0722 986225,
www.provincia.ps.it/comune.piobbico
Sant'Angelo in Vado IAT, Piazza
Umberto, T: 0722 818498,
www.comunesantangeloinvado.it;
Tourist Information Bureau, Località
Pratello Santa Maria, T: 0722 88455,
www.mostratartufo.it
Urbania IAT, 21 Corso Vittorio
Emanuele, T: 0722 313140,
www.marcheweb.com/urbania; Pro
Loco Casteldurante, 27 Corso Vittorio
Emanuele, T: 0722 317211, www.
montefeltro.info; Comunità Montana
Alto e Medio Metauro, 25 Via Manzoni,
T: 0722 318681, www.cm-urbania.ps.it;
for information on trekking and bike
tours; also bikes for hire.

HOTELS

Acqualagna
€€€ **Albergo Il Furlo**. Historic hotel
with excellent restaurant. 66 Via
Flaminia, T: 0721 700096.
€€€ **La Ginestra**. Tiny, welcoming
hotel near the gorge, with a delightful
restaurant, pool and tennis. 17 Via
Furlo, T: 0721 797033,
www.ginestrafurlo.it
€€ **Birra al Pozzo**. Simple building in
a good position, opposite the abbey of
San Vincenzo, close to the Furla Gorge;
restaurant serves appetizing local dishes. 12 Via Pianacce, T: 0721 700084.
Borgo Pace

€€ **La Diligenza**. Small inn with good
restaurant, in the town centre, excellent
value for money. 9 Piazza del Pino,
T: 0722 816021.
€€ **Oasi San Benedetto**. In a 9th-cen-
tury monastery between Mercatello sul
Metauro and the boundary with Umbria,
a tiny hotel for a really relaxing holiday—no TV, no phones in the rooms,
the restaurant serves organic food, vegetarian on request, with abundant servings. 7 Via Abbazia, Lamoli, T: 0722
80133, lamoli@oasisanbenedetto.it;
Cagli
€€€ **International Cagli**. In a lovely
position, surrounded by woods; good
restaurant. 5 Strada Civita, T: 0721
781883, besthotelcagli@libero.it
Fermignano
€€€ **Hotel Bucci**. Just out of town,
very nice little hotel, with garage, but
no restaurant. 13 Via dell'Industria,
T: 0722 356055.
€€€ **Serra Alta**. Charming hotel on
beautiful wooded hill, pool, restaurant
and pizzeria; car park. 28 Via Serra
Alta, T: 0722 332525.
Piobbico
€ **Montenerone**. In centre, very simple,
excellent restaurant. 30 Via Roma,
T: 0722 986282.
Sant'Angelo in Vado
€€€ **Palazzo Baldani**. ■ Small hotel
with excellent restaurant in an18th-cen-
tury palace, elegantly furnished; gym
and sauna. 4 Via Mancini, T: 0722
810101, www.palazzobaldani.it
€€€ **Santa Chiara**. Lovely rooms in
an old monastery; excellent restaurant.
26 Corso Garibaldi, T: 0722 818874,
www.santachiarahotel.it
€€ **Da Lucia**. Friendly, comfortable
hotel, with a good restaurant; car park.

33–35 Via Nazionale, T: 0722 88448.
Urbania
€€€ **Bramante**. Small old-fashioned
hotel, restaurant, central. 92 Via Roma,
T: 0722 319562.

BED & BREAKFAST

Cagli
La Maestade. Comfortable rooms with
private bathroom, sauna, and bowls.
English, Spanish and Russian spoken.
36 Via San Paterniano, T: 06 3314283.
Montescatto 12. House outside town,
with a car park. French and Spanish
spoken. 12 Località Montescatto, Cagli,
T: 0721 799275.
Fermignano
Garden. Comfortable house with gar-
den, tennis and a car park. English,
French and German spoken. 35 Via
Martin Luther King, T: 0722 330007,
b-bgarden@libero.it;
Piobbico
Rosanna Marinelli. Very comfortable.
62/a Via Ca' Bernardo, T: 0721 861333.
Urbania
Maria Bianchi. Countryside location,
with a garden. 15 Via Bembo, T: 0722
318494.

FARM ACCOMMODATION

Apecchio
Chignoni. Panoramic 16th-century
farmhouse, organic food, cookery
courses; pool and lake. English and
French spoken. Località Chignoni, T:
0722 99205, www.chignoni.it
Pieve San Paolo. Beautiful position,
ideal for ramblers or cyclists (bikes
available). The farm produces berry
fruits and flowers, strictly organic,

English French spoken, Italian language
courses arranged.Località San Paolo di
Fagnille, T: 0722 99772,
www.pievesp.it
Cagli
Ca' Belvedere. Ancient farmhouse surrounded by trees, convenient position
for Urbino and Gubbio. Cereal crops
and farmyard animals are raised using
organic methods; vegetarian meals on
request. Pool, archery, table tennis. 103
Strada Pigno-Monte Martello, Località
Smirra di Cagli, T: 0721 799204.
Casale Torre del Sasso. 15th-century
country house with watch tower, cereal
crops and forage, offers comfortable
self-catering apartments, pool, archery.
12 Strada Civita, T: 0721 782655,
torresasso@info-net.it
Fermignano
Locanda della Valle Nuova. ■ A lovely place in a strategic spot. Farm produces organic wine and cereals. Home-
made bread and pasta. Pool, bowls,
horse riding. 14 Località Sagrata La
Cappella, T: 0722 2888,
www.vallenuova.it
Mercatello sul Metauro
Ca' Betania. For an interesting holiday
and excellent food; learn how to make
bread and pasta, or repair straw-seated
chairs. Children welcome; they will love
the animals. 34 Località Ca' Betania, T:
0722 89902, www.agriturbetania.it
Grotta dei Folletti. Small farm with
magical atmosphere, panoramic position, meals on request. 29/a Località
Bruciata, T: 0722 89120,
www.lagrottadeifolletti.it;
Piobbico
Ca' Licozzo. Apartments to rent, pool
and gym in wooded area. English and
French spoken. 19 Via Manzoni, T: 0722

985032, www.agriturismocalicozzo.it
Candianaccio. Large farm raising cattle
and honey bees, growing sunflowers,
sugarbeet and cereals; guests can help
on farm. A seven room farmhouse just
right for large families or groups of
friends (up to 14), meals on request,
pool. 6 Via Candigliano, T: 330
883402, gsm.mochi@libero.it
Sant'Angelo in Vado
Ca' Camone. Apartments to rent, pool
and thermal springs, in a lonely wooded valley. English spoken. Via
Candigliano, T: 0722 99370.
Urbania
Cal Terrazzano. Comfortable welcoming farmhouse about 4km from
Urbania. Organic farming methods,
meals on request, pool, tennis, horse-
riding, cookery courses. The farm raises
horses and produces walnuts and forage. 7 Via dei Fangacci–San Giorgio,
Località Cal Terrazzano, T: 0722
319529.
Mulino della Ricavata. Ancient water-
mill and farm producing flowers for
drying, vegetables and poultry. In a very
peaceful position on the River Metauro
which once carried gold; interesting
local food. Closed Jan–Feb. 5 Via Porta
Celle, Peglio, T: 0722 310326,
www.mulinodellaricavata.com
Pieve del Colle. Old stone farmhouse,
bright and colourful rooms, delicious
local food, horse-riding. English and
French spoken. 1 Via Pieve del Colle, T:
0722 317945, www.pievedelcolle.com

RESTAURANTS

Acqualagna
€€€ **Furlo**. ■ Mussolini loved this
restaurant, where he always made a
point of stopping, and cooking his own
tagliatelle, followed by 12-egg omelettes
with truffles. Nowadays chef Alberto
Melagrana prepares exquisite dishes
using the local ingredients, including
the world-famous truffles; the wine cellar is a delight. Closed Mon evening
and Tues. 66 Via Flaminia, T: 0721
700096.
€€ **Ginestra**. Famous for the cuisine,
this restaurant is also a banqueting hall;
at the same time there are small rooms
with an intimate atmosphere for those
who don't like crowds. Besides truffles,
rabbit and lamb are the specialities;
lengthy wine list. In the garden is a
pool and tennis courts. 17 Via Passo del
Furlo, T: 0721 797033. Closed Mon
and Jan, always open July–Aug.
€€ **Il Tartufo**. Truffles of course, also
cheeses, hams and salami, *ciauscolo*,
fresh potato gnocchi. Also wine bar in
the evenings. Closed Mon. 1 Viale
Risorgimento, T: 0721 797195.
€€ **Il Vicolo**. Booking advisable for
this tiny restaurant, famous for grilled
meats and truffles; excellent wine list.
Closed Tues and July. 39 Corso Roma,
T: 0721 797145.
Borgo Pace
€€ **La Diligenza**. Three generations of
taverners, a long tradition for simple
dishes with something of nearby
Tuscany about them. 9–15 Piazza del
Pino, T: 0722 816021. Closed Wed.
Cagli
€€ **Guazza**. Home-made pasta, good
service, traditional local dishes. Closed
Fri. 1 Piazza Federico da Montefeltro,
T: 0721 787231.
Cantiano
€€ **Tenetra**. Welcoming atmosphere in
this traditional restaurant, occupying

the cellars of an old convent. Home-made bread. Closed Mon. 1 Piazza Bartolucci, T: 0721 788658.

Piobbico

€ **Montenerone**. Renowned restaurant, marvellous *antipasti*, ravioli, vegetable dishes, grilled meats. Closed Wed. 28 Via Roma, T: 0722 986282.

Urbania

€€€ **Big Ben**. Romantic restaurant in town centre, try the duck cooked with morello cherries, or the local cheese with figs. Closed midday and Wed. 61 Corso Vittorio Emanuele, T: 0722 319795.

€€ **Da Doddo**. Traditional trattoria in the heart of town, good house wine. Closed Sat. 4 Via della Cereria, T: 0722 319411.

€€ **Mulino della Ricavata**. Charming atmosphere and interesting food, all grown on their own farm. Closed Jan–Feb, open evenings only. 5 Via Porto Celle (old watermill between Urbania and Peglio), T: 0722 310326.

€€ **Osteria del Cucco**. ■ Old tavern, no menu, brown paper tablecloths, marvellous food served with care. Closed Sun evenings and Mon. 9 Via Betto dei Medici, T: 0722 317412.

CAFÉS, PASTRY SHOPS & ICE CREAM

Acqualagna

Bar Furlo. Mussolini stopped here 40 times in all. Closed Tues. 54 Via Furlo.

Cagli

Caffè del Teatro. Attractive coffee house in the centre. 34 Via Leopardi.

Mercatello sul Metauro

Caffè Rinaldi. An historic coffee house in the most beautiful square in Italy. Piazza Garibaldi.

Urbania

Caffè del Teatro. Good coffee, home-made ice cream, cakes and biscuits. 4 Piazza San Cristoforo.

FESTIVALS & EVENTS

Acqualagna National Truffle Fair dedicated to the black truffles, called 'black diamonds'; Info: 0721 796741, last-but-one Sun in Feb. National Truffle Fair in Piazza Mattei; Info: T: 0721 796741, events for the celebrated white truffles, mid-Oct–early Nov.

Cagli Feast of St Gerontius, procession and fireworks, 9 May. *Il Giuoco dell'Oca*, a kind of large-scale snakes and ladders, carried out in honour of the patron St Gerontius, with splendid costumes, pageants, 16th-century atmosphere; Info: Associazione Giochi Storici, 5 Via Marconi, T: 0721 781646, 2nd Sun in Aug. Drama, concerts and opera at the Teatro Comunale, T: 0721 781341, Oct–March.

Cantiano *La Turba*, the people of the town dress in costume to portray the Passion of Christ; tradition going back to the 13th century, culminating in a dramatic torch-lit procession to a hill representing Golgotha, Good Friday.

Fermignano *Palio della Rana*, the 'Frog Race'; to celebrate their independence from Urbino, declared in 1607, a race between representatives of the seven city districts, each with a frog in a wheelbarrow; the point is to reach the finish with the frog still there; Info: Pro Loco, 3 Corso Bramante, 1st Sunday after Easter. Parade of 19th-century-bicycles; Info: T: 0722 3321542, 1st weekend in Sept.

Mercatello sul Metauro Feast of St

Veronica, traditional summer fair, 9 July. *Palio del Somaro*, donkey-race between the four town districts for the traditional banner; Info: Pro Loco T: 349 2361138, 22–24 July.

Sant'Angelo in Vado Feast of St Michael Archangel, with traditional fair, 29 Sept. *Mostra Nazionale del Tartufo Bianco Pregiato*, a real festival for the precious white truffles, weekends Oct–Nov.

Urbania *La Befana*, parades, shows and games for children, to celebrate the benevolent witch much loved in Italy; Info: T: 0722 317211, www.labefana.com, 6 Jan.

LOCAL SPECIALITIES

Acqualagna
Marini Azzolini Tartufi, 26 Viale Risorgimento, is the best place for truffles: fresh, frozen, freeze-dried, or preserved in oil. **Pietro Sorcinelli**, 18–20 Via Marconi, Pietro prepares hams and salami from local livestock, including boar. **Tartufi Tofani**, 37 Via Bellaria, another good place for truffles.

Cagli
Pipe Don Carlos, 4 Strada Fontetta, his workshop is not easy to find, but it is worth the effort. Music lover Bruto Sordini, the only Italian member of the Pipe Club of London, makes some of the finest pipes in the world, and he is an interesting person.

Cantiano
Amarena Furiosi, 18 Via dell'Industria, for morello cherries, syrups and jams. **Robertino Furiosi**, Via IV Novembre, has typical cakes and sweets of the area. **Romitelli**, 40 Via Catria, Chiaserna, for the famous Monte Catria sourdough bread: large loaves, inimitable flavour.

Mercatello sul Metauro
Pacio, Corso Garibaldi, a renowned pastry shop for local cakes and biscuits.

Piobbico
I.M.M. Antiche Manifatture Artistiche, 84 Via Roma, is the place for hand-woven rugs. **La Bottega delle Essenze**, 63 Via Dante Alighieri, for rust-printed cloth.

Sant'Angelo in Vado
Fabiano Martelli, Via Papa Clemente XIV, for truffles, fresh or preserved. **MP Laboratorio Orafo**, 38 Via XX Settembre, is where Mara Pradarelli, one of the last exponents of an ancient local craft, makes jewellery.

Urbania
L'Antica Casteldurante, 4 Piazza Cavour, for the beautiful local pottery, an ancient tradition. **Ravaldo Longhi**, 55 Corso Vittorio Emanuele, for yet more truffles, and the condiments derived from them.

SAN LEO & THE MONTEFELTRO

The name Montefeltro derives from *Mons Feretrus*, the rock on which San Leo stands, and it refers to a vast area in the northwest of the Marche region, between the Adriatic and the central Apennines; very hilly, and with several enormous limestone outcrops with castles on the top of them—of which San Leo is one—rising sharply and dramatically from among their more modest brethren. This characteristic landscape is the result of ancient subterranean upheaval, which forced to the surface a great plaque of limestone, the bed of a primeval sea, fracturing and tormenting it in the process. Several rivers flow through the Montefeltro: the Conca, Foglia, Metauro, and Marecchia are the most important. The River Marecchia, once known as the *Ariminus*, and which gave its name to Rimini, is 70km long, and one of the most interesting of central Italy for its mountainous course. The Foglia, the ancient *Pisaurus*, gave its name to Pesaro.

HISTORY OF SAN LEO & THE MONTEFELTRO

The wild character of this area made it attractive for prehistoric populations seeking the security of isolation, and they left many traces of their passage. Later came the Romans, who built a road through the mountains to Rimini. Then came the monastic communities of the early Middle Ages, followed by the powerful families who alternated in controlling this part of the region: the Montefeltro, the Malatesta, the della Rovere, and the grand-dukes of Tuscany, who built the lonely fortresses and the magnificent castles. San Leo was once a rock worshipped as sacred by the primitive people of the area. It was chosen as a place of refuge by the runaway Christian Dalmatian slave St Leo, companion of St Marinus (after whom the republic of San Marino is named), in the late 3rd century. From here Christianity spread rapidly, and soon Montefeltro (the old name of the town) became an important diocese. The impregnable rock also made it an important military base; in 962 Berengarius II even declared it to be the capital of the Kingdom of Italy, and it was consequently besieged for months by Emperor Otto I. Later it became a key position during the struggles between Guelphs and Ghibellines. In the 13th century the counts of Montefeltro appeared—as dukes of Urbino, they would play a fundamental role in bringing the Renaissance to central Italy. With their extinction in 1631, San Leo passed to the Papal States, and its castle became a prison—the pope's preferred 'high security jail', where many prisoners would languish, including Cagliostro (*see p. 338*). Among the famous visitors to San Leo are Dante (who commented on the stiff climb up), and St Francis of Assisi. In fact, in 1213 St Francis received here, as a gift from Count Orlando of Chiusi, the mountain of Verna, where he would build his convent.

Federico da Montefeltro (1422–82)
A warrior who became a prince, Federico was born in Gubbio in 1422, the illegitimate son of Count Guidantonio of Montefeltro and Urbino. When he was five his father had a legitimate son, Oddantonio; to protect him from his stepmother he was betrothed to Gentile Brancaleoni (aged 10), and sent to live with his future parents-in-law. It was an excellent turn of events for Federico. He was encouraged to study and to travel, and spent long periods in Venice, Mantua and other cities, learning the arts of diplomacy together with an appreciation of literature, painting, architecture and music. At the age of sixteen he married Gentile and went to Milan to learn the art of soldiery. He soon became the *condottiere* of the Visconti, earning himself considerable respect—especially when he captured the Malatesta stronghold of San Leo in 1441, thought to be invulnerable. Even after becoming lord of Urbino and Montefeltro in 1444, when Oddantonio was assassinated, he never gave up his military campaigning on behalf of the various great powers of the day—

Portrait by Pedro Berruguete of Federico da Montefeltro and his son Guidubaldo (1480–81). After losing the sight of his right eye and sustaining a disfiguring wound to that side of his face in a joust, the duke was always portrayed from the left.

the Visconti, Francesco Sforza, the pope, Venice, the King of Aragon, Florence— gaining an enormous fortune, but also a reputation for being absolutely trustworthy and a man of his word. Edward IV of England even awarded him the Order of the Garter. In 1460, having lost his first wife, he married the thirteen-year-old Battista Sforza, a girl of character and learning. She convinced Federico to turn Urbino into a unique 'ideal city', where the palace became a meeting point for artists and intellectuals, and gave him six daughters, one after the other. At last, in 1472, she produced the much-desired son, Guidubaldo. She died not very long after.

EXPLORING SAN LEO

Worn stone, brisk winds, friendly cats, and appetizing cooking aromas drifting from welcoming open doorways: San Leo (538m, population 2,700) stands on a limestone crag, almost inaccessible, with an eye-stopping castle perched on the top, dominating the Marecchia valley.

Entering the town through the south gate, which is the only access, you reach Piazza Dante; on the left is the **Palazzo Municipale** (16th century), once the residence of the Montefeltro counts and of the dukes of Urbino; next to it is a beautiful church, the oldest in the town, the **Pieve** or Basilica (*open 9–1 & 3–6*), perhaps built in the 8th century, and modified in the 11th. Inside are some columns and capitals from Imperial Roman temples. In the presbytery, which is raised over the crypt, is a 9th-century ciborium supported by slender columns with medieval capitals. At the beginning of the south aisle is a narrow stair leading to an underground chamber, said to be the first church, founded here by St Leo in the 4th century. In the absolutely perfect, peaceful little square, is an octagonal fountain where birds swoop down to drink. A little further along, on the right, is Palazzo Nardini, where St Francis of Assisi stayed in 1213.

On the same square is the Palazzo Mediceo (1521), housing the **Museo di Arte Sacra** (*open 9–6; Aug 9–8.30; T: 0541 916306*), a collection of works of art from local churches, including a panel painting by Luca Frosino of the *Madonna and Child with Sts Leo and Marinus* (1487), and a *Deposition of Christ* by Guercino.

The duomo

The duomo (12th century) is in the highest part of the town, built entirely of mellow ivory sandstone, with graceful apses decorated with little blind arches, lancet and double-lancet windows, revealing Lombard influence. The interior is solemn, a central nave and two side aisles, divided by pilasters; the date of construction (1173) is carved on the fourth south one. There are also two Roman columns, with 3rd-century capitals. The presbytery is particularly interesting, quite high, and curving to form the three apses. In the central apse is a 13th-century Crucifix. Under the presbytery is the crypt, with more ancient columns and enigmatic capitals, and the lid of St Leo's sarcophagus. At the back of the cathedral is the isolated, superb 12th-century bell-tower (*open 10–12 & 3–7*), 32m high, and a good viewpoint for the famous panorama over the Marecchia valley and the Marche, and to San Marino, Romagna, and sometimes even the mountains of Dalmatia. Between the bell-tower and the cathedral you will find a mysterious rectangular hole carved into the rock; it could be a prehistoric altar, or (when filled with water) an astronomical observatory; it may have been used as a baptismal pool by early Christians.

The Rocca

The fort of San Leo or Rocca (*open 9–6; Aug 9–8.30; T: 0541 916302*), thought by many to be the most beautiful castle in Italy, is reached by taking Via Leopardi to the right, just after the south gate. The glowing, almost magical construction owes its present aspect to Francesco di Giorgio Martini, architect to Federico da Montefeltro, who adapted a medieval fortress (probably originally Roman); he devised the immense cylindrical towers, and the triangular fortification at one end, like the prow of a ship, ideal protection against the powerful cannons of the time. In the castle is the **Museo della Città** (*opening times as above; T: 0541 916233*), with a collection covering the 3rd century BC to 1866, with particular information on Berengarius II, Otto I, St Francis, Dante, and the Montefeltro family. There is also an art gallery with old masters and contemporary paintings, and a section with pottery and furniture.

A PRISONER IN SAN LEO

Giuseppe Balsamo, count of Cagliostro, was born in 1743 Palermo, the city from which he fled after being accused of theft; he went to Rome, but soon became restless, and went to London. An alchemist and an intellectual, he was soon much in demand among the European aristocracy, for his skill as a healer and his esoteric knowledge, but he also claimed to be a medium, and to foresee the future. He founded a Masonic lodge, inspired by Egyptian pharaohs and the goddess Isis, appointing himself as its head. This was too much for the Church. Betrayed by his wife, in 1791 he was sentenced to death for heresy by the Inquisition, but Pope Pius VI spared his life, condemning him to spend the rest of his days in solitary confinement. Cagliostro was sent to San Leo, where he died four years later, in a tiny, dank dungeon (into which he had been thrown from above; his food and water arrived the same way); all he could see through the barred window was a church, and all he could hear was the sound of church bells; a terrible sentence indeed, for a man who valued his freedom above anything else, and who was an avowed atheist. It is said that nobody dared bury his body, which in fact has never been found.

Sant'Igne

A pleasant walk leads c. 2 km north of San Leo to the convent of Sant'Igne, founded by St Francis in 1213, with a lovely Gothic cloister; 'Igne' derives from *ignis*, fire, because of the comforting blaze which miraculously sprang up on this spot, on 7th May 1213, during a terrible storm, to light and warm the saint.

THE MARECCHIA VALLEY

Talamello

Talamello is opposite San Leo on the other side of the Marecchia, on a crest of Mt Aquilone, and protected by the high peak of Mt Pincio. The name of this delightful little town derives from *thalamos*, Greek for 'secluded room', a reference to the numerous caves carved into the limestone tufa by the population through the centuries. Talamello, in fact, goes back at least to the 9th century, and was seat of the bishop of Montefeltro during the 14th and 15th centuries. In the central Piazza Garibaldi, with its lovely fountain, is the church of **San Lorenzo** (17th century), with a remarkable painted wooden Crucifix (14th century), said to be the work of Giotto. It attracts many pilgrims, especially for the Monday after Whitsun, when a traditional procession takes place in the afternoon, and the Crucifix is carried through the streets.

In Piazza Saffi, housed in the old 19th-century Amintore Galli opera house, is the **Museo Gualtieri** (*open April–Oct Wed–Sun 10.30–12.30 & 3.30–7; winter Sun and holidays only; T: 0541 920036; www.gualtierimuseum.com*), with a collection of paintings by the local artist Fernando Gualtieri (b. 1919), who now lives in Paris. At the cemetery of Talamello is the **Cella** (*normally open in summer; T: Municipio 0541 920036 to request a visit*), a small chamber entirely frescoed by Antonio Alberti in 1437, with charming pictures of saints, angels, the *Nativity* and the *Resurrection*.

AMBRA DI TALAMELLO

Among the delicious cheeses produced in the Marche is *formaggio di fossa*, pit-matured cheese from Talamello, made with a mixture of cow's and sheep's milk, rightly described as 'amber', and protected by the *Denominazione d'Origine Protetta* label. In early August the cheeses are wrapped in cloths and buried in straw-lined pits or caves, carved into the limestone, and the entrances are cemented over. In November the pits are opened, and the cheeses are recovered and cleaned, simply by scraping with a spoon. The results are rather deformed in shape, but with perfect consistency and flavour, having lost all their excess liquids. This tradition developed with the necessity of hiding various kinds of food from the surprise attacks of bandits; now it provides a true gastronomic delight.

Novafeltria and Maiolo

Talamello is only a stone's throw from **Novafeltria**, one of the most important towns of the Montefeltro, known as *Mercatino Marecchia* until 1941, and famous for its summer fairs, which attracted merchants from all Italy. Now it is a busy commercial centre, with industries for the manufacture of shoes, building materials and clothes. In the central Piazza Vittorio Emanuele, with an elegant 19th-century fountain, is Palazzo Segni (1661), now the town hall, a cream-coloured building with a portico. To the right of it, at the top of a stairway, is the quaint little 14th-century chapel of Santa Marina, with a 16th-century belfry. This square has been the market place for about 1,000 years; the market still takes place every Monday.

East of Novafeltria is the conical hill of Maiolo (624m), with beautiful diagonal ridges giving it almost the aspect of a seashell, the ruins of a castle perched dramatically on the top, and the houses of the village of Maioletto on the steep hillside; the town of Maiolo on the northern slope was carried away by a landslide in 1700, and now the town centre is at nearby **Serra di Maiolo**, which is called Capoluogo. For centuries Maiolo was a rival to San Leo, and was bitterly contested by the Malatesta and the Montefeltro. This town is among the 21 places in Italy said to prepare the best bread; until recently there were still over 70 bakeries. Fifty of these wood-fired stone ovens are still in use—about one for every 12 inhabitants, but only about 10 are lit every day. The local economy is based on farming and forestry.

Sant'Agata Feltria

The road from Novafeltria towards the boundary with Romagna passes along the top of a crest, and is very panoramic. Under the imposing Monte Ercole (937m), sacred in the past to Hercules, is Sant'Agata Feltria, instantly recognisable by its picturesque castle. Once inhabited by Umbrian tribes, then a Roman settlement in 206 BC, it became an important medieval fortress belonging to the Malatesta and the Montefeltro families, and finally seat of the Fregoso, an aristocratic family from Genoa, who claimed it through marriage.

Just south of the town is the convent church of **San Girolamo**, built in 1568, with a stunning *Madonna with Sts Jerome and Cristina* by Pietro da Cortona (1640) over the main altar. In the central Piazza Garibaldi is the Palazzone, built by the Fregoso family in 1605, and now the town hall, which encloses the oldest opera house in the region (and one of the oldest in Italy; 1660), **Teatro Mariani** (*T: 0541 929613*), still in regular use, built of wood, and exquisitely decorated. Continuing up the steep Via Vittorio Emanuele, you reach the castle (10th and 15th centuries; Francesco di Giorgio Martini), high on the rock, made even more photogenic by the rich colours of the brick used in its construction, with an inaccessible tower perfect for Rapunzel: the **Rocca Fregoso** (*open 10–1 & 3–7; T: 0541 929111, www.roccafregoso.it*). Inside is the civic museum, with some interesting collections: manuscripts dating from the 15th–19th centuries, antique furniture, 16th-century frescoes, and displays describing alchemy and tailoring.

Southeast of Sant'Agata, c. 6km along the secondary road to Pennabilli, is the romantic medieval village of **Petrella Guidi**, still perfectly intact around its 13th-century castle; another lovely old castle is at **Rocca Pratiffi**, c. 6km south of Sant'Agata.

Pennabilli and the southern Marecchia

Pennabilli, richly colourful and peaceful, dominated by Mt Carpegna, was formed in 1330 by the union of two fortified villages, Penna and Billi (the latter thought to be the older of the two, perhaps on the site of an Etruscan temple dedicated to the god Bel). After belonging first to the Medici, then the Malatesta, and then to the Montefeltro, in the 16th century it became the seat of the bishop of San Leo, and was declared a city. It lies between two peaks, Roccione (once Penna; the castle has disappeared) and Rupe (once Billi; a few ruined walls and a Crucifix are still there). Via Roma leads up under the impressive, decrepit 16th-century monastery of the Suore Agostiniane, on the left, once the castle of the Lucis family, donated by them to a cloistered order of nuns (who still live there), to the central Piazza Vittorio Emanuele, with the 15th-century Palazzo della Ragione and the Loggia dei Mercanti built by the Medici, and the 16th-century cathedral; in the centre is the Fontana della Pace, the fountain erected in 1350 to celebrate the peace between Penna and Billi. The ancient Via Carboni leads up to the Roccione, through the oldest part of the city, passing through two gates, Porta Carboni (1474), and Porta Malatesta (13th century).

On the right is the side of the church of Sant'Agostino, or Santuario della Madonna delle Grazie, housing a museum of objects relating to the cult of the Virgin Mary. The church was built in two parts, one in the 15th century and the other in the 17th. The organ is very old; it is signed *Cyprianus Bononiensis* and dated 1587. Over the north altar, in a marble frame, is the much-venerated 14th-century fresco of the *Madonna*, in good condition. In this part of town (Via Teatro) is the charming Art Deco opera house, Teatro della Vittoria (1922), and, in Vicolo Somina, the Museo Diocesano A. Bergamaschi (*to request a visit T: 0541 928415*), with a rich collection of paintings, vases, furniture, reliquaries and other religious items, coming from various churches of the Montefeltro. Pennabilli attracts many artists, some of whom become permanent residents; one of these, the poet Tonino Guerra (Fellini's favourite screenwriter), has created a series of **Musei minimi** (*those inside buildings can be visited from 9–12.30 & 2.30–7.30; T: 0541 928578; www.montefeltro.net/pennabilli/orto.htm*), best described as places for reflection. For example, in the centre of Pennabilli is the 'orchard of forgotten fruits', *Orto dei Frutti Dimenticati* (Via San Filippo), once the garden of a convent, with a mulberry planted by the Dalai Lama in 1994, and an orchard with about 80 fruit trees: almost forgotten varieties of plums, cherries, apples and pears, once frequently grown in the Apennines, but without the intervention of Tonino, destined to disappear from the face of the earth. Along the streets you will see many different sundials, inspired by famous works of art; here and there, Tonino's verses give new significance to commonplace things.

Just outside town, at Ponte Messa, is a museum, unique in Europe, the **Museo dell'Informatica e Storia del Calcolo** (*open 3rd Sun of month 10–12.30 & 3.30–6.30; other days on request; T: 0541 928563, www.museoinformatica.it*), an interesting comparison between ancient and modern mathematics, calculus, and information technology. Near the museum is a little Romanesque church, the 11th-century **Pieve** (*to visit, ask Pro Loco*), with a crumbling façade decorated with geometric motifs; inside, the altar is a Roman sacrificial stone. Other carved elements, some from the 9th century, lead experts to believe that this was first a Roman temple, and then an early Christian place of worship.

Casteldelci, immersed in the forest, on the mountainside not far from the source of the Tiber, overlooks the Senatello stream, full of trout. Honey-coloured stone houses surround the bell-tower. This fortress-town was originally built for the bishops of the Montefeltro, who gave it to the della Faggiola family. In the course of time it passed to Cesare Borgia, Lorenzo de' Medici, and finally, in 1522, to the dukes of Urbino. A story is told here of Count Rapaché, paladin of Charlemagne, who once raped all the virgins in the village, a terrible event which has never been forgotten; the local people still use the word *rapasceto* to indicate a disaster. In an old house in the centre is the Casa-Museo (*to request a visit T: 0541 915423*), with a collection of finds relating to archaeological investigations in the valley. The Gothic church of San Nicolò is very photogenic, with its bell-tower; in the church of Santa Maria in Sasseto there are some frescoes of the Giotto School of Rimini. There is a wonderful Roman bridge over the Senatello, and several tiny, enchanting hamlets in the surrounding woods, such as Campo, Gattara and Senatello.

THE CONCA VALLEY

Sassofeltrio and the border towns

Sassofeltrio, close to the border with Emilia Romagna, is a fortress going back to 756, rebuilt by Francesco di Giorgio Martini for Federico da Montefeltro; some traces of the surrounding fortifications are still standing. The view from Sassofeltrio is exceptional—the entire Conca valley as far as the Adriatic, San Marino and Mt Carpegna.

Mercatino Conca stands at the point where the road to San Marino crosses an ancient road from Cattolica to Tuscany, and meets the confluence of the Conca with the Tassona. It is an important commercial centre (in spite of its small size; just look at the shop windows), as suggested by its name, and by the splendid five-arched bridge over the Conca, wide and gravelly at this point (but it can flood at times). The town was destroyed by Federico da Montefeltro in 1462, but in 1508 his son Guidubaldo granted the inhabitants the right to hold a market every Friday, a tradition which is still respected.

West of Mercatino is **Montegrimano Terme**. The name derives from *germanus*, brother, because this castle was one of a pair: the other 'brother' was the castle of Monte Tassi, now under the jurisdiction of Montegrimano. The two castles were built in the 11th century, and were often contested during the disputes between the noble families of Urbino and Rimini, until Federico da Montefeltro made this one the seat of his representative in the area, and the fortress was enlarged and embellished. After that (fortunately for the inhabitants) history ignored Montegrimano, until in 1861 it became part of the Kingdom of Italy. The little town stands in a wonderfully panoramic position, and enjoys a mild climate throughout the year. The steep, narrow streets, enclosed in the area of what was the fortress, lead up to a spectacular 15th-century bell-tower, once the keep. The beneficial properties of the sulphurous springs on nearby Monte San Paolo were particularly appreciated in the Middle Ages.

Macerata Feltria and environs

Macerata Feltria, once the Roman town of *Pitinum Pisaurense*, nestles in the woods on a hillside around the high clock tower, overlooking the Apsa stream; this was one of the first independent communes of central Italy. It is formed of two parts, the old medieval town called Castello, and the lower Borgo, founded in 1500. Although very small, the town has some remarkable old buildings and interesting works of art. On

Via Antimi, the main street of Borgo, is the parish church of San Michele Arcangelo (19th century), inside there is a marvellous painted wooden Crucifix by Carlo da Camerino (signed and dated 1396). The Terme Pitinum, the spa, is famous for its sulphurous waters. After crossing a bridge, Via Gaboardi leads to Castello; just before entering the old gate, Arco dei Pelasgi, on the right is the church of San Francesco (1376), the convent of which houses an interesting collection of old, still functioning radio sets, Museo della Radio d'Epoca (*to request a visit T: 0722 742244*), then a steep cobbled street continues up to a little square. On the left is the high tower (over 1,000 years old) of the Palazzo del Podestà (11th–12th centuries), seat of the Museo Archeologico e Paleontologico (*open May–Sept 10–12.30 & 3.30–7.30; T: 0722 73231*); a large collection of local finds, ranging from prehistoric flints to Roman remains, medieval tombs and Renaissance pottery. Just west of the town, on the Apsa, is the site of *Pitinum Pisaurense* and the 11th-century Romanesque church of San Cassiano al Pitino (*to request a visit T: 0722 73231*), one of the oldest churches in the Montefeltro, built on top of a Roman temple to Saturn.

Around Macerata Feltria there are over 50km of trekking trails; an interesting walk leads c. 4km northeast to **Certalto**, a medieval township, now practically abandoned, very photogenic and offering views over the Foglia Valley.

Pietrarubbia is a scattered township, administered from Mercato Vecchio. From here, a short road leads up to the ruins of the castle (11th and 14th centuries); try to be here at sunset, when the strange rocks of this mountain take on a reddish tinge—*petra rubea* means 'red stone'. Here and there are sculptures in stone or metal, some the work of Arnaldo Pomodoro, who founded a local academy for the artistic application of metals. This is a good point of entry into the Sasso Simone and Simoncello Park (*see overleaf*).

Another scattered township is **Montecopiolo**, administered from Villagrande. A busy ski resort in winter, the inhabitants raise cattle; every Monday in September, there is a cattle market in Pugliano which has been held for over a thousand years. The ruined castle, built in 962 on an almost inaccessible crag over 1000m high, was destroyed by Lorenzino de' Medici in 1520; it was the cradle of the lords of Urbino, because it was here that Frederick Barbarossa in 1140 gave Antonio of Carpegna the title of Count of Montefeltro, and that is how the illustrious family began. Montecopiolo forms part of the Sasso Simone and Simoncello Park. A pleasant walk leads to the lake of Villagrande (974m), source of the Conca; full of fish, the water is 5m deep in places.

Overlooking the River Conca is **Monte Cerignone**, consisting of two parts, the picturesque old fortress, called Castello, and the lower town, called Borgo. The castle is now used as the town hall. Close by are the 17th-century church of Santa Caterina, built for the Knights of the Order of Malta; the church of Santa Maria del Soccorso, which houses some paintings by Bartolomeo Vivarini, and the 17th-century church of San Biagio, the patron saint of Monte Cerignone, with a 12th-century Crucifix in the interior said to have been left here by crusaders returning from the Holy Land, and much venerated in the village. Umberto Eco, author of *The Name of the Rose*, spends his summer holidays in Monte Cerignone, where he owns a house.

THE HEART OF THE MONTEFELTRO

Exactly in the centre of the Montefeltro, and capital of the area, is **Carpegna** (748m, pop. 1,600). Thanks to an ancient privilege, the town enjoyed the status of an independent county for many centuries. It is a quiet place, but sometimes strange things occur—they had a mysterious spate of church bells ringing by themselves a few years ago, a phenomenon which attracted curious people from all over the world; no explanation has yet been found. In the centre is an old public fountain, whose tank is an enormous sarcophagus carved out of a block of limestone, big enough for a knight in full armour. The little square, used for the market on Wednesday, is dominated by the impressive Palazzo Carpegna (1675), built for Cardinal Gaspare di Carpegna; the great doorway is approached by a double stairway in grey stone.

THE SASSO SIMONE & SIMONCELLO REGIONAL PARK

Visitor centres: Via Rio Maggio; www.parcosimone.org; Ponte Cappuccini, Pietrarubbia, 157 Via Montefeltresca, T: 0722 75350.
Carpegna is an excellent base for exploring the park. Thick woods of conifers, beech and Turkey oak, rich in wildlife, surround two splendid limestone crags with flat tops, thought of as sacred by the primitive populations. Judging by archaeological finds, they were perhaps sun worshippers; in fact, the sun rising between the two hills is the symbol of the park. On the largest of the two, Sasso Simone (1204m), Cosimo de' Medici built a town in 1560, which was abandoned after a few years because of the prohibitively cold winters. The smaller, Simoncello (1221m) is a little higher, but when seen from the east or from the west, they look like a mirror image; there is no other similar formation in the world. They are both easy to climb; from Carpegna the walk would be c. 2hrs, to reach the top of one or the other. The area is home to a huge variety of mammals, birds and reptiles.

Frontino

Frontino, on a rocky spur overlooking the Mutino valley, and within the boundaries of the Sasso Simone and Simoncello Park, is the smallest town in the province of Pesaro, but its position is such that its castle was frequently disputed between the Malatesta and the Montefeltro. Still surrounded by robust walls, with a pentagonal tower to give added protection, Frontino is built entirely of mellow stone, clean and tidy, with lots of flowers. There is one long main cobbled street, with steep and narrow alleys leading off from it. In the centre is the aristocratic Palazzo Malatesta; a long tunnel connects the cellars of the palace to a 14th-century mill (still functioning) outside the walls, to guarantee the supply of flour in case of siege.

A beautiful panoramic road leads up 3km south of Frontino to the peaceful Franciscan **convent of Montefiorentino** (*open Mon–Fri 8–12 & 3.30–7; T: 0722*

The tiny walled town of Frontino.

71202), surrounded by woods, and well worth a visit. First built by St Francis in 1213, and later enlarged, the convent is used every year in October for an important literary prize-giving ceremony. To the right, on entering the little church, is the splendid Cappella dei Conti Oliva, designed by Francesco di Simone Ferrucci in 1484 for Carlo Oliva, count of Piagnano. An excellent example of restrained Renaissance elegance, with a floor of majolica tiles, there are several interesting works of art. Over the altar, in its original frame, is Giovanni Santi's finest painting, signed and dated 1489, the *Madonna with Christ Child and Sts Jerome, Anthony Abbot, Francis and George*, with angel musicians and the donor. Against the south wall is the magnificent tomb of Gianfranco Oliva (Francesco di Simone Ferrucci; 1478), father of Carlo; while opposite is the tomb of Marsibilia Trinci—his mother—by the same artist (1485). Don't miss the beautiful inlaid wooden kneelers, made by the famous craftsman Maestro Zocchino, signed and dated 1493, and the 17th-century organ and choir-stalls. To the left of the church is a small rectangular cloister, with two 18th-century well-heads.

THE FOGLIA VALLEY

The border with Romagna

North of Urbino is the township of **Tavoleto**, on the boundary with Romagna, frequently the scene of fierce battles for control of the territory. Formerly it had a castle designed by Francesco di Giorgio Martini, on the orders of Federico da Montefeltro; it was pulled down in 1865, and replaced with a neo-Gothic private home, Castello Petrangolini. Napoleon destroyed the town so thoroughly that for years the inhabitants were known as the *Bruciati*—the Burnt Ones. Even during the Second World War Tavoleto was an important stronghold along the Gothic Line, and strenuously defended by the Nazis, until Gurkha troops freed the town on the night of 3rd–4th September 1944, using only their knives.

Closer to the River Foglia is **Auditore**, built on a rocky outcrop. The name derives from the Latin *auditorium*, a reference to the fact that both the Malatesta and the Montefeltro families used this place to listen to the complaints of the population, and resolve disputes. The old centre is still intact, and surrounded by medieval walls; there is an interesting clock tower, with a round lower part and a hexagonal top (15th century). Auditore was once famous for its production of church bells, which were exported all over Europe. In the modern district of Casinina, at the foot of the hill, there was heavy fighting during the German retreat in 1944; an interesting museum, Museo Storico della Linea Gotica (*open 9–12.30 & 3–7; Jan–Feb closed Sun; T: 0722 362170*), documents those dramatic moments with a series of photographs, maps, newspapers, school books, and prisoners' letters.

Sassocorvaro and west to Tuscany

On a spur of rock, along the road between San Marino, San Leo and Urbino, is **Sassocorvaro**, dominating the Foglia valley, and overlooking Lake Mercatale, formed by a dam on the river. The old town, with its pastel-coloured houses, is still partly surrounded by the walls, and several of the medieval towers are still standing. It is easy to understand why this position was so often fought over by the Malatesta and the Montefeltro; when the latter finally took control, it was given to Ottaviano Ubaldini, Federico's right-hand-man, closest friend, and perhaps brother, as the seat of his county: he entrusted the job of building the castle to that genius of military architecture, Francesco di Giorgio Martini (1475). The splendid result is the Rocca Ubaldinesca (*open April–Sept 9.30–12.30 & 3–7; Oct–Mar Sat and Sun 9.30–12.30 & 2.30–6.30; other days on request; T: 0722 76177, www.arcarte.it*), housing the L'Arca dell'Arte museum, dedicated to works of art in danger; during the Second World War more than 10,000 masterpieces of Italian art were brought here for safety. The exhibition includes life-size replicas of the works of art saved in this way, a section dedicated to masterpieces now in danger, and a display of local handicrafts which are in need of support. A prize is awarded annually to those who, anywhere in the world, effectively do something to 'save art'. The Pinacoteca (civic art gallery), is also here at the castle, and on the first floor, reached by a spiral staircase, is the exquisite little theatre, Teatro della Rocca (18th century). The fortress itself is shaped like a tortoise, with massive towers, and was specifically designed to resist attacks using the ferociously efficient firearms of the late 15th century. In the castle's underground chambers, magnetic distortion has sometimes been observed: electronic devices behave strangely, compasses don't point north— rather like the phenomena reported at the

Bermuda Triangle. The distortion is not constant, but only occurs sometimes: no explanation has been found.

In the upper Foglia valley, surrounded by chestnut woods, **Lunano** developed at the foot of the 13th-century Castello degli Ubaldini, now a romantic, ivy-clad ruin. Most of the inhabitants are carpenters and furniture manufacturers. An easy path leads from the centre of the village to the castle, and from there to the Convento di Monte Illuminato, with a beautiful medieval bell-tower, said to have been founded by St Francis in 1213, consecrated by seven bishops in 1222, and called *illuminato* because he miraculously restored sight to a blind woman on this spot. Inside the convent are some 15th- and 16th-century frescoes.

Behind the hill of Lunano, within the boundaries of the Sasso Simone and Simoncello Park (*see p. 344*), is the attractive town of **Piandimeleto**, the ancient *Planus Mileti*, dominated by the imposing castle of the Oliva family, reconstructed in 1480 on a preceding fortress, perhaps built by Charlemagne. The castle (*open 9–12.30 & 3–7; T: 0722 721528*) now houses the town hall, and two interesting and well-organised museums: the Museo Scienze della Terra, a geological collection with a botanical section and a library; and the Museo del Lavoro Contadino, a display of tools and equipment used by local farmers, and a description of their way of life. Close by is the Gothic church of Sant'Agostino (*open 9–7*), where you will find the tombstones of members of the Oliva family who died of the plague in the 13th century.

Belforte all'Isauro, a characteristic little grey stone and russet brick village, stands on the River Foglia, close to the border with Tuscany. A bridge over the river unites the modern district with the old town, dominated by the strong lines of the Castello, first built in the 6th century, and later modified by Francesco di Giorgio Martini for Federico da Montefeltro. It was purchased in 1874 by a noble Prussian, Baron Beaufort, whose ancestors had once lived here—he later donated it to the town council of Belforte. Now the castle, a robust three-storey construction, with access over a narrow bridge, has been completely restored, and houses a school of Italian for foreigners, which organises month-long courses. In the main square is the parish church of San Lorenzo, with some paintings by local artists in the style of Barocci, and an old Crucifix, said to be miraculous. By the cemetery is the ancient chapel, Pieve di San Lorenzo, first built in the 8th century, with two well-preserved old frescoes inside.

PRACTICAL INFORMATION

GETTING THERE

• **By train**: The nearest station is Pesaro, with express bus connections to Urbino, Urbania, Apecchio (AMIBUS, T: 0722 350738, www.amibus.it).
• **By bus**: AMIBUS (see above), operates services connecting Urbino, Auditore, Sassocorvaro and Tavoleto. Autolinee Baschetti, T: 0575 74361, runs services connecting Arezzo, San Sepolcro, Pennabilli, Novafeltria and Rimini.
Ferrovie Emilia Romagna, T: 0541 25474, operates services connecting Pennabilli, Novafeltria and Rimini.
Salvatori, T: 0541 820194, operates services connecting Pesaro to the Montefeltro, including Sassocorvaro, Lunano, Piandimeleto, Frontino, Carpegna, Pennabilli and Casteldelci.

INFORMATION OFFICES

Useful general websites to the region are www.montefeltrotour.it and www.montefeltro.net
Carpegna Pro Loco, 1 Piazza Conti, T: 0722 77326, www.carpegna.it; Comunità Montana del Montefeltro, 34 Via Amaducci, T: 0722 727003, www.cm-carpegna.ps.it; Parco Regionale Sasso Simone e Simoncello, Via Rio Maggio, T: 0722 770073, www.parcosimone.org
Frontino Municipio & Pro Loco, 16 Corso Giovanni XXIII, T: 0722 71135.
Macerata Feltria 10 Via Antimi, T: 0722 728208, www.comune. maceratafeltria.pu.it
Novafeltria This town, together with Gubbio, Pesaro, Senigallia and Urbino, forms part of the association La Terra del Duca, dedicated to the Montefeltro; Info: www.terradelduca.it. Tourist Information Bureau, Municipio, 2 Piazza Vittorio Emanuele, T: 0541 927059, www.comune.novafeltria.pu.it; Comunità Montana Alta Valmarecchia, 11 Piazza Bramante, T: 0541 920442, www.cm-novafeltria.ps.it
Pennabilli Pro Loco, Piazza Vittorio Emanuele, T: 0541 928659; Tourist Information Bureau, T: 0541 928070, www.comune.pennabilli.pu.it
San Leo IAT, Piazza Dante, T: 0541 916306 & 800553800, www.comune.san-leo.ps.it; Pro Loco, 10 Piazza Dante, T: 0541 916231.
Sant'Agata Feltria Pro Loco, 12 Piazza Garibaldi, T: 0541 848022, www.santagatainfiera.com; Tourist Information Bureau, Museo della Rocca, T: 0541 929111, www.roccafregoso.it
Sassocorvaro Municipio and Pro Loco, 2 Via Roma, T: 0722 76873, www.montefeltro.net/sassocorvaro; Tourist Information Bureau, Via Crescentini, T: 0722 76177.
Sassofeltrio Municipio, 3 Piazza Municipio, T: 0541 974130.
Talamello Municipio, 2 Piazza Garibaldi, T: 0541 920036, www.cm-novafeltria.ps.it/talamello

HOTELS

Carpegna
€ **Locandina**. Small inn, open summer only, with good cooking; children welcome. 22 Via Amaducci, T: 0722 77125.

Frontino

€€ **Rocca dei Malatesta**. Charming hotel in the smallest village of the province of Pesaro, with lots of atmosphere, very good restaurant. On request there are courses in Italian language, cookery or pottery. 1 Via Giovanni XXIII, T: 0722 71121.

Macerata Feltria

€€€ **Pitinum**. Small, modern hotel with a good restaurant. 16 Via Matteotti, T: 0722 74496, www.pitinum.com.

Mercatino Conca

€ **La Pineta**. Restaurant with rooms, friendly atmosphere and good food. 31–33 Via Pineta, T: 0541 972020.

Montecopiolo

€€€ **Villa Labor**. Beautiful Art Nouveau building designed by Sacconi in 1906, very panoramic; good restaurant. Madonna di Pugliano, T: 0722 739025.

Montegrimano

€€€€ **Villa Di Carlo**. Comfortable hotel with pool, fitness centre, internet, restaurant, at the spa. 1 Via Martiri della Resistenza, T: 0541 972128, www.montegrimanoterme.it

Novafeltria

€€ **Del Turista**. Comfortable inn with good restaurant. 7 Via Ca' Giacessi, T: 0541 920148.

Pietrarubbial

€€€ **Locanda Il Vicariato**. Charming inn with restaurant, in the 15th-century Palazzo del Vicario. 10 Via Castello, T: 0722 75390.

San Leo

€€ **Castello**. Small hotel with restaurant in old palace, family-run. 11–12 Piazza Dante Alighieri, T: 0541 916214, albergo-castello@libero.it

€ **La Rocca**. Comfortable inn with an excellent restaurant. 16 Via Leopardi, T: 0541 916241, www.paginegialle.it/laroccasanleo

Sant'Agata Feltria

€€€ **Falcon**. Countryside location for this modern, comfortable hotel, with garden, tennis and a car park. 30 Via San Girolamo, T: 0541 929090, falconhotel@tin.it

€€ **Perlini**. Family-run inn, good restaurant. 4 Piazza del Mercato, T: 0541 929778.

SPAS

Macerata Feltria

Spa centre Pitinum Thermae. Sulphurous thermal springs, offering excellent anti-stress or chronic catarrh treatment. Open March–Dec. 18 Via Antimi, T: 0722 73245, www.pitinumthermae.com

Montegrimano

Terme di Montegrimano. Known since Roman times, the waters are drunk or inhaled for various cures; they were publicised in the 16th century with the Latin motto *qui cute, qui stomaco, qui rene et splene laborat, vallem ubi potatur plurima linpha petat*, 'he who suffers from skin, stomach, kidneys and spleen, should run to the valley where the water of many properties is drunk'. Open all year. 1 Viale Martiri della Resistenza, T: 0541 972128, www.montegrimanoterme.it

BED & BREAKFAST

Novafeltria

B&B Pietra Solara. Country location, beautiful villa with garden, pool; help offered for trekking and gathering medicinal herbs. Closed winter. 22 Via Pietra Solara, Località Secchiano, T: 02 97290244.

Perticara (near Novafeltria)
B & B Pandolfi. Charming accommodation in mountain village near border with Emilia Romagna. Open summer only. 132 Via Trieste, T: 0541 927013.

San Leo
Residenza Sant'Apollinare. Old stone farmhouse, wonderful views, very good breakfasts. 325 Via Sant'Apollinare, T: 0541 926298.

Sant'Agata Feltria
Borgo del Sole e della Luna. Old house in beautiful hamlet. 33–38 Via Petrella Guidi, Località Petrella Guidi, T: 0541 929814.

Tavoleto
B & B Alberto House. Very comfortable, with garden; children welcome. Painting lessons on request. Car park. Closed winter. 35 Via Giordano Bruno, T: 0722 629238, www.albertohouse.com

FARM ACCOMMODATION

San Leo
La Cegna. Comfortable accommodation in two old farmhouses, one 15th century, the other 17th. The farm raises prize-winning horses; good restaurant. Via Monte, Ca' Fantino, Montemaggio, T: 0541 924204.
La Lama. Close to town, home cooking, generous portions; horses, sheep, pigs, goats and poultry are raised, also production of fruit, cereals and vegetables; pool. 4 Strada per Pugliano, T: 0541 926928.
Locanda San Leone. ■ Gorgeous old

water-mill, where according to legend the noble Federico da Montefiore used to make love to the miller's wife. Now luxurious accommodation, the farm produces olive oil, wine, wheat, sunflowers, sugarbeet and fruit; excellent restaurant. 102 Strada Sant'Antimo, Località Piega di San Leo, T: 0541 912194.

COUNTRY HOUSE

Frontino
Residenza San Girolamo. Listed 16th-century monastery, quiet countryside location, good restaurant, health and beauty treatments on request, courses in music. Via San Girolamo, T: 0722 71293, www.sangirolamo.com

RESTAURANTS

Lunano
€€€–€ **La Gatta**. Beautiful stone house comprising restaurant, pizzeria and tavern; varied and appetizing menu, imaginative desserts, good local wines. Closed Mon, Tues and Jan. 13 Via XX Settembre, Località Brugneto, T: 0722 700024.

Macerata Feltria
€€ **Pitinum**. Unusual hotel restaurant specialising in kitsch dishes, such as prawn cocktail, Russian salad, gammon with pineapple, chicken salad, trifle; but they have an exceptionally good vegetable *antipasto* table too. For the nostalgic. Closed Mon and Nov. 16 Via Matteotti, T: 0722 74496.

Novafeltria
€€ **Da Marchesi–Ristorante del Turista**. Specialising in pasta dishes and meat, with truffles when in season,

along the road from Novafeltria to Perticara. Closed Tues. 7 Via Ca' Gianessi, T: 0541 920148.

€ **Due Lanterne**. Country inn, delicious food, especially the pasta. Closed Mon and Jan. 215 Via Torricella, Località Ca' del Vento, T: 0541 920200.

€ **Trattoria Savina**. Old tavern in town centre, serving simple, satisfying dishes; the *zuppa inglese* (trifle) is very good; drink the local Sangiovese. Closed Sat. 3 Piazza Roma, T: 0541 920091.

Pennabilli

€€€ **Il Piastrino**. Try the local hams, salami and cheeses, or the various thick and satisfying soups, or the vegetable quiche (*torta salata*). Very courteous service, just outside town. Closed Tues in winter. 9 Via Parco Begni, T: 0541 928569.

€€ **Al Bel Fico**. Fascinating tavern open evenings only, serving the best local wines and lovely home-made pasta or polenta; the fungi are out of this world. Closed Wed. 24 Piazza Vittorio Emanuele, T: 0541 928810.

€ **Il Giardino**. ■ This little restaurant in a convenient spot in front of the castle-monastery, makes an ideal lunch stop; the lasagne are perfect! Also coffee bar and ice cream parlour, pizzeria in the evenings. Closed Wed. 29 Via Roma, T: 0541 928436.

€ **La Peppa**. Lovely little restaurant opened a century ago in the old centre, delicious, carefully prepared food. Open lunchtime only. Closed Sat. 7 Via del Prato, T: 0541 928583.

Piandimeleto

€€ **Ristorantino del Castello**. Fungi appear frequently on the menu, but don't miss the *formaggio fuso*, cheese melted in a terracotta pot in the oven.

Closed Sat in winter. 4 Via Giovanni XXIII, T: 0722 721714.

San Leo

€€ **La Rocca**. Restaurant of a long tradition; local ham and salami, roast shoulder of lamb, no concessions to modern frivolities, good wine list. Closed Mon and Jan–Feb. 16 Via Leopardi, T: 0541 916241.

€ **Il Bettolino**. ■ Friendly coffee bar and restaurant, serving also pizza in the evening, try the delicious *ravioli con formaggio di fossa* (with pit-matured cheese), followed by *tagliata con lardo di Colonnata*, an unusual beef salad with pit-matured lard (scrumptious). They also make their own mascarpone (clotted cream). Closed Wed. 4 Via Montefeltro, T: 0541 916265.

Sant'Agata Feltria

€€ **Perlini**. Excellent local cuisine, central position. Closed Sat. 4 Piazza del Mercato, T: 0541 929778.

€€ **Trattoria Bossari**. A charming tavern where pensioners spend the afternoon playing cards; wonderful pasta; try *lombo al vapore*, steam-cooked pork, served with fungi and truffles. Closed Mon. 2 Via San Girolamo, T: 0541 929697.

Sassocorvaro

€ **Nido del Corvo**. High on the hillside over the castle, this is a good place to come in the evening, to eat pizza or *crescia*, cheese and ham, accompanied by the local wines; it is always packed with locals, because there is a dance floor, open-air in summer. Always open in summer, in winter open evenings only, Sun lunchtime only, closed Mon and Tues. 22/b Via Colle Igea, T: 0722 76334.

CAFÉS, PASTRY SHOPS & ICE CREAM

Mercatino Conca
Caffè Verdi. Try the delicious *belmoro*, traditional cake. 29 Piazza Verdi.
Novafeltria
Caffè Grand'Italia. ■ Gorgeous Art Nouveau coffee house, a real institution. Piazza Vittorio Emanuele.

FESTIVALS & EVENTS

Belforte all'Isauro *Festa del Miele*, annual honey festival, 2nd Sun in Oct.
Maiolo *Festa del Pane*, when this picturesque village in the woods celebrates its delicious bread; Info: Pro Loco, T: 0541 920012, last weekend in June.
Monte Cerignone *Fiera di Santa Croce*, traditional fair dedicated to the Crucifix in the church of the patron San Biagio (St Blaise), 1st Sun in May.
Novafeltria Feast of the One Hundred Bowls, celebrations for St John include the sale of bowls of flower petals along the streets, fireworks, a witches' dance, and impromptu open-air entertainment, 23–24 June.
Pennabilli *Artisti in Piazza*, buskers from all over the world perform in the streets and squares; Info: Pro Loco, T: 0541 928659, June. Antique Market, well-known open-air exhibition and sale of antiques; Info: Mostra Mercato Antiquariato, T: 0541 928323, July.
Perticara (near Novafeltria) *Mostra-Scambio Minerali & Fossili*, exhibition and swapping of minerals and fossils; Info: Pro Loco, T: 0541 927576 or 0541 927212, 2nd Sun in Sept.
Sant'Agata Feltria White Truffle Fair; Info: Fiera del Tartufo, 1 Piazza Garibaldi, T: 0541 929314, Sundays in

Oct. Christmas Market; Info: Pro Loco, T: 0541 848022, Sundays in Dec.
Talamello *Festa del Crocifisso di Giotto*, perhaps the oldest and the most important celebration of the Montefeltro, Monday after Whitsun. *Fiera del Formaggio di Fossa*, celebrations dedicated to the famous pit-matured cheese; Info: T: 0541 920036, 1st two Sundays in Nov.

LOCAL SPECIALITIES

Belforte all'Isauro is renowned for its production of honey. The traditional market takes place on Saturday.
Carpegna
Carpegna Prosciutti, Via Petricci, for particularly good hams, such as *prosciutto San Leo*, just right for eating with figs or melon, and *prosciutto La Ghianda*, stronger flavoured, nice in sandwiches.
Due Sassi, Via Pian dei Roghi, for the renowned aromatic Carpegna ham.
Maiolo
Mini Market, 141 Via Capoluogo, for the famous bread (and many other good things).
Pennabilli
Bosco dei Regali, Piazza Vittorio Emanuele, for your artistic souvenirs.
Il Forno Panangeli, at 13 Via Cinzia Degli Olivieri, for bread, cakes and biscuits.
Piandimeleto
Dominici, in Via delle Due Chiese, sells delicious local bread, at Easter and Christmas traditional cakes. Ernesto Riccardi, 14 Via del Macello, for honey and royal jelly from his own bees.
Pietrarubbia
Le Ricette di Anna e Gabri, Via Ca' Rosso, for the best *bustrengo* (bread

pudding). **Panificio Brizi**, 6 Piazza Municipio, using a stone oven, Clara bakes her famous bread, also *torta brusca*, loaves enriched with raisins and walnuts.

San Leo

Giorgini, 17 Via Leopardi, a baker using traditional wood-fired oven, prepares local cakes and biscuits, and Tuscan bread (no salt). **Giorgio Moretti**, 3 Via Montefeltro, a sculptor who creates delightful naif works of art in stone, wood, or iron. **La Bottega di Mario**, 26 Via Montefeltro, for wild boar sausage, and cheeses matured in walnut leaves or in wood ash; also honey and olive oil.

Sant'Agata Feltria

Prodotti del Montefeltro, 9 Via Vittorio Emanuele, for all the best local hams, pasta, cheeses, and *lardo di Colonnata*. The inhabitants of Sant'Agata are skilled at finding white truffles, called *trifole*, in the surrounding woods; the season is Oct–early Nov.

THE REPUBLIC OF SAN MARINO

San Marino (pop. 29,000) stands on Mount Titano (749m), which rises abruptly from the gentle rolling hills of central Italy, in an ideally strategic position close to the Adriatic coast—17km from the sea. Extending over only 61 square kilometres, it is the smallest nation in the world after Monaco and the Vatican, and the oldest republic in Europe, dating back to AD 301. Although tiny, it offers a variety of landscapes, and stunning views over a large part of central Italy and the Adriatic. The Republic consists of the mountain and its surrounding slopes, which are forested or intensely cultivated (wheat, vineyards, orchards). The old city of San Marino (*Città*) occupies the summit of the mountain, while lower down there are eight ancient townships called *Castelli* and some smaller villages.

HISTORY OF SAN MARINO

The security offered by the mountain's rocky heights was known and appreciated by the prehistoric inhabitants of the area, as well as by the Etruscans and the Romans. During the reign of Diocletian, towards the end of the 3rd century AD, stonemasons were brought from Dalmatia to work on the reconstruction of the port of Rimini. Some of them, who were Christians, escaped; led by Marinus (Marino), they came to Mount Titano, where they founded a community. San Marino dates the creation of its Republic to the year of their settlement—3rd September 301 is the date celebrated. In the year 754 a *Castellum Sancti Marini* is listed among the possessions of Pope Stephen II, indicating that the community was becoming a fortified township surrounded by farms. A significant event took place on 20th February 885 when the *Placitus Feretranus*, a papal document, assigned ownership of lands on Mt Titano to the abbot of San Marino. Total independence was probably obtained in the course of this century. From 1243 San Marino was governed by two captains-regent, chosen by a council of families, called the *Arengo*. The statutes were written down in 1353: no interrupting during meetings, no gambling, no throwing rubbish into the streets. Murderers and traitors were hanged; swearing could be punished by a sentence of 150 days in prison. Those who were robbed were entitled to compensation from the guards if the thieves were not arrested, and fugitives and refugees were guaranteed asylum. In 1440 war broke out between Guido Antonio Montefeltro of Montefeltro and Sigismondo Pandolfo Malatesta of Rimini. Montefeltro, San Marino's traditional ally, emerged victorious in 1463. As a sign of gratitude, Guido Antonio persuaded Pope Pius II to issue a decree naming San Marino a republic and listing the territories under its jurisdiction. Its boundaries have not been extended since that date.

Administration of San Marino

Today San Marino proclaims itself to be independent, democratic and neutral. Italy maintains an embassy in the Republic and there are no customs formalities at the frontier. The administrative and legal systems of modern San Marino are basically still those of the 14th century. Voting takes place every five years to choose a council and an executive committee; heads of council are the two captains-regent, who maintain office for six months. Female representatives are often chosen for the post. The death sentence was abolished in 1859; for serious offences, criminals serve their term in Italian jails. The official language is Italian, although most people speak in dialect among themselves, a resonant mixture of Marche and Romagna terms. Since 1981 the country has been able to produce a limited amount of its own coinage, first lire and now euros, which are much sought-after by collectors. The economy, once dependent on farming and quarried stone, now flourishes, thanks to tourism: San Marino receives more than 3 million visitors a year. The Republic is defended by a small army called the *Militia*, now mostly ceremonial, although one of the ancient statutes declares that every citizen between the ages of 16 and 55 and of healthy constitution can be called upon to defend the country 'in case of need'. The police force is called the *Gendarmeria* and consists of Italian officers, while traffic offences are dealt with by the *Polizia Civile*, formed entirely of San Marino-born officers.

THE CITY OF SAN MARINO

San Francesco and the Museo di Stato

The old city of San Marino (pop. 4,500) stands on the mountain top, defended by three walls one inside the other. The main entrance is through the third wall at Porta San Francesco, also called *Porta del Loco*, with its ancient oak doors still in place. In front stands the stark church of **San Francesco**, built in the 14th century by craftsmen from Como, with a little loggia in front. Its simplicity is typical of Franciscan buildings of the time. The wooden Crucifix on the main altar is early 14th century. The two wings of the cloisters house the Pinacoteca e Museo di Arte Sacra San Francesco (*T: 0549 991157*), with panel paintings, canvases and a precious fresco from the church of St Francis, showing the *Adoration of the Three Kings* by Antonio Alberti of Ferrara (1437), vestments, church furnishings and hangings, indicating that the Franciscans played a significant role in the artistic evolution of the Republic.

From San Francesco Via Basilicius leads to the attractive Piazzetta del Titano. At no. 1 is the 17th-century Palazzo Pergami-Belluzzi, which houses the **Museo di Stato** (*T: 0549 883835*), displaying more than 5,000 objects in four separate collections. The ground floor is dedicated to archaeological finds from the territory of San Marino, and Renaissance elements from the ancient basilica. On the first floor is a rich collection of paintings and sculptures, many from the old convent of St Clare. There is an important painting by Guercino (1656) of *St Philip Neri*; a particularly sensitive portrait of *St Marinus Helping his Republic to Rise*, painted in Rome by Pompeo Batoni in 1740; and a sculpted bust of St Agatha, co-patron of the Republic. The second floor displays in three rooms Byzantine icons, porcelain, paintings and other works of art which have been donated to the Republic. There are rare Limoges enamels and a group of 18th-century paintings from Latin America, donated by an emigrant. Further donations consisting of archaeological objects of prehistoric, Egyptian, Greek, Etruscan, Roman and southern Italian origin are to be found on the lower first floor, with a valuable collection of some of the oldest coins minted by the Republic in 1864.

Piazza della Libertà

From the museum, Contrada del Collegio leads past the **Agenzia di Stato Filatelica e Numismatica**, the official agency for philately and numismatics, and rises steeply to **Piazza della Libertà**, heart of the city, called *Pianello* by the local people. Along the way, on the right, the street called Contrada Santa Croce was the ancient Jewish quarter. The panorama over the Apennines is impressive. Here is a white marble statue of *Liberty* (1876), gift of Otilia Heyroth Wagener of Berlin, a great benefactor of San Marino, who was made Duchess of Acquaviva. Facing west is the post office, a 20th-century reconstruction in 15th-century style on the site of the old *Domus Parva Comunis*, or Small Town Hall. At the foot of the bell-tower is an ancient stone giving the official sizes and measurements for tradesmen. Facing south is a series of ancient palaces, including in the far northwest corner, the Casa dell'Arcipretura Vecchia (15th century), the old law courts. Dominating the west side of the lovely square is the **Palazzo Pubblico**, seat of government, surmounted by a clock tower. It is the late 19th-century reconstruction of the original of 1380, known as the *Domus Magna Comunis* or Large Town Hall. The façade includes the heraldic devices of several of the castles of San Marino, while over the clock in three niches are the mosaic portraits of the saints Marinus, Agatha and Leo. It is possible to visit the interior when no ceremonies are in progress. Inside are the busts of all the protagonists of the history of the Republic, from St Marinus himself to Garibaldi (a great admirer), from Pope Clement XII to Abraham Lincoln (made an honorary citizen after he abolished slavery). The council chamber is magnificent, with 60 thrones for the members. One wall is taken up by a painting of St Marinus offering an open book with the words '*relinquo vos liberos ab utroque homine*' 'I set you free from every man', in tempera by the local artist Emilio Retrosi (1890).

Basilica di San Marino

From the Palazzo Pubblico steps lead up to the **Basilica di San Marino** (*T: 0549 882380*), dedicated to the patron saint. This modern building, completed in 1838, takes the place of the ancient Pieve di San Marino, a much smaller church. Neoclassical in style, it is preceded by a portico with eight Corinthian columns. The bell-tower, possibly 12th century, rebuilt in the 16th, holds seven bronze bells. The interior has a central nave and two side aisles. Over the high altar is a marble statue of St Marinus (1838). Under the altar is an urn containing the bones of the saint, while on the right, in a marble monument, is the silver reliquary which holds the skull and which is carried in procession for the feast of 3rd September. To the left of the altar is the throne of the captains-regent, used during ceremonies. Among the finest paintings in the church, over the first south altar, is a sombre *Noli me tangere* by Elisabetta Sirani (1661), while over the second north altar is *The Holy House of Loreto Transported by the Angels*, by Bartolomeo Gennari. The organ is signed and dated *Opus Bazzani Jacobi-Venetiis*, anno 1833, and has 26 registers.

To the right of the basilica is the little **chiesetta di San Pietro**, built in the 16th century over the 4th-century original, and much reduced in size in 1826 to make room for the new basilica. The apse is carved into the mountainside; there are two niches indicated by popular legend as being the beds of Marinus and Leo, and said to have miraculous healing powers. They are probably tombs of the pre-Etruscan Villanova culture. The 17th-century altar, of inlaid marble, is magnificent, and surmounted by a white marble statue of St Peter (1920). Under the church is a crypt, created in 1941: the bas-relief on the altar shows St Marinus working as a stonemason protected by his tame bear.

THE BELLS OF SAN MARINO

In a tiny country like San Marino church bells were very important: the chimes could be heard by the entire population, so various bells were used to communicate different messages. The basilica bells are each dedicated to a particular saint: the largest is that of St Marinus, and is rung for funerals, St Leo is rung to warn of storms, St Agatha's is rung for her festivities, the fourth is St Peter's; the fifth that of the Madonna of Mercy; the sixth is of St Quirinus and is called *paro cruentes* ('prepare for blood'), because it was tolled when someone was sentenced to death; the seventh is dedicated to the saints Sebastian, Roch, Francis and Mustiola. The great bell at the Guaita tower, with its distinctive tone, now informs the people that council meetings are about to begin, but once it warned of imminent danger of invasion.

The towers of San Marino

A narrow little street, partly stepped, leads from the basilica up to the three towers which are the symbol of San Marino. They were built on the three peaks of Mt Titano and appear on the national flag (which is blue and white), surmounted by three ostrich plumes representing liberty. This is the oldest inhabited part of the Republic and you will find many medieval doorways and arches. Under the houses is an ancient aqueduct carved into the rock, called *Fossi*, where in 1897 a fossil whale was found. The **first tower** (*T: 0549 991369*), *Rocca*, *Guaita*, or *Prima Torre*, goes back to the 10th century and was an important watch-tower—*guaita* means 'guard'. The views from this tower (751m), are stupendous. Restored many times, it housed the prison until 1970. Originally access was over a drawbridge. Over the inner wall are the bell-tower (16th century) and the so-called 'tower of the feather' (15th century). The path to the **second tower** (*T: 0549 991295*), known as *Cesta*, *Fratta*, or *Seconda Torre*, is spectacular and should not be missed. *Cesta* stands on the highest peak of the mountain (756m). From here most of central Italy can be seen, and sometimes even the Dalmatian mountains, 250km away. The tower was probably built in the 13th century, but the upper part was added a century later. It stands on the spot where the Romans had a look-out post. The Museo delle Armi Antiche is now here, displaying a collection of armour and ancient weapons dating from the 14th to the 19th centuries. The **third tower**, called *Montale*, or 'of the mountain', is not accessible to the public. There is a terrible underground dungeon, and traces of a wall built of great blocks of stone, thought to go back to the Villanova period (9th–8th centuries BC). From Montale there is a lovely walk down the wooded slope to Piazzale Gandhi and the Congress Centre.

Other sights of the city

From Piazzetta del Titano, Contrada Omerelli leads west, under an archway. Almost immediately on the left, you will spot the **Oratorio di San Giovanni Battista**, an attractive Baroque building with lavish stucco decoration, paintings and sculptures inside. It is often called *Oratorio Valloni* by the local people, because it was the private chapel of the Valloni family who lived next door. The family arrived in San Marino from Carpegna in the early 18th century, building their palace in Contrada Omerelli; they were to become one of the most influential families in the republic. **Palazzo Valloni** now houses the state archives and the Biblioteca (*open Mon–Fri 8.15–6; T: 0549 882248*), with more than 60,000 beautifully-kept books, manuscripts and incunabula. The palazzo was completely rebuilt in 1953, after a Second World War bombing raid destroyed it. Continuing along Contrada Omerelli is a series of buildings, several of which still show their 16th-century origin. No. 145 is Palazzo Braschi or Palazzo Maggio; next to it is the handsome Palazzo Begni. Opposite is the monument to the volunteer soldiers who fought for Italy.

By taking the steps which go up on either side of the monument, it is possible to reach the Giardino dei Liburni, a small public garden. In this part of town and also elsewhere (they move them around), you will see bronze statues by the contemporary artists Francesco Messina, Emilio Greco, Bino Bini, Venanzo Crocetti, Antonio Berti and others. Over the archway leading down to Contrada Omerelli is the **Galleria Nazionale di Arte Moderna**, open in summer for temporary exhibitions of modern art. The gallery faces Cava dei Balestrieri, where a crossbow contest is held every year on 3rd September.

Returning to Contrada Omerelli, on the right is the barracks of the Militia. A little further along on the left is an ancient covered passage, *androne delle Monache*, and on the right is the **Monastero di Santa Clara**, of the Franciscan order of the Poor Clares. The beautiful late 16th-century building is no longer used by the nuns, who transferred to a new convent at Valdragone in 1971. It is now the seat of the University of San Marino. Part of the building, at 24 Contrada Omerelli, houses the very interesting **Museo dell'Emigrante** (*open Apr–Sept Mon–Fri 9–6, Sat 9–1, Sun closed; Oct–Mar Mon–Fri 9–12 & 2–5; T: 0549 885171, www.omniway.sm/emigration*), documenting the stories of all those *sammarinesi* who in the 19th century and again after the Second

World War, were forced to leave their country and face the unknown, when the economy ground to a halt. Contrada Omerelli ends at **Porta della Rupe**, where there is a small fortress. This was the ancient entrance to the city for those coming from Borgo Maggiore and Rimini. It is possible to see some of the old bulwarks along the walls here. From Porta della Rupe there is a lovely stepped path down to Borgo Maggiore, called *Costa dell'Arnella*; an excellent shortcut, it was once the main road.

THE SURROUNDING TOWNSHIPS

The eight ancient castles of the Republic are Borgo Maggiore, Serravalle, Domagnano, Acquaviva, Fiorentino, Chiesanuova, Montegiardino and Faetano.

Borgo Maggiore and Valdragone

Panoramic Borgo Maggiore (pop. 6,000) was an important trading centre by 1244, when it was known as *Mercatale*. Now the San Marino weekly market is held here every Thursday morning. Here is the lower station of the cableway (with ample car parks) which takes passengers to San Marino city in just over a minute. In a modern building is the **Museo Postale e Filatelico**, displaying all the stamps and coins issued by the Republic. In the same building is the interesting **Mostra Garibaldina**, with memorabilia of Garibaldi and his wife Anita, illustrating their time in San Marino (Gariblady and his troops were offered refuge here in 1849). At 21 Via Valdes de Carli is the **Centro Naturalistico Sammarinese** (*to request a visit T: 0549 883460*), with displays illustrating all the natural aspects of the Republic, from geology and palaeontology to the flora and fauna. Borgo Maggiore was severely damaged during the Second World War, and the parish church was completely destroyed. The new sanctuary of the **Beata Vergine della Consolazione**, in Via Salita Ugolino da Montefeltro, is the work of the Tuscan architect Giovanni Michelucci (best known for Florence's Santa Maria Novella railway station).

At **Valdragone** (signposted from the superstrada), under the jurisdiction of Borgo Maggiore, is the church and convent of Santa Maria (2 Via Castellonchio). In the 16th century this was the most important religious complex of the Republic. It was, however, drastically restored in 1938 and very little of the original structure remains. Inside the church there are some remarkable works of art, such as the ancient wooden Crucifix. Attention is drawn, however, to the 15th-century *Annunziata* polyptych, an anonymous tempera painting on canvas, of the Madonna offering a pear to the Christ Child, with Sts Catherine and Barbara, the Archangel Gabriel and the Virgin Annunciate. The painting is thought to have been brought from Siena.

Serravalle

When arriving from Rimini, Serravalle (pop. 9,350) is the first of the townships to be encountered, and incorporates Dogana, the old customs point. It was once known as *Olnano* and was a Roman settlement, but is mentioned for the first time in the Middle

Ages in 962, and became part of the Republic in 1463. It is now the largest of the townships, with industries manufacturing furniture, paint, garments and foodstuffs. The centre and the old castle, the Rocca Malatestiana, are very picturesque. Close to Dogana is **Falciano** (signposted), which forms part of the castle of Serravalle, and which houses the well-known **Ferrari Museum**, Maranello Rosso Collezione (*open Mon–Fri 10–1 & 2–6; Sat–Sun by previous arrangement; T: 0549 970614, www.maranellorosso.com*), displaying all the most famous red Ferraris, and also a collection of 36 cars designed by Carlo Abarth.

Domagnano and Acquaviva

After Serravalle the road reaches **Domagnano** (pop. 2,700), probably founded in 1300. According to the inhabitants, this was the birthplace of Bramante, but this is disputed by the nearby towns of Urbania and Fermignano, in the Marche, both of which claim the great sculptor and architect to be theirs. From here the views towards San Marino and the sea are spectacular. Close by, at **Paderna**, a hoard of more than 2,000 Roman coins was accidentally discovered in 1893, and not far away, a cache of jewels and gold buckles, perhaps from the tomb of a 6th-century Ostrogoth prince. The coins were lost, but the other objects are now in various museums of the world.

Acquaviva (pop. 1,700) takes its name from an abundant spring of mineral water, which emerges from the bare rock. This is where Marinus baptised his converts: the scene is represented in a painting of unknown origin in the tiny church of Sant'Andrea. Acquaviva is surrounded by attractive countryside, and is close to the wooded Monte Cerreto wildlife reserve. The nearby village of **Gualdicciolo** is the point of entry into the Republic when arriving from the Novafeltria road, and houses most of the industries: paper, playing cards, garments, pottery, motorcycles and bicycles, dairy products.

Faetano and Fiorentino

If taking the quiet secondary road from Rimini, you will come to **Faetano** (pop. 4,100), on a spur, dominated by the spire of the 19th-century church of San Paolo. From this clean and tidy little town, the three towers of San Marino look like the crest on an angry wave. Once part of the domain of the Malatesta, it was the last township to form part of the Republic, in 1463. **Fiorentino** (pop. 2,100) is the point of arrival of the road from Cattolica, San Leo, Pesaro and Urbino. Once part of the Malatesta domain, it joined the Republic in 1463. Many important archaeological finds have been discovered in the area. There were three castles at Fiorentino: the medieval Castellaccio, the ruins of which can be seen on Mt Seghizo; the Castrum Pennarossa (1069), now surrounded by a nature reserve; and the 12th-century Torricella on Mt San Cristoforo, unfortunately defaced by post-war quarrying activities, but still offering a wonderful view.

Chiesanuova and Montegiardino

Chiesanuova (pop. 1,000) has a pleasant rural atmosphere, despite its thriving industries (office accessories, lingerie), and beautiful views towards San Marino city and the mountains of the Montefeltro. Its restaurants attract plenty of visitors, especially on summer weekends. The narrow little streets and the simple old houses of **Montegiardino** (pop. 800), founded in the 14th century, but perhaps much older, make it one of the most picturesque townships; the castle is no longer standing, but the imposing old portal gives a good idea of its former importance. The parish church of San Lorenzo (1865) is worth a visit for its paintings: in the north aisle is a 17th-century *Crucifixion* by an unknown artist, and a *Madonna of the Rosary* by the school of Palma Giovane, showing St Dominic and St Anthony praying in front of the Madonna, with Mt Titano in the background. The 15 roundels surrounding the painting represent the mysteries of the Rosary. In the south aisle is a late 16th-century *Madonna and Child with Saints*, where the young St Marinus can be seen to the left of the Madonna, holding Mt Titano in his hands.

PRACTICAL INFORMATION

NB: Winter is a good time to visit; temperatures are mild and it is not so crowded. For most of the year the prevailing south wind, called the *garbino*, helps regulate extreme temperatures. July and August are the busiest months, with thousands of visitors every day.

GETTING AROUND

• **By air**: There are international airports at Rimini Miramare (24km), Forlì (74km) or Ancona (130km).
• **By train and bus**: From the railway station at **Rimini** on the Milan–Bologna–Pescara line there is a regular bus service.
Fratelli Benedettini, T: 0549 903854, runs bus services within the Republic and to Rimini.
Bonelli Bus, T: 0541 372432, runs services to and from Rimini Miramare Airport.
• **By car**: A particularly beautiful approach is over the mountains from Urbino, along the secondary roads, or from Rome on the SS258 through the Montefeltro. Tortuous but quiet secondary roads lead from Rimini and San Leo. Visiting San Marino by car is easy (but not in July and August, when it is too crowded) and there is an admirable series of numbered car parks (T: 0549 883808) in strategic positions.
• **By cableway**: Borgo Maggiore station (T: 0549 883590) to San Marino Città station; service available daily from 7.50, last evening time varies month by month.

INFORMATION OFFICES

Ufficio di Stato per il Turismo, 20 Contrada Omagnano, T: 0549 882998, www.omniway.sm; www.sanmarino2000.sm; www.visitsanmarino.com; **Tourist Information Bureau**, Contrada del

Collegio, T: 0549 882914. You can have your passport stamped here (just for fun).

OPENING TIMES

San Marino state museums are open daily from 8.50–5 in Jan, Feb, March, Oct, Nov, Dec, and from 8–8 in April, May, Jun, July, Aug, Sept. They are all closed on 25 Dec, 1 Jan and the afternoon of 2 Nov. Info: Musei di Stato, 2 Scala Bonetti, T: 0549 882670, www.museidistato.sm mds/index.htm. For guided tours, T: 0549 883835. It is possible to buy combined tickets. Times for private museums are indicated in the text.

HOTELS

San Marino Città
€€€€ **Cesare**. Newly renovated hotel, with good restaurant; internet access. 7 Salita alla Rocca, T: 0549 992355, www.hotelcesare.com

€€€€ **Grand Hotel San Marino**. Pleasant situation, beautiful views over the Apennines; garage. 31 Viale Antonio Onofri, T: 0549 992400, www.grandhotel.sm

€€€€ **Titano**. Attractive hotel founded in 1894, well situated in the old city. 31 Contrada del Collegio, T: 0549 991006, hoteltitano@hotmail.com

€€€ **La Grotta**. Central but quiet position, small hotel with good restaurant. 17 Contrada Santa Croce, T: 0549 991214.

€€€ **Rosa**. ■ Lovely rooms, marvellous restaurant and ideal position make this hotel a good choice. Garage. 23 Via Lapicidi Marini, T: 0549 991961.

€€ **La Rocca**. Small but comfortable, with a restaurant. 34 Salita alla Rocca, T: 0549 991166.

€ **Bellavista**. Tiny hotel a stone's throw from the cableway station. 42–44 Contrada del Pianello, T: 0549 991212.

Acquaviva
€€€ **Rio Re**. Attractive modern building with pool, garage and internet access. 11 Via Genghettino, Gualdicciolo, T: 0549 999216, www.riore.sm

Borgo Maggiore
€€€ **Hostaria Da Lino**. Right in the market place, a short walk from the cableway station; restaurant. 47 Piazza Grande, T: 0549 902300.

€ **La Fonte**. Very small inn with cool garden, restaurant and pizzeria, comfortable rooms, and sea views.

Chiesanuova
€ **Pensione Da Tina**. Basic accommodation but there is a pool, a popular dance hall, a restaurant famous for home-made pasta dishes, and a car park. 46 Strada Fontescara, T: 0549 998029.

Domagnano
€€€ **Gasperoni**. Comfortable rooms, restaurant, car park and internet access. 121 Via V Febbraio, Fiorina, T: 0549 900282, www.tradecenter.sm/hotelgasperoni

€€€ **Rossi**. Family-run hotel with garage, restaurant, modern comfortable rooms, bus to Rimini beach and San Marino city centre. 13 Via XXV Marzo, T: 0549 902263, mrossi@omniway.sm

Montegiardino
€€€€ **Relais Locanda dell'Artista**. ■ Exclusive accommodation in the ancient Palazzo Mengozzi,

every room with jacuzzi; excellent restaurant with good wine cellar. 18 Via del Dragone, T: 0549 996024, www.locandadellartista.com

Serravalle

€€€ **Dogana**. Rather incongruous modern hotel, good position on main Rimini–San Marino bus route. 65 Via III Settembre, T: 0549 905317, hoteldogana@omniway.sm

RESTAURANTS

Restaurants in San Marino present fairly simple cuisine, using ingredients from the surrounding countryside and fish from the Adriatic. Traditional recipes are influenced by the nearby regions of Emilia Romagna and the Marche. The dishes are carefully prepared and the home-made pasta is particularly delicious. You will probably eat the best lasagne of your life here. Local wines are good.

San Marino Città

€€€ **La Fratta**. Elegant restaurant close to the inner walls, specialises in grilled meat or fish, home-made pasta and authentic flash-baked pizza, good wine list. 14 Via Salita alla Rocca, T: 0549 991594,

€€€ **Righi La Taverna**. Smart restaurant and a snack bar too, high standard and good wine list. Closed Wed in winter. 10 Piazza della Libertà, T: 0549 991196.

€€ **Panoramica da Rosa**. ■ Very good cooking, outside terrace and pizza in the evening in summer. 27 Via Lapicidi Marini, T: 0549 991961.

€€ **Grotta dei Nani**. Homely atmosphere and good simple dishes. Closed Thur in winter. 7 Contrada dei Magazzeni, T: 0549 992636.

€€ **La Spingarda**. Breathtaking views over the rooftops from the terrace. 30 Contrada dei Magazzeni, T: 0549 992306.

€€ **Vecchia Stazione**. This delightful little restaurant was once the railway station. 38 Viale Federico d'Urbino, T: 0549 991009.

Acquaviva

€€ **Parco Verde**. Delightful countryside restaurant; car park. Closed Mon. 51 Strada di Montecerreto, Santa Mustiola, T: 0549 992695.

Borgo Maggiore

€€ **La Grotta**. Typical local cuisine and good wine list; small car park. 2 Via Valdes de Carli, T: 0549 906434.

€ **La Rupe**. Self-service; car park. Closed Mon in winter. 103 Strada Sottomontana, T: 0549 903301.

Domagnano

€€ **La Fiorina**. Very pleasant atmosphere; veranda and car park. 80 Via V Febbraio, Fiorina, T: 0549 900409.

€ **Due Soldi**. Self-service; car park. 9 Via XXV Marzo, T: 0549 907236.

Montegiardino

€€€ **Locanda dell'Artista**. Excellent food, good wine list, booking essential. 18 Via del Dragone, T: 0549 996024.

Murata

€€€ **Piccolo Restaurant**. Charming little restaurant in a cave, fish dishes a speciality, good wine list; comfortable rooms also available. Closed Mon. 17 Via del Serrone, T: 0549 992815.

Serravalle

€€ **Il Castello**. Splendid position on the old walls. 11 Via Elisabetta da Montefeltro, T: 0549 904232. Closed Mon and Sun lunchtime.

FESTIVALS & EVENTS

San Marino Anniversary of the Liberation and Feast of St Agatha, co-patron saint of the Republic, 5 Feb. Pageant in medieval dress to celebrate the Anniversary of the *Arengo*, 25 March. Investiture ceremonies of the Captains-Regent, with processions and costumes designed by Raphael, 1 April and 1 Oct. Medieval Days, with parades and competitions in medieval dress, 27–31 Aug. Anniversary of the Republic and Feast of St Marinus, which includes the famous crossbow contest called *Palio dei Balestrieri*, and is concluded with a magnificent firework display; Info: Federazione Balestrieri Sammarinesi, 51 Contrada Ombrelli, www.federazionebalestrieri.sm, 3 Sept. At Christmas and New Year the streets are animated with handicraft markets and impromptu entertainment.

Townships Feast day in Valdragone is the second Sun after Easter, when white roses are taken to the Madonna. Other feasts: Borgo Maggiore 1st Sun in June; Serravalle first Sun in Oct (Madonna of the Rosary) and 30 Nov (St Andrew); Falciano 29 June (St Peter); Paderna 2 July; Acquaviva 1 Oct (Madonna of the Rosary); Gualdicciolo first Sun in May; Faetano 25 Jan; Chiesanuova 2 June; Montegiardino 10 Aug (St Lawrence).

LOCAL SPECIALITIES

San Marino has low VAT on many articles. Cameras, binoculars, DVDs and CDs, perfumes and cosmetics cost less than in Italy. You will also find bootleg CDs, and rare, long-lost recordings at very favourable prices. Wines and liqueurs of local production, such as the Moscato di San Marino (a sweet dessert wine) or the liquorice-flavoured Mistrà, are worth taking home. A useful address is the Wine Point at Porta San Francesco, www.consorziovini.sm. There are three national cakes: the t*orta Titano*, layers of wafer biscuit and fine dark chocolate, the *torta Tre Monti*, light and fluffy, and the *ciambella paesana*, a kind of sponge cake. The cake factory is in the township of Fiorentino: **La Serenissima**, 7 Via La Doccia.

Attractive pottery is made in the local workshops. Italian tourists like to buy good quality packs of playing cards as souvenirs. At 10 Via Giacobini, Città, **Silvana Mariotti** makes the traditional San Marino rust prints on linen for tablecloths, cushions and curtains. A collector's paradise, the little Republic is famous for beautiful stamps and coins, but if you want a set of San Marino Euros, be prepared to spend about 40 times the face value. Lovely gold coins called *scudi* are also minted, and are legal tender. Contemporary artists are invited to design coins and stamps; they have included Annigoni, Guttuso, Greco, Messina and Manzù. The official outlet is the **Azienda Autonoma di Stato Filatelica e Numismatica**, Piazza Garibaldi, T: 0549 882370, www.aasfn.sm (Mon–Fri 8.15–1, Mon and Thur also 3–5).

PRACTICAL INFORMATION

PLANNING YOUR TRIP

When to go

Spring: This is the best time for the wildflowers in the Sibylline Mountains. It is also the season for *bianchetto* truffles at Fossombrone, black truffles at Acqualagna. There are also particularly impressive Easter celebrations at Cantiano and Sassoferrato; fireworks at Ripatransone; the Frog Race at Fermignano and a St George's Day procession (23 April) at Porto San Giorgio. In May, special events in Camerino (sword race), Sarnano (antiques exhibition), Cagli (9 May, procession for the patron St Gerontius), Jesi (*palio* contest for St Florian) and Monterubbiano (ancient Picene celebration).

Summer: Most of the historical pageants and firework displays take place in summer. The hottest month is July, when the sunflowers are in bloom and the wheat is harvested. For Corpus Christi (June), the streets are covered with flower petal designs at Castelraimondo, Amandola and Servigliano. There is a Palio contest for St John the Baptist at Fabriano (24 June); Maiolo celebrates its bread (end of June); and Opera Festivals at Macerata (July) and Pesaro (Aug). Treia organises a match of the traditional game of *pallone al bracciale*.

Autumn: This is the season for the kite-flying contest at Urbino, and for the procession for the Madonna at Macerata, with offerings of wheat and flowers. October is the month for celebrating truffles, at Apecchio, Sant'Agata Feltria and Acqualagna. The grape harvest and wine-making are celebrated at Camerano, Loro Piceno, Rosora, Cupramontana, San Marcello and Corinaldo.

Winter: This is a pleasant time to visit the Marche, but it can be rainy and cold. The rainiest month is November. Ancona celebrates chestnuts and wine; pit-matured cheese is presented at Novafeltria; and truffles again at Acqualagna. In December there are *tableaux vivants* of the Nativity at Acquasanta Terme, Genga, Treia and Porto San Giorgio. Loreto celebrates the arrival of the Holy House. The *Befana*, a friendly witch, the Italian version of Santa Claus, makes her appearance at Urbania in January.

Websites for the Marche

General information:	www.turismo.marche.it, www.cultura.marche.it.
Beautiful villages:	www.borghitalia.it.
Castles and fortresses:	www.incastro.marche.it.
Exhibitions:	www.artonline.it.
Folklore:	www.macina.net.
Food:	www.slowfood.com.
Historic theatres:	www.amat.marche.it.
Roman cities:	www.marcheromane.it.
Theatre programmes:	www.stabilemarche.it; www.infopointspettacoli.it.

Wildlife parks:	www.wwfitalia.it/marche; www.parks.it;
	www.lalupusinfabula.it; www.lipu.it
Wine, cheese and olive oil:	www.cittadellolio.it (the oil-producing centres),
to orderproducts on-line:	www.esperya.com

Websites for San Marino

General information:	www.omniway.sm; www.sanmarino2000.sm
	www.visitsanmarino.com
Coins, stamps and phone cards:	www.aasfn.sm
(for collectors)	
Museums:	www.museidistato.sm/mds/index.htm
Wines:	www.consorziovini.sm

Maps

Detailed town plans are included throughout the book, providing easy navigation around towns and ancient sites. For those requiring more detailed maps, the best are published by the Touring Club Italiano (www.touringclubitaliano.com). They are constantly updated and are indispensable to anyone travelling by car in Italy. Their *Grande Carta Stradale d'Italia*, on a scale of 1:200,000, is divided into 15 maps covering the regions of Italy, including the Marche and San Marino. The road maps are also published in the handier form of a three-volume atlas called the *Atlante Stradale d'Italia*. The one entitled *Centro* covers the area.

Health and insurance

It is always a good idea to take out a comprehensive insurance policy before going on holiday. Remember to keep all receipts (*ricevute*) and medical report (*cartella clinica*) to give to your insurer if you need to make a claim. Citizens of EU countries have the right to claim health services (free treatment and low-cost prescriptions) in Italy, if they have the E111 form (available from post offices). Thefts or damage to property must be reported immediately at the local police station; you will need a copy of the *denuncia* to claim insurance.

Disabled travellers

The region is fast applying current legislation, which obliges public buildings to provide access for the disabled, and specially designed facilities within. However, many churches have imposing flights of steps in front of the entrances as their only means of access, not to mention the stepped streets and alleys which are the norm in hundreds of hilltop towns and villages. In small towns, access to toilets in coffee bars or restaurants is often a problem because they are situated on the first floor, and lifts are rare. In the annual accommodation list published by the local tourist offices, establishments which can offer hospitality to the disabled are indicated. Airports and railway stations now provide assistance and certain trains are equipped to transport wheelchairs. Access for cars with disabled people is allowed to town centres usually closed to traffic, where parking places are reserved for them. For all other information, contact the local tourist offices.

GETTING AROUND

By car

Motorways (*autostrade*) are indicated by green signs, normal roads by blue signs. At the entrance to motorways, the two directions are indicated by the name of the town at the end of the road, not by that of the nearest town, which can be momentarily confusing. They are a fast and convenient way of travelling around, often providing panoramic views of the countryside, crossing difficult terrain by means of viaducts and tunnels, and in places they are spectacularly beautiful. Beware: always lock your car when parked, and never leave anything of value inside it. If purchasing fuel or oil at a motorway service station, always check that you have been given the right amount, that the seal on the oil can is intact, and that you have been given the correct change. Unscrupulous staff know that it is difficult for a tourist to go back if a fraud is discovered.

By train

The Italian Railway Company, Trenitalia, www.trenitalia.com, runs various categories of train: ES (Eurostar), international express trains (with a special supplement, approximately 30% of the normal single fare) running between the main Italian and European cities (with obligatory seat reservation since no standing passengers are permitted), with first- and second-class carriages; EC and IC, international and national express trains, with a supplement (less than that for the Eurostar); Espressi, long-distance trains (both classes) not as fast as the Intercity trains; Diretti, slower than Espressi, although not stopping at every station; and Inter-regionali and Regionali, local trains stopping at all stations, mostly with second-class carriages only.

Buying tickets and booking seats: Many stations are now unmanned, and tickets can be purchased in the nearest coffee bar, tobacconist or newsagent. Valid for two months after the day sold, they must be bought before the journey, and date-stamped in the machines you find on the platforms, otherwise the ticket-collector will make you pay a stiff fine. If for some reason you fail to do this, try to find the ticket-collector before he finds you! Once stamped, the ticket is valid for six hours for distances of up to 200km, and for 24 hours for longer distances. It is much easier to buy your tickets at a travel agency.

Discounts and railcard options: Children under the age of 4 travel free, and between the ages of 4 and 12 travel half price. If you are planning a lengthy journey through Europe starting in Italy, then a Eurodomino pass (www.eurodomino.it) is useful, with a voucher for each country you intend to visit. Also for journeys starting in Italy, the Carta Verde and Carta Verde Railplus allow discounts on tickets. Non-European train lovers can purchase a Eurail pass from their travel agent before departure. Europeans with a Senior Citizen railcard can buy a Carta Argento, allowing 15% discount on tickets; a Carta Blu is available for the disabled. Cars, motorcycles, bicycles and wheelchairs can be transported only on certain trains (not on the Eurostar, for example). Prior booking is obligatory, except for bicycles. Prices depend on the size of the vehicles. A day ticket for a bicycle costs €3.50 on a slow train, and €7 on an Intercity (IC), but for a short journey which would cost a passenger less than €3.50, you can simply buy a passenger ticket for your bicycle.

Left-luggage facilities are now available only in main stations, they are usually open 24hrs a day.

By bus

Inter-city and inter-village services in the Marche are capillary, punctual (although perhaps infrequent) and fairly comfortable. Services tend to finish in the early evening. Detailed information on the bus companies and the routes they serve will be found in the chapter listings. Tickets can sometimes be purchased on board, sometimes at the nearest coffee bar or tobacconist; to be on the safe side, check before you travel.

ACCOMMODATION

In the text we have indicated many places to stay in every locality, endeavouring where possible to offer a choice within each type and price range of accommodation. Establishments were chosen for one or more of the following reasons: charm, historical interest, value for money, convenient position and comfort. For Blue Guides Recommended, see p. 373.

Hotels

Hotels are grouped into five categories according to the services offered, and are classified by stars, as in the rest of Europe, from one star for very simple comforts (corresponding to the old definition pensione) to the luxuries of five stars. However, prices can vary considerably, even within the same star category, according to the time of year or the locality. Nowadays all but a very few establishments offer en-suite baths or showers. Generally speaking, stars are an indication of services, not of beauty, comfort or charm. The more stars an establishment has, the more services there are in the rooms, from private telephone, hair dryer, colour or satellite TV, minibar, internet access, jacuzzi etc. Not all hotels have restaurants, but continental breakfast is usually included. Service charges are included in the rates, but beware of extras on the bill which can be extremely expensive: drinks from the minibar, breakfast in the room, phone calls from the room, pay-movies, laundry, and so on.

Price categories

NB: Prices are decided by individual managements and communicated to the tourist offices for publication in their brochures. Prices given here are only intended to give a general idea.

★★★★★L	single €195–350,	double €295–600;
★★★★★	single €100–285,	double €150–350;
★★★★	single €70–190,	double €90–300;
★★★	single €30–110,	double €50–120;
★★	single €25–70,	double €45–90;
★	single €20–65,	double €40–75.

Bed and breakfast

There is a wide choice of bed-and-breakfast accommodation in the region, mostly in the countryside. Legislation in Italy has been relaxed, making it much easier for people to offer rooms for visitors: bed and breakfast in the Marche is a particularly good way of gaining a better understanding of the places you visit. The inhabitants are extremely hospitable, and their homes are comfortable. Most provinces classify this type of accommodation according to the star system: one star means you will have to share the bathroom with the family, while three or more star establishments can be like luxurious small hotels. Not all homeowners speak English or French, but they are invariably helpful.

Prices range from €15–20 per person in a simple family home, classified one star, to well over €100 in an aristocratic villa.

Farm accommodation

Known as *agriturismo* in Italy, there are now hundreds of working farms in the Marche which offer accommodation, highly recommended for travellers with their own transport and families with young children, as an excellent way of visiting the countryside. Terms vary from bed and breakfast to full board or self-contained flats; some farms require a stay of a minimum number of days. Cultural or recreational activities are sometimes provided; on some farms you can help with the work on a voluntary basis, milking sheep or cattle, gathering fruit, harvesting, etc. Again, the star system is used to classify the standards;

★★★★★	single €110,	double €250;
★★★★	single €50,	double €90;
★★★	single €40,	double €80;
★★	single €35,	double €60;
★	single €30,	double €50.

Country houses

These are simply houses in the country without a working farm; some of them are luxurious aristocratic villas, others are quite basic. Recommended for independent travellers who enjoy the countryside.

Monastery accommodation

Many convents and monasteries have rooms available for visitors. These are very basic, but always with private bath or shower. Sometimes meals can be taken in the refectory. It is not required of you to be a Catholic, but obviously Catholics enjoy the experience more. It always represents very good value for money.

FOOD & DRINK

In each chapter we have indicated a range of restaurants for all pockets. Our choices reflect personal pleasant experiences and an endeavour to allow travellers the possibility of sampling the very best local dishes and wines. Remember, service is often slow (that's the way Italians like it). Service charges are included in the bill unless otherwise stated (some places add a cover charge), so tipping is not an obligation, but always much appreciated. Here is what you can expect to pay for a full meal without drinks: €€€ means a luxurious restaurant, over €35 a head (sometimes well over); €€ means a good restaurant, from €20–35 a head; € means a trattoria where you will pay €10–25 a head.

Food and wine

Italian gourmets consider the Marche one of the most stimulating parts of the country for eating and drinking. Some cooks have achieved international recognition. Restaurants in Senigallia and Cartoceto are said to be among the best in Italy (but you will find sparkling jewels elsewhere in the region). Lunch is usually the main meal of the day, especially in the interior; pasta followed by salad is a standard. The pasta is almost always freshly-made, sometimes with the addition of eggs. A favourite dish is *tagliatelle alla papera*, with a dressing of duck ragout. Ravioli stuffed with ricotta, sometimes together with spinach, often appear on the menu, and sometimes you will find *vincisgrassi*, the exquisite local version of lasagne. Salads are quite imaginative, often consisting of beef (*tagliata di manzo*) or fish (*insalata di mare*). Along the coast, fish soup, prepared to different recipes from place to place, is justly renowned. You will also find *stocco*, dried cod: they are famous for this in Ancona. Meat is usually grilled or roasted, and the preference is for farmyard animals, such as rabbit, lamb, chicken, turkey, duck and pigeons. If you like truffles, this is one of the best places in the world to find them—at Acqualagna they are collected throughout the year.

Local varieties of apples, peaches and pears are very good, but the universal dessert in the Marche is *panna cotta* (literally 'cooked cream'), or occasionally *tiramisù* ('pull-me-up'; clotted cream with sponge cake, coffee, liqueur and a powdering of cocoa), but young cooks are starting to offer all kinds of imaginative and irresistible creations. Most people like to start or finish their meal with assorted cheeses, invariably served with a selection of honeys and home-made preserves: plum jam is particularly good with cheese. The soft *casciotta d'Urbino*, for example, tastes wonderful with chestnut-blossom honey; pit-matured cheese from Talamello is good with morello-cherry jam.

Bread in the Marche is absolutely delicious, and treated almost reverentially—at Senigallia and Maiolo there are annual celebrations in its honour. The large, golden sourdough loaves of Cantiano are said to be the best. In the evening, especially at weekends, people flock to restaurants offering *crescia*, soft flat loaves studded with various tasty morsels, depending on where you are: lard and cheese, for example, or *ciauscolo*, the soft salami of Macerata, or the classic dark red salami made in Fabriano; *crescia* is accompanied by a glass of wine. In Pesaro, Gabicce and Tavullia the *piadina*, the unleavened bread of Romagna, is preferred as a snack, together with ham and salami, salad or cheese, and eaten with beer, like pizza.

Olive oil is excellent, again varying in flavour according to where you are. In the 13th century, Venetian merchants were prepared to pay more for oil from this area, because of its superior quality. Many experts maintain that the oil of Cartoceto is the finest in the world. Near Civitanova Marche they produce *cilestra* oil, from a local variety of olives which give a delicate flavour. Another special variety is the *coroncina*, found near Tolentino and Serrapetrona; the oil is bright green and slightly bitter. Ascoli Piceno is famous for sweet and tender olives, which can be prepared in different ways, stuffed and fried, for example.

Many Marche wines are guaranteed by the DOC label: *Denominazione d'Origine Controllata*. The reds include Rosso Piceno, Rosso Piceno Superiore, Lagrima di Morro d'Alba, Rosso Conero, Esino, Offida Rosso, and the distinctive, sparkling Vernaccia di Serrapetrona (the only wine in the region where the quality is also guaranteed, DOCG). The whites include Verdicchio dei Castelli di Jesi, Verdicchio di Matelica, Falerio dei Colli Ascolani, Colli Maceratesi, Colli Pesaresi, Offida Passerina, Spumante and Pecorino, and Bianchello del Metauro. In certain areas wine is also made with cherry juice: *visner* or *vino di visciole*. A special condensed wine called *vi'cotto piceno* can be found at Loro Piceno. *Vinsanto*, sweet wine made from grapes which have been allowed to wither during the winter, is rare. *Sapa* is condensed grape must, used as a flavouring and for dressing certain dishes. The most famous liqueur is the aniseed-flavoured Mistrà.

ADDITIONAL INFORMATION

Emergency numbers

Police: 113 (Polizia di Stato) or 112 (Carabinieri).
Medical: 118.

Telephone and postal services

For all calls in Italy, local and long-distance, dial the city code (for instance, 071 for Ancona) then the phone number. For international and intercontinental calls, dial 00 plus the country code followed by the city code (for numbers in the UK drop the initial 0) and number. To call Italy from abroad (not USA) dial 0039, then the city code and number. From the USA, dial 00139 followed by the city code and number.

Stamps are sold at post offices and at tobacconists (*tabacchi*, marked with a large white T). *Posta ordinaria* is regular post, *posta prioritaria* receives priority handling, including transport by air mail, and is only slightly more expensive. Correspondence can be addressed to you while in Italy c/o the post office, simply by writing 'Fermo Posta' followed by the name of the locality, on the envelope after the name of the addressee.

Museums, galleries, archaeological sites, churches and theatres

Many museums and galleries are not permanently staffed; a phone call the day before, or a visit to the Tourist Office or the Town Hall when you reach the town, are normally sufficient to gain entry, especially in the morning. The same goes for the historic theatres and the archaeological sites. It is often possible to buy cumulative tickets. Some of the most interesting works of art are in the churches; entry to these is always free of charge. You will find that some stay open all day, even when the sacristan is not there—apparently, honesty is not a lost virtue here in the Marche. When a church you particularly want to see is closed, just ask nearby, and someone will find the sacristan, the priest, or the custodian; and don't be surprised if you are trusted with the key, to give back after your visit. In many places you will find bright, well-informed students to show you around, or enthusiastic local historians. Nothing seems to be too much trouble for these people, who are intensely proud of their heritage, and are only too happy to 'show and tell'. A gratuity is not normally expected, and in some cases would even cause offence.

BLUE GUIDES RECOMMENDED

Hotels, restaurants and cafés that are particularly good choices in their category—in terms of location, charm, value for money or the quality of the experience they provide—carry the **Blue Guides Recommended** sign: ■. All establishments recommended in this way have been selected by our authors, editors or contributors as places they have particularly enjoyed and would be happy to recommend to others. We only recommend establishments that we have visited. To keep our entries up-to-date reader feedback is essential: please do not hesitate to email us with any views, corrections or suggestions.

GLOSSARY OF ARTISTS

Agabiti, Pietro Paolo (Sassoferrato, 1470–1540), painter and architect; besides painting canvases, he worked in terracotta.

Alberti, Antonio di Guido (Antonio da Ferrara; Ferrara, 1390–1449), painter. Influenced by Ottaviano Nelli and Gentile da Fabriano, he has left very few works, the most notable are the frescoes in the cemetery chapel at Talamello.

Aleandri, Ireneo (San Severino Marche, 1795–1885; www.ireneo.aleandri.sinp.net), architect employed for many years as chief engineer at the town council of Spoleto. He is remembered for his churches, villas, and town halls, but above all for his theatres: the Sferisterio of Macerata (his masterpiece) and the opera houses of Ascoli Piceno, San Severino, Pollenza, and Sant'Elpidio, all practical buildings with elegant lines and good acoustics. He also worked on civil projects; part of the Ancona–Rome railway is his.

Alunno (Niccolò di Liberatore; Foligno, 1430–1502), painter. After growing up in the Gothic atmosphere of the artists' studios in Foligno, he went to the Marche, where he was inspired by Antonio Vivarini's Venetian-style polyptychs and the work of Carlo Crivelli.

Amorosi, Antonio Mercurio (Comunanza, 1660–1740), painter; founder of the so-called Bamboccianti school, noted for humorous scenes of peasants and humble people in the relaxed atmosphere of taverns or country feasts, and especially children at play. He worked for most of his life in Rome, where his style was in complete contrast to the rigid atmosphere of the papal court, but he received many commissions from foreign dignitaries, who wanted him to paint their children's portraits.

Andrea da Bologna (Andrea de' Bruni; Bologna, fl. 1369–77), miniaturist and painter, he illustrated manuscripts written by his brother Bartolomeo (one of which is in the museum of Chantilly), and also frescoed churches.

Andrea da Jesi (Andrea Aquilini; Jesi, 1492–?1526), little-known outside his native town, this painter came from a family of artists.

Andrea di Bartolo (Siena, fl. 1389–1424), painter, renowned for his luminous colours; he also gilded wooden statues.

Angeli, Fra' Marino (Marino d'Angelo; Santa Vittoria in Matenano, fl. 1443–48), priest and painter – although active only a short time, he started an artistic school in his area.

Annigoni, Pietro (Milan, 1910–88), painter; he lived for a time in Britain, and is famous for his portraits of the royal family.

Antonio da Fabriano (Antonio d'Agostino di Giovanni; Fabriano, fl. 1451-89), painter; his work shows the influence of Flemish art, also that of Piero della Francesca. Few of his works survive today, among which the masterpiece is undoubtedly the Crucifix in the Piersanti Museum of Matelica.

Antonio da Faenza (Antonio di Mazzone de' Domenichi) (Faenza, 1457-1535), painter and architect; he probably arrived together with Benedetto da Maiano and his brother, to work on the sanctuary of the Holy House at Loreto.

Antonio da Pesaro (*see Giovanni Antonio da Pesaro*).

Apollodorus of Damascus (2C), Greek architect favoured by Trajan, he followed the emperor on his campaigns; besides his famous bridge over the Danube, his most representative work is the arch of honour in the port of Ancona.

Arcangelo di Cola (Camerino, fl. 1416–29), painter, one of the foremost exponents of the Camerino school. He was influenced by the Rimini artists; an excellent diptych of his is now in the Frick Collection of New York.

Baglione, Giovanni (Rome, 1571–1644),
Mannerist painter and art historian, great
admirer of Caravaggio, with whom he had
a furious fight, which ended with a trial.
He was very popular in his day, not only in
Rome, but throughout Europe.

Barili, Andrea and Antonio (Siena, fl. late
15C), brothers; architects, sculptors and
engravers. Followers of Francesco di
Giorgio Martini.

Barocci, Federico (Federico Fiori; Urbino,
1535–1612), painter. After Raphael, critics
believe him to be the finest artist of the
Marche; his paintings are unmistakable for
their luminous quality, and the joyful use
of colour.

Baronzio, Giovanni (?Rimini, ?1300–62),
painter; a much-admired artist, who successfully combined the rich chromatism of
Byzantine colours with the naturalistic figures introduced by Giotto.

Bartolini, Luigi (Cupramontana,
1892–1963), painter, engraver, writer and
poet, author of *Bicycle Thieves* (1948), a
neo-Realism film by Vittorio de Sica.

Batoni, Pompeo (Lucca, 1708–87), painter;
son of a goldsmith, Pompeo opened a studio in Rome, where he became famous
throughout Europe for his realistic portraits.

Bellini, Filippo (Urbino, ?1550–1604),
painter; descendant of Giovanni.

Bellini, Giovanni (Giambellino; Venice,
1430–1516), painter; extremely painstaking artist. His background settings,
although often a combination of various
places, were always painted from life; he
was one of the first to use oils.

Benedetto da Maiano (Maiano, nr. Florence,
1442–97), sculptor, architect and engraver;
apprenticed to his brother Giuliano, he
excelled in wood-carving (ceilings of
Palazzo Vecchio in Florence); he also
worked in Naples; as architect he worked
in Arezzo and at Palazzo Strozzi in
Florence.

Berentz, Christian (Hamburg, 1658–1722),
painter noted for his exquisite still-lifes.

Berruguete, Pedro (Paredes de Nava, Spain,
1450–1506), painter; one of the many
artists who flocked to the court of Federico
da Montefeltro, where he worked together
with Joos van Ghent. On returning to Spain,
he was able to put his Italian experience to
good use, carrying out an innovative series
of frescoes for the cathedral of Toledo.

Berti, Antonio (San Piero a Sieve, nr.
Florence, 1904–90),one of the Fascist
regime's official sculptors, he carved several
statues of Mussolini, earning himself a reputation from which he found it impossible
to escape after the war.

Bini, Bino (Florence, 1916), sculptor and
goldsmith.

Boccati, Giovanni (Camerino, fl. 1443–80),
painter and musician; the most famous
exponent of the Camerino School,
although he lived and worked in Perugia.
Influenced by the Siena painters and by
Piero della Francesca, his pleasing, original
style provided inspiration for Raphael.

Boscoli, Andrea (Florence, 1560–1607),
painter; follower of the early Mannerist
style of Florence.

Botticelli, Sandro (Alessandro di Mariano
Filipepi; Florence, 1445–1510), painter. At
the age of 15, after working in the ateliers
of Filippo Lippi, Verrocchio and Pollaiolo,
he opened his own studio, and immediately found fame. Liked and protected by the
most powerful families of Florence, he left
Florence only from 1481–82 to paint the
Sistine Chapel. One of Italy's most fascinating painters, for his intensely expressive
works, precisely drawn, with luminous
colours chosen to awaken an emotion
rather than express reality.

Botticini, Francesco (Florence, 1446–98),
painter. Apprenticed to Verrocchio, he was
an excellent artist, but he never knew
fame, probably overwhelmed by the great
masters of his generation.

Bracci, Virginio (Rome, 1737–1815), architect; he often worked for the pope.

Bramante (Donato di Pascuccio;
Fermignano, 1444–1514), Pope Julius II's
favourite architect, he was also a skilled
painter.

Bramantino, il (Bartolomeo Suardi; Milan, 1455–1536), painter, sculptor and architect. In order to achieve the right effect, he carefully arranged folds of wet cloth or paper, before reproducing them in marble or on canvas.

Brandani, Federico (Urbino, ?1525–75), moulder and sculptor, the greatest stucco worker of his day.

Brandi, Giacinto (Poli, nr. Rome, 1623–91), painter. Apprentice to Guercino, he became famous for his historical scenes.

Bucci, Anselmo (Fossombrone, 1887–1955), painter. He spent his formative years living a precarious existence in Paris, where he made hundreds of sketches of daily life, with a journalistic style, almost like snapshots; he was a friend of Dufy, Utrillo, Modigliani, Severini and Picasso. In 1922 he founded the artistic movement Novecento Italiano; he also wrote for *Corriere della Sera*.

Caffè, Nino (Alfedena, nr. L'Aquila, 1909–75; www.ninocaffe.com), internationally known and acclaimed artist; he has a very pleasing style.

Callido, Gaetano Antonio (Este, nr. Padua, 1727–1813), skilled organ-maker, perhaps the finest in Italy; after learning his trade as apprentice in the workshop of Pietro Nacchini, in Istria, he lived for 30 years in Corinaldo.

Canova, Antonio (Possagno, nr. Treviso, 1757–1822), sculptor and painter. Very popular in his day, he is remembered especially for his pleasingly erotic statues of Paolina Bonaparte, and the *Three Graces*. Also for his part in negotiating the return of many Italian artworks purloined by Napoleon.

Cantalamessa, Carlo (Rome, 1909–82), sculptor and medal designer, he also produced some very good etchings.

Cantarini, Simone (Pesaro, 1612–48), painter and engraver much influenced by Guido Reni, to whom he was apprentice. Their relationship was stormy, so Simone opened his own atelier in Bologna.

Cantatore, Domenico (Ruvo di Puglia, 1906–98), self-taught painter and art critic. One of the most important contemporary Italian artists; his easy, pleasant style leans a little towards abstract art.

Capogrossi, Giuseppe (Rome, 1900–72), painter; he left a career in law to paint, following Carrà, Picasso and Modigliani. On his return from Paris he settled into an abstract style, with a characteristic 'fork' or 'trident' as his graphic sign.

Capponi, Mattia (Cupramontana, fl. late 18C), brilliant architect, perhaps a pupil of Vanvitelli. Practically all his works are in the Esino valley.

Caravaggio, il (Michelangelo Merisi; Caravaggio, nr. Milan, 1573–1610), painter; one of Italy's most extraordinary artists, with a vigorous, realistic style quite in contrast with the Mannerist art which was popular in his day. Dirty, eccentric, and often violent, he spent a lot of time on the run—even escaping from his prison cell in Malta by shinning down some knotted sheets, and reaching Sicily in a rowing boat. In Sicily he painted some of his finest works, the enormous dark canvases which gradually reveal the story he has to tell: the *Burial of St Lucy*, the *Resurrection of Lazarus*, and two exceptional *Nativities*, one of which was stolen from a church in Palermo in 1969, and never recovered.

Carboncino, Giovanni (Giovanni Carbone; Albaro, 1614–83), painter, he excelled in portraits.

Carlo da Camerino (Camerino, fl. late 14C–early 15C), painter. After recent studies, it is thought that this artist never existed; paintings formerly attributed to him are probably by **Olivuccio di Ciccarello**, an artist of the same period, born in Camerino and active in Ancona.

Carnevale, Fra' (Bartolomeo di Giovanni Corradini; ?Urbino, late 15C), Dominican friar and painter; apprentice to Piero della Francesca. A shadowy figure about whom little is known; he was Bramante's first teacher; an exhibition of his works has recently been organized in Milan (2004).

Carnevali (or Carnovali), Giovanni (Il

Piccio); Montegrino, nr. Varese, 1804–73), painter. He started working with his father when he was eight, for an aristocratic family, who called him *il piccio*, the 'little one'. He drew a bunch of keys on the wall of their villa, which were mistaken for real ones. At the age of 11 he was admitted to the Academy of Bergamo. He was a lonely person, extravagant and unpredictable. He drowned when he fell into the River Po at Cremona. A great landscape artist, he also excelled in portraits, and enjoyed painting Biblical and mythological themes.

Carolis, Adolfo de (Montefiore dell'Aso, 1874–1928), painter, engraver and illustrator, influenced by the Pre-Raphaelites and Art Nouveau.

Carrà, Carlo (Alessandria, 1881–1966), painter. An early exponent of the Futurist movement, he soon returned to a more traditional style.

Carracci, Annibale (Bologna, 1555–1619), painter; an influential artist with a strong personality, who meticulously studied the work of his contemporaries. Together with his cousin, **Ludovico Carracci** (1555–1619), he set up a studio, whose output hastened the transition from Mannerism to the Baroque.

Cassinari, Bruno (Piacenza, 1912–92), prize-winning Expressionist painter; deeply influenced by Picasso and Modigliani.

Chirico, Giorgio de (Volos, Greece, 1888–1978), painter. Certainly the most imitated artist of his day; and the most falsified: hundreds of fake de Chiricos were circulating even during his lifetime; probably many important galleries of the world still have them on display. He described his style as 'metaphysical': deserted squares, classical architecture, statues and columns.

Cialdieri, Girolamo di Bartolomeo (Urbino, 1593–1680), painter, architect and engraver, follower of Barocci.

Cignani, Carlo (Bologna, 1628–1719), rather slow-moving fresco painter (it took him 20 years to decorate the dome of the chapel of the Madonna in Forlì cathedral), he also painted many altarpieces.

Cola dell'Amatrice (Nicola Filotesio; Amatrice, nr. Rieti, ?1480–1559), painter and architect.

Conca, Giovanni (Gaeta, fl. 1706–54), painter; younger brother of the more famous Sebastiano, active in Rome as a fresco painter.

Contarini, Giovanni (Venice, 1549–1603), a notary public who turned to painting in his later years, when inspired by Titian, Tintoretto and Palma Giovane.

Coxcie, Michiel (Mechelen, modern Belgium, 1499–1592), Flemish painter and designer of tapestries and stained-glass windows, he lived in Rome; influenced by Raphael.

Crivelli, Carlo (Venice, 1430–1500), highly esteemed painter; he died in Ascoli Piceno. His paintings are unmistakable for the delicate colours and accurate design; the abundant use of symbolic fruits, flowers and vegetables; and the lingering care with which he depicts his subjects: the faces are often so elongated they are almost caricatures, with elaborate ringlets and long slender hands. He liked the International Gothic style, which was already passing out of fashion elsewhere in Italy. Some historians say he was attracted to Fermo by the favourable cultural atmosphere, others say he fled Venice after spending 6 months in prison for having seduced a fisherman's wife. Whatever the reason, his arrival was a good thing for the Marche.

Crivelli, Vittore (?Venice, 1440–1502), painter, brother of Carlo, very prolific in the Marche. Until recently considered vastly inferior to Carlo, he is now receiving credit in his own right.

Crocetti, Venanzo (Teramo, 1913–2003), sculptor and painter (bronze was his favourite medium) with a pleasing style; in Rome there is a museum of his work.

Damiani, Felice (Felice da Gubbio; Gubbio, 1530–1608), Mannerist painter of the Counter-Reformation. His work is perhaps too heavy for modern tastes.

Daretti, Lorenzo (?Ancona, fl. 18C), architect and fine painter.

Depero, Fortunato (Val di Non, 1892–1960), Futurist painter, sculptor and poet, one of the most representative exponents of the style in Italy.

Domenichino (Domenico Zampieri; Bologna, 1581–1641), painter and architect. Apprenticed to Annibale Carracci, with whom he worked in Rome, he went on to work for the aristocracy, decorating the interiors of villas and palaces. In 1621 he was appointed architect for the pope: many of the plans he drew up in that period are now at Windsor Castle. In 1630 he was invited to decorate a chapel in Naples Cathedral, but envious local artists destroyed most of his work, embittering the end of his life.

Donati, Alessio (Offida, fl. 18C), wood carver; his work is exquisite.

Fabiani, Giovanni Battista (Mogliano, fl. mid 18C), wood carver, sculptor and painter, who worked almost exclusively in Mogliano.

Fanelli, Pier Simone (Ancona, ?–1703), painter.

Fazzini, Pericle (Grottammare, 1913–87),known as *lo scultore dell'aria*, sculptor of air, for his fanciful creations.

Ferri, Giovan Francesco (Pergola, 1701–75), painter. Besides working in fresco for churches, he also enjoyed painting theatrical backdrops and safety-curtains.

Floriani, Pompeo (San Severino Marche, 1545–1600), architect. A great favourite of Pope Sixtus V, Floriani designed the towns of Loreto and Montalto delle Marche.

Folchetti, Stefano (San Ginesio, fl. 1492–1513), painter; admirer of Carlo Crivelli.

Fontana, Luigi (Monte San Pietrangeli, 1827–1908), painter, sculptor, but perhaps best known as architect.

Francesco di Gentile (Fabriano, fl. late 15C), painter; follower of Gentile da Fabriano, he was perhaps his son.

Frosino, Luca (Florence, fl. late 15C–early 16C), artist, apprenticed to Botticelli.

Genga, Bartolomeo (Cesena, nr Forlì, 1516–59), painter and architect.

Genga, Girolamo (Urbino, 1476–1551), painter, architect and sculptor, father of Bartolomeo; strongly influenced by Signorelli and by Raphael.

Gennari, Bartolomeo (?, 17C), painter, apprenticed to Guercino, but with his own particular approach.

Gentile da Fabriano (Gentile di Niccolò; Fabriano, 1370–1427), painter; one of the finest exponents of the International Gothic. While familiar with the work of French, German and Flemish artists, he was able to condense his experiences into his own unique style, which would in its turn influence Pisanello, Giovanni Bellini and Jacobello del Fiore.

Gentileschi, Orazio (Orazio Lomi; Pisa, 1563–1638), painter, follower of Caravaggio; he lived in England for a while, where he was court painter to Charles I.

Gessi, Francesco (or Gianfrancesco; Bologna, 1588–1649), painter, apprenticed to Guido Reni.

Ghiberti, Lorenzo (Florence, 1378–1455), sculptor, goldsmith, architect and painter, one of the greatest figures of the Florentine Renaissance.

Ghissi, Francescuccio di Cecco (Fabriano, fl. 1359–95), painter. Apprenticed to Allegretto Nuzi, he chose almost exclusively the Madonna as his subject.

Giacomelli, Mario (Senigallia, 1925–2000), photographer, with his own distinctive style, revealing the personality of his subjects.

Giacomo da Recanati (Giacomo di Nicola; Recanati, 1390–1466), painter. His elegant style and careful attention to detail, deriving from the Venetian style introduced by Jacobello del Fiore, are characteristic.

Giambologna (Jean Boulogne; Douai, France, 1524–1608), Flemish Mannerist sculptor. He went to Rome to study ancient statues and the work of Michelangelo, and ended up working in Florence for the Medici.

Giambono, Michele (Treviso, fl. 1420–62), painter and mosaicist, who worked in

Venice, attracted first by the exuberance of Jacobello del Fiore, then by the Gothic style of Gentile da Fabriano and Pisanello.

Giorgio da Como (Mastro Giorgio; Como, fl. early 13C), architect and sculptor, he was one of many stonemasons from Como and Lugano to work in the Marche at that time, but he was the only one to sign his works – the cathedrals of Jesi, Fermo, Penna San Giovanni, and perhaps the porch of San Ciriaco in Ancona.

Giosafatti (Ascoli Piceno, fl. 17C–18C), family of gifted architects and sculptors, who worked in many of the churches of their city. The most prominent among them was **Giuseppe Giosafatti** (1643–1731), who built the distinctive cave church of Sant'Emidio alle Grotte, at Ascoli Piceno.

Giotto (Giotto di Bondone; Vespignano di Vecchio, nr. Florence, 1267–1337), perhaps the most important figure in the history of Italian art, this innovative and courageous painter and architect introduced completely new concepts on the use of colour and space in his works, and the arrangement of the people in the scenes depicted. He succeeded in awakening emotions in a way no other artist had done before, not even Cimabue.

Giotto School of Rimini (fl. Rimini, early 14C), the atelier of Pietro da Rimini and his apprentices, followers of Giotto.

Giovanni Antonio da Pesaro (Antonio da Pesaro or Giovanni Antonio Bellinzoni; Pesaro, 1415–77), Gothic-style painter, who worked exclusively in Pesaro, Fano and Ancona.

Giovanni da Camerino (or Giovanni Angelo di Antonio da Camerino; Camerino, fl. 15C), painter. This artist has only recently been officially recognised, by the art critic Federico Zeri; his work was previously attributed to the Maestro dell'Annunciazione di Spermento. He is one of the most interesting exponents of the Camerino School.

Giovanni Battista da Lugano (Ticino, d 1538), architect; he came to an untimely end when he fell from a church he was building near Visso, just when he thought he had at last reached fame and fortune.

Giovanni dell'Opera (Giovanni Bandini; Florence, 1540–98), sculptor who worked a lot in Florence, especially for the duomo. His masterpiece is considered to be the *Pietà* he carved for the cathedral of Urbino.

Girolamo di Giovanni (Camerino, fl. 1449–73), painter; exponent of the Camerino School, his eloquent paintings show the effect of his formative years in Padua, and his admiration for Piero della Francesca, Mantegna, and Filippo Lippi.

Giuliano da Rimini (Rimini, fl. 1307–46), painter influenced by Giotto and by Duccio di Buoninsegna.

Greco, Emilio (Catania, 1913–95), controversial sculptor, initially inspired by the Dalmatian-born medieval master Francesco Laurana. While his monument to Pinocchio at Collodi (Pistoia) was appreciated, the bronze door he made for Orvieto Cathedral in 1964 was bitterly contested; it was, however, mounted in 1970, against the wishes of the regional council for antiquities and fine arts. Angered by the indifference with which he was always treated in his home town, he left Catania nothing in his will.

Guercino, il (Giovanni Francesco Barbieri; Cento, nr. Ferrara, 1591–1666), painter. Like Rubens, this artist had a pronounced squint, a fact which probably enhanced his work. Certainly chromatic effects were more important than perspective for Guercino. In the course of his prolific career, he painted more than 100 altarpieces.

Guerrieri, Giovanni Francesco (Fossombrone, 1589–1657), extremely refined painter of tense, dramatic works.

Guttuso, Renato (Bagheria, 1912–87), controversial Sicilian painter, noted for his bold brush strokes and use of colour.

Hayez, Francesco (Venice, 1791–1882), painter. As a young man he moved to Rome, where he became the friend and follower of Antonio Canova. Thanks to this friendship, in 1850 he was invited to become head of the Brera Academy in Milan. His early works are academic and Neoclassical in style, but his romantic nature soon begins to show through. He remains famous for his dramatic historical scenes inspired by medieval episodes, and for his portraits. His most famous work is the extremely sentimental *The Kiss* (1859).

Induno, Gerolamo (Milan, 1827–90), painter. As a soldier, who took part in many campaigns, including the Crimean War and the expeditions of Garibaldi. His paintings are mostly patriotic, or of a sentimental nature.

Innocenzo da Petralia, Fra' (Fra' Innocenzo da Palermo; Petralia Soprana, ?1592–?1648), sculptor. A Franciscan friar like his more famous contemporary Fra' Umile (who was born in the same village), Innocenzo left Sicily for the Marche when still very young. He was renowned for his impressively realistic Crucifixes, all life-size, carved in wood and then painted, said to cause fits of uncontrollable weeping and even convulsions, especially among the female members of the congregation. A fast worker, each Crucifix took him only a week to complete.

Jacobello di Bonomo (?Venice, fl. 1385–early 15C), painter; a faithful follower of Paolo Veneziano, with a few Byzantine touches here and there; few of his paintings survive.

Jacobello del Fiore (Venice, 1380–1439), artist who cleverly combined sculpture and painting in his works, to obtain a three-dimensional effect, and a particular dynamic quality.

Jacometti, Pier Paolo and Tarquinio (Recanati, late 16C–17C), brothers; sculptors, painters and architects.

Joos van Ghent (Josse van Wassenhove; fl. Urbino 1471–80), painter of Flemish origin, he was invited to Urbino by Federico da Montefeltro, where he left some beautiful paintings, some of which were taken by Napoleon.

Kostabi, Mark (Los Angeles, 1960), innova-

tive painter, sculptor and composer; www.markkostabi.com.

Labruzzi, Pietro (Tommaso Pietro Labruzzi; Rome, 1739–1805), painter. He had a successful career in Rome, where he painted a portrait of Pius VI, which pleased the pope; his younger brother Carlo was also a painter.

Latini, Giambattista (Mogliano, fl. 19C), moulder. His stucco, indistinguishable from marble, was prepared to a secret recipe.

Laurana, Luciano (Zara, modern Zadar, Croatia, 1420–79), architect. He probably worked in Naples and Mantua, where he met Federico da Montefeltro, for whom he built the exquisite palace of Urbino (his only documented work), considered one of the masterpieces of Renaissance architecture. Scholars believe he also designed the castles of Tarascon, Villeneuve-les-Avignons, Gubbio and Pesaro.

Lazzarini, Giannandrea (Pesaro, 1710–1801), Neoclassical painter and architect, who studied with Carlo Cignani in Forlì. He was also a writer, and taught for many years at the Pesaro Academy.

Licini, Osvaldo (Monte Vidon Corrado, 1894–1958), Italy's finest abstract painter. He lived for a time in Paris, where he made friends with Picasso and Modigliani. Many of his works are inspired by the tragic figure of Queen Amalasunta of the Lombards, who was drowned by her enemies.

Ligabue, Antonio (Zurich, 1899–1965), impressively shocking naïve painter, much inspired by animals, especially ferocious ones. He characteristically added *trompe l'oeil* insects to his portraits.

Lilli, Andrea (or Lilio; Ancona, fl. 1571–1631), painter,. He worked for a long time in Rome for Pope Sixtus V, where he was influenced by the Mannerist artists, especially Barocci. He returned to the Marche in 1597.

Lorenzo d'Alessandro (San Severino Marche, fl. 1462–1503), painter. His Madonnas are so beautiful people used to say the angels had painted them.

Lotto, Lorenzo (Venice, 1480–1556), deeply religious, good-natured, unhappy, but with a strong sense of humour, Lorenzo Lotto is perhaps the most humanly accessible of all the artists of the Marche. Pietro Aretino says of him rather caustically that 'Lorenzo is as good as goodness, and as virtuous as virtue'. He spent much of his working life in Bergamo, in Rome (where he worked with Raphael), and in the Marche, where he died (in Loreto). 23 of his works are still in the region, in Ancona, Jesi, Loreto, Recanati, Cingoli, Monte San Giusto and Mogliano (it is possible to buy a cumulative ticket to visit all the art galleries containing his works). It has recently been discovered (Sept 2004), after thorough cleaning, that many of the frescoes in the Apostolic Palace in the Vatican, previously attributed to Raphael, were in fact carried out by Lorenzo Lotto. His style is so individualistic that many critics say he must have been self-taught, but others say his first master could have been Alvise Vivarini; certainly Dürer influenced him greatly. Until the early 20th century he was considered a second-tier artist; today he is considered one of the very finest.

Loves, Matteo (Matthew Lowes; England, 17C), English painter who was apprenticed to Guercino, nevertheless maintaining his own particular exotic touch, giving his works a fairytale quality.

Luca di Tommè (Siena, fl. 1356–95), painter. Influenced by Simone Martini, he worked mostly in Siena and Pisa.

Maestro di Offida (fl. late 14C), fresco painter.

Maestro di Staffolo (fl. 15C), painter, probably apprenticed to Gentile da Fabriano.

Maestro di Verrucchio (Bartolomeo Silvestri da Verrucchio; fl. early 14C), painter.

Magini, Carlo (Fano, 1720–1806), painter; a skilful artist, little known outside his native Fano; his still-lifes are superb.

Magistris, Giovanni Andrea de (Caldarola, fl. 1529–55) and **Simone de** (Caldarola, 1534–1612), brothers; painters, sculptors and moulders. Little known outside the Marche, they were prolific at home, and much in demand. Simone in particular was an admirer of Lorenzo Lotto.

Mancini, Antonio (Rome, 1852–1930), painter, inspired by the poor, but dignified, inhabitants of Naples, to whom he dedicated almost his entire production. Invited to Paris, he did not enjoy the experience, which ruined his health: afterwards, he had to spend four years in a clinic. He lived his last years in Rome, happily experimenting with his colours, which he enriched by adding bits of tinsel, glass, mirror, and mother-of-pearl.

Mancini, Francesco (Sant'Angelo in Vado, 1679–1750), Mannerist painter; well-known for his carefully designed altarpieces.

Mantegna, Andrea (Isola Mantegna, nr. Padua, 1431–1506), painter. When he was 10, his father, a carpenter, gave him in adoption to the artist Francesco Squarcione: his genius was soon recognised, and he was working on important commissions from an early age, together with the best-known painters of Florence, Padua and Venice, but he maintained his own personal way of presenting a scene (as if seen from below), which makes his work unique. He married Nicolosia, daughter of Giovanni Bellini, and went to Mantua, as official painter to the court of Ludovico Gonzaga. A famous group of nine paintings, *The Triumphs of Caesar*, is at Hampton Court.

Manzù, Giacomo (Giacomo Manzoni; Bergamo, 1908–1991), sculptor and painter. Self-taught, he admired Gothic and Romanesque art, Donatello and Picasso. Bronze and wax were his preferred materials. He made the bronze side door of St Peter's in Rome ('Doorway of Death', 1962) and that of Rotterdam Cathedral.

Maratta, Carlo (Carlo Maratti; Camerano, 1625–1713), painter. He learned his art in Rome, where he served as apprentice to Andrea Sacchi; a fervent admirer of Raphael. He was appreciated for his portraits.

Mariani, Cesare (Rome, 1826–1901), painter, noted for the series of frescoes on the Life of St Emygdius in Ascoli Piceno cathedral.

Martini, Francesco di Giorgio (Siena, 1439–1502), brilliant and prolific architect, and also sculptor, painter, and inventor of war machines. Federico da Montefeltro often chose him to build his elegant palaces, impregnable castles and foolproof defensive systems. His beautiful, practical constructions can be seen at Urbino, Sassocorvaro, Sant'Agata Feltria, San Leo, Urbania and Fossombrone.

Maso di Bartolomeo (Arezzo, 1406–56), sculptor and architect. Influenced by Donatello, he preferred working in bronze, creating gates, candelabra, and doors for several churches in central Italy.

Mastroianni, Umberto (Fontana Liri, nr. Frosinone, 1910–98; www. fondazioneumbertomastroianni.it), prize-winning sculptor. His works evoke a strong emotional response; he started at the age of 14, under the guide of his uncle. Much appreciated in Japan.

Mattiacci, Eliseo (Cagli, 1940), painter and sculptor; an early exponent of Pop Art, which gradually evolved into his personal 'vibrating' style. You can see some of his works in the courtyard of Cagli Town Hall, and in the tower.

Mazza, Giuseppe (Bologna, 1653–1741), sculptor and moulder. He was clever at creating large, quite complex scenes, using only stucco: full of movement and interesting details.

Melozzo da Forlì (Melozzo degli Ambrosi or Marco Ambrogi; Forlì, 1438–94), painter. Little is known about his beginnings; he was perhaps apprentice to Piero della Francesca, before going to Rome, and from there to Urbino. You can see the influence of Piero in his work, but the people in his paintings look warmer and more human.

Messina, Francesco (Linguaglossa, nr Catania, 1900–95), sculptor. His bronze studies of young girls and dancers are unmistakable for their graceful abandon; he also liked to portray horses; his study of a *Fallen Stallion* caused an outcry in Catania, where it stands in a central square, when the council blacksmith was ordered to provide the animal with a pair of iron knickers to avoid embarrassing the ladies. The story appeared on CNN, and the ridiculous 'panties' were immediately removed.

Michelucci, Giovanni (Pistoia, 1891–1990), architect. His interest was inserting modern constructions into ancient contexts. Perhaps his most successful work is Florence railway station.

Milione, Vincenzo (Offida, fl. mid-18C), this little-known artist lived most of his life in Rome, where he painted portraits for the aristocracy.

Monachesi, Sante (Macerata, 1910–91), Futurist sculptor and painter, thought by many critics to be one of the finest exponents of the style.

Morandi, Giorgio (Bologna, 1890–1964), painter and engraver. He particularly enjoyed painting still-lifes, which he said were 'A way of being, a way of observing, a way of living our daily existence'.

Morelli, Cosimo (Imola, 1732–1812), architect. In spite of temptation he managed to avoid the excesses of Rococo; the elegant lines of his churches and palaces are very pleasing to the eye. His masterpiece is probably Palazzo Braschi in Rome, with its sumptuous Renaissance-style staircase.

Morettini (Perugia, fl. 19C), illustrious family of organ manufacturers, whose work was in demand all over Italy.

Nacchini, Pietro (Istria, fl. 18C), organ maker, one of the best of his day. He taught the great Gaetano Callido.

Nanni di Bartolo (Il Rosso; Florence, fl. 1419–51), sculptor. The portal of the basilica of San Nicola in Tolentino is perhaps his masterpiece.

Nelli, Ottaviano (Gubbio, fl. 1375–1444), painter. His frescoes are imaginative, with graceful figures and good use of colour.

Nespolo, Ugo (Vercelli, 1941, www.nespolo.com), Pop Art exponent whose paintings often look like theatre sets, with exciting and amusing events taking place.

Nobili, Durante (Caldarola, ?1508–?78), painter; apprentice and follower of Lorenzo Lotto.

Nuzi, Allegretto (Fabriano, 1315–73), painter. After serving his apprenticeship in Florence with Bernardo Daddi, he returned to the Marche, where he worked for the rest of his life. In his later years he came under the influence of the artists of Siena.

Oddi, Muzio (Urbino, 1569–1639), architect and engineer for the della Rovere family.

Orsini, Giorgio (Giorgio da Sebenico; Juraj Dalmatinac; Dalmatia, d. 1475), architect and sculptor, assistant to the great Florentine Michelozzo in Dubrovnik, and also much in demand in Ancona, where he settled down and married.

Paci, Antonio, Giovanni and Vincenzo, (Ascoli Piceno, 19C), organ makers of acclaimed quality.

Pagani, Lattanzio (Monterubbiano, 1515–1602), painter, son of Vincenzo.

Pagani, Vincenzo (Monterubbiano, 1490–1568), painter who worked almost exclusively in Ripatransone. Strongly influenced by Crivelli, he later came under the spell of Umbrian masters like Bernardino di Mariotto. Towards the end of his life, his inspiration came from Raphael.

Palma Giovane (Jacopo di Antonio Negretti; Venice, 1544–1628), painter; protégé of Duke Guidubaldo II della Rovere.

Palmezzano, Marco (Forlì, 1456–1539), painter. Some critics believe he was apprentice to Melozzo da Forlì, later working with artists from Ferrara and Venice. He was certainly strongly influenced by Giovanni Bellini.

Pandolfi, Giovan Giacomo (Pesaro, ?1570–?1650), painter; one of the most important Mannerist artists of the region.

Panfili, Pio (Porto San Giorgio, 1723–1812), painter, engraver and architect. He grew up and lived in Bologna, before returning home to carry out the decorations in the cathedral of Fermo, and making etchings for artistic publications, now in the city library of Fermo.

Pannaggi, Ivo (Macerata, 1901–81), Bauhaus-group Futurist architect and painter. He studied with Walter Gropius in Vienna.

Paolo Veneziano (Venice, fl. 1333–62), painter noted for his abundant use of gold, influenced by Giotto.

Pardo, Vito (Venice, 1872–1933), sculptor and painter, capable of creating really enormous monuments in bronze.

Parmigianino, il (Francesco Mazzola; Parma, 1503–40), Mannerist artist with a happy sense of colour, much influenced by Rosso Fiorentino. He was the first Italian artist to make etchings.

Pasti, Matteo de' (?Verona, fl. 15C), architect. He also designed medals and coins: certainly the finest of his time.

Perugino, il (Pietro di Cristoforo Vannucci; Città della Pieve, nr. Perugia, 1445–1523), painter. His crystal-clear landscapes, forming the background for religious scenes, were widely imitated.

Peruzzi, Cesare (Montelupone, 1894–1995), painter. Some of his work is strongly reminiscent of van Gogh, especially when he is inspired by humble peasants eating their simple food; he was 101 when he died.

Picchi, Giorgio (?Urbania, 1550/60–1605), Mannerist-style painter and ceramicist, noted for his clear, bright colours. A follower of Barocci, he came from an illustrious family of potters.

Piergentile da Matelica (Matelica, fl. 1515–30), painter. He liked to work with Venanzio da Camerino, with whom he had a close relationship.

Piero della Francesca (Sansepolcro, 1415/20–92), influential painter, with a very individualistic style, a strong sense of perspective, and a strange, almost impersonal approach. Tragically, he was blind for the last years of his life.

Pietro Alemanno (or Alamanno; Gottweich, Austria, fl. 1470–1498), painter and goldsmith; follower, perhaps apprentice, of

Carlo Crivelli.

Pietro da Cortona (Pietro Berrettini; Cortona, nr. Arezzo, 1596–1669), painter and architect, eternal rival of Andrea Sacchi, with whom he had a love-hate relationship.

Pietro da Rimini (fl. early 14C), fresco painter from Romagna, influenced by Giotto, and founder of the so-called 'Giotto School of Rimini'.

Pinturicchio, il (Bernardino di Betto; Perugia, 1454–1513), painter. He worked with Perugino on the Sistine Chapel, where he came into contact with Florentine artists such as Botticelli and Ghirlandaio; a cultural shock for him. The people in his paintings, always in the foreground, look fragile and delicate in their sumptuous costumes, always meticulously portrayed. '*Pinturicchio*' can be loosely translated as the 'Fussy Painter'. Art critics are often ambivalent as to whether they admire him.

Piranesi, Giovanni Battista (Mestre, 1720–78), architect and engraver. His famous etchings are still much sought-after by collectors.

Pisano, Nicola (Pisa, fl. 1349–1368), sculptor, goldsmith and architect. Certainly one of the finest sculptors of his day; his sensitive works are immediately recognisable.

Podesti, Francesco (Ancona, 1800–1895), in the course of his long and prolific career he produced at least 1,000 paintings, besides numerous drawings and sketches. He preferred romantic themes.

Pomarancio, il (Cristoforo Roncalli; Pomarance, nr. Pisa, 1552–1626), painter. He decorated several rooms in the Vatican for Pope Gregory XIII, but his masterpiece is the work he carried out for the sanctuary of the Holy House in Loreto.

Pomodoro, Arnaldo (Morciano di Romagna, nr. Forlì, 1926), and **Pomodoro, Giò** (Orciano di Pesaro, 1930–2002), brothers, sculptors, painters, goldsmiths and designers. Arnaldo is fascinated by symbolic shapes and archetypes, like spheres (Dublin, New York, Brussels—he says they represent the corrosion of modern civilisation). Giò won several prizes for his elegant bronze monuments, such as that at Milan's Malpensa airport.

Pontelli, Baccio (Florence, 1450–95), architect, sculptor and carver. After designing the choir for Pisa Cathedral, he went to Rome, and from there to the Marche, where he designed many castles and churches.

Preti, Mattia (Il Cavalier Calabrese; Taverna, nr. Catanzaro, ?1613–99), painter of predominantly religious themes; much influenced by Guercino.

Raffaellino del Colle (San Sepolcro, 1480–1566), painter, apprentice to Raphael.

Ragazzini, Giovanni Battista (Ravenna, ?1520–89), painter. He spent most of his artistic career painting for various churches in Fano.

Ramazzani, Ercole (Arcevia, 1536–98), studied with Lorenzo Lotto until 1552, when they quarrelled, and Ercole went to paint in Tuscany and in Rome, where he was strongly influenced by the Mannerists and the Counter-Reformation movement. He soon returned to the Marche, where he spent the rest of his life, painting for the little towns in the area of Ancona and Macerata.

Raphael (Raffaello Sanzio or Santi; Urbino, 1483–1520), one of Italy's finest and most influential artists, and great exponent of the High Renaissance. He served his apprenticeship under Perugino, when little more than a child. He is buried in the Pantheon in Rome.

Reni, Guido (Bologna, 1575–1642), Mannerist-style painter who considerably influenced 17th-century Pesaro artists, such as Simone Cantarini.

Ribera, Jusepe de (Lo Spagnoletto; Jativa, Spain, 1588–1652), painter. He came to Naples as court painter for the viceroy of Spain. Influenced by Caravaggio. He was also successful with etchings.

Ridolfi, Claudio (Verona, 1570–1644), painter who spent his entire career going backwards and forwards between his native Veneto (where he had learned his art in the atelier of Paolo Veronese), and the Marche, where he worked with Federico Barocci in Urbino. He had a house in Corinaldo.

Robbia, Ambrogio, Giovanni, Luca and Fra' Mattia della (Florence, fl. mid-15C–early 16C), a talented family of architects, sculptors and ceramicists; noted for their round moulded ceramic portraits of the Madonna, often surrounded with fruits.

Romogni, Vettor (?Cremona, early 18C), little is known about this artist, author of exquisite, intensely spiritual *trompe l'oeil* works.

Rondelli, Francesco Antonio (Urbino, 1759–1848), painter, commissioned by the town of Petriano to restore the paintings in some of their churches

Rondolino, il (Terenzio Terenzi; Pesaro, 1575–1621), painter. Protegé of the della Rovere family, this little-known artist probably started his career in the atelier of Federico Barocci; he might have worked on the Sistine Chapel.

Rosa, Salvatore (Naples, 1615–73), painter; one of the most representative Mannerist artists of his city.

Rosso Fiorentino (Giovanni Battista di Jacopo de' Rossi; Florence, 1494–1540), painter. His tormented figures and strange chromatism, inspired by Dürer and Pontormo, were misunderstood in Italy, so he went to France, where he was immensely popular, and helped found the so-called 'Fontainebleau School'. According to Vasari, he committed suicide.

Rubens, Sir Peter Paul (Siegen, Germany, 1577–1640), painter; noted for his earthy, opulent, colourful, almost three-dimensional figures. Some critics maintain that he achieved this effect because he had a squint. In 1608 he visited Rome to paint an altarpiece for a religious order, after which he was invited to paint the *Adoration of the Shepherds* for the church of S. Filippo in Fermo, finished in only three months. A fast worker, in Italy they called him *Furia del Pennello*, 'Paint-brush Fury'.

Sacchi, Andrea (Nettuno, 1599–1661), painter and eternal rival of Pietro da Cortona. They worked together in Rome, at Palazzo Barberini, but Sacchi, much slower and more painstaking, could not keep up the pace. He was happier painting panels for churches, an activity in which he excelled.

Sacconi, Giuseppe (Montalto delle Marche, 1854–1905), architect. His most famous work is the *Altare della Patria* in Rome, the monument to Mussolini.

Salimbeni, Lorenzo (b 1374, fl. 1400–20) and **Salimbeni, Jacopo** (fl. 1416–27), brothers. Influential painters from San Severino Marche; they were among the first to break away from the rigidity of the Gothic style. Their frescoes are like richly detailed tapestries.

Sangallo, Antonio da, the Younger (Antonio di Bartolomeo Cordini; Florence, 1483–1576), sculptor and architect. The architects Luca and Francesco were members of the same family.

Sangallo, Giuliano da (Giuliano Giamberti; Florence, 1445–1516), architect, engineer, sculptor and engraver. He started in his father's wood-carving atelier, making models of buildings for architects. He later specialised in military architecture, designing many forts and castles, before creating the lovely dome for the sanctuary of the Holy House at Loreto in 1499.

Sansovino, Andrea (Andrea Contucci; Monte San Savino, nr. Arezzo, ?1460–1529), sculptor and architect. After serving as apprentice to Pollaiolo, in 1491 Lorenzo de' Medici sent him to Portugal for 10 years. On his return, he worked in Florence and Rome until 1512, when Pope Leo X appointed him sculptor-in-chief at the sanctuary of the Holy House in Loreto.

Sansovino, Jacopo (Jacopo Tatti; Florence, 1486–1570), architect and sculptor, and a close friend of Lorenzo Lotto.

Santi, Giovanni (Colbordolo, 1435–94), the father of Raphael, and an excellent painter in his own right.

Sassoferrato, il (Giovanni Battista Salvi;

Sassoferrato, 1609–85), Mannerist painter of gentle Madonnas, in recent years much more appreciated than formerly.

Sassu, Aligi (Milano, 1912–2000; www.aligisassu.it), important painter, ceramicist, engraver and sculptor of Sardinian origin. He began as a Futurist, but soon his works were expressing such strong political statements that he was imprisoned under Mussolini. He liked rich, sensual colours, and to paint people engaged in activity: cyclists, battle scenes, bullfights. He often worked as set-designer for the theatre and the opera; in 1989 he was appointed Italian ambassador for Unicef.

Schayck, Ernst van (Ernst de Schayck or Schaichis; Holland, fl. 1567–1631), painstaking Flemish artist and follower of the Bologna School.

Scoccianti, Andrea (Raffaello delle Fogliarelle; Cupramontana, 1640–1700), carver and stucco moulder, envied by his fellow craftsmen for the skill with which he could reproduce foliage.

Sebastiani, Sebastiano (Recanati, fl. 1593–1626), sculptor. He often used papier-mâché for his works.

Sebastiano del Piombo (Sebastiano Luciani; Venice, 1485–1547), painter. Apprenticed to Giovanni Bellini, he was influenced by Giorgione, Raphael and Michelangelo. Noted for his deeply personal portraits, towards the end of his life he concentrated on religious subjects.

Seitz, Ludovico (Rome, 1844–1908), painter. He carried out a series of remarkable frescoes for the sanctuary of the Holy House in Loreto, with many delightful details, such as a little German girl in a *dirndl* skirt carrying a basket of fruit, and some tormented Gothic knights. He probably made use of members of his own family as models.

Severini, Gino (Cortona, 1883–1966), Futurist-style painter, he started in Paris with the Neo-Impressionists (Seurat), before experimenting with Cubism. He also frescoed several churches in Italy and

Switzerland.

Signorelli, Luca (Cortona, 1441–1523), painter. Apprenticed to Piero della Francesca, he later came under the influence of the Florentine painters, especially Pollaiolo. In 1482 he participated in the decoration of the Sistine Chapel, but his masterpiece is the work he carried out in the cathedral of Orvieto.

Sirani, Elisabetta (Bologna, 1638–65), painter and engraver. Although she died young, she was a prolific artist and a fast worker: when she was 17, she already had her own studio, and could paint a Madonna in less than a day (more than 200 works are attributed to her, completed in only ten years). She opened a school for female artists, where she taught for several years. When she died, the family servant was accused of having poisoned her, and was sent away from the city. Now it is thought that she probably suffered from a gastric ulcer, made worse by her frenetic activity. Her mysterious death added to her appeal; in the 19th century she was something of a cult figure. She is buried next to Guido Reni, in the church of San Domenico in Bologna; her city has recently (2004) organised her first-ever solo exhibition.

Solario, Antonio (Lo Zingaro; Venice, fl. 15C–16C), painter. He probably started painting in Vicenza, before going to Naples, and finally Venice: he is noted for his use of warm, luminous colours.

Spazzapan, Luigi (Gradisca d'Isonzo, nr. Gorizia, 1889–1958), abstract artist and designer, noted for his use of brilliant, glittering colours.

Stark, James (Norwich, England, 1794–1859), painter; exponent of the Norwich School. He loved painting forests, using wonderful subtle greeny-blue watercolours.

Stefano da Verona (Stefano da Venezia or Stefano da Zevio; Verona, 1374–1438), supreme, refined exponent of the International Gothic. Little is known about his life: he appears to have travelled in

Germany and Bohemia in the early 15C.

Stomer, Matthias (or Matteo Stom; Holland, 1600–50), painter. Little is known about his youth, or even exactly where he was born. He started his career in Rome, probably attracted there by the works of Caravaggio, and where he made friends with another Dutch artist and Caravaggist, Gerrit van Honthorst. After a long stay in Naples, in 1641 he went to Sicily, and lived in Palermo for the rest of his life.

Tamburi, Orfeo (Jesi, 1910–95), painter and engraver, famous for his Parisian skylines: simple and effective, just a few lines and a little touch of colour here and there.

Tedeschi, Pietro (Pesaro, 1750–1805), painter, well known for the altar panels of St Emygdius which he carried out for the cathedral of Ascoli Piceno.

Tibaldi, Pellegrino (Pellegrino de' Pellegrini; Puria di Valsolda, nr. Como, 1527–96), architect, sculptor and painter. His Mannerist style owes a lot to Michelangelo, of whom he was an admirer. He worked for many years in Milan, especially on the duomo. Towards the end of his life he worked with Federico Zuccari as a painter at the court of Philip II of Spain.

Tiepolo, Giambattista (Venice, 1696–1770), painter and engraver; renowned for his enormous, scenographic frescoes. He was the father of **Giandomenico Tiepolo** (1727–1804), who was his father's chief assistant, inheriting his talent to a large degree.

Tintoretto, il (Jacopo Robusti; Venice, 1518–94), painter and engraver. His nickname, the 'Little Dyer', was given to him because his father dyed silk cloth. It is said he studied with Titian, but the master was envious of his pupil's skill, and they broke off their agreement. He was a prolific worker and his paintings can be found in many of the world's museums: interesting portraits of richly-dressed aristocrats and prelates, or dramatic religious episodes, sometimes with accurately portrayed architecture as a setting. Of his eight children, four went on to become acclaimed artists.

Titian (Tiziano Vecellio; Pieve di Cadore, nr. Belluno, 1487–1576), painter, and one of the greatest and most influential of all European artists. He is thought to have studied under Bellini, and certainly inherited that master's skill at rendering a portrait. His paintings of religious subjects are no less celebrated. After Bellini's death he reigned supreme as the greatest painter in Venice, and important patrons flocked to his atelier. Most celebrated of these are Pope Paul III (Alessandro Farnese), and Philip II of Spain.

Tito, Ettore (Castellammare di Stabia, 1859–1941), painter, well-known for his romantic views of the bay of Naples and Vesuvius, and the lagoon of Venice.

Tosi, Arturo (Busto Arsizio, 1871–1956), painter with a compact, refined style. His works are almost metaphysical, emanating a sense of solitude and loneliness.

Uccello, Paolo (Paolo di Dono; ?Florence, 1397–1475), painter. An interesting artist, controversial even among his contemporaries, with a difficult, introvert personality. He was obsessed with perspective and the use of colour.

Unterberger, Christopher (Cavalese, nr. Trento, 1732–98), Neoclassical painter. One of a large family of artists, he had a particularly strong sense of colour; he reached his maturity while working in the Vatican.

Valadier, Giuseppe (Rome, 1762–1839), architect; one of the best of his time. He enjoyed a number of papal commissions.

Valentin de Boulogne (Louis de Boulogne or Le Valentin; Coulommiers, France, 1594–1632), Baroque-style painter and great admirer of Caravaggio. In the Dresden Gemäldegalerie is a famous work of his known as *The Cardsharpers*, freely inspired by that artist.

Vannini, Pietro (Ascoli Piceno, 1413–1496), engraver and goldsmith. His incredibly delicate reliquaries are witness to his painstaking workmanship.

Vanvitelli, Luigi (Naples, 1700–73), illustrious architect who learned to design in the atelier of Filippo Juvara, and carried out many works in the Marche, before going to Rome in 1735 to work on St Peter's, and then to Naples for Charles VII of Bourbon, for whom he designed his masterpiece, the royal palace of Caserta.

Varlé, Gioacchino (?, flourished in the Marche, 1734–1806), sculptor; frequently requested by religious orders to assist in decorating their church interiors, for his skill in creating the Rococo stucco details, carved wood choirs, and especially angels and cherubs, for which he was considered unbeatable.

Vedova, Emilio (Venice, 1919), self-taught painter, noted for his strongly dynamic works. He has also designed sets and costumes for theatre productions, also for the Scala in Milan.

Venanzio da Camerino (Camerino, fl. 1518–30), painter; close friend and associate of Piergentile da Matelica.

Vici, Arcangelo (Palazzo, nr. Arcevia, fl. 18C), architect; one of an illustrious family.

Viti, Timoteo (Urbino, 1465–1523), painter; he was Raphael's first master.

Vitruvius (?, 1C BC), architect, engineer and architectural theorist whose studies retain their validity to this today.

Vivarini, Alvise, Antonio and Bartolomeo (Murano, Venice, 15C), painter brothers, from a prolific family of artists. It is thought that Alvise may have been Lorenzo Lotto's first master.

Viviani, Antonio (Urbino, 1560–1620), painter. Afflicted by deafness, hence his nickname, '*Il Sordo di Urbino*'. His first commissions were in the Vatican. Later he travelled to Genoa, Urbino, and finally Pesaro, Rimini, Fano and Fossombrone.

Webb, James (Chelsea, England, 1825–95), painter. Although he lived all his life in London, he travelled on the Continent, where he painted delightfully romantic watercolours. He preferred coastal and port scenes, which transmit feelings of tranquillity and harmony.

Zoppo, Marco (Cento, nr Ferrara, 1433–78), painter who worked in Ferrara, Bologna and finally Venice, influenced by Mantegna and Giovanni Bellini.

Zuccari, Federico (or Zuccheri; Sant'Angelo in Vado, 1542–1609), and **Zuccari, Taddeo** (Sant'Angelo in Vado, 1529–66), brothers who made their fortune in Rome as much acclaimed painters.

GLOSSARY OF TERMS

Aedicule, originally a shrine; used to describe the frame of a door, window or other aperture, usually with columns or pilasters bearing a lintel

Ambo (pl. *ambones*), pulpit in a Christian basilica; two pulpits on opposite sides of a church from which the gospel and epistle were read

Amphora, antique vase, usually of large dimensions, for oil and other liquids

Arca (*pl. Arche*), a tomb, usually in the form of a monumental stone sarcophagus

Architrave, lowest part of the entablature, resting on the columns

Archivolt, moulded frame carried round an arch

Atlantes (or Telamones), male figures used as supporting columns

Atrium, forecourt, usually of a Byzantine church or a classical Roman house

Attic, topmost storey of a Classical building, hiding the spring of the roof

Badia, *abbazia*, abbey

Baldacchino, canopy supported by columns, usually over an altar

Basilica originally a Roman building used for public administration; in Christian architecture, an aisled church with a clerestory and apse, and no transepts

Biroccio, the traditional farm waggon of the Marche

Borgo, a suburb; street leading away from the centre of a town

Capital, the top of a column

Calanchi, natural gullies formed when the topsoil is eroded, leaving the underlying clay exposed. They are a particular feature around Ascoli Piceno

Cardo, the main street of a Roman town, at right-angles to the decumanus

Caryatid, female figure used as a supporting column

Cassone, a decorated chest, usually a dower chest

Cavea, the part of a theatre or amphitheatre occupied by the rows of seats

Cella, sanctuary of a temple, usually in the centre of the building

Chiaroscuro, distribution of light and shade, apart from colour in a painting; rarely used as a synonym for grisaille

Ciauscolo, soft salami from the Macerata region

Ciborium, casket or tabernacle containing the Host

Cimasa, the topmost, crowning panel of an altarpiece

Cipollino, onion-marble; a greyish marble with streaks of white or green

Cippus, sepulchral monument in the form of an altar; a stone marking a grave or boundary

Crescia, soft bread with pieces of cheese, lard or salami pressed into it

Cryptoporticus, a semi-underground covered portico used in Roman architecture for the construction of terraces or as a covered market

Decumanus, the main street of a Roman town running parallel to its longer axis

Diptych, painting or ivory tablet in two sections

Dossal, an altarpiece

Duomo, cathedral

Entablature, the continuous horizontal element above the capital (consisting of architrave, frieze and cornice) of a Classical building

Etruscan, of, relating to, or characteristic of Etruria, an ancient country in central Italy, its inhabitants, or their language

Exedra, semicircular recess

Ex-voto, tablet or small painting expressing gratitude to a saint; a votive offering

Forum, open space in a town serving as a market or meeting-place

Fresco, (in Italian, *affresco*), painting executed on wet plaster. On the wall beneath is sketched the sinopia, and the cartoon is transferred onto the fresh plaster (*intonaco*)

before the fresco is begun, either by prick-
ing the outline with small holes over which
a powder is dusted, or by means of a stylus,
which leaves an incised line. In recent years
many frescoes have been detached from the
walls on which they were executed.

Graffiti, design on a wall made with an iron
tool on a prepared surface, the design
showing in white. Also used loosely to
describe scratched designs or words on
walls

Greek cross, cross with the arms of equal
length

Grisaille, painting in tones of grey

Grotesque, painted or stucco decoration in
the style of the ancient Romans (found
during the Renaissance in Nero's Golden
House in Rome, then underground, hence
the name, from 'grotto'). The delicate ornamental decoration usually includes patterns
of flowers, sphinxes, birds, human figures
etc, against a light ground

Herm (pl. *hermae*), quadrangular pillar
decreasing in girth towards the ground,
surmounted by a bust

Hypogeum, subterranean excavation for the
internment of the dead (usually Etruscan)

Iconostasis, a screen or partition, covered
with icons, that divides the public part of a
church from that reserved for the clergy

Impost block, a block with splayed sides
placed above a capital

Intarsia, inlay of wood, marble, or metal

Intrados, underside or soffit of an arch

Krater, antique mixing-bowl, conical in
shape with rounded base

Latin cross, cross with a long vertical arm

Lancet window, tall narrow window with a
pointed arched top. A feature of early
Gothic architecture

Loggia, covered, arcaded or colonnaded
gallery or balcony, usually at ground or
first-floor level

Lunette, semicircular space in a vault or
ceiling, often decorated with a painting or
relief

Mandorla, tapered, almond-shaped aura
around a holy figure (usually Christ or the
Virgin)

Municipium, a town hall

Narthex, vestibule of a Christian
basilica

Nymphaeum, a sort of summer house in the
gardens of baths, palaces, etc., originally a
temple of the Nymphs, decorated with
statues of those goddesses, and often containing a fountain

Opus reticulatum, masonry arranged in
squares or diamonds so that the mortar
joints make a network pattern

Pala, large altarpiece

Palaeochristian, from the earliest Christian
times up to the 6th century

Palazzo, any dignified and important building

Pediment, gable above the portico of a classical building

Pendentive, concave spandrel beneath a
dome

Peristyle, court or garden surrounded by a
columned portico

Picene, pertaining to the ancient inhabitants
of the Marche region, before the arrival of
the Romans

Pietà, group (usually featuring the Virgin)
mourning the dead Christ

Pietre dure, hard or semi-precious stones,
often used in the form of mosaics to decorate cabinets, table tops etc.

Pieve, parish church

Pinacoteca, an art gallery specialising in the
exhibition of painting

Pluteus, a low wall that encloses the space
between column bases in a row of columns

Podium, a continuous base or plinth supporting columns, and the lowest row of
seats in the cavea of a theatre or amphitheatre

Polyptych, painting or tablet in more than
three sections

Pompeian, art, especially wall painting, in
one of three or four styles found at
Pompeii

Predella, small painting or panel, usually in
sections, attached below a large altarpiece

Presepio, literally, crib or manger. A group
of statuary of which the central subject is
the infant Jesus in the manger

Prostyle, edifice with free-standing columns, as in a portico

Pulvin, cushion stone between the capital and the impost block

Putto, figure of a child sculpted or painted, usually nude

Reredos, decorated screen behind an altar

Rocca, citadel above a town

Rood screen, a screen below the crucifix dividing the nave from the chancel

Rostra, ships' prows, captured in battle, used to adorn the front of a speaker's dais

Scagliola, a grey stone (selenite), occurring near Cingoli, used to imitate marble or *pietre dure*

Share-cropper, The share-croppers (*mezzadri*) are the tenant farmers of the Marche. Their rent was all paid in kind: in return for a small plot of land for their own poultry and vegetables, they had to give most of what they produced on their landlords fields to him, and were also responsible for maintaining farmhouses, farm equipment and for looking after livestock

Sinopia, large sketch for a fresco made on the rough wall in a red earth pigment called sinopia, because it originally came from Sinope on the Black Sea

Situla, a water bucket, for ceremonial use

Soffit, underside or intrados of an arch

Spandrel, the triangular space on either side of an arch

Squinch, small arch thrown across an angle as support block for a circular dome above a square space

Stele, upright stone bearing a monumental inscription

Stemma, coat of arms or heraldic device

Stoup, vessel for holy water, usually near the entrance door of a church

Telamones, see *Atlantes*

Tessera, a small cube of marble, glass or brick, used in mosaic work

Tetrastyle, having four columns

Thermae, originally simply baths, later elaborate buildings fitted with libraries, assembly rooms, gymnasia, circuses, etc.

Tondo, round painting or bas-relief

Trabeation, a construction system whereby verticals (eg columns) support horizontals (eg lintels) rather than arches or vaults

Transenna, open grille or screen, usually of marble, in an early Christian church separating nave and chancel

Triglyph, blocks with vertical grooves on either side of a metope on the frieze of a Doric temple

Triptych, painting in three sections

Trompe l'oeil, literally, a deception of the eye. Used to describe illusionist decoration, painted architectural perspectives, etc

Truss-beam, system of roofing held together by trusses, that is beams tying the supporting structure together, mainly in a triangular form, to prevent it from splaying outwards

Tympanum, the face of a pediment within the frame made by the upper and lower cornices; also, the space within an arch and above a lintel or a subordinate arch

Vincisgrassi, Marche-style lasagne

INDEX

Explanatory or more detailed references (where there are many), or references to places where an artist's work is best represented, are given in bold. Numbers in italics are picture references. Dates are given for all artists, architects and sculptors.

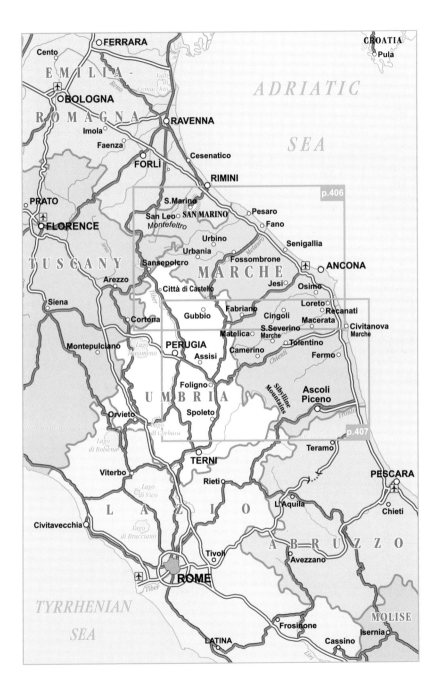

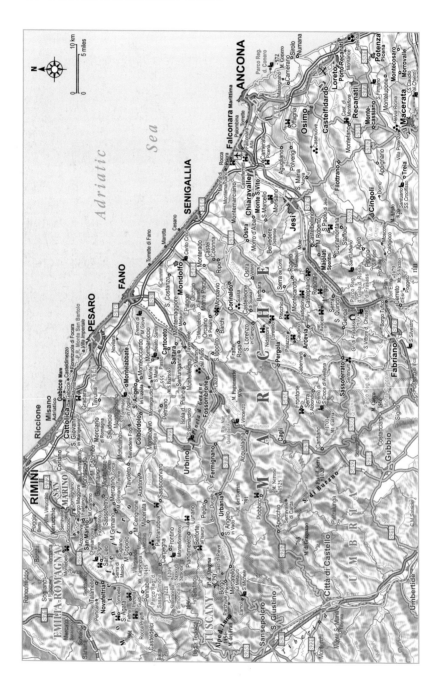

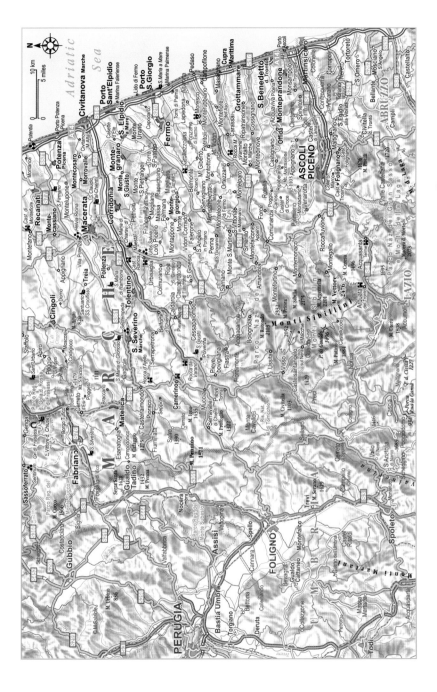

contd. from p. 4

Editor-in-chief: Annabel Barber
Assistant editor: Judy Tither

Contributor (wine sections): Joseph Kling

Layout and design: Anikó Kuzmich
Maps: Dimap Bt and Imre Bába
Floor plans: Imre Bába
With special thanks to Richard Robinson

Author's ackowledgements:
'Grateful thanks go to all those who have helped me prepare this guide,
generously lending time, energy, knowledge and enthusiasm. It has been infinitely rewarding
putting this book together, and I hope it will be both useful and enjoyable.
Very special thanks go to the Touring Club Italiano, the Biblioteca Egidiana of Tolentino,
the staff at all the tourist offices of the Marche Region and the Republic of San Marino, and to
Sandro Abelardi, Eraldo Bagnetti, Grazia Barbagallo, Teresa Bellesi, Giovanni Carnevale,
Moreno Cedroni, Andrea Cherchi, Maria Stefania Conti, Stefano d'Amico, Daniela Giannini,
Graziano Ilari, Anna Longhi, Cinzia Marcotullio, Cristiano Massari, Giacomo Mazza,
Diana Mazza Rampf, Anna Migliori, Samuela Moscati, Loretta Mozzoni, Silvia Orlandi,
Shuslie Vania Perozzi, Gerhard Rampf, Werner Rayé, Marina Ricci, Milena Scola,
Luigi Vannucci; and to Fabio Filippetti and Elsa Ravaglia, for their
Guida Insolita delle Marche (Newton & Compton).'

Photography:
Photo editor: Hadley Kincade
Giacomo Mazza: pp. 3, 12, 16, 27, 28, 41, 43, 59, 85, 88, 102, 109, 113, 129, 135, 142, 162, 165,
181, 187, 209, 213, 214, 220, 228, 252, 263, 275, 288, 289, 304, 319, 324, 326, 345, 354;
Geoffrey George: p. 73; Alinari Archives/Bridgeman: pp. 306, 308; Alinari Archives, Florence: pp.
53, 336; Archivio Seat/Archivio Alinari: p. 115. Other images courtesy of Comune of Pergola:
p. 250; Musei Civici of Pesaro (photos: Giacomo Mazza): pp. 288, 289; Museo Civico of Urbania
(photo: Giacomo Mazza): p. 319; Museo Brancaleoni of Piobbico (photo: Giacomo Mazza): p. 326;
Pinacoteca Civica of Jesi (photo: Giacomo Mazza): p. 41; Pinacoteca Civica of Recanati
(photo: Giacomo Mazza): p. 228; Province of Ascoli Piceno: pp. 144, 156; Quadreria Cesarini
(photo: Giacomo Mazza): p. 275; Regione Marche, Servizio Attività e Beni Culturali, Sport,
Marchigiani nel Mondo: pp. 21, 79, 117, spine

Cover images
Top: Villa Buonacorsi (photo: Giacomo Mazza)
Bottom: Landscape near Ripatransone (photo: Giacomo Mazza)
Spine: Detail from an altarpiece by Carlo Crivelli, in Ascoli Piceno
Title page: Detail of the *Annunication* by Lorenzo Lotto (photo: Giacomo Mazza)

Printed in Hungary by Dürer Nyomda Kft, Gyula

ISBN 1–905131–14–3